GOOBERZ

LINDA GOODMAN

IMAGE 10

HAMPTONROADS
PUBLISHING COMPANY, INC.

Copyright © 1989 by Linda Goodman

Hampton Roads Publishing Company, Inc.
891 Norfolk Square
Norfolk, VA 23502
Or call: (804)459-2453
 (FAX: (804)455-8907

If you are unable to order this book from your local bookseller, you may order directly from the publisher.
Call 1-800-766-8009, toll-free.

Library Of Congress Cataloging-in-Publication Data

Goodman, Linda
    Gooberz / by Linda Goodman
        p.   cm.
      ISBN 0-9624375-0-6
      I. Title
      PS3557.0584G6   1989   89-27704
      811'54 — dc20   CIP

10 9 8 7 6 5 4 3

Cover art by: Charles Frizell

Printed in the United States of America

For the Lion, Robert A. Brewer

ζ

the co-author of this book
from the Alpha to the Omega

who transmitted it to me through the wakefulness of his sleep,
on a higher level of awareness, spanning Time and Distance,
until it was conceived within the sleep of my wakefulness . . .
then grew into his likeness . . . and was born at its full term
in the form of words, which left me then, as now, with but
little conscious memory of their shaping.

as always . . . . also for

Robert and Annette Kemery — Pauline Goodman

and my own four elves

Sally . . . Bill . . . Jill . . . Michael

there is

out there

somewhere

a golden haired and magical messenger of the gods, named Victor Z.
who is from the OOber galaxy of stars, by way of Mars
a galactic poet and sculptor of truth, who knew that I would write this book
and when and why — what it would tell — and much more too
long before I ever guessed or knew

*. . . and the light shineth in the darkness
and the darkness comprehended it not . . .*

John 1:5

I believe that he — or that part of him who knew
has returned to his own asteroid . . .
so I take this way of telling him that I do know now
yes, I know who
and also when . . . and how
why it took so long for me to learn . . .

and to let him know, in druid talk
that the Little Prince will soon return

* * * * * * * * * * * * * *

"If some people think Love and Peace is a cliché
that should have been left behind in the '60's, that's
their problem. Love and Peace are eternal."

John Lennon
December, 1980

I would like to thank

Sam O. Goodman

without whom I could not have channeled this book
for he spent many patient hours helping me look
within myself, for answers

also . . .

Ruth Cook

who does not know the exact time of her birth
but who definitely has her Moon in Sagittarius . . .
because she believes in telling the Truth
so help you God — even though it may kill you

Aaron Goldblatt

A Sun Sign Sagittarian, who also preaches and teaches
that one should tell the Truth, no matter how much it hurts
even about the carelessness of St. Peter . . .
and who reminded me, from time to time
not to forget my rhyme and meter

Nona Stodart

an Aquarian apostle of druidic Oneness with Nature
and devoted protector of Francis of Assisi's beloved birds
who taught me that Truth must be discovered alone
in silence
before it can be shared with others
through words

and

Dr. Charles Muses
whose wisdom never fails

a special acknowledgement to him . . .

he, who said:

"suffer the little ones to come unto me
and forbid them not
for of such as these . . . is the kingdom"

and a bushel of bunny hugs

for

Toby and Wendi

because in such as these small druids . . .

. . . are the teeny-tiny seeds of magic planted
to grow into tomorrow's kingdom of miracles
on Earth . . . even as it is in Heaven

my eternal gratitude
and a shower of stars from the Oober galaxy

for

Aquarian publisher, Robert Friedman
whose faith
manifested *Gooberz* into your hearts

also for

Com Com druids

John Rehus ☆ Ruth Davitt ☆ Christopher Hickey

and their leprechaun helpers
Tina Berg, Jerome Tauber, Michael Dichysyn, Alice Wimmer
who waved their magic wands
with awesome efficiency and saintly patience

" . . . the writer who possesses the creative gift owns something of which he is not the master — something that, at times, strangely wills and works for itself.

Be the work grim or glorious, dread or Divine, you have little choice . . . but quiescent adoption. Your share in it has been to work passively under dictates you neither delivered nor could question — which would not be uttered at your prayer, nor suppressed at your caprice.

If the result be attractive, the world will praise you, who little deserve praise; if it be repulsive, the same world will blame you, who almost as little deserve blame.

He wrought with rude chisel, and from no model but the vision of his meditations."

Charlotte Bronte as Currer Bell

from her description of the work, *Wuthering Heights*, written by her sister, Emily Bronte, under the pen name of Ellis Bell, in 1847

Spring owes me something

so far, she's pulled off a few splendid sparklers
   a plump, rosy angel, who stayed for awhile
      a make believe tree house
and once, a shiny gold ring

but not a real Sky-Rocket-Block-Buster Miracle
like she always promised . . .

      maybe this year, unexpectedly

from *The Song of the Ram*

Linda Goodman's Love Poems
published by Harper & Row

for those curious reviewers and readers
who will inevitably question
whether or not this work is autobiographical
the answer is : partly yes, and partly no

I found this tale told itself more smoothly
by using the first person narrative form

the events themselves did actually occur
and are as real as the paper of the page
you now hold in your hands
but . . to *whom* did they occur ?

        it shouldn't matter about *whom* the truth is written
        as long as what is written is truth

        so never mind *who* !

this book may — or may not — have been written about me
        but it very well may have been written

        about you

it is properly classified by its author as fiction
because the dictionary defines fiction as . .

        an invention of the imagination

of course ! isn't Life ? isn't Love ? isn't Death ?
isn't everything on Earth, in reality

        an invention of the imagination ?

        it is

and that simple, unguessed mystery of magic
is what this book is *really* all about

        the simple secret of all magic and wonder
        each of you once knew yourselves
            when you were gods and goddesses
                possessing great powers
        you have too long forgotten

                L. G.

TABLE OF CONTENTS

PART ONE — STAR QUEST

Canto Twenty   847

Canto Twenty One   1019

PROLOGUE

all children's hearts contain the Serpent wisdom
                                                      of coiled secrets
never dreamed of nor suspected
by those who do believe the wells of childish minds are shallow
and thus careless, then may overlook some ancient mystery
                                                      lying silent, fallow

sleeping there unseen, invisible . . beyond the ken of all those unaware
that children meditate and dwell on things O !   never told
when their thoughts are brushed with fleeting gold
by passing angels, rustling silken wings, and murmuring low
above these softer forms of clay
too recently exiled from Heaven to pass judgement . . and so
who harken with still open souls
as yet not sealed by the ponderous gravity of Earth experience

only later, after trials of torment and temptation
are the doors to Truth slammed shut, and firmly locked
by the flesh inheritance of fixed opinion, engraved while in the womb
then do such shining spirits become the self-imprisioned, final minions
of the Body Temple's narrow, echoing tomb
crumbled from a promised alabaster . . into a common dust

        yes, children . . all

contain fragmented prisms of these bright and shimmering secrets
which magic they keep hidden, even from themselves
and buried deep within the heart, till slowly, they become a part
of subconscious memory's haunted whispers, waiting latent
                                                      to be rediscovered

        secrets spun . . .

from the gossamer threads of a faint remembered Sunrise
tangled in the cobwebbed recollection of Sun-Set's separated tears
that left an anguished heritage of loneliness and fears
these not uncovered, so for many Moons to rest
                                                      till they come forth, insistent
beckoned by the pain of some familiar strain of music
or rise up bidden by a single chord of bursting joy, heard
                                                      crashing through the constellations

PROLOGUE

sung by Nature's acapella choir, in deep-deep-deep-green woods
or in a concert hall, bringing déjà vu recall
of the peace that passed all understanding . . a flashing glimpse
                                                    of someone's face
before the Fall, that blotted out the light of grace
to cause the dark night of the soul , now wandering, lost
storm-tossed, and struck by aeons-old amnesia of its former goal
for millenia neglected, Free Willfully rejected

yes, secrets . . called to resurrected recogniton
by an errant word, or by a name . . perhaps a phrase
a sentence accidently overheard
played back then, through a swirling blend of all the senses
in mad confusion, bringing swift the yearning for a twin-soul fusion
        firm-forbidden, not allowed
by religion's dreary disciplines of dogma, long since blind
neither wont to be permitted by the educated intellect
                            nor the so-called sane and stable mind

. . . or maybe stirred, and soft 'roused to remembrance
by some nostalgic passing scene, like a negative reversed
viewed with a startling surge of inner sight, almost as though rehearsed
melting Present into Past . . oft times to form, at last
a path toward the Future, believed unknown — but known
and well remembered still   O ! well remembered

since my own April's messianic symphony of spring
wherein lies the mystery of eternity's glowing ember
has long been muted by the icy blasts of winter's cold December
I cannot say for certain that all this was so with me

        though I do know my deepest, untold childhood secret
        was rocked gentle, near a tall and humble tree . . pine scented, fir
        swaddled softly in a Christmas cradle
        later buried 'neath an Easter crypt of silence, stained with myrhh
        then shrouded with a veil of misty growing-knowing
        around a Pyramid-shaped Truth, too filled with glory and elation
        to penetrate completely in this present, struggling incarnation

                    but I listen to the music

        and I remember . . .

GOOBERZ

LINDA GOODMAN

IMAGE 10
Hampton Roads
Publishing Company, Inc.
Norfolk/Virginia Beach

Part One

STAR QUEST

CANTO ONE

My Verses Don't Always Scan

Ram that I am, and ruled by Mars — I am cursed with curiosity
concerning the maybe-miracle of tomorrow's newborn sunrise
                                    promising a brighter spring

therefore, I mistrust sedatives in any form
from pills to religious platitudes . . prescribed by medicine men or monks
for neither can tranquilize the pain threshold of loneliness
until it reaches its final, suicidal stage of longing for permanent oblivion
which would only leave unsolved . . the mystery of approaching April

    and so . .

tonight I tried to fight insomnia the hard way
by watching one of those group therapy talk shows on television
            now I may never sleep again
a couple of guest stars were rapping with the host, in the round
and the subject they rapped was the nitty gritty of poetic expression
then one of them tossed out this literary pearl of wisdom

      . "I've always felt," she cooed and simpered

      " . . that poetry is the creative artistry of genius
      plus a knack, of course, for rhyme and meter
      in its essence, poetry is the subtle alchemy
                of a sensitive soul"

    like hell it is

      poetry is what squeezes out of you
      when you've been squashed by Life, like a bug
      and if I had suspected what was involved
      in developing the knack for poetic expression
              "in its essence" — years ago
      I would have chosen a safer career
      like riveting or truck driving
      maybe fighting cynical science, tooth and nail,
      with Cleve Backster's polygraphed philodendron plant,
      testing faulty parachutes
      or even lady police work, on the narco squad

but I guess it's a bit late for hindsight to help me

my "sensitive soul"
has already sopped up too much of that . . . what did she call it ?
. . . that "subtle alchemy"

Magic !

without any warning, not even enough time
to make one last, starry wish

. . . or *was* there time ?

I died unexpectedly while I was sleeping
and the last thing I remember is the sound of angels weeping
as they mourned my loss in Heaven, whispering a final blessing
to protect my immortal soul on its descent down into hell
a lonely prison of three dimensions . . . on a spinning ball called Earth

then, from out of the darkness and dearth . . of the night
that followed my death
immersed in the floating sensation of falling, sans all conscious will
I thought I heard, through the mist, a familiar voice calling . . .

*"be still, my love, be still
somewhere . . a clock is timing us"*

and felt comforted by the promise, like a soothing prayer
as I wondered — who is "us" ? I am only me
sinking once more beneath oblivion's blankets of deep-blue-velvet-peace

until I awoke suddenly one morning, struggling frantically for air
to the sound of muffled moans, and my own frightened screams
during a thunderstorm streaked by lightning, that blotted out my dreams
yet soon apologized for its violence, and softened my mother's pain
with the lilac-scented breeze of a fresh spring rain
scattering tiny drops of diamonds
through the open bedroom window of a house on Kingwood Street

I was born naked and bald . . . on an April day

which isn't so bad — lots of babies are
but, although they covered my nakedness right away
I remained completely bald till I was nearly four
and a dozen times a week, or maybe more, my mother said
they rubbed and massaged by hairless head . . with olive oil
hoping it might perform some kind of growing magic
since a bald headed girl child was considered more or less tragic

2 ☆ Canto One

then, just as I made it to the age of two months
I almost died again — down here
from a highly contagious epidemic of medical fear
coming very near to being born again in Heaven
when several doctors gloomily prognosed I couldn't possibly survive

and I must admit that I looked more dead than alive
in the snapshot they took of me in the backyard, at the time
wrapped in my mother's arms . . lids half closed, mouth open
                                    like a dying baby robin

my mother, of course, did not believe the doctors at all
so she fed me miracle milk from a friendly nanny goat called Sue
owned by a neighbor in town, Mr. Earley
who assured her it would not only make me live . . .
it would also abracadabra my hair to grow in *curly*

                he was wrong about the hair — but I lived
                    yes, magic !   here I am !

                and I find it odd that the milk of a Goat
                should have saved the life of a baby Ram

Trinity

in the accepted spritual tradition of most every western faith and belief
I was given the mystical insurance and religious relief
of having my eternal soul sanctified and saved
                        long before there was any chance to lose it

which is probably just as well, since I am careless by nature
and have a habit of losing things — or giving them — or throwing them
                                                    away

so, duly swaddled in lacy-white, and hopefully blessed by Holy Light
I was baptized from the marble font of Trinity Episcopal
as instructed by John . . and also as insisted upon
by my very proper, paternal Capricorn grandmother, whom I adored
and called Nana, after the St. Bernard dog in Peter Pan

there was, I'm told, a minor fuss about the sprinkling ceremony
springing from the fixed fact that my stubborn Taurus mother
had once been a Baptist Sunday school teacher . .
naturally, my majestic Leo father won the denominational battle
                                    for my soul

one does not argue with the royal Lion and win — not often anyway

but all's well that ends well
as Shakespeare, Newton or Bacon, whichever one was the plagiarist
once wrote

and after the storm calmed down, I was saved — symbolically at least
to become a bona fide member of the Trinity Episcopal Church
though it was years before I comprehended exactly what that meant

it meant that I had become a leafy shoot
on a sturdy branch of the Church of England
which was itself an ancient, broken-off root
of the awesome, powerful Church of Rome
pruned rather ruthlessly
when Henry decided to divorce his Queen
for the love of Anne with an 'e'
although none of that English history
mattered much to me
at the tender age of two or three

it also meant something far more tangible — it guaranteed
that I would be quite acceptable, according to prevailing social rule
at all the 'right' birthday parties, not to mention
the 'right' kindergarten and nursery school
but I somewhat diluted the dubious distinction, you see
by manifesting myself as an invincible individualist, at an early age
indelicately obvious in my Aries insistence on being "me"

in most small towns like mine, where church affiliation is a 'must'
the Episcopal Church is considered the genteel Protestant stronghold
of the society leaders and religious upper crust
who form the **WASP** blind faith . . . and dogmatic creed
which is but one of the cross-bred garden varieties of the Prejudice seed
that is, well — if you're an Episcopalian, you'll pass
it gives you a certain class

of course, all this has undergone a gradual change
since Bishop Pike and others began to see astral ghosts
and dared to challenge the spiritual infallibility
of the Episcopal spokesmen for the Heavenly Hosts
with their own independent mystical experiences
which some of the stuffier religious abbots
saw fit to label blasphemy

there seems to be a decided snob appeal for most Americans
to anything linked with "merrie auld England"
whether it be Oxford, Dickens, Eton collars or Parlimentary Procedure
which is why even the snootiest American music critics
found it difficult to pan the Beatles on their "very first telly show"

"they are, after all, quite British, old chap, you know ?"

as a Cancerian country, traumatically torn from the maternal breast
in the dawn's early light, by the rocket's red glare
it's understandable that we all still share
somewhat of a Freudian mother hang-up about Britain
nostalgically clinging to mama's familiar accent and apron strings
fascinated by Sherlock Holmes, and the mysteries of Scotland Yard
thrilling to the colorful pageantry of the Changing-of-the-Guard
and secretly longing to be presented to the Queen
                              . . . insecure infants are difficult to wean

so the Roman roots of the Episcopal Church, therefore, perchance
had less appeal for American Society
than its subliminal association with the Anglican branch
back then, when such ancestral pomposity was relatively important
before the reckless, candid youth of the protesting and questing
                                        Aquarian Age
began to stick pins of truth in the hypocritical balloons
of each snobbish religious fraternity and sorority

and just to prove the deep-rooted Episcopal sense of superiority
to the doubters named Thomas or Dick or Harry
or to anyone who's especially wary of calling a spade a spade
I believed for years that the Holy Trinity
                      was exclusively designed and Divinely made
for Episcopalian worshippers like me
who were baptized by, and attended my church — by that I mean
the Father and the Son and the Holy Ghost lived there

              where else ?

after hearing the lovely chords and lyrics of . .

        praise God from Whom all blessings flow
                    praise Him all creatures here below
              praise Him all of ye Heavenly Hosts
                    praise Father . . Son . . and Holy Ghost

impressed on your heart and mind and soul
        once a week, from infancy on
one is quite likely to literally accept that these Holy Three
might visit, from time to time, "lesser creatures down here below"
but most certainly go home to sleep at night in an Episcopal Church

        especially, for goodness sake, in one called Trinity

or so I firmly believed, being thus lyrically soul-washed
which is nearly the same as being brain-washed, but a shade more subtle
and upon this Rock of Exclusivity I built my faith for ages
        at least it seemed like ages
during those slow-moving, dream-like, snail-paced formative years

since my paternal grandparents were pillars of the Episcopal Church
I was given no chance to avoid the engraving of Trinity — no inkling
of any other Holy Grail from which I might drink
                              to quench my burning spiritual thirst
still, my membership in the religious elite suited me just fine, at first

              yes, it suited me just fine
              mostly because the Trinity nursery Sunday school

was absolutely divine !

              it had perfectly marvelous rainbow colored chalks for drawing . . .
              bright yellow smocks to wear, to save your good clothes
                                            from smudges

              white enameled tables and chairs, just my size — and best of all
O ! best of all

              hanging on the wall, splashed with sunlight
              a life size painting of Jesus
                        with gentle brown eyes, flecked with green
              and a soft brown beard
              wearing a snowy robe . . barefoot, his toes peeking out
              holding white-wooly lambs in his lap

              and smiling a wistful, glad-sad smile

I adored singing the songs, after learning the words as well as I could
and getting a shiny gold star for being good
drawing pictures of Jesus and Mary, on my childhood religious search
while the steeple bells rang, calling the grown-ups to church
as the Sun streamed through the stained glass windows
of that beautifully architectured, old stone Trinity building

                    . . . and being carefully taught that Jesus thought
                    we were all perfectly marvelous too !
                    because he "suffered the little ones to come unto him"
                    and forbade them not

O ! he was definitely on our side, against the grown-ups
who were forever forbidding us, by saying **NO** day and night
and so . . . every last one of us believed
                    that Jesus was "all-*right* !"

he was kind to animals too, which made me especially trust him
since I unfortunately knew an older boy, named Chester
who liked to frighten kittens by tying tin cans on their tails
I didn't dare tattle to his father, of course
so I threatened to tell Jesus on Chester instead — and it always worked !
because when I frowned at this boy, and glared
then sqeezed my eyes shut and started to pray — he got scared

and ran away . . . and the kitties went free

but Chester may have had more faith in Christ and the Trinity — and me
than I . . since I was never really sure that Jesus heard my prayer
when I looked up into the clouds and saw no one there
no one to answer, or even care . . which made me feel strangely alone

I didn't understand why I couldn't call Jesus on the phone
when I was all full of hurt, like the time I fell in the dirt, playing Red Light
and skinned my knee, running out so fast from where I'd been hiding
                                        behind the big Oak tree
after hearing the leader
who was closer to my age, and liked kitties too . . . yell

                        "Green Light ! Green Light !
                        Come on home free !"

and everyone made fun of me
for being dumb enough to get caught, but you see
I didn't know how to play the game, and I thought — well, I thought
that if you were told it was time to "come home free"

            it ought to be the truth

or the time I was extra-special sad and blue
because the faerie forgot to leave the money for my tooth
and it was my *front* tooth too !

if she was really-truly-druid-honor a faerie
you'd think she could somehow magically see
how ugly-ugly-ugly you feel
with nothing but a big hole where your front tooth used to be

        and I always used to wonder . .

even though Jesus lives so high in the sky
        shouldn't he know when things make me cry
and I need so much to speak with him ?
surely a place as big and important as Heaven
            should have a telephone number

yes, I worried a lot about that every night
when I 'layed me down to sleep' and 'prayed the Lord my soul to keep'

        just in case the baptism
        wasn't enough to be safe

but sometimes I skipped the last line of the prayer I'd been taught
because it was positively not . . well, you know, not at all what I believed
I mean the line about . .

if I should die before I wake
I pray the Lord my soul to take

by 'Lord', I supposed they meant God Himself
and I found that a frightening way to pray

                              to an Omnipotent Almighty

why should I give God my soul — to keep or take
if He lets me die — before I even wake ?

                    just as, years later, I pondered
                    why mortals should succumb
                    to the darkness of unnecessary death
                    before awakening to the light of Truth

it seemed my soul would be much safer
in the care of gentle Jesus — who would never allow me to die in my sleep
so I gave my soul to Jesus to keep — at least I knew what he looked like
and I had never seen a picture of God — not in Sunday school or anyplace

          God wouldn't let anyone draw His face — I wonder why ?
          and I wonder — does God ever cry ?

                              Jesus wept

A Chocolate Bunny, Honey

when I was very small, oh ! extremely teeny-tiny . . somewhere
between the age of three months, when I could not cry real tears
and the age of three years, when I could — my mother became quite ill
and I was delivered to a nearby town (by Chevrolet, they said)
to live with relatives, until
                              . . . until my mother was better

I was told this many years later, and it sorely puzzled me
for I thought I remembered someone saying that I had been born
in the town where I was taken to visit — in that very same house

there was something about it all . . sort of half forgotten and strange
some remembered refrain . . a pouring rain
and gazing through the steam-fogged window of a train

                              "oh, no ! that couldn't be"
                              I was firmly told
                              "you were never on a train
                              till you were six years old"

still . . I remember that train . . and the rain
the frightening smoke and fire from the engine
                                        and the pain
on someone's face

my new home was a happy place
living with my Aunt Maud and my maternal grandmother I called Nanoo
                        to rhyme with sky-blue
which was the color of both her eyes and her disposition
for she was as calm as a cucumber, and as cool — yet as warm as . . oh !
her cheeks were as warm as feather pillows to kiss
yes, I remember this so clearly, her warm cheeks . . like feather pillows
                                to kiss

I guess Aunt Maud and Nanoo spoiled me quite a bit
I was somewhat over-protected
the most persistent memory fragment of the period when I started to talk
is the recollection of everyone fearing I'd come down with pneumonia
from running out into the rain . . after I'd learned to walk
            (before that, I crawled out into it, in pure bliss)
they were forever saying
                "you are sure and certain to catch pneumonia !"
only they said it pronouncing the 'p' so I would laugh
and for years I called it that — pee-nee-monia

        "you'll catch pee-nee-monia for sure and certain !"
        I would shake my finger and tell my dolls

when my mother finally came to take me home with her
                        I did not know her at all
she was a lady who was pretty
with dark hair — and sweet and nice and slim and tall
but I did not know her at all

        so I hid behind Nanoo's long skirt and starched blue apron
        that hung all the way to the floor
        then peek-a-booed out at the strange lady
                        near the kitchen screen door
        but refused to go to her when she coaxed me

                until she said . . "come here, honey
                and see what I've brought you . .
                        a fat chocolate bunny !"

then I ran straight into her outstretched arms
and she gave me a bear hug . . but I thought it was funny
that she was laughing so hard
        at the same time there were tears in her eyes

it has always been a surprise, to remember that day so clearly
and the tears on her cheek

when I sometimes have trouble remembering, even nearly
the things that happened last year . . or last week

The First Time

the first time my eyes ever gazed upon the icy face of death
the finality of it was gently hazed and misted
for I was approaching only three . . when death first came to visit me

    and I was led by the hand
        and taken in to see . . Nanoo
    who had just . . died

I do not believe that I cried
when I was led inside the bedroom to gaze upon her face
in that familiar place, the house I knew and loved

    I only remember how cold she felt
    she . . whose cheeks had been so warm, like feather pillows

so warm . . to kiss

    and I thought they should cover her
    with more fluffy comforters, more cozy grandma quilts
    or she was sure and certain to catch pee-nee-monia

                that's all . .

I did not think about the mysterious Holy Trinity
as I first gazed upon the face of death
except . . that night I had a scary dream about one of them
                    . . the Holy Ghost
and someone, maybe Aunt Maud
made me cinnamon toast and peppermint tea
that time when I was scared in the night
                  and nearly three

The Land of Love

my paternal grandfather, Dadoo — who rhymed with Boo and Love You
was a very special kind of man, with twinkly eyes and silvery hair
who used to rock and rock in his old rocking chair
and when I was there, he let me climb up, and sit on his knee
while he was wearing his horn rimmed glasses, and reading
                  the evening paper

so I could listen to the soothing tick-tock
of his perfectly marvelous, old fashioned, gold pocket-watch-clock
with delicate flowers of pink and blue etched on its porcelain face
I was never scolded when I dropped it on the floor
Dadoo just said he'd get it fixed
                              by the ancient elf at the pocket-watch store
then wink-blinked at me

he was a quiet, gentle man, so soft spoken
who never raised his voice in anger
he always wore a vest — a garter on his sleeve
and a funny hat, with a green shade, when he worked late at night
to make his bank book balance and the figures come out right

he owned a huge, oval shaped picture of Abraham Lincoln
in a mahogany, carved antique frame — a lithograph
signed at the bottom, in faded ink, with the President's name

                    Yours truly
                    A. Lincoln

which had belonged, he said
to his mother, Ella, when he was just a little fella

Dadoo allowed me to borrow his picture to take to school on February 12th
when I was nine or ten, and had been chosen to recite, at assembly
                              the Gettysburg Address
which he had patiently taught me to say
and somehow, that day, in English class — I dropped it
breaking the frame and shattering the glass
but Dadoo didn't scold me, or even frown — he just said

                    "that's an awfully big thing
                    for a little tyke to carry around"

he and I both adored the sound of music
pouring out of the old Victor Victrola
with the picture of the RCA dog listening, his head bent to one side
we played it together by the hour — and I thought
that deep back inside the golden horn
was a perfect place for the singers and musicians to hide
I remember every time I said that, Dadoo would laugh till he cried

          but the most magical thing Dadoo ever did
          was when he, himself, hid — every single year
                              on Valentine's Day

he'd ring the doorbell loudly, on the front porch — on 8th Street
then run and hide somewhere outside
while I rushed to answer the door — and there in front of the screen
were the most glorious gifts I had ever seen !

sometimes lacy hearts of snow white, or bright red
tied with satin and velvet ribbons
sometimes heart shaped boxes of red cinnamon candies — and always
mysterious square envelopes, with Valentines tucked inside
      never signed, except . . *"Guess Who ?"*

if I questioned him about these later, he would only shrug
and say it must have been the Valentine Man
with happy messages and surprises for me — from the Land of Love

once, as I reached the door, I saw someone with a garter on his sleeve
disappearing around the corner of the front porch
then I knew — and couldn't be fooled anymore
but he didn't lie — no ! it was still true, what Dadoo said . . .
the lacy hearts of snow white and bright red
                really *were* from the Land of Love

I used to save the satin and velvet ribbons to tie in my hair
before I jumped up to sit in his lap in the old rocking chair

    because Dadoo was the only, only one
    who ever told me my straight hair . . was pretty

The House on 8th Street

sometimes when my parents were traveling out of town — or ill
instead of being sent to Aunt Maud's
I was left to visit with Nana and Dadoo on 8th Street
in my own home town

Nana did so many lovely things, like teaching me to make dandelion rings
and she was forever coaxing me to eat a banana
for, she said, fruit made your hair curly — so did carrots
but never, never chocolate candy or soda pop junk
or too much rich gravy, or three helpings of whipped cream
                they made your hair straight

she brushed my hair, to help the bananas and carrots make it curly
and she let me read in bed when I went upstairs early
over and over again — *Little Women* and *Little Men*
and *Emmy Lou — Her Book and Heart* (that was really the title)

Nana always allowed me to keep the kittens I brought home to feed
    she let me tame them and name them
and she bought me little red collars, with silver bells
to fasten around their necks, so the baby birds would be warned
    by the silvery tinkle, to fly away — just in time !
there were several I loved

one was a girl kitty named Pat, short for Patricia
. . Pat stayed the longest
when Nana kissed me goodnight
she smelled of Hinds Honey and Almond cream
Rose Glycerin and Jergen's lotion — she wore all three
on her hands and face, when she went to bed, for she said
that the skin must be protected, and kept smooth and creamy
I thought the way she said that was dreamy — those words
"smooth and *creamy"*
Nana was a trifle vain, I guess

she was considered a Great Beauty
not just when she was young, but even when she was very, very old
as old as thirty !
when men looked at her, they always acted a little flirty and bold
but Nana was quite proper, and never flirted back
even when she was **POSITIVELY ANCIENT** — at forty and fifty
people still said she was a Great Beauty
and even years after *that* — in fact, she was called beautiful
her whole, entire life
everyone thought Dadoo was terribly lucky
to have Nana for his wife
well, he was, of course, but I always thought she was lucky too
to be married to a man who rhymed with Boo and Love You

yes, Nana did so many lovely things . . she let me help her
sprinkle the rose bushes . . and fill up the bird bath in the backyard
so the wrens and sparrows, bluebirds and robins
could take their morning showers

she made the most fantastic grapefruit rind candy on holidays
and she showed me where to find the sparkling, cobweb necklaces
of dew-diamonds . . left carelessly behind by the wee druids and faeries
when they'd danced in the lillies-of-the-valley the night before

once she allowed me to choose a shiny gold ring
for my very own — from the magical Woolworth's store
when I proved I could remember how to multiply nine-times-four
arithmetic was my very worst subject in school
I could never seem to master a single rule . . although
I made 100 or A plus every time, in reading and writing
somehow, those subjects were always more intriguing and exciting
yet Nana said . . . "numbers are just as important to learn"
and many years later, I found that numbers *are* as magical as words
I even discovered they're sometime winged . . and can fly, like birds !

many, many years later . . I learned this

I suppose Nana was somewhat of a class conscious Society Dame
acutely aware of her D.A.R. standing and status — and name
rather a bit of a social snob about what she referred to as "breeding"

when I brought a new friend home to play with me, Nana always asked
           "but dear child, who *is* she ? what is her background ?"
'background' you see, meant Family Tree

      she let me swing for hours and hours . . and hours
      on a rope swing Dadoo made for me, on the upstairs back porch
      the back porch just off the big bedroom . . . .
I used to love to sit alone . . all by myself, in the dark
in that big, cozy-warm bedroom, when there was a fire in the fireplace
and just watch the snowflakes fall past the street light
through the lacy curtains at the window
and hear the carols drifting upstairs from the radio
                      when I spent Christmas there
making a wish on each falling flake
that very soon I would awake and discover . . oh, joy !
                      that I had curly hair !

Nana allowed me to play with my Aunt Peg's delicate doll dishes
but never-ever with her Haviland china
which I was not permitted to touch, not even at dinner . . .
I had my own Goosey Gander plates, which I could break without
                                        the danger
of being spanked in front of . . a visiting stranger

          that dining room had the most **MAGICAL** thing !

there was this spot on the floor, under the table, beneath the rug
where Nana sat — and when you pressed your foot **EXACTLY** on the spot
like that ! what a musical sound it played !
it rang a bell in the kitchen, for the listening maid
so she would know it was time to bring the dessert — when she heard
                      the silvery ding !
oh ! I thought that was a truly, truly marvelous thing

sometimes I hid under the dining room table
and pressed the spot with my thumb as many times as I was able
until I got caught and was not allowed to finish my dinner
then was sent upstairs to bed **THIS MINUTE !** and not even allowed to play
but I honestly didn't mind all that much
because Dadoo always sneaked my meal up later on a tray
and it really tasted better that way, when he wink-blinked at me
with his kind, wise eyes . . and I wink-blinked back at him
which was our secret signal for a special surprise
      then he would sit with me for awhile, as I ate
to watch the windmill go round and round
the one on top of the service station across the street
so my punishment became a special treat
because he'd tell me stories, then — about Jesus and Lincoln
and Tom Sawyer and Huckleberry Finn, with his bright-kind-wise
                      Dadoo grin

and whisper, when he finally kissed me goodnight
that I had a dimple in my chin, which meant, he said
                    I had an angel within

I loved that, because everyone else always said
                    "dimple in chin — devil within"
I much preferred Dadoo's version, although the other may have been
closer to the truth . . . and thought that angel was the same
as the good faerie, who left money when I lost a tooth
but who lived inside me the rest of the time

          the loveliest thing Nana ever did, I believe
          was to let me munch apples and read . . in the attic
          the whole day long, when it rained
          she allowed me to rummage through the old trunk up there
          and play with the bits and pieces of sequined materials
                    mother-of-pearl combs for your hair
          and scraps of satin or velvet from the gowns she wore
          when she was the Belle of the Ball, and first falling in love
                              with Dadoo

but very best of all — oh, **VERY BEST OF ALL !**
she let me try on, as often as I liked, my Aunt Peg's wedding veil . . .
it was so heavenly, all lacy and snowy white
                    and trimmed with tiny orange blossoms
so, with secret blushes of pride
          I could pretend I was a really-truly bride
as I examined everything hidden away, on a grey rainy day
in that lovely, cedar-smelling old trunk . . things Nana called "junk"
but which I knew were fragile treasures of olden day pleasures

          . . most especially that wedding veil
          trimmed with baby orange blossoms
          that made me look like a bride . . and gave me
          such a smooth, creamy feeling inside, that sometimes I cried
          when I wondered if I would ever be
                              a really-truly bride
yes, Nana
      was lovely
and beautiful
          and good for you
like a banana

          she would always say to me
          when I was very, very bad — or very, very sad
          either one . . . . . she would say

                    "now, just remember who you *are*"

and I wondered about that a lot
I mean . . . well, you see

Short Prayer

is there anyone of any faith — or lack of faith
is there any saint or sinner, loser or winner — esoteric mystic
or spiritual beginner, whether metaphysically timid or bold
who has not, at some time, heard or read about the experiences
                                        of levitation
literally known to the saints of old ?

I've always pondered what it might be like
to be so miraculously transformed as to levitate my body
or to know the magic of transfiguration — to feel like a shooting star !
and the closest I ever came to comprehending
such a certainly sensual religious scene
was twice . . not more than that . . at least, that's the score so far

> the first time, as I recall, was when I was six
> or thereabouts — and spending the summer
> as I did, 'most ever year, with my Aunt Maud
> in the house where my mother . . . (and I ?) . . . had been born

it was a magical kind of place, where you could have such fun, and run
and race . . with the wind in your hair, most anywhere
    buy penny licorice sticks at the store, and swing on the cellar door
or play jacks in the alley, when you'd learned to count to four . . or more
there was a honeysuckle vined front porch, with a creaky swing
and in the large backyard was a really perfectly marvelous thing
an e-n-o-r-m-o-u-s apple tree, with branches that invited you
                                        to climb them
there was a rabbit pen too
near the tall sheaves of growing corn-on-the-cob
with real live, honest-to-goodness
fluffy-snow-white-pink-eyed bunnies I was allowed to pet
while they were munching their lunch of carrots and grass
and a delightfully wood-and-grease-smelling tool shed
next to a likewise delightfully grease-smelling garage
where my maternal grandfather, Dado, pronounced like Dad-*oh* !
lived like a hermit, day and night
after he and my maternal grandmother, Nanoo
had some sort of fight
    . . and he had such wonderful stories to tell !

> Dado used to un-snap his old, worn purse
> and give me a penny
> warning me not to spend it all at once

then tell me tall tales about a small girl named Yellow Wax
who absolutely **NEVER** stopped to count to ten
and who, therefore, fell into trouble, over and over again

he meant *me* — when I was bad

but when I was good, Yellow Wax and I
were always rewarded with an extra penny
and on special days . . a long walk up the hill
                                        to the cemetery
with ice-cream-on-a-stick
on the way back home

there was a garden, of course, in Aunt Maud's backyard
with corn . . and leaf lettuce and tomatoes
all the ordinary . . and extraordinary . . garden things

next to it was a flower bed, with petunias and bluebells
forget-me-nots, bachelor's buttons, zinnias and four o'clocks
and best of all, pure, heavenly smelling **SWEET PEAS !**
        if you have never smelled sweet peas, wet with rain
then you simply have not lived
I mean, you really-truly have not lived
                        you have only existed

once, on this day near the 4th of July
there was an incredible, e-n-o-r-m-o-u-s storm
with the most mountainous rolls of thunder **CRASHING !**
and bright yellow zig-zag lightning streaks **FLASHING !**
all through the dark grey sky, frightening the white cotton clouds away
and sending the noonday Sun on the run
. . also scooting Aunt Maud and my cousins,
                Barbara Jean, Charles and Freddy, into the house

anyway, on this summer day
when the storm came rumbling and grumbling
and fiercely exploding in the sticky air
they all ran inside, and cried out for me to follow them
to escape the danger of being struck by lightning

they ran with their hands over their ears, to dull their fears
of the crashing crescendos of thunder, sounding like Rip Van Winkle
rolling cannon balls at celestial ten pins
but when they called for me to "come along in !"
I did not follow

I was quite busy, you see
searching for elves, in the hollow of the old apple tree
where there might be . . . . not only elves
but gnomes, faeries and actual druids waiting to play with me

they called and they called, in mounting fear
"Alice-Mary . . Mary-Alice . . Mary-Mary-Quite-Contrary
come into the house **THIS MINUTE,** this **VERY** minute, do you hear ?
before you get all wet — or maybe hurt
an electrical storm is coming up
                    and it's going to pour cats and dogs !

oh, that was a big mistake for them to make
for, after I heard that warning, certainly no one was going to persuade me
to come inside that day — no way !
they called and they called and they called, but how foolish they were
                                    to imagine that I
would miss seeing kittens and puppies fall through the sky
      because of a few noisy fireworks
which exhilarated me far more than they frightened me

          there was . .
                    a strange, sulphur-like smell in the air

almost like I imagined the brimstones of hell
Dado discussed with me now and then . . . would smell

the strong, sharp odor . . the brilliant lightning flashes
blending with the electrical crackling sound, and the mighty pound
                                    of thunder
made me truly wonder if Jesus might possibly be
at long last, ready to personally speak with me
after remaining silent and distant
and unreachable by telephone for so long — oh, yes !
the crash of that unexpected storm
shocked the very marrow of my bones with excitement
                                    and expectation

      so I didn't go inside when I was called
      but ran instead, with sudden glee
      fast ! like a jack rabbit, into the garden
      and hid behind the tallest corn stalks, so they couldn't see me
                                    or find me

in a moment or two, it came — the cloudburst
drenching me to the skin, until my red and white sun suit
stuck to me like wallpaper

      I looked up expectantly, holding both arms out wide
      as wide as they could reach
      waiting for a kitten or puppy to fall down into them
      from God . . up there in the Land of Love
      but there were none
      only a splashing waterfall, like a heavenly Niagara
                                    fell from above
not a single cat or dog — not one

then I forgot my disappointment suddenly, because . .

oh ! the rain and the storm and the warm
of the humid summer air, now breathing again
was so beautiful . . so beautiful
that I kicked off my new Buster Brown sandals, dug my bare toes
into the dark, squishy-squashy earth
drinking in the rain and the storm and the warm
like cherry soda pop

and as I burrowed my feet in the dirt in a spasm of ecstasy
oh ! oh ! oh ! the smells !
the indescribable smells of damp earth and wet grass

sending steaming scents of Nature's perfume
into my quivering nostrils

I buried and smashed my nose into the pink-velvet petals of a rose
then into the sweet-sweet-sweet **SWEET PEAS** . . grew dizzy
and nearly fainted with happiness
while silvery needles of clean, fresh rain beat down on my head
and the thunder rolled, and the lightning flashed — "**OH BOY ! OH JOY !**"
I screamed aloud, in unadulterated-by-adults pure joy

then, as suddenly as it had begun — the rain stopped
as the Sun came bursting through the clouds
spinning and whirling them into white cotton candy once more
and at that very same second — oh ! oh ! oh !

OH !   I saw a wild streak of colors
                          stream in a glorious arc
OH !   across the top of the apple tree . .
        OH !   every color in my Crayola box
                          . . every one I had ever seen !

pink and red and violet and orange and yellow and blue and green

as though God had smeared a giant paintbrush through the sky
it's truly a miracle that I didn't die — from the sheer awe and wonder
while, from far, far away, I head a remembered voice speak
within a final, deep rumble of disappearing thunder

I fell down, then, into the ozone-soaked dirt and grass
and saw tiny raindrops . . glistening and sparkling like faerie necklaces
on the petals of every flower
while the scent of sweet peas floated in my head
until I honestly believed I was dead
and had floated up into Heaven, with the angels

I glanced once more at the glorious arc of Crayola colors
smeared by God on the wide Blueboard of the sky
and began to cry, as I whispered

"thank you, Jesus . . . Amen"

it was, I believe
a short prayer of simple gratitude for beauty
for I had seen my very first rainbow

and, just as I whispered "Amen"
sensing I had experienced something sacred and holy
I felt the strangest lifting feeling
as if I were flying, but very, very . . slowly . . gently lifting
softly, slowly . . . unmistakably drifting
then floating back down in the grass again
hearing the faintest choir music sound

      a few moments afterwards
      I was *literally* levitated from the damp ground
      by a pair of strong hands, belonging to my Aunt Maud
      and told to march into the house **THIS MINUTE !**

of course I was punished for hiding and getting wet
for ruining my new sandals, and nearly catching pee-nee-monia
    immediately plopped into a tub of hot water and Ivory soap
then ordered to take a nap

      or just lie in bed . . and meditate on my shortcomings

oh ! but it was worth the imprisonment of a nap
for the awe and wonder which had passed my way
and caused me to say
          "thank you, Jesus . . Amen !"

another strange thing . . . so strange
I discovered later that Dado, who rhymed with **OH !**
had been watching me the whole time
from a window in back of his wonderful, grease-smelling garage
and he told me that Yellow Wax had been very good that day
he also said that, if I ever wanted to really pray
the very best way was during a storm, to speak up loud and unafraid
and tell Satan to go — just shoo him away — then talk directly to God

         wasn't that odd ?

but anyway, that summer when I was five or six or so
was the very first time I sensed the glow of the transfiguration of levitation

     or believed I did . .

the second time I felt myself levitate or lift from the ground
was years later, in another season — winter
and for a somewhat different reason
        to do with Lost and Found

The doors are many
but the key is one
and the end lies there
where naught is done:
that space has room
for a winged and wondrous child
(like the magic womb beguiled
a spark to substance
with her rounding word,
and whirled a little world to being
by insistent life untombed the void's reality).

that child alone
shall fly the abyss
and seek the Double Flower
and reach the Second Sun.
Myráhi is his name
whom those may claim companion
who have done the same:
Companions of Myráhi.

Kyril Demys (Musaios)
*Wings of Myráhi

* *Wings of Myráhi* and *Prismatic Voices* with verses by Kyril Demys (Musaios) may be ordered
from *Golden Sceptre Publishing* — 109 Mendocino Place — Ukiah, CA. 95482

Sticks And Stones

I suppose the reason it always puzzled me so when Nana would say
                    "now, remember who you *are,* dear"

is because I never knew just who
this person called 'me' might be

I could never completely identify myself, leading as I did it seemed
a sometimes half-way-in-the-middle life
predicted at my birth by my somewhat afflicted planet in Libra

blessed, however, by trines from Gemini, Neptune and Mars
and the graceful conjoining of certain Fixed Stars
                    such as Spica and Arcturus
as though some angry witch, not invited to my Trinity christening
had touched my bald head with her serpenty wand
and mumbled a curse of silvery Twins and golden Scales
dipping and swaying back and forth in an April breeze
never quite perfectly balanced
                    and sometimes frozen lopsided, in winter

given by others strange, false identities and labels
              like *Old Catholic Dyer*

because I wore a small gold cross around my neck, to school
in the grammar grades — and crashed into a snowbank, at recess
on a Flexible Flyer, to attract the attention
of a lad named Richard Dyer . . . for no more reason

              and *Jew Lover*

because I once investigated the Law of Moses and the Chosen Ones
           through a pre-teen friendship of undenominational loyalty
with a beautiful biblical heroine named Judith, in my class

              and *Dirty Old Trash*
                throw-her-in-the-river-and-hear-her-splash

because I changed grammar schools
from one called McKinley to one called Nash

              and *Stuck Up Snob*

when I attended birthday parties at the homes of children
whose parents were friends and bridesmaids of my Charleston Aunt Peg
on the paternal side . . . with ancient Family Trees

              and *River Rat*

when I walked home from school against the unspoken rule

with friends who lived on the wrong side of the river
                              and were called "dirt poor"

                and *Aunt-Jemima-Black-Face*

when I defended my love
for a negro couple named Bob and Grace

             and the most persistent label of them all

                  Crazy Daisy

when I said what I liked and did what I chose
and one day bit off the petals of a rose
then spit them out in the street . . in front a funeral parlor

             but none of these identities

                  were *me*

Growing Pains

when I was growing up and down
and spinning around the lilac bush in my small home town
I wanted so — *oh ! I wanted so*

                    to be a real Brownie

             Brownies are a bunch of little sprouts
             in the 'waiting club' for the big Girl Scouts
             kids too young to go camping in mysterious tents
             or learn to start fires, by rubbing together two sticks
             and other perfectly marvelous tricks
             because they are still scared, you see
             of meeting the Three Bears in the woods

I wasn't scared of that myself — oh, no, not me !
meeting the Three Bears would have been terribly exciting
                              not frightening
but you know how some little kids are . . .

to be a real Brownie, you had to be officially nine years old
not just eight-going-on-nine
nine years old was ancient — **POSITIVELY ANCIENT**

             I was impatient when I was eight
             and couldn't possibly wait for all that dumb red tape
             so I started my own Brownie group

and made my own club pins for the troop — a small elf
painted pink and gold, like the sunrise glow
fastened with a tiny safety pin
                    to your collar, where it would show

not wanting to be a copy cat, I called my dozen or so Brownies — *druids*
with a small 'd' — and the reason why
was because druids are wee, shy Nature Spirits, who hide from humans
so a capital 'D' would have made it too easy for grown ups to find them
                    and spy

naturally, I was the Brown Owl (the President)
and I initiated druids of eight years, all the way down to five and four
I discovered the first day I could get lots more members that way
by not being fussy about age and stuff
except for one iron-clad rule: **NO BOYS** — boys ruin everything

the official Brownie motto was: *we're the Brownies, here's our aim*
                    lend a hand and play the game

but we druids were not fascinated by such un-marvelous goals
as the ordinary lending of hands, and playing the same old games
with us, it had to be far-out, or what was the point ?

the motto I made up was far more inviting
and surely much more exciting

            we're the druids, here's our wish
            to wave our wands, and make Magic Fish
            who can swim through the sky
            and mysterious mountains, who know how to fly !

of course, wishing is one thing — pulling it off is something else again
                    I don't recall that our skinny wands
ever coaxed any minnows out of their ponds — or unearthed any hills
who gave us chills and thrills, by soaring through the sky
                            like giant birds
no matter how many secret, magical code words
we muttered, in our daily druid incantations — at recess
sometimes we even used our abracadabra mantras to try to stop the rain
and it gave me a sharp hurting-pain
                    when the rain . . wouldn't stop

still, I kept the faith, baby — oh, I kept the faith !
and never considered magic a flop
the druids never lost their enchanted charisma for me
I just told myself they worked all their marvels at midnight
at the foot of an old oak tree, while I was sleeping — and One Fine Day
I would awaken to catch them making miracles
                    like mountains who could fly !

24 ☆ Canto Two

. . I hadn't studied pronouns yet
in third grade English grammar . .

eventually, when I made nine years old by the skin of my teeth
                         . . I thought I would be stuck in eight forever
I was duly invited
to join the really-truly Brownies — who had only modest ambitions
no Magic Fish — nor even any especially marvelous wish
like stopping the rain . . or making mountains fly
                         just "lending a hand, and playing the game"
    it was never the same

        I was no longer a Brown Owl — no longer in charge
        so I didn't enjoy it much, I guess
        since I was never very **WOW** about teamwork
        was I a loner even back then, when I was nine-going-on-ten ?

nevertheless, I was proud — oh ! I was button-busting proud
of my tan cardboard, official Brownie certificate of membership
imprinted with mysterious silhouettes of owls and squirrels and elves
bunnies and leprechauns . . and other marvelous creatures of the forest
leading a small boy, who looked like Peter Pan
to the secret magic-midnight circle at the foot of the old oak tree

        and most thrilling of all

bearing my full, complete name, written neatly in brown ink
my own personal identification to the world-at-large
it proved who I was . . . a Brownie

            and it also identified me

                to me

Altar

that strange, mysterious home of the Tabernacle, Covenant and Host
and the eerie hiding place of the powerful, unseen Holy Ghost

                the *Altar*

in any church, whether mystical Catholic, familiar Protestant
or distant New York Synagogue
drenched me in wonder — it awed me — oh ! how it trembled and awed me !

that mysterious Altar, high above me
from where Jesus himself, sometimes looked down to love me
where deep, unthinkable magic existed, in misty rain

silently materializing, like incense . . . .
magic much more awesome than any mere druid could hope to attain
far too holy for pilgrim feet like mine
wearing unsanctified, shabby Buster Browns, sadly in need of a shine

none but a Rabbi, Minister, Reverend Father or Priest
was permitted by God the precious privilege of walking softly there
where even the Heavenly Hosts of angels feared to tread
mere mortals of common clay were allowed such sacred honor
only lying in their caskets, after they were dead
                              and somehow, purified
no longer so unworthy in God's eyes
once their living breath had been transmuted into death
and the sinful clay could no longer pray in any way
which might displease the Lord on High

                    . . it almost made me wish to die

for years and years and years
I trembled and tremored and shook with unnamed fears
when I thought of the Altar . . .

          the foot of the old oak tree, where the druids performed
          their secret rites, on enchanted moonlit nights
          was but a pale, diluted imitation of this Abracadabra spot
          sanctified and sanctioned, oddly, by friendly Jesus
          who had so tenderly said, "forbid them not . . . .

     forbid them not to come unto me . . the little children"

                O ! that awesome Altar !

it beckoned me from afar, like some forbidden star
shining out its invisible light all through the bright, white day
                    and darkened purple night
but I never would have dreamed . . of attempting to approach it
                              before I died
no ! never would I have ever tried
I would not even have dared to contemplate such blasphemy
privately, in bed, within my own room
certain that such a sacrilegious wish would surely seal my doom
and the stone door on my tomb
would bear the scary letters that clearly spell — **HELL**

          this unreachable Holy-of-Holies gave me such a complex
          at a tender age
          that, until I was twelve years old or so, I could not . . no !
          I simply could not force my intimidated tongue
                              around that frightening word
          and I remember how hard I cried when I tried

but it was a useless deformity of speech to fight
for it would absolutely refuse to come out right, no matter how often
I heard that word pronounced
           by Minister, Reverend, Pastor . . Priest or Nun

and so, for the longest, longest time
I pronounced the strange word to make it rhyme with . . *star*
placing the emphasis heavily on the first syllable
and calling it *Al*-tar, matching the inflection of *All*-star

    O ! how that mysterious, mystical *Al*-tar
enthralled me . . and beckoned me
it filled my mind with wonder, swelled my trusting soul with worship
and caused my very soul to pound with thunderous curiosity

       forbidden *Al*-tar
All-star of promised holiness and grace

       of Love and Peace

         everlasting

Golden Chariots and Trains

sometimes, when my mother and father had to go away somewhere
and my paternal grandparents were not at home either
I was left to stay and play with two angels of mercy
on 19th Street

                 named Bob and Grace Carpenter

overnight, over a week-end
occasionally for several weeks at a time, which was terrific
for, the longer I could stay with them, the better

Grace was full of Peace and Love, that seemed to stream up
                    from her heart
and shine through her gentle, dark eyes like moonbeams
her name suited her just right
since I'd always heard that *grace* meant "pure, white light"
and every time I hear the Catholic rosary prayer
            . . *Hail, Mary, full of grace*
      I see her face

framed in the delicate Irish lace of the collars she always wore
               and crocheted herself

as for Bob, he was the most perfectly marvelous man

in the entire world — and next to Dado, who rhymed with Oh !
and Dadoo who rhymed with Boo and Love You — and my own father

      I loved Bob most of all

yes, I dearly loved them — Grace, who rhymed with lace
and Bob, who rhymed with gold watch fob
but . . both names together, Grace and Bob . . I soon learned
           rhymed with secret sob

for you see, Bob's skin was a beautiful brown ebony
and Grace's skin was the exact shade of hot chocolate, with whipped cream
oh ! what lovely, creamy-tan skin Grace had !

     but people said they were "colored"
     then whispered that was bad

I never told Grace and Bob about this secret sob I carried inside
since, though it was clearly not true, it would still make them sad
if they knew that people thought they were bad

    I was always very, very careful
so they would never find out

    I knew that Bob and Grace were good, not bad
    and I wept about it privately, when I was smaller
    desperately wishing I could grow taller
             so I would understand

    when I thought about people rhyming those two words
    it seemed to me they had pulled down some kind of blinds
    over their minds . . and then had forgotten to raise them again

    bad and good ? those two words rhyme ?
    I was simply unable to see how they could, or why they should
    no, bad and good do not rhyme, for any reason, at any time
                 Period.
    nowhere on Earth . . nowhere
    was I ever as happy as I was there
    at Grace's and Bob's, who rhymed with secret sobs

nowhere . . not even in my own home on Oak Street
and later, on Spring Street, with my mother and father and Pat
               my calico cat
not even at Nana's and Dadoo's, on 8th Street
swinging on the upstairs back porch, playing in the old cedar trunk
with gorgeous junk . . and wink-blinking with Dadoo
           watching the windmill go round and round
not even at Aunt Maud's with family reunions
deep in the woods . . and hot biscuits and home-made chocolate cake
playing with Dado in his wonderfully grease-smelling garage

with all the mud pies I could possibly bake
                              no, not even at my paternal Aunt Peg's
having dinner by candlelight, in Charleston
the gentle life, with gleaming silver and Fostoria . . and sometimes
the Governor of the State and his wife for company
all those Christmas trees in the front yard . . even a wading pool
                                        on the stone patio
        I loved all these people, places and things
        but summers, winters, autumns or springs
        a visit with Grace and Bob
        was the most toe-squeezing, tickled-pink pleasure of them all

        I guess it was the sight . . and the sound . . and the smell of these two
        and the sights and sounds and smells of their house
        when I was given the jumping-bean joy of being allowed to stay

                "oh, glory be to Jesus ! Amen"

as Bob used to say
to be allowed to stay for more than one night . . !
"glory be to Jesus ! Amen"
he said it that way every single time

I thought about Jesus being a carpenter too
and maybe being somehow related to Grace and Bob Carpenter

        yes, the smells . . I remember the smells

Bob smelled of foamy shaving-cream lather and Ivory soap
when he kissed me good-morning, and sent me off to play in the yard
                Grace smelled of lilac water and love
when she kissed me goodnight, and sent me off to sleep, in bed . . .
my very own bed, in my very own room, that belonged to me there
the bed itself smelled exactly as I imagined Heaven must smell
with snowy-soft sheets, sun-soaked and scented with fresh air
and feathery-light quilts, whiffing faintly of moth balls

then, too, there were the smells of baked apple pies
or fragrant spices and cinnamon sticks

                        . . and the sounds
                oh ! I remember the sounds

Grace humming, as she went about her work
sometimes singing the words, in her clear soprano . . miracle songs
about climbing Jacob's ladder, climbing higher . . higher
and some mean old Pharaoh, letting her people go . . at last

        and dreamy songs

about sweet, golden chariots, driven by bands of angels

who swing down low, then carry you home — straight up to God !

> the sound of Grace's bell-tinkling, raindrop-sprinkling laugh
> and her soft, whispery voice telling me, by the hour
> the most perfectly marvelous faerie stories
> > you ever heard in your whole, entire life
> the tick-tocking Grandpa clock, in the front parlor
> and the copper tea kettle
> whistling a merry, bubbling-soon, tinkle-tune
> before it grew into a cheerful, peep-boiling-now-peep

> Bob's voice, booming low and deep
> like the ocean, or like friendly thunder
> his huge, belly-rolling laughs, when we were all three singing
> and he said he couldn't carry a tune in a bucket
> > from-here-to-Nantucket
> which was positively the funniest joke I ever heard
> then . . his Bible reading voice — quiet, steady and rich
> when he read aloud from the Holy Scriptures each night

oh ! the sights in that house . .

> watching Bob creak, in his old wicker chair
> while I hugged my pinch-pillow
> > the one I pinched as I fell asleep

how I loved to see his gold rimmed glasses slip down on his nose
as he sat there, in his old wicker chair
under the warm, yellow glow of the lamp, reading all those pages
about the Rock of Ages . . all those begats and begots
dearly familiar names, like Moses and David . .   James and John
> > > the beloved
and the things Jesus said . . every evening
just before Grace tucked me into bed
with the lamplight blessing her silvery hair
which she wore in a neat bun, at the nape of her neck
> > > but, oh ! surprise, surprise !
at night, she brushed it down
long and wavy, till it hung below her waist . . and with her rosy cheeks
when she kissed Bob goodnight, she looked exactly like Snow White
> > > kissing her Prince
> or Cinderella . . or some fairyland Queen

if I had been an artist, I would have painted the bright colors
of the afghans Grace knitted, the way they looked
against the crispy-white organdy ruffled curtains at the window
I loved seeing her wearing her starched aprons
with a big bow in the back — and a pocket in front, with a lace hanky
I especially liked to feel the pale, blue silk of the dress she wore to town
or when she and Bob took me to the Baptist Church with them
> > > on Sundays

which made my mother grin, and everyone else in the family frown

and my favorite sight of all . . .

the long tapering fingers of Grace's hands
always busy with yarn — or needle and thread
or lighting a fire in the oven
to bake golden, sweet-smelling loaves of bread

winter mornings were best, when it was freezing-cold outside
oh, freezing-cold ! sitting there in the cozy-warm kitchen
listening to Grace sing and hum, and telling me
those perfectly marvelous faerie stories
                    while she bustled around, getting breakfast

    . . . she and Bob believed in druids too, like me
        and they knew all about the magic circle
        at the foot of the old oak tree, where they hid . . .

the big bowls, with tiny, painted blue flowers
filled with hot, yummy-tummy oatmeal, covered with thick cream
crunchy brown toast, buttered-to-the edges, just so
                    with rich, country butter
and peach marmalade . . fluffy scrambled eggs
and icy-cold, freshly squeezed orange juice
                    served in her rainbow glasses
    I called them that, because they were cut glass
and reflected the light . . Grace kept them all washed and polished
in the dining room china closet — but she didn't waste them
    "just for good" or company
she used her sparkling rainbow glasses every single day

I used to curl up there, in my sky-blue chair Bob painted for me
because it was my all-time-favorite color
on those freezing-cold wintry mornings, with pure contentment oozing
half snoozing . . wiggling my toes, near the fire
with it still dark outside
watching the snow fall past the pantry window . . as I loved to do
                    in Nana's big upstairs bedroom
but it was even more magical to watch the flakes fall
in that warm-scented kitchen, so early . . at dawn
            then Bob would come down the back kitchen stairs
to eat his breakfast . . . kiss us both goodbye on the tip of the nose
and tell me I was his "special rose" — it was only when he was leaving
for work that he called me that — other times, he called me
                                    Little Potato
        and I called him Big Potato

Big Potato worked for the big railroad, the Baltimore and Ohio
everyone called the B & O — and made sure the trains

were never too fast or too slow

he had a Very Important Job as a Porter
and wore a marvelous, dark blue uniform, with shiny brass buttons
a wonderful hat, with a bill on the front
and carried a pocket-watch-clock, like Dado's, with his initials, R.C.
carved on the gold case, at the end of a golden chain he called
his watch fob

hanging from his pocket

oh ! Bob looked gorgeous when he went to work !
he exuded a mysterious train mystique that delighted me
wisps of thrilling, far-away places
trailing all around him . . . little puffs and traces of engine smoke
when he sang

 "down at the station, early in the morning
see the little puff-a-billies standing in a row
see the engine driver turn the little handle
CHOO CHOO ! WOO WOO ! off we go !"

everytime I hear the lyrical call of **ALL ABOARD !**
even today, in Grand Central, I always think of Big Potato
and how he kept the B & O running, all by himself

once, when I was having breakfast in the dining car
on the Metroliner to Washington . . I saw a man in a dark blue uniform
with brass buttons, wearing a gold watch fob, walk toward me
swaying with the movement of the train
and when he grinned, and called out "good morning !"
I burst into a sob, from the sharp memory-pains
trains . . and porters . . affected me that way, with sudden tears
for years and years and years

Big Potato liked to Pontificate About Politics, Grace used to say
Pontificate-About-Politics . . . that's what she said
and Bob would say, "aw, go soak your head !" . . . then they would laugh
and I would roll on the floor, and wiggle and giggle
for, of course he didn't mean it, when he told her to go soak her head
they loved each other just like the Prince and Princess
in the faerie stories I'd heard and read — I knew this was true
because, at night, when she was tucking me into bed
Grace would smile a dreamy smile, then sigh . . . and say

"oh, I love that man so !
I guess I loved him before I was born
and I'll love him after I die . . . "

I could never understand the part about before she was born
and after she died — but it sounded so lovely

I always sighed along with her, each time

then Bob would whisper in my ear
when Grace couldn't hear, and was nowhere near

> "oh, I love that woman
> with all my heart — so much
> it sometimes makes me cry . . "

and a big, shiny raindrop would fill up his eye
but he'd blink it away, thinking I couldn't see, then sigh — "ah, me . . "

I never tattled on either of them
I mean, the secret of how they loved each other
because they would always wink, and say, "now promise not to tell"
and I truly never did, though I knew perfectly well
> they probably guessed each other's secret anyway

as I grew from smaller to taller, it puzzled me greatly — when I moved
to larger cities than my own home town
to see that people were still rhyming bad with good
even when I said I didn't think they should, or see how they could
some called them colored, some called them negro, some called them black
> the ones like Grace and Bob
and one man said to me, with a smirky sneer on his red, ugly face

> "the only good one is a dead one"

and he used a word that rhymed with "bigger"

> "they don't know how to keep their place
> that's why they're bad"

OH ! that made me **RIP ROARING MAD !**

and then, when I was a little older, people became even bolder
in the things they said about folks like Bob and Grace
they told me the colored were sexually promiscuous

SEXUALLY PROMISCUOUS ?

when Grace and Bob were as truly in love as Romeo and Juliet ?
they told me that negroes were slothful and lazy

SLOTHFUL AND LAZY ?

with Grace always scrubbing and mopping and polishing
her kitchen floor so sparkly clean, the window panes shining like diamonds ?
and Bob working so hard to keep the B & O running, all by himself ?

they told me the blacks

were slow and stupid and ignorant

STUPID AND IGNORANT ?

the way Big Potato memorized the Encyclopedia and the Bible
and most of Shakespeare . . by heart ? and the words they taught me
long words, like 'incidentally' and 'consequently'
                            and 'pontificate' and 'denigrate'
the way Grace and Bob both helped me with my homework every night
in spelling and grammar and arithmetic
                    and I passed every test when they tutored me ?

they told me next, that people who were shaded mahogany
or chocolate, or creamy-tan . . . . . were sneaky and dishonest

SNEAKY AND DISHONEST ?

with Big Potato always teaching and preaching
that you have to tell the truth, or it would make Jesus cry ?
and my parents always leaving the key to our house with Grace
when they went away, so things would be safe, my mother would say
and the only time . . . . the only, only time Bob ever scolded me
was one day when I took a dime from the little boy next door . . because
it fell from his pocket, and rolled on the floor

                    Bob said

                        "taking a dime that isn't yours
                        leads to taking a dollar, or three or four
                        then leads down deeper, all the way to hell"

        and then he said — "this is true, without equivocation"

I have a vivid memory of his teaching me, then, to spell it — **EQUIVOCATION**
that big, long word I had never before heard
not even at Aunt Peg's, from the Governor of the State
who also liked to Pontificate-about-Politics . . . like Big Potato

                promiscuous, ignorant, dishonest and lazy ?
                I finally decided that the world was crazy
                and the Earth is God's asylum for the insane

to this day, I feel a sharp loving-pain
when I think about Grace and Bob who rhymed with secret sob
and cannot understand why people still want to rhyme bad with good

one day in school, when I was in the higher grades
I tried to help people pull up the shades they'd drawn across their minds
so the light could get in — and wrote a kind of poem
the teacher let me read it aloud to the class . . . . it was called

and it went like this . .

"no ! I would not — certainly not ! because I knew a girl once who did
and it ruined her whole, entire life, to be this colored man's wife
he had a bright red temper, purple passions
                              and dark green jealousy
also a yellow streak of cowardice
oh ! and terrible, dark blue moods . . and cloudy grey thoughts
but his colors were all painted over with white
so everyone believed he was very good, and terribly bright

you see, colored people rhyme with bad, and it's very sad
but that's how it is . . . . no, I wouldn't want my sister — if I had one
to marry a colored man
and I avoid colored people like *that* . . whenever I can"

but, do you know what ? not a single person in that room
understood my poem
                    not a single one . . not one

many years later, after I'd grown from small to big
I wrote some speeches for a good friend
        who was President of the National Urban League
a tall, proud Lion — a Leo, named Whitney Young

and in one of the speeches, I suggested that maybe — just maybe
the planet Earth is like a small baby
only crawling, not yet walking — or perhaps a candle
                              God is just now lighting
        and Whitney said to me

"listen, if I go on talking
and you go on writing — and we all
stay in tune

we might make bad
rhyme with passing-away-fad, someday soon
and even make good — rhyme with
                    finally understood
in a happiness poem
        colored with truth, for my people
you just keep on writing the truth
and I'll keep right on telling the truth
because truth, repeated over and over again
is really the only sure way"

oh, how I wished that Grace and Bob
could have been there with me, that winter twilight
so I could have heard Big Potato say . .

"glory be to Jesus, Mister Young !
you are, without equivocation
                    absolutely right"

Peg-O-My-Heart

maybe because I was a lonely, only child
somewhere between the fourth and sixth grades in grammar school
I got lost for awhile, like a falling star — I mean, I lost my way
and nearly forgot how to spell words like pray
and faith — and happy — and trust — and good — words like that

from the very first day in school, my best and truest friend — Boy
was Charles Tuttle . . for two reasons only
I was lonely . . and Charles was the smartest boy I had found
which meant he could help me with arithmetic problems
and he was also the tallest boy around — not just tall in size
but, you know — tall inside too
like, he never-never broke promises he made
                        and he always loaned me his brand new pencils
then just smiled, and said, "that's okay"
when I lost them, or broke them, or forgot to give them back
sometimes he bought me eskimo pies
                and he simply never-never-never
                    ever told any lies

        and . .

from the very first day in school, my best and truest friend — Girl
was Peggy Johnston . . for two reasons only
I was lonely . . and Peggy was a druid too, like me
she was absolutely the only one in my druid club, who believed
                                    as hard as I
that fish could really swim through the sky
and mountains really knew how to fly
if you could just wake up some night to catch them doing their tricks
and anyone who didn't believe in magic was just plain dumb
that's what Peggy and I used to tell each other

well, this falling-star time, between the fourth and sixth grades
when I forgot to spell words like happy
                this time, close together . . two things happened

        the first one . .

was that Charles started liking a girl named Mary Jean Corbitt
who had curly black hair and button-brown eyes
and peaches-and-cream skin . . and who was also a whip with — oh !

the very hardest tables, like eight-times-nine
and seven-times-eight in arithmetic
she lived next door to him
and he liked her a million-trillion times better than me
so, after awhile, Charles stopped punching the boys at recess
when they called me Crazy Daisy, on account of the druids and all
he never had any more spare time
to help me with pronouns and multiplication tables
he stopped loaning me his pencils, and buying me eskimo pies
mostly because, well — he was always and forever
over at *her* house playing

he even . . walked her to school

I didn't mind the eskimo pies, but I caught him telling occasional white lies
like, this one morning in June, he told me he didn't have any extra pencils
then loaned his best bright blue one to *her* — that very afternoon

he winked at her — and I saw him too
he even loaned her his own notebook, one day when she forgot hers
the one with his name printed on the front
naturally, all this made me see
how positively unlucky and ugly you can be
when you have straight, mouse-colored hair, like mine
instead of curly black

and skin that freckles and burns, and gets duck-bumps easily
instead of peaches-and-cream
and plain, medium blue eyes, instead of button-brown
also, dumb, dumb parents, who rent a dumb house
on the other side of town
on Spring Street — when I told them and *told* them
before we moved from Oak Street
about the house across from his being empty — and for rent

I didn't care if he liked her better than me, not really
it was just kind of lonesome, because I was used to having him there
to take up for me and stuff . . . .
the other boys were not tall at all — they got mad
and yelled at you, if you borrowed their pencils
and broke them or lost them
but it wasn't so bad

because I still had . . Peggy

and then the second thing happened

Peggy didn't have anyone but me
to punch the boys when they teased her

she had pale, silvery hair, like moonbeams
and large, deep lavender eyes
the same exact color as the violets she and I used to pick
enormous bunches . . in a field behind the school
when we talked about druids and things
and sometimes, made leaf whistles and dandelion rings

I thought Peggy was beautiful, all fragile and flower-like
with those violet-lavender eyes, and pale moonbeam hair . . so delicate
she reminded me of Queen Titania in a Midsummer's Night Dream
yes, her hair was the shade of a silvery moonbeam . . exactly !
but sometimes, the boys would tease her, on the way home from school
when I wasn't there, that is . . . when I was there, they didn't dare
for I wasn't afraid of them, you see
                              except when they were teasing me

they would yell at her, "hey ! Peg-O-My-Heart, I love you !"
and then they would laugh and laugh
they meant it as a mean joke, because . . well

because Peggy was so very, very thin — as thin as a pencil
hardly even making a shadow
so frail . . and kind of white and pale, her skin

the gooey-mush song about *Peg-O-My-Heart*
from my parents' courting days, was being revived about then
I wish it hadn't been . . . . because
all the rest of that year, the song made me cry when I heard it
not because it was so sentimental — and not because
the boys sang it so loud, to be cruel and tease her . . . no
that's not why that song made me cry

    it was because, one day — it was summer — Peggy and I
    had been invited to a birthday party
    but when I stopped to pick her up, at her house
    her mother said she was sick in bed, and couldn't go
    because she had pee-nee-monia
    only Peggy's mother said it right, of course
                            pronouncing it new-monya
    and that night, they took Peggy to the hospital

they wouldn't allow me to see her or talk to her
when I went there to visit the next morning — it was raining
and . . three days later

                just *three days later*

    Peggy died

that's why I cried when I heard that song, for ever so long after

the evening my mother and my English teacher
took me to the funeral home to see Peggy
it was not at all like gazing on Nanoo's frozen features
veiled by the merciful hazing and misting of the innocent grace
                              of nearly three
it was different, and scary

Peggy's faintly smiling face was framed in violet-lavender lace
to match her eyes . . which were closed tightly
so no one but me could see
how perfectly they matched the lacy collar on her dress

she was white — and still — and icy cold
and she looked, somehow, old
lying there in all that quilted pink satin . . thinner, even, than usual
her hands folded like she was saying her prayers
and as I stood there, looking down on her
                              with the scent of lilies heavy in the air

I thought I heard her say

      "goodbye . . . . I'm sorry I had to be so dumb as to die"

then my heart pounded and pounded and pounded in my chest
and I don't remember any of the rest, except that I couldn't cry

                              and my mouth was dry

      but I do remember later, the next day
      when I told my teacher what I had so clearly heard Peggy say
      that she didn't really want to be so dumb as to die
      and how I was certain I had heard her whisper, "goodbye"

my teacher said — "no wonder the boys
                  all call you Crazy Daisy"

then she told me that I must never-ever lie
about things which were obviously not so
and that made me cry, at last . . because I had believed
until then, that everyone knew
it was impossible to lie about something
you were so absolutely-positive-sure
                              was true

With This Gold Ring, I Thee Wed

Saint Raphael's was a convent home for nuns
who lived and worked and prayed there quietly, with manner mild
not open to prying public eyes

          especially not open to the curiosity of a child

      positively no one

who was not visiting on urgent Catholic business
save the laundry man and maybe the baker
               and an occasional beeswax candle maker
was allowed to pass beyond those forbidding gates
let alone permitted to walk through the mysterious portals
of the convent's heavy wooden doors

        no one but me

for I had made friends one fine spring day, in a quiet way
with a gentle, soft-spoken Sister, who was watering a rose bush in the yard
she was dressed in the snow white and light blue of the novice
not clothed in the stern and scary black robes
            of the others who had frowned at me

I smiled at her and she smiled back
then we spoke, and she invited me . . . **O !** choirs of angels !
to come inside the chapel, if I sat very still . . . .
to watch the nuns at prayer, saying their daily rosaries
counting each well worn and lovingly fingered bead
which would then lead . . . into the meditation of his final passion

I was hovering somewhere between nine and eleven
and filled with such a swelling pride, to be so honored and so blest
as to be singled out from all the rest of the curious outsiders
and permitted to stay, to watch the nuns pray

for years and years . . well, at least for three or four
I slipped past that mysterious, carved and arched wooden door
and the nuns would simply smile, not speaking a word
allowing me to stay and kneel in their chapel, where the sounds I heard
and the sights I saw with youthful eyes
filled me with an ancient peace and adoration of ritual
                that lingers still
a blend of the senses, which sent my spirit soaring
and made the paler Protestant services
          seem dull and plain and boring

the low and dulcet murmurings of the nuns, whispering Latin phrases
and the muted hazes of light, transmuted
      by the chapel's stained glass windows into rainbows

passing across those incredibly young and smooth and tranquil features

made that convent — even more than the Trinity Episcopal Church
truly an appropriate home for the Holy Ghost
and all of the Heavenly Host — especially when you counted in the incense

. . and the haunting and melodious
melting-into-velvet-silence chants

in addition to the Sisters, I ran into an occasional priest or parishioner
there on some sort of secular business — yet, not once did anyone
in or out of habit — attempt religious coercion
to convert me, or entice me with the lure of Catholic faith

I, of course, coerced, enticed and allured myself — and who knows ?
perhaps the nuns anticipated this
but no matter, for my slowly growing bliss . . was the awakening kiss
of self-discovery — never coaxed by words or dogma
only feeling, warmly stealing over my heart . . and mine alone

in my rare and whispered talks with the novice Sister
who had first permitted me to enter . . I assume, with private permission
from the Mother Superior . . I learned a truly mind-shattering
but absolutely fascinating thing !

I discovered that each nun
was a bride of Christ — every single one !

oh, this was a polygamous puzzlement indeed
that made me ponder the creed of multiple wedding bonds
which I believed only Mormons were allowed

but . . each nun . . a true bride . . of Jesus himself ?

it was a startling revelation, that caused me wonderment, each night, in bed
after my prayers had been duly said
and left me with burning questions, unanswered, yet unburied

at first, no matter how I tried
I simply could not imagine Jesus married
any more than I could imagine him eating corn-on-the-cob
or sneezing . . blowing his nose . . or freezing his toes in the snows of winter
or taking a bath, and scrubbing himself with soap
and drying himself with a towel . . or swimming, and doing a belly smacker
or, you know . . having hiccups and catching poison ivy
scratching a mosquito bite . . or any of the ordinary things that people do

not even . . . laughing

although I could easily imagine him sleeping — or weeping
since the Bible said, according to all my Sunday school teachers

Canto Two ☆ 41

and I verified this later with the Sister
whom I trusted somewhat more
when it came to biblical lore

but married ?

no, for a long time, I could not imagine Jesus of Nazareth married
especially not to all those women at once !
it was difficult enough to imagine him married
to just one wife . . kissing her goodnight
and in the beginning, it gave me quite a spiritual fright
but I gradually grew accustomed to this concept
sometimes being able to picture him giving a devoted wife
an affectionate and husbandly good night embrace
as Nana and Dadoo, my mother and father — and other grown ups did

after all, the nuns had a better-than-Brownie-Honor proof of marriage
for each one wore on the third finger of her right hand
a plain gold wedding band
and it was no secret that, when they took their vows
they became his really-truly brides

"it is something the Church allows . . "
Sister told me gently

since, as she said, it's only a symbolic marriage, not real
just a mystical link to make them feel . . somehow
a closer bond with him . . like pretend or make-believe

still, I used to wonder anyway, to myself . . real or not
and mystical maybe
because, I mean, well, you know — they never had a baby
or anything like that
still, what was the gold ring a symbol of — really ?
was it perhaps a ritual of remembrance
for an honest-truly, one-time marriage, in the olden days of Palestine ?

oh ! do you suppose that Jesus had a girl
he once called his very own Valentine ?

from what I'd been told of symbols, they had to symbolize *something*
something once actual and real
about the way people used to act, and the way they used to feel
and so, I privately decided that the nuns were acting out
mystically and symbolically
a real marriage of long ago
but Jesus later deserted his wife, to roam around barefoot and teach
and try to reach the multitudes with miracles
. . . and the nuns were pretending or make-believing the loneliness

his poor wife must have felt when he deserted her
because God called him out to wander the hot, dusty roads
                              leaving her weeping behind

or maybe she didn't really mind — maybe she wasn't angry with him
for leaving her alone, all sad and blue
if she was religious, like him . . and believed in miracles too

gradually, I developed the certain idea
that the Vatican, in Rome
that far-away place all Catholics call home
held a deep and enormous mystery — which was
      The Greatest Religious Secret of All Time
buried beneath some huge rock . . or moss-covered stone
under the Pope's golden, jewel-encrusted chair
                          which I always pictured as a royal throne

      and . . oh ! I trembled when I imagined this . .

and beneath that huge rock or stone — was buried
a yellowed and crumbling piece of paper
which was the legal marriage license of Jesus and Mary Magdalene !
yes, the Magdalene . . . the one with whom he fell deeply in love
after he forgave her all her scarlet sins, and made them white as snow
and very few people were allowed to know
because it was kept a deep, dark secret in the musty vaults of Rome
since, when Jesus walked away from his married life, to wander around
it amounted to a sort of marital separation
and who would worship a man who deserted his wife ? oh !
even if God told him to go, did I not surely know
that men who did such a thing today — not that different from yesterday
were considered weak and bad — not very nice ?
      yes — wife desertion, even back then, must have been called a vice
no wonder the Catholic Church keeps it a secret !

was not Mary Magdalene the one — the very first one
                    at the tomb, on Easter morning ?
and did not such loyalty and devotion prove
that she was more worried about him than all those others
who were always claiming they loved him, then hiding
when they were the most needed to stand up for him — defend him

                    and believe in him ?

of course, I didn't dare to breathe a word
about my private theological theories
especially the one about the priests of the Catholic Church

I had heard they were never allowed to marry girls they loved
and raise a family — as Ministers of other Faiths and Jewish Rabbis
                    were permitted to do

and I thought that maybe the priests, too
were somehow acting out the same mystical symbolism
of Jesus' desertion of his bride
and that the Church also kept hidden inside the mysterious Vatican
the secret of the true reason the priests were forbidden to marry
which was — that they had to bear this loneliness as a punishment
or a symbolic retribution for wife-desertion
since everyone who ever went to any kind of Sunday school
or studied the Old Testament rule
knows that the sins of the father are visited down
                              from generation to generation
              in perpetuity

and perhaps the Church rightfully thought it only proper
that this shameful sin be atoned for, right down to this very day
by anyone who wanted to preach, or teach God's Holy Word
as a kind of post-mortem purification

no, I dared not speak of these strange wonderings
born of discovering the vows between the nuns — and him
speak of them **OUT LOUD ?**   oh, never, never !
it would have turned my relatives white-haired overnight
whether my theories were wrong or right
conceived, as they were, from the mating of logic and learning
in the literal, yet imaginative and ever-burning childhood mind
not so insensitive and blind as the minds of adults
to the seeds of truth

as my conviction grew, I was no longer so confused
                              by this new ideal of Jesus
no, I was not disturbed, but rather, lulled — and somehow, sure
that he was just as true as ever — and as pure
I felt even nearer to him than I had before this spiritual blow
when I thought of Jesus being human . . and loving someone so
it was warmly comforting to know that he
might make a mistake or two, or three . . like me
which made me feel more acceptable, both to him . . and to myself

I longed for the courage to whisper of these things to Sister
but I never did, fearing she might be as indignantly shocked
as I was absolutely certain my own family would be
and I would find those great portals once more locked
losing my precious privilege of praying in St. Raphael's chapel

so I contented myself, in private
with my own imitation of the nuns' symbolic marriage
and saved my allowance, hoarding it till I had enough to buy
in the yard goods department of Dils Brothers
some foaming white net material for a veil
then I carefully selected a dime store wedding band
which I placed reverently on the third finger of my right hand

where the Sisters placed their own
and wore them to bed, sometimes at night
when I knelt on the floor . . and quietly said

"with this ring, I thee wed"

whispering all the other vows too
promising to love, honor and obey Jesus
with all my heart, till death did us part

and the truly marvelous, really lovely thing
about my secret veil and ring
was that no one in the whole world ever knew
that I was married to him too

except, naturally, the Almighty
who performed the ghostly ceremony, as I knelt in my flannel nighty
after which, I blessed myself each time
with a sweeping sign of the cross

but the secret I treasured within most of all
was the mysterious surprise of one special Christmas Eve
when St. Raphael's smelled of cool, green pine and spruce
while the nuns were singing, a capella . . . *silent night, holy night*

and *Oh ! little town of Bethlehem*

. . above thy deep
and dreamless sleep
the silent stars
go by . .

so magical and whispery-soft, and wondrously holy
with the snow falling silently outside . .
the candles flickering little red glows in the dark
and the incense smoking, hazing the air
like ancient frankincense and myrrh
. . . I felt some memory stir

when I first walked into the fragrant warm, my nose freezing-cold
little snowdrops in my lashes and hair, glistening on my red wool scarf
wearing my new Christmas mittens, made of soft, white
imitation bunny fur — the Christmasy feeling of deep mystery and joy
from the sound of the chanted carols
and the mingled scents of sweet bayberry wax and pine
poured richly through me, like wine . . intoxicating, yet also stilling
my soul

I was standing in the chapel's vestibule
my cheeks damp with melting snow, mixed with glad-tears
staring in awe and wonder, at the life-like manger scene before me
the little Lord Jesus, asleep in the hay . . real straw, smelling musty

Mary wearing a really-truly, gauzy blue veil . . and Joseph
dressed in a rough-woven, brown cloth robe, smiling down at the baby
wrapped in swaddling clothes . . . the heralding angels
with their golden wings, nestled in the pine boughs all about

    I could almost hear the shepherds shout !
        the three Kings, wearing sparkling crowns of jewels
oh ! so real it was . . all the animals seemed to move and nod
at the tall, Wise Men
           sent there by a sign from God

timidly, I joined the other voices, singing
as I leaned over the crib . . and touched the tiny hand

  . . . *all is calm, all is bright*
        holy infant, so tender and mild
    sleep in heavenly peace . . .

then I looked up . . .

    high up . . at the shimmering, five-pointed star
    on the very tip-top of the Christmas tree
    suddenly smelling cinnamon and oranges
        from somewhere in the air

and . .

    O ! holy holy holy night !

the soft spoken, gentle Sister, smiling — glided up smoothly behind me
then, bending down, she whispered . . "Merry Christmas, little one !"
kissed the top of my head, and said

        "I have a small Noel gift for you"

as she pulled out something from beneath her billowing sleeve
with a swift, flowing motion
like some oddly dressed magician, pulling forth a rabbit
or a never-ending strand of colored ribbon
as I had seen them do on stage, at school, on special assembly days

    it was . .

        a sparkling, blue and silver rosary
        she placed in my trembling hand
        murmuring tenderly . . so low and clear

        "this is for you, my dear . . .
        because you believe in miracles . . .

it is for you to keep, to always use
when you say your prayers
                  so you will never-ever lose
your love for Jesus
who believed in miracles too, like you"

Brownie-Honor, that's what she said !

and her smile, as she spoke, was so full of light
it made a sort of rainbow around her head
her eyes had the strangest, burning glow — she looked
well, she looked like an angel
                  O ! was she ? I thought so . . .

that was, I shall always believe, the happiest, holiest Christmas Eve
I have ever known, or ever will — nothing could equal the magical thrill
of that shining strand of silver and blue beads
with its glittering crucifix at the end, given to me by my gentle friend
like a secret druid wand, with the mystical power
to bring me nearer to the one who had said

                  "forbid them not — to come unto me"

          for such a simple gift of love

               is rare

later, when I left the convent, and stepped outside
the snow was deep and crisp and even like on the feast of St. Stephen

          . . and I walked in the moonlight
                  through falling, lacy snowflakes

as the nuns' sweet voices followed me
still echoing in my ear . . so near . . so clear

          . . and gathered all above
while mortals sleep . . . the angels keep
                  their watch of wondering love . . oh !

          morning stars together . . . . . .
                  proclaim the holy birth
     and praises sing to God, the King
               . . . . . . and Peace to men on Earth

one gold-brushed afternoon, in early fall
I was sewing doll clothes at Anna Margaret Frost's house
around the corner from my own — on Thirteenth and a Half Street
so named, I guess, because it was only one block long
and next to Thirteenth Street — what could be more logical ?

there were six of us — Caroline Fay and Judy Witte
Mary Jean Corbitt, Ann Rich, Anna Margaret . . and me (and I ?)

we were all in the same secret L.O.Q. club, and we had a coded yell
we would shout **AHH-EEH-AHH !** trying to imitate Tarzan
to call each other out to play
    it was absolutely forbidden, on the pain of ex-communication
not to answer that Tarzan yell, even if we were taking a bath
or sound asleep — once I got caught, when they yelled, in the tub
and **BOY-OH-BOY !** did I ever give my big toe a stub
        running over to the open window to answer

that afternoon . . though I guess it was closer to evening
    late afternoon, near dusk or twilight
we had been sewing away all day, and my fingers were numb
from needle pricks, since I refused to wear a thimble
too much bother — besides, I hated to sew — sewing is so dumb
but the rest of them loved it, and I had this thing
about anyone doing anything better than me — I mean, than I

Carolines's mother was an English teacher in high school, you see
which made us all a little nervous about grammar
she had taught my aunt and my father
and would also someday teach me — since I hoped maybe to someday be
a real, honest-to-goodness writer
that is, if I ever managed to make it to high school English class

    bored with sewing, I was turning somersaults in the grass
        some cartwheels and back bends too
    feeling my bones growing . . a little tense, and needing to stretch
    when I saw, over near the hedges, by the fence

                  a dead bird

    a baby robin

dead and stiff and cold

        we all voted, with the official club Tarzan sign
        to give the baby bird a proper funeral
        so I quickly suggested a Mass for the dead

Anna Margaret then went inside to get a match box

emptied out all the matches — and Judy lined it with a scrap of red velvet
she'd been saving to make into a ball gown for her doll
which I thought was a perfectly marvelous sacrifice on her part

tenderly, we placed the teeny-tiny robin
in the red-velvet-lined box, and carefully sprayed his feathers
with Anna Margaret's mother's very best perfume
then tucked small rose buds all around him . . and the six of us
began the sad Processional for the Dead
tearfully, yet somewhat enjoying the glamour and beauty of the rite

　　　we marched slowly, circling the house
　　　our solemn ritual accompanied by a hymn I'd taught the others . . .
　　　after all, I was the only one who worshipped at Trinity
　　　where the Holiest-of-Holies obviously lived
　　　　　they were mere Methodists and Presbyterians
　　　so it was only right that I be allowed to choose the music

　　　　　　　　　. . as the only Ram in the group
　　　　　　　　　I sometimes got away with things like that . .

we marched single file, with Judy, I believe
carrying the tiny casket, as official pallbearer
all singing at the top of our lungs

HOLY, HOLY, HOLY !　　　　
LORD GOD ALMIGHTY
GOD OF THREE PERSONS
BLESSED TRINITY !

I know the lyrics don't sound like much
without the melody and the organ, and the choir
but it was really rather grand and glorious
quite dirgy and very funereal, believe me
you just go to an Episcopal service some Sunday, and you'll see

we proceeded to march, in mournful procession, eyes raised toward Heaven
for a long, long time . . . until we all grew chilly
it was autumn — football weather — and quite nippy by seven

then we buried the baby bird, with a tablespoon to dig the dirt
　　　　　　　prayed the Lord his tiny soul to take
sadly covered the grave with pink rose petals — and broke up the wake

since supper at our house was at five thirty
　　　　　　　. . can you *believe* that ? it really was
as you might guess
I arrived home for my evening meal more than a little late
but thanks to a blessed fate, Nana was there, visiting my folks
and her presence somewhat cushioned the blow

still, my parents were in a snit — and it didn't help a bit
when I told them I had been attending a funeral
they told me not to be funny, and I told them it was the truth
so they called Judy Witte, but the line was busy
and still in a tizzy over what they believed for certain was a lie
they called Anna Margaret, whose mother confirmed my alibi

then they asked, ominously

"where did you hear that Catholic business
about Masses for the dead ?"

I stubbornly refused to answer any of their questions
about our Catholic ritual, with roots in Rome
I guess I didn't think they would understand the glory
of the whole story — of St. Raphael's
and when they persisted in asking where I'd heard
about Masses for the dead, I just said

"I'm starving" . . edging closer to Nana

it worked — as I knew very well it would — because
Nana was forever and always on my side, whether I was bad or good
she spoke in her holier-than-thou
combination Capricorn-Episcopalian tone, and stated firmly

"well, if anyone cares to know how I feel
I do not believe the child should be made to eat a cold meal
simply because she has buried a dead bird

I've always heard
that God also cares about the fall
of a single sparrow — is this not true ?"

and I thought, in a rush of affection
"oh, Nana-banana, I do love you !"

my parents agreed with her, as they always did
no one ever dared to disagree with Nana, especially Dadoo
who rhymed with Boo and Love You — he was not there at the time
or he would have defended me too, even more emphatically
for Dadoo was not only always on my side
he even cried when I cried — which made me cry even harder
because I loved him so
so, my mother and father
who really were very nice sorts, even if they were not
every single time, on my side — then allowed me to eat my supper
and, oh, joy ! they even let me have an extra dessert
of chocolate pudding, with two scoops of whipped cream
and Nana said . .

"all that rich food will be certain to give her
a bad dream — but I guess it won't hurt, this once"

it was . . . kind of a happy ending to a funeral

but later, upstairs alone, in my bedroom
as I was trying to fall asleep
I felt as though I might be going to weep . . because
the Mass for the dead that we had said
somehow didn't seem so glamourous and beautiful anymore
it seemed, instead, very sad and frightening

suddenly, I remembered Nanoo . . . and Peggy Johnston
and I got up, and went over to the open window, raising it higher
to look out and make a wish on the evening star
but I only got as far . . as, "twinkle-twinkle little star
            how I wonder what you are . . "

        and didn't finish

I just sat there, wondering, "what you are"
in the purplish light, and whispering aloud to myself

"yes, and I wonder, too, what You are, God
are You *always* right ?"
            I asked the deepening night

"well, if You are so good, and always right
then why do You let birds — and people — die ? oh, You can't deny
that You do let things die, while You sit up there
way above the world so high, like a diamond in the sky . . "

then I realized that I was repeating to God
the end of the star verse, the one I always followed with

        "star light, star bright — I wish I may, I wish I might
        have the wish I wish tonight"

remembering that, surprisingly often, the twinkling star
came through for me, to grant what I sought
when God, so cold and remote, had not . . . and thought

"well, maybe God is a Star Himself . . . maybe He is
maybe the biggest, brightest one up there
or did Dadoo tell me that was the Sun ? I don't care
because, if God is a Star, then He has to be
        whichever one is the **BIGGEST** and **BRIGHTEST** . . . "

then an unexpectedly cool autumn breeze blew through my hair
until I shivered in my nightgown, and closed the window
all but a tiny crack — but the dumb thing wouldn't stay open

at exactly the place I wanted, so I propped a book on the sill
and climbed back into bed, to think about the twilight Mass

                                        for the dead
and the tiny robin
who would never trill a note of spring . . ever, ever again

I wondered about searching for the reason
somewhere out there, among the bright, shining stars
but before I began my star quest for truth
I thought it safer to say my night-time prayer . . because
I was a little frightened of the sudden, shivery chill

                                        I felt in the air

and began . .
            "now I lay me down to sleep . . " then stopped

"I don't *believe* that prayer anymore !" I cried aloud

as I thought . . whether God is a beautiful Star, up high in the sky
                or just an old man with a beard
                I think I'll obey His will, just a little longer
                until I find out for sure why He lets things die

and had a sudden inspiration

maybe it's not God, after all, Who lets things die — maybe its His son
the middle one, of the Holy Trinity
oh, no ! that's Jesus, and he's too kind and gentle
well, if it's not God's son then maybe it's the Holy Ghost . . yes !
I'll bet a thousand-million stars
that spooky Holy Ghost up there hiding in the sky
is really the one Who lets birds and people die . . but, I wonder why ?"

it was growing more difficult all the time
to try to make Life and Death rhyme
or to think in any terms but the one-two-three of the Trinity
but the dying part . . . yes, about that

        sometimes, I wanted to scream and shout
        like when the boys played baseball

OKAY, GOD ! THREE STRIKES, AND YOU'RE OUT !

            You and your Holy Trinity

and thought that night . .

        if He makes me see three
                and Nanoo and Peggy are already two
        I just don't know what I will do

my parents were so anxious for me to spend the night with Ann Rich
I had every right to be suspicious . . . something was obviously wrong
Ann was one of my very best friends at school
but this was against a strict house rule
you don't sleep over with friends on a week night
                         too much homework — it just isn't right
so why this sudden permission ?

oh, I thought of several things it might be
my parents were having a private quarrel or fight
that had nothing to do with me — if not that, then maybe a party
with too much grown up fun and noise
where I wouldn't be welcome — I had so little poise
back then, when I was ten, going-on-eleven
                      and someday might make twelve

somehow, I felt that Ann knew
so I begged her to tell me, and not to lie

"I won't let my parents know you snitched
cross-my-heart-and-hope-to-die"

strange, that I should have said that

                   "allright," Ann sighed, finally

                   "they told me to keep it a secret
                   and at least I tried
                   it's Pat, your calico cat
OH !   she was hit by a car — and she's dead"

         Oh

              oh

NO ! NO !

"but Pat's not dead, she *can't* be dead !
she's going to have babies the first week in May
it was just last month she got married to Tiger
the big yellow kitty next door . . "

                 "well, she's dead for sure"
                   Ann Rich said flatly
                 "and your folks didn't want you

to see her buried"

she's dead for sure, she's dead, she said

they put her in the ground, when I wasn't around
to see that no one hurt her ?
my very own kitten who needed me ?

oh, Pat ! will you ever forgive me for that ?
I ran out in the rain to find you that night
but they had already taken you . . . somewhere

>they forgot to tie on your favorite red bow
>I saved it for years . . did you know ?

Which Way to Heaven ?

my non-optional membership in the Episcopal Church
where the Father, the Son and the Holy Ghost slept each night
after briefly visiting lesser creatures down here below
suited me fine, it really did, for a number of years — for I loved to go
>to the stained glass, bell ringing Nursery Sunday school show

but, at Trinity, there was no Sunday school all summer long
from the ages of six to twelve or so . . no Sunday school, the *whole summer* !

you were actually expected, each summer Sunday
to sit in a pew in church, with all those grown-ups

in the sticky, prickly heat — and stay positively-perfectly neat
and absolutely never scrape your Mary Janes on the seat
of the pew in front of you . . and not twist your hair ribbon into a string
or do a single, solitary thing to distract the Reverend
or to attract attention . . under threat of receiving a religious detention

you had to sit very still and quiet, like a church-mouse
and try not to wiggle and squirm, like a worm
through sermons which were illuminating, I'm sure — but which seemed
to last for forty days and forty nights, at the very least

it was an eternity of exemplary behavior — once each week
all through the lazy summer season — and a season, at certain ages
may last anywhere from two to three centuries
I just simply did not have that many centuries to waste
>>>>>>playing church-mouse
there were times when I thought

that I would literally burst, like a balloon **PING ! POP ! PING !**
from the overpowering urge to twist my hair ribbon into a string

    but, oh ! when the choir began to sing . .

that sweet-voiced choir of grandeur and glory
I firmly believed for years and years
were actually the angelic Heavenly Hosts
fluttering down into the choir loft on Sunday mornings
and ever so much more enticing and beautiful
than the scary, elusive, peek-a-boo Holy Ghost . . yes, the choir !

    when the choir sang to the deep, mellow music of the organ
    I sat stiller than still . . and listened with a completely surrendered will
    and felt such an indescribable thrill
    oh ! the choir could always inspire me !
    the feeling was next best to the one I experienced at St. Raphael's
    although the convent visits were a deep, dark secret
                         I could share with no one

if I had been given a choice
I would surely have embraced Catholicism as my faith
after that miracle Christmas Eve . . and my blue and silver rosary
but it never occured to me to dream of such disloyalty
for, to my staunchly Protestant family
it would have been tantamount to my joining a Witch Coven

Protestants have had hundreds of years of practice in protesting
and they would have protested powerfully
true, they believed in the axiom of "live and let live"
                    but not too close for comfort
nevertheless, something had to give
sooner or later, under the rubber-band strain of sticky summer stuffiness
which was slowly smothering my soul and strangling my freedom
to wiggle and squirm like a worm — I mean
there are times when you simply **MUST** wiggle your toes
even if it shows

the choir might have successfully stuck me to Trinity
with the mystical glue of music and angel imagery
                  maybe . .
but I stopped picturing the choir as angels fluttering down into the loft
the shocking Sunday that the boy who liked to tie tin cans
                to pussycat's tails
was graduated into the choir ranks
first-row-front . . white robe, lace collar, floppy black bow
but his angelic face and thrush-like voice did not fool me for a single instant
this boy of noise and cruel intent was **ABSOLUTELY NOT AN ANGEL !**
not by any stretch of the most sensitive imagination . .
and the Sunday morning I saw his face, framed in foams of white lace
all shiny-scrubbed, with cheeks like rosy apples

sweetly curving lips and golden-chestnut curls masking his secret sadism . .
the bubble of celestial music and angel imagery burst wide open

  it was while the choir was singing
                    praise God, from Whom all blessings flow
            praise Him all creatures here below . .

that I decided, *it is not true* !
the Trinity choir is not composed of singing angels
it is made up of creatures down here below
and some of them really creepy too

this was definitely, without equivocation
not the church where I wanted to go — oh, no !
not even any Sunday school in the summer, for goodness sakes !

        the other Protestant churches enticed me with the lure
        of Sunday school all summer long
        and to make the temptation even stronger . . . my Brownie pack
        met in the basement of the Methodist Church
            truly, my conversion could not wait a moment longer !

and so, against the wishes of dear Nana, who was deeply distressed
also to the acute embarrassment of my proud Leonine father
but to what I believe was the secret delight of my Baptist mother
I ex-communicated myself from the home
        of the Father, the Son and the Holy Ghost
and tried to ignore the family fuming, feuding and fussing

I became a Methodist, not through indoctrination or dramatic dogma
but as a desperate reaction to the disillusion of realizing
that the musical choir of Trinity's Heavenly Hosts
harbored the Viper of a Kitty-Hater in its bosom

        not long after my switch, I discovered something odd
        so very odd . . . about the Protestant Church I had joined
        through my rebellion against my childhood faith
        in the home of the three-times-three of the Holy Trinity

my new place of worship was called by everyone, simply, the First M.E.
at least, that's what it was to me
and to all the other Brownies and Junior Scouts
who knew it was a Methodist Church, but had no special inclination
to probe its hidden mysteries in depth
including its familiar and taken-for-granted name
carved in stone, over the door
and so, I'll never forget the sharp sting of shock I felt
the Sunday morning my new Methodist Sunday school teacher told me
that the full, formal name of my newly adopted church
                            called the First M.E.

was really the First Methodist **EPISCOPAL**
that's what the initials stood for

I privately shivered a tiny shiver of fear
this was, indeed, a strange thing to hear — for, the Holy Ghost
white sheet and all . . had obviously followed me
to this brand new place I had found to pray — to what purpose ?
I knew it was what people call a coincidence
                                    still, I wondered anyway
just exactly what "coincidence" was trying to say

it was downright spooky, like the feeling you get on Halloween
sometimes, in the dark . . when the leaves are rustling.
and a screen door bangs . . and a black cat yowls and howls
suddenly running in front of you, brushing your legs
then it's all still and quiet . . and you can't find any of the kids
who started out trick-or-treating with you

because they are all hiding somewhere, to scare you
and the Moon goes behind a cloud . . and you hear whispers behind you

              like that . . you know ?

the sturdy branch of the Church of England
with its ancient, Roman roots
seemed to have a Catholic clutch on my leafy religious shoots
but . . was it the Church itself ?
or perhaps some deeper, still sleeping mystical memory
of the three-times-three of the Holy Trinity ?

Whatever or Whoever pursued me, the Methodist stop
was my first, uncertain step down a winding path of religious wandering
to end, I still don't know exactly when or where
although, I remember I was happy there, at the First M.E.
except for those occasional twitches of suspicion
that the Holy Ghost was somehow, stealthily, silently following me

observing every private prayer

              like a spiritual F.B.I

without even telling me why

        it can make you nervous inside
        even when you only imagine it might be true
                          I believe that was about the time
        when I began to be touchy and self conscious
        about my personal identity
                    "remember who you are"
        but who was I ?
        what did I believe ?

and who — or what — was I destined to be ?

a mystical drop-out ?

Ribbons For My Hair

one purplish day, in a quiet way
to match his gentle manner

Dadoo

who rhymed with Boo and Love You

Dadoo died

this time, it was the house on 8th street
where I was taken to view another casket, except by then
I had stopped looking . . I was ten

not a single memory do I recall
of how Dadoo looked when he was dead
nothing at all — not a solitary thing
only that I am sure and certain
that Dadoo was wearing his wedding ring
he loved Nana so . .

my sense of sight was somehow blocked, as my heart was locked
that purplish day . . and blackish night
but not my sense of touch — oh ! not my sense of feel
for I do recall, and the memory is painfully, vividly — real
how icy cold his fingers felt . . . and how they . . .

. . . how they just would *not* bend, when I tried

I was scolded sharply for doing that, before some visiting strangers
and I cried, but only inside, where no one but me could see . .
the rest of that misty, hazy time, I was very, very bad
and made everyone very, very, sad . . by my behavior at the funeral
for, as my beloved Nana related a hundred times, over the years
while her eyes invariably filled with tears

"all that child did, the entire time she was there
was to drive us crazy, by rocking and rocking
in his old rocking chair
and asking, every five minutes or so, at least
if she could have all the colored ribbons
on the baskets of flowers — to tie in her hair

saying, over and over and over again
              that he surely wouldn't mind, or care
since he was so obviously sound asleep
and not once, mind you — not once did I see her weep
after she and her Dadoo had been so close . . such good pals"

oh, but Nana, dear Nana-banana
what you never knew — and I'm so sorry
I never found a way of telling you

          was that I had stayed up very late, the night before
          kneeling on my bedroom floor — with paste and crayons
                                        and paper
                                         and glue
          making an enormous, lacy red heart Valentine
          for Dadoo to hold in his prayer-folded hands

          but I tore it up, because it wouldn't come out right
          and cried so hard that star-less night
                        there were no tears left the next day
          so I couldn't even cry, or say goodbye
          when Dadoo went away

although I thought I heard him whisper, from somewhere up above
      "it's allright, honey — I've only gone to the Land of Love
                           where the Valentine Man lives"

          that's why I needed the ribbons for my hair
          I just *knew* Dadoo could see me from up there

          and I wanted so — *oh ! I wanted so* . .

              to look pretty for him

CANTO THREE

Hymn to Shakti

As dawn first burst against my opening eyes,
I dreamt a last dream ere I woke to earth —

On golden air your fair form did arise,
And fused my soul with light to give it birth.

One instant lived as I a new-blown breath,
As fresh as that from soulless sylphs out-breathed,
In vernal fires my doubting died a death
That left my brow with wraiths of heaven wreathed.

Then every atom, lustreless and dim
Within me, drank your splendid smile and rose
Upon the morn, — a golden-chorused hymn
Of perfumed pollen to the heavens' rose.

Thus daily turns my dross to gold by Thee
Thou and the dawn: divinest alchemy !

Kyril Demys (Musaios)
Prismatic Voices

the spring I listlessly arrived at the unexciting age of eleven
or maybe it was twelve ? I wrote my first poem
squeezed out of me, not by the "creative artistry of genius"
but by the alchemy of my carelessness

I had been chosen to read a verse about the Resurrection
in church, on Easter Sunday, just before the sermon
in front of the world at large — the entire congregation of the First M.E.
and I wondered . . is this really happening to **ME ?**
will I actually be allowed to stand so near the awesome *Al*-tar ?

(still rhyming it with *all*-star)

     I was thrilled, but then, running around the lilac bush
     daydreaming . . and caught up in other matters of great consequence
          I forgot to select a poem to read
     and with some strange blotting out of mind and senses
     didn't realize that I hadn't until Easter Eve
                too late — the library had closed

have I ever known such panic ? no ! never-never-never
I thought I could procrastinate as late as I chose
because I was so clever-clever-clever
and I couldn't even tell my parents, or ask them for help
because they wouldn't understand . . . oh, never-never-never !

     but wait . . reprieve !

maybe there might be an Easter poem in some book
on the shelves holding the stacks of volumes
which had belonged to Dadoo, who rhymed with Love You
       . . bless his heart, he loved to read too, like me
quickly, I ran to see

I found verses and poems there allright
about Bethlehem's still and holy night — even funny ones
about other holidays, like Halloween
          some fascinating stories by Mark Twain, in prose
and some intriguing rhyming verses about a rose
but no poem, no verse about the Easter gladness — not one

my panic truly approached a form of madness
as I pictured myself standing before the mysterious *Al*-tar

           of red velvet and rosewood
with church scents and the sound of organ music all around
staring at the stained glass window of Mary Magdalene at the tomb
          through glazed, frightened eyes
with not a word to speak, not a single line to squeak

to the waiting, shamed faces of relatives and friends
or to the accusing glares and stares of strangers in the front row pews

and how would the Methodist Minister take this news ?

there was no way out, for my picture and name
had already been printed in the Church Bulletin on the previous Sunday

no way out . . no way

and so, truly terrified, I cried all night, and couldn't sleep
thinking the unthinkable — the embarassment I would surely reap
for the seeds, already carelessly sown
of laziness and unforgivable procrastination

how would I be punished
by the Almighty — the Minister — and my parents — in that order ?
how would I be chastised, when I had procrastinated this way ?

as the unforgiving night ever-so-slowly crept toward
an inconceivable dawn, I tried to pray — but what could I possibly say
to God ?
and how could even He
find a poem now, this late, for me ?

I sat at the open window in my back bedroom of the red brick house
on Spring Street, where we had moved from the magical Oak Street
and shook and wept, and waited for my Fate
with no less fear, I believe, than I might have felt
in my cell, on Death Row
and the hours went by so slow
oh, they went by so slowly . . . so slow
until the dawn came

and I watched it come, nearly forgetting my awful fear
for it was . . so very beautiful
this was the first time in my life I had ever seen Sunrise
and the glory of it filled my eyes
trembling my heart with sheer wonder

it was even more overwhelming than the thrill I always felt
in a sudden and unexpected electrical storm
when I ran outside to bathe in rain, and feel delightful shudders
at the thunder's **BIG BANG** noise, and see the lightning **FLASH !**
with every mountainous, booming **CRASH !**
singing along, with each **BOOM** — "rain, rain, go away
come again another day"
. . . and sometimes, it really stopped

but this new miracle of dawn . . . .
this cool, peaceful poise of Sunrise

was more marvelous than the storm's violent noise
        more trembling to my spirit
than the lightning flashes and thunder crashes

        its beauty misted over my soul
        like a delicate blanket of soothing quiet
        until I forgot the pounding, troubled sea
        of the panic churning inside of me

the fresh smell of the dew-drenched grass
and the lilac scented spring breeze
wafted through my straight hair, stirring it softly . . softly

        oh ! that lilac scented breeze !

and the lovely shade of pink-gold
the sleepy-waking Sun brushed on the window sill, and on my arms
tracing little patterns, and streaming across the room
                                in ribbons of light
it was such a heavenly shade
of pink-gold-sunny, just like my druid pin
and tiny glad-tears sprang into my eyes, from the pure beauty and wonder
of my very first dawning, golden Sunrise
                . . . from all that ecstasy
                        of sight and smell and sound

the birdsong sounded like elfin choirs . . and the bells
were ringing the early Mass, from St. Raphael's, around the corner
such a symphony of all the senses !
I felt so strangely complete — all whole — in one piece inside
as if I had died, and gone to Heaven

yes, all whole
in one piece inside
        complete

            I couldn't possibly hold so much gladness
            and still retain a drop of sadness
            the two sensations just wouldn't rhyme
            inside of me, somehow — one simply had to go

    and so . .

I felt the hell of my approaching agony recede
and pale into the distance . . far away
as I watched the pink-gold morning dawn
            of this perfectly marvelous Resurrection Day
bathing me in cool waters of peace, like a green ocean of serenity

                I knew . .

that my big bunny basket, wrapped in yellow cellophane, or pink
making the jelly beans look like jewels
would be waiting outside my bedroom door by now, as a surprise
as always, each year . . jammed with chocolate goodies
marshmallow chicks and candy egglets . . with maybe a special gift
                              tucked inside an egg, like a charm bracelet
        and I knew too

that I would half-pretend I believed the Easter Bunny had been there
still clinging to a faint wisp of childhood magic
knowing the truth, yet reluctant to lose the old dream
that made all holidays seem . . somehow more wondrous, exciting
                              and awesome
we played the game, my parents and I
                    they never got out the dye
for the eggs . . until after I'd gone to bed
then coloring them rainbow-streaked
purple, green, blue . . orange, yellow and red
so my father could hide them all over the house
sometimes on the front porch, in nests of play grass
for me to find, and make believe I didn't know who hid them
            . . like when I was little

my eyes filled, then, with the Easter sights around me in the room
the glory-of-arising-from-the-tomb perfume
            of the purple hyacinth on the dresser

the hyacinth my mother never failed — but once — to place there
                              each year
the night before, so I could wake up and smell it
in the morning, while I was getting dressed
                    to go to church and be blessed . . and
my shiny-black-brand-new-patent-leather shoes
new, white-lacy petticoat . . . panties and anklet socks
the dress my mother had made for me herself, sewing at night for weeks
pale-pink-whispery-silk-organza
smocked in front, with a full, full skirt
and small, embroideried forget-me-nots and violets all over it
            my cream colored straw Easter bonnet
with the long, blue-violet-velvet ribbons hanging down its back
the very same shade of the blue-violet-purple
as my richly scented hyacinth
coaxing me, with its perfumed-bower smell
to pop up from out of my sadness shell
                    into a misty-melting-miracle of joy
        OH BOY !

        OH WOW !

a bright, flashing light burst through my brain
                    it's not too late, it's not too late !

I'll *write* a poem to recite — yes ! I'll *write* an Easter verse myself !

that will make everything allright . . . . oh ! why didn't I think of that
                                                                last night ?
how hard could it be to write a poem ?
didn't I always get S for Superior on everything I wrote in English class ?
I glanced quickly into the looking glass

      "I'll write an Easter poem all by myself"
      I told me — and smiled

of course it has to rhyme — a poem just *has* to rhyme
let's see now, how will I begin . . . how on Earth do I start ?
with pounding heart, and pencil and paper, I sat near the window
looking out at the Sunrise, wrinkling my forehead
                                        and concentrating hard
    how shall I begin ?

      . . . and at that very moment, saw a lone robin
      hip-hopping across the wet grass in the yard
      with a worm in his tiny beak
      then heard him trill a single note of spring

as he dropped the worm
carried away, I guess, by sheer beauty . . like me

    when I heard that teeny-tiny robin trill its single note of spring
    a shower of words sprinkled suddenly in my head
    and I hastily scribbled them down on the lined tablet
                                        I kept beside my bed

  . . . *the Sun rises over the hilltops*

      actually, it was rising over the roof of the grocery store
      at the end of the block, but no matter

. . . *the Sun rises over the hilltops*
the dawn of another day

      day, day — oh ! what word rhymes with "day" ?

. . . *the Sun rises over the hilltops*
the dawn of another day
 so silently the mist drops . . .

      hilltops — mist drops
      OH, BOY ! that rhymes — it really rhymes !

 . . . *the Sun rises over the hilltops*
the dawn of another day
so silently the mist drops

we see the Sun's first ray

> ray rhymes with day ! I shouldn't use Sun twice
> in the same verse — but that's okay
> because it's what I really want to say — so why not ?

> and I wrote on
> scribbling in a fever of growing excitement

. . . but this morn is more glorious than any
for, on this bright day

> is it allright to use day twice, I wonder ?
> oh, and what rhymes with any ? pennny ? Jenny ?

. . . for, on this bright day
JOY ! is in the hearts of many
and like the angels of old, we say

> any — many ! that's it !

. . . and like the angels of old, we say
ALLELUJAH ! to God in the Highest

> in the Highest what ? oh, well — I'll leave it in
> it has a nice, holy sound

ALLELUJAH ! to God in the Highest
ALLELUJAH ! to the lowest of creatures
ALLELUJAH ! to those who sighest

> sighest ? is that a real word ? I never heard it
> never mind . . . it rhymes

I was using poetic license in a perfectly dreadful way, that day
> such awful verse, it was
but how beautiful I believed it sounded at the time
overwhelmed and carried away by the miracle of making rhyme
I read over what I had already written on the pad
feeling so inspired, so bubbling **GLAD !**

> *the Sun rises over the hilltops*
> > *the dawn of another day*
> *so silently the mist drops*
> > *we see the Sun's first ray*
> *but this morn is more glorious than any*
> *for on this bright day — JOY ! is in the hearts of many*
> *and like the angels of old, we say*
> *ALLELUJAH ! to God in the Highest ! ALLELUJAH to the lowest*
> > > > *of creatures*
>
> *ALLELUJAH ! to all those . . .*

Canto Three ☆ 67

I felt uneasy . . was I stealing that line
from the Trinity hymn about "all creatures here below" . . . ?
so I crossed it out, and re-wrote the line

ALLELUJAH ! to God in the Highest
ALLELUJAH ! to the lowest of men
ALLELUJAH ! to all those who sighest
for Jesus shall say unto them

     does *them* rhyme with *men* ?
     well, except for one letter, that's all
     no one will notice — it rhymes nearly
     'm' sounds almost like 'n'

     then I crossed out the line, and wrote instead

. . . for Jesus shall comfort them

     oh, that's much better ! yes, Jesus comforts
     he is like . . a comforter . . cozy sounding word
     I'll leave it in . . it belongs

. . . on that first Easter morning, when Jesus arose
all the Earth was happy and glad
and no beautiful line of poetry or prose . . .

     arose — and prose ! they rhyme too !
     should I work in the word *rose* somewhere there ?
     no, I'll leave it alone — it's perfect

. . . on that first Easter morning, when Jesus arose
all the Earth was happy and glad
and no beautiful line of poetry or prose
should on this day make us sad

     I knew it ! I don't need 'rose'
     glad and sad rhyme just right ! that is, they rhyme
     but . . glad and sad are such different *meaning* words
     I wonder, why should they rhyme ?
                  glad . . . and sad ?

I felt vaguely disturbed
then suddenly, unbidden, vividly and clear
I saw before me an instant image of Pat, my calico cat

I stared at the corner of the room, where she always sat, after breakfast
and remembered the Easter morning I first tied on her red bow
   how she loved it, and pushed a jelly bean
                     around the floor, with her paw
   for a moment

my heart lurched, with a sharp loving-pain . . then I finished hurriedly
scribbling the next words through a film of tears
                              choking back a sob

    . . . *oh, Beautiful One, way up above*
please shine on us today
and let our hearts overflow with love
as we bow our heads to pray

                I had hit a double rhyming jackpot, with *above* and *love*
                and then again, with *today* and *pray*
                yet, somehow, it didn't elate me like the other rhymes
                I had made — or forced — that morning

        the thought of Pat, coming so unexpectedly
        had diluted my exuberance, and some of my delight was dimmed

it was a corny, tipsy-metered poem, strangely scanned
really an awful verse — and there was no time, of course, to rehearse
but I read it in church that morning anyway, loud and clear
so everyone in the very back pews could hear
and later, when people crowded around me outside
saying they just couldn't believe I had really written it myself
I guess I felt a slight tickling of timid pride

        the odd thing is that — today
        I don't recall at all how it felt to stand there
        on that sacred spot, before the Altar
        whether I was nervous with stage fright or not
        or anything I may have sensed or thought . . .
        the scene is completely blanked out in my mind
        and the only thing I remember is how loudly I read
        in a voice which, some girl who was jealous of me cattily said
                        would have awakened the dead
                              for sure

she was a little brat, to say that
my friends told me afterwards, to cheer me up
they didn't know I didn't care if she had acted like a brat
because, you see, I was still thinking about Pat

        the Minister seemed very pleased, then asked me
        if I had shaky knees — and I said, no — my knees never wobbled
        but I just made that up
        like I said, I didn't know whether I wobbled or shook or not
        because I wasn't at all aware, standing up there, of any sensation
        it was as if such nearness to the AL-tar
        had frightened all impressions out of my mind, leaving me blind
        to everything but the necessity of speaking out loud, to reach the crowd
        with the words I thought Jesus wanted me to say that morning

out on the Church steps, before he left
the Minister patted me on the head, and said that I was very bright
	I think he was just being kind and polite — still
they did print my Easter poem on the following Sunday
in the Methodist Church Bulletin . . . every single word
with my name — and age — and grade in school
and I guess I was slightly puffy-proud that I had been allowed
the honor and distinction of actually being published

	yet . . the thought of those two words, glad and sad

glad . . . and *sad*

	they removed the edge of my happy, and even caused some of the glory
	of that perfectly marvelous Sunrise to fade away . . .
	I simply could not stop thinking about Pat, and I wondered

		if the Resurrection really means what they say
		and if Jesus truly arose on that first Easter day
			then why can't *she ?*
		if the story of Jesus conquering death is true

	then why can't Pat rise from the dead too ?

oh, it deeply, deeply troubled me — and what troubled me the most
was that maybe I had written and spoken a lie, in my poem
making people believe something — for nothing
				yes, that troubled me the most
even more than my secret, imagined fear
that I was constantly being spied upon by the Holy Ghost

		for, if people who die — really die — and kittens too
		and the Resurrection can't possibly come true

then Easter is a lie

		and what about dear Dadoo
		who used to allow me to listen to the soothing tick-tock
		of his old fashioned pocket-watch-clock ?
		and Nanoo . . and Peggy . . and
		well, none of them are here anymore — and so
		even if Jesus truly did arise — then what for ?
		if they can't rise too
		then what does it matter whether Easter is true
					or not ?

yes, the Easter gladness brought a haunting sadness
that tortured me for years with its inscrutable mystery . . or deception
I kept thinking, over and over again . . . . if Jesus arose

why can't she ?   *why can't he ?*

        oh ! gladness should not rhyme with sadness

I don't like poetry

A Matter of Pride

it was all really rather amusing
my Easter poem eventually made the home town newspaper
following its duly accepted publication in the First M.E. Bulletin
I believe the paper even carried my picture
but I'm not sure about that — it may be retroactive wishful thinking

of course, you must remember that small town newspapers
do not have a surplus of home-grown celebrities to feature
so they do the best they can with the material on hand
it doesn't take much genius to be News Star of the Week
sometimes, it's the fellow who just broke out of jail
or the chap who batted the most home runs of the season
just about any old reason will give you a claim to fame

so I was favored briefly, on a back page, which was more than I deserved
for my poorly scanned and metered verse
about the questionable gladness of the Resurrection

still, the small flurry of publicity, minor as it actually was
caused the dignified Reverend Waterman, of Trinity
to call on Nana, as soon as he was told — and suggest casually
that I be allowed to sneak back into the fold

dear Nana ! it warmed her Capricorn heart, I'm sure
to be hostess to this Trinity capitulation

as for me, I was spinning in a trauma of sorts
trying to figure out if I was being labeled a Little Lost Lamb
      rescued by the Good Shepherd
or maybe a Black Sheep, being welcomed back
through unspoken publicity blackmail — into the fold again

      but Nana surprised me

she told the Trinity Shepherd
that his Little Lost Lamb — Black Sheep — whichever
was perfectly happy praying in the Methodist pew, thank you
with typical Saturnine grace — coolness and courtesy
and a Capricorn relish for winning the final round

later I heard her sniff . . . "Hmmmmph !
now they want her back, do they ?
well, I didn't see anyone from Trinity
                        rushing over here
to talk her into staying
when they first heard she had left
it serves them right for ignoring our family"

I believe Nana was somewhat miffed because no one at Trinity Episcopal
had seen fit to send out a spiritual posse to lasso me back, initially
and this was her chance to make the elders of the Church eat crow
            . . . she may have had her Moon in Scorpio !

yet, it troubled me perhaps even more than Nana
that no one had tried to contest my desertion from the beginning . . .
what she had said was true, though she had worded it courteously
because my hasty departure and self ex-communication from Trinity
            caused not a ripple in the stream
            not a scratch on the ancient, hard-backed Episcopal shell
            let alone any noticable cracks in the steeple bell

            truthfully, it was sort of like deciding to go straight to hell
            then discovering that no one in Heaven cares — or misses you
            or even notices the absence of the flutter of your wings

I remember eavesdropping from the upstairs landing one night
during a family confab about the sticky religious mess
and overheard my mother state emphatically
in the no-nonsense tone female Bulls use to make a point

            "I don't see why everyone's making such a fuss

                        she switched churches for the simple reason
                        that she gets more attention at the First M.E.
                        and she's not happy
                        unless she's grabbing center stage"

my Taurus mother was a wise woman
who possessed the uncomfortable habit
of painfully hitting the Bull's-eye

            with the truth

Poetry is a Knack for Rhyme and Meter

I seem to have always nurtured a compulsion to rhyme both poetry and Life . . .
once I wrote a Mother's Day verse — I came across it the other day
and in the second verse, I had written

> *my Mother's eyes remind me of spring*
> *and on her finger, she wears a bright, gold ring*
> *OH ! a Mother's hands are a bless — ing*

I actually split the word, then underlined the second syllable in red
carried away by my brilliance in rhyming spring with ring
                 I was determined that no one should miss
my triple poetic jackpot of spring and ring and "ing"
                 so I forced *blessing* into rhyme
after awhile, I learned, more or less
that you can't make poetry by dividing blessing into bless   ing
but I never blessed myself, I guess, with a more important rhyming lesson
and still haven't acquired the knack of understanding
that you can't force Life and people to rhyme — all of the time
only when they blend naturally
           into the same phonetic symphony of sound

<u>April Fool</u>

somewhere betwixt and between the Junior and Senior Scouts
when I had outgrown both the Brownies and the druids
not outgrown them in my heart, just chronologically

        one mysterious April, full of promise
        I became really — not nearly, but *really*

TWELVE YEARS OLD !

the magical clock-strikes-midnight age . . twelve ! ding-dong !
I hummed it for years, like a song
the miracle-Cinderella-clock-strikes-midnight age
next year, I thought at eleven — next year, silk stockings for Sunday
and pink lipstick for parties — **OH, WOW !**
just one more year to wait to be a Full Grown Woman

and so . . I waited for the magic of twelve
I waited for the miracle of twelve

              I waited . . . .
            and waited

          for the magic
   . . . . for the miracle

but the clock-strikes-midnight age brought no magic, and no miracle
I was still not a woman, in any secret way I could tell, inside
nor in any outward way the boys could tell

the secret way within was what everyone called the curse
and some of the girls in my Tarzan gang were cursed as early
                                              as eleven
the outward way, that boys could tell
was an absolute, positive *must* — the miracle
                              of a visible bust

but the mysterious, midnight age of twelve
brought me no such luck — not even a trace, to save face
though I waited . . and waited . . and waited

there I was, that mysterious spring . . waiting for nothing
treacherous April, leading me nowhere all year
not even . . the year after
except down the same, well-worn paths of childhood

        no magic
          no miracle

the clock-strikes-midnight age of twelve . . . ding-dong !
brought me no secret Lunar curse — or outward blessing
no pride of possessing the *must* of a visible bust

        twelve . . ding-dong !

the poems and books and songs are all wrong, I used to cry
I might as well die — twelve is a lie
      twelve is a big-fat-zero-nothing flop

        I wasn't sure I even wanted to try

            for thirteen

Merit Badges and Demerits

if I were a daisy or a rose — or some kind of flower
you would say I was a late bloomer
so late, I had to resort, at Scout camp, when I was twelve-and-a-half

        . . to stuffing socks under my sweaters

our camp had such a romantic Indian name — *Kiashuta*
and there was this time, when the Boy Scouts who camped near there
were invited to spend the day at *Kiashuta*, playing organized games
and teaching the weaker sex their older scout magic tricks
like tying square knots in ropes . . and building fires
                            by rubbing together two sticks

of course, their grown men counselors came along with them
which I suppose is why our lady counselors
were even more excited about the approaching activities than we were
and, oh ! were *we* ever excited !

on this particular evening, at sunset, we were all gathered
on the bank of the Kiashuta River
singing this wistful song, and sailing our wish boats
with lighted candles in them . . down the river

naturally, the boys were there with us
and some of the lady counselors were secretly holding hands
with the grown men counselors
thinking we wouldn't notice — but we did
or that we couldn't see — but we could

> then, when we got to the verse
> with the words . . .

> *. . on down the river*
> *a hundred miles or more*
> *other little children*
> *will bring my boats ashore . .*

I leaned over to look out across the water
to make sure my wish boat hadn't sunk — that it was sailing onward
toward those perfectly mavelous far-away lands

> but I leaned over too far in my V-neck sweater

> and my crumpled-up socks fell out

in front of everyone

> in front of all those boys

oh ! pure and pounding panic . . panic-panic-panic
mortification to the end all mortification
> *in front of all those boys*

> that night, I ran away . . . into the woods
> and when they checked my tent
> they got all silly-fussy worried, like grown ups do
> and called in the Sheriff from a neighboring town
> then they all came tramping through the trees
> > with flashlights

                    they found me of course
                    someone always does . .

sound asleep, under a gnarled oak tree, growing all by itself
in the middle of a dense clump of dark green fir

I was lying on a sweet-scented blanket of spruce and pine needles
lovely, soft moss . . and fern
when I was jarred into consciousness by bright lights flashing in my eyes

                    "here she is ! over here !
                    we found her ! she's over here
                                        under this tree !
                    can you see ?
                    here, I'll shine the light . . "

        unspeakably frightened
at being so violently awakened by the white glare
and the noise . . and strange voices
my heart thumping in sudden alarm and fear
I knew, then, how the animals in the woods must feel
each year — in season

                    when the hunters
                    bear down on them

            the rabbits
                                    quail
            the gentle deer

yes, I knew exactly
how they must feel — the hunted

                    their terror
                    and sudden fear

        the rabbits

    quail

        the gentle deer

WE'VE GOT ONE !

        SHINE YOUR LIGHT OVER HERE !

WE'VE CAUGHT ONE !

            HERE IT IS !

OVER HERE !

my terror that night, I suppose, was partially due to my genuine surprise
at being hunted down — because, you see, I hadn't expected anyone
to come searching for me . . until morning
I had left my tent after everyone was asleep, stealthily, on tip toe
with no best friend to tell — I had no best friend
and I didn't go very far into the woods — it was dark, and I was afraid
thinking only that I could lie there, and rest my eyes for awhile

> that's all . .
> just rest my eyes

and by sunrise, when they had discovered my disappearance
I would walk deeper into the woods, I thought
where no one could possibly find me — and live on berries, until . .

> . . actually, I hadn't planned that far ahead
> I only wished that I were dead
> no detailed plan of action . .

just the tearing hurt, the loss of poise
over the gales of laughter from the boys . . . on the river bank
and their snickers, later, when they were loading into the buses, to leave

> just the pain and shame reaction
> no detailed plan of action

I would live on berries, until . .

and so, not expecting to be missed, or searched for until daybreak
lying there asleep on the moss covered ground
then so suddenly awakened, by the unfamiliar sound
> of shouting voices, loud and unreal

I knew . . yes
I knew the terror and shock the hunted must feel
the ones who rest their eyes . . in the wilder wood

I understood

and all my life, since that night, I have never forgotten
nor will my heart ever be seasoned to the "sport" of hunting

> that summer, I lost all my hard earned merit badge credits
> because I had left my tent without permission
> it hadn't occured to me that a Brown Owl needed to ask permission
> but then, it also hadn't occured to me
> that no one knew I was a Brown Owl — besides myself
> it was my own private identification

                              and I had no way of proving it
                              to the-world-at-large

the thing I still recall most vividly about that warm July night
is how slowly the hours passed, in the forest
waiting for the druids to come out and tell me how silly I was
for wanting to die over a pair of dumb socks
for hours and hours I waited, while the night was cautiously crawling
into a so-far uncommitted dawn

                    I waited the longest, longest time
                    but they never came . .

I remember how sweet-clean and fresh, how deep-deep-green-cool
the woods smelled . . with the moss, so velvety soft
as I chewed on a pine needle, to make it Christmas . . then pretended
I was an Indian Princess
waiting under the pale, New Moon for her strong, handsome Brave

                    her tall, brown lover

          lover . .

then I thought about that word for awhile . . lover
and tried to decide what it meant . .
I didn't believe it could possibly mean what some of the Senior Scouts
were whispering and giggling about one night, after Taps
which was entirely too silly to be true
                         . . or could it be ?

no, that was just simply, positively ridiculous
          they had used funny sounding words to describe
          what a lover is — and does
and I thought they were fooling me, with some sort of gibberish talk
                                        like pig latin
     dumb words
          dumb talk
     dumb girls
        and dumber boys

                              lover . .
                    . . lover

     it rhymed with cover

I finally decided, as I fell asleep on the pine and spruce needles
and moss . . that lover had something to do with the Bible verse that says

                    thy Comforter shall come

because, when I was five or six or so

I'd been asked one morning in nursery Sunday school
to repeat the verse we'd studied about . . "fear not . . thy Comforter
                                                    shall come"
and I hadn't been paying close attention to the lesson
so, recalling the cozy-warm comforter Nana always tucked under my chin
on frosty winter nights, on 8th Street, I squeaked nervously

      "Jesus said to the man . .
      don't worry, you'll get your blanket"

it was the source of family hilarity for years . . .
like the time I was singing out loud, at the top of my lungs
in Trinity Episcopal Church, one boring Sunday morning, in the summer
somewhere between the ages of four and five
the line from the old Trinity hymn, *Onward, Christian Soldiers*

      "Christ, our royal master
           leads against the foe"

and I bellowed out my own understanding of the words
since I had first heard them sung

      "Christ, our royal master
           leans against the phone"
   more hilarity

in one way or another, I kept everyone supplied with chuckles
for a number of years — and I suppose, more or less, I still do today
   the habit of permitting ridicule — and pretending you don't mind it
            isn't easy to break
   I guess it's allright
   if the people who are laughing
   really-truly love you

        some did . . some didn't

but anyway, even today, I still believe "thy Comforter shall come"
has a nice, snuggly-warm, grandma quilt sound

    with or without a lover

    that's incidental

And He Gave Me a Rose

I duly went to Anna K. Neal's ballroom dancing school — and I say 'duly'
because truly . . . . everyone who was anyone at all
went to dancing school all year long, in my home town

if you didn't go to dancing school, you were considered a fool
at birthday parties, where people laughed at you
and treated you like a circus clown, if you were a boy
or the crazy lady in the side show, if you were a girl

both sexes usually started as young as eight or nine
and continued till they were around twelve or thirteen
by then, the boys had started to feel silly, and dropped out
and the girls were not far behind — because
the girls followed the boys
not just on the dance floor, but everywhere else

after that, the chase took place, with little change
at basketball and football games, instead of at dancing school

but while it lasted, dancing school was a weekly Cinderella ball !
especially when you got to dance with a boy who was tall
or taller than yourself, at least
who did not step on your feet, and whose clothes were neat

I was floating somewhere between a wish and a dream
and had been there only a year or so . . when a miracle happened
the third miracle I ever knew
the rainbow was the first . . and the blue and silver rosary
                                                made two
I secretly admired a boy named Jerry Jones
first cousin to a friend of mine, named Betty Jones
      and one afternoon
he closed his warm, strong hand
over my own trembling hand, in its white cotton glove
and we danced together . . and fell in love

      only . .

well, I didn't have the slightest idea, at first
that it was love I felt for Jerry — no, not in the beginning
and I can't speak for him, of course, at all
I simply knew that he was tall — at least two inches, maybe three
taller than me — I mean, than I
he was terribly neat, and he never stepped on my feet
and his hair . . . his hair was exactly the color of wheat
the way he brushed it made it sparkle with gold
      and he was mysteriously old
at least six months older than me — I mean, than I

he was a little shy, but so quiet and gentle
not unpredictably temperamental, like most boys — who rhyme
                                                with noise

once he even told me, kind of bashfully
that I had pretty hair
although it was poker-straight and baby-fine, not thick at all
and dreary, mouse-colored too
but afterwards . . after he said that . . I liked it better
and I brushed it more at night

                    he had the strangest
                    ocean-green-silvery-wise eyes

and he was going to be a real doctor someday, he used to say
he wanted to learn how to heal — and his very best subject was biology
one Saturday afternoon, he was late to dancing class
because, somewhere along the way, he'd found a baby bird
who was trying to learn how to fly, and had fallen from the nest

he did his best — he really tried to make it live
but it died, right there in his hands — and his eyes were red, he said
because he'd cried so hard when it died
but he made me promise, druid honor, not to tell a single person
                                        that he had wept

oh ! as if I ever would !
as if I would ever tell anyone a secret of his
not a special, inside-secret like that
I mean, there are some things you can say and tell
but there are other things you know very well
you must not ever — no, never, never-ever tell anyone
very secret, very special, shared-kind-of-things

                    he was so gentle and kind, Jerry Jones
                    so calm — so polite

and he always behaved, somehow, just right
    he never talked back to the dancing teacher, smart-alecky
like most all of the other boys did
    and he never tossed spit balls around
or stuck chewing gum on chairs, where the girls sat down
    he positively never acted like a silly clown
and yet . . well, sometimes he could be as crazy as a daisy

                    like me

we always used to do these crazy-daisy things together . . like
oh, like trying to make it snow, by just wishing it so, you know ?

he bowed very low — and spoke very low too . . and clear
when he asked me for a dance
maybe I didn't know what to call it back then

Canto Three ☆ 81

but it was surely a genuine story book romance !

     yes, his voice was low and clear
     and one day, he bought me a ten cent root beer
     he had an orange juice, I remember — he said it was healthier
     and better for you . . . because it had no sugar
     he was always saying things like that

it was in a little store across the street from dancing school
next door to a funeral parlor
I was nervous about that place, but when Jerry saw my face
looking all sad and scared, he made me laugh

             "we should say a Halloween Witch prayer
             to that spooky goblin Holy Ghost over there"
             he said, nodding toward the funeral home

so we both giggled, then
and sprinkled each other's heads with the root beer and orange juice
as we whispered, dramatically . . "I baptize thee — eternally"

        first, me-to-him
        then, him-to-me

and I had this strange thought that we were taking — or making
a kind of private Holy Communion — or a Forever vow

unlike the other pesky boys, who thought they were so smart
Jerry never broke my heart
by making fun of me for things I couldn't help
he never teased, or even snickered when I sneezed
one of those wet-spraying sneezes
he just said "Geshundeit" — or God bless you
only he pronounced it "Geshoonlight" . . . but I never laughed
I didn't know how to pronounce it either
then he always gave me his big, white handkerchief to use
                    that smelled of him

sometimes, Jerry Jones would just stare and stare
at my hair . . or into my eyes
and I would feel funny, and look away
except for this one particular day . .

     we were sitting near a window, waiting for the others
     because we had both arrived early for dancing class — and
     the Sun was shining through the glass
     on his hair . . making a kind of rainbow glow all around it
     a sort of misty light, the same shape as his head
     and I laughed, and said

"you look like someone out of the Bible"

    but . . he didn't laugh back like I thought he would
    he just stared and stared — and I did too . . . . for the longest time
    until suddenly, I felt frightened
    and got up . . and went to the cooler to get a drink of water
    wondering why there were tears stinging my eyes

one autumn afternoon, we were all told to dress in our very best clothes
for a formal dance the very next Saturday coming up
and when Saturday finally arrived, after waiting about a hundred years
I wore my shiny, patent leather Sunday Mary Janes
and a pink tafetta dress my father insisted that my mother buy
when he heard me sigh . . that I owned nothing special enough to wear

the dress made a whispery-rustling sound when I moved
and I was allowed one splash of cologne
not only that, I was also allowed this time — to go there alone
without a parent for a chaperone — **OH, PURE JOY !**

      every boy . .

had already been told, the week before, to bring flowers
and to give them to the girl he chose as a partner for the first dance

well, my tafetta dress had this *awful* orange velvet flower
artificial — near the sash that tied around my waist
                            . . such terrible taste !
and so, as soon as I was out of my parents' sight
walking down the street, I ripped off that ugly orange flower
and threw it away . . . but it left a big hole in my dress
                   . . . . I prayed it wouldn't show
                     I mean, I *really* prayed !
when the music started . .
first records, then the piano lady — they took turns
I didn't see Jerry anywhere, and I was sure he wasn't there

                oh, black day !
so I began to fiddle with my hair
making it look worse, instead of better
and trying to cover the hole in front of my dress with my sash

        then . . I saw him

he was walking straight toward me . . and I thought my knees
would crumple into tissue paper
                when he stopped
in front of me, and smiled
that's all . . just smiled
then bowed low, and handed me

a single red rose

I buried my nose deep down into the petals of that rose
and wiggled my toes . . in pure, purring-kitten-delight

    then I saw that same strange light
    around his hair . . as he was standing there
    while the Sun streamed through the window behind him
    seeming to form a golden halo over his head
                as he very quietly said

        "I would like to have the first dance
        and all the rest — with you
        you know, your eyes are so blue
        I just . . well, I've been wanting
                to tell you that
        for the longest time
        and I really mean it — honest, I do"

    and then I knew

I knew I loved him

    but I also knew I could never-ever tell anyone how much
    that it must always be a sacred secret between myself and me
    but I wondered if maybe he loved me too
    and was keeping it a sacred secret between himself and him

        which would make it a secret shared

           between

            us

Be Still

when he was there at dancing school on Saturdays, I never felt alone
because Jerry Jones was not like any boy I had ever known
and I used to wonder what he would be like — when he was grown
I wondered and wondered about that, because . .

I guess because there was a kind of knowing-thing about him — yes
a knowing-thing that was, somehow, more than just a growing thing
he was so truly different from any boy I'd known before
in my whole, entire life
I knew him — and loved him — for not quite two years
and I wanted so — *oh, I wanted so !*
                to watch him grow

that I shouted one day

I HATE YOU, GOD ! I HATE YOU !

that was the Saturday afternoon I went to dancing class
and Jerry wasn't there to smile at me — to make my knees
go tissue paper weak, by just barely touching my cheek
                              with his . . when we danced

he had been sick all week, for seven days
with some mysterious illness . . I couldn't find out
what it was — and I really didn't care
all I knew was that Jerry wasn't there . . . that afternoon

and I knew too, that God was not true
oh, I knew that God was a lie !
because, when I asked my dancing teacher why

        . . why Jerry wasn't there

    she said

        SHE SAID . . in a voice as flat as an iron

                              she said

    "Jerry is dead"

                    "Jerry is dead," she said, she said
                    he died this morning, in his sleep . . .
                    we are all going to call at the funeral home
                    tomorrow . . together
                    it's the one across the street
                    and now, we will all say the Lord's prayer
                                              for Jerry"

            just across the street . . next door to the place
            where he bought me the root beer
                        that Holy Communion day ?

AND THEY EXPECTED ME TO PRAY

TO A DUMB GOD LIKE THAT ?

while they were all praying for Jerry's soul, I gritted my teeth
and hummed aloud to myself — then the teacher glared at me

        AND I GLARED RIGHT BACK AT HER

the next afternoon, everyone in dancing class filed into the funeral parlor
like stealthy Indians
                        one-by-one   on tip-toe

we were each told, as we entered, to remain . . by the remains
that's what they called Jerry, I **swear !**

    we were told . . . to remain by the remains
    only half a minute, no more
    so we wouldn't disturb the family

in that allotted thirty seconds, I did not gaze on Jerry's face
against the white quilted satin in the casket
                        or upon his hands, folded, praying
or even listen to what he might be saying
                        maybe whispering to me
I was too busy whispering to myself, over and over and over

    "I hate You, God — and I hate the Holy Trinity too
    even more than I hate You
        I hate every single one of the Heavenly Host
    and I *especially* hate the Holy Ghost"

suddenly, I was frightened — and sorry for what I had said
and I opened my eyes, to once more gaze . . upon the silent dead
but before I could really see his face
or memorize his features for the very last time — or listen for his voice
maybe whispering to me . . a final secret between us

                        I sobbed aloud

then someone grabbed my shoulder
pinching it so hard, it hurt — and hiSSed
                        like a Serpent
                                in my ear

        "be still, be still
                    do you hear ?"
        be still !"

I felt an icy chill . . kill all tenderness in my heart
as the unseen hands belonging to the hiSSing voice
pushed me firmly away from Jerry's face
and when the girl behind me took my place, I wanted to scream

    "oh, **PLEASE !** let me see him
    for just one minute more — oh, **PLEASE !"**

but I ran out the door, instead
I ran out of that murmuring mortuary for the dead

and as I ran, I reached forth blindly
                    to grab a rose from a wreath

                        one rose

then I did a very bad, insane thing — I bit the rose hard, with my teeth
spitting out the petals right there on the street
and knew, at last, that I was going to cry, because I did not know why
I had done such a terrible, terrible thing

        . . . after awhile, I picked up the spat-out petals
            and wrapped them in his big, white handkerchief
                            that still smelled of him
one I had kept . .
after I sneezed in it one day

                    and I walked away

Spendthrift

each year, when I visited Aunt Maud, my parents sent me an allowance
from two to five dollars a week
depending on my age, during any particular summer vacation

I could count on receiving it each Friday, to spend as I liked
which they, in turn, could count on my doing without fail
usually within a few hours of the time it arrived in the morning mail

I spent it on things like souvenirs from the dime store
stamped in gold with the names of the Town and State
a giant Barometer, a Key to the City — or a miniature Capitol Dome
sometimes, Three Monkeys — seeing, hearing and speaking no evil
to take my friends when I went back home

I also spent it on Eskimo Pies, occasionally a fresh peach or pear
and when I was younger, for chances on the dart board at the grocery store
to win a doll with real hair — or a terrific, red and blue bike
the doll was breathtakingly beautiful
but by the time I was thirteen and fourteen — and past
I was really too old for dolls
after all, I went to ballroom dancing school . . that is, I did for awhile
        I never went back again
                after that Saturday Jerry Jones . . died

so, if I had been lucky enough to win, I would have chosen the bike

it would have given me such glorious independence
riding it all around town, as free as a bird, with the wind blowing my hair

my relatives said I was sinfully extravagant
a real spendthrift, they called me — to get rid of my allowance so fast
they told me I should try to save some each week, to make it last

                    maybe they were right

for, one day, I made a big mistake — and after that
I never had a penny to spend for anything, which caused me some grief
since I had to do silly, lonesome things
like pretend I was eating an Eskimo Pie, when I was only chewing
                                        a lettuce leaf

my big mistake took place the summer I was thirteen-and-a-half
though it left its mark on my vacation there for the following
                                        several years
and by the time I was between fourteen and fifteen
I knew the scar would be permanent, even though it might be invisible
                    to everyone but me

but that thirteenth summer . . . . yes

it happened one Leonine August morning
a beautiful day, all sky-blue-sunny, with warm breezes
and fluffy white clouds . . not a hint of tragedy in the air

there was this neighborhood boy, whose claim to fame
was that he could do such a perfectly marvelous imitation
          of Donald Duck
if you closed your eyes, you really believed you were at the movies
watching a cartoon — he was that good, honest he was

      well, anyway, on this beautiful, sky-blue-sunny August morning
      this boy accidently stepped on an ant hill, in the backyard
      and squashed the juice out of all the ants
                    some of them were only . . half dead

          and they just lay there
                    squirming in pain and terror

oh ! I had seen it, I had seen it with my very own eyes !
as one-by-one-by-one, the squirming ants expired
      I learned, first-hand, of the agony of an ant, when it dies

              for I had been witness
              to cold blooded murder

when he saw the look of horror on my face, the boy laughed
and the more he laughed, the harder and louder I cried

I yelled and I screamed and I wailed — and I made such a fuss
that my aunt came running up from out of the basement
where she had been wringing clothes through the washer

but, when she observed the cause of my storm of anguish
even my gentle, compassionate Aunt Maud
thought I was agonizing all out of proportion to the crime
not comprehending, I guess, the dreadful dilemma
            of my struggle to make Life and Death rhyme

nor do Death and Laughter rhyme
any more than Glad rhymes with Sad

                "after all," she said, "these are only ants"

she spoke quietly, softly
as she tried to make me see

                "if some human had been hurt or killed
                it would be cause for sorrow — but ants ?
                really, child — here, take my hanky
                you are making much ado about nothing
                                    are you not ?"
then, to the grinning, blushing, ducking boy
she turned and said — with one hand placed tenderly on my head
and the other shaking a warning finger of admonition at him

                "she's too soft hearted for her own good
                but stop clowning around, do you hear ?"
                or you may not come back to play
                ever again — is that clear ?"

        he promised earnestly
        to behave himself in the future

but no sooner did Aunt Maud disappear
to finish the laundry, back down in the basement
than he threatened to do it again
to kill more ants — for the sheer fun of hearing me scream

so I offered him a quarter, a shiny, new quarter
if he would swear to leave the ants alone
        money — to him — was always a large concern
because you have to watch Donald Duck cartoons ever-so-often
at the movies . . if you expect to imitate the quack as cleverly as he
therefore, knowing this very well
I was fairly certain the money would tempt him

                it did

and from that day forward, it was down-hill-sledding all the way

for the neighborhood boys, who rhymed with noise
when they needed their allowance padded with extra cash each week

for some reason, Donald Duck never did it again
which was honorable and kind of him, more or less, I guess

still I always wanted to rhyme his first name of Fred — with dead
as funny and friendly and nice as he was, even though I liked him lots
and was grateful when he let me ride his bike, because I said "please"
and didn't laugh when I fell off and skinned both my knees
even so . . . I couldn't help rhyming Fred with dead
because, although Donald Duck remained true-blue to his promise
the neighborhood grapevine soon started swinging
as the news leaked up and down each street and back alley

the other boys soon found — that, when I came around
                              they had it made-in-the-shade
they knew all they had to do, to earn a quarter or two
was to threaten to kill ants in front of me
then I would cross their palms with silver — sometimes
                                   even with green paper
they worked out among themselves
a complicated cost-accounting system, based on the law
of supply and demand — and, of course, the ants on hand
as all things are priced for barter, in every marketplace

        the death of one ant — was worth a dime
        two ants, or more were worth a quarter
        to save them from death, that is

        an ant hill brought a whole dollar
        and pulling the wings from flies — oh ! to stop that
        was worth, they soon discovered
                        a dollar and fifty cents

then one kid of great ingenuity, a real mental giant of originality

                . . . I'm sure he later became a General in the Army
                or a big Corporate Executive
                some kind of a Billionaire — or maybe
                an important World or Community Leader . . .

this boy . . like a walking Think Tank . . used his brains
and thought up a new strategy, that made him immensely wealthy
                            for his age
while it threw me into a periodic hysterical rage
besides draining me of every penny I owned — every single summer
as I grew, not smarter and smarter
but more and more sensitive — and therefore, dumber and dumber

he built a Fort of matchsticks — the kind they call Kitchen Matches

that come in a big box — and he stocked his Fort with dozens of ants
then, while they were all frantically trying to escape
he reached into the pocket of his overall pants, for the final, fearsome match
to set the Fort afire, in a blaze — and I watched, in a daze
as the teeny-tiny, helpless, squirming ants

                              were burned
                                        to a crisp

   OH !
       Oh !
          oh !

my torment that day, as I tried to pray, must have been delicious
                                        to observe
I remember one small boy
rolling over and over in the grass, clutching his stomach
he was laughing so hard — and even . . . . even the girls laughed

then I began hitting, striking out blindly with clenched fists
but they all ran away, shouting their taunts from a distance
hiding where I couldn't find them, or see them — just hear them
so I sat down at the foot of the apple tree, pounding the trunk
in an agony of angry frustration — and bruised my hand badly

that night, I didn't eat any supper at all
though they had iced tea and sliced, red-ripe tomatoes
from the garden . . and fresh leaf lettuce
     corn-on-the-cob, with the country butter I loved
vanilla ice cream, with Aunt Maud's home-canned peaches
she kept in the basement, in the dark, on a shelf
and my very all-time-favorite toasty-warm biscuits
                              I called hot cross buns

     but I wasn't hungry

after that, the charge for building a matchstick Fort
stocking it with ants — and *not* setting it ablaze was a flat
                                        two dollars
     I paid it

and there went my birthday money from Nana, each spring
twenty dollars, every April, to take with me on my summer vacation
and spend only for something really-truly special
some marvelous, magical kind of thing — once a genuine
                              gold plated charm bracelet

which some bully who lived in the alley took from me one day
but I told everyone I lost it — and they scolded, "careless child"

     because, to be known as a tattle tale
     tattle-tale-stick-your-head-in-a-wormy-pail
     was a social catastrophe

and no one would ever have played with me again

one cannot have a thin skin, and win — at the game of childhood
that sweet, innocent time of roughness and toughness
adults tend to see only through rosy-posey colored glasses

since the Donald Duck episode occured when I was about thirteen — two years after
I started in dancing school . . continuing throughout the next
                                    three or four years
every summer, the twenty dollars from Nana trickled away
like my weekly allowance from my parents
two and three dollars at a time . . . .
after that first August
no one bothered with Single Murders anymore
they had graduated into the world of Big Business

it was kind of a team effort — they pooled their energies
                                    and split the profits
naturally, I never told — only sissies do that
and I am a Ram — no sissy

it took hours and hours to catch the ants
plus a great deal of patience to properly build the escape-proof Forts
and they took some pride in that . . it became
            quite a competitive thing, whose Fort was biggest and best

but the endeavor was not without bottlenecks
like, they spent lots of time chasing away this red-headed pest
a small boy, freckle-faced
who kept drowning the ants with his grape pop
just when they had collected enough so they could stop for the day
                        he was too young, you see
to have enough sense to threaten to drown them in front of me
                                    for money

which is just as well, I suppose — because, goodness only knows
what might have happened to him
if he had gone into the ant drowning business for personal profit
competing against the Fiery Forts of the already organized

            Ant Murders, Incorporated

he was too little to protect himself against the certain retaliation . . . .
most likely, he grew up to be a poet — or some other useless thing
being, obviously, no business man

I guess the older boys figured all the trouble was worth it
although it was surely not worth it to me — financially
I never got to see any movies
except on those rare occasions when Donald Duck treated me
to a double cartoon, Saturday matinee

I suppose he thought it was the least he could do
being the original cause of my poverty
which was, in a way, kind of sweet — but nevertheless
my Nana birthday money and parental allowance
were both eternally in the red, as I bled
                                   for the ants

          saving ants — or people — from a fiery furnace
          can be a decidedly prohibitive expense
          whether in a small town in Virginia — or in Germany
          so the Catholic Church has claimed . . . and who am I
          . . to deny the cost ?

I remember how all the mothers in the neighborhood would complain
"well, I just can't understand where all these matches have gone
already the box is half empty, and I only bought it last week"

then they would claim that the grocer — or the match company
                         was trying to cheat them
and threaten to boycott him if he didn't do something about it

I felt bad about that — I mean, the grocer having to take the blame
for my out of proportion sensitivity . . .
he was Italian, and I believe his last name — yes, his last name
was Benveneuto — and he was always very kind

but I didn't dare tell my aunt, for the very good reason
that, even if she didn't spread it around that I was a tattle tale
she might have snitched to my parents
and I would have been punished by having my allowance cut off
with no way to stop Ant Murders, Incorporated anymore
and I used to wonder — if I were ever caught and punished
                                   what would I be punished for ?
for stupidity and extravagance ?
or for over-sensitivity . . which one ?

I thought about telling Dado, who rhymed with **OH !**
but I wasn't quite sure what his reaction might be
Dado was a very strange man . . . he even wrote poetry secretly
and never told anyone in the family but me
one day, he read me one of his short poems, about a rock and a tree

but Dado, you see, had bright, ice-blue-sapphire eyes
that sometimes twinkled, in fun . . and at other times
shot out flames of ice-blue-sapphire anger
and he had very large, floppy ears, that wiggled when he laughed
but turned fiery red when he was mad

     I didn't want his big, floppy ears to turn red

in anger — only wiggle in fun
and I didn't want those ice-blue-sapphire eyes to spark flames
                                        in my direction
so I didn't tell . . and also, well . . the truth is
I was more than a little afraid of what he might do to the boys
if he chose to be on my side, against them
for I'd always been told that Dado had
                        a terrible, terrible temper
when he was aroused enough
to be really fighting, fiery angry

I wondered a lot whether he would have said to me
that Yellow Wax was bad — or good
if I had ever gotten up enough courage to tell him about the ants
and, even though I knew that he considered wasting money foolishly
to be a Great and Evil Damnation of the Soul
                        . . even though I knew all that
still, there was a secret part of Dado
I felt I understood
so I made it up to believe that he really-truly would
                        have said that Yellow Wax was good
instead of bad . . . and that he wouldn't have been mad

        that's what I pretended anyway

A Song Without Words

my expensive experience with Ant Murders, Incorporated
taught me some valuable lessons

        I learned that sometimes . .

you can stop people from hurting
by giving them money

        and during those traumatic years
        when I was buying, with cash and tears
        the right of ants not to be burned

I also learned

        that there are some people who do not like to hurt
        and even if you offer them money — they will never take it

there was this boy . . one summer
when I had jumped from twelve to nearly fourteen overnight

          . . although the ant killers still bullied me
          not even noticing that I wasn't a little kid anymore

there was this one boy, whose name was Charles
I believe it was . . Charles Hollingswell . . . or something like that
and he wore the funniest thing on his head
          he called his old hiking hat . . because he liked to hike in the woods

one summer when I was visiting Aunt Maud
          one bee-buzzing-lazy-daisy-crazy afternoon
we were fooling around, racing each other to the Moon
which was actually the apple tree — and back again, to the rabbit pen
and he accidently tripped — then slipped
                         and fell smack on the top of an ant hill
                         squashing the juice from hundreds
                              of baby ants

I tried hard not to cry — because, well, I guess I kind of liked him
and I thought I would die, if he should happen to laugh
after all, I wasn't a baby of ten or eleven — I was too old to cry
almost a woman . . nearly fourteen . . almost

so I squeezed back the tears, on account of my fears of his ridicule
and asked him, in what I hoped was a dignified way
if he would promise never to do it again — on purpose, that is
if I gave him five whole dollars

          I said five dollars
          instead of the established price of three
          that current summer
          because . . well, like I said
                         he was sort of special to me

immediately, it became suddenly quiet between us
he was sitting in the grass, where he had fallen . . and I was
so close to him . . . I could see a tiny lady bug, walking on his chin

          but he didn't make it go away
          he just let it stay

it was so quiet . . and he was so close . . and the only sound
was a buzzing bee, in the grass
then I realized my hair was a mess, all sweaty and stringy and tangled
from racing and running and funning around
so I added, right after the five dollar offer, the silliest thing

          I said

"oh, gosh, my hair . . . my hair looks like a witch's head
like that witch called Medusal
with snakes all twisting and curling . . I'll bet

well, I'll bet it looks just awful"

I'd read about the witch in Dadoo's books, on 8th Street
but I was never sure how to pronounce her name
so I called her Medusal
just the same, oh ! why didn't I stop
after I offered him the money ? that was silly enough
without mentioning my tangled hair, and all that dumb witch stuff
oh, *why* did I say that about my hair ?

    I remember . . his stare
    he looked at me so strangely, then — with sea-green eyes
    kind of like the ocean, yes . . vibrant, somehow
    like the ocean in the sunlight, I thought
        though I had never seen the ocean

eyes that seemed so deep and wise, for a boy his age and size
then he took off his old hiking hat . . . . he had bright, blond hair

    and he . . continued to stare and stare
    the Sun was behind him, making a pale golden light
    around his head . . like that other one . . like
    the rainbow reflection at dancing school
        around Jerry's hair

it was so quiet, so very still . . . the stillness was everywhere
and he was so near . . and that buzzing bee sounded so far away
like the only sound anywhere at all . . like the world
        was silently spinning around
without a single sound . . except that bee
and I kept looking at the tiny lady bug on his chin
        as he stared at me
he just kept on staring
until I nervously twisted my bare toes, in the grass
oh ! I remember twisting my toes . . yes, I remember that too

        and finally, he said

        "no — I won't take money from you"

        then he said . . . "but I promise anyway
        never to step on ants, or fall on them again
        like I did just now — at least, I promise
        never to do it on purpose"

        then, unexpectedly, he commanded
        "stop twisting your toes"

    and I stopped
    twisting them
    suddenly

then, after a long moment, he said, kind of low

>he said . . "don't you know
>it doesn't matter how you look ?
>I think your hair . . well, I think
>it always looks great . . . hey, wait !"

and do you know what he did ?

while his words . . . "*it doesn't matter how you look*"
floated within me, somewhere near my breast
he ran over to the flower bed, and looked around
and didn't find what he was looking for, I guess . . because then
he went over behind the rabbit pen
>leaned over to pick up something . . and brought it back
>>and handed it to me

>it was . . a daisy

small and skinny, and kind of wilted, but . . a daisy
and he blushed from a bright pink to a rosy red
>>as he said

>"this is for you, because I think
>you're crazy — like a daisy"

but when he saw my eyes
mist over with sudden hurt

>he said . . "please don't start to cry
>don't you know why I gave you the flower ?
>I thought . . . you would guess why
>it's because . . well, because
>we're *both* crazy like a daisy ! see ?"

>I saw . .

and I kept that daisy for years and years
pressed, for some reason, between the pages of my Bible

>and . . he said something else

>he said . . "that witch — her name is Medusa"

he pronounced it exactly right
the way Dadoo had, and my teacher

>" . . . her name is Medusa . . and
>you don't look like her at all"

I remember . . . oh !

my heart, then
flip-flopped, like a rabbit

not so much because of the awkward compliment, though it pleased me
but because he knew ! he had read about her too !
and I never thought anyone else cared about old books
and things like that
the same as I did

at least, I had never met any kids
who knew about Medusal — but *he knew*

and then too, there was his firm refusal
to take the money I had offered him
and promising not to hurt ants anyway
. . all those things
and of course . .
the being crazy-like-a-daisy, saying that he was crazy too, like me
made me feel all happy and suddenly free !
and light . . and bright . . and somehow, just right
not dumb and silly, like I usually felt

and there was this one other thing
about him — the song
a sort of . . song

everytime I thought of Jerry Jones, I remembered how I used to hear
. . . this song
with no words — just music
inside myself, whenever Jerry smiled at me
or when he simply said hello

and the funny thing is, that I know
it was never a song, or any piece of music
they ever played at dancing school
it was different from any of those
almost like I had made it up . . in my head, you know ?

or . . like I had heard it . . oh ! lots and lots of times before
but I couldn't remember exactly where . . or when
and when I tried to hum the melody aloud
it would always go away

well, that day — with this boy

when Charles took off his hiking hat, the sound of that very same song
was humming in my ears . . while the bee was buzzing in the grass
and after that, every time I talked with him
or when he grinned at me
I could hear that music

well, to be honest, I didn't really hear it . . I just remembered it again
sort of, inside my head — and it almost
                              made me feel . . like Jerry wasn't dead
            . . sometimes

it made me wonder, all over again, where I had first heard that music
and what were the words ?   I kept trying to hum it
so I could ask people, "what's the name of the song ?" . . but
            I could never remember it that long

            I mean, this boy didn't look like Jerry
            not at all — except for the wheat colored hair
            and the sea-green eyes
            but I kept *thinking* he did — that they looked like twins

and then, at night, I would take out Jerry's wrinkled photograph
when I was alone . . the one in the group, at dancing school
where he was sitting next to me . . the one that I'd cut out
                              so there were just the two heads
            his and mine

and then I would see that Jerry and Charles
                        looked nothing alike
and I couldn't understand why I kept on *thinking* they did

            I suppose it was that song . . . that made me think
                  they looked alike
            when they actually looked so very different

            yes, I guess it was the song I remembered when I was with Charles
            that made me believe they looked so much the same
            but that music made me sad . . and sometimes, it made me mad
            like, when I just couldn't remember it long enough
            to ever ask Charles if he knew the words
            or if he had ever heard it before . . because, well

            somebody had to have heard it before, besides me
            so I gave my song a secret name
            I called it *Forgotten Melody*

      yes, I kind of liked him

      once in awhile, he would chase away the other boys
when they were building their ant Forts — which was comforting
almost as good as having a brother to say
                        . . you leave her alone, do you hear ?
but he couldn't do it all the time
because he worked a lot

            he worked to make money, not to spend on Eskimo Pies
            and stuff like that — but to save, he said

Canto Three ☆ 99

                                        for college someday
        since his parents maybe couldn't pay
        what it might cost to go . . and so
        he was gone a lot, working . . . . . .

I used to think — college someday ?
    it sounded so strange, and far away

he had an afternoon paper route each day, and sometimes used to baby-sit
and deliver for the grocer . . and do all sorts of odd jobs
like cutting grass . . and even fixing broken glass
                                    with really strong glue
one time I asked him to
when the mirror in my music box got cracked
and I paid him a quarter for fixing it

        and he took it — he said it was allright to take the quarter
        because he had earned it — that's what he said
        still, his cheeks turned sort of red
                        when he took it from a girl

most of the time, he was too busy to play, or keep chasing away
the members of Ant Murders, Incorporated, every single day
    but he made them stop whenever he could
and that was . . good

        yes, it was good, just to secretly know
        that he always would, whenever he could
        whenever he was there

            I remember once he said to me

                    "I know how you feel about hurting
                    and I want to heal things myself
                    not hurt them or kill them"

I asked him, then
"are you going to be a doctor someday ?"

                    and his answer was very strange

                    he said . . "well, maybe — maybe a doctor
                    or maybe somebody who makes music
                    or a painter . . an artist — or
                    somebody who writes books
                    it doesn't matter, they're all the same"

for years, I tried
to figure out what he meant . . . although
not wanting to seem dumb
I didn't ask him that day

                    100   ☆   Canto Three

he said he wanted to heal things
but how can a doctor be the same as a writer
and someone who makes music
                or draws, or paints pictures ?
I could never understand what he meant
        it bothered me intensely, but I never asked

and then one summer . .

    his family moved away
    to another town — and I never . . . .

        . . . I never saw him again

eventually, I grew old enough to chase away the boys, without his help
so I suppose I didn't miss him an awful lot . . . not really

        except, sometimes . . oh
        when kids said they'd never heard
        of Medusal . . times like that

    that's all

and, as I said, the entire Ant Experience
taught me some valuable lessons I've never forgotten
things I will remember . . like

        there are people
        who will stop hurting
        if you give them money

and there are others
who don't like to hurt
and who won't take money
even when you offer it

                    and those last ones . . . .
                    if they ever do hurt
                    it's never on purpose

        like . .

                    when they have to go away
                    for some reason they can't help

And Yellow Wax Went Away Too

not too long after the boy with the eyes
so deep and wise
moved away with his family . . somewhere

      Dado died

Dado, who rhymed with **OH !**

      the funeral was at the Baptist Church
      in the town where Aunt Maud lived
      and I was taken there, to view the . . remains

           by my mother

   yet, somehow or other . . I can't

remember Dado's face at all

      how it looked against the quilted satin
           or if his huge, pink, wiggling ears
      had maybe shrunk
           or whether his work-worn hands
      were folded in prayer or not
           or if his ice-blue sapphire eyes
      might have still been visible to me
               through his lids
      after they had closed in his final sleep

after he had laid himself down
and prayed the Lord his soul to keep

          somehow, I can't seem . . . to

            remember

      all I recall is that it was so very humid and hot
      in that room where his casket stood
      made of light brown wood
      and . . was it carved with angels ?

Oh, I thought so !
      I thought it was . . . .

      the heavy perfume in the room, from the lilacs and roses
      and other summer flowers . . made my senses numb
         nothing seemed quite real
     except the flower smells . . and the humid, stifling heat

and there is this other
tiny-memory fragment . . . .

it happened after the long sermon
by the Heaven and Hell and Brimstone Baptist Preacher
which made my mother cry
and cry and cry and cry

because of having been, years before, a Baptist Sunday school teacher
and I guess she got scared, somehow, by the Preacher . . .
usually, Baptists don't say Minister or Pastor — or Reverend
it was most always . . Preacher

as I was standing there, while everyone else was moving . . whispering
and murmuring low, as people do in a funeral parlor . . around
sounding like buzzing bees, humming on a hot day   the
I heard this Baptist hymn begin to play . .   dead

. . . with organ music . . and it's so strange
because I don't really know for certain
whether everyone there was singing that hymn
or if I just . . heard it in my head
and somehow, I've never wanted to ask

once Dado told me it was his all-time-favorite song

it was a hymn my mother used to sing all the time — oh !
over and over again, when I was little
and so did Aunt Maud — and Nanoo, who rhymed with
sky-blue

and the words went

. . I come to the garden alone
while the dew is still on the roses
and the voice I hear
falling on my ear . .

 the Son of God disclo — oh ! — ses

(. . discloses, but you
draw it out when you sing)
. . and He walks with me
and He talks with me
and He tells me I am His own

and the joy we share, as we tarry there . .

none other . . . . has ever known

Canto Three ☆ 103

the words seemed to remind me
of something about Dado . . long ago
and something about me

                what was it ?

then I remembered

        as I smelled sweet peas . . strongly . . in my nose
        drowning out the other flower scents in the room

there was only the heavy, unbearably sweet
perfume . . of the invisible sweet peas
                damp earth and wet grass
and the crackling
        electrical smell of the thunder
and lightning
        . . and the rainbow

        like the July day, in the sudden storm
        when I had felt that gentle, drifting . . lifting
        and thought nobody saw me
                oozing delight, out there
        smelling . . and laughing . . and crying — and then
        finding out that Dado had been watching me
                all the while . . and never told

        and what he said to me later
        about speaking right up to Satan — or God
        what's on your mind
        and a storm, with thunder and lightning, he said
        is the best time to reach Heaven or hell without fear

another tiny memory, then
fluttered its wings
        and flapped at me

    . . . my mother's voice
    saying to someone — maybe my father ?
    talking about Dado, and calling him Papa . . funny name

        yes, my mother, saying to someone

        "*the whole time we children were growing up
        we never had a Christmas tree
        Papa would never allow one in the house
                . . and it made Mama cry*"

        Mama was Nanoo

    "*. . but Papa stubbornly refused to give in
    'no Allie,' he would say — 'absolutely not*

it's extravagant foolishness, a tree, and that's that'

Allie was also Nanoo
Mary Alice, really . . like me

" . . . *and then when she was there*
staying with Mama and Maud, while I was so ill"

by "she", my mother meant me

" . . *her very first Christmas, that December*
before she was even one year old — much too small
to notice things like that — eight months, mind you
Papa came lugging in this huge pine tree
the first Christmas tree in that house . . ever !

he was determined
that she have a big pine tree
her first Christmas

not for us — he never allowed it, oh no !
but for her — eight months, mind you — for her
he brought home a Christmas tree"

then, suddenly, from somewhere . . came an image
so vivid and so clear, I knew it could not be only . . imagination
from somewhere deep inside me
somewhere
deep within

came the scent of pine — overwhelming
the prick of sharp needles
scent of cinnamon and oranges
immense, giant ocean of dark, green pine
prickly, sweet-smelling needles

immense ocean
of green cool

Dado's rough hands
on my face . . gently
touching my cheek
gently . . gently

see, Yellow Wax ?
see the pretty tree ?

. . . . *pretty snow*

snow falling . . . .

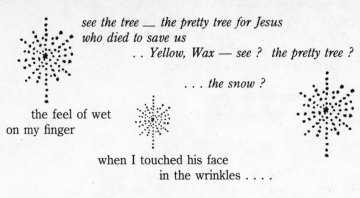

see the tree __ the pretty tree for Jesus
who died to save us
                     .. Yellow, Wax — see ? the pretty tree ?

                          . . . the snow ?

        the feel of wet
on my finger

                    when I touched his face
                          in the wrinkles . . . .

        deep, dark green

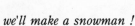   the scent of pine

first snow !

        we'll make a snowman !

                     . . . . see the pretty snowflakes ?

            oh, no !
                    not too small
                at all

                        there are things
                    about the memory
                             people do not yet
                    understand

                    oh ! I remembered, I remembered !
yes, God and I both knew I remembered . . that it was true

                    a memory . . buried deep within the dark recesses
                        of my mind . . always there
                                    now fluttering and flapping
                    its wings at me

no ! no ! not too small at all
yes . . there are things about the memory
people do not yet understand

                        see, Yellow Wax, see ? the tree ?

                    . . . . the pretty Christmas tree

snowflakes

         deep dark green
           scent of pine . . . .

   feel of wet
on my finger
     as it touched
his cheek
      . . . . in the wrinkles

first snow !

we'll make a snow man !

      . . . . see, Yellow Wax, see ?

the pretty Christmas tree ?

I wanted to cry — I wanted to cry for a thousand years
but I blinked back my tears . . hard
    and I swallowed and I coughed, and cleared my throat

   and I did not cry

        . . I did not cry

I was trembling over in a corner . . alone
by myself . . as the hymn died away in my ears
        Dado's all-time-favorite song

   unconsciously pulling
      the petals from a rose

   pinching them hard — the petals of the rose
and I did something that made some relative whisper to another
    "I wonder what she knows ?"

as I spoke out loudly — to no one in particular
I spoke quite clearly and distinctly . . . . and I said

    "no one in this whole world
    ever *understood* Dado — not really"

then my mother whispered Shh ! Shh ! — took my hand
and led me out the door of the funeral parlor

   later, we were back at Aunt Maud's house once more
   and I thought . . maybe what I said had been right
   when they were all talking about the money

and didn't know I was listening

everyone was so surprised, because they hadn't known
this thing about Dado . . thousands of dollars
                                        they found

tucked and hidden around
in that big, wonderfully grease-smelling old garage
where Dado mostly stayed . . even sleeping there at night
taking his bath in an old iron tub
                        and cooking there too
making strong, fragrant coffee
            and working with his hands

            yes, hundreds and hundreds of wrinkled, old bills
        money hidden there, where Dado and Yellow Wax and I
                                and my cousins . . . had played
some of the larger bills stuck in between
the yellowed pages of old Farmer's Almanacs . .

            and the biggest secret of my whole, entire childhood
                    at least, the *deepest* one

was what I found the day after Dado's funeral
when I wandered into the garage alone
                    to smell the grease . . and to
        remember

up high on a shelf, where he used to hide licorice sticks
for me to find, when I was good . . . up so high
I had to climb on a chair to reach
because Dado wasn't there to reach for me . . I groped to see
if he might have left a licorice stick there for me
                                one last time
which would have, somehow
            made him come alive again . . for a moment
like it was before . . with nothing changed

            but I found no licorice — instead
            I found a dirty, old white envelope
                all smeared with grease
            under some of his tools — and nails

            it had not been sealed — and inside it
            was a very wrinkled, crumpled, grease-stained
                twenty dollar bill

and I felt the strangest chill, when I stared at the envelope
because, written on the front, in Dado's familiar
                        squiggly-spidery scrawl . . . were the words

For Yellow Wax .. and the Ants

I cried, then, at last — oh, I cried and cried, for the longest time
and my tears were fresh and clean . . . they gave my soul a bath
for I had been right, all along, about Dado
                    when I made it up to believe he would
  . . that he really would have said
                              Yellow Wax was good — not bad
          about the ants

            I knew . . that he had been watching me, from somewhere
            like he watched that time in the storm

and I did this strange thing
I truly do not know why

        I went to the store, to Benveneuto's grocery
        and traded the twenty
        for five crisp and new one dollar bills
                          plus one five — and one ten
            and then . . . .

        I walked down the back alley, smelling the cinders and tar and heat
        to where some kids lived — there were twelve in the family
        and my folks had always called them "dirt poor"
                a phrase which had vaguely troubled me

          and these kids — the oldest one especially
        they were among the ones who used to tease me unmercifully

                "your grandfather
                has bunnies in his head !"
                              they said
        "crazy, crazy, crazy !"

          then they would laugh, and run away

and sometimes, too . . throw rocks in his windows, and break them
            and trample his tomato vines
                  and run through his garden
        until he stormed out of his garage . . to shake his fist at them
            and threaten Hell and Brimstone

                        "crazy, crazy, crazy !"

        I gave those kids that money — all of it — every dollar
        and they were so excited, so overwhelmed
        they turned cartwheels and handsprings and somersaults

I remember so vividly
the strong smell of tar and cinders in my nose
as I told them, firmly

"before he died . . my grandfather left this money for you
to buy Eskimo Pies and things like that
my grandfather was the smartest man in the whole, entire world
and he was *not* crazy"

they grew very quiet, then
and one of them — the tiniest one — said
"gee ! tell him thanks !"

he really meant it — because he was only
about six or seven
and maybe believed you could talk to people
after they had died . . . and gone to Heaven

finally, the biggest, oldest boy said

"yeah . . . your grandpa was really okay
and I'm sorry I broke his window with the rock that day"

then I felt better
and walked away

but I never told a single living person

about my ant money
from Dado

not a single . . . . living person

CANTO FOUR

Come quickly, Lord,
if come you will !

We wait on failing strength
We faint upon the window-sill
of time's great shadow's length.

Kyril Demys (Musaios)
Wings of Myráhi

> her name was Judith
> and she was beautiful

I shall never forget the first hour she strolled
languidly, gracefully — confident and cool
into our humdrum home room at school

> her name was Judith
> and she was divine

I shall never forget the day she was assigned
the very next seat to *mine* — Oh, Joy !

> her name was Judith
> and she was from New York

New York ! that magical place of miracles, rainbows and Times Square
the positively *hugest* city in the whole wide world
home of St. Patrick's and Rockefeller Center — Broadway too
where *anything* could happen — any kind of dream could come true !

> her name was Judith
> and she was Jewish

Oh, Double Joy ! Double Boy ! and Wow !
I was in a seat position now . . . to solve a twin mystery
the secrets of Judaism — and Manhattan
not to mention the benefits of such close exposure to Glamour

> and such inviting glamour it was
to have a genuine New Yorker, who was also Jewish, in our school
because, you see, we had not seen enough of these strange folk
to be able to view them with casual detachment

years later, I became good friends with twin boys
> named Hank and Jerry
from another Jewish-Manhattan-Exodus family
but, although darkly handsome Hank (Henry) looked properly biblical
his twin brother, Jerry — had green eyes, red hair and *freckles* !

> he was really very appealing, in a way
> the most popular girl in school, Helen Frances — Hennie for short
> was madly, but *madly* in love with him !

still, Jerry's Nordic, nearly Gaelic features and coloring
did seem to spoil the Jewish charisma somewhat

> Judith's appearance did not

Judith was Jewish charisma and mystique personified
she had hair like a raven's wing, with inky-blue highlights
and not brown, but glittering, black-diamond eyes
framed with a fringe of starry lashes
and the smoothest, creamiest olive-tan skin
which only deepened in the summer Sun
and absolutely never burned or peeled — or broke out
                              with horrid little bumps, never !

yes, her face, arms — and legs, in snowy anklets
were all smooth, creamy olive
she wore moccasins, with beaded Indian designs
not dumb, clod-hopper oxfords, like mine
and sometimes her mother allowed her to wear . . Oh !
                                 silk stockings
on Saturday, which was her Sabbath

her clothes were all so *different* . . bunny soft angora sweaters
in shades of yellow, pink and robin's egg blue
                each one obviously brand-spanking new
knife-sharp pleated Scotch plaid skirts, and crisp white blouses
monogrammed with her initials on the collars — J.L. in red letters
        and she carried her homework back and forth
in a book bag of real leather, with such a heavenly, expensive smell

        although, back then . . I didn't realize
          that there's nothing 'heavenly' about the scent of the skin
            of our slaughtered animal brothers
                          and sisters

Judith also wore a delicate charm bracelet
with charms that were — each one — solid 14 karat **GOLD !**
flashing on her creamy-smooth, olive-tan wrist
that made little tinkling sounds when she wrote in her notebook
                 . . like faerie bells

        not that the 14 karats surprised me

they thrilled me, but they didn't surprise me
because just everybody knew that, if you were born a Jew
you were simply immensely wealthy — Period.

        actually, Judith's family was rather well-to-do
        since her father had moved to our town from Manhattan
        to manage an exclusive dress shop — or did he own it ?
        I believe he owned it, it bore Judith's surname
                     . . but whatever
        his store almost immediately
        became the prestige place to shop

the very air in there, as it assailed your nose

was softly scented with sweet perfumes and exotic oils
wafting and drifting . . from the cosmetics counter, I suppose
even my staid Nana, on rare occasions
deserted the perfectly adequately scented Dils Brothers Department Store
owned by friends of our family . . . for the seductive, silken lure
                                        of Glamour
which hinted of Easter Parades on Fifth Avenue
but which did not necessarily hint of the resurrection

    it wasn't long until Judith succumbed
    to my obvious puppy-dog adoration of her mystique
    and we became such close friends that I was permitted
        to call her Judy

naturally, I allowed the news of such intimacy to leak
since it gave me a certain distinction at school — just about everyone
                                        envied me
even those who retained a slight touch of prejudice
were, at the very least, curious — and mildly furious
because they still had to call her Judith

among the kids in my group, prejudice was a nebulous thing . . . some of them
called everyone they didn't like a Jew
even before they ever actually met or knew one — I mean
it was nothing personal, you understand, but how dumb can you be ?
as for me, I wanted to know the real meaning of any word
                                        I was using
otherwise, I felt, language can be totally confusing
so I never called anyone a Jew . . only because
well, you see, I suppose I was what you might call a Word-Snob

    all prejudice is not religious or racial, by any means
    those who make straight A's in English
    can get tied to the rails of the Superiority Track too

I stopped in to visit at Judy's elegant house 'most ever day
                                        after school
and began to sop up a lot of Jewish culture . . .
I thought it behooved any intelligent person to do the same
because, by then, I definitely approved
of anything with even the slightest Semitic flavor or name

I adored the lighting of candles at Judy's, on Jewish holidays
    Yom Kipper, Passover, Hanukkah and Rosh Hashona
        . . not necessarily in that order
seemed to cross right over the border
to Heaven . . . without requiring a passport from St. Peter

    I also quickly absorbed
    the Hebrew respect and worship
    of learning and education

which, to a Word Snob
                 was most assuredly admirable

and gradually, I felt that, somehow, all Jews — everywhere
contained a deep wisdom in their very veins
that others could never dare hope to possess — oh, yes !
I was soon fairly burning to convert — so that I, too, could be hurt
by being called a Jew, with a scornful sneer
and hold my head up high, making it clear — without equivocation
that "sticks and stones may break my bones"
                         but words are puny weapons
against those who have been so awesomely Chosen by God
as Judith did, in the face of snide whispers
reminding me of every mysterious, olive-tanned
black-diamond eyed, raven-haired heroine in the Bible
when she merely shrugged, with a faint smile, those times the kids
                                                    whispered
that the borsht she sometimes ate for lunch
was made from the blood and flesh of sacrificed infants

Judith never condescended to explain that the white and crimson soup
was actually a blend of beet juice, boiled potato and sour cream
why bother to instruct such peasants of ignorance ?
she also only shrugged, with that same faint, enigmatic smile
when the kids taunted her with shouts of "Christ-killer, Christ-killer !"

because, well — it was just so stupid
since, not only was she obviously not the murderess type
     she wasn't even *there* on Good Friday, you know ?
so Judy never wept when they teased . . although
sometimes I saw her hands tremble, ever-so-slightly
as she tossed her blue-black hair, in a fine, careless gesture
not even glancing at her tormentors

yes, she reminded me of every proud, raven-tressed heroine
in the Bible — Old Testament, that is
but isn't it considered true — that the Old is always superior to the New ?
it was to one like myself, reared in the bosom of a Republican family

the Chosen Ones, of course ! did I not know
that God Himself told Moses of this honor He wished to bestow
in the Burning Bush — and then once again
when the two of them were alone together, high up on the Sinai mountain ?
with no Saints in the middle to confuse the issue ?
                              He surely did !
so every single Sol and Irving and Sid
is a direct descendent of Moses — also every Rebecca and Ruth
and that's the **GOSPEL TRUTH !** I mean, what's fair is fair
it has nothing to do with the color of eyes or skin or hair
     for, had I not assuredly already seen
a pure-blooded, directly-descended-from-Moses

red-headed Jewish boy with eyes of green ? and with freckles yet !
oh ! there was no doubt that His word was not second-hand, or third
no, God definitely told Moses all this **IN PERSON**

and since the Almighty does not joke
it should be obvious to everyone that, when He spoke
to those whom the Egyptians believed were inferior and odd
and told them right out, with a **FIERY SHOUT**
that they were to be . . the Chosen Children of God
He meant exactly what He said — and He proved it too !
by magically providing shelter, water and bread
when they were roaming around, "dirt poor" on the hot desert sands
with nothing but time on their hands . . to pray
and pay strict attention to anything He might choose to say
to show them the way . . to Heaven
which they called the Promised Land of Milk and Honey

maybe that was at the same time God told them the secret
of how to make lots of money . . so they wouldn't have to be "dirt poor"
anymore

yes, God meant what He said to Moses, on the Mount
for God always makes every word count — and so
those who dared to persecute the Jews were surely in dire danger
of Dado's Fire and Brimstone
how can there be a worse curse than eternal Damnation to Hell ?

I could almost hear the Almighty yell — and shout to the Pharaoh

"these are my Chosen Ones
and if you harm a single hair on the head
of any of my People — or cut off their bread
*you can just **GEH-EN-DRED** !"

naturally, before I informed Judy of my intention to honor her people
in my own personal way
by converting to their Faith
I had to resolve the problem of Jesus in my mind
and try to find an adequate reason for what might seem to be
desertion to the enemy camp
which is what placing my stamp of approval on Judaism could mean
to him — who liked to lean
against the phone . . . as well as lead against the foe

I remembered my sudden shock when I had first learned
that Jesus was a Jew
I was absolutely astounded !
for I had always had it pounded into me
that he was part of the Holy Trinity — the middle one — the Son
and the good Lord knew

* Trans: go to hell

I mean, God knows . . that an Episcopalian could never-ever be a Jew !
although I secretly felt he might possibly be a Catholic
yes, they seemed to have room for argument there
with all those nuns being married to him, and taking it so seriously

        but . . a Jew ? it couldn't possibly be true !

eventually, I got it clear, though it took the better part of a year
to sort it all out in my head
and even before Judith entered my life, I had decided
there was no more to be said
Jesus was Jewish, and that was that, Period.

        he, too, had belonged to the Chosen Race

    it was just too bad, and so sad, that his own people
    had nailed him up there on the cross
    not even guessing that he had come from their own Almighty
                        and to save them yet !

you see, the Protestant churches back then
didn't stress the Roman soldiers much
they just talked about the Jews not accepting the Lord, and such
then glossed over the rest, in emphasizing that Jesus was
                            some kind of test
the Jews flunked — and the Gentiles passed
with flying colors, like the red, white and blue American flag

finally, after much soul-searching, the answer came to me
I would join up with Judy's church — in New York !
        or Synagogue, as they called it
oh ! even the name of their place of worship was glamourous !

yes, I would join the Jewish Synagogue
and dedicate my whole, entire life to making the Jews see
that Jesus had come to set them free
just the same as he tried to free Pilate, and those thieves
and Mary Magdalene, and Saul-turned-Paul, and best of all — me

it was just ridiculous of the Jews
to have such an inferiority complex about a Saviour
who, after all, was descended from their own blood line

        yes, my justification for conversion to Judaism
                suited me just fine

I chose a bright, sunny, April afternoon — the day after my birthday
and wore my very best Scotch plaid skirt and angora bunny sweater
from Judy's dad's store — and after school
I invited my beautiful, biblical friend to have a soda, treat-on-me
so I could announce to her the perfectly marvelous news

that I was going to set her people free
by joining the Jews, and spending my life to make them see
that Jesus was truly a legitimate shoot of the David root
                              of their very own Family Tree

          . . even if it should mean the sacrifice of a week-end train trip
          to New York — oh, joy ! — to meet her Rabbi, in the Synagogue
          that wonderful, magical word that rhymed with log
                              and mystical fog

I told her it might take some time, even as long as five or ten years
to erase all those ancient fears — but if she and I worked together
we would somehow, someway, some day, surely . . find our Holy Grail
of leading the lost Semitic Race down the blessed trail
                              to shining Truth !

          Judith just sat there, in the booth
          calmly sipping her strawberry soda, and listening

     I was never very easy
     to interrupt . .

                         and when I was all through
                         she stated cooly

                         "you can't be a Jew"

what did she mean
I can't be a Jew ?

                         then she continued, still calmly sipping
                         still cool, and somewhat bored . .

                         "Good Lord ! don't you know
                         you can't be a Jew ? how do you think
                         we keep our bloodlines pure ? oh, sure
                         sometimes they make an exception
                                        I guess, but . . . "
          and she went on
          in her creamy-smooth
          olive-honeyed voice

                         " . . but that almost never happens
                         and even when it does
                         you have to go through a cleansing . . "

          I believe she used
          the word *Mikvah*

"a cleansing ?" I asked, my Mars temper rising
and my voice rising too — "**A CLEANSING ?**"

"well, you're not a Jew"
          said my ex-friend, Judith
"and everybody knows
          that Gentiles are impure, and so . . "

     this was not at all what I had expected
     oh, black day ! my gift of *me* had been rejected !

and somehow, suddenly — I felt dirty
even though I had bathed that morning, as usual
using Judith's scented, birthday-gift soap
and patting on her also scented, birthday-gift powder, and . .

          . . was that why she had given
          such a luxurious gift to me ? was **THAT** why ?
          and I had scrubbed my nails, and washed my hair . . .
          oh ! I was mortified enough to die

then I exploded in anger, and I'm afraid I shouted at her
in front of the druggist, who looked somewhat astonished
as I blessed myself dramatically, with a defiant sign-of-the-cross

          and cried . .

"just forget everything I said ! *geh en dred !*
who wants to belong to a church where the people are so blind
they didn't even recognize the little Lord Jesus
when he was born under the Star of David ?
not even when he grew up to be tall
and passed every single one of their dumb tests of prophecy
not just one of them — oh, no ! he passed them all !
why, you . . you don't even have . . . a Christmas tree !"

my voice broke, then as I realized what I had done
                              for it was easy to see
that this was the end of the friendship
between my beautiful, biblical heroine and me

          but as she left, and paid the check — she turned
          at the door . . walked back to the booth, and smiled
          her beautiful, calm, confident smile . . once more

               and said . . "don't hock mir a cheinick"

          then walked away, this time to stay

     you must remember that our misunderstanding
     took place long before the Chosen Ones
          welcomed Sammy Davis and Elizabeth Taylor Todd into the fold
. . as well as before I had read *The Robe*, which, years later

educated me to the fact that there were, indeed
even back then, many fine Jewish scholars
who felt that this sad, gentle man, riding a donkey
instead of leading a Great Army
might possibly be the One promised by God to set them free

.. also before I had learned to be tolerant of the convictions of others
considering that I can be blind to the truth rather often myself

and over the years, I would almost have admitted
that the Jews might be wrong — or they might be right
since no one can be sure, on either side, of the true source of Light

except, well .. there was Jesus

and if I went that far, I would have been denying
that he was the Son, the middle one, of the Holy Trinity
wouldn't I ?
I mean, wasn't he ?

although I sometimes wondered if both Jesus and God
must not have had some trouble, when they tried to be fair
in choosing up sides and bloodlines

still, the Jewish mystique and charisma lingers — and even today
I still find myself unable to see a Jew
as anything other than brighter and wiser
more steeped-in-ancient-tradition, and safer from perdition
than paler Gentiles
the men more handsome, and the women
more beautiful

than ordinary mortals not Chosen by God

later, when I delved into astrology, reincarnation and metaphysics
where I still stand .. and learned more of the man, Moses
who led the Jews to their Promised Land .. and discovered that Jesus
in an earlier incarnation, was none other than Moses' ancestor, Abraham

.. I felt as though all theories
led straight through the Looking Glass
to Wonderland and the Mad Hatter ..

I mean, if Jesus was also Abraham, and Abraham knew the truth
and Jesus did too — and each was a Jew
but one of them said one thing, and one said another
and one had a wife — while the other had a virgin mother

well, it seems to have been a more complicated muddle
than the ordinary magic of the three-times-three
of the traditional Holy Trinity

and where does God Himself stand — in the middle ?
whose side is He on ?
the Catholics or the Protestants or the Jews ?
where do Buddha and Mohammed come in ?
and the Krishna Guru — or the High Lama, of Tibet ?
yes, where do they all come in ?

which one is responsible for the real Original Sin
of all this tangled, holy cross-purpose ?

it seems like a cop-out to place all the blame
on a poor, innocent snake
who just told Eve how delicious the apples tasted, from the tree
and what about Adam ? after all . . . .
he didn't have to bite into the apple . . unless he wanted to
didn't he have Free Will, the same as me ?

maybe, instead of blaming it all on the snake
it should be blamed on the apple itself
if an apple may be thought of as a guilty god
it was most likely the Serpent, I guess
but *someone* is guilty of misrepresenting the truth
and it wouldn't surprise me if it turned out to be
that sneaky Holy Ghost
because he is the one I mistrust the most !

I realize now, to my shame, that I was not qualified to be a theologian
and solve the riddles of religion, back then, when I offered Judith
my gift of instant conversion to her Hebrew faith . . with such pride

no, I was really not that well versed, or rehearsed
in the ritual or the dogma of either side
as must have been shockingly evident to Judith's family
when they read what I hoped was my cool and dignified
farewell note to her — the next morning

Dear Judy — I mean, Judith,

how can something Moses taught is the only thing
which is right and true — be something I can't believe or do
unless I was born a Jew, like you ?
after all, I try to practice his Ten Commandments too

I never let the kids say things like "jew-him-down" around me
no, never-ever ! and I always defend your People
by reminding everyone of how you are all so bright and clever
and telling them it's no wonder you're all so intent on getting rich
the way dumb Gentiles treat you — and have for so long
but I just can't help thinking it's wrong
for you to be as snooty in your own private club
as they are, when they won't allow you to join theirs

I'm sorry if I hurt your feelings — or if I sounded mean
but, actually, I'm very happy at the First M.E.
and I'm sure I could never give up my manger scene
                                        or Christmas tree
even though I believe your Synagogue
that rhymes with log . . . and mystical fog
is a perfectly marvelous place to go !

just to prove there are no hard feelings
I still believe you're the prettiest girl in the whole school
                                        Scout's Honor !
thank you for being my friend
and just to show you I'm not really mad
I hope you'll invite me when your mother and dad
give you your circumcision party

                    Yours Truly

                    "me"

One Summer

Nana's dearest chum since girlhood was a lovable lady named Sallie
who was married to a lovable man named George Bruce
and even though we had no connecting bloodlines, I called them
                                        Aunt Sallie and Uncle George
with easy, familial familiarity
as my father, aunt and uncle had done, before me

Aunt Sallie looked like a Grand Dame, and when she laughed
she actually twinkled all over with kindness

Uncle George had snow white hair, and looked for all the world
                        like a huge, St. Bernard puppy
with soft brown eyes, wearing glasses — floppy ears
and a crusty, brusque exterior
covering a heart that fairly panted with shy warmth and friendliness

        they lived in a perfectly marvelous house
        in a place called Indianapolis, Indiana
        and the summers Nana took me there to visit the Bruces
        on the exciting B & O Railroad . . were truly magic

yes, if anything
was ever magic . . . . those summers were

the Bruce house was like a dream . . . I'm sure it wasn't real
it was an etching, or a steel engraving — not real, no
that house was too charmingly Dickensish and Louisa May Alcottish
too altogether delightful and wonderful — to be real

the family lived as though they still existed
amid the elegance and grace that made Life rhyme
at the turn-of-the-century, paying slight attention
to the passing of Time

oh ! I was all for that — I have always wanted Time to stand still
for one magical reason or another . . except unhappy moments
no, maybe not stand still, but just be able to turn it back and forth
like the dial on a radio . . . switching it to Yesterday's station
when Today's has too much static

Aunt Sallie's house was so lost in Time, I nearly anticipated
the sight of Queen Victoria herself, gliding majestically down the stairs
holding out her royal, jeweled hand, to be kissed by a footman
. . or maybe by Albert

it was a house crammed and jammed to the rafters with love and wonders
warmth and security . . crackling fireplaces . . and surprises
a house steeped in tradition, and saturated with memories . . . .
one of its surprises, the cut glass door and beveled, prismed windows
casting unexpected rainbow splashes on rugs and walls
brilliantly colored, spectrum-hued . . quivering
dancing rainbows

I remember . .

a huge front yard, with hedges and bright flower beds
. . such perfect places for druids to hide !
a rambling front porch, with a proper swing at one end
and the apple tree in the back yard, much taller than Aunt Maud's
where I would walk through the dew-damp grass, barefoot
in the soft, summer twilight, picking up golden apples
from the ground
and biting into the deliciousness . . oh !
surely Eden contained no finer fruit than this — not even
the rosy red apple used by Eve to tempt Adam with secret knowledge
no wonder he could not resist !

there was a grand, glowing, rosewood Player Piano in the parlor
I pretended to play by the hour . . inserting my favorite melodies
then watching the actual ghosts press the keys up and down
to create the sound of music
. . what indescribable magic that was !

did you ever see a ghost play the piano

Canto Four ☆ 123

with invisible fingers, causing the black and white keys to move
and no human hands anywhere near ?   oh ! what magic !

I simply adored selecting tunes for the ghosts to play
choosing from rolls of old-time songs, like . .

  Dear Old Girl, the robin sings above you

      Dear Old Girl
          . . . . it sings of how I love you

     Swanee River
       . . way down upon
and so . . far, far away

           Massa's in the cold, cold ground . .

      oh ! freezing-cold

 . . hear that mournful cry

            . . . . Mighty Like a Rose
                . . Summer Time
    . . oh, your daddy's rich
           and your Ma is good lookin'
       so sleep, little baby
           don't you cry . .

all the barbershop quartet favorites

       Let Me Call You Sweetheart . . .

  . . That Old Gang of Mine

I knew all the words from listening to Dadoo's RCA Victor records
back home, on 8th Street . . so I could sing along, as the ghosts played

   it was a house of polished bannisters, and a winding staircase
   begging for a ball . . rich, red and blue toned Oriental carpets
   plump, stuffed couches and chairs, with delicate doilies on the arms
   and ornate Tiffany lamps, that seemed, somehow, at dusk
   to send out a softer, more golden glow
   than any other lamps I knew — or still know
   and some of the lamp shades had picture scenes on the stained glass
                that came to life at night
     more magic !

angel-carved and gilt framed
photographs of children and grandchildren
babies . . laughing in someone's arms

tapestries hanging here and there, and draped
with dangling silk fringe and crystal beading

heavy, rich drapes at the windows
were they velvet ? Ming vases, intricate alabaster pieces
and tiny miniatures, painted on porcelain

huge bathrooms, with old fashioned fixtures, smelling like Ivory soap
and gleaming white and green . . . fresh air, pouring through casement windows
four poster beds, some with canopies
fluffy, embroidered pillow cases . . . feathery-light quilts
lace curtains . . . and hand crocheted, creamy heirloom spreads

I would wander through this fairyland of polished woods
rainbow splashes, ghostly music . . . sweet-smelling flowers
golden lamplight, paintings . . and shelves
of musty books, all classics

listening peacefully . . contentedly
in the low murmuring of well-bred grownup talk
in dulcet tones . . warm, soft and gentle . . and never raised
in anger or excessive emotions
always pleasant, cheerful
musical voices — except on those occasions

when someone mentioned Roosevelt — Franklin D.
then . . oh, my ! oh, me !
Nana and Dadoo, like the Bruces, were what everyone called
dyed-in-the-wool Republicans
and I remember how they laughed once, at a joke
Uncle George told, about a thing called the National Recovery Act

. . something about the initials, N.R.A.
standing for Nuff Roosevelt Already

"nuff", of course, meant "enough"
even at a tender age, I caught that subtle nuance

the only time I can recall any of these warm and cozy, graceful people
being especially cross or cranky with me
was one afternoon, when everyone was on the porch, drinking iced tea
and I spoke up loudly, stating that I believed Roosevelt
to be a nice, grandfatherly sort of man
WELL !

you could have heard a tiny gold safety pin drop on the thick carpet
you could have cut the icy-silence with a knife
then someone spoke, in freezing tones — oh ! freezing-cold tones

"now, child, don't speak of things
which don't concern you — go play a roll on the piano"

it was lovely, waiting there in Aunt Sallie's embracing house
for dinner to be called, with a gorgeous gong
that sounded deep musical tones of **DONG ! DING ! DONG !**
then served by a pair of smiling lovebirds
                              named Brooks and Mary
            who ran the house

and who, I used to believe, actually owned it — because
Brooks and Mary were the only ones who always knew
                                        where things were kept
like extra white, fluffy towels
and elderberry jam . . . . . they worried so when anyone
tracked muddy-feet-all-over . . or when the silver wasn't polished
and Brooks was forever driving into town
                        on important, mysterious missions
yes, dinner was surely an enchanting experience
often, with candlelight and fresh baskets of flowers from the yard
with the crystal sparkling, and the silver gleaming
and soft, damask napkins, that felt like clouds against my cheek

    . . here at Aunt Sallie's
    I was allowed to eat right off the china
    not from my own plate, like a child . .

                              but . .

      what attracted me most
      about the Bruce house

        was Cousin Bob

          one of the sons of the family

Cousin Bob did not look Victorian, like Albert
he looked exactly — I mean *exactly* like Errol Flynn !
just like his twin, with flashing grey eyes — and dimples
and tanned skin, from golf and tennis
                        . . wearing turtleneck sweaters
with brown, wavy hair
and a smile that made me nearly faint
each time I saw it coming in my general direction

not understanding at first, that the aunt and uncle terms
I had been encouraged to use . . did not signify bloodlines

I used to lie awake at night, and cry
and cry and cry — because I believed we were related
and therefore, could never be married to each other

I didn't care a ginger snap that he was elderly
somewhere between twenty five and thirty, I guess

I would nurse him, I thought, in his old age
and be his devoted wife — until Death did us part
if only I could win his heart . . . if only we weren't blood relatives

by the time I realized we weren't really related
I was too bashful to propose marriage to Cousin Bob
but I dreamed about it — oh, yes, I did !
I truly did . . and I hid my eyes, staring down at the floor
so he couldn't see the love welling up inside them

it was that intense, and maybe even deeper — my silent
but absolute, pure adoration and worship
of this handsome, tall and tan — strong and sure
and gentle, smiling man . . . who would never frown or scold

once, when I was flying somewhere back and forth
between thirteen and fourteen years young — or old ?
he took me to a place where they played a game at night
              under bright lights . . called Miniature Golf

. . and showed me how to hold the club
by standing behind me, and putting his arms around me
my hands in his . . as he placed them . . just so
                        on the golf club
and the nearness of him
made my heart spin dizzydizzydizzy
tears filled my eyes . . till I couldn't see
the ball or the green grass . . and I trembled
hoping he wouldn't notice

              yet, at the same time
                    hoping he would

knowing then that we could
oh ! we truly could be married . . if he loved me
because we weren't really cousins, Cousin Bob and I
that was only grown up make-believe

the golf incident happened the same summer
that Bob had promised, druid-honor, to drive me to the station
to board the B & O train back home

and I had made up my mind firmly
to tell him, on the way — when we were all alone, in the car

that I loved him

I practiced my speech for days, shaking at the thought of it
but nevertheless determined to see it through
                  . . and just say it right out

Canto Four ☆ 127

just say, "Bob . . I love you

and I don't care how old you are
I'll love you till I die
however old you are . . . . even
yes ! even if you're thirty"

         and I wished very hard, on a star
         that he wouldn't laugh, when I told him

then, the evening before I was to leave Indianapolis
after I was all packed, and had said goodnight to Nana, at the Holloway
         the apartment building owned by the Bruce's
where Nana was living for a year or so, following Dadoo's death
which had cut her, like a knife, in half
         I mean . . she no longer seemed whole, ever again

that evening . . I took a deep breath, and went into my bedroom
and closed the door to pray what I knew would be
                         the most important prayer of my life
yes, indisputably, the most urgent prayer of my life

         for Nana had given me the crushing news at dinner
         the news that . . Bob had found a girl he deeply loved
         and wanted for his wife
                         her name was Patty

and since Patty, Nana said, would be in town to stay
the next day . . Bob might have to remain with her
and not be able . . probably not be able . . to drive me
                                 to the train
              like he promised
                    because *she* was in town

I had met her just once, at the Bruce house, for dinner
and remembered only that her eyes were bright . . and button brown
and her hair was lovely, dark . . and crisply curly
I believe she was Scotch or Irish — her cheeks were pink
and she was **BEAUTIFUL** . . sweet, and rather shy

         and quite old — around twenty-three

I said nothing to Nana
but I knew Bob would never-ever break a promise
                    he had made to me

he would be there, I was certain, in the morning
just exactly as he had said . . to drive me to the train station
and — Patty or no Patty — I would propose
I would somehow make him see — that our love was fated to be
at the moment each of us had been born — never mind how many years apart

silly calendar numbers can't interfere
with the destiny of the heart

I was sorry for not having told him sooner — because
I truly did not want Patty to be hurt, you see

> yet, secretly inside, I knew that Bob loved only me
> and was probably marrying Patty on the rebound

I knew because . .

> because at dinner . . . across the flowers on the table
> when everyone else was chattering about this or that
> Bob would always catch my eye . . and wink
> and no one ever saw — but us
> he would wink at me, then grin — to share our secret
> as I grinned shyly back
> > . . and no one else ever noticed our secret code

and . . when I was younger, before he realized how much he loved me
when we were just sort of beginning to fall in love
and someone, for some reason, would scold me, or speak crossly to me

> Bob would put both his arms around me
> protectively, and say — "leave my girl alone"

then he would wink at me, or kiss me on the cheek .
and whisper . . . "don't mind them"

> later, when he was even taller, and I had grown up
> grown into a woman . . like now, this summer
> sometimes, when he looked at me, his eyes seemed so lonely
> so searching . . misty . . as if . . . .

> > . . . oh ! I knew he loved me only
> his eyes . . yes, his eyes were so searching
> so quietly sad, sometimes . . though they usually sparkled
> > > like Errol Flynn's
> > and I thought maybe
> > he knew too, like me

but was afraid I might think him too old . . to love

too old to love ? oh, I simply had to let him know !
I had to tell him he would always, always be young to me
somehow, I had to make him see . .

> then too, there was that miracle moment
> just a few nights earlier
> when he put his strong arms around me

on the Miniature Golf course
maybe he was trying
to tell me he loved me then
and lost his nerve

later, when he drove me back home to Nana, at the Holloway
in his car . . he put his sweater around my shoulders
                                        so I wouldn't be chilly
and he placed it there . . so tenderly

then, when he said goodnight, at the door
and made the promise about taking me to the train
I thought I saw rain
            in his twinkle-star eyes
and I just had to turn that rain to Sun — oh, I had to tell him
he was the only one . . the only man I could ever marry
and that, to me, he would always and forever
                                        be young
it hurt me to see the rain in his eyes

and so . .

this night, I knelt on the floor, beside my bed
and said the Lord's Prayer . . certain that tomorrow would bring
a shining rainbow, to last Forever After

I had decided to say the prayer one hundred times
believing that angels sometimes slumber
and feeling a mystical power in that number — to awaken them
                    to hear my supplication

on a forbidden sheet of Nana's monogrammed, engraved stationary
kept in the drawer of the night stand
I marked off each prayer . . . each time around

I got as high as sixty-seven . . then black velvet covered me
        and I fell asleep, dreaming of the heaven of Bob beside me
                    alone together, in his car
    . . and woke in the morning
to Nana's cheerful breakfast call, her tap-tap-tapping on my door

    . . still lying there, on the floor

my neck was stiff, and my back was sore — but my heart was light
somehow, deep down inside, I knew it was going to be allright

we were having poached eggs, and buttered toast
and orange juice, Nana and I
            and she had just remarked
that the air was not so much like summer this morning
as it was like a balmy spring

when the telephone gave a quick, sharp ring

Nana answered
and it was Cousin . . it was Bob

I heard her say his name, in greeting
and hardly knew what I was eating . . but kept on swallowing
                                                    automatically
        then . .

                        I heard Nana say — "oh, that's too bad !
                            I know she will be disappointed — but
                        she'll understand, I'm sure . .

                        yes, I'll tell her you said goodbye
                        and — what was that ? oh, you're a dear . . .
                        now you and Patty have a happy day
                        and, say ! why don't you bring her over here
                        for lunch next week . . . ?"

    a few more words of farewell, then

        "here, honey — Bob said
        to give you a kiss on the cheek"

and she kissed me

    "he said to tell you he loves you a million bushels
            but he's all tied up today
    and can't see you to the train, as he promised . . . .
    he said he knew you would understand
                        and to be sure to write to him
    as soon as you get back home — and, let's see
    oh, yes ! he asked if you planned, that is, he *hopes* you plan
    to come back to visit next summer
    so he can teach you how to play golf . . you know, it's odd
        . . . I have a hunch he and Patty may have quarreled the other night
    did he seem especially sad, when he left you at the door ?
    but now everything seems to be allright once more
    dear me ! young love is sometimes so full of pain
    don't you think Patty is a charming, beautiful girl ?
    so right for Bob — Sallie and George are simply delighted . . "

"oh, Nana . . Nana . . I . . will you
        excuse me for a minute, please ?
I think I swallowed a piece of toast
down my Sunday throat . . I'll . . I'll be right back"

and I ran into the bathroom, through a mist of black . . closed the door
fell down on the cool, tile floor — and cried my heart out

        then got up, and washed my face

slowly . . and brushed my hair

"are you allright, dear ?"

"yes, Nana-banana
I'll be right there . . . "

I slipped into my blue silk dress
with the white Peter Pan collar

and my dumb anklets . . .
Nana didn't think
I was old enough, yet
for silk stockings

buckled my shoes

fastened my gold charm bracelet
on my ugly, skinny, freckled arm

and I . .

"dear, you'd better hurry !
it's time to call a taxi
I'll ride with you to the station"

and I . .

tore the paper with the sixty-seven criss-cross marks into tiny pieces
and flushed them down the toilet . . stared for a long moment
into the bathroom mirror
at my straight, limp, mousey, dishwater color hair
and my pink-rimmed eyes, all swollen . . pale blue . . and bloodshot
my odd-shaped nose, now bright red on the end

then . . I walked out into the kitchen
and smiled at Nana

"oh, honey. just look at you ! good gracious
your eyes are all red from tearing up
when you choked on the toast
you really shouldn't eat so fast — although
I know what a dreadful feeling it is
to swallow something down your Sunday throat

poor child, here — take this extra hanky
you may need it on the train
now isn't that the most exasperating thing ?
this morning started out just like spring
and now it looks like rain

here's a bag with some Brownies in it
in case you need something to munch
before they serve lunch in the dining car

the humidity must be rising . . well
maybe the rain will cool the air
        oh, child — your hair !
it looks so limp
do you suppose if you got a permanent wave
that would help ?
your hair is lovely, dear — so nice and fine
but thin — not much body to it
here, I've tucked twenty dollars in your purse
so when you get home, tell your mother
to call Miss Grueser
        you remember Leitha ?
and get a nice wave — not too much in front
I hate to see children your age
with their hair artificially curled — but
yours is so straight — I guess it won't hurt
just make sure she doesn't allow it
        to get too frizzy on the ends

my ! that's a pretty dress !
I haven't seen you wear it since you came
why on earth did you save it
to wear on your last morning here ?

do you have your white gloves ?
yes . . good . . now, don't forget them, dear
and lose them, like you did before

what are these ? oh, I see, ticket stubs
from the golf course the other night
just drop them in the wastebasket over there

is that the taxi already ? hurry, honey !
stop fiddling with your hair
you don't want to miss your train
oh, good heavens, wouldn't you know ?
it really has started to rain
        now where is my umbrella ?
I do wish Bob had come along — we need him
to help us with these bags
run out and ask the driver . . hurry, now"

Honey . . .

I mailed a small package out to you today
some grapefruit rind candy — and your Bible
did you know you left it on the night stand ?

we were in such a rush that morning
but I was surely lucky — because
after your train pulled out of the station
I turned around to look for another taxi
and guess who was standing there behind me ?

Cousin Bob !

poor dear, he looked so sad and disappointed
when I told him your train had already gone

he said he'd been thinking about it all morning . . .
that he had made you a promise . . .
and he wanted to come and tell you goodbye himself

Patty was in the car, waiting — and they drove me
back to the Holloway, which was certainly a blessing
I don't know how long it would have taken
to get a taxi in such a downpour

Cousin Bob said he had something special to tell you
he didn't say what it was, but he said it would wait
until he sees you next summer

he and Patty are definitely going to be married
next month, I believe they said
we're all so pleased — she's such a lovely girl

if you haven't had your hair done yet
tell Leitha not to give you too much curl — just the ends

this is only a short note, dear
Bob is picking me up to drive to Aunt Sallie's for dinner
I'll write a longer letter later — did you leave your gloves
on the train ? I hope not

all my love, as always

Nana

Hope calls from the flying cries of birds:
Someone else and better than posturing, hateful-
                              hearted men
Made these, and gave them flight.

Hope springs from the smallest stalks of blue-eyed grass
One stem taller than an oil-well tower
    than a towering building's shaft.
And mightier than the maker,
Artist, engineer and knower,
Greater the maker of the blue-grass stalk
  than any man who ever built, or shall.

My hope flies with wings
Beyond what hate or ignobility could make
And grows in the earth with the blue-eyed grass,
Lies beyond the worst — or the best — of men.

Kyril Demys　　*(Musaios)*
Prismatic Voices

I Pray the Lord in Latin

my curious interest in the roots of Rome
extended gradually beyond its Anglican branch
where I had grown as a leafy shoot, until I pruned myself
                                        into the First M.E.

        . . . leading me eventually
        down a path toward the Vatican itself

            oh, but I kept this quiet, quiet . . .

not wanting to start a minor riot among my family members
who bore sufficient concern over my streaks of social eccentricities
without also being troubled about my leaning in the direction
                            of the rigid doctrine of the Pope
in fact, had I ever openly announced
that I was even considering a Catholic conversion
I might very well have had my mouth washed out with soap
at least, I might have, when I was small enough not to know better
which was at any age under sixteen
after that, no one would have minded as much
or made such an undue fuss
since Nana herself had some dear, close friends
who were of the Catholic persuasion

        the main objection during my early, formative years
        would have been that I was changing too many philosophies
        in mid-stream, making it seem
        as though I were choosing churches and faiths
        like a religious game of musical chairs, when I'd barely graduated
        from comprehending Goldilocks and the Three Bears

of course, Nana's oldest friend, Sallie Bruce
was neither Episcopalian or Catholic — not even a protesting Protestant

        she was a Pillar of the Christian Science Faith
        back in Indiana — a worthy apostle of Mary Baker Eddy's creed
        and sometimes . . I wish Aunt Sallie had tried harder
        to convert me to her Faith, because in those flower-scented days
        I could have been easily persuaded
        that her church was the one holding the key
                            to common sense and sanity

but her Church was not the kind to proselytize, with zeal and fervor
preferring to allow any lost lambs, seeking the way home
to wander into the comfort of its fold themselves . . the long way

        one reason she didn't try harder may have been her reluctance
        to become the center of an unpleasant family dispute
        since I had always heard it said that Nana and Sallie
        never allowed religious differences to harm their treasured friendship

. . which was really only another way to say
that there *were* deep-felt differences

nevertheless, needless to note
I would have gladly espoused, by rote, any creed Bob Bruce embraced
and would have happily faced ten legions of angry angels
if Cousin Bob had, in even the slightest way, beckoned me into his Faith

for, the older I grew, and the more I learned
about Aunt Sallie's Church believing in the Power of the Mind
as the means to the miracle of healing
assisted by God and one's Higher Self, rather than by surgery or drugs
the more I suspected that, had I wandered through that spiritual door
when young enough, I might have stayed
and prayed their stronger prayers . . . forevermore

    yes, I might have remained, to see my soul re-claimed
    into a Faith which comprehends fully
    at least the basic truth that the word itself
                means exactly what it says — *faith*

but such a peaceful path of non-resistance was not to be — for Fate
had charted a longer journey for me, to make me see
whatever Truth might be visible for the seeking — or the taking

    there are some
        whose spirits need more breaking
    and I was surely one of these

so, since the next step on my wandering hegira of mystical learning
was an intense burning to penetrate the mysteries of Catholicism
          and discover just what made it tick
I did not follow the road to Aunt Sallie's Faith
using the power of mind-over-matter to heal the sick
             in body or soul

besides, there was no Christian Science Church, at the time
in my home town — and then, too
after that broken-hearted Indianapolis summer, I suppose
anything even remotely connected with Bob Bruce . . only hurt
and made me remember what I knew I had to forget

    funny . . . many years later
    when I mentioned the Miniature Golf game to "Cousin" Bob
    during a casual telephone call, just to say hello
    he had no recollection of the event — none at all
    but that's logical, when you think about it
    because, although one might recall each vivid instant
    of meeting the President — or a King
    neither President nor King recalls every adoring face

or clasp of hands

it's a matter of degrees
        or levels of caring
everything is relative to the sharing
    of the reason
for the season . . of remembering

  following my exposure to Catholic liturgy and ritual, at St. Raphael's
I investigated all highways and byways, as well as short cuts — to Rome
although I was always wary, lest my family sense
I was about to switch spiritual horses again, in mid-stream
from the now front running Methodist entry
        to the religion of the "lace curtain Irish"
and the "emotional Italians"

who were the ones most small town Protestants believed
made up the entire congregation of Catholic worshippers, from Rome
           to Pago Pago
adding to that sweeping reference
all the ignorant and superstitious savages from the barbarous jungles
where pushy Catholic Missionaries arrived first
ahead of the more pious and reserved Protestant Evangelists

I must admit I tended to go along
with this Irish-Italian lumping of Catholics

    since most of the children I knew well at school
    who ate fish on Friday — took communion wearing lacy veils
    and made the sign-of-the-cross on their foreheads
    when they were wishing very hard . . as a general rule
    did have melodious names, like Pangallo, Pompilio and Lichello

and those who told dreamy tales of leprechauns in the schoolyard
picked them up, in the usual way
from immigrated Gaelic grandmothers at home, still somewhat fey

    also, Kelly was the surname
    of my longest lasting female friend, in later years
    who was very, very Irish
    and she went to Catholic Mass each Sunday

        even to the nine-nights-in-a-row
        Saint Francis Xavier Novenas

and so, with such evidence surrounding me
I, too, believed that most Catholics
were either superstitious Irish or emotional Italians

I missed out on the Polish prejudice
there being no Poles in our home town
that anyone I knew had heard about, at least

                    except for maybe
an itinerant Polish Priest, passing through the Parish

        there was, however, one Syrian Catholic family
        and that was nearly as good for being different, odd and strange
                    as Polish would have been
        but later, I became close friends with one of the girls
        in the Syrian family — named Evelyn
        and she turned out to be
        as disappointingly normal as . . . . well, as normal as me

            and she . .

        and an Irish-Catholic girl named Ruth — and I
        talked far into the night, over the years
        solving some of the world's Greatest Problems
        but unfortunately, none of our own, that I can recall

as for Nana, she was less disturbed, it sometimes seemed
by my religious promiscuity — than by my stubborn refusal
to pick up my D.A.R. papers, dating from her side of the family
and have them framed, hanging proudly on the wall

it was because I'd heard the Daughters of the American Revolution
would not give their permission for the black singer, Marian Anderson
to sing her glorious gospels in their sacred D.A.R. concert hall

        and that somehow seemed to me, not to be
        exactly what the forefathers those nice ladies are so proud
        to call their ancestors — had in mind
        when they wrote those words about Freedom and Equality
        and the inalienable right of each individual
        to his or her own pursuit of happiness

        I felt the Sons and Daughters of the American Revolution
        ought to be more dedicated to both upholding and uplifting
        the clear and plainly stated intent
                    of a Declaration of Independence
        in which they so fervently believe they have exclusive membership
                    absorbed, somehow, through genes
                                    and chromosomes

        it's all very well and good, I thought, to be proud
        of dating back to the mating of those Revolutionary heroes
            who fought so bravely beside Washington, George
        as long as one does not forget the true cause
        for which they crossed the icy Delaware
                    and froze their toes at Valley Forge

had I picked up my D.A.R. papers of pedigree

they would have served as a kind of identification, I suppose

    but, as desperately as I was searching for a personal label
    which might identify myself to me — and to others
    I was not overly anxious to be identified as an accomplice
    to the prostitution of the Constitution

        it would have been both false and useless
    to glue on the intials of D.A.R., in labeling the contents
    of the odd-shaped jar — called "me"
        calling a bottle of pickles by another name, such as roses
    will still not make slices of Dill . . smell like an American Beauty
    for, a pickle by any other name, is still — a pickle
    and the Trinity of the initials D.A.R. gave me no thrill
    of belonging — ancestrally or otherwise

    names and labels were beginning to throw me off balance
    in all categories — wherever I turned, it seemed I learned
    a new distortion, a new slanted image in the funny-house mirrors
                                    around me

    the Syrian family I knew, was quite well-to-do
    wealthy, by small town standards
                and I used to wonder why it was

    . . . when those who were foreign-born
    managed to accumulate a pile of money — they did so
    because they were wily, cunning or shrewd

    whereas, those whose great-greats were born over here
    became financially fortunate, because they were clearly imbued
    with extremely brilliant brains — and very clever minds

        but . . . name does not rhyme with brain
            it only seems to — if you don't listen closely

the game of rhyming Life
was becoming more complicated
every year I lived

    one thing that impressed me about the Catholic Church in my home town
    was that there were two black families
    who were not only members, but also communicants at Mass
    and this color acceptance of Saint Xavier's
                      . . or Saint X, as we called it
    appeared to me to be
    extraordinarily commendable

    because I truly did not know of any other local church
    where folks with skin the shade of Bob's and Grace's
    were wont to show their bright faces, of a Sunday morning

. . except the Baptist, which everyone but my mother
thought was just "so-so, as churches go" — although
they never dared to say that in front of *her*

knowing those black families were welcome to worship
at the Mass in Saint X, each Sunday morning, and week days too
I felt a secret respect for Catholicism being born
in both my heart and my mind
conceived, I'm sure, from my own private worship
of Grace and Big Potato, not too far removed

from the grace . . . of God

it gave me an undeniable, private thrill
to walk past the weathered stone edifice called Saint X . . and
on any thin pretext, I managed to pass there
as often as I could, when my errands should have taken me
down other streets

Saint X stood imposingly on the main thoroughfare called Market Street
forcing the Protestant shoppers to face daily
the reminder of Papal Infallibility . . . .
another matter, which, at the time, arrested me
and attested to me
the Catholic supremacy of holiness

I had heard it rumored and whispered
that the Pope was an actual descendent of Peter
and therefore, could do no wrong
he was, in fact, Infallible — unable, even if he *tried*
to commit a religious goof or spiritual faux pas

and I considered this the ultimate in religious insurance policies
for Jesus, after all, actually did say to Peter
that, upon this rock . . . the rock of Peter's strong faith . . .
he would build his very own church — and all the devils of hell
could not shatter Peter's rock . . . or prevail against it

oh, yes . . . Peter had D.A.R. papers
dating back to Palestine
not just back to Paul Revere

symbolically, Peter's rock also referred to that resplendent Rock in Rome
I still believed to be the hiding place
of many Great Religious Secrets and Spiritual Mysteries
not the least of these being that yellowed piece of parchment
. . . the official marriage license
of Jesus and Mary Magdalene

certainly it all seemed theologically sound
when you tossed it around — in a teen-age mind

I decided the Catholics simply had to be the ones who were right
never mind what God said to Moses on the Mount
Moses evidently misunderstood — or else God later changed his mind
after the Chosen Ones hurt his feelings
by not believing that His only Begotten Son was the One
sent to deliver them from bondage to the Gentiles

something else which magnetized and drew me further
into the depths of Roman mystery and Catholic history
was the hypnotically chanted, lilting liturgy of the Latin Mass

    it possessed a flowing poetry, almost a rhyme and meter
    especially when blended with the flickering red glow
    of the candles . . clouds of incense . . Dominus Vobiscum
    and those fascinating secrets about the infallible descendents of Peter

    God had always seemed to me, poetic — shrouded in ritual
                      by Divine design
    not to be described, much less discovered
    where just plain, one-two-three Trinity talk prevailed
    and so, it appeared to me that the true Light shone
                    in the Catholic Mass alone
    in no other service or worship

however, that was back then
today, Rome has made a most fallible decision — indeed unwise
in the opinion of many a member and potential convert
by dropping the Latin, and modernizing in other ways
leaving a place of worship not all that different from the rest
no more the murmuring Sanctuary, somehow lacking
the Cathedral charisma . . missing some indefinable facet
of its former mystique

and could it be but mere coincidence
that the dropping out of its members, as well as priests and nuns
so closely coincides with the elimination of Latin from the Mass ?
no longer is it true, as it once was
that Catholic Churches everywhere in the world
possess the same vibratory note of precious recognition
to stir the heart with the powerful chords of familiarity

yes, the renouncing of Latin was surely a "fallible" decision
and a rather difficult one to retract
    the Vatican perhaps underestimated the magnetic appeal of mystery
for both Initiate and layman
and now the damage to the poetry has been done

    still, there was no inkling of such dreary shadows to come
    when I entered my teens — and I thought then
    there was simply no comparison — as indeed, there even yet is not

between the unearthly, haunting beauty of *Ave Maria*

and garden-variety, ordinary hymns of other churches
not even . . *praise God from Whom all blessings flow*

down here below — it was the Catholic Church
where the Heavenly Host lived, Period.

and when I learned that almost every Christmas carol is Catholic
because there were no other churches around when the majority of them
were composed
my conversion within was complete

I may not have had the courage to openly and formally
join this new Brownie pack of what I now believed to be the only
Legitimate Angels . . . but I was a member in my heart

one of my most persistent memories
of Catholic impression
which left me with an inner confession
of loyalty to Roman ritual

was the funeral of a Nun
at Saint Xaivier's one April morning

and I doubt if I shall ever forget . . .

at least
I haven't
forgotten
yet

the Great Bells ringing and chiming and gonging
as if they, too, were wistfully longing
to express their sadness . . yet, a sadness which seemed
somehow, more glorious than funeral-dead and chilling-cold
more old . . and ancient
I stood there, soaking in
the sounds and scents and images . . and thrilling
to the soaring sight of the flight of the birds overhead
winging and dipping over the steeple of the Church
against a sky of bright blue
as the nuns and priests filed out, through the huge carved doors

a moving stream
of black and white
their pure, uplifted faces, touched by rainbows
of misty light

                        the spring breeze gently billowing their robes
                rosary beads dangling from their waists
                                                here and there, a crucifix
                        glittering brightly
                                in the Sun

great swells of organ music
                        and the chants of the choir
                pouring out from the dark cool within . . behind them

                it was all so beautiful
        so holy
                        and so lovely . . I wept

standing there, and wishing so . . that I could share this day with them
wishing I was really-truly Catholic too . . as I watched the glory
                                                        sweep past me
                hoping to catch a glimpse
                of the smiling, soft-blue robed Sister of St. Raphael's
                but she was nowhere in sight . . that day

                I listened to the sweeping song of death
                                that seemed more like a breath
                of heavenly incense

        than the funerals
                                I was used to seeing
                                        and smelling
                                                and hearing

        somehow . .

                        with more hope of gladness
                                woven as bright gold threads
                        through the grey wool of sadness

        yes, poetry

                        not quite, but nearly . . making Life rhyme
                        as in some other, long-forgotten Time
                                        I half-remembered

Snow Diamonds

when I was fourteen-going-on
        fifteen
                        I never said I was fourteen

I always said that I was
fourteen-going-on-fifteen

nearly every year
from twelve through twenty
I was never any age
but that age, going-on-the-next

I was lingering mistily
in a sort of No Man's Land of years
not belonging
to the one behind — nor yet
to the one ahead

it was like making Time stand still
like floating somewhere, suspended in Space
not any age at all

no age at all

no Time

when I was fourteen-going-on-fifteen
I was a Full Grown Woman in every way
only, no one knew it besides myself — and that was lonely

I spent the Christmas holidays
of that particular standing-in-the-middle
of-no-age year
in Charleston, with my bright-eyed Aunt Peg

Aunt Peg was on my father's side
I mean on his side of the family

being Libra-born, she never took sides
but balanced people in the middle
of her Scales . . no
never either right or wrong were you
with her
but always half of each — a little of this
and a little of that — just so
it all came out even, or as even as possible

Aunt Peg suited my own mood exactly
during those half-and-half years
of going-on-the-next
for, like her, I was hanging in the middle

I was walking back to Aunt Peg's apartment

from somewhere, this particular Christmas Eve

.. the apartment where Aunt Peg and Uncle Bill lived
while their new home was being built . . . which made me as sad
as they were glad . . because I had so loved their old house
                      with its beamed ceilings and dormer windows
dozens of Christmas trees alive in the yard
      and a balcony on the upstairs landing
where I could lean over the rail
            look down on the enormous living room
and recite the lines from Romeo and Juliet
                        which began . .

        Romeo, Romeo . . . wherefore art thou, Romeo ?

      many years before, when I was only a child
Nana had made for me a Juliet cap, of seed pearls and rhinestones
                              all cob-webby
to wear when I was acting out my balcony scene
though I had no long, flowing hair to match its beauty
just my silly-straight-dutch-bob-with-bangs

            oh ! how I hated my ugly, short-straight hair !

      but anyway . .

        on this particular Christmas Eve

the snow was drifting down in little flurries of softness
      piling mounds of whipped cream
                  and powdered sugar
   atop the roofs of houses and parked cars
                  and making the trees and plump bushes
         look like giant frosted lollipops
the sparkling scene around me reminiscent of fairyland
                        or the way, I believed, as a child
         fairyland would look
an image I still held, now that I was a Full Grown Woman

      Mother Goose had been shaking her feather quilts
      in a frenzied fury of falling flakes this way, all day

it had just turned dark, a black-velvet-winter dark
               and I was walking home through the baby blizzard
                        of snow feathers
to Aunt Peg's warm, pine smelling
      tangerine and nut-filled apartment
where she was probably mixing an egg nog at this very moment
with extra cinnamon on top, the way I liked it
               wondering what was keeping me so long

what was delaying me
was the way I was walking . . for I was walking . . so slow
through the snow
　　　this Christmas Eve
　　　　　　　in the just-turned-dark
　　and crying
crying very hard
and the tears froze on my cheeks

　　　　　　feeling like little slivers of ice

I had been in Charleston three days . . and the first morning I arrived
somehow, someway, somewhere
either on the way to — or on the way from town . . or the store

　　　I had lost my precious blue and silver rosary

　　three days now, it had been gone
　　my Christmas gift from the smiling, blue clad Sister
　　on that magical Noel, at St. Raphael's

the gentle Sister, who had, since, died of pneumonia
the previous April, just one week past my birthday
it had been . . her funeral
I had watched that spring day, at St. Xavier's
　　　　　　　　　from across the street

and I hadn't been told about it
until Thanksgiving . . long after she'd been buried

　　　like Pat, my calico cat . . they told me after she was buried

OH, HOW COULD I HAVE BEEN SO CARELESS !
HOW COULD I, HOW COULD I ?

that rosary was so much more than just a sparkling strand
of silver and blue beads, with a crucifix at the end

　　it was a gift of love, from a precious friend
　　　　　a part of the haunting sweetness
　　of those stolen, mysterious moments
　　　　　of kneeling in the cool and quiet convent chapel
　　and the childish game of playing bride . . with Jesus
　　which had left a Christmas-Easter haze
　　　　　of inexplicable, indefinable comfort
　　very personal, intimate — and private
　　I could sometimes hide behind, as behind a cloud of grace
　　when I was daydreaming
　　　　. . and the silver-blue beads had made it all real

Canto Five　☆　147

but all that was gone, forever-and-ever
with no more personal rosary ritual to make my dreams come alive
and all because of my awful, unforgivable Aries carelessness

there was no hope of finding it now — no chance
I had been frantically searching, silently wild, these past three days
                                                    so pained
with everyone asking, what could be wrong with the child ?
she is so morose, they complained — so uncommunicative and glum

        how can people who love you be so dumb — and so blind
        when they believe they are being kind ?
        I was not a *child*, but a *woman* — oh ! why couldn't they see
                                    the Woman in me ?

    I searched in silence, keeping my agony to myself
covering every square foot of snow-patched yard
in front of my aunt's apartment building . . . every square inch
of sidewalk . . from there to town . . and back

        perhaps it had slipped from my winter coat pocket
        in some store, while I was Christmas shopping
        or perhaps . . but what was the use of wondering
        how or where . . or when I had lost it ?

                            it was gone

and so much was gone, that Christmas
along with my rosary

            . . . the blue beads
        of old dreams and illusions . . .
        my trust in goodness and elves
                and wishing stars
        one by one, dropped along the way
        from my pockets of faith

        . . . the silver beads of miracles
                that never really happened
            outside of books

        and lost . . along with the shining silver crucifix
dangling at the end of the beads
                the most marvelous miracle of them all
the resurrection of gladness
            from the Easter tomb of sadness
                            . . gone forever too
        because I had discovered
            for certain
        that the dead don't rise

. . . that the resurrection simply was not true

as I walked, and heard . . and felt . . my boots crunching
on the hard-packed snow, it seemed to grow
somehow . . . unearthly still
so still, so quiet, that I choked back my sobs

lest the sound carry
all the way inside Aunt Peg's apartment

> *so still it was . . so very, very quiet*
> *. . so unearthly still*

whereas, moments before
there had been the noise of traffic
but now it was . . so still
I shall never forget that strange stillness . . and how very dark it was

the only sound . . . .

the crunching of my boots
in the snow

> I looked up into the black-velvet winter sky
> and saw the stars, winking and twinkling at me
> like teeny-tiny lights, peeking through the holes
> in the floor of Heaven
> celestial pinpoints
> of glittering glory

then . . in that sudden, holy stillness of the street I walked along
the words of the angels' ancient caroling song
rose gently, from somewhere deep within me
till I began to sing them softly . . in the darkness
to the pure, white night

and almost believed myself to be walking along another darkened street
in a far-away place . . and long-ago time
when the herald angels sang to the shepherds
of peace on earth
and mercy mild
with God and sinners reconciled

> *. . oh, little town of Bethlehem*
> *how still we see thee lie*
and thought . . .
what a wonderful thing
to imagine one could
actually *see* stillness !

♪ *. . above thy deep and dreamless sleep*
the silent stars go by

. . yet in thy dark streets shineth
an everlasting Light
the hopes and fears
of all the years
are met in thee tonight . .

I stopped singing, as my voice broke
and strangled into another sob
and I prayed, then
in a burst of genuine grief and anguish
for all . . I had lost

oh ! please Jesus — little Lord Jesus
asleep in the hay
let your light on *this* dark street
shineth . . . now

please, Jesus . . some way, somehow
will you help me find my rosary ?

it meant so much . . .
I could never explain it — or make anyone see
but *you* know how much it meant

it was like a secret, that rosary
yes . . . . . a secret between you and me

then suddenly, without a sound

the street lights turned on

not lit by the Old Lamplighter
but by some brighter angel, pulling a switch
back at the electrical Power plant of Heaven

and the soft glow
from those street lamps
made such a glorious transformation in the snow
at my feet . . O ! the snow !

the snow was shimmering and shining and sparkling
like millions of glittering diamonds

millions of delicate snowflake diamonds
                                    no two alike

oh ! the shimmering-shining
sparkle of snow diamonds !

        bathed in the soft glow of the street light
        on that still and silent, holy night
        was such a lovely, beautiful
        breathtaking sight, all silvery-white . . . .

        OH ! OH ! OH !

oh ! oh ! oh !

        and lying there . . lying in the snow
        at the foot of an old oak tree, by the curb on the street
        the kind of oak tree where druids like to meet
        there at my feet — at the foot of that tree
                                on the frozen ground
        sparkling among the snow diamonds

                . . . was my blue and silver rosary !

The Lost Has Been Found !

                        O ! JOY to the world !
                        let Heaven and Nature sing !

        it was for all the world, for all of Heaven
        as though Jesus had heard every word of my prayer
        and told the Heavenly Host to shine a flashlight down there
        on that spot — to make it glow and shineth
                                like the everlasting light
        on Bethlehem's streets
        that other holy, starry night . . when he was asleep in the hay

to show me that the way
was to first
                look up !
at the sky

                        then, with clearer vision, look down
                        to see how the lost can be found

maybe he even asked St. Anthony to help
the saint in charge of all things ever lost

and I sent up a quick rush of thanks
to Anthony . . and the switch-pulling angel

but it was really Jesus to whom my heart poured out
its overflowing gratitude — Jesus knew just what to do
to make it a bell-ringing, choir-singing Noel for me
at the foot of that Christmas tree
                              untouched by any tinsel
                              but the starry snow diamonds
                                        sans gaudy trim

        yes, it was him !
        Jesus always knew exactly what to do

                at just the right moment of Time
                    to make things rhyme

and I whispered, through my tears of pure joy
a childish prayer, for an already Full Grown Woman
of fourteen-going-on-fifteen

        "thank you, little Lord Jesus
        wrapped in swaddling clothes, in a manger
        with no room at the Inn
        and no crib for your bed . . I kiss
                        your sweet head"

then, standing there
whispering that prayer
on the Charleston streets of Bethlehem

        I thought of the time in Aunt Maud's garden, in the storm
        when I had felt this same kind of joy, overflowing
        and the cup of my heart runneth over with happiness

        as the remembered scent of rain-soaked sweet peas
        mixed crazily in my nose . . with the sharp, clean smell of snow
        and the cold winter air seemed to contain the odor
                                        of damp, warm earth
        suddenly, all oddly blended

        the celestial pin points of glittering glory in the sky this night
                that long-ago rainbow
        electrical thunder and flashing lightning
                these shimmering, sparkling snow diamonds

wet sweet peas . . sweet peas
        apple tree
just Jesus and me . . . .
        and for an instant

                for just one suspended moment
                I had that same, strange *lifting* feeling

as before . . when I had seen my very first rainbow
                            as a child of six or seven

        it was my second time of glowing-knowing
        my second wondrous sensing of the transfiguration
                            of levitation
        whatever the word means — and
                whatever it meant to the saints of old
it meant to me, at those two moments

        which were seemingly unconnected, even by season
        one summer, one winter — and with apparently no reason
        nor did the Heavens open up

        but my levitation seemed so real
        there was . . . that strange, lifting sensation I could *feel*

and I made a vow to myself that night
that if, ever in my life, these two miracles
unrelated to each other
                        . . the sweet-pea-rainbow-summer-rain miracle
                            of the electrical storm

        and this shimmering-snow-street-lamp-glow
        glittering-diamond miracle of the lost being found

should ever come to me
both at once — at the same time

        it would be a sign that Life was, at last, going to rhyme
        and a truly gigantic, biblical type miracle
        was about to take place, in a mist of grace
        which would transfigure me into a complete knowing
                of who I was, and why
        this magic performed, somehow, by Jesus — to prove
        that the Easter story was true

                not nearly . . but *really* true

of course, it seemed a hopeless vow
for how could all these things
happen at the same moment of Time ?
unless maybe both seasons converged
at the end of the world

        still, logical or otherwise
        these two minor transfiguration and levitation experiences
        combined, fused together
        and remained inseparable in my heart
        for the rest of my life representing the requirements of a miracle

not just an ordinary miracle — no
the miracle to surpass all miracles
and to end my search . . my quest
                              for a star
        of truth

yes, I guess that's the kind of miracle I meant
the search for something lost . . long ago
        but just what it was, I did not know

    standing there that night
    in the falling, feathered snow
        nor do I yet

                        and perhaps
                        I never will

Scattered Creeds

            I spent so many hours alone
            wondering who I was . . and where I was going
            while I was growing

    and still not knowing
    I made one final attempt to identify
        with God . . and people

and switched again

            from the First Methodist Episcopal Church
                the First M.E.
            to the protesting Protestant Presbyterian Church

    where they had heaps more fun
    bobbing for apples in the church basement
    on Halloween, than the Methodists did
    and cuter boys in the Young People's League

                        and prettier lyrics
                        to their hymns

for no more reason
    . . no more

    but underneath it all . . was still
    a secret druid, like before

a Brown Owl, unrecognized

and unidentified by God

    still waiting
    and listening

                for remembered music
                and the Light of Truth

CANTO SIX

Where is the sky that I dream of,
Where are the fields of the heavens,
Where is the love that I sing of,
Where is the heart I adore ?

Friend of mine, friend of old,
Where is the pathway you follow ?
Come, — I see your laughing eyes,
I know that we shall meet —
While we journey toward tomorrow.

Where are the hills of the faer-light,
Where are the songs of the morning,
Where is the home of the sunset ? —
Where lies my heart evermore !

Kyril Demys   *(Musaios)*
Prismatic Voices

Mother Nature didn't hate me after all

at the proper time . . . the Charleston year of the Lost and Found
I collected my dues as a female
and was finally cursed

it was all I could do not to announce the monthly Lunar achievement
with a note tacked to the school bulletin board
so I did the next best thing
for a couple of semesters, I stayed home
or was late for class on at least one day out of each twenty-eight
as regularly as clockwork
with excuses more or less spurious

and on my return to school
I would be very mysterious
about the reason for my absence
when questioned by the curious

I'm sure most of them, especially the boys — were secretly convinced
that I'd contracted some rare form of periodic bubonic plague
missing the whole point, and shattering my newly acquired feminine
poise
in addition to being finally cursed
I was also blessed with the absolute must
of that long-awaited miracle of a visible bust — and so
thus honored with my womanly dues
I billowed into respectable bloom, within and without
about the same time — the same spring
I bloomed into the right age to become a Senior Scout

fourteen-going-on-fifteen-almost-sixteen

all three accomplishments
the curse — the blessing — and the Senior Scouts
represented a promotion of sorts, I suppose
but they were disappointing miracles
lacking any lasting magic

why is success always such a failure ?

even with three brand new identifications
the Cursed — the Blessed — and Senior Scout
I was never again quite as sure of who and what I was
as the day I started my own druid pack
and made myself Brown Owl

for, you see . .

these were all identifies I shared with millions of others
and I was looking for myself — for *me*

having already being discouraged at Kiashuta Camp
of my incentive to earn merit badges
eventually, I dropped out of the Girl Scouts
and like my earlier departure and self ex-communication from Trinity
they sent no searching parties
                    . . hardly noticing that I was gone

  nor, was there much of a fuss made
when I decided to depart the first M.E. church
for the Presbyterian protestors

        it followed the same pattern
    as my desertion of Trinity and the Senior Scouts

as before, it was like deciding to go to hell
then discovering that no one in Heaven cares
    or even notices your absence

the Holy Ghost seemed to be
                    the only one still interested in me
    continuing to haunt my dreams sometimes . . at night

unsure of which of Life's skeins were colored wrong or right
first, a religious drop-out, now a Girl Scout drop-out
                I had become a loner again

we didn't have *school* drop-outs then — at least
            I couldn't imagine such action
being punishable by anything less than death by hanging
so I was stuck scholastically, like it or lump it
                            I lumped it

        by the time I had graduated into the world-at-large
        of Senior High School — I had no identification at all
        until I made Big Red Cheerleader, one fall
        but for one season only, as a substitute
        I never got called out to lead a single cheer
                    except for one football game, late in the year
        that got rained out at half-time

the scout merit badge I didn't earn that stung me the most
was the badge of Official Scout Lifeguard
oh ! how I hungered after that !

    so, for awhile, I identified myself — as Lifeguard
    at the City Park swimming pool
    neglecting to add the minor detail that it was

                                        the baby pool
            two feet of water at the deep end

the cheerleading episode, however, wasn't a complete loss
since it allowed me to meet a local football hero
whose first name was Charles . . but he was nothing like

                              Charles Hollingswell
                              my summertime, buzzing-bee
                              friend — who chased
                              the ant killers away
                                        when he could

this Football Star, Charles
evidently hadn't heard — or maybe ignored
the rumors of the dangers involved in becoming a Swain
of the Original Straight and Number One Scatterbrain

one night at a party I believe I somehow crashed
where everyone present — except me — was absolutely smashed
on some smuggled-in blackberry wine
he decided, this Charles, to make me his comic Valentine
when he observed I was the only one at the swinging soiree
who didn't smoke, and who refused to listen to an off-color joke

and he told my best friend, Kelly
something which turned my knees to jelly — he told her

                    "I'm going to marry that girl"

        he meant *me* !

        and he sealed that hasty vow a few months later
                    on the 4th of July
        with a genuine, one-sixteenth karat diamond ring

but then he took it back that very same year
and wouldn't even let me keep it as a souvenir — because
he found a girl who, although she smoked and joked
nevertheless, played better touch football at half-time intermission
and who knew how to spell thrill

        his pet name for me was "Chicken"
        I never quite knew what he meant by that
        I told myself it was affectionate, but still . .

and then there was Jim . .
        I still hear faint music
when I think of him . . . . . the lyric of a song

                    160 ☆ Canto Six

with a depressing last verse
                                    that warned

. . someday, I know that Jim will surely leave me
but, though he'll always hurt me and deceive me . . .

    the hints were all there, in the music — but
        I was too bemused, too bewitched
    to see that I had hitched my hopes and dreams
    to the fragile star of self delusion

I was overwhelmed with the heart leaping happenings
of a secret smile, an intimate glance — or a cheek-to-cheek dance
each glamourous illusion of young love . . completely unaware
that the male definition of romance
                is not quite so ethereal and misty

when I hear his name . . or that song, called "Jim"
                I still remember a snow white taffeta gown
with a full, full skirt
all covered with sparkling diamonds
             that glittered like stars, when we danced

    well, actually rhinestones
    but they looked like diamonds
             . . from a distance

one enchanted night, while they were playing *The Anniversary Waltz*
during his fraternity Prom at W.V.U . . . . a night that trailed stardust
Jim gave me, to wear on a gold chain, an official Phi Sigma Kappa
                            locket
I engraved his initials, J.M. — on the back, with a safety pin
then scratched mine beside them — naively believing
        that would identify the locket as my very own
                forever after
and also identify me as his girl
for approximately the same length of time

        it didn't work . . the forever incantation

    which hurt
    more deeply than
    I like to recall

        Jim's last name rhymed with end-it-all
        and one day — he did
        like the football Swain and his ring — Jim
        took back my locket . . and gave it to a girl named Emma
        who evidently didn't mind wearing stolen property

weaving quietly, gently, in and out

and around and through all the others . . like Jacob's ladder
rising higher and higher, in my eyes
was a boy named William, who was deep and wise . . . sometimes
he took me to Sunday Mass, at Saint X
and we lit a few candles together

William was the kindest, and the most perceptive of them all
we used to walk home from school together
shuffling our feet through red-gold burnished leaves
in the autumn
and he listened to my dreams patiently
for hours . . even believing in most of them
but it didn't last long, because, after awhile
he began whistling a song
called *Margy* — and that wasn't my name

William and I were only playing a Jacob's ladder-higher-and-higher
Friendship Game
keeping each other protective company . . I guess
still, I may have secretly liked him best
in a longer-lasting kind of way
and I really missed the Friendship Game we used to play
crying occasional tears he never noticed . . .

then there was Calvert, a boy who was handsome and tan
and perfectly dreamy — he even played the piano
but Calvert and I had too much in common — our families
his parents were close friends of my Charleston aunt Peg
which is one of the surest way to kill passion
I mean, who wants to marry someone approved of
by your relatives ?
it removes all the taste
of forbidden fruit . . and the excitement
of defiance

so Calvert, too, eventually drifted away
not that I ever really believed he would stay
because he called me "Sunny"
and never noticed the times I was blue and rainy

I had learned, with Jerry Jones, how to dream and how to dance
maybe even how to love . . .
but I was an eternal failure at casual romance
I could never master the required light touch
all through those growing years
I tried too hard, and I cared too much

the world of multiple dating, with picnics and hay rides
and mid-winter sleigh rides . . collecting Hi-Y pins and hearts
to dangle on charm bracelets

was alien to me

I was a stranger, in a strange land

it seemed so phony-baloney to pretend purple passions I didn't feel
and permit exploratory excursions
just to prove I wasn't an artificial bloomer, but real
to guarantee a Saturday night movie once a week — with boys
who demanded considerably more than a kiss on the cheek
or invitations to the bigger proms and parties . . . and football games

basketball was too loud and sweaty
                                        and unromantic
        who needs an escort to Bedlam ?

such predatory opportunist tactics were beyond my thespian talents
I was helpless to cope with the ground rules
                                of this new Brownie pack

so I didn't "lend a hand, and play the game"
as the Brownie motto used to go — nor lend any other part of me
to panting boys in parked cars
                or in the last row, at the late show

I might have been willing to try something more thrilling
if the rules hadn't been so changeable, right from the start
                that I was always afraid to loan my heart
and I didn't want to lend-or-lease just a piece of myself

        my heart went along with the rest of me
    inseparable, undetachable — an integral, odd-shaped
    piece of the puzzle of my intimate Beingness

yes, I may secretly have longed to lend a hand
and play the new Brownie game — but no one wanted to borrow
                                        my heart
along with my hand, and the rest of my anatomy

        all the rules . . were so insensitive

like, just casually going steady, with Kimball or George or Freddy
then switching partners for the following Saturday night
                not even because you'd had a fight
but only because the double-date had caused the chemistry to bubble
                        in a different test tube

        . . trading dances, as a matter of courtesy
                mandatory ethics, hiding each hurt tear
    while watching the absolutely only boy in the world
            with his arms around the school Beauty Queen
        chewing on her perfumed ear . . .

Canto Six   ☆   163

till it was half-time again . . change sides !

when in doubt, punt ! and go-go-go- for that touchdown
                                    over the goal line !
        Rah ! Rah ! Rah !
        we want a touchdown, Sis-Boom-Bah !

oh, blah, blah, blah — is how I felt
about those touchdowns on dates
and sometimes I had to kick to make my point
kick up a fuss, that is
            to tie the score once more

yes, decidedly, the view is better from the bleachers — and safer
far away from the athletic ground
if you really want to check the score at half-time
and watch the quarterbacks call the signals of On and Off
                            and Out of Bounds
        . . like the unwritten law
                about breaking up

breaking up being about as inevitable and periodic
as the Lunar curse — and no blessing — because possessing
was strictly against the rules

you had to expect to break up before the romance was even broken-in
and no sniffling about it either — that was neither cricket
                            nor good form
it was considered a cardinal sin
to cry when you didn't win . . at the glittering game of romance . . . .
oh, maybe a few star-crossed lovers were permitted
                        the luxury of agony
when they broke up — made up — broke up
but they were almost legendary gods and goddesses, the golden ones
like Betty and Marvin, and Helen and Fred, and Babs and Bud
    maybe I've forgotten and scrambled the names
having such a poor memory for those teen-age romantic games
the ones I was always losing before they even started
ending up alone and broken-hearted . . not over real boys
just over shattered dreams, that never saw the light
                dreams that never even got kissed goodnight
    just kissed goodbye

        I was left to rhyme
        sigh and cry with . . . why ?

because I continued to rhyme hello with no
not go-go-go ! make a touchdown, Rah ! Rah ! Rah !

        Sis-Boom-Bah !

no, I wasn't a goddess

>like those others I worshipped as star-crossed
>and may have mistakenly named
>   for all I know, their coupling names may have been
>Betty and Fred . . Judy and Bill . . Marvin and Nancy
>or Helen and Julian — or was it Steve ?
>whatever they were called, they were undeniably
>   the golden ones
not being a goddess myself
I never met any gods from Mount Olympus

>we mere peasants were expected to play by the rules
>and learn that breaking up was not allowed to be unduly tragic

maybe it was a sprinkling of left-over druid dust
that made me feel things had to be magic — or forget it, Charlie
and you too, Mike — or was it Don ?

when I loved — or thought I did — I Loved For Keeps

>and that sort of intensity gives boys the creeps
at almost any age you can mention . . . .
permanency was not the tender intention of any of the lads I knew

the ones who gambled on taking me out to a movie or a dance
spent most of the time trying to prove to me
and their curious macho-minded buddies
that they were men — real men — with my seduction
                              as the final proof
none of them wanted to sit on the roof
eating Goober's Peanuts . . and counting hailstones
and I didn't run into any tall ones
with a rainbow hanging behind their left ears

>. . which was sort of a druid yardstick
>I had made up — more or less pessimistically

no, none of them had rainbows draped behind their ears
their chief ambition was to have a few short beers
then park in lover's lane — and collect their dues for the night . . .
it always ended in a struggle, or an outright nasty fight
until eventually I earned a brand new identification — *Seabiscuit*

nicknamed for a race horse, who had, years before, been put out to pasture
                    why ? because I was so *fast*, get it ?
it was one of my early lessons
                    in the sharp sting of social sarcasm

there were only those few, over the years, who shared with me

a couple of smiles and some genuine tears
instead of just a parked car tug-of-war
and who might have been brushed with the pale shimmer

of . . maybe not love
                              but a gentle pink-gold

just those few

        like Jim and Charles
        and William, who climbed with me
        up Jacob's ladder
                    to occasional truth

and . . . . Jimmy Lee

        I can never remember how old we were
        perhaps somewhere around two or three — or maybe
        much older, like seventeen or so
                                yes, Jimmy Lee

he used to chase butterflies with me, and lightning flashes
and rainbow splashes . . and the thunder of wonder
once he joined me on an elf hunt, during a fine spring rain
behind a far-off, violet shaded hill
and he almost taught me how to spell thrill
behind that far-off violet shaded hill, where elves and rainbows hid

        yes, he really-nearly did
        and he wasn't so bad at lending his hand
                        and a tiny piece of his heart
        to play the Brownie game
        but I was never able to guess his secret aim
        and the trouble with Jimmy Lee
        was that his last name rhymed with dream . . in the beginning
        and still . . behind that violet shaded hill
                                at the end

the boys I thought I loved — or who may have thought they loved me
grew up to be doctors and dentists — and lawyers
and, I believe, one became a physicist
                    . . his first name, Kimball, rhymed
                        with silent cymbal

        but none of them grew up strong enough, or brave enough
        or tall enough — or crazy enough
        to make fish swim through the sky — or even try
        to learn how to make a mountain fly
        they didn't even understand a mountain who could fly

or was it only that I . . . . was a willow

who couldn't seem to learn how to bend ?

and let's see . .

I guess that's the end
of the short list

of my Knights
in shining armour

Except For One

after high school was over

there were no more Knights in any kind of armour
shiny or dull — riding horses or donkeys

except for one
years later

except for just one . .

who helped me catch
a bunch of baby druids
though three of them flew away

he never really grew up at all, but he was always very tall
as long as he was around
sometimes, he would look at me, and stare — and stare
and I would see a sort of glow around his hair, like a light
did I imagine that glow . . or was it really there ?

he was forever trying to reach a star — or ring a far away bell
like the Carnival Bill, from Carousel
his last name rhymed with apple-cider . . and he loaned me
his name — and his hand — and his heart
as we tried very hard to play love's Brownie game

together at first
then at last . . apart

yes, the Carousel Bill nearly taught me to spell thrill — and
if only he could have remained long enough to grow
he could have tossed off a few miracles, I know . . like
making it snow, by just wishing it so
. . like Jerry Jones

Oh ! what dreams the Carousel Bill could weave !

he was a druid too, exactly like me — a twin
        like half of my soul
and he was always saying . . . "shall we make believe ?"

    one night, he said

                "now just try to imagine
                what it would be like . . . . if I loved you"

    then we'd pretend

it's true, he was magic !

        but it hurts too deeply to remember him now

        so I'll wait . . and remember him later

Shifting Gears

in my teens, when I should have learned how to drive
my Leo father regally commanded, "absolutely not !" placing a car
in my hands, according to my paternal Lion — would be tantamount
to placing a deadly weapon in the hands of a maniac

it flattened my ego, and somehow, after that dire prediction
my desire to learn to drive was stifled

                I felt small and incompetent — a chastised maniac

now I'm a more or less permanent pedestrian
at the mercy of friends and strangers — sometimes, even enemies
yes . . once, years later, driving as a passenger
                        to Newport Beach, California
definitely at the mercy of enemies

but my father was probably right
for I am careless and impulsive — and I daydream a lot
you can miss plenty of Stop Signs that way, even on foot
I remember one sunny morning when I'd just turned seventeen
                        with no traffic in sight
I rushed headlong into a busy, crowded heart
when I thought I saw a **Green Light** in someone's eyes

                I should have waited
                        the light was changing . .

    I have my doubts about passing a driving test today
after all those years of ignoring Sharp Curves Ahead

and Falling Rock warnings
I can never tell Forward from Reverse
I always strip my emotional gears when I'm shifting
from High to Low — or from Low to High
                    and mechanically speaking, it's the same
I guess I'm a confirmed gear stripper both ways
no matter how hard I try

I have a Capricorn friend named David . . . also a Goat named Steve
who think I shouldn't give up driving entirely
and have offered to teach me . . but they think I should learn
on the old fashioned kind of stick shift
and develop my own automatic transmission
                              so, who knows ?
I may end up in the driver's seat yet, behind the wheel at long last
with nothing to stop me
from speeding down the highway to Freedom !
both emotionally and mechanically matured, with finally a Driver's License
making it easy to properly identify myself — to everyone but me

              I still won't know who I am
                    or why I try

Getting High

someone once said — I believe it was Sinatra or McKuen
that being a loner and being lonely . . are not the same thing

        well, I don't know

I guess it's a safe enough answer to give
when people probe into your life style — at least it cuts off curiosity
from friends, strangers and enemies . . . . sometimes one person
                                        can be all three
I walked home this morning about two a.m. or so
which is kind of late to stroll Broadway, even for a loner

it was raining . . and all the taxis had disappeared, as usual
but I wasn't really lonely, or even afraid of muggers
by that hour, they're home in bed
or hanging around Howard Johnson's, drinking coffee

              New York muggers are a spoiled bunch
              with millions of victims to pick from
              they can afford to be choosey about working conditions
              and who wants to hack out a living in a drizzle ?
              they have a lot in common with Manhattan cabbies

it was good to have the Great White Way all to myself
I love to walk in the rain — it's like stepping into a giant shower
I always feel like singing, and scrubbing my mind with Ivory Soap

      what is that thing in the air
that makes the pavements smell fresh and sweet
                  when they're wet ?
I drank it in this morning
through my nose and my skin
while the moisture-drenched breeze blew affectionately
                  through my hair
and tangled my mind into wispy little cobwebs of nostalgia

      rain smells better on the grass, of course
      in a small town, or in the country
      where they still have happy, healthy trees
      I remember that much . . even after twelve years in Fun City

   . . and I remember other things

oh ! it was marvelous, the times it rained when I was a child
I could put on my red-and-white-striped swim suit
run outside and splash through the puddles at the curbs
squint my eyes, and tilt my head back . . let the rain fall on my face
open my mouth to drink the drops
               and sniff that ozone smell
until I felt like screaming with joy — just to be me, and alive
with maybe chocolate pudding for supper

      it's not much like that anymore

for one thing, now I know that chocolate, especially Rocky Road
                      ice cream
     clogs up the body's freeways

besides, if I had slushed barefoot
this morning, through the puddles at the curb
throwing back my head to drink in the sweet-smelling raindrops

      the narcotics squad would have appeared out of nowhere
      and hauled me in as a junkie
      getting high on Life — and drugs — is so similar
      people can't always tell the difference at a distance

still, little spurts of chlorophyll
managed to make it, somehow, this morning, through the smog
soaking my senses, and tugging at my heart, as it always does
with the old, familiar call
      of wild, impossible dreams and alleluia choruses
or maybe a miracle tomorrow . . on a windswept hill !

and I felt that same delirious surge
of indefinable, uncontrollable happiness . . I felt as a child

it lasted until I remembered the question
my driving instructor asked me in Colorado last week
"why are you lonely ?

who's lonely ?
these are raindrops, not tears . . on my cheek

Take Me To Your Leader

after awhile . .
my flaming worship of Judaism's traditional, ancient wise
and emphasis on learning — stopped burning
when I began to realize why the Jews of old failed to recognize
the man from Galiliee . . as the one from whom they awaited deliverance

my former awe condsiderably cooled, when I saw how they'd been fooled
by their own High Priests — those self-serving Rabbis
who feared the Golden Rule would expose their lies
and their teachings . . as brass
and so ridiculed and rejected
the humble carpenter from Nazareth
when he rode into Jerusalem on a lowly ass
not at the head of a powerful Army, on a snow white steed

after all, a Messiah's business is to lead, not to plead
and surely not to bleed — on a cross.

this man was a freak, who championed the weak
defended the meek — and turned the other cheek to Caesar
it certainly had not been Moses' fashion
to show enemies compassion
Moses parted the Red Sea — and set their people free
what kind of Messiah spends all his time forgiving miserable sinners ?
Abraham and David and Moses were winners
but Jesus was a loser, whose promises proved impotent, empty and hollow

no god — only a man

for other losers to follow

a crucified prophet is a Saviour for fools
and Jesus broke all their messianic rules

then, following my Hebrew disillusion
came the end of my Inner Pilgrimage to the Vatican

my fascination for the Catholic ritual's deep mystery
buried somewhere behind Roman Church Law
ceased to magnetize me, when I clearly saw
that the Church is hiding more than mystery from the light

such as, the reason for the marble tiles, in the Pope's bathroom
inscribed with the twelve signs of the zodiac, from Aries through Pisces
                                        from the Ram through the Fish

the real reason behind the sacrilegious surgery of 300 A.D.
      the murders of the bloody Inquisition
and the Council of Constantinople, in 430 A.D. — that time
                                        of misguided dedication
when those allegedly infallible ones, in Rome
performed the shameful spiritual castration
of removing from the Bible all previous reference to reincarnation
carving away their own foundation
leaving dull, sterile dogma . . to replace former faith

      not to mention . .
                        the well kept secret of the true symbolism
                        behind the mystical marriage of the Nuns to Jesus

yes, Catholicism's ritual hides much mystery
behind Church history
                        and has also hidden Truth

      but disillusioning me

even more than Catholicism's light tossing away
of the logic of the Cause and Effect of the doctrine of Karma
contained in the ancient precepts of reincarnation

                  was the attitude taken by the Roman Vatican
                  toward Hitler's Nazi nation
                  when the Jews — and others — were being tossed into
                                        fiery furnaces
                  like so many helpless, struggling ants
                              tossed into flaming Matchstick Forts
      and so . .
                  the growing bubble of religious delusion
                  of the babbling dogmatic confusion
                  of Judaism's blindness — and Catholic hypocrisy
                  swelled even larger with my observation
                  of the Protestant protesting bureaucracy
                  and the sterility of ritual, lacking mystical symbolism
                  in those plain-Jane churches
                              of methinks thou dost protest too much
                  then finally burst wide open
                              POP !

172 ☆ Canto Six

leaving me with the limp, rubbery pieces
of my former balloon of trust . . in all these faiths
with seemingly, nowhere to turn
yet, still burning to learn — the Truth   . . consequently

      after skipping and hopping
           and starting and stopping
    and tiptoeing and gliding
            and walking and floating
    and swimming and running
           and crawling and falling

in and out of Synagogues, Catholic Masses — and Protestant classes
                        in empty theology
I wandered next through Egyptian Mythology
and during that lingering spiritual crisis . . was deeply stirred
by the tragic fate of those Twin Souls
               known as Osiris and Isis
an unsolved mystery
of ancient history . . that still haunts me
in a strange, inexplicable way
            . . then one fine day

I stumbled on a brighter path, far from the Holy Ghost's invisible wrath
and far from a vengeful god's angry retribution of
          "an eye for an eye, and a tooth for a tooth"
a path which still leads me
slowly . . . toward enlightenment and Truth
through the time-tested teachings
of re-birth and astrology . . even containing a hint

    to the final solution of all the confusion
    in the Isis-Osiris mythology

  yes, I wandered, at last, on the path of the stars
  and there I stayed — and there I remain, through Sun and rain
    part-time mystic, and full-time agnostic, guided by Mars

yet . . still secret druid
    chanting deeper rites
       on moonlit nights

CANTO SEVEN

Birth of cataracts that pulse the Nile
Ancient Mausoleum of deluged temples
and the Prophet's sacred graves
Hiding-place of old drowned voices

Hieroglyphic stones
speaking once from
black rocks and russet green-blue water
Lapis sky

and the skimming dhow
seeking Sudan and Wadi Halfa
southward to the end of upper Egypt . . .

There perched on a single carven rock beyond the prow
stately and still an Ibis stands
Holy emblem of thrice greatest Thoth
                                    . . the Wise

while the motley rowers
chorus wild:

Hállai am Wáfi !
Hállai am Wáfi !

God give us strength !
O strength, Allah !

Kyril Demys   (Musaios)
Wings of Myrahi

Birthdays

I don't recall exactly when it was that I first learned — or knew

.. maybe a few centuries
or even a few million years ago ..

that each human is meant to exist in the same flesh Body Temple
sans all signs of illness and aging — for thousands of years — *or eternally*
and if one should choose to clothe one's self in a different body
through Free Will choice . . . for complex karmic purposes
this may be done in much the same manner as changing sweaters
eliminating the need for sadness or tears
accomplished with full knowledge, and wide awake
both consciously and unconsciously
without the coma of "death", as we know it
the coma itself being the most feared facet of the dying process

in changing Body Temples, both the departed and the bereaved
may be made aware of the identity of the new temple chosen
but before this kind of transition can be mastered
one must first master the difficult lessons of Love and Forgiveness

and Faith — not weak hope

gravity is the most formidable obstacle in conquering "death"
for those choosing to retain the same flesh body forever . . .
and eating, of course . . and thinking
because, what one eats, and what one thinks, with every breath
is what one *is*

but with the insurance companies constantly bombarding our minds . . .
seeding their illusionary, arbitrary "life expectancy" statistics
into the collective, mass subconcious
already seeded in childhood with the weeds
of the same lies
it may be some time before each human wins such a longevity prize
although such achievement is definitely attainable now
to those select few with both the formula and the Faith of Knowing

available, yes, if one can bear the loneliness of such an eternal existence
for it is lonely to recall, from literal experience
events and places no one else remembers . . or shares
remembering is achingly sad, when the recalling itself finds
no answering echo
in the eyes . . and hearts . . and minds . . of contemporaries
only in one's fleeting dreams and private prayers

and those who have acquired this magic
.. called Gurus, Avatars or Master Adepti

bear the additional burden of deception
being forced by the disbelief and unawakened awareness
of Society and Science in every Age and Era
to periodically require new identification

.... bearing a bizarre symbolism
to our Government's infamous "witness relocation program"

for, after an aspiring Avatar has reached a chronological 'age'
when current mores . . and "life expectancy" charts
dictate that the "average" man and woman really should die

.... it's considered bad form to refuse

then, to avoid being burned at the stake — imprisoned
committed to an asylum as a lunatic
or merely suffering the sting of ridicule and social rejection

.... depending on prevalent custom of the time

one must carefully adopt
a new name — as well as a new and suitable place and date of birth
with a new group of memorized ancestors — and believable parents

then arrange to "die" in some manner, so that the body
is never found — or seen

then re-appear, as unobtrusively as possible
in some new geographical location
on the planet Earth . . . preferably a different nation
which, of course, makes the mastery of several languages
a most important study for an Avatar

in truth, it's a weary and intricate process — although
undeniably worth all the time and trouble
for otherwise, no great discoveries or giant leaps could be made
for the advancement of the human condition
since one needs many more years than a hundred or so
to master wisdom, through experience

enough experience, that is
to be capable of creating lasting contributions to Earth

except for those extremely rare ones, in every Age
who make their lasting contributions in art, music and science
not because they have lived
in the same flesh body for centuries or longer — this time
but because they have, already, in past incarnations
achieved such longevity and its resulting enlightenment
and have elected, through Free Will choice
to return to Earth . . and "soothe the savage beasts"

through stirring symphonies, inspiring paintings
                          or the higher Math of Relativity
these called by society and science
          prodigies
but metaphysical teaching reminds us of their origin
as ancient legend instructs us that . . .

          "new knowledge, easily gained . . is old knowledge"

a scattering of these artists, composers and scientists
being, not the above
but Avatars in the metaphysically literal sense . . . from distant "Earths"
in other solar systems

which are which, few can say
but they know themselves — and each other
though they're not likely to discuss it over an afternoon cup of tea

some claim Nicola Tesla
Shakespeare, Bacon and Newton fell into the latter category

odd, that brain-washed masses fail to see this simple Truth
as the Adepti themselves ponder — yes, the Adepti
those strange ones who wander among us, even today — clear eyed
perfectly aware that they are merely players on Life's stage
amused at the blindness of other players who take it all so seriously
          not realizing that they cast themselves in the Drama
even as did the Avatars . . and may change the next Act
anytime they please or choose . . after they've paid their karmic dues
not by just wishing it so, although wishing it so . . is a beginning

no, I can't recall when I was first aware of all these mysteries
but it was surely not while I was cast in that chronological drama
called The Teens . . that play in which every actor and actress
                                        is a Star !

the sudden blossoming of the calendar Eighteen
held no more magic than the clock-strikes-midnight Twelve
or the highly over-rated Bittersweet Sixteen

Eighteen — the age of Freedom ! but legal freedom only
old enough to be held responsible for public action
yet not fulfilling a fraction
of the average birthday pilgrim's expectations

so I tossed away, with no regret, as worn out clothes
which bored and tired me — the tempestuous and temperamental teens
then I discarded Twenty One, as an age not quite the proper size
too large for some dreams — too small for others
too young for some ambitions, too old for others — called illusions
and passed this uninspiring milestone too

now adding birthday candles to my carrot cake each year
with a deeper wisdom, born of the new-found truth that miracles
do not belong to any age, but only to the heart
not numbered 12 — 16 — or 21
nor guaranteed by any calendar of chronological delusion

       but not restricted by it either

miracles have a mind of their own — and happen when they happen
never pre-arranged, or pre-dated
created by Desire and Will and Heaven, working as a Trinity

     and so . . slowly, but surely . . yet also impulsively
                      and impatiently
     I grew past the midnight-Cinderella 12
     past Bittersweet 16 — past Freedom labeled 18
                and boring 21
     and grew until I knew
     I was, at last, a full grown Woman . . with inalienable rights

        among them, lonely nights
        and questions still unanswered

nevertheless entitled to the benefits of mellowing
past the One and Twenty marker — after which, stale custom
has ceased to pick on any one particular year as a *happening*
until the number 40, when Life is presumed to begin anew

     oh ! I was going to begin my own Life
     long before *that* number !

for the 19 years between the disappointing 21 and Life-Begins-at-40 mark
are left alone, sans false labels, pompous predictions
                     and purely imgainary qualities
I will enjoy these 19 years
I thought, at one and twenty

     in fact, if I were the one in charge of gumming labels
     on illusionary chronological mileposts
     these 19 years, as yet untouched by superstition
     would be the ones I would christen truly Free !

     free, at least, from mass pre-judgement and pre-conditioning
     quite as likely to contain a miracle
         and far more likely to deliver one

for . . a quality of miracles
sometimes forgotten by those who like to label things

     is the quality of . . the unexpected

yes, finally, through the metamorphasis of repeated disappointment
I emerged a Woman — free of numerical cocoons and intense anticipations
                              based on certain years alone
      my hopes . . . desires

          based instead on what I could actually attain
          through the ingenuity and individuality of — *me*
          no longer depending on 1-2-3
                    or any other impotent figures

that is . .

          I was a Woman biologically
          chronologically and intellectually
          if not yet spiritually and emotionally matured

child-woman
I once was

                    woman-child
                    I had now become

there is a wide, wide difference, when you really ponder the two
for, when Nature forces upon you, the label *Child*
you need not also choose to be
          Woman, longing

just as, when Nature forces upon you, the label *Woman*
the choice of remaining *Child* is still yours to make

          only the first half of the label is non-optional
          the second half is pure Free-Will — on either level of awareness

so . . Child-Woman
      that I once was

                    Woman-Child
                    I had become . . reversing polarities

not choosing then
to be Child-Child

      nor choosing now
      to be Woman-Woman

looking on the pock-marked face of the agonized and terminal planet
                                        Earth
being ravaged systematically, piece-by-piece
lake-by-lake and stream-by-stream
wood-by-wood and mountain-by-mountain . . . screaming
an unheard lament as she dies

seeing the world through Woman-Child glasses
I saw the same distortions as before, now sharpened into focus
no longer softened by the earlier innocence of Child-Woman

> . . sensing the adjustment
> would have been even more difficult
> had I formerly chosen to be Child-Child

to avoid, as much as possible, these disturbing distortions
I chose tinted lens for my symbolic bi-focals
> I chose . . . the gentle pink-gold of dreams
to tone down the glare of reality
that causes both eye-strain and heart-strain

> to the more near-sighted soul

> for only the far-sighted can bear to gaze
> through clear, untinted glass
> upon Madness, climaxing

> and watch the aging children dancing . . .
wrapping faded ribbons
> around North-South May Pole axis
> slowly slipping
> in brown and withering grass

I saw then

> through my tinted lens of gentle pink-gold
> that the planet Earth and I — equally old
> > in disappointed hopes
> had, at least, these 19 years
> before Life Began Again . . forced by wasteful carelessness

> to start all over

> from the beginning Genesis

Me Tarzan — You Jane

I haven't joined
a Women's Lib group — yet

> that's not to say I don't dig Gloria's cool — and her tinted shades
> or Germaine's brain — it's just that, in my own personal domain
> there's never been the slightest doubt about
> what is 'hers' and what is 'his' — and which word comes first

however, if the fact that I'm a Ms
should ever cause a male chavinist Mster to give me the biz
by insinuating that I'm worth less than a man
financially or intellectually
or, to make one word from two — worthless in any other way
the Mars temper of this Ms would fizz
and I'd start my own protest parade

but at the moment
I shall leave
what I consider
        well enough
    alone

        I'm not much good at marching in parades
        led by other Brown Owls
                . . . . we're the Brownies, here's our aim
                lend a hand, and play the game . . . .

        I always get socked with demerits
        for being out of step
        and arguing with the Parade Master
        let alone each different drummer

I'm an Aries Ms

        (I'm glad you asked)

        and all Rams were born liberated
           from male dominance
        or anyone else's dominance . . me and Lucy

if you don't believe that
just ask Charlie Brown
or Linus . . or Schroeder

My Center of Gravity is Slipping

Pat, my calico cat
and her faded, favorite red bow

the fancy ladies-of-the-evening
in Colorado Pleasure Palaces, long ago

the hard working hookers
along Broadway today

the original prototype Magdalene

wearing, in Palestine
robes of Virgin-Mary-blue . . yet not true
                              till she met him
the Swingers and the Straights
wrong or right ?   cursed or blessed ?

expected to pass, blindfolded
some ancient karmic test

lonely men, who mine the Earth's treasures
of turquoise and gold, out west . . and what for ?

a Mass for the dead . . **O !** holy holy holy
for a tiny baby robin, who will sing of spring no more

a blue and silver rosary
sparkling through the blue and silver rain
that splashes on my cheeks tonight

> how can these fragments of memory from burning and learning
> help me to mine the treasure of Truth from a silent Universe
> while I stand here, precariously
> trying to keep my balance . . on a waning planet
> slowly slipping on its axis . . as I am slowly slipping on my own ?

are we both preparing . . . the Earth and I
to reverse our North and South Poles ?

my soul is weary

my soul is lost
and lonely

but more than this . . my soul
does not know what it yearns for

to whom it calls
or even why
it seeks the way back home

back home
to where ?

why do I
         still reach
for a star that hides
in the wide night sky out there ?

shall I blame my lost and lonely
weary quest — like all the rest
on the thunder of the Aquarian Age ?

that's the popular scapegoat of the day
for those who don't know
or who have forgotten how . . to pray

> at least in that, as each dream fades
> I shall be in step with the Times
> not breaking step
> as I do in all other parades

Challenge

do not listen
to those smug prophets and Cassandras
who argue endlessly and monotonously
that the Aquarian Age is, technically, not yet upon us

> and who babble and quarrel among themselves
> about the stern astronomical Precession of the Equinoxes
> ignoring the Procession of Children
> walking through the loneliness with lighted candles
> chanting *Peace*

all we ask . . is give Peace a chance

we are well within the orb
of those unpredictable Uranus vibrations

> as a matter of fact . . . .
> a matter of both astronomical and astrological fact
> we are as close to them now as the Earth was
> to the trembling vibrations of the Piscean Age

> when the symbolic fish of Christianity
> first swam into the muddy streams of ignorance
> on this dark and dreary planet
> at the time of Mary and Joseph's weary ride into Bethlehem
> to the teeming Inn, where there was
> no room
> with the same over-population problem

> no room

> for the hungry, or for the despairing oppressed and homeless
> in our selfish, seeking hearts

> no room for those who wear the robes of a different skin
> or who hear the call of a distant drummer

no room for those who follow a different star
whether it be the Star of David
or the Hopi Indian Star of Harvest Faith

and do not forget

as that Piscean vibration struck the Earth
and the Neptune ray beamed into our collective unconscious
                                        two thousand years ago
we also felt the reflected influence
of the sign *opposite* Pisces — Virgo, the Virgin

first manifested in the rumored virgin birth of him

        later, also felt

under the puritanical reign of stiff, uptight Victoria
and then in the Virgo hair-splitting shouts of science

        "give us the facts, the facts, the facts !"

astronomy and science

each unable to see the great metaphysical forest of Knowledge
through the trees of lower mathematics and physics, sans the 'meta'
meta meaning, in Greek, *beyond*

        . . beyond the fiction of fact lies Truth ?

and so . .

the Pisces Age contained Neptune mysticism — versus Virgo realism
symbolizing the Law of Polarity
but now we stagger in confusion, under the restless rays
        of the Aquarian Age

sounding the chords of humanitarianism and individualism
in the human symphony
                . . and yes, the flat notes of insanity too

once again
under the ancient Law of Polarity
feeling the reflected influence
of the sign *opposite* Aquarius — Leo

Leo, the Lion Hearted
the Lion of Love
of Idealism and Youth

        Aquarius, the Water Bearer — Seeker of Truth

the unpredictable advocate of Change, whatever the cost
through violent revolution, if necessary
                    as a means to justify the end — of prejudice

the eccentric, half genius, half mad
Uranus vibrations of Aquarius
blending a compulsion for Progress

        with the hot rays of Leo's ruling sun
                reflecting back the Lion's firm hold
                    over Youth and Love

                    "we *will* have Change !
                            we *will* have Brotherhood !"

                    rings out the clarion call of the Water Bearer
                    insisting upon the individual's right
                            to do his — or her — own thing
        and . .

"let's make love, not war ! let's worship Youth !"

roars the fierce, hot-blooded Lion
as he rolls in sensuous ecstasy with the Lioness . . his mate

        is it any wonder, then, that we're having a sexual revolution
        that we shake under the Uranus-Aquarian thunder
        of individuality of hair styles, clothes, politics and religious
                                            convictions
        with women clamoring to be Ministers and Priests
        and riots on campus, introducing the Seventies, taking their toll ?

        didn't you see it all coming, Mister Gallup and Mister Poll ?
        didn't you feel Kent State coming ?
        or do you scoff at the stars — and ignore the planets too
        as blind astronomers and other scientists are wont to do ?

        Einstein might have explained it to us
        in its Relativity of Time and Space
        yes, Abstract Al could have perhaps made it all more clear
        than Columbia's Professor Owen Ratliff, or any similar peer
        who knocks and raps astrology
        if its fashionable to do so, during any particular year

        or than the shrinks and sociologists, stubborn astronomers
        and the frightened astrologers themselves
        who wrangle with one another, in unceasing competition
        refereed by prejudiced, pre-judgemental, know-it-all science
        wearing the dark glasses of dogma

                            I see them squatting

in their Kindergarten of Knowledge

      the professors and the shrinks
the scientists and astronomers
         the sociologists and poll takers
and an occasional politician

      playing with Truth
as children play with colored blocks
         lettered **A B C**
for Apathy — Blindness — and Cop-out

then, when their blocks topple over
from too much emphasis on Equatorial Equinoxes and such
they rage in childish petulance
         and bang each other over the head
with the offending chunks of wooden facts

      do not bang *me* over the head with your **A B C** blocks
colored with half-truths
you disciples of Thomas, the Doubter

      you will not break the Ram's tough horns !

The Aquarian Age is here !

      and its pulsating, powerful, unpredictable orb
mixing with the Sun rays of the roaring Lion
         is ominous, if not heeded

locking the New Age in your scientific closets
with boring, tiresome technicalities
         will not make it disappear

yes, the vibration of Aquarius is here
and much too close for comfort

            it burns my soul
            and sears my mind
            with unanswered questions

It All Depends

there are a considerable number of volumes, making an impressive case
to support the authenticity of Visitors, not invited guests, from Space
these waning Twentieth Century days

some of them even suggest, in various ways
that God Himself was an astronaut — yes, God
is that not odd, in the extreme ?
like some sort of science-fiction bad dream ?

is a humane and educated, bright and apple pie, normal man
like Scott Carpenter, then — Omnipotent
to cringing Earth Worshippers . . somewhere out there ?

my own personal view of God
has always been . . somewhat larger

one of the volumes, I believe, is called *Chariot of the Gods*
or is it Chariots ?
plural, I guess, yes — because the author writes of many gods
from many planets, not just from poor Mars
who takes the inter-planetary travel blame for all the stars

whether discussing U.F.O.'s in present, past or future tense
the books make a lot of sense
not only scientifically, but also metaphysically
     in a sane and logical, geological kind of way

                              . . except for one mistake
mystical legend — and also
spiritual common sense . . which is not so common
makes it clear — that, if any visitors from Space are here
they are not from other planets, on which there is no
                                        human life
but from other Earths
in other Solar Systems of the Universe
some, perhaps . . from the hollow, inner Earth
it's but a minor difference of opinion
not minor to "science", nevertheless — minor in the long run

however, today . .

I read a new book of this kind
called *The Gods Who Made Heaven and Earth*

and although certainly, it too contains
both a scientifically and metaphysically sound point of view
its author spoke of these Masters from Space
as possessing a trace, I felt, of sadism
a kind of coldness of heart, like Earth Scientists
                         . . a seeming lack of compassion
as I read this book, I shook
with a sudden chill of apprehension — at the same time, feeling
a sudden flash of comprehension
a blend of polarized impressions I couldn't seem to define

he, the author — in nearly every line
insinuated, and nearly proved by fact-after-fact

that the planet Earth is but a seeding place
like an experimental garden — or greenhouse
for gods, who plant the human seeds of us
then observe the growth, study our actions and re-actions

. . occasionally seeing the necessity
to pull up a weed — sometimes even the need
of destroying the entire garden
to begin again
and again . . and again

what troubles me
about some of these books, and their authors
is not that they suppose us to be a mass experiment
for gods from another planet
or two or three, or more
even though I believe that to be false
. . it still doesn't trouble me

no, what troubles me is the frequently repeated, further suggestion
that these allegedly highly evolved entities
who explore and search each planet in Space for its possibilities
as a flourishing garden
look upon humans
as we look upon ants

and therefore, feel no more real concern
for us, as individuals — for our personal tribulations
and hurts and fears, or for the pain of our desperate tears
than human beings feel for ants

no more than we feel
for a colony of ants

as I ponder Voltaire's words, in his published *Philosophical Dictionary*
those words he wrote, perhaps
as a secret message of some kind to us today, in a coded way

those words, which say

" . . in the beginning, God created Heaven and Earth
that is how it has been translated
but the translation is inaccurate — there is no man
with even a little education, who does not know
that the text reads . . in the beginning, the *gods*
made Heaven and Earth . . . . . "

yes, as I ponder Voltaire's statement, though I know the man was a cynic

to whom much of Life was a clinic — with often, a sterile heart
to match his sterile opinions
as revealed in the obvious biting . . and caustic sarcasm of his writing·

    I feel, nonetheless, that his statement may be
    something more than a cold, but educated guess

yes, Voltaire and the others may be quite correct — yet, somehow
I still elect to speak up in defense of these Masters — or plural "gods"
these inter-galactic Visitors from outer Space
perhaps because I always try to chase the truth
                         or perhaps because I happen to see
a different expression on the face
of each of these various gods or Masters . . . imaging them as individuals

                    some good, some bad
              some cruel, some kind

    traveling their own higher spiral of evolvement and involvement
    toward the larger Light . . some already wise
                    and some . . still blind

twinkle, twinkle, little star
          how I wonder what you are

yes, today, I wondered
what is a star ?

    it may very well be true that these gods
    consider us to be like unto ants

    but it may *not* be true that every god who tests the sod
    for seeding — fails to see the pain on a human face
    or ignores the pleading . . and private needing
                  of individual human souls
    even if we are as ants
    to gods gazing down on us — yes, even supposing
    this is how we are truly seen
    it does not necessarily mean . . . that we, here on Earth
    are looked upon as having no personal worth

              it all depends

             on how one feels

             about ants

             does it not ?

I thought this today, and I wondered
how many souls the gods from Space have bought
                              away from anguish
and at what cost
so they would not burn — and how long
it takes human ants . . to be taught . . . to learn

Choosing up Sides and Horses — Post Time !

    prejudice is a subtle vibration
    whether it be racial, cultural, religious
              or sexual

    the seeds are always there, waiting to sprout
    if tended carefully, and watered . . . . seeds planted
    in the garden of the mind, by the accident of Birth

              accident ?

    Birth is no accident — nor is Death
    both are charted by the Supraconscience — the Angel of the Higher Self
              between the two Doorways

    as the necessary means, to justify the end
              . . as the only way to escape the re-birth wheel
    and eventually leap off
              the spinning Carousel of Life
into the brightness of enlightenment

after all the karmic debts
are finally balanced and understood
and your credit rating with God is good

    but, whoever planted them, with motive cruel or kind
    for whatever reason — and however they were buried in the mind
                              the seeds are there
    the seeds of the Little Prince's
    dreaded baobob trees of blindness and intolerance

like . .

    you take a woman — a soul born into the body of a woman
    in this particular incarnation — like mine

              when I was a teeny-tiny woman
              called a child

                        called a child
                        yet, still . . a woman

Canto Seven ☆ 191

a teeny-tiny woman

I used to watch the spinning Carousel in the park
and wonder and wonder and wonder . . about the painted horses
how to tell the Boy from the Girl horses

> I finally decided
> that the prettier, brighter-colored
> yet stronger and sturdier horses — were the Girls
> and the scratched and chipped
> smaller, dismal-colored horses — were the Boys

that's the way it is with every teeny-tiny woman, called a child
and of course, the reverse is true
                with every teeny-tiny man, called a child

> then they both grow up, and each of them pursues
> the horse judged as inferior, in childhood
> perhaps, as Nature's subtle way of teaching that even horses
>   of a different shape and color
> are still, after all, bound together on the spinning Carousel of Life

> for, a horse is a horse is a horse
> and a soul is a soul is a soul — like a rose is a rose is a rose
> by any other name, or in any game between the sexes

> when it comes to catching the brass ring
> and the final goal — of leaping off the Carousel
> into the greener pastures of enlightenment

only by enough of us pursuing the horse of the opposite sex
can the Owner of the Carousel be sure of having enough new ponies
to keep the rides spinning . . even though no one seems to be winning
                        the game of catching the brass ring
Carousel ponies
have such a short life span
on this Earth — compared with the ones
who spin and win, in other galaxies

> but this is the Aquarian Age !

Aquarius, the Water Bearer of Truth
Aquarius, the sign of the Uni-sex
teaching that the two sexes are the same
                        in the Universal game
out there on the Big League Carousel

teaching that the higher forms of Einsteinic equation
is — two equals one . . . yes, $2 = 1$

when it's all said and done . . and also teaching
that men and women are all sisters under the skin
                    or the opposite — brothers

for a soul is a soul is a soul, like a rose is a rose is a rose
                    as everyone knows
and a painted horse is a painted horse, whatever color or sex
                                        it chose
this time around
whatever race or creed — or whatever
chronological or psychological age it is

            in the clearer vision of the Carousel Owner

                    Who is not spinning

although, I will say this
the teeny-tiny riders are the ones who find more bliss
in whirling around any kind of merry-go-round
                    than the grown ups, who get dizzy

of course, if you learn certain special magic tricks
                                from the druids
you can be teeny-tiny at any chronological age
and enjoy the spin — not curse it
possessing the knack of leaping off more quickly

            . . not before your ride is over, mind you
            but more quickly

                    whoops ! whee !

                    lope and leap off !

                    we're all home free !

                    oh, WOW !

                    whoops ! whee !

                    let's get back on

                    and try it again . .

                    let's see if we can

                    come home free !

Canto Seven ☆ 193

I wish they had taught me more of their magic, the druids
about how to remain a teeny-tiny rider
                as you grow taller — how do you stay smaller
and remain both at the same time ?
I never quite learned that perfectly marvelous knack from them

        although . . they taught me this much
        with some sprinkles of druid dust . . it begins with Faith and Trust

        for the teeny-tiny riders on the Carousel's ponies
        really . . not nearly, but *really* believe
        that Santa will come
                        and he does !

    children are forever questing for a star . . oh !
    they really believe there are such things as invisible friends
    and magic rings . . and there are, there are !
    if you wish on a star, these things are as real as can be

            but a star is so hard to see
                        through the smog today

as for the male-female polarity
I don't believe the druids had a hang-up
        over the Boy-Girl hex
no . . . druids had no difficulty in 'divining' either sex

        but in this New Age of Water Bearers, the whole question is a puzzle
        telling dark from light —   black from white
        or day from night . . especially in the fight for might
                        between the Girl and Boy horses

    the basic thing responsible for stampeding the riders
    on their painted horses — if anyone should ask *me*
    is the strange fact that a horse of any color
    as strong as he or she may be — or as swift and sturdy

            is terrified into a panic

            by a *mouse*

    and certainly wouldn't want to be one
    no matter how horses rare, and kick their hind legs in the air
                        when they see one
    it's less alarming to *see* one
                    . . than to *be* one

        and run the danger of being caught in a trap that snaps shut
        on freedom and self respect

            Woman — or Man — or mouse

which one is brave
which spouse is the slave in the house ?

the one who toasts the bread
and brews the tea
or the one who *earns* the bread
                              and runs free
                              or freerer

which one is right — which one is wrong
which one is weak, which one is strong — and
right or wrong, weak or strong

                    which one is the mouse ?

Woman — and Man — and mouse
when they are all three are playing house
or playing musical horses on the Carousel
which spouse in the house is the mouse

                         he — or she ?

oh ! 'tis a puzzlement which side should win, which side should lose
yes, 'tis a puzzlement, as the male chauvinist King of Siam used to say
while he refused the right of his wives to choose
a puzzlement indeed — who has the deeper need to be freed
who should be punished, and made to pay ?

     which one wants to break away — and break away from what ?

          with all of this tumbling around in the hay today
          it's getting so you can't tell the Cubs from the Brownies
          it used to be so simple
          the Cubs wore blue socks — and the Brownies wore pink
                                                  . . . . I think
               or did they both wear green ?

but I wore my socks
stuffed in my sweater, instead of on my feet
so, where does that leave me ?
still sleeping under the druids' old oak tree
in the woods, I guess . .

     I've spent my dreams, and I don't have many left
     since dreams burn a hole in my pocket — like I've spent my Life
     which burns a hole in my soul
     in the kind of musical horse game that helps the Carousel Owner
     keep the new ponies spinning around
     and always shall — as long as I have the fare
          yet I also firmly believe

that a rose is a rose . . and a horse is a horse
and a soul is a soul

and it takes two of them
two long-ago separated Twins

to make a whole

yes, it takes two Twins
one soul plus one soul — to make a whole

whether those twin souls are riding painted horses
of the same — or a different color
racially — or chronologically — and in some incarnations, sexually
on the Carousel

for, to the Carousel Owner
Who is *not* spinning

a rose is a rose — a horse is a horse
and a soul is a soul, longing and yearning
and seeking to be whole

as to the Little Prince
his rose was unique in all the world
different from all the other roses — only because
he — alone — had tamed her

yes, they were two of the lucky ones
the Little Prince . . and his rose
who discovered the magical formula
for becoming whole and free

the secret

of how to make one "us"

from a lonely and separated

you and me

Astrologers Don't Go to Shrinks

am I the innocent victim
of a new kind of psychological circumlocution
or am I suffering the pangs of paranoid persecution ?
    why do I feel these strange solar plexus sensations

as I ponder the acute schizophrenic implications
of this frenetic, kinetic and peripatetic Aquarian Age ?

where is the enlightened and illuminated page
in Freud's Electra-Oedipus text
that will hint what I might expect next
in this perplexing pattern of non sequitur human behavior ?

how would Sigmund psycho-analyze the Jesus freaks
who murmur about the rebirth of a mystical Saviour
wearing beads and crosses and ankle laced sandals
with this pyro-maniac complex about incense and candles ?

and what would he mandate should be made of the Moonies
who sell flowers for hours ?
would he label them wild-eyed fanatics, with toys in their attics
or call them the most sincerely religious and serious youth of the day ?
would he psyche them out as collecting their cash for the Dove of Love
or for more politically oriented Birds of Prey ?

could he explain why the Born Again Christians
are so confidently pure, yet so absolutely sure
that the rest of us are not
as they chant their "Jesus Saves" deliverance mantra
while condemning all those who think differently — to hell
with a courteous, pleasant smile of regret
            less like a blessing than an unspoken threat ?

and how would Freud employ the quirks of Oedipus Rex
to solve the growing mystery
of this confusing Aquarian Age hang-up about sex ?

all those people who sneak into films
showing hard-core, nude topography

                                . . and the ones who don't

all those people who peek into books
to see hard-core, lurid pornography

                                . . and the ones who won't

would he say that the ones who do
are hiding an incestuous lust for their sisters and brothers
and the ones who don't
are secretly in love with their fathers and mothers

            or vice versa ?

would he say it's true that the ones who do
are lonely, frustrated and scared

and the ones who don't, are sexually well mated
and already happily paired ?

    or would he claim
    it's the other way around ?

and what would Herr Freud have to say
about this Aquarian interpretation of marriage ?

    all those liberal couples, who permissively share
    whatever — and whoever — is there
    to be communally fair

    and the conservative ones
    who just wouldn't dare ?

all those free lovers, who choose not to get wed
until they go to bed — and try it

    and the romantic traditionalists
    who simply won't buy it

all those quick-passioned pairs
who play musical partners under the sheets

    and the old fashioned squares
    who make love by reading each other
    the verses of Browning and Shelley and Keats

would Sigmund pontificate
on these spanning-all-generations gaps
by tapping his academia, and serenely explaining
that the former are trying to prove they're superior
because the latter have made them feel inferior ?

    or would he explain it in reverse ?

and what, pray, would he deduce
after watching hundreds of couples rehearse
the same Act, over and over and over
as those voyeur love-birds, Masters and Johnson did
in their peek-a-boo research
of each volunteer exhibitionist gander and goose ?

    would he say that abnormal is slow and uptight
    and normal is fast and loose ?

are all these different attitudes toward sex
based on casual promiscuity . . . . versus rigid frigidity
or is the whole problem infinitely more complex ?

why doesn't psychiatry
ever call on God ?

or is it only to be expected that the Almighty would be neglected
in the unholy study of the Id by the Odd ?

and what have the Sweethearts of the Alma Mater of Sigma Freud
uncovered and discovered, as they've tinkered and toyed
with this Aquarian Age hang-up on drugs ?

all those people who trip acid
and shoot heroin — either a little or a lot

and the ones who will not
those who'd rather be shot than ever be caught
having a sniff of coke or a whiff of pot

would it be obvious to Herr Siggy, that this little piggy
who does — is seeking an emotional fire escape

and this little piggy — who won't
is reluctant to bend his straight mind out of shape ?

and what about this little piggy
who went to market — to push ?

and this little piggy, who was a bad little piggy
a hopped-up little piggy
who hid, with a gun, behind a bush ?

or this little piggy, who was a sad little piggy
and cried "wee-wee" all the way home . .
all the way home from a bad acid trip, that caused him to slip
out of a 20th Century window
and fall into oblivion ?

would Father Goose Freud tell us
that the ones who do — are trying to be entres nous and "in" ?

and the ones who don't — are consumed with the fear
that a pseudo high is a cardinal sin ?

I must confess . . . .

that the astrologer is quaffing the same quandry
as the shrink

and as the former, how can I be sure what I think ?
since there's nothing to be gained from consulting the latter
and getting more Oedipus-Electra chatter

I'm stuck in my own cosmic groove, trying to decide if I agree

                                     or disapprove

of the pro and the con . . with no magic druid wand
to help make these mumbling mountains fly away
and no stars in the smog to wish on today

      must I tranquilize the manic of each religious fanatic
      and exorcize the depression of each atheist's secret panic
      when they stop me on the street
      with a query about each theory of every known theology ?

      what do I say to these wondering ones
      to these staggering and tripping Uranian dancers
      who are convinced that astrology holds all of the answers ?

am I qualified to hear the traumatic confession
of those souls left shell-shocked by the unexpected exposure
of a nude group therapy session ?

      am I a member of the Priesthood
      or the astrological profession ?

when I'm asked to supply through astrology's art and science
all the missing links
by those disappointed in churches, and dissatisfied with shrinks
should I go into a trance, and make like a Sphinx ?

should I murmur magical druid incantations
or bless the wine . . when they invite me to dine ?

       and what about my own personal manic-panic ?

I do the best I can . .

      while the psychiatric Solomons are making copious notes
      on which patients were fed on the breast
                   and which ones were fed on the bottle
      I continue to consult Plato, Jung and Aristotle
      not to mention Newton and Bacon . . who each tried to warn
      that our actions are fated, and somehow related
                       to when we were born
(not fated *entirely*, but . . that delves deeper)

I ignore the snide, scientific sneers
as I follow the ancient wisdom of the occult seers

      "were you born at midnight or noon ?"

carefully rectifying each hour and minute of birth
while grumbling to myself . .

>   "we've been to the Moon
>   now when are we going to get it together
>   down here on Earth ?"

I make no apology for astrology
to the arrogant medical dictators, who like to say
through the holy communion
            of their sacred A.M.A.

                    . . . genuflect, please . . .

that my art and science should be berated and negated
by all the 20th Century rules of logic and sanity

        as I wonder at the dangerous vanity
        of an erudite group of white coated saints
        who pay to astrology only the homage of complaints
        and who have not the slightest interest in Venus or Mars
        nor the patience to even try
        to discover exactly why
        their own High Priest, Hippocrates, studied the stars

is it more sane and ethical to allow people to die
                            and call it mercy ?
to allow people to die, when they might live . .

        to resort to giving morphine, for an easing of the pain
        and call that mercy — then call astrology insane ?

oh, no ! I make no apology for astrology
to the sanctimonious medical profession
I just pray for the day they unbend enough
to take a few lessons from the valid medical astrology notes
of their own founding Father — and not dismiss this healing potential
as too much of a bother and unnecessary fuss to even discuss

        and yet, and yet . .

                there are still some urgent questions
                the stars coyly refuse to answer

        stars . . fair weather friends

always blinking at you on a balmy night
when the weather's just right
then out there somewhere playing hide-and-go-seek
with the Heavenly Host — or the Holy Ghost
when the storm clouds gather . . and you need them the most

            where do the wise stars run
                when bereavement darkens the Sun ?

Canto Seven ☆ 201

yes, where do they run
.. then ?

reincarnation is the common astrological comforter in death
but what solace — what relief from grief
may be found in such a doctrine, true though it may be
what comfort is there in such abstract thought

if reincarnation means only what has *thus far* been taught ?

what genuine solace is there in the suggestion
that someone's newborn infant may answer the question
of where the loved one may next be seen ?

there are no final answers one may glean
in the Tibetan Book of the Dead
or in any other books I've ever read

when someone they love has chosen to go .. do I tell the bereaved
"you must bow to Fate, and wait
a few hundred years or so
or a few thousand ..

until you see the glow .. of the remembered brown or blue
of tender eyes you once fiercely loved and knew
until you hear again a voice grown dear
and feel the warmth once more
of the protecting arms that held you before .. ? "

what do I say to those
who expect me to take the spiritual lead
when they plead and plead ..

"oh ! tell me how .. please, please tell me how
I can see and feel and hear
those eyes, those arms .. that voice
those lips .. those hands
that comfort I once knew . . .
tell me how I may find my love again — *here and now*
show me how to *believe* in the Life Everlasting
how to believe in it *now* and *here*
not in some dim future .. "

how shall I calm their fears, and dry their tears
by telling them only — "have courage, have faith"

have faith in *what ?*
have courage until *when ?*

how can I dry their tears
by chanting monotonously

"have courage, have faith
you must endure
and I promise — for sure
you will, you *will* see him — or her — again

in just a few thousand years"

how can *that* dry their tears ?

what good is the lonely search to find your own twin soul
if the final goal . . is but once more
eventual and certain loss
whichever one goes first . . ?

what good to find
your own twin soul

only to face
a renewed separation ?

how can reincarnation
make death . . or any other kind of loss of love
easier to bear ?

what do I say
to the lonely, grieving ones out there
who defy Fate — and still wait ?

what unseen Galaxy of Stars
holds the true wisdom of the Easter gladness

and the answer to all this other madness

of the Aquarian Age ?

The Subtle Alchemy of a Sensitive Soul

there are things . . oh ! there are things
so many things I do not understand

as I spin around on this Carousel of Life
reaching frantically for the brass ring
the Serpent's Circle of Eternity

a ring . . a key ring ? to hold the keys of Truth

I spin and I spin . . and as the discordant din of the calliope
strikes an occasional familiar chord in my heart and mind

I know there is something
                    . . something I still must find

            I have been blessed by Heaven with a full set of keys
            to the ancient wisdom of the stars and planets
                                and they open many doors

but where are the Keys to the Kingdom ?

            where are the Keys to the Kingdom of Heaven
            the gentle Nazarene placed in Peter's care ?

            within the darkness and dearth
            of happiness on this Earth — where is the Light ?

        who has glimpsed the dazzling sight
                            of those precious Keys of the Kingdom
                cast in the metal of pure gold
                from the energy forms of blood . . and tears
                solid granite . . nails and thorns
                by the Essenic formula for the transmutation of matter ?

            where are the Keys, transformed by Essenic magic
            into Victory over Death . . through the alchemy
                                of his suffering ?

    the alchemy of the suffering of his sensitive soul
    squashed, like a bug — by Life

    squashed by Life, yes — squashed like an ant
    a deep well in his heart, of pain
    carved out . . as the hollow is carved in a clay jug
    then placed in the potter's furnace

    mashed flat by Herod . . wounded by the kiss of Judas
                            forked-tongue Serpent kiss
    smashed by the desertion
    of even Peter . . . . . even him

    at that dark hour, when the cock crowed thrice
    to synchronize the triple denial

                "I do not know him of whom ye speak"

                    I do not know him
                    I do not know him
                    I know him not

                                three times

204   ☆   Canto Seven

mashed and smashed and squashed, like an ant
and mortally wounded, his sensitive soul
nearly torn assunder by the torture of Temptation
during forty long days and nights . . alone

his sensitive soul, bleeding
from the stabs of fear and doubt . . and the inner rebellion

of Gethsemane

yes, he was squashed
by Life, like a bug

humble . . yet stern enough

to lash the whip of outrage
at the greedy money changers
in the marketplace

and sensitive enough . . to weep

oh ! Jesus wept

those two sad words

yet, for all of that . . strong enough
to conquer the finality
of death

stern

sensitive
strong

but also tenderly compassionate enough
to care for Pat, my Calico cat
the Colorado miners
and the Broadway Magdalenes
all Earth bound riders
on the Carousel of Life

and even care for me

poetry is the alchemy
of a sensitive soul ?

he was the Poet-of-Poets, then
a Master of the genius of creative expression
taking a rear seat, on a donkey
as he rode the spinning Carousel . . . reaching calmly

not frantically, for the brass ring

     the Serpent's Circle of Eternity and Truth
     and caught it — then turned it into gold
     by the mystical, mysterious and strangely beautiful
     alchemy of his suffering . . . for us

     but . . the golden Serpent Circle ring, transmuted into gold
     holding the Keys to the Kingdom

            where is that key ring now ?

where are the keys that unlock the Carousel
to reveal the inner mechanism — and the switch
that makes it stop spinning ?

where is the secret formula of chord progressions
that can turn a whining calliope of music
                      into the Music of the Spheres
and brush the grinning, painted horses
with all the glorious colors of the unseen Spectrum
making them flash with prisms of rainbows and light ?

where are the Keys cast in gold by Perfect Love
which casteth out all doubt and fear
the Keys which unlock the Easter joy and gladness
     remove all sadness — dry every tear

          where are they — now and here ?

          where are they — *now and here ?*

sometimes I think that golden ring of Keys slipped out of the pocket
of Peter's homespun robe, when he was crucified upside down
         and were lost forever

while the keys we are offered today
  of religious dogma and ritual
  are hanging on a ring of cheap brass
  that sparkles with sufficient glow and glitter
  to fool us into thinking they are the purer metal we are seeking

         we are seeking ?

     it is not "we" walking here
     through the valley of the shadow
     of my Gethsemane of doubt

     there is no "we" — there is only "me" — a rusty key

shaped in a strange design

that will not open any door

I reach for the brass ring, and it eludes my grasp
but what matter ?
I do not possess the alchemy of spirit
to transmute it into gold

it would remain as brass — a child's ring of make-believe
in my fumbling, frantic, manic hands

there is something I still must find
.. something I must find

buried somewhere
in the back of my mind
something .. I must find

I stare into the blank expressionless eye
the blank expressionless eye
the blank expressionless eye

of the painted horse I ride

and she does not speak
she does not speak
she does not speak

I listen to the monotonous notes
of the off-key calliope
and try to sing along, but cannot stay in tune
I hear, not just a different drum — I hum
a different melody

I am a different hummer of the calliope's song
even daring to profess the distant drummer is wrong

the Carousel sometimes
spins backwards ..

and the things I saw before me
are now behind me ..

and the things I saw behind me
.. are now before me

and the fragments, oh ! the fragments
of lost pieces of the puzzle .. perhaps also
bits of metal scraped from those lost keys

```
fall
      through
            the
                  air
                    around
                        me
```

like shreds of colored confetti
from Heaven's distant Mardi Gras

    or splintered shavings of stardust
    drifting down around my head and shoulders
    from some unknown, brighter Galaxy

      or pastel snowflakes

        no two alike

When You Wish . . . . .

during my teens and early twenties
all the high school girls and college women I knew
were searching for love . . in a crowd
with too many false starts
changing their favorite songs
each time they changed partners
      in the romantic game of musical hearts

while I walked through those growing years
      more or less alone
failing each attempt I made to . . . belong
as I hummed the melody to my own secret song . . . like

    "*when you wish upon a star*"

or was it . . "*someday my Prince will come . . .* " ?

how corny . . how square
to believe that love should, somehow . . be fated
how silly . . . how childish

      but . . . I waited

there are lots of things
I couldn't talk about
      while I was waiting
    fat and dimpled pink smelling babies, clinging to my skirts
    while I baked golden loaves of bread, and maybe even
    churned the butter . . . . clear cool water drawn from the well
                          in wooden buckets
  clean fresh winds
  whipping the clouds of a storm

                and the warm of him

                bringing in the logs
                    for the long, cold winter
            and making me tremble
              with the promise in his eyes
                      . . of later

    there are lots of things
    I couldn't talk about
        while I was waiting

walking barefoot through dark, silent woods
green fir trees . . dark brown eyes
              shiny black braids
bride red feathers
          turquoise beads
smoky prayers
around a campfire . . my fine white horse
swifter than the north wind !

                and the warm of him

              strong, handsome brave
                  and favorite of the Sun god
              soft hot breath against my breast
                      lips murmuring
              arms clinging, blood churning
                      loins burning
              while the rain beat gentle on the tent
                    near the lake
              and the pale Moon faded into dawn
              at the moment when the wild birds cry

there are so many things
I never told
while I was waiting

      silver ships with swelling sails

the music of the Nile, crashing chords of glory
emerald serpent with ruby eyes
      Pharaoh's tomb . . Egyptian skies

     and the warm of him

       lying naked . . dead beside me
           in the shadow of the Pyramid
       gleaming white in the Moon's pale light
          buried secrets in silent desert sands
       myrhh scented skin . . familiar hands
                . . and oh !
       the Nile is blue . . so blue

there are lots of things
I kept inside
while I was waiting

brass gongs ringing through violet hills
oceans rolling thunder . . nights filled with wonder
hot humid breezes
     blowing over beaches
wet eyes shining
    catching sunbeams . . and

the warm of him

      teaching me to match
         the rhythm of the sea gulls
     move and sway, back and forth
           move together
      back and forth
         explode in fire !
     then cool green water
     floating . . floating . . floating . . explode
          in fire !
     cool green water
       again and again . . . and again

misty fogs, on Scottish bogs
Irish meadows, starred with shamrocks
rocking softly, as voices keen
Kathleen, Kathleen
        . . . I'll take you home
to where your heart
    will feel no pain

the White Cliffs of Dover kissed by foam
       three infants' faces

fine white laces
     satin breeches, golden crown
London towers, falling down
       so many walks near Notre Dame

déjà vu . .

             oh ! déjà vu

so many things I never told

    and then he came . . . . and he knew

Part Two

CAROUSEL

CANTO EIGHT

The title leapt before my eyes
Olde Ballades, Tales, and Faerie Wives
It was on vellum old and scarred
The corners dogged and the pages marred,
Written in silvery blackish ink.

Flickering like the brackish clouds on the brink
Of the horizon when their lightning's all
but spent; and like coals the letters brent
into my brain until I only saw
that antique book and nothing more.

Olde Ballades, Tales, and Faerie Wives
there's something there that sly connives
and cuts and fools the thoughts
from long-accustomed ruts.
A ballad, yes, or a tale is told and heard.
But to *read* a maid of faery is absurd
I mused and whispered to myself:
one does not read but rather meets an elf.
No sooner thought and spoken of than done;
the vellum volume gleamed all red in the sun
that was dissolving far away.

Late it was getting and cold outside the cave
You must be bold I told me
And invoke the female knave.
But why a knave, the thought rushed up,
When she could a damsel be
Shining like copper and like gold
All foaming from the sea.
Maiden come,
I cried aloud,
My damsel princess
Sweet and proud
And tender too
To me.

The last rays shone
And the vellum turned to bone
As I stood there by the sea;
the cave then hummed, grew thickly black

I turned my back
To see, and when I turned again
I saw the maiden standing free.
O fairest, awaited many lives,
I sang as I caught her to me.

O lightsome winsome lovely one
O faerie wife for me.

And they said we died there side by side
in the cave made by the sea.
All bliss and pain they both were there
in the gates to Ever-Be.
And just as we passed beyond the gate
One last pain stabbed like knives
My eyes saw back through the lower air
the vellum title lying there:
Olde Ballades, Tales, and Faerie Wives

Kyril Demys (Musaios)
Wings of Myrahi

And We Were One

yes, it's time to remember
it has started to rain . .

never mind the pain, never mind it
I remember . . . .

       for the first time since my own Brownie pack, I was properly identified
       by him — the one always trying to reach a star
                       or ring a far away bell
      the one so like the Bill from *Carousel*
he knew exactly who I was — from the moment we first met
                       and I knew him too
      as the Bible tells
      we *knew* each other . . . *"and Abraham knew his wife Sarah*
                    . . . and she conceived . . . "

he wanted to be a composer . . a writer or a doctor . . maybe an artist
to heal, he said . . people's bodies, minds and souls
it didn't matter which, just one of the three
and the healing of the other two
            would surely follow, he believed

   . . . oh, darling
you healed *me*
    you healed *me !*

he never quite made it — he tried, but somehow
something always interfered
      he started — then stopped — in medical school
at two different universities
    as for composing, the closest he ever came to that dream
was listening to symphonies for hours — and to operas
Tschaikovsky, Madame Butterfly, Der Rosenkavalier
                  . . and others
but he did finally become a writer
at least, I thought so . .
his letters to me were poems
needing only to be placed in stanza form
              and scanned
yes, to me . . his letters were poems

         in one of them, he wrote

         "I send you a message from Einstein
         about the relativity of Us
         darling, I love you more at this moment

than I loved you tomorrow
and more than I will love you yesterday"

then, in the Postscript
he asked, anxiously . .

"does this letter confuse you ?
do you understand ? I was trying
to explain in which way — and direction
Time moves for Us — in an Eternal Now
like the Serpent Circle of Eternity
the snake, eating its own tail
but since we've been apart
Time is crawling like a snail . . .
oh, I miss you ! and I love you so"

and I wrote back
    "I know, darling, I know"

he seemed to say it better each time, the Forever thing
in every letter from Stuttgart, Germany, written as an Army Sergeant

    . . there were no trenches
    no notes scribbled under enemy fire
            no wading through rice paddies in Korea or Viet Nam
    thank God for that
        he had no stomach for war and killing

during a week-end in Switzerland, in another letter, he wrote . .

"I am like a bird, swelling and expanding
into the Universe
        skiing down these snowy mountains
is such a magical challenge and thrill !
I'll bring you here someday — and together
like druids, you'll see
        we'll make these mountains fly !"

yes, he loved Tschaikovsky, Puccini . . Nature . . the woods
and especially — later, in California — the ocean
walking for hours along its shore
he knew exactly how to make a dandelion ring
                . . most people don't, you know
and once, he did a very enchanted thing
            at the movies, watching *Carousel*
he went to the lobby
and brought back a box of chocolate covered *Goober's Peanuts*

        then whispered in my ear
        "here's something for you to munch

these are mystical peanuts
                    manufactured in another galaxy
and when you eat them, you become
                        extremely small
very teeny-tiny
        you grow smaller . . and smaller
till you're no larger than a mouse
with a faint, inaudible squeak . . so
                            be careful !"

I laughed, gobbled them down — and
all the rest of that night
he pretended he couldn't see me, or hear me
with a perfectly straight face . . oh, he was magic !

we rode Life's Carousel, side by side, and hand-in-hand
                            . . familiar hand
our painted horses grinning, dipping up and down
in crazy rhythm, seldom synchronized
first, his horse rode high . . . and I looked up to him
then his horse dipped gracefully lower
                as I rose higher, looked down on him
and blew him a kiss

rising and falling, to the rhythm of the calliope
the music now pouring out smooth melodies, now screeching
sometimes tinkling brassy notes, but never stopping
around and around . . and round and round
they matched perfectly, the two fine horses we rode

                    so did their secrets match

all the other Carousel horses seemed, to us, grotesque or comical
wild, unfamiliar stallions and fillies, with oddly measured gait

        yes, my twin soul and I

walked together, along the painful path of evolving and learning
and shared the burning lessons of growing
but also shared the ecstasy of each deeply *knowing* . . the other

    we quarreled bitterly, sometimes violently
    as we cut and lashed each other with cruel whips of words
    occasionally dropping the reins
    and nearly falling off the Carousel
    or pushed by one another, during some unbearable hurt

we raged . .

    but we loved — and so we forgave

I forgave . . even her . . the cool, sure one
so different from me, so unpossessing . . so permissive
with small, daintily dimpled hands
and soft feminine voice . . unlike my own

   so unafraid, she was

so confident . . so un-teared by uncertainties or self doubt
oh ! why could he not see what I feared ?

   she was so *sure* . . she was so un-*teared*

yet, after awhile, I forgave him . . even her
and he forgave in me, too, so much
different kinds of things, but still . . so much

   I have forgiven too — though not forgotten
   another minor, hurting-thing
   but, if minor — then why do I still remember ?

         yes, if minor . . *why can't I forget* ?

it was in the beginning
      . . . in the beginning, Love created "Us", needing — but we waited
and on the seventh day, a Sunday — of the seventh month after we met
we faced, for the first time, the seductive serpent of our original sin

we were not wed

   and the lumpy bed in that shabby hotel room, was sagging
                                    the spread was thin
   old and torn
the carpet faded, cheap and worn . . a musty odor
lingered in the bedclothes, and in the mended drapes at the window
permeating the close, dank air — oh ! why did we go there ?

it was so ugly ugly ugly . . but I was drawn
like a helpless wooden puppet, manipulated by his eyes
my arms and legs dangling awkwardly, awaiting instructions
or a pull on the strings from the puppeteer . . to make it clear
               what was expected of me
it was a hasty, ill considered decision of passion . . therefore
I had no gown to wear
and not sufficient brazen courage . . or trust ?

   for love's honest, naked offering

so I slipped over my head his wrinkled shirt
the one he'd been wearing all day, in the hot Sun
measuring with precision instruments, the roads outside St. Mary's

. . tiny town of three or four hundred souls

he had become an engineer, and secretly despised it
the Highways of the State employed him . . as the Pharaohs employed
                                                    the slaves
to lift and measure stones, to build their silent tombs

dusty roads . . are so unlike sterile medical laboratories
nor do ditches much resemble a vaulted concert auditorium
or the polished hallways of an art exhibit

    but he did save up enough cash
    to buy a typewriter
    one-two-three dreams, you're out !

        and who is the umpire — Fate ?

the shirt . .

    was miles too large, over my trembling nakedness
    and khaki colored, like an army regulation
    I slipped it on nervously . . then, for no reason at all
                except pure, raw tension

I remained in the bathroom, with its cracked mirror and stained wallpaper
for what must have seemed to him, hours
hating my uneven, shoulder length, straight hair
and, hoping it would look neater short
I cut and slashed away at it, with a razor blade from his shaving kit

    stalling for time-time-time

    my hands shook so, I nicked my ear lobe
so I drew dark-winged raven arches on my brows
smeared blue shadow on my lids
bruised my lips with fuschia-scarlet gloss . . and on my cheeks
the corpse-colored pink foundation
called Sun-Kissed by some insane, blind Madison Avenue copywriter

    . . . . as compensation for shredded wheat hair
    and bleeding ear, and shaking hands . . . .

the stern, army regulation of the mud-colored, long tailed shirt
revealing one bruised knee, no thigh . . . . firmly buttoned up high
to forbid my swelling breasts from shaming themselves
              with any suggestion of surrender

    ugly, coarse nightgown

oh ! but it smelled of him — Sun-soaked and musty
sweet, like a nest for birds

made of straw, caked clay . . . and dampness
I could feel baby robins fluttering their wings
somewhere deep within me
                              they were hungry

I walked into the bedroom slowly, unsure . . . uncertain
knowing-knowing-knowing
I was a peeled onion, with a stinging, smarting ear lobe
my blue shadowed eyes swollen, under the black raven arches of brows
eyes bleared with criss-cross red lines, from weeping in frustration

         I hesitated

then walked toward the bed . . . to my Comforter

         and he laughed

                         he laughed, and said

                         "hey ! take off the Dracula mask
                    and that Bride of Frankenstein wig
                    you'll never catch a husband that way"

oh ! what a dumb thing to say
what a dumb, dumb thing to say
and I thought he was a poet . . . .

my heart broke, and I wept . . humiliated
then he told me he was sorry

                    "I'm sorry, I'm sorry, I'm sorry"

                    over and over again, against my sore ear
                    and murmured hoarsely, swallowing hard

                    "it is I who is the Monster, not you
                    I am the Frankenstein-Dracula Monster
                              for teasing you
                    you are . . oh, you are, you are
                    a beautiful woman
                                   and you have lovely hair
                    it smells like raindrops . . and it feels like . .
                    gauzy butterfly feathers"

then we both fell down on the lumpy mattress
and rolled and tumbled, doubled up with fits of uncontrollable laughter
laughing so hard, the tears ran down his cheeks and mine
until my fuschia-purple lipstick, pink pancake and blue eye shadow
streaked into crazy rainbows
on both our faces, turning us into clowns
turning our hearts suddenly sunny . . banishing my tears

as we laughed and laughed . . . oh, it was so funny !

trying to imagine
                    a butterfly with feathers . . .

suddenly
    we stopped laughing

                    suddenly, we stopped

        it was so still between us
        I could hear his thumping heart

as he stared deeply into my rainbow-hued eyes, all stained
for a long, long moment . . his lips so near
I could feel and smell his breath
                    hot and musty, like jungle grass

then he reached out . . . slowly . . . and stroked my cheek
with his fingers, then cupped his hands around my face
                    so gently . . so very, very gently

and I felt an unaccustomed, throbbing ache
                    that hurt in the back of my ears
in the spot where you first feel mumps
an incredible mump-lump of inexpressible longing
                            no words can describe
as we kissed deeply deeply deeply
clinging, clinging . . . both moaning softly, low
then melted together like cocoa butter . . . and loved
                    again and again and again
until we fell asleep, damp and exhausted, in each other's arms

        it was . . the first time ever

for both of us

    the next morning, I awoke . . reached out to him
    but touched only an empty pillow
                        he was gone
    not there
            . .   just gone

fingers of fear clutched tightly, then, into a hard-knuckled fist
and thrust a sharp cramp into my belly, like a curse of shame
causing crimson streams to flow across the love rumpled bed
as I lay there, a pale clown, sans greasepaint
staring at an empty tent . . a ludicrous clown, with no audience
                            to applaud my antics
no one to cheer — the audience had walked out

Canto Eight ☆ 223

indicating distaste, disapproval of the clumsy, inexperienced grossness
of my unfunny, un-touching tumbling act

I had lost my seat on the Carousel for fumbling the reins
and was slipping off my painted horse, never to catch the brass ring now

      oh, who cares ? I was weary of the spinning anyhow
      nearly falling . . and thinking of a painless way
                        to end the ride

        but falling off the Carousel is an art

ask those who try . .

      I started to cry, swallowing the ache in my throat
      as I realized he hadn't even left a note
                        not even a thank-you note
           to thank me

how did the other girls successfully perform this tumbling act ?
    how did the other girls tumble, and never fumble
holding the audience breathless and spellbound ?
I had no practice . . no rehearsal . . and I had thought
there would be a net to catch me, if I fell
              a safety net to catch me . . his arms

      his arms were my safety

then the door
opened suddenly

        as he exploded into the room !
        fell on the bed beside me, in one great leap
        and scooped me up into his arms
        smelling of fresh air and March winds, rain-washed

          . . kissed the tip of my nose
                  handed me a toothbrush, in a blue case
      and a spray of pink-and-white apple blossoms
      from the tree in front of the drug store, on the corner

oh, that lovely, lovely tree !   *

    *   *   then said, his eyes tear-misted

       *   "darling, will you marry me ?"

  *   *
        *   *
    *

                                    *

        magic magic magic magic magic !
                        *   *
        *
                                        *
                *

I tried an experimental tumble through a hoop
and laughter and applause roared all through the tent
as we swung out higher and higher, soaring on a silver trapeze

            then floated
                    floated
                            floated

down into the safety net of each other's arms
                                . . like gauzy butterfly feathers

        If I loved you

                . . if I loved you

        I loved you

                I love you . .

                            "oh ! I love you !" he said "I do, I do !"

                            like the Carousel Bill

"but . . you should have left a note"
I whispered, trembling still
        the fist of fear relaxing slowly

"you should have left a note
to tell me where you went . . because
I almost fell off the Carousel
I really, nearly did

                    . . I really, nearly did"

And We Were Three

        we eloped

            strange word — who needs the extra 'e' ?

antelopes lope
        through deep-deep-green-cool woods

as we 'loped'

no misty white cascading foam of veil
   . . . orange blossoms or organ music

     just a sleepy, unshaven Justice-of-our-new-Peace
     and his sweetly smiling spouse, bespectacled
     carpet-slippered and hair-netted

him . . in his new blue cashmere sweater
smelling of Seaforth shaving lotion . . my Comforter has come

me . . in my chocolate brown halter dress
white strap marks criss-crossed on my sun-tanned back
smelling of Chanel . . and Jergen's lotion on my hands
so they would be worthy of the gold ring
to be placed there . . engraved *Love is Eternal*
the same words Abraham Lincoln
               had engraved inside Mary Todd's wedding band

      . . I had no ring for him
      the jeweler didn't even want to give us
      credit for the one . .

  I was not . . a bride
no wedding veil or bridal gown
but it didn't matter

    yes, we 'loped' ! no wedding cake or bridesmaids
but confetti ! we had confetti-confetti !
               daisy-pink-and-purple-tulip-confetti !
it was so quick, so impulsive
in the spring, in April . . we picked daisies, and pink and purple
                        tulips
in front of the courthouse, where we went to pick up our license

we gathered confetti blooms of flowers
to toss at one another, like delighted children
loping across the Easter-green grass, dizzied and dazzled by spring
and my gold ring

   and began to sing . . *If I Loved You*
   like two mad maniacs

our happiness was illegal, of course
we were caught — and fined ten dollars
fined on our wedding day
ten dollars — for our happiness

   it was against the law to pick the flowers . . and so
   he gave the cranky custodian a crisp, new twenty dollar bill
   our last twenty . . it left us with seventeen dollars to last the week

saying merrily . .
"ten for the flowers, and ten for you !"

then we saw a miracle !

the cranky custodian creased his frown wrinkles backwards
into the crinkles of a smile . . returned the twenty
                              and wished us well

later, he ducked into a doorway, my Comforter
and soon reappeared, with a bunch of violets
and a square, white card, with his printed words

                "we are deep-deep-purpley blue
                and freshly picked — and velvety soft
                     and shy, like you
                but perfectly legal violets, so you are
                permitted to kiss us and love us
                              . . it's perfectly legal !"

I buried my nose in the violets
feeling the salty sting of glad-tears
but quickly blinked them back inside

          . . it's unlucky to weep
                on your wedding day

he had given me his heart to share, and his German Snyder surname to bear
now I, too, would rhyme with apple cider, forever after

          ring the bells of St. Mary's !

we are married, we are married ! too long have we tarried
and now we are married . . in the wood where the piggy-wig stood
what a beautiful druid, you are-you are
                what a marvelous druid you are !
with a kiss on the tip of your nose, your nose
                with a kiss on the tip of your nose !

holding hands and touching hearts . . . afterwards
we breezed into a little coffee shop, to say hello
to the rest of the Highway chain gang
                other slaves of the Pharaoh, having their lunch
and showed them my ring — and the violets

     they grunted and grinned, and blushed, and said . . "Good Luck !"

then came the night . . .

and our unspoken date for a flight . . together
on butterfly feathers again
it was a deep-blue, softly clouded place
                of flaming red rockets and open petaled flowers
not as shy as before, with cool green woods within me
then . . midnight velvet peace around us

    the next morning

I was watching him while he shaved
the yellow-white brilliance of the Sun crocheting delicate lace
across the white heirloom bedspread and sky-blue quilt . .

        . . bless her heart forever-and-three-days !
        that lovely lady with her cheerful welcome house
        and its perfectly marvelous antique room for rent

  . . his face was covered with foaming bubbles, and I snuggled in bed
in a surge of delicious joy, watching him
                my tall, tan Comforter . . bare back rippling
with shaving arm movements

wearing a towel around his waist . . . bare feet
with funny-shaped, now dear, familiar toes

    I lay there, sniffing his Seaforth shaving soap scent
    mingling with the ozone spring breeze
    wafting in through the windows, and ruffling the organdy curtains
    curling my toes . . and squeezing my lashes together
    to keep the happy tears from escaping

                then he turned
                looked deeply into my eyes . . and smiled

            that's all . . just smiled

"oh, hurry," I whispered
"come here and kiss me this minute !"

    he loped across the bright braided rug
    splashed with small patches of dancing sunlight rainbows
        into the snowy-white-soft bed
    and kissed me deep and long
    smearing my face with sweet-smelling bubbles of foam

                "darling, good morning"

"good morning, darling"

    then suddenly . . we both trembled and shook
my knees crumpled into tissue paper

        his warm, strong hand, full of fever, lightly touched
the ivory satin over my breast . . pressed harder, and lingered

     our eyes spoke to each other, yes yes yes
as I slipped out of my new, bride-beautiful, whispering silk and satin
whipped cream gown . . . and we loved again

    this time, a mysterious gentleness drifting through
                           our rhythmic urgency
both felt it . . a strange glow
spreading across our faces, suffusing our bodies
blending with the intensity of our passion
and unexpectedly creating tiny pearls of tears
                to mix their moisture on our cheeks
like a dew-drenched cloud it was
        . . drifting so softly

          misting . . enfolding . . enveloping our consummation
          with tenderness
               . . then lifted, almost visibly

        the bright Morning Star
        last to reluctantly leave the sky at dawn
           must have been watching us
        nodding and twinkling a cosmic approval
                  of our loving
        then blinked out
        and streamed all the way to Heaven . . to tell her
          "the time has come, at last !"

          because she flew down
          nine months later — to the day
          our Anne, with an 'e'

Thank You, Morning Star

           Anne with an 'e'
                star-kissed eyes
           silken hair . . tiny smile to share

she is so new, so very dear
tumbling here
       and reaching there
for a clover or a violet

                              so new
                         so dear
                    so small a druid

oh, whisper to her gently, spring
she is too fragile, small and vulnerable
to stand against your slightest breath
let alone your raw March winds
                    and April thunder storms

              she has only newly learned to find
              the magic thrill of walking . . so please be kind

              blow tenderly on her trembling, dimpled knees
              kiss her softly, April breeze

              or she might fall
              and tumble over in the starry grass

sing enchanted elfin songs
              through the silken ruffles
of her baby-druid hair

                         but please take care !

     she is so dear, so new
     to Earth

                    she is such a tiny prayer

And We Were

              one languid August afternoon
              I tip-toed into the room where Anne was sleeping
              with the two newer druids
              who had come to play with her, as sister and brother

and unexpectedly caught him fumbling in a drawer . . . .
he turned quickly, startled . . when he saw me

"what were you doing ?" I asked, curiously

              then he closed the drawer, and spoke casually
              though a blush stained his cheek

              "have you seen my blue cahsmere sweater anywhere ?
              I can't seem to find it — and I thought perhaps

                         230   ☆   Canto Eight

you might have sent it to the cleaner's last week"

so I let it go . . although
I felt somehow, uneasy — and was certain
that there was something he didn't want me to know

      the next morning, when I opened the drawer
      looking for a ribbon to tie back my hair
              I saw it there . . a note

    with a crazy-daisy
    crookedly drawn in the corner
               and the words . .

        "dear spunky wife
        while you and the babies are bathing
              in scented oils

        and I'm out building dusty roads
        remember that a Pharaoh's slave loves you
        and I shall be wealthy and famous someday
             and bring you rubies
        then we'll bathe in grape juice
            and drink raindrops . . "

    oh, he was magic !

Paul Was a Glib Gemini Poet

      ever has it been, and ever fated shall it be
      that all lovers ask themselves

is this an emotional infatuation
a mental attraction — or merely a chemical reaction ?
Is it only a physical need we feel
        . . or is it *real* ?

before St. Mary's
and also later, after we were married lovers
especially when we quarreled
we spent a lot of time asking each other those questions
mutually wondering
if we were truly real and forever

    and one day
    when it was my turn
    to ask him

he pondered the question for a while
then said
"love is an inexplicable emotion
and as far as I know
the only reliable yardstick
for measuring the true depth of devotion
is in the Bible
St. Paul summed up love's definition
in just two words, when he said . . **"love lasts"**

unexpectedly frustrated
at being given an emotional yardstick
to which I had no way of measuring up
nor did he — which was worse
I told him bitterly, tense and terse

"well, that's certainly a cop-out to end all cop-outs
it's almost as sneaky as your quote from *Carousel*
if I loved you — *if* again !"

and I continued, my voice and anger
both rising

"I guess I'm supposed to hang around
and wait till I'm on my death bed — then
if you should just happen to still be there
I can close my eyes in peace — and go
because, by then, I'll know

St. Paul must have been a Gemini, like you
such glibness, such clever twisting of words !
I can't imagine a more deceptive . .
a more meaningless, empty way to measure
a relationship — then that"

he looked at me, then . . .
for a long, eternal moment
his eyes full of movement
as though seen through a rushing
stream . . the expression in them
luminous and magnified

but he didn't answer, he only sighed

several months later
one evening, while he was painting our kitchen chairs blue
with a yellow tulip decorating the top
his face smeared with colors . . a bright blob of yellow
dotting the corner of his nose

I snuggled up against him, and surrendered the argument

"darling, I've been thinking about what you said
and to give credit where credit is due — Paul was right
there's no honest way you can promise me
                              or I can promise you

that our love is true
in the present or the past — only in the future
because, as Paul said
          if it's love . . it will last"

                         he grinned at my capitulation
                              squeezed me hard, in the middle
                         then winked, and said

                         "you see ? it's like I've been saying
                         there's nothing we can do — or try
                         but trust each other
                                        till we die"

And We Still Were

oh, why do I lie ?

                    why do I, even now, tell myself
                    that I forgave him . . . her ?

I did not — no

                    I did not forgive him that hurt
                    not the cool, sure one
                    I did not — could not
                                   forgive him . . . her

                    she was my friend
                    my best friend, I once believed
                    the cool, sure one . . he confessed making love to her
                                   not before — but *after* we were married

               three times
               three times
               three times . . . she was my *friend*

I gave him cause, he said . .

          I gave him cause — gave him reason
          by becoming angry over nothing — I accused him falsely, he said
          so often . . over nothing, nothing, nothing

so often, he said — that he made the lies come true
I always claimed, he reminded me, that one should be careful
    of what one expects, for one is sure to get it
well, I did, he said . . . I got what I expected, what I had imagined

        he made the lies come true, he said, with the help of vodka
        an ocean of vodka . . . because he was so hurt, he said
                so **HURT ?**

        yes, so hurt, he said — and weary
        of being falsely accused, unfairly suspected
        he was hurt and desperate, he said
        and needed to hurt me back as I had hurt him
                    . . to cause me matching pain

        he needed to prove to me, he said, that he was a man
        a man he said — and not a mouse
        yes, to prove that he was a man, and not
        a squeaking mouse

"get out of this house
you double-faced Gemini
with your forked tongue
and lying Twin hearts

    . . . get out, get out
get out of this house !"
    I screamed

                    "I am a man — not a mouse"
                        he replied, quietly

        I gave him cause, he said
        because I . . turned him away

                "you gave me cause, you turned me away
                        you denied me our love for weeks
                with your continual accusations
                for nothing, nothing, nothing at all !
                you wounded me, you killed me
                        you murdered my manhood
                            oh ! can't you see
                how deeply you wounded me ?
                all for nothing-nothing-nothing
                I had good cause to do what I did !"

"I did not give you cause
no cause — for **THAT !**
there is no cause for **THAT !**

        GET OUT !"

no . . . I did not forgive him . . *her*
I could not forget
the wound cut too deeply into my soul
and the scar has not healed yet

. . I am still not whole

if my suspicions were unfair, each lonely night
if I accused him unjustly . . if I was wrong . .

but, no ! I was not wrong, I was right !

how could my suspicions have been **WRONG**
when they were finally proven to be, **RIGHT** ?

over and over, I asked my tortured mind this question
scarce dreaming or suspecting then — how soon I was to learn
that the answer to it contained the Truth of all existence
                                        on this Earth

"oh, no, oh, no ! you are wrong and I am right !
I was right all along
and it was you who were wrong !
get out — **GET OUT** !"

            she was . . my friend, my best friend
            and he was my . . Comforter

oh, God !

        no, I did not, could not
        forgive him . . . her

but he forgave me — yes, he forgave me, when I said
                        . . oh, did I really say it ?
when I said I had never wanted the three small druids anyway
and shouted at him . . . that I wish they would all return to
                                . . wherever they came from

                even . . . . . . Anne with an 'e'

"yes !" I cried . . . . "let them return to wherever they came from
to the fake oak tree, in the fake woods — as all false dreams die
I wish I had never seen those druids ! . . and I wish
                        I had never seen *you* !"
        the baby druids are a lie

they are not magical anymore

you have made them — and us — a lie
shabby and ordinary, no longer marvelous
and you **ARE** a mouse — yes, you are, you are
a mouse, and not only that — you are weak !

then more softly
with more dangerous venom
in a voice low and clear
I repeated . .
      "you are weak"

                    then he shouted at me
                    shouted at me . .

                    "you *reek* of unforgiveness !"

and I spoke softly again

      "you are weak"

                  a single tear
                  rolled down his cheek

                  "please don't," he pleaded . . "oh, please
                  don't smash everything we love
                  with ugly words of unforgiving hate
                              it's not too late

                  to begin again
                  don't kill everything we love with ugly words
                  please . . don't hate so hard
                  just try to understand . . please, darling
                  give me your hand . . "

                        and he wept

but I stared at him in stony silence
my very soul torn to shreds
and would not forgive . . *could* not forgive

      my twin soul and I . . walked hand-in-hand
      on the painful path of evolving and learning — and shared
      the burning . . of the terrible agonies of growing
      but also shared the unspeakable ecstasies of knowing

            and comforted each other through our pain
                            . . as one little star
                one tiny druid
        fell through the dark of the wide night sky
        and was lost . . somewhere in the mist out there

later, I said
I forgave him, but . .

    and he said
    he forgave me, but . . by the end of the following two years

        one

           by one

                by one

                    the remaining two of the three baby druids left
                      each one . . all

the one with an 'e'
not many months after
she had learned to walk

            she was so new
                so dear
        so small

Saturn in Scorpio

    I have made the dreary trip, the slow, winding route
    of melancholy and despair
    with blank, unseeing eyes . . stern, tight lips
    and gushing torrents of scalding tears

        I have closed my weary ears
        to the dirge of murmuring, hollow voices
        and stood, with stiffened spine and aching lungs

in chilling winds

        that freeze the marrow of the bones
        and rob the heart of its last drop of warmth

I have drawn long, shuddering sighs . . controlled my trembling spirit
beneath dark grey and leaden skies
    felt a warm, strong, dear familiar hand

        "my love, my love, my only love
            be still, be still . . . I'm here"

and clung to this, while kneeling
before a tiny flower covered bier

as crashing chords of *Ave Maria*
washed over our bowed heads

Ave Maria . . Maria . . Maria

"*my love, my love, I'm here*
. . *be still*"

I have forced my shaking legs to carry me
down an endless, grassy hill
to watch a tiny, withered wreath of violets
placed gently on the ground

three times
three times
three times

as one . . by one . . by one

. . . . they went away

my heart remained as granite, for a time
then, at last, relented
in a bursting waterfall of cleansing tears
and I stroked his cheek with tender
and he touched my tangled hair
with gentle

as we locked eyes
in a deep, deep knowing

and loved each other

and forgave once more

Drowning

the thrill and challenge of skiing down snowy slopes
and occasional hopes of swelling and expanding into the Universe
to the music of Tschaikovsky, Puccini . . and Rachmaninoff

moving into a new apartment, swept clean of memories
with crisp, white ruffled curtains

me . . writing poetry
behind a veil

                    he . . writing magazine articles
                    and receiving only rejection slips in the mail

  the sunny and the rainy days
  prayers and disappointments

                        some bright moments

    scattered, cooling kisses

           none of this could
           make the mountains of grief
           fly away for him — or for me

nor could anything else we tried
after the three . . . died

               so I drowned myself

I drowned in a sea of memories and dreams . . .
in an ocean of recrimination, bitterness and mistrust

              and he drowned himself too

                in rivers of vodka
                and a sea of new faces, smiling
                with scented hair

   until we had nothing left to share

and the three-times-three
    of us

              became two

          and finally   one . . and one

each drowning alone
in a different kind of ocean

     and so . . I did the only thing left to do

          then came the day I stared, unbelieving, at the legal paper
          telling me that the State of Virginia
          declared our marriage to be over . . ended

         the State of Virginia declared it, the paper said

        but the State could not separate our hearts
        no matter how profusely they bled

nor could the several thousand miles between us
stretching from the east coast to the west
keep our souls apart . . through this final test

oh ! but it separated . . kept apart
our bodies and our minds

no longer bearing the same name
we waited through the dream of loneliness

but morning never came

CANTO NINE

Your dark eyes flash mysterious discontent,
Your head is turned, as though you smiled in vain —
Your curving lips are sweetened with the scent
Of ancient splendid blossoms, alive again

For these few moments of remembrance in your heart,
When you look into my own —
As the seething flames wind rapturous about the echo
                                    of your name . . .

Kyril Demys (Musaios)
Prismatic Voices

One Night

one night, several years later . . .

oh ! years of inner thunder

> after the State of Virginia imagined
> it could split our souls asunder, with a knife
> fashioned from a simple piece of paper

> but did not succeed

this night . .

> I could not sleep — I'd gone to bed around ten o'clock, but . . .

> no matter how I tumbled and tossed
> how hard I tried — I could not sleep

> until I heard the twelve chimes of midnight
> then fell sound asleep, at last
> but continued to awaken, periodically . . every hour or so

> six different times I awoke that night
> between midnight, when I first fell asleep
> and the cold grey light
> > of an October dawn

> I had been so very, very restless
> between ten and midnight . . for no reason I could fathom

I'd gone to Colorado, to rent, for a few months
a haunted, antique house, on a barren plot
to rest, near mountains who might soothe me

> they did not

> > instead, surprising me, they flew
> > oh, they flew, like bats ! like dark winged bats
> > or the dark-winged ravens of my painted brows
> > on that butterfly feathers night . . so long ago

I awoke on this Halloweenish October night
this goblin-filled, black-cat-screeching-screaming night . . every hour

and each time, thought it light
believed it to be morning
> each time . . thought it to be
> > dawn . . .

but it was not

it was still dark, still black outside
velvet black . . . . . as, to match the night
a black cat cried

> I jolted awake from uneasy slumber
> sharply . . sitting up in bed

abruptly

> morning ? dawn ? time for coffee ?
> breakfast time ?

no . .

> black cat . . neighbor's mewing pet
> then looked out the windows . . old bay windows
> of this antique, haunted house

black outside
still dark

> not morning yet

> each time I awoke startled . . sitting up, looking out the windows
> it was still night
> and each time, I felt a fright
> a sudden fright . . because I thought I saw

> I did not think
> I nearly-really *knew* I saw

a shadow on the wall

> and more real, even, than the shadow — much more real
> was the absolutely distinct

sensing

that someone stood
just outside my door

> and once . . stood at the foot
> of my bed
> in the dark
> faintly outlined, with a pale, barely visible, silvery light

> and each time, I called out
> cried out sharply, loudly — his name
> the Bill, from Carousel

"is that you ?"

    "are you there ?"

"is that you ?"

                by this, I knew
                that he was intensely needing, wanting me
                out there on the lonely Laguna Beach
                            in California

                where he had gone
                to drown, in his vodka ocean

                although, lately . . for more than a year
                he had not tasted a sip of beer
                    . . he had written to me, just last month

yes . . because my subconscious, the deeper me-of-me
had called out, cried out his name
I knew it must somehow be the Carousel Bill I sensed
standing there, outside my door
                and once, at the foot of my bed
it must be . . he

        needing, wanting me . . astrally, in his sleep
        as I needed, wanted him

                were our astral bodies loving maybe ?
                oh ! I hoped they were !
                I hoped our astral bodies were clinging in the night . . . .

                as I fell asleep again, near dawn . . .

                I must call him, phone him in the morning
                and tell him not to visit me, to kiss me astrally
                without my permission . . . I thought

only teasing myself
playing a joke upon myself
knowing I would never, never call him
fearing rejection

    no, not true . . not fearing rejection
but fearing that I could not — even yet — forgive

for years, and especially in recent months
I knew he wanted, needed me
but I was afraid . . I still could not forgive

    . . . somehow, the night went by

and when I next awakened, it was already day

but grey — no Sun

I arose, slipped on a robe
and went downstairs, to pour a glass of orange juice
too tired and weary, feeling too dreary
for any larger breakfast

and took my orange juice into the den, sitting there
wondering . . . and thinking
many intimate thoughts of him
and of us

was it really he, I wondered . . was it he I had sensed so strongly
standing there, in the black night behind me ?
was it he, who had given me such a fright — who woke me
suddenly, every hour . . all night ?

was it my own husband . . needing, wanting me
intensely . . astrally ?

or perhaps the Holy Ghost, still
still relentlessly pursuing me ?

which ?
or . . . both ?

oh, was it the Carousel Bill I sensed so vividly ?

wait ! *what was that* ?

I could swear I saw a shadow on the stair !

I went, then, to the stairway — looked up to the landing

no one there

but . . what was that shadow on the stair ?
I was certain I had seen it
yet, there was no Sun this day . . . all the clouds
outside the window . . were colored dull grey
no Sun to make a shadow there

and then, unbidden
I felt an overwhelming lonely

a sweeping, overpowering lonely . . a longing
for his arms around me, his kiss on my cheek
his lips on mine . . . once more only

a need so deep, so deep . .   like no need I'd ever felt before

no, not ever — not even those times
when we had clung together in the dark, fused into one
those remembered nights of blending
                               . . deeper even than then, was my need
surprising me
with its waves of sudden passion

I thought . . he must be sensing it too
this sweeping, overwhelming need
he must feel it as deeply as I
                         which is obviously why
           he broke through
the curtain of my conscious awareness last night
                               . . so many times

      oh ! our love still rhymes !

           I could not bear our separation one hour longer
           no ! not one more minute
           we have both, I thought, been wrong and blind

then rushed to find . . in the desk
my small address book
with his telephone number

             and read there, as if in slumber . . what I had forgotten

yes, I had forgotten
until I saw it there, in my own writing

      he had moved from Laguna Beach . . recently
      to Salem, Virginia
      the California number was written there clearly
      but, for Salem . . where he now lived, alone
      I had only his address
                      . . no phone

he had written it to me . .
his new Salem telephone number
but I had not yet transferred it into
this address book
and his letter . . was back in New York

      oh, well

           I shouldn't call him anyway . . it was merely
           an impulse of the moment, I thought
           I had been saved from making a serious mistake
           by my own carelessness

. . then, suddenly . . unexpectedly

his face

as real as flesh . .   as real

      his face flashed vividly before my vision
      smiling his old, remembered crooked grin
      I could even see the tiny scar beneath his chin
      from a dog bite, as a child

      his long, starry . . unusually long . . lower lashes
         his lips . . teeth . . hair

      it was so clear, the flashing image of his face
      it was truly as though . . . oh !
      as though he were there . .   *really* there

and the sharpness of his image

    was so real

that, with it came an uncontrollable longing
to hear the sound of his voice
with the old, familiar laughter in it, warm and tender

   just to hear him say "hello"

      I simply had to call him
      I must find a way to locate his number

and maybe . . maybe I might ask him
if he would fly out here
and help me haunt this antique house

   we could be sitting here, drinking orange juice
   together . . as soon as tomorrow morning !

   why did I wait so long ? I knew he needed me, but now
   could I be strong . . and could I — forgive ?
   he had suggested, in letters, often . . that we try once more

   and I had repeatedly refused
   was I wrong ? but maybe . . maybe

I knew he would come — this I knew
he had wanted so to see me, to talk it over
              to try again

      yes, I knew he would come, and . . he could fly
      of course — he could fly ! I heard myself cry aloud

Canto Nine　☆　247

and be here in just a few hours !

                my heart began, then, to pound with long-denied joy
                and excitement . . and spring
                                the forgiveness I had postponed
too many years . . the happines
I could have fed to my heart, in its lonely hunger
and had so many times refused

        now I would not refuse my heart its nourishment
        of touching . . seeing . . hearing him again
        his hands, holding mine . . together . . no more pain

        and had a swift thought, that made me laugh aloud
        I'll ask him to bring some *Goober's Peanuts* with him on the plane

I laughed joyously aloud again

        yes ! *Goober's Peanuts* !

I'll ask him to bring along a box of them
so I can gobble them down, and grow smaller . . and smaller
until he can't see me at all
or hear me speak or squeak . . a single word

        no, this time, I'll make *him* eat the magical Goobers
        and let him, not me . . grow teeny-tiny
                        smaller . . smaller
        and then pretend
        as he did with me . . that I cannot see him or hear him
        oh ! that will be such fun . . that is so funny !
        we will both eat them, and grow teeny-tiny together

                        . . disappear together
        how funny !
                . . like butterflies with feathers

a warm, cozy feeling . . a breath of tender, gentle warmth
filled me like a balloon, with memory and gladness
                        . . no more sadness
        oh ! no more sadness . . .

                I felt glad-tears sting my eyes
                then came the lump behind my ears
                in the spot where you first feel mumps
                        . . the indescribable mump-lump of longing
and the baby robins
        fluttered, singing
after so long
        their hungry song
in my breast

softly, I began to hum our words from *Carousel*
*If I Loved Yo*u

                as I dialed the operator . . . .
                Long Distance Information
                for Salem, Virginia

      no number

    oh, no — not this — when I so need his kiss
    and am so filled with love and forgiveness
    not now . . when he needs me too . . after he tried last night
    to reach me astrally . . six times
    oh, God, don't make me wait another day or week—to kiss his cheek
    . . . to tell him I still love him . . and forgive him
                           . . . and need him so
"but, Operator, Operator !
try again — please check again !
his name, it rhymes with apple cider
and his first name is . .
like the Bill from *Carousel*

. . maybe you're spelling it wrong"

    and I spelled it for her . . slowly, carefully
    "it rhymes with apple cider" . . oh, she must find his number
    I suddenly needed so desperately to tell him
                     " . . . darling, I forgive you"
    I so needed to hear
      the tenderness in his warm, familiar voice
    when he said, as I knew he would . .

"you silly Goober Peanut !
you perfectly marvelous druid . . I love you
and I need you
I'll catch the next flight to Colorado . . will you meet my plane ?"

    "I'm sorry," said the robot voice in my ear — "yes
    there is a number for him here
             I didn't see it before"

oh, thank you, God !

    " . . however, it is unlisted, and I am not permitted to . . "

"oh, Operator, **PLEASE**
please, Operator
look, he is my husband — and you could
call him yourself
just call him, and give him my number
so he can call me back"

"sorry, we are not allowed to do that . . "

"but, Operator
this is my husband — and
it is . . an emergency"

CLICK

she had
cut me off

      he had an unlisted number
      his phone — unlisted
      I sat there for a moment
      wondering what to do

then decided to try again, and reach the Chief Operator
she would, somehow, see that I got through

      but . . just as I touched the receiver of the telephone
      before I had a chance to lift it
                it rang

a clear ring
like a robin

      trilling a single note of spring !

oh, miracle, miracle, miracle !
I *knew* he was thinking of me too !
we always crossed telepathic wires
like this . . I blew the telephone
             a kiss
then lifted the receiver

      knowing . . knowing . . knowing

waiting to hear his voice — rejoice !
oh, darling, darling, darling
you *heard* me try to call you, in the same astral way
you came to me last night . . and you've called me back ! I thought

   "hello ?"

 a bad connection . . clicking . . buzzing in my ear
oh, *why* hadn't I called him last night ?

why didn't I call him last night — not now
and tell him to catch an early flight
he could be beside me this minute . . without
            all this bother

click . . buzz . . click

       it was Long Distance . . "hello ?" the Operator said
       "hello ? I have a call for you . . from Salem, Virginia"

I knew it, I knew it !
I miracled inside
old dreams, awaken !
it's time ! he received
my message astrally

       "hello ? go ahead — there's your party now"

"HELLO ?"

       it was . . a mutual friend of ours

he said . .

      he said

           he spoke his name
           and he said . .

"I called to tell you — Bill is dead

he passed away last night, in his sleep
or rather, about three o'clock this morning
he is gone . . he is dead"

       he is dead . . he's dead . . he said

he is dead

          "he went to work yesterday, as usual
          after having dinner with a friend
                 the night before
          but he wasn't feeling well, and so . . about four
          he left work early
          and stopped in to see a doctor he knew
          who told him he had 'walking pneumonia'
          I believe that's what he called it — and
          the doctor told him
          he should be home in bed . . and asked
          if he had anyone there to take care
                 of him
          he laughed, and said . . 'no
          there's no one there — I live alone
          but I have a telephone
             so it's not really like being alone
          besides, I can take care of myself,' he said

and the doctor told him then
'I'll stop by in the morning, to see how
you are — my office is not very far
                   from your apartment
but there really should be someone
there with you
walking pneumonia is no joke, you know

then he went home . . to rest
he took a phone call from a friend
                 a neighbor . . a lawyer
shortly after midnight
and said he felt drowsy — and was
                  going to try to sleep

they found him this morning, in bed
and he . . was dead

they're not certain exactly when he died
all they know is that he was alive
                at midnight . . . .
that's all they know
hello ? hello ?   are you there ?"

Goodbye

now I have placed a larger wreath
of autumn flowers, red and gold
on freshly turned and frosted earth

        cried out . . "oh, no ! don't go, don't go !"

and knelt beneath the crushing weight
of the echoing organ's choruses of *Ave Maria* . . .
           which had filled the funeral chapel earlier

Ave Maria, Maria, Maria

tearing once more through my quivering soul . . each roll
of music over my head
thundering a deep, insistent promise . . with every chord

be still, be still . . he is not dead

I have pressed a final, tender kiss
on numb, blue lips

and placed, too late, a golden band
on a cold white dear familiar hand

then heard, impossibly, but clearly
a distant robin sing
a single, trilling note of spring

through October's
autumn chill

and walked away

alone

. . . be still, my love, be still . .
somewhere, a clock is timing us

To be sung to the tune of *Londonderry Air*

If I should dream
That you were gone,
My dearest love,
I would despair of all my heavens' gain,
And I should look
With darkened eyes
Upon the world
That would be empty of the one I love . . . and vain.

O dearest heart,
My light and love and laughter,
I could not weep or sigh
if you did go —
But I should smile
While throned in time thereafter,
When you return, O love,
In love's own light and glow.

Kyril Demys *(Musaios)*
Prismatic Voices

the day following his dream-like funeral
after he had been duly chanted over
with the cruel mantra . . *dust thou art*
. . . and to dust thou must
return

I thought . . . **OH, DAMN !**

what great spiritual lesson is the one bereaved supposed to learn
from this frail graveside testament of comfort
dictated by all holy churches, to be delivered at the final curtain
to diguise the hollow sound of their theology
. . . to whitewash the emptiness of their dogma ?

what lesson

from . . *dust thou art*
and to dust each must return ?

the druids never incantated such bleak prophecy
no Stonehenge druidic Nature Spirits
ever dribbled such impotent mumbo-jumbo over any grave
no magical creature could have originated or spoken
such icy-cold and clammy pseudo-comfort

those who held the secret of making mountains fly
would surely have invented something
more miraculous to say . . . when fellow druids had to die

I knew, just *knew* that this was true

damn it, damn it !

then felt immediate regret
for druids also . . do not ever

. . . *druids do not damn*

I knew that, too, was true . . from misty memory
no, druids do not, for any reason, ever damn

but . .
on the day following his funeral

.. the day following the funeral, like a rushing river of grief
threatening to flood the spirit, and sweep it on toward Hell's
                                                    waiting
                                                    whirlpool
                                                    and even
                                                    further.

            on that day ..

         I sat alone, at last, and found it impossible, nearly
         to accept what I recalled so clearly
         impossible to believe my secret behaviour
         beside his casketed body, cold .. two nights past

yet, it was real, it had truly happened
for I could still feel the anguish of that moment
when, kneeling beside the casket, all alone — except for him
with no one near .. long after midnight
                        for more than an hour

when he and I were by ourselves
in that flower scented room, together

            I . . . .

I . . . .

            softly, yet audible
            to anyone who may have been
            listening ..

softly, I sang to him
to his closed eyes, sweeping lashes
on his cheek .. faintly smiling lips

         sang the lyrics
         of our song to him

            If I Loved You

                                 oh, darling !
                                 if only I had known *how*
      .. time and again   to love you
         I would try to say
   all I'd want you to know ..

      .. if I loved you

words wouldn't come in an easy way

Canto Ten ☆ 257

.. 'round in circles I'd go

longing to tell you ..

but afraid and shy

      .. I'd let my golden chances
                  pass me by ..

. . . but Operator
you must have him listed, you must !
his name, it rhymes with apple cider . . .

**WHY DIDN'T I CALL
AT MIDNIGHT ? WHY, WHY, WHY ?**

.. *soon you'd leave me*

      .. *off you would go, in the mist of day*

never, never to know

        how I loved you . . .

   if . . .
     I loved you

then sobbed into his icy ear
"no, not *if* — not *if*

    that was a bad song, a sad song
    not a glad song .. for us to choose as ours

      no, not If — because I *did* love you
      yes, I did, I did .. I truly loved you

and you loved me
and you loved me

        not If

then could hear the voice of the *Carousel* Bill
on the record .. the one
we used to listen to, together .. over and over
saying to her, to Julie, the one he loved

> *"well, anyway, you don't love me*
> *that's what you said, wasn't it ?"*

and Julie's
hesitant answer

> *"yes"*

> *"say, are you trying to get me*
> *to marry you ?"*

then her soft sigh
to him . . *"oh, no !"* she said

> *"then what's put it into my head ?"*

and as the memory
of the *Carousel* record
       we played and played
began to fade
    I sobbed aloud again
into his icy-cold ear

> *"not if, not if . . . . . . I loved, you, I did"*

then stopped, suddenly
aware of the tense I'd used
and whispered . .

> *"no, not did . . I do love you . . now*

> not past tense — present tense — I *do*

and . . I know you did . . but
do you, even *now,* this moment
do you still love me too ?"

>   . . and then

> I swear, I swear, I swear !
> oh ! I swear, not on this worthless life alone
> I swear on all future incarnations before me
> and on all those lives long past
> in whatever Body Temples, surely far more valuable
> than this present one — yes, I swear on all these !

I swear
    I heard him
not imagined — but *heard* him

                  answer
"yes"

            so softly

                        his whisper . . I know his whisper
                        have I not heard it, felt it sending loving words
                        into my ear, upon our single-shared pillow
                        on . . how many nights, how many ?

it was not
imagination — nor was it
the magnified imagery of grief
no — it was real
                  . . a physical voice
I heard

        I swear he whispered faintly

                              "yes, I do love you still"
then, being driven
slightly mad, I guess
by those clear, however faint
    distinct words

    I assumed that he could hear me too
    and cried out to him, in that flower scented room

wondering, even now
if I was heard by the undertaker
somewhere in the hall

                    cried out . .

"then listen to me, listen !
if you truly love me . . and you spoke
and you can hear my voice speaking
listen ! hear what I say
open your eyes, this very moment

    this very moment
              only open your eyes
    and show me that you are not dead . . that
    you are not clay . . or dust

                    please . . you *must* !"

and tears streamed down
the cheeks of my soul

        "please show me you are not dead
              so I will know the voice I heard

                    260 ☆ Canto Ten

was not just within my own head
         . . please prove to me
you are not dead
                  come back to me . . *come back to me* !
and if you will, I promise
druid honor . . honor bright . . I promise on my honor
                  on my sacred, sacred honor
I swear to God . . no, I swear to Jesus, who knows me better
I swear to Jesus
                  if you will prove to me you are not dead
                  by coming back to me

      I will forgive you . . *her*
      yes, I will, I will, I promise I will
      I will forgive you . . her

      and never again suspect you
      or be cold to you
                  or deny you our love again
      or shut you out . . or make you leave
                        or tell you to Get Out !
      never, never, never again

I will never doubt you, never mistrust you
oh ! please — if you truly love me . . open your eyes
come back to me, and I'll forgive you, I will !
please, please . . do not be dead"
                        . . . I said

and was almost certain that I saw
his long, sweeping lower lashes
tremble . . . tremble . . . for one instant

      I thought his eyes . .

                  but no, they did not open
                  although . . his lashes faintly trembled

I saw them tremble

                  but his eyes . . did not open
                  to gaze into mine again

then, as I clutched the blanket of roses, draped across the casket
the flowered Comforter . . I had sent there . . to cover him

      a single red rose

                  fell into my shaking hand
                  and remained there
                              . . a single rose

Canto Ten   ☆   261

. . . I would like

to have

         this first dance

with you . . .

     my mind a blank tapestry of nothing
     I took his dear familiar hand
             wearing now the gold band
  we could not afford, in St. Mary's . . . I had placed there
         . . . . held it gently in my own
    then fell asleep, kneeling there beside him
               holding hands
and did not dream
while I slept

      no . . did not dream

how soon he would prove to me
   that he had heard my pleading call
       and had already answered
    in a voice
      too low for me to hear

but heard, and answered . .

     "yes, I will come back to you
     I will come back . . "

no, as I slept there, so near
I did not dream he had heard
each pleading word

    I did not dream
    that he would keep his promise to me
    made at that star-crossed moment
           from somewhere beyond
    as I had sobbed
      and begged him to

    but that I would break *my* promise
          my forgiveness bond
    made to *him*
     anew

in my dreamless sleep . . .
later awakened by the undertaker

I had no . . . knowing

           that I would break my promise

Fragments — Finale

    there were so many things
    I never told
        while I was waiting

so many faces, so many tears
    fragrant lilacs, falling snowflakes
locked iron gates . . crystal fears

so many flickering candles
    in the shadow of the cross
chiming bells . . dark, stone cells

    and three brown monkeys
    carved in a circle

see no sorrow — speak no evil — hear no sadness
    joy and gladness, grief and pain
        sun and snow and wind and rain
déjà vu
    déjà vu

    so many things I never told
    and then he came . . and he knew

but stayed only such a little while
to hurt me and help me, curse me and bless me
sharing, evolving, growing, knowing
        in love and light
then, left alone to face the night
he held her picture, one of the three
        Anne with an 'e'
after writing a note to me
found later . . in the pocket of his sweater

    . . the wind blows soft
        the night grows kind
    sleep's not far off
      peace fills my mind . . .

a verse he wrote himself
or memorized ?

bringing a sharp stab of pain each autumn season

>   we loved . . and why ? . . we loved
>   because it was he . . . . . and because it was I

oh, God !

>   why did You let him die

>   . . . again ?

Even in a Seventh Heaven

>   it was a wind-chilled, long ago September
>   when we first met, in an unexpected rain

a hazy-blue and early spent October
when he left for California
to try to drown his pain, by fading into sunset's beaches
>   of promised anonymity

>   and then, again October
>   when he lay down to rest alone — on a bed
>   we never shared, believing no one really cared
>   and went to sleep forever . . . .

but I cared . . I cared !
please, God, wherever he is now
tell him . . let him know how *much* I cared
and how much I wish
we could have shared all the tears
of those last drowning years . . together

>   was golden autumn, then — our season ?
>   the time of fading beauty, bittersweet nostalgia
>   and the burning leaves of memory — yes
>   autumn was our loving time
>   as well as our time of goodbye
>   . . and now
the smoky season
is here again

>   . . this vaguely restless, blue-grey November twilight
>   smells like football weather
>   that's what we used to call it, in school
>   when I was an almost cheerleader
>   turning cartwheels in my mind

264   ☆   Canto Ten

poets call it Indian summer
I wonder what the Colorado Ute tribes named it ?

    he would know

    like he knew about phosphorite and polar bears
                          physics and phonetics
    as befitted a man of such catholic interests

    but, somehow, he never quite knew what to do
    with all his knowledge . . he thought a lot
                  about so many things
  and amused himself
  by debating with the authors of the books he read
imaginary confrontations, he sometimes shared with me

                my smaller mind
                amuses itself
            with more mundane
            and minor matters
                of the moment

    across the street, eight tousled lads
    are playing Red Rover — let Jimmy come over
    and Jimmy breaks the line . . .
    I used to be afraid they wouldn't call my name
    when I played that game . . and once they didn't

  down the block, near the big oak tree
  at the corner, where the kids park their bikes
  someone has lit a smoky golden bonfire

    and the scent of burning leaves
  hangs heavy-heavy over my head
                like some nostalgic incense
  Madison Avenue would market
        under the name of déjà vu

    oh, God, will I miss him this painfully
    every autumn season ?
    and . . wherever he is, in time and space
    does he miss me too ?
    can he see these tears on my face ?

Minor Memory

I don't remember how soon
I was able to eat and drink
or what I consumed
after those three times of grief
              when the three baby druids . . left

but I remember
after he had gone to join them

it was five days before I could swallow food
and the first thing I ate
              was a piece of pecan pie

and I remember
how it shocked me that I could be
so hungry

I guess I thought that I would never be
hungry or thirsty . . ever again

and I would sustain my body
on vitamins and memories

Running and Scanning

I had been trying to write a Happiness poem
and unsuccessfully attempting to make Life rhyme
since childhood . . yet had not completed
              even the beginning stanza
maybe if I should fly . . . once more
to Colorado, I might try . . oh, not to write it now
but to forget, somehow, the reasons why it could never be
                    completed

then it might be, hopefully, diminished
    eventually exorcized to finally disappear
this, my secret fear . . that the inner peace I sought
was a gift the future did not hold for me

my earlier three month escape to the mountains had been too brief
perhaps this time, I could return to the same rented antique house
and remain awhile, I mused

but when I arrived in the State

where some once thought the streets were paved with gold
I found myself to be still obsessed
                    with the same unexpressed, unspoken fear
and wondered what magnetic power
                had tugged on me, to pull me here

as those great remembering beasts are silently drawn
to find the elephant's burying ground
where they might lay themselves down to die
                        knowing they will not be found

and who could find me now
in this teeny-tiny cobweb
gold mining, ghost filled town
out west ?

        not even my most relentless pursuer
        that chief of the spiritual F.B.I. — the Holy Ghost Himself
        would think to seek me
        in such a slipping-off-the-time-track town
        with buildings falling down, like the London Bridge nursery rhyme

yet, even so . .

        which I had grown to love — the more, perhaps
        because it was not new, but old
                    and seemed to hold a finer gold
than the kind they once mined out here beneath the ground

                        ground bruised and pitifully scarred
                        by man's greed — the need for wealth more desperate
                        than possessing Nature's beauty for his own

a town whose people still believe and act
more like children . . than children

and this, their un-touched and touching
childlike faith . . even that the mines
will open up and pour out gold again . . "just any day"

reached my heart
apparently not yet robbed
of all belief in magic

                and made me want to stay

no, the Holy Ghost could not pursue me here
it would not occur to Him that I might hide my face in this lonely place
for it was more like me to bury myself
                        as a needle in a larger haystack
            beneath the glare of brighter lights

than the kerosene lamps that flickered peacefully
                      recalling another age or bygone time
   here, in a haunted, antique house
that made the Present scan and rhyme . . I thought
                      with a warmer, lovelier Past

   and felt, despite my mournful brooding
   that I had found my way back home, at last

   sadly and ironically too late to write a Happiness Poem
   yet comforted, as the pachyderms are soothed
   when they find that sought, familiar spot
                      for here, perhaps
   I could lay me down to rest
   lullabyed and rockabyed by ghosts
   some holier-than-thou, some unholy

      breathing cool, clean mountain air
      and watch the children playing there
      who still believed in miracles

          as I once did

Polarity

   my thoughts scramble

      they ramble

they tangle into knots

      no rhyme or reason, logic or sense

   no Future
   all Past Tense

      it is as if I were, in some way, haunted
                     still wanted
      by my spiritual pursuer
          the Holy Ghost

      does He still follow me ?

      and what if . . . what if *He* is a *She* ?

   odd thought, weird idea to entertain
   that the Holy Ghost should track me down

to this little mining town, dressed in a white lace nightgown
instead of in the billowing, sheeted robes
I had always imaged before

at Trinity

but the notion
stayed with me — why ?

with woman's intuition to guide Her
would not She find it easier, by far, to follow me ?
and, if full of wrath, because I had wandered from the path
of my childhood faith — would not a feminine wraith
feeling, then, such a Holy spurn
answer the familiar description of a Female — and burn
with a fire which Heaven hath no rage to equal ?

I was dwelling, meditating on nonsense, purely
for surely, there was no point in such wild conjecture
and yet, and yet . .

there was some wisp of recall . . some wisdom
from ages . . or eons . . past
something which whispered in my inner ear . . hold fast !

hold fast to this thought, for it is not
pure nonsense — it is fraught
with deeper truth

but how could there be any secrets revealed
or wisdom contained . . in wondering whether the Holy Ghost
might be named John or James — or Rebecca or Ruth ?

how could this lead to any deeper truth ?

finally, the wisp faded away
drifting back into the depths of consciousness
somewhere in my sleeping mind . . . although

where that place might be, buried in forgotten memory
I did not know, nor care to ponder or to find

I was finished with the Holy Ghost

and so, I made myself a pot of tea and cinnamon toast
recalling, perhaps, Aunt Maud doing this to comfort me
after Nanoo died . . when I was three
before I knew to either love or hate — or fear
this dim essence of the Holy Trinity

then found I was neither hungry nor thirsty
but . . feeling suddenly

Canto Ten ☆ 269

                        . . so sleepy

and though it was only seven, hardly dark
I went to bed, and slept . . perchance to dream ?

                                    . . dreaming maybe

but not consciously guessing
what deep secret might lie behind the beckoning mystery
of the sexual polarity I had pondered — what truth lay hidden
in whether the Holy Ghost answered to the call
                    of John or James . . Rebecca or Ruth

polarities . . opposite poles of North and South, East and West

man and woman . . rich and poor . . black and white
day and night . . woman opposes man . . Adam and Eve
                                    . . and Serpent ?
sexless Serpent ? boy or girl Snake ?

        Serpent SexleSS ? hiSSing Serpent SexleSS ?

waking in the black dawn, toward morning
and then . . falling back to sleep

                    I dreamed of Eden

            with meadows green, and shamrock starred
            hearing a familiar voice . . whose ?

                                    singing

        . . dreamed I heard it keen

    I'll take you home

        I'll take you home again, Kathleen

And If My Face Turned Green

    I played a foolish game of desperation this morning
    a game with myself — the Universe — and him

    hunt and choose, to drown the blues . . win or lose
                                place your bet
    when there's something your heart and mind

won't let you forget

a game left over from childhood fancy — make a blind choice
then see if some sort of answer might lie
in what the inner eye . . . . has chosen

like flipping over the pages in the Bible
or in any book . . and allowing your finger to linger on a word
a sentence or a phrase
which could hold some underlying
or symbolic meaning on a conscious level

. . or like Chinese fortune telling sticks
of which only the I Ching
has any true validity

just one of those pathetic magic tricks
the heart turns to, when all other doors to truth
are closed and locked

stop a spinning coin
before its spin is through
and which side stares up at you . . heads or tails ?

the experiment usually fails — at least, it did for me
in younger, more trusting years
whatever the hopes or fears or needing
that made me turn to games of chance

I played it now in a mystical way
as a substitute gesture of pleading and supplication
having been unable to pray . . for weeks

instead of dice or coins, I used old love letters — his
placing them in a heap on the floor, in the den
then . . knelt before them reverently, as before an altar

. . yes, in reverence, as before the *Al*-tar of childhood

letters from Germany, Stuttgart . . Switzerland
Fort Campbell, Kentucky . . Laguna Beach, California
letters of love and longing . . and occasional misunderstandings

quarrels and reconcilliations on paper
letters of friendly content and humorous intention
of poetic invention . . some erotic-from-missing
letters lonely-for-kissing, describing intimacies
and familiar secrets

some containing paragraphs of wise, some wistful
bearing words of affection . . tender words, kind and gentle

some angry accusations, scattered traces of sarcasm
                    sparks of doubt and suspicion

   letters outlining some private ambition
   hope — or despair
   letters written from the heart, using the mind
                              as a powerful pen

   often mightier than the sword of face-to-face confrontation
   but pale beside the communication of physical touching
   when attempting to substitute for Love

perhaps between the lines of one of these . . . hidden within
his declarations of love and hurts
written in spontaneous spurts of both happiness and disappointment
I might discover a message I could decode
                    as an answer to my question

   my two-part query
   concerning survival

      how could I survive alone
      and what reason for doing so ?

      yes, survival
                    part one — *how* ?
                    part two — *why* ?

I had little hope for enlightenment from words written so long ago

                    but I could try

I closed my eyes, in the attitude of prayer
not praying, though
and stretched out my hand, groping . . and hoping
toward the scrambled pile of letters on the floor of the den
bearing his familiar script

     curiously, trusting in an unsolicited Fate or Deity
                    to guide my hand's trembling search

   . . and touched a letter

a thin one . . not as plump as many others
maybe only a note . . still, something he wrote
which might guide this moment of desperate seeking

   I lifted it from the pile of correspondence

                    slowly . .

the envelope told me nothing
then removed the two sheets of greenish-blue
air mail paper
with writing on both sides
and read each word with mystical x-ray vision
magnifying every nuance, lingering over each syllable

for some clue

with the very first line, I remembered this letter
written, wounded . . after he'd received an impulsive epistle of mine

I tried to read it now with different eyes
hoping it might disguise some coded message
sent by him
from whatever Heaven
he might now call home — to me

left alone and lost
on this lesser planet
spinning faster
every hour

in an earlier letter, he had sent a proud snapshot of himself
from Germany, standing tall, and holding skis
wearing an unfamiliar hair cut — crew
and I had furiously scribbled back
that he looked like a Nazi Storm Trooper
no longer like my husband — unlike any man I loved
or even knew
I recalled writing to him
"I do not know you — who *are* you ?
I cannot recognize the man
in this picture . . and if that man came near me, here and now
I would run away, as from a stranger
please allow your hair to grow back again . . so I will once more know you
as the man I love"

it wasn't very kind or tactful of me
but outraged Rams are rarely noted for their subtlety
or second thought — and must be loved for other virtues
such as courage, honesty . . innocence of intent
and intensity of passion

I regretted the impulsive words
the instant I had sent them winging to him, overseas
like birds, bearing daggers in their beaks
to stab his pride and wound his sensitive sense of self respect

but by then . .
as with all Mars-ignited, rash rockets of fire

Canto Ten ☆ 273

whether written or verbal
             it was too late

words once penned or spoken may be painfully regretted
but may not, without appropriate atonement, be cancelled out
once carelessly conceived, and given hasty, ill-timed birth

    except through gradual drowning in the soothing ocean
       of an extra measure of love and clear devotion
       given for an indeterminate length of time
                         to the one so hurt
this a deep need of the human heart
to heal . . and learn to trust the thoughtless one
                    who wounded it . . . anew
which both sides in any lover's quarrel
should heed and remember — but sadly, seldom ever do

in real-life Love Stories, as opposed to fiction and film
love *does* mean saying you are sorry . .

    I read his letter now
    with fresh eyes of searching and sorrow
    scanning it for some message sent from Yesterday
    into Today — giving hope for Tomorrow

baby wife
spunky mouse-spouse

    who is it you love, some image of myself — or me ?
    what has my hair to do . . with the way you feel inside ?

        why should you feel so unfamiliar with the man you love
        because of an outward thing like that
                          . . unless you lied
        when you first said you loved me

and the letter
      continued . .

        I'll let it grow in again, of course
        to please you — and you may be right
        a crew cut doesn't suit me

        but I can't help wondering now
        if it's really me you love — the inner me
        since you say you do not recognize
        the man who loves you . . anymore

as I read on
I concentrated on every word
and tried to see some

invisible meaning . . not just *within*
but *between* . . every line

as the words wavered, then grew
luminous . . upon the paper

what if I should decide to grow a beard ?
would you avoid me then
and not love me as before, because of my appearance ?

I am the same man, always and forever
my soul even still the same
           after Death . . and longer
my heart yours for all of Time — and yours mine
also for Eternity — isn't that the way it is ?

that's the way I thought it was . . with us

if my skin should change color
                   and if my face turned green
or my nose reversed itself
to be relocated, where my eyes are now
I might look like some weird monster from outer space

but . . whatever mutation might overcome me
and change the appearance of my physical being . .
oh ! don't you see ? I would still be me
the man who promised he would love you
                   all through Eternity . . and after

but, do you love me as much ?
     I honestly wonder, since your letter

then I turned it over
the greenish-blue, thin paper
and read what was written
on the back side . . of the second sheet

I'm sorry if my words sounded crabby
           I don't mean to scold you
I realize you wrote impulsively
as you do most things — not thinking really
or meaning half of what you wrote
                   no more than you mean
half of what you say
but . . it's been a stormy, lonesome day
and your letter arrived to depress me
                   just when I was needing most
to know you cared

I'm so worried about this test we're taking
you and I
it's such a hard test
I know I shouldn't worry about it, but I do
and the later it gets, the more I worry
if we're going to pass the test

                              of being apart

still, I guess I can seem insensitive at times too
and blind to your needs . . and I'm sorry
that I had to hurt you again, or seem unkind
it's only because I'm so worried about the test
will you forgive me, if I've hurt you again
by trying to explain how I feel ?
                    I miss you terribly
and it's so lonely here, without you

          . . your adoring, but slightly angry husband

                    "me"

P.S.

don't worry, darling, we'll pass this test together
if we keep remembering that we love each other
and I do understand why you wrote as you did

I always understand
                    . . everything you do

I folded the letter, placing it gently
back inside the envelope, which was still as crisp and new
as the day it arrived
only the letter itself was crumpled
and tear stained . . . from a hundred readings
                              over the years
          and tried

          to find some message in it
          but could not see
          how these words could now apply

          written before he knew how soon
          he was going to die
          and leave me lonely . . longing only

                    to join him

A------makes merely 'place' a 'palace'.

A what ?

Why A itself, of course !

Ah, but what is A ?

The beginning and end of your entire question.

O teacher, thanks. I see !

No, only eye sees, but U see.

What is this U ?

It is what you call I.

Then is U . . I ? Are you ?

Not interchangeably,
but I and U *are* one whenever you tell me you see.

I am silent with understanding that leaves no words.

Then, empty of words, you are filled; but not yet fulfilled.
Go whole; this holiness has no flaws, no holiness.

Kyril Demys (Musaios)
Wings of Myráhi

one dreary grey
        and unexpected wintry day . . in Colorado
as the wind was moaning
                through the eaves
and whipping frightened leaves
                to scurry past the window

I was mourning, listening to the chimney groaning
in my rented, crumbling antique house
                . . every shadowed nook and corner
haunted by probable ghosts I never met
nor cared to know . . yet did not try to chase away
wishing almost they would stay
                to keep me cobweb-shy and silent company

yes, I was mourning, numbly
seeking, needing only to be left alone

refusing to pick up the phone
                for, even its insistent ringing
blended with the dirge in minor key my soul was singing

                        as its constant theme

        my empty soul

now left bereft of every dream, robbed of all
it once held true and sacred
        by the endless visits of the always hungry thief
                        called Death
who had, this time, devoured every flake of faith
and crumb of caring
        I had long been hoarding
against the emotional poverty I feared, at last, was coming
                        instead of spring

down deep within, I heard the fearful drumming
of this emotional barreness — oh ! surely coming
at the end of one more winter season
                of my heart

which had survived, already
too many bitter-cold and lonely Decembers
of watching the glowing coals of memory embers
dying slowly, one by one
                threatening to leave it buried
beneath the opaque ice of frozen hopes

then melting, under the blessed warmth
of April's reincarnated promises
to rise once more from its wintry tomb, to sing again
as from the bursting womb of spring
                    the golden-daffodil bells still ring
their maybe-a-miracle-tomorrow chorus of crocus buds, soft scented
                                        hyacinths
          rain-drenched lilacs

and sweet peas . . .

          but April would be late this year
          and might be planning never to return

O ! this final visit of Death
was the last straw in the broom of doom
          brushing each room of my heart with indigo
sweeping its cupboards bare, and leaving there
                    no wishing stars
or magic I could share
          no shreds of rainbows I might wear
to transform my locks of mousey hair
          into raindrop-smelling butterflies with feathers

     no scrap of happiness
     or morsel of joy to give

                    to any other, ever

in this haunted setting . . stern, dry eyed, I was content
and reconciled, I thought, to wait
for bitterness to seal my fate . . at last to roll
the final, heavy stone of being eternally alone
against my weakened faith, and crush it

          now believing it too late
          for spring to bring her optimism winging back

so I was mourning her, lost spring
and truth, lost too — and the three — and, yes . . me
all the others gone
               and him

staring at a snow-bird, perched stiffly on the limb
of a naked tree, whose branches
like starved and scrawny arms, reached out to one not there
needing Nature's nourishment, and finding only
                    wintry emptiness . . . .

               . . . . I begged my own withering clutch
of too much hungry need, I could no longer feed

with the seeds of faith and hope
to loosen its strangling grasp
with a desperate plea, to let me be — oh, *let me be* !

       let go !

   and die in me, my need
       please die

like all things mortal

   as the whining wind was sighing, crying like a loon
on this moody afternoon, so soon to turn
               to the darker shades of approaching twilight

   I was dwelling in trance-like numbness
on the obvious, absolute dumbness of remaining alive
and attempting to survive — for what ?

unfairly, unduly pessimistic, perhaps — and unnaturally so, for me
who could usually see the silver lining behind each cloud
but I was not to be allowed, it seemed, to see a light shine through
this gathering, dense November nimbus
until I dreamed of something more
     than weary, dreary chants and mantras
till I looked up to promised sunnier skies . . and remembered
more powerful prayers
not born from helpless, hopeless cries . . but from the serenity
                        of *knowing*
yet was unable to stop the ticking clock in my head
with the hands set on half-past dead
and stuck there, unmoving, the timepiece being wound too tight

            with this un-named dread

   which was causing me to dwell
on the inevitable and atheistic futility

      of being conceived — and born — and dying

     the utter uselessness of trying, or crying out
expecting anyone to hear — or care

for, I thought, what is Life's goal
but a final destruction of both body and soul ?

   the spirit destined to disintegrate
into an eventual grave of impersonal ethers
as surely and as certainly as the dusty earth-grave
wherein the body, called its Temple . . lies
            when it, too, dies

these two inseparables

synchronizing their extinction, like Romeo and Juliet
or any lovers . . and sometimes missing this appointment
by but a single heart beat
during which eternal-seeming instant
                    one is forced to watch the other go

the Spirit or Soul, to see its Temple linger
or the body, to view its Soul, lost first
                    take leave ahead
each praying, inconsolable, then
also to be dead, like its companion — whichever one
has left the other behind
                    the Body Temple . . or its Spirit
oh ! this wintry day I needed someone, somehow
to reach me, and to teach me a truth
which would not crumble into clay dust, when I tried to hold it
                                    in my hands
    . . some way I could *believe* again

and cringing there, curled in my chair numbly
I continued meditating glumly, on the continuous circle
of free rides on Life's Carousel
                    free rides ?

free will, perhaps — but, oh, not truly free !
for you had better see that you have the karmic fare in your pocket

                    to pay for . . nothing

yes, a free ride only for the will
but staggeringly expensive for the soul and mind
of anyone not too deaf and blind to notice
                    the lack of any destination

what final destiny for this endless circle of karmic rides
but none, at last ? monotonous, leading nowhere
save around and around . . and around
                    the spinning Carousel of Life
in the circuses
and carnivals of various incarnations
                    all unobserved

the distant Owner of the Carousel
oblivious to its increasingly dizzy speed
not seeing its whirling colors, blending into grey
nor even hearing
    the broken-whirring-humming sound of His musical plaything

    . . let alone ever glancing

at the ant-like faces of the riders
perched crazily upon their grinning, painted horses

some glued, some
falling

all hanging on precariously

no, the Owner does not even note
the slipping-on-its-axis, or pending pole reversal
of His forgotten, useless toy
opened after seven days and nights
with little boy joy
on some long past Cosmic Christmas morning

. . now tossed aside
discarded and neglected
in the excitement of some brighter planet . . not as cracked
as worn and chipped, or faded . . all shiny new
. . and who

is ever loyal to toys
when the holidays are over ?

certainly not the Universe-size Child
Who owns all toys

and plays with them, displaying no less brief
wonder and delight — and no more cruelty
than terrestrial children, as they play with theirs

and with no less final, discontented boredom
when they begin to show the signs of wear and tear

or need . . repair

like both real and toy autos
and other bright-turned-boring
Earth objects, of fleeting
obsolescent appeal

. . . . and as I brooded on all this

there came a pounding
sounding at the back porch kitchen door
causing me to jump ! turn on a lamp

which quickly cast a cheerful glow upon the carpet
to cancel out the greyish streaks of the gloomy afternoon
and lightened the room, if not my still foreboding
and lingering sense of gloom

              reluctantly
I answered the knock

              and when I turned the lock
              not knowing who — or what — was waiting outside the door
              I shivered in an unanticipated blast of chilly air

then saw standing there

              not some Skeleton, rattling bones, bleached white
              or Grim Reaper of the night, bearing scythe and sickle
              no Scrooge-haunting type of Spirit
                    clanking the chains of Christmas Past
              or unknown Christmas Future

I saw standing there
only another cheerful, lamp-like glow

       . . her dark and wind-blown hair
              dusted lightly by the falling snow

my Pisces neighbor, dropping in for a cup of tea
but mostly, I guess, to check on me

              her name was Ruth
              and she was vaguely reminiscent of Ruth-in-the-Bible
              the one so devoted to her mother-in-law

for, like that Ruth, this one seemed to always say
with a gentle glance of Neptunian compassion
to family, friends and lonely strangers

                    . . wither-soever thou goest
                           . . into the valley of trouble
                    or into the shadow of sorrow

              there goeth I also . .

and I had found that, to this next-door-neighbor girl Fish
       as to her biblical namesake
love meant loyalty in time of need, and so . . did friendship

       I felt a happy lifting from this gracious gesture
       of warm and sympathetic company . . .
       projected back into the brighter world-of-the-living
       by this woman who was forever sharing a cup of cheer
                                   and a listening ear
       and who resembled a ghost
       only in her uncanny and spooky perception
       of the exact moment when you needed her the most

but . . no sooner had she filled for me
my whistling tea kettle in the kitchen
while I was rattling cups and saucers, than we heard
another pounding, sounding this time . .

                              at the front door
sharp, sudden and unexpected

then, a shrill ring
  of the creaky bell

          and when I answered
          there stood a man . . a stranger

a stranger had come a-knocking
on my closed-to-friends-and-strangers door . . a disturbing intrusion
not just because I did not know his face or name

        but because he did know mine

          yes, he knew mine
          and even seemed to flash some sign
          of deeper recognition . . into my eyes

    reflected for an instant only
    then gone . . or did I really see it ?

          I tried to make him understand — or did I truly try ?
    that I was not seeking any sort of company
    why did I hold out, then, my hand . . in greeting ?

    why did I invite him to come inside ?

          he was the very image of a staid and bland
          and proper businessman
          with silvery-grey hair, wearing horn-rimmed glasses
          a dark blue suit and conservative tie
          so mild of eye and manner, so dignified and subdued
          and so obviously imbued
                        with a well-bred, quiet courtesy
          that somehow, I could not be rude

          or make him feel . . . unwelcome

I could never seem to lose the memory that all truly religious Jews
believe that . . when one entertains a stranger
one may be entertaining also . . an angel . . unaware

since they are certain that the Christ, their Saviour
has not yet been born — and
therefore, some Herald of his coming . . might knock
at any time . . anywhere
to announce that the Old Testament prophecies

                    are soon to be fulfilled

a deliverance
announced by a heralding angel

was it, then, that old childhood memory, from knowing Judith
or was it something more . . that made me choose to invite into my house

        this quiet stranger, who came knocking on my door ?

then suddenly, another memory fragment flashed
across my mind . . at the thought of the word *deliverance*

half-remembered words and phrases I once had read
                            in a book about the dead
containing also, some secret, esoteric lore
about those Avatars or Adepti
        of that ancient society of the White Lodge
some called Rosicrucians . . who can come and go, at will
in their astral bodies
            to heal, at night

and to bring some inner Light to souls, while they are sleeping . . . .
those who possess some mystical way of teaching
                    never completely explained

        . . . and this book had stated
that these strange Masters or Initiates
                    often hold a respectable, responsible position
in the community where they live
emanating a quiet, soft spoken manner . . to disguise
their true business on this Earth
        and . . unless one caught their eyes unguarded
their identities might not be guessed — and
                    I could not recall the rest
but this stranger . .

seemed to hold no different a light or expression behind his eyes
        than I, myself — or than my next-door-neighbor, Ruth

and was truly so unimposing, so completely ordinary
that I felt a flush of foolishness
for dwelling on such wild occult imaginings

this was surely no angel, monk — or guiding Guru

he bore not the slightest resemblance
to a Herald of the First — or Second Coming

and looked like nothing so much as a polite, small town
                                                    Rotarian
shy of speech, with hat-in-hand
awkwardly attempting to make me understand
why he had intruded upon me, uninvited

he said he was a fellow traveler
on the spiritual path of Light

        and that he had heard, while passing through
        this tiny town, from someone — he could not remember
                                                    . . who
that I was interested in astrology
telepathy and astral projection — as well as
the human aura, levitation
                        and . . . reincarnation

all subjects
he had studied extensively
he said, and smiled

        he had learned my name from this person
                                    he could not recall
        and also where I lived
        so he could bring to me a gift of some books
        some books which, perhaps, I had not yet come across
                                                    or read
        some esoteric works . . to leave with me

                and that was really . . all

        no more than that, he said, standing there
        seemingly so uncertain, behind a heavy curtain
                                    of humility and reticence
    . . no more
                no more than that . .

and so, I took his coat and hat
as I invited him to stay and chat awhile

he said he would be delighted, though only for an hour or so
then he would have to go, lest there be a heavier snow by nightfall
causing the highways into Denver to be icy

meanwhile, he said, he would very much like to stay
to share some tea and conversation
if he was not inconveniencing me in any way

I introduced him to my Pisces friend, who smiled
somewhat nervously, I thought
then nodded, and excused herself to make some peppermint tea

leaving the stranger alone with me

feeling inexplicably uneasy, I told my visitor
to make himself at home . . and followed Ruth
wither-soever-she-goeth into the kitchen

her hands were trembling slightly
which surprised me — and
as I placed small cookies on a plate
I asked her why

. . we whispered, so he wouldn't hear

although the front room parlor was really not that near
being two full rooms removed
from the kitchen pantry, where we stood

"I feel the strangest inner trembling"
Ruth whispered in my ear

"because this man is here ?"
I whispered back

"yes — there is some powerful vibration
I am picking up . . . I seem to sense
some telepathic pulsing in the air
I know this sounds absurd
but I really believe this stranger . . . . "

she hesitated

"do you think he brings
some kind of danger ?"

"oh, no — that is, I'm not sure
I can't tell whether these strong currents
I'm sensing . . are bad . . or good
I only feel that I . . somehow I believe I should
remain until he goes
though goodness knows
it could be only my imagination . . yet
I can't shrug off this odd sensation
it's simply something . . . I cannot explain"

she finished, lamely

"you Pisces Fish are all alike"
I grinned at her
"but I would feel much better too
I think, if you . . well
if you would sit back in the den
while we are talking — or join us"

> "no, I will not intrude that way
> he came to speak with you, not me
> I'll just read a book, back in the den
> and we can pretend . . if he should ask
> that I'm waiting for a telephone call"

I agreed, and was oddly relieved
that I would not be alone in the house
    with this stranger
although I did feel we were both, perhaps
making much ado about nothing . . still
I knew better than to disregard a Piscean's psychic chill
however illogical it might seem to be

> too often I had observed Ruth's intuitive premonitions
> manifest into actuality
> with apparently neither rhyme nor reason
> based only on some inner warning bell
> over which she, herself, had no control
> as far as I — or she — could tell

> for Neptune murmurs secrets into the Pisces inner ear
> with tones too whispery soft and far-away
> to be detected by any other, save by one born also
> > under a Water Sign
> but I am Fire

therefore, I couldn't help but wonder
what Ruth was sensing here
I found nothing in the man to fear
> as I grew . . to know him better

in that strangely haunted, antique house, while we spoke together
we discovered many things to discuss, of mutual interest
> and concern
and I found myself hoping that Ruth
was paying close attention too
because I felt this stranger knew
> . . so very much, from which we both might learn

> our talk was neither ominous
> nor frightening — merely enlightening

and I was not to know

till after I had seen him go

> that a Fish may need no ear to hear
> some things unspoken, clear

yet . .

> a stranger may choose to build a wall
> of silent sound
> when someone is around . .
> > someone he does not wish to climb
> the ladder of words he is building
> to a higher level of awareness

for it was only I . . . oh ! only I
who heard the hiSSing of a Serpent WiSdom
Snaking and coiling itself around my Third Eye

> only I who heard the Serpent's hiSSing
> and who thought it was some Minister of the Sinister
> who had come to steal away my reaSon

believing mySelf to be poSSeSSed by Some mad MaSter of Infinity
not bleSSed by the myStic touch of divinity

> oh, I recoiled in mistaken mortal terror
> from the Subtle Eden-Snake of knowing-growing
> > that nearly stole my sanity away

> on that dreary grey
> > and unexpected wintry day
> in Colorado

Travel Talk of Mountain Scenery

> since that day the quiet stranger came a-knocking, uninvited
> my life has never been — nor ever will be — quite the same
> but richer, in a growing-knowing sense

> > filled with wiser, new incense
> > to wind around my consciousness blue-scented
> > > > trails of smoke
> > which were to whisper to me
> > over the next few weeks
> > > the *why* of all the things of which he spoke

teaching me to reach far out of sight . . to know

that the Past lies just ahead
                    the Future lies behind
and the Present is only Now
                    because it contains the other two

        for all three are but One
        and may not be separated from this Oneness

        as the Beginning is the End . . and the End is also
                                    the Beginning

                as in all trined Holy Trinities
                            so be it done
                            as One

I now confess, the stranger
came to bless

        yet, for some time after he had gone, I wavered, disturbed, in disbelief
        fearing his visit was a curse, manifested through my grief
        brewed of herbs and secret spells
        unknown to any but apprentices of Merlin
        believing him, the Stranger, to be a Sorcerer
                                    of the blackest kind of magic
        frightened at the mere idea
        that I had sheltered him

it was not until much later that I finally understood
comprehension gradually creeping into my awareness
                    with the reasons, whys and wherefores
                                    of his intent

but at first, I felt an unrelieved . . and undeniable
foreboding sense of terror
followed by a silent-screaming type of manic panic
difficult to share, even with Ruth

        . . certain she would think I'd taken leave
        of all me senses . . as the Irish are feyly wont to say

        . . not that I had many to 'take leave of' — or to lose
        in that dark period of the Moon, when my very soul had lost
                                            its way

        yes, although his appearance at my door later proved
        to be a blessng in disguise, flowing from
                                    his knowing eyes
                    yet, unnoticed by me
during that tranced two hours or so . . .
from the time commencing after his farewell
when I had watched, as he drove slowly down the hill

and disappeared around the bend
then turned, to analyze his visit with my Pisces friend

from that moment . . it was a nightmare

before that, more like a prophetic dream
as I was to discover, sooner than I knew or guessed

my conversation with the stranger had commenced
in such an ordinary way

with predictable small talk
and gracious courtesies of speech between us
all the expected social amenities
both knowing how to keep our places
I, as hostess — he, as guest

which soon, however, became a different kind of game
with he, as Guru, mild-eyes-then-burning
and I, as student
thirsty for knowledge
yet still stubbornly, reluctantly learning

I first asked why he should have given
. . as I so often do myself
such a generous gift of books to me
and he answered, simply, that in a recent dream
he had been told he would soon hear of one
who, through sorrow, was yearning
and whose heart and mind might be, therefore
ready to unfold, now to hold
a deeper ember of wisdom . . not illusion

having been somewhat startled and embarrassed at the intrusion
on my personal privacy of this telling of his dream
and needing to quickly hide behind a change-of-subject

my second conversational gambit
was to describe how much I loved the mountains of Colorado
the greenery of the scenery . . . the murmuring pine and aspen woods
surrounding this tiny town, itself a ghost

a travel monologue
lasting, possibly . . a few minutes, at the most

then suddenly, with no warning

we plunged into deeper waters
where we swam, and sometimes floated . . for the balance of the time
that he was there

in a mystical dialogue we cautiously began to share

    we spoke of seeing auras, and much more
    as of colors, which rhymed
                      or vibrated to certain odd and even numbers
    and to certain planets
               also to certain musical chords
    or notes of sound
                a tangled blend of chromatic scales
    and spectrumed music of the Spheres

we discussed the mysteries of levitation, astral travel
extra-sensory perception . . and the current prevalance
                            of psychic deception
    I wonder now that I did not marvel then
at the depth of those mysterious waters
and the multitude of subjects we were covering
in such a brief and crowded time

    eventually . . I don't remember when or how
    I told him of my bereavement, my loss . . my seeking
    my disillusion with Life's Carousel
               and the lack of destination for its riders
    hoping he might offer some spiritual relief
    to my unconsolable grief

      and he did . . oh ! he did
      but I strongly resisted this — resisted, yes
      with all my strength of will
      not comprehending what he said
             about the living . . or the dead
as we talked further
    diving deeper into mystery waters
I saw more light shine upon the darkness of my initial disbelief
but failed to see all of its brightness while he remained
only guessing later, long after he was gone
how hard it rained on me — the truth, that day

I looked directly into his eyes as we spoke
yet not really seeing
so intent was I — on listening

"you are telling me many things
I thirst to know, and have been longing so
these recent weeks
to discuss with one enlightened, such as you
which seems too good to be entirely true" . . I said

    . . wondering how he would then explain
the coincidence of our meeting
for I did not, despite my curiosity

believe it to be, in any way, predestined
no, I believed it nothing more than an accident
of fate .. but wondered this to myself, and not aloud

      as he said . . .

           "are you not aware of the ancient promise
           murmured by Tibetan monks
           about this sort of meeting ? which is, you see .. "

           and he smiled

           " .. not quite the accident of fate
               you are presently thinking it to be"

understanding that he had read my mind
      but blind to any deeper implications
of this psychic trick of his
and curiously un-surprised, I asked ..

" .. of what promise do you speak ?"

           "I speak of the ancient promise
               or the Essenic saying
          that ..
            when the student is ready
            the teacher will appear . . . "

"Essenic ? Essene ? . . . you must mean
the Dead Sea Scrolls, and all that
but it's hard to see how this can be
or how it can .. just happen"

           "after an Earthling has reached a certain level
           of awareness — it has long been told
           as I have said
           that, when the student is ready
           the teacher will appear, then to unfold
               some needed truth
           and one need not call or seek

           when such time next arrives for you
           much will be made more clear
           by still another kind of teacher than I
           who will very soon appear .. yes
           very much sooner than you now guess
               and quite suddenly"

"suddenly appear
without my calling him
or seeking him ?"

"did I not come to you today, in this same way ?
yes, without the need of your beseeching
save through a silent call
which he will clearly hear . . within himself
through a sensory perception
                              other than the physical human ear"

"how can this teacher know
what truth I need — if I do not know myself ?
how, then, shall he be aware
of those things he is to teach me ?"

            "some teachers are aware, some not
            you will have more than one teacher
            sharing a different type of relationship
                                          with each
            for different lengths of time
            but the one who comes next to you . .
            he will *know* — yet, *not* know
            from where he comes . . . and why
            his knowing will come and go . . .
            . . . sometimes guessing
            still, within himself will lie the answers
            he is to bring to you"

"I do not understand"

            "the eyes of wisdom open slowly
            your teacher shall be . . as wise as
                                          a Serpent
            yet as harmless as a Dove
            with human fraility, much like your own"

"but I have always heard it said
      and I have also read
that these teachers — Adepti or Avatars
are either saints or gods"

            "some are, some are not
            as all may be . . and all may not . . be
                        as I have said
            some dwell among the living . . some
                                          among the dead"

            he paused . .

      and I shivered, then hastened
      to fill the sudden silence

as my questions, and his answers bounced back and forth
      in unbroken rhythm, like ping pong balls of instant wisdom

sent across a net of understanding and new trust
  stretched nearly visibly, between myself and this kind
                    almost painfully shy stranger
how could I have believed
he brought the threat of any danger ?

    the only danger, possibly in the opening of my mind
    to things which one may not dismiss too lightly . . and which
    in turn, open up the spirit to thirst for more

                    yes ping pong balls . .
          . . .   . .
              . .   . . .
        . .   . .
                    from me
              . .   . .
                . . .
        and back   to him
              . .   . . .

"this . . teacher, you say . . this next one
who will soon appear
do I understand that all these things will not be clear
to him . . on a conscious level . . only sometimes ?"

              "you will teach him also
              are not some things clear to you already ?
              on several levels of your own consciousness
              you are aware of some mysteries
                    of some you still are not
              there is much, mutually, between you, to be taught"

"I — a teacher ? I ?
but I am not an Avatar"

              "each holds within himself — herself — a star
              we are, in some ways, all teachers
                    of each other
              the one of whom I speak
              carries strong vibrations of Saturn
              not a seventh dimensional planet, as some
                    textbooks claim
              but eighth dimensional
              and know . . that he chose, for reasons
                    I may not disclose
              to incarnate at this time . . .
              it was his own decision . . . and not a necessary one"

"this must mean he is quite evolved
beyond this Earth plane — if he chose
I mean having already paid his karmic debts

on the Carousel down here . . . "

> "perhaps, perhaps not — it is not my place
> to say just now
> perhaps more — or less — or equally
> as evolved as you
> I am not at liberty to tell . . but I will
> say this
> that even angels
> have been known to fall, when they return
> to the temptations of this particular Earth
> all should help one another, but especially these
> should help each other not to fall
> and be forced to begin the climb again
>
> one does not want to be responsible
> for the fall of any angel — of whatever rank
> from any heaven . . "

"when the student is ready
the teacher will appear . .
how comforting ! and how clear"

> daydreaming, mistily
> of the sheer poetry of the concept
> I heard little of what he was saying
> just then, being lost in wondering

and mused, murmuring aloud

"would it not be a happy thing
if one's own twin soul . . . one's true lover
or Comforter
could also come in this way, when needed
not called by lips, but only
by the heart and spirit . . . "

> he smiled then
> a cryptic smile

> "at special times, under certain conditions
> certain karmic vibrations
> these may be the same
> one may be both a teacher — and
> what you call a Comforter"

"NOT THIS ONE !
not this one you say will come to me . . **NO !"**

I was aroused from my dreamy musing
suddenly scorched by fierce flames of loyalty

which no spiritual mystery could extinguish
and cried out to him . .

"I was only thinking aloud
not wishing at all, not wishing

because, as I have already explained
the one I love is dead — and
I *will not* accept another in his place !"

> "the body is but the Temple of the soul
> is it, then, only the Temple which you loved
> and not the soul, the spirit — or the Higher Angel
> of that house of flesh ? *think* !"

"no, that is
        I loved — or I love . . "

he was confusing me unfairly, and my mind
was muddled — numbed already as it was, by grief
    not as alert as I needed it to be
        to answer his riddles
            but I tried

"yes, it was the soul, or spirit
residing within the body Temple which I loved
and still love — but which cannot return
for a hundred years or more . . . .
or even if not that long — even if through
an instant incarnation
    into the Body Temple of an infant . . . .
and what comfort can I find in *that* . . however long
or however brief a time away
his next incarnation may be . . what comfort ?"

> "what you say . . is not true"

"*what* thing — *which* ?"

> "concerning the Body Temple of an infant
> this is not . . exclusively . . true"

"but a soul, once passed
from its own Temple, surely may not
move back into a body
        . . except that body be unoccupied
is this not true ?
such as the body of an infant, newborn . . "

> he did not answer

"I do not see what you mean
even using the simplified metaphor of houses
here on Earth — literal houses
one cannot just move into a house already owned
and occupied by another
I do not see what you mean . . . "

> but still
> he did not answer

"I am weary of hearing and reading about
and thinking about the soul, the soul, the soul !
weary, weary, weary ! for, don't you see ?

whether I should find the one I lost
tomorrow, in the body of an infant
and with some psychic flash
recognize him there
or whether I should find him in an unfamiliar
and newly designed adult body Temple
in some future life, hundreds of years hence
what good is either possibility to me ?"

> "the coming together once again
> for a new attempt toward permanent blending
> that is the good, of course . . "

"but you do not understand !"
I cried, in tortured inability to project
the intensity of what I felt and knew
> was true
not just of me, but of others too

I could not seem to communicate my meaning
and repeated, in frustration . .

"you simply do not understand !"

> "I understand much better than you suspect . . .
> using the painted horses on the Carousel
> as an example — you are claiming it is the horse
>
> comparable to the body . . . which you now miss
> and not its rider
> > is this not so ?"

"you are unfair ! you are making it sound
somehow . . *wrong* to feel this way
and it is not ! I am an Earthling, made of flesh
even if containing Spirit
> and I do not seek a shroud

yes, of course it is the essence
of his soul I miss — but I am made of clay
even my heart is made of clay
        not made from ethers, or from some misty cloud"

                "yes, I comprehend what it is that you are saying . . . . "

                and he momentarily
                closed his eyes
                as if he might be praying
                for some guidance

"no ! you do not understand at all !
how can a new Body Temple heal my grief
        in some future life ?
I will still be me, be me, be *me* !
and he is still — to me — he is, simply *himself* !
        not some etheric essence
even if there were some way to tell
in which Temple he resided — even so — which I doubt
even then I would miss . . . . "

                and I felt tears on my cheeks
                dry these many weeks

" . . . what I miss . . is this . . "

                and caught a quiet sob
                forbidding it to escape

" . . the sound of his voice . . the way he said my name
no one else ever said it quite the same — my name, no . . oh
his eyes, his ears, his cheeks, his hands   no
fingers . . yes, even his nails   one
his hair . . the way he walked . . his laugh . . oh !
his laugh, like no other laugh
                upon this Earth

yes, his hands, his face . . his smile . . his kiss
no other Body Temple could replace all this
and this is what I miss
                the tangible, *touching things*
so warm and dear
                so . . familiar
don't you see ?
        even his nose, his toes
the warm, tangible, familiar *touching things*

and you speak to me of spirit essence ?
this is the fallacy of all religions everywhere !
telling the bereaved who have truly, truly loved

Canto Eleven ☆ 299

then lost — to death
telling them **GHOST STORIES !** yes ! **GHOST STORIES !**
this is the only thin and watery comfort
offered by all churches, all dogmas — all faiths
                              and now I see
it is also the only icy comfort offered, even by astrology
and reincarnation . . . **GHOST STORIES !**

how can they heal a human ache, ease a human pain ?

sending ethereal promises of visiting ghosts
on some future day, a thousand years or so away
will not stop such anguish, or halt such pain !
it is like . . trying to stop the rain
yes ! like trying to stop the rain by mumbling some
                                    religious mantra
        I am tired
        of both religious and spiritual abracadabra

the churches have failed
can't you see that *the churches have all failed ?*
and the biggest ghost story of them all
the biggest ghost-hoax of all Christian Churches
is the Easter resurrection conception
                    which is nothing but a cruel deception !
        a cruel deception !

a joke played upon the broken-hearted and bereaved
            a joke of . . such poor taste
and I tell you — **I SWEAR** that I will not be so deceived !"

my voice then shattered into bitter splinters
of remembered cold and lonely winters
and I could not continue . . .

                he slowly shook his head
                but his tone was tender, gentle
                his voice low and soft
                        when he spoke . .

                "no, the resurrection of Jesus is not a joke
                        it is literal
                more tangible and real than you feel
                at this moment
                        Easter is Truth"

but I was too distraught
to allow myself to be unresistantly taught
too disturbed, even, to consider Ruth
then sitting in the den
and perhaps listening to this Serpent's hiSS

. . or what she might be thinking
of my shameful breaking down like this
before a stranger . . not like me at all

"Easter is a joke, a joke ! can you prove it is not ?
well, prove it then ! ghost stories — all
I cannot make you understand the *need of flesh*
to hear a voice, once loved
to see a smile — surely, surely you must know
that all Body Temples are not the same
like fingerprints — yes, and like snowflakes
no two alike . . "

          "no . . you are wrong . . not like a snowflake
          only the individuality of the soul or spirit
          Higher Self — the seed atom — ego
          call it what you will
          is like unto a snowflake — but not the
                    Temples, called bodies
          this is *not* true of them !"

"but there are no two Body Temples
on Earth — which are exactly alike — no two !
so why do you say that my analogy is not true ?
how can you say this ?"

          again . . he did not answer

"is this not true ?" I persisted
"there are no two alike !"

          "I can see and understand . . "

          then he very lightly touched my hand
          with such infinite compassion . .

          "I can see that this is true to you
          there is nothing which can comfort your grief
          except his own, exact Body Temple
          I see this now — and I see why
                  please do not cry
          I truly understand your words
          about his smile, his walk
          his warm and dear, familiar hand
                  . . I understand"

    somehow, his voice
was so soothing, so lulling — gentle, mild
like a father, speaking to a child
so kind and so truly, deeply understanding
with almost, it seemed . .

almost a hint of some sort of promise

and I had a wild, insane-with-hope thought . . . oh !
sudden-soaring, daybreaking !
           I felt, somehow, like a child
who was being told — it's allright now
you may have this thing you hurt for — yes
you may have it, if you need it so

       oh, oh, oh !

but I must not allow myself to dwell, I thought
on such a thing — even for an instant
how could I attribute such an impossible dream
to the compassion in his eyes
and the kind things this stranger had said ?
for the man I loved — his body
           my own twin soul — was dead

his Temple already crumbling into dust
oh, I must, I *must* . . stop conjecturing such an impossibility

this man is not Jesus Christ — and even if he were
who knows if even Jesus
ever truly brought back Lazarus — or himself
from the grave
no, this stranger cannot produce
such a glorious Easter miracle for me . . . .

but, somehow, I felt a warmer glow
     a strangely calming comfort
that he should even *want* to make that miracle
and I knew that this was true
from the look upon his face — yes, he would, if he could
restore to me the Body Temple I had lost

 . . after a moment, I spoke aloud
apparently believing he could read my mind
and said, sincerely, with all my heart
not feeling quite so alone as I'd felt before . .

"thank you anyway . .
     thank you . . for wanting to so much"

                          and then . .

               he answered slowly
               his quiet eyes gazing into my own
               so tender-wise and gentle-kind

               "you must not grieve — or fear

for there is a Law at work down here
which always was — and always shall be . . .
God possesses an eternal integrity
as does Nature Herself
.... you need not be lonely
Life has joy and color
if you will only look to the rainbow !
and not below . . to the clay dust
at your feet"

"his body was **MORE** than clay dust !
his Temple was a thing I knew and loved — still love !
how can you tell me not to dwell on this
that his body was — is — only dust, only clay ?
I cannot agree with what you say"

"look up ! look to the stars above you !
especially, look unto Saturn . . the planet of Karma"

"oh, what do the stars really mean anyway ?
and what has Saturn to do with this
or Venus or Mars — or the Sun or Moon ?"

"raise your eyes to the skies — do not cast them down
to see only the stones and pebbles
of rigid prejudice against the real Truth of the dead
for, as the one called Jesus said

seek the Truth — and it shall set you free !

you need not accept all this from me
Jesus said these things too
and do you not believe the words he spoke were true ?"

"but even Jesus, whom I truly love
and want so much to believe in — even he did not explain
how one could possibly feel the same
about a Body Temple with a different shape, a different name
without the same familiar voice . . eyes
and hand

I simply will not ever understand
not in this present lifetime — neither will I understand
when offered the same small comfort
in some hazy future life"

"the physiognomy of features . . the structure
of Body Temples
is not what you believe it to be"

"I cannot disregard the dear familiarity, don't you see ?

Canto Eleven ☆ 303

of this particular Temple — and **CANNOT** find solace
in the thought of its inevitable and permanent destruction — no way !"

                        "a Maker of images of clay . . clay images
                        like unto clay pitchers
                                        the Architect of the Body Temples
                        may He not create these images *in duplicate*
                        and many times over . . if He should so choose ?"

"create them in duplicate ? many times over ?
He may, I suppose
but if He did, it still would not bring me solace
because He could not create a clay image
exactly like the one I lost — no, not so exact
                                that I could be fooled
into believing it to be . . he"

                        " . . and may the Maker not also
                        destroy His own molds
                                        if He should so wish ?"

"may ? *may* ? He does *just* that !
and this is the very thing I cannot understand
this cruel, uncaring caprice of Divinity
which nearly shatters my faith in God completely"

                        "is it the shape and design
                                        of the clay pitcher
                        that cools the thirst
                        . . or the water within ?"

this time it was I who remained
silent — and did not answer right away

"will you . . . repeat that question ?"

                        "as the poet wondered . . .

                        is it the shape and design
                                        of the clay pitcher
                        that cools the thirst
                                . . . or the water within ?"

"but . . . . . he was not a clay pitcher !
and even if he was, symbolically
it *did* cool my thirst . . the shape of his mouth
                        the design of his eyes
the touch of his hand !

even in Nature, all seasons are individually beloved
the beauty of winter's frosted landscape is not the same

as spring's silvery rain . . autumn's red gold leaves
or summer's green carpeted and flower showered meadows

they are all lovely, but each formed differently
each snowflake, each raindrop is different
not the same — and I need the **SAME** !

not a different Temple, whether now
or a thousand — a million years from today
I shall miss, I tell you — forever
his own, individual design — and shape — in clay
I am only *half* spirit — yet still half *flesh*
can you not see ?"

                    "the one you now so tenderly miss
                    is a vibration, as a chord . . of music"

"oh, **GOD** !
do you mean that as consolation ?
how can a chord of music
be as individual as he ?
    there are not enough music notes to make
so many chords as he is made of
can't you see ? he was my *husband*
I am his *wife* !"

                    "if you will listen to what I say
                                        you will find him again
                    in this present Life

                    he is not one single note of music
                    but an individually coded chord vibration
                    inter-twined and complex
                        totally individual — truly, I tell you this
                    his emotional vibrations
                    constitute the mass chord of music
                                        on the chromatic scale
                    which is his, and his alone . . .
                    and these vibrational patterns are limited
                    only by the gamut of his conscious awareness
                        in each lifetime
                    these being gathered on every ride
                                        around the Carousel
                    on different horses
                    which were not his, but borrowed only
                        nor was that Temple in which you knew
                                        him recently, his own

                    he is a mass chord of emotional vibrations
                    formed of why — and when

Canto Eleven ☆ 305

and how many times he caught the brass ring
and transmuted it into gold, on his
                                        spinning rides
just as you have been to him
            many brides . . . before
I understand your need for his individuality
but it is not lost to you
it can return, if you so desire
in a way you are not yet prepared
                            to comprehend

humans have such an exaggerated
sense of the geometric
but, there is a geometric reality
in the true recognition of one soul for another
especially for its twin"

as I tried to grope for comfort
I was almost finding solace in these words
some inexpressible hope . . .

something sounded . . somehow . . right in what he said
at least more solid than the average ghost story
about the dead
        almost . . nearly . . but not quite

            his voice continued
            softly speaking . .

                    "the one you are seeking
                    is also a mass color vibration — which is
                    as individual as his chord of music . . .
                    but, whatever his individual color hues
                            or harmonic identity
                    you must remember this
                    that, behind colored glass — always

                            is a *Light*

                    shining through the colored glass or prism
                    to create the rainbow spectrum

                    there are no colors cast at night
                        without the Light
                    which must shine through the tinted glass"

and I thought of the stained glass windows
in the chapel, at St. Raphael's
and how . . dark . . the chapel seemed at night
when no light was shining through

to cast lovely rainbows on the faces of the nuns
so bright, so inexpressibly sweet

                    "you cannot ever find his individuality again
                    in this life — or in any other
                    if you continue to dwell on the clay at
                                    your feet
                        I tell you
                    he *is* an individual !
                    and recognizable literally as this
                    but I warn you — if you wish to ever find him
                    either now — or in the future . . . "

"now ? how can I possibly
find him *now* ?"

                    "you must look to the stars ! and pray
                    for you have closed your eyes
                                to his color vibration
                    and you have closed your inner ear
                    to his mass chord of music
                    by your insistence in dwelling on dust
                                  and clay"

"what you tell me does seem to be
more real than ethereal
more tangible than mystical
something, at last, I might *hold*

but is it not, essentially, the same
as the churches have all told . . . to the seeking
only stated in different words ?
the churches, too, say that somewhere
out there is . . *something*

but this "something" . . or whatever
or however it is described
must, nevertheless, find a Body Temple
if I am to recognize it, and . . . "

                    "this is true, yet it is urgent for you to do
                    what you still don't realize — to *recognize*
                    his chord of music, his color code
                    in whichever new Temple he should choose
                                  to reside
                          and this is never easy
                    no, much more difficult than you may believe
                    if you are not truly looking and listening
                      for what lies *within*
                    otherwise, many sad and sorry mistakes
                                  may be made

Canto Eleven ☆ 307

and enlightenment will fade . . "

"oh, now we are back to Temples
and ending up as we began
like all religions . . . with more ghost stories
I must wait to recognize him in a new Body Temple
a hundred or a thousand years from today
isn't this what you are trying to say ?"

        "no, as I have already stated, but you were
                                    not listening
        you need not wait that long
        to hear his song — his chord is quite clear

        . . . . let those who have eyes — see
          let those who have ears — hear . . . . "

"see what ? hear what ?"

        "when you see his color . . hear his music
        then you will have found the one you love"

"how can I reach so far above ?
do you mean, in an infant's face
in a newborn baby's cries ?"

        he did not answer
           for a long, long moment

        then said . .

        "do not forget — and *mark this well* !
        the Body Temple's windows . . are its *eyes*
        through which both the soul and spirit look out
                            upon the world
        in any Temple
        where they may briefly — or longer — reside"

"I do not see what you mean
because I still . . . "

        and he interrupted . .

        "but *you will* — and now, since I must soon
        be leaving
            I would like to leave with you
                          a message"

I felt swiftly disappointed
and let down — at the thought
of his leaving . . .

there were still so many things to ask

"a message ?"

           "in this dream . . . " and he hesitated

           " . . . this dream I did not think to be a dream
           but more a vision . . I was told to say unto you
           that you will someday soon
               be with one
           you will love . . and know . . from long ago"

"you mean, he — who died ?"

           "yes . . . and no"

"what kind of answer
is *that* ?"

        but he ignored my question, and said . .

           "this one — he will *know*
              and he will come — and go"

"yes — and no ? come — and go ?"

           "he will first come, then go
        then come again . . . even so, as I have
                    stated"

"is there some way to . . well
I mean, do you know . . . "
and I thought of a foolish thing to ask

"do you, by any chance, know his name ?
the one who comes . . and goes
then comes again ?"

           "I only know his spiritual name is *Al*-tar
           I do not know his Earth name
           but you have met before . . over many, many
                    centuries
           and . . even in this lifetime
               in a curious way . . "

"in this lifetime ?
but how can that possibly be ?
this teacher . . one I have already known ?
impossible, unless he is someone
I knew when I was small — and who has since been reborn
        as a child

he cannot be the one I lost . . .
I am so confused
is this Al-tar teacher, then, someone
who has been reborn as a child ?"

> "you were once an Essene — you knew him then
> also, of course . . . "
>> he paused

> "you knew the Essene . . . called the Nazarene"

"**HIM**, oh ! truly *him* ?
you mean, I once spoke to Jesus himself
and saw him with my very own eyes . . . .
that is, with the eyes of another Body Temple
but still, it was me — and I saw him ?"

the idea . . the image he presented
was overwhelming
for I had not meditated much upon Karma
>> or past lives
having been too occupied in meditating
upon present deaths, since childhood

"and did this . . this *Al*-tar know him too ?
did he also speak with Jesus ?"

> "one might say . . . he knew him too
> yes, this is true"

"is Al-tar . . . "

> I noted that he had pronounced it to sound like All-star
> as I did — with the accent on the first syllable

"is this Al-tar the teacher you say
will appear, when I, the student, am ready ?"

> "yes — and no
>> maybe not — maybe so"

"what does that mean . . .
yes and no, maybe not, maybe so ?"

> "he will, as I told you, come . . and go
> there is a coming and a going thing about him
> for, when he comes, he leaves
> and when he leaves . . he returns again"

"you mean that I shall run across him
. . that he is some person I may meet

who will be my friend
then I won't see him for awhile
but run into him again . . once a year or so ?

I know people like that already — friends
who move away, or become quite busy
then pop up, oddly and unexpectedly
when you need them
will Al-tar be this kind of sometimes-friend
since you have not said for certain
that he is the teacher about whom you spoke ?"

          "something like that . . you will be friends"

              and he smiled

"will he know
that his spiritual name is Al-tar ?"

          "no, he will not, at first — and may not
                              ever

          it depends
          the river flows . . and bends"

"depends upon what ?"

          "upon his own Free Will
          his own seeking of himself
              and his thirst for truth"

"but, if he doesn't even know
himself — and I can't be sure that he is
the teacher who will appear . .
then how will I know him ?"

          "you will know — for he will come . . . . . . and go
          look to the rainbow ! look up to the stars
          hear God's music, His symphony of Life
          and remember that the eyes
          are the windows of the soul — if you
              remember all this
          then you will know with every breath

          you have seen, in your lifetime
                    much death
          but there has been a plan
          a destiny behind it . . a reason
          why you have been fated to meet mortality
                  so often"

"a destiny ?

worked out for me . . by God ?"

        "a destiny planned elsewhere
        in another galaxy — by none other than yourself
        by you, who chose this path . . "

"chosen by myself ?"

        "by your own Higher Self . . and also chosen by
        the one you shall be with soon
        such a spiritual choice has a name — it is called
        The Thunderbolt Path of Accelerated Karma"

"The Thunderbolt Path . . .
a path leading where ? and
if I chose it myself — or we chose it ourselves
then why do I not recall the choosing ?"

        "you will . . if you listen to your spirit
        when it is singing to you
        I can tell you this — you began your
                       self-planned destiny
        when you were very small
        and set its final mold when you were twelve"

"when I was so troubled
about the Easter resurrection story ?"

        "perhaps it was that troubling of your heart
        which was the first verse
        of a Happiness Poem you shall write someday
           making sadness rhyme with gladness
        bringing new Light to the Easter story
        for those bereaved, whose hearts are full
                          of pain
        but first, you must learn
        to wipe the tears from your own eyes
        so that you may see more clearly"

. . so he knows
about my Happiness Poem too
I thought

then an image flashed of the peripetetic, traveling friend
I was to meet — Al-tar, the All-star Avatar
it made me smile
and I meditated to myself . . even though I must be alone
without love . . until I find the one I lost
in some future incarnation . . it won't be quite as lonely
with a sometimes friend, like Al-tar . . . . . . "

abruptly, he interrupted
my thoughts

"and now, I really must go . . .
thank you for the tea and hospitality
God bless and keep you, lost one"

then, almost so swiftly
as to seem shockingly rude
.. after his former courtesy
without another word
not a single word more
only a smile and a nod

he stood up, took his coat and hat
from the rack near the door

and simply . . . left

before I could even murmur — "oh, thank *you* so much *too* !
and when will I see you again ?"

he was gone

I watched his car drive slowly down the hill, and turn the bend
at the corner . . . then excitedly ran back into the den
to ask my Pisces friend what she had thought of this strange
discussion

of which she must not have missed a word during the past hour or two
since our voices could be easily heard
from one room to another — so close they were, yet private to the eye
the den snuggled back a few feet from the parlor

I could hardly wait to talk with Ruth
who rhymed with truth
and flew to her, fairly bursting with the anticipation
of sharing this new and glowing kind of knowing

"oh, Ruth ! did you hear ?"

and she smiled a wry smile
of Piscean self depreciation

"yes," she replied — "I heard"

then shrugged, and went on

"I guess my Neptune powers of psychic
perception

are waning
I feel so foolish for being alarmed
and wasting a perfectly good twenty minutes
when I could have had dinner ready at home"

I trembled suddenly, then
with a growing dread
as the full import of what she had said
gingerly sent little wiggles of warning
to tickle my spine

she noticed my trembling, and asked

"are you chilly ? shall I make a fire ?
sit down and finish your tea
I'll bring in some kindling from the porch"

"no, please don't . .
I'll make a fire myself in a few minutes
after my mind has cleared
but first — did you hear what he said ?
and wasn't it all very strange and weird ?"

she smiled . . "I heard what *you* said, mostly
he hardly spoke the entire time
what a dull man ! very nice and sweet
but certainly no social butterfly . . . .
it must have been annoying for you
to try to keep the conversation going
well . . at least he didn't stay the full hour
it was barely twenty minutes he was here . . "

she glanced at her wrist watch
then her grin widened

"I didn't know you knew so much
                         about Colorado !
you sounded like a member
of our local Chamber of Commerce
that was quite a twenty minute
                         monologue of a travelogue !
and him of no help

with his polite monosyllables
of 'yes' and 'no' — and a rare 'yes
                              that's so . .
it is very lovely around here' . . . ."

abruptly, Ruth stopped speaking
in mild surprise, noticing my stricken look
but tactfully pretending nothing was amiss

as Pisceans tend to do . .
          she continued, somewhat hesitantly

                    "you know, that speech about
                    the beauty of Mount Pisgah
                              and the Sangre de Cristo range
                    the murmuring pine and hemlock woods
                    or whatever . . it was quite poetic . . "

she stopped again
when she noticed I was not responding
or smiling back at her

          then went on
          her voice a tone lower

                    "you don't look at all well to me
                    just sit here on the couch
                    let me make some fresh tea, and start a fire
                    see ? I was right !
                    that man didn't cheer you up in any way
                    I didn't want to be rude, but I really felt
                    you shouldn't have invited him to stay
                    it's been such a gloomy day
                    and you've been so sad these past few
                                        weeks
                    certainly not in the mood
                    for the strain of entertaining company
                    especially not a stranger
                    who can't even carry on an intelligent conversation
                    except to ask, every two minutes, it seemed
                    if it was snowing any harder

                    I would have come in and rescued you from boredom
                    but you know how timid we Fish are . . "

I didn't smile
in response to her mild attempt at humor
was this some secret occult test ?
I felt as though I were strangling
unable to swallow, my throat dry and parched
my eyes burning and stinging
my heart thumping madly in my chest

                    "you're too friendly for your own good
                    if you ask me . . .
                    do you want honey in your tea ?"

I entertained a swift and comforting thought
she was joking — just making a joke
teasing me, to make me laugh

but, no — Ruth rhymes with truth
and my friend would never allow a joke
        to go this far
for now I could see real concern on her face
as, at last, the tears gushed forth
a steady flow . . and I sobbed aloud . . truly terrified
        for my sanity

                "my God !" Ruth cried, who seldom swore
                    "what's wrong ? what happened ?
                did I say something to upset you ?"

                as a strong gust of wind
                rattled the back porch kitchen door
                and swept through the chimney
                                with a roar

"oh, it's nothing, nothing"

I managed to answer, between shakes and sobs
with a mad cackle, and morbid humor

"only that I've lost my mind, that's all
just that — nothing more
you'll have to visit me at the funny house
as soon as I've been assigned a room and a shrink"

                at first, Ruth did not know what to think
                then her instinctive Neptunian wisdom returned
                and she said firmly, sharply
                        "stop crying"

shocking myself
I did

                "take a deep breath"

I did

                "now, tell me what happened
                with that stranger
                I just *knew* he vibrated danger !

                did he hypnotize you . . and somehow
                simultaneously cut me out
                so I couldn't hear what he had to say
                like some voodoo black magic trick ?
                witchcraft is not simply an "old wive's tale"
                it's a reality, you know

                stop doubting your sanity this minute

there's a logical explanation
for whatever happened in there — oh !
why didn't I come in and join you ?
I should have trusted my inner warning bell"

no, her Neptunian psychic powers
were not waning, after all
and I felt a warm rush of gratitude toward this woman
who jumped so instinctively to a conclusion
of respect for me — and mistrust of another
who had hurt, in some way, a friend of hers — she had not
        as others might have done
even for an instant imagined she was dealing with someone
driven into hallucinatory experience by bereavement

    . . I could tell that Ruth believed me
    whatever I might have to tell her, and however
    bizarre it might seem . . she knew
                I would tell her the truth

then I poured out the whole story
strangely . . not a word had I forgotten, not one
it was still as vivid and clear as when I had first . . first what ?
imagined it — or heard it ?

and when I was through, I sobbed again
"oh, Ruth, it is not my imagination, I swear !
that's what he said while he was sitting there
in that rocking chair — every word I heard
with my own ears, I did !
please believe me — every single word !"

        she wrapped her sympathetic Pisces smile
        around me, along with her shawl
                        answering quietly

            "yes, I do believe you heard
            every single word"

we talked, then, far into the night, over mugs of hot soup
                        and some toast
trying to decide, between us
if the stranger had been some sort of astral ghost
or a hypnotist, with an ulterior motive
perhaps one who knew more than a trace
            of voodoo black magic arts
and discussed a book we both had read
about certain visitors from space
who can, allegedly, program the human mind
even in a crowd . . without speaking a single word aloud
through tuning — or locking in

Canto Eleven ☆ 317

to one's individual vibratory thought wave frequency

over and over we pondered and puzzled the enigma of the stranger . . .
how had he managed to remain
for a time which appeared to me to last at least
                    two hours or more

but which to Ruth had seemed
to be somewhat short of a full twenty minutes ?
and how had he managed to tune Ruth out of awareness
so that she heard nothing at all
of our shared conversation — including my own words
save for those initial
                    few comments we had exchanged
about the Colorado scenery
                    and the mountain greenery ?

finally, physically exhausted, and emotionally pretzel-twisted
from the tangled reactions of curiosity and excitement
                              mixed with tears and fears
I fell half-asleep on the couch in the den
dozing in the middle of a sentence . . or a question

        and Ruth covered me with a quilt
        like a proper protective friend
                    . . . or like some friendly Neptune elf

I closed my eyes
        so she would think
I was sleeping soundly
        and get some rest herself

then she tip-toed through the dark parlor
closed the front door gently, as the lock snapped shut
and went home, next door, to her patient husband, Lowell
and two Huck Finn-Tom Sawyer sons
        aged nine and eleven, going-on-ten-and-twelve

    leaving behind, I felt
the biggest baby of the lot — me
for, to Rams
        maturity comes hard

                the grandfather clock chimed out four times
                reminding me that it was four o'clock in the morning
                four o'clock . . . . like the flowers
                in Aunt Maud's rain swept, grassy back yard

 . . four o'clocks
        sweet peas . . rain

. . and rainbows

       yes, she reminded me of the biblical Ruth
       and sometimes, of the St. Raphael's Sister . . .
       the moment she was gone, I missed her cheerful voice
       for I was still too full of ghost
       to go to bed — or even go-to-couch

I sat there, staring at nothing, for more than an hour, I guess
wondering if the stranger had come to curse or to bless

       listening to the grandfather clock tick-tock
       keeping perfect time with the ticking in my head
       of the clock of dread
       with the hands still set on half-past-dead
       and still too tightly wound

as my thoughts chimed themselves around and around
on a Carousel of craven horses
spinning to a mass chord calliope vibration

       until I saw the rosy fingers of the Sun
       wave dawn at me, through the dining room window

and was finally able to fall into a deep sleep

. . then dreamed of a Thanksgiving football game in Heaven's Rose Bowl
with St. Peter making the touchdowns
                  . . Saturn playing tackle
myself leading the cheers
              Rah ! Rah ! Rah Heaven !
 Ra ! Ra ! Ra !

       rooting crowds of Holy Ghosts and Heavenly Hosts
with Go, Go Go ! Go, Serpent, Go !
          Serpent-Seven-Come-Eleven ! ringing through the sky
as Al-tar, the all-star quarterback
             kicked the point for a final tie

the numbers on the Pyramid-shaped scoreboard reading
                          Score: 7 to 7
7 to 7 ? seven plus seven equals 14
   what does that mean ?

       hiSSed by a Snake from Eden

                SSSSSSSeven to SSSSSSSeven
   score tied
         he died — Satan lied

   God cried

my mind . .

        had been programmed
        as a computer

   by the stranger

              to pour forth to me . . in code
              the information
              he had placed within its data bank

     . . . . later

        back in New York

but I did not suspect this
nor comprehend what I had been taught

           for I control my *own* mind

              as *all* do

    do I not ?

CANTO TWELVE

Love, not learning finds the way,
Opens the eyes to the Doors of the Day,
Uncovers the wonders of undreamed sights,
And leads the way to the Wisdom Lights.

Kyril Demys (Musaios)
Prismatic Voices

321

Snake Eyes

I no longer weep

    I have cried all of the tears
out of my heart . . . my tears have all been spent

        it is nearly a month, by the incandescent Moon, since he died
and my eyes have released all the waterfalls
from the flowing rivers of grief

    they are purged now, my eyes
and they are dry

        but there are still un-shed tears
        which remain in my soul
        more burning than the common kind

    my eyes do not weep
but neither do they sleep

        they stare, in their sockets
        on this purple-shadowed night

                    they burn . . so deep
                        so deep
                        so deep

oh ! why can't I sleep ?

        I ask myself now, what the others asked me
        when they used to beg and plead
        for me to lead . . the way
                    lead the way ?
        I could no more have led them
        out of their valley of the shadow . . then
        than I can lead myself now
        I was the blind, leading the blind
        with compassion, but no wisdom — no keys
                to the Kingdom

"please tell me how," they each would ask
    "please tell me — what about here and now ?"

  "ease this fear"
they cried

      "what about the *now* and *here* ?"

"where are the lips, the voice, the hair, the eyes

the hands — warm dear familiar hands
how long must I wait for a return ?" they begged, like the Pleiades

    yes, tonight they burn
    the un-shed tears in my soul
    I was the blind, then . . leading the blind
        and still am blind

I am blind, and cannot see
it is so dark
in this room . . so dark . . so still

      how far did he go, how far ?
      beyond which star or unseen galaxy . .

        how far ?

. . . on down the river
      a million miles or more
   other little children
    will bring my boat ashore . .

      seven-seven-seven . . . seven rhymes with Heaven

seven *why ?*   *why ?*
seven
      seven rhymes with Heaven
      seven rhymes with Heaven
          a voice within cried twice
toss God's dice !

    seven-come-eleven

    seven-come-Heaven ?

how does seven come Heaven
on a roll of God's — or Fate's — dice ?

      seven-come-eleven
      how does seven come Heaven ?

777 seven 777

      bright Heaven-Heaven-Heaven . . Light
              777
why did I dream of Saturn
last night ?

Canto Twelve ☆ 323

yes, why Saturn ?
the stern, stony and silent
planet of Karma
of death and discipline
why did I dream of . . Saturn ?

in the few brief hours I am able to sleep
why are my restless dreams about Saturn ?
Saturn does not bring reprieve . .

and in this tortured wakefulness
as I still grieve — why do I think about seven ?

why does seven rhyme with Heaven ?

seven-come-eleven — toss God's dice !

but, *how* does seven come Heaven ?

when I first learned to draw
the astrological symbol of Saturn
stern, stony, silent planet
I found a trick, so I wouldn't forget
how to draw it

what was that magical
Saturn symbol drawing trick ?

oh, yes, I remember !
now I remember

you just draw the figure seven — you draw a 7

then you make it taller — like this ♄

and you take the taller 7 . . . being now   ♄

and place upon it, a small hat
♄ like that !

7 7 taller   ♄ ♄   then a hat ♄ ♄

add a small tail . . . ♄

and you have it !

♄ . . . the symbol for Saturn

a faint light broke through the veil clouding my mind . . . yes !

the ancient astrological symbol for Saturn
planet of Karma, Discipline and Death

not to mention patience, waiting
                          and common sense . . is ♄

         but

      what has Saturn to do with seven
      other than my magic-memory astrological drawing trick ?

Saturn-seven-Heaven
seven-Saturn-Heaven

                          does Saturn come to curSe or bleSS ?

            seven and Saturn
            both words begin with the letter S
            yes, both *begin*
                          with the letter
                              S

S . . it looks like a Serpent
   yes, it looks like a Snake
a Serpent

         so, S is . . Serpent

         Serpent begins with "S" too

         Saturn-Seven-Serpent
         Seven-Serpent-Saturn
         Serpent-Saturn-Seven

and Heaven
what about Heaven ?

toss God's dice !
God's . . Free Will dice ?

               Seven-come-eleven
                 Seven-come-Heaven
                   Saturn-come-Heaven
                     Serpent-come-Heaven
                       Serpent-come-Seven

               Saturn-come-Serpent ?
roll the dice again !
snake-eyes-snake-eyes-snake-eyes

Snake-Serpent

         toss God's dice again !

Canto Twelve ☆ 325

Snake-eyes Zero — **O** — in a dice game's score
but . . . there is something more

the Serpent, eating its own tail
is the symbol for Eternity . . . . . **O**

> the symbol for Eternity
> Serpent-Seven-Saturn
> > Heaven . . Eternity
>
> what does it mean ?

I do not see
what it all means

> three words — three
> three-times-three

three ?

three is the Holy Trinity
the Holy Trinity of what ?

> the Holy Trinity of the three-times-three

> of me ?

 now encased in pain, now numb and blind

the Supraconscious or spirit — the Mind — and the Body
> the least of the three

the holy trinity of me ?
the three-times-three
> of the me-of-me ?

Seven-Seven-Seven
Saturn-Saturn-Saturn
Serpent-Serpent-Serpent

> Heaven-Heaven-Heaven
> Seven-Seven-Seven
> > . . . . Eternity

do the druids know
the secret ?

> do the druids know ?

Eternity — the keys
the Keys to the Kingdom of Heaven
the lost Keys

326 ☆ Canto Twelve

I heard inside my head a voice, a sigh
which seemed to whisper

"what did you used to tell yourself
when the mountains refused to fly ?
did you not tell yourself
that the druids work all their marvels
                              at midnight

              under the old oak tree
                    while you sleep . . "

yes, Eternity . . the secret of the Keys
Jesus gave to Peter, to keep

        the Keys to the Kingdom
              Snake eyes

my eyes no longer weep

              SEVEN COME ELEVEN
                    SEVEN COME HEAVEN
                    Seven come Heaven
                          seven come heaven . .

        I am weary . .
              . . I must sleep

The Keeper of the Keys

I listen to the drowsy autumn rain
sounding a silver symphony on the old tin roof
as it pitter-patters silver splatters
                              in my brain
but I remain
awake

why am I aloof to the rain on the roof tonight ?
        at other times, it brings me peace
and the blessed release from awareness, called sleep

that sends me out of this world of illusionary reality
into the world of dreams — and true reality
where the spirit and soul, are free to fly . . so why
                    do I lie here awake ?

somewhere, within the silvery splatters

of this slumber song
I hear a gong . . a silver chord that once did bind
calling brown-robed monks to pray
far, far away . . . and hear their musical chants
echoing through the vaulted monasteries of my mind

. . . this is the world of illusion
this is the world of illusion
this is the world of illusion . . .

 a world of illusion ? perhaps it is
but there is one thing I know, you monks of Tibet

I would like to forget-forget-forget
                that this is a world of confusion

not merely illusion

        and still the rain
        goes pitter-patter in my brain

pitter-patter, what's-the-matter, pitter-patter, what's-the-matter
silvery-sleepy-making melody
        pitter-patter, pitter-patter, what's the matter

silvery-slumber song . . what's wrong ?

        pittering and pattering
        silvering, splattering and smattering
        in my brain, this autumn rain

oh, what does it mean, what does it all mean ?
this silvery-slumber-song, what's wrong
this silvery-sleepy-making-patter ·
        this what's-the-matter-silver-splatter
what does it all mean ?
and what can I glean from the pitter-patter
of Serpent-Seven-Heaven ?

        the silvery-mystical-pitter-patter
        of an occult song, oh-what-is-wrong ?

this silvery-Serpent-Seven-Heaven-patter

what silvery Serpent
slithers and snakes through my mind ?

 with this Seven-Heaven-patter
        this Seven-Heaven-Saturn matter

Serpent come Saturn

Saturn come Seven

Seven Come Heaven

toss God's dice — roll Snake eyes !

the silvery Serpent
      snakes through my mind
oh ! why am I still blind
          to its meaning ?

then, at last

    my pitter-pattered-smattered brain
    so long confused, darkened and dulled
    and numbed with grief
    brought me an astrological relief

as I remembered what I already knew, by heart
through my memorization of the art — and science
of the study of the stars and planets
              called astrology

how could I have forgotten
the basic Saturn-Seven astrological cycle ?
how could I not have remembered
        the astrological basics
hammered into my brain ?

             the rain . . has stopped
  so suddenly

. . and now my mind is clear

yes, my mind is clear
and I'm wide awake
what clue is there here

 to the mystery of stern, unyielding Saturn ?

approximately every seven years, in the life of every Earthling
give or take six months or so on either side
the planet Saturn moves ponderously and profoundly through
            the Heavens
and aspects — that is, forms an angle
by conjunction, square or opposition — to his own position
in that individual's natal horoscope
which is merely a picture of the planetary pattern
at the moment when the infant drew its first breath

* and these periodic, seven year, cyclic Saturn conjunctions
    squares . . or oppositions
all symbolize the time for varying kinds of contemplation
        a need for guidance from the planets, and their wisdom
for, these periods in the life are for the testing of the soul

    so the ancient texts do say

a time for one to pray for Light — to re-assess one's true goal
and purpose for being . . . the need for seeing the truth
         and for discerning wrong from right

among others, the Mercury-ruled, Gemini astrologer, Grant Lewi
hero of the mathematically inclined seers
wrote many words and hints
about Saturn's demand for "housecleaning"
       approximately every seven years

and the great metaphysicians, Goethe and Steiner
each in his own way . . quite agreed

housecleaning
cleaning house — why ?

        for company, maybe ?
        guess who's coming to dinner !

who, in the house of the spirit
called the Temple of the soul

        . . the physical body
is coming to dinner ?

if Saturn orders us to clean house
every seven years or so . . is a guest expected ?

who's coming to dinner — who ?
the Brown Owl ?

fish or fowl, man or beast, why must I prepare for a feast
by cleaning and sweeping out my Body Temple
      at Saturn's rigid, cycle-of-seven demand ?
and, even though Saturn may sternly command
        must I obey ?
what did Grant Lewi say ?
I can recall, not all . . . but much
of Lewi's big, Mercury-clever Saturn aspect interpretation

<hr>

* Note to amateur and professional astrologers: This Saturn-to-Saturn 7 year cycle is not the
same as the approximate 30 year Saturn Sun Sign cycle : Editor

his often inspired pitter-patter
and silvery Mercury chatter
about this silver-Serpent, Snake-eyed matter
of Saturn's Seven-come-Heaven
conjunctions, squares and oppositions

　　　. . though I may scramble a bit
　　　the juxtaposition of these three aspects
　　　I may twist into some minor tangles

his descriptions of these three Saturnine angles
but never mind, if I get what comes before, behind
it's a far deeper truth I seek from Saturn

　　　. . "*a time when one may be twice born*"

twice born ?　dear God, isn't once enough
　　　　　　　　　　　　for any lifetme ?
who needs to roll the karmic dice twice — or more
in this game, in which a distant Deity is keeping score
and the rules change every century or so
as to whether you lose or win
will depend upon obvious sin — or hypocritical virtue

this century I'm stuck in, at present
contains — or has created
some strange rules for salvation
between church and nation

like, singing the virtuous song
of my church — or my country — right or wrong
and trying to learn the confusing Golden Rule
of . . being taught, in Sunday school
 it's wrong to kill
then growing up, to be taught by your country
that killing is good, and should bring a patriotic thrill
when you slay to defend the Freedom way

twice born ?
Good Grief !　who needs it ?

Charlie Brown, good buddy — old pally
maybe you should ponder your favorite sally . . "Good Grief"
grief is not good, it's a sin — it's sad, and it's bad
what's good about it, Charlie ?

but wait . . is grief truly bad ?
undeniably, it hurts, and it's achingly sad
　　　　　　　　　　but is it bad ?
maybe it's good for the soul, and helps us reach some goal

allright, until all the votes are in
I'll go along with you, Charlie Brown
     grief may not be a sin
it may be good for something . . but Good Grief ! good for *what* ?

we'll wait and see
    Lucy and me

               " . . *a time when one may be twice born*
                             or more"

a time to ask Saturn the score ?

               " . . *a tme for reorganization of the ego . . for*
               by the time this aspect has passed
               you will be a new person . . "

a new person — new ?

               " . . *you will have abandoned old ideas*
             and perhaps struggled hard
                       against the abandonment"

of course ! and why not ?
who wants to lose himself — herself ?

               " . . *for it is here . . .* "

at the seven year Saturn cycle ?

               "*that Free Will operates . . as free*
             and untrammeled by circumstances
             or outside environmental influences
                       as it ever will be"

so the will is free — to choose what ?

               " . . *a new mastery over Life is yours*
                     for the taking
             when Saturn thus aspects his birth position"

a new mastery over Life ? I'm all for that !
but how can I be Brown Owl of myself
if stuffy Saturn is still boss over me . . ?

               " . . *the choice made now will forge your fate*
             for a long time to come
               change your basic thinking
             and revise your aims and purposes . . "

well, yes, I suppose if I did all that

I would be a new person . . . . . no doubt
if I chose it myself, that is
without being pushed or forced by Saturn

> " . . *you will stand free*
> *at this periodic Saturn cycle*
> *of many . . erstwhile restrictions*"

and who releases me from jail ?
Brown Owl Saturn ? does he hold the key
to my 'erstwhile restrictions' ?

> " . . *you will be given a chance to shift*
> *but if you have refused to be twice-born . . .* "

refused ? ah ! so old man Saturn
is not Brown Owl after all !
if I have the right to accept or refuse
being 'twice born', then I am Brown Owl
over the holy trinity
                    of the three-times-three
        of the me-of-me
        but, should I refuse . . then what ?

I couldn't seem to recall the rest
and was not sure how it might be linked
to the lost Keys of the Kingdom
    . . though I continued to ponder it

is Saturn, then, perhaps
the Keeper of the Keys ?

Saturn is the ruler of the Sun Sign Capricorn — also
the symbolic, traditional ruler of Jewish culture and Hebrew
                                        covenant
which keeps the secret of ancient Kabala wisdom
and guards it with blood, even today

and Saturn is too, of course, the ruler of all Goats
        the Cappies themselves
Capricorns — undeniably stamped with Hebrew traits
whatever their individual religious persuasions might be
all Goats harbor a secret love of learning
plus a most healthy respect for achievement and financial
                                        security
they're also quite attached to their relatives
social status . . and they , not always, but usually revere law and authority
whether it be the Law of Moses — a small community, or a nation

yes, Capricorns, those odd people — so strict and rigid and stuffy
but with a playful twinkle in their steady, serious eyes

Capricorns — with their strange, Reverse-Aging twist
born as wrinkled little old men and women
            as children, more mature than their own parents
yet, curiously growing younger in appearance
and more youthful in action . . as they grow older

does Saturn tell us, then
that, after birth and sorrow, experience and grief
have aged our spirits . . hearts . . and bodies
we must then, somehow, go into reverse — reverse gears ?

      . . no wonder I'm having trouble
              getting it clear
     if it's in any way analogous to shifting a gear !

perhaps Saturn is trying to teach us that we must go into reverse
to transform all the crinkles and wrinkles
of the soul and heart, and the body's wear and tear
into the smooth, sunny face — and innocent laughter and faith
                              of childhood
which contained, for us, the wisdom
from the very beginning
until we threw it away . . and spent its shining coin
for the Fool's Gold of growing up . . adulterating the magic
                              with hypocrisy
yes, *adult*-erating the magic . . . .

our minds pre-conditioned by insurance companies . . and our 'elders'
to accept an arbitrary life span
along with the acceptance of the supposedly unavoidable
disease and disfigurement of age
brought about by the supposedly unavoidable process
                      of slow death and decay
yet, none of it
necessary in the least, except as *believed* so

is this what Capricorns
are here to teach us
through their ruler, Saturn ?

well, if Saturn was trusted to hang on to the Keys — I confess
there's no one I'd trust more than a Capricorn
especially the Brown Owl of *all* Capricorns — to handle
                      such a responsibility

 but was it Saturn ?

        was it not Peter to whom Jesus gave the Keys ?
        and "infallible" Peter was an idealistic
        but rather rash Aries Ram

prone to losing things, through carelessness
　　　　　　　　　　　　　　like me

surely the Keys of the Kingdom
would be safer, for a longer period — like Eternity
with old man Saturn
　　than with Butterfingers Peter

although I must say
it was surely a lovely and perfectly marvelous gesture
for Jesus to allow an impulsive Ram, like Peter
to experience the joy of possessing them
　　　　　　　　　even if only briefly

　　　　　　　so . . Saturn has the Keys
　　　　　　　but Saturn isn't talking

Capricorns are a taciturn lot
little wonder it's so difficult to get at the truth

　do the keys Saturn holds
　work in the lock of Life ? and how do they unlock the door
　where the switch is located
　that stops the Carousel from spinning ?

　　　what good is it to discover, in this Eternity game
of button-button-who-has-the-button
who truly might be the one holding those lost Keys
if that one happens to be Saturn
　　　　　　　　　　and he won't talk ?

and what is all this about being twice-born
when Saturn drops in for a formal visit
in the Temple of the soul — the body
　　　　　　every seven years or so ?

why are we warned to clean house in our Body Temples
each seven year cycle ? who's coming to dinner ?

　　　　　　　. . a new person . . with a shift
　　　　　　　　　of ideas . . and a new perspective . .

　a new soul ?

　　　　　　a new soul ?

　　　a new soul ?

　　　　　　　is *that* who's coming to dinner ?

I felt myself grow still within

as I allowed the enormity of this possibility
to wash over my mind . . roll over my consciousness
like waves, surfing the shoreline
                              of awareness
but . . how could this be
oh ! how could this be ?

if the present me-of-me
entered into this Body Temple
at my most recent Saturn-Seven-cycle

and was not in my Temple . . . .
did not reside here in my body before
not even in St. Mary's

then why does this present me-of-me, this *maybe*-new soul
still remember the Brownies . . the druids
the socks in my sweater at camp . . Jerry Jones
the loping happy of our wedding day
and the millions of other bits and pieces
                              of kaleidescope memories ?

no, no — this must be still the same 'me'
who — which ? resided in this Body Temple
then and now
              although . . somehow . . I do

            feel different

in ways I can't really explain
I feel — I think — differently about many things
    than I did then
and than I did . . during so many 'thens' of the past
but more emotionally than mentally
                              more . . spiritually ?

yes, in those ways, I can believe
I might be a new me-of-me

and yet . . I still recall every Christmas
I remember every December and Easter . . the letters I wrote
every case of poison ivy and sore throat

                      so, if I am not the old me
                      then who can I be ?

if I am not still the old me
then how am I able to recall

every summer, spring, winter and fall
of my early youth and childhood ?

oh, I would like to believe, I so need to believe
                              that all this is so
because, maybe . . just maybe !
the him-of-him might enter a new adult Body Temple
and I could find him again

even the merest possibility of such an improbability
made my head swim, my eyes dim with tears . . oh, if . . maybe !

but — enter the Body Temple
of an adult, not necessarily a baby ?

no, I could not permit myself to dwell on such a thing
it was too torturous for my heart to image
                    that I might see . . find . . recognize a part
of him . . again

if this were true . . . . . . I tried to stabilize my thoughts
to pin them down to logic and rationality
but the nearness, the concept of this being a reality
made them flutter, instead, like butterflies in my brain

or like . .

        butterfly feathers
        in the rain . . . .

please, God
please, no . . . .

                    this hurts too much, brings too much pain
                    to even consider that it might be so

if I were to hope, to look, to search — yes, to quest
                              for the star of him
to reach out for his arms, his voice
his hands, his eyes . . the inner spark, familiar glow
                    of the him-of-him I knew, and know

if I were to believe this really, not nearly
but really — could be so

then there would be no reason anymore
for anyone to ever grieve

no reason to grieve over death
for death would not be final

if this Seven-come-Heaven dream could be true
it would signal the end of sadness — and bring forth the glory
of the Easter story, in all its **GLADNESS !**

oh ! if I could truly know
I might see him again . . and hear him

                        touch him

physically

      not a ghost or a spirit — but flesh

if this could be, and if he could, somehow, then — make me see
let me know, in ways no other ever could
through some look, some word . . some sign leaving no doubt
                    telling me for certain
that the soul within the new Temple he chose was *really*

          the him-of-him

O ! the awesome wonder of it
thundered in my blood, pounded in my veins
and flooded my very beingness
with the ecstasy of surging hope . . answered prayers

        recaptured dreams

   if he . . . .

       if he could but return to me

    death would have no sting
          and a robin could be heard to sing
of springtime . . in the winter !

like a wave sweeping me out to sea
     . . yes, like a wave sweeping me out to sea

if he could
return to me . .

   O ! what a story to tell !
what a joyful bell to ring, of spring !
an Easter bell
        of truth and gladness
ending forever the ominous sadness
           of tomb and grave

   O ! the broken hearts
the shattered faiths I could then save !
if this were true
and he could, somehow, *let me know* — in his new Body Temple

what peace to the lonely

   if only . . this could be so !

but no . . . .
   such a thing could not, could not be
   for, the present me-of-me still remembers Nanoo
   so cold . . needing Comforters
            cold cheeks . . when I was
   only three

no, no, no !
   I still remember each memory ember
               of the past
   and this Saturn-Seven-come-Heaven miracle
   is but a cruel joke my daydreams
                  have played on me
   there is no such miracle possible
   no such Easter magic — and death is just as tragic
   as it was before

why do these mad thoughts scramble
through my brain . . like butterfly feathers in the rain ?

      I must forget
   I even dreamed of such a thing

there is no Saturn-Seven-cycle of the soul
no Easter goal, for the heart to reach
no new lesson Saturn has to teach . . oh !

   how could I have tortured myself so
   when I know . . when I *know* — he is dead

not to be risen
not ever . . to be risen

   what is that verse . . what are those lines
   from the Rubayiat of Omar Khayam ?
   then I remembered . . .

         Up from Earth's Center
               through the Seventh Gate
         I rose, and on the throne of Saturn sate

         and many a knot unravelled by the road
         but not the Master-knot of human Fate

oh, true, true words
of the Rubayiat !

   the Seventh Gate . . the throne of Saturn . . . should it not be the Eighth Gate ?
               may unravel many knots
   but not the Master-knot of human Fate
                  . . it is too late

for miracles
                    too late
            for druid magic

too late
for Seven-come-Heaven

this has been merely a joke, played upon my mind
by old man Saturn himself — but I am not a fool, so blind
that I do not see there is no such enlightenment ever to be
for me . . or for others, simliarly grieved and bereaved

this errant theory is empty, empty
as my heart is empty . . and my arms are . . empty
my dreams have all lied
the Master knot has already been tied
                            and he is dead

        the Saturn-Seven-Heaven
HiSSing Serpent secret
  cannot untangle, nor unravel this knotted thread

he is . . . dead

            he is

                    dead dead dead

        . . . isn't he ?

Vital Statistics

occasionally, a public servant
will make a careless mistake — that hurts

    is it because they aren't paid enough
    as servants of the public — to be careful ?

    or is it because the public itself
                        is apathetic and insensitive ?

I am not the public
I am sensitive

I sit here and remember . . oh ! I remember
as I face this bleak November

staring at his death certificate, duly mailed to me
                              by the undertaker
as his next-of-kin

yes, we were kin
he was, in fact — my twin

you public servants, did you know that ?
we were twin souls
separated by the surgery of sudden death
with no anesthetic to ease the pain
did you know that ? do you care at all ?

then I stared at his name, after the printed word *Deceased* :
and after the printed Cause of Death :
                         was typed a single word : *pneumonia*

it was a kindness — kind of the doctor
to write pneumonia in the blank space, when the cause of his death
was really — drowning
                    drowning in an alcoholic sea

. . or was it grief
for the three

or was it . . me ?

yes, kind doctor, with a strange sort of name
written in a dwarf-like scrawl
at the very bottom of the page, where it was printed
Signature of Physician :

that's where they should have printed
his name — *his* name !

he wanted so, oh ! he wanted so . . to heal
and he always felt that, had he remained in medical school
he could have healed and saved them — all three

                    "but I couldn't even heal myself"
                              he said

          strange name

this kind doctor, who wrote the word 'pneumonia'
strange name, though perhaps not uncommon — except to me
a name with six letters — rhyming with truer
and three dimensional viewer — I wonder if it's British — Brewer ?
or maybe Scotch or Irish ? I had never met anyone with the name
though, of course, that meant nothing . . I'm not much of a traveler

oh, well, what's the difference ?

  it wasn't the doctor who was insensitive
  no, it was the clerk, who filled out the form

  in the blank space, after the printed words
  Date of Birth of the Deceased :

                    . . . after the words *Date of Birth*
                  this public servant had typed

December 7th, 1970

what a stupid, blind mistake !
they tell me this ? they tell me now
that the date of his birth
          is December 7th 1970 ?

they tell me this, on a bleak November in 1970
as I sit here mourning his death, only a few weeks ago ?

they tell me the date of his birth is this coming December ?
that he hasn't even been *born* yet ?

don't they care how that makes me feel ?
as if he . . wasn't even real

          not ever *born* . . . not even *real* ?

oh, what an unkind winter's April Fool
how careless, cold and callous

          how very, very cruel

CANTO THIRTEEN

Washed upon the sand I lay
among those hills like combed hair,
and poured my listlessness into the sea.

Sky hid the sun —
Gulls did not move the air —
There were no birds to move that air.

Quiet . . . no wailing rent awareness.

Without willing I remained there,
became quite unaware
of unwept thoughts
and still-born tears.

I stayed . . .
Beyond all wistfulness
that time had told could be.

Kyril Demys (Musaios)
Prismatic Voices

November and December
             are unreal in California

who can conjure cranberries, or jingle jolly holly
in such an alien atmosphere ?
only those born here, who do not have different memories

to these, perhaps, the quiet beauty of graceful gulls,
riding crested waves of snow capped clouds
in a sea of rosy sky, tinted by the Sunrise glow
high above the Moon-tugged ocean's tides
                 of emerald ebb and flow

compensates for missing happy winter sleigh rides in the snow
over the hills and through the woods
to grandma's house, for hot mince pie and merry mistletoe

       who can celebrate Thanksgiving
       in a land awash with painted Indians
       but short on Pilgrims, making Progress ?

       not lacking hordes of naked savages
         worshipping the Sun god
       and trading strands of colored beads

       but with hardly a Puritan in sight
       especially at night
       along the gaudy, neon-lighted, hard-core-porno-Strip

or where any vision of a New World Ship

       is blurred by the swarming pestilence
       of motorcycles bearing down on screaming dunes
       leaving trails of noxious fumes
                and belching noisy back-fires

not that I miss the Puritans all that much

          I never really knew one

       but I used to like to draw them
       with their stiff, white collars — and tall, buckled hats
       cutting them out in silhouette
       or painting them in water colors . . hands folded, praying
       thanking God for Nature's blessings
                    before they feasted
       somehow, I just can't fool myself
       into imaging Big Sur as Plymouth Rock

not even when Nepenthe
features pumpkin pie and stuffing on the menu

the most exotic tropical blooms
which still survive in Beverly Hills
        and creep their vines around the swimming pools
of Los Angeles hotels
     in the City of Lost Angels

      do not bear much resemblance
to glittering tree balls, etched with elves

and palms, of course, even those not brown from smog
make unsatisfactory trimmings
nor did I ever see one masquerading as a Yule log
and burning brightly, crackling cheer
                  out here

O ! it's hard to catch a glimpse of prancing reindeer
on the twisting L.A. Freeway
          teeming into Mulholland Drive

or hear the clear and joyous ring
         of any kind of Noel bell
in the lazy, balmy air
     of the bored, half-hearted spring
Californians manufacture out of winter wishes
to make their oranges grow
          . . . not even any snow

let alone a William Brewster

    or a partridge in a pear tree

still, I had to go away
somewhere

to find a quiet, private shore
where I could listen to the ocean's roar
and watch the waves roll in
        maybe even try once more
to write my Happiness poem
since I had failed in Colorado and New York

but . . much more than the writing
there was this restlessness of spirit I was fighting
something nameless I was striving to discover
before it was too late

something I was desperately trying to reach

.... a seaside town called Laguna Beach
was the first restless, rest-stop

on my unsuspected date
with a long ago predestined fate

I planned myself, as all do
but retained no conscious memory
of its shaping

Beaches and Boulevards — Tuesday

arriving in Laguna lonely, out of season

I found a small beach front hotel
with a tiny wishing well . . in a shaded patio nearby
where I tossed some dimes and quarters, out of habit
just for luck . .

but made no wishes

and changed my room three times, the morning of the first day
undecided as I was, if I should stay
which brought some snickers from the bellman
until I tipped his ill concealed suspicions of my stability
into wide, gratuitous smiles, each time he moved my luggage
        the cash seeming to suffice
as a sufficient leveler for my eccentricity

    plus my explanation that a room must have
    the proper numerological vibrations

although I overheard him whisper to the maid — "say !

that new one who checked in last night
she's really out of sight !"

and I thought, grimly, to myself
oh, bellman, bellman !
you have no idea how close to truth you are
or just how far
out of sight and mind I am these days

    I finally settled on the Dolphin Suite
    because its name, for some obscure reason

appealed to me

yes, *The Dolphin*

facing the beach
and overlooking western sunlight . . not the eastern

I should have remembered
that Sunrise seems to have some special magic way
of stirring in me sudden gladness
while Sunset seems to have some special tragic way
of stirring in me sudden sadness

Sunrise, Spring and Easter, all being part of
and belonging to the Aries essence

but autumn's burnished gold
is more likely to bring peace to Virgo
and Sunset's harvest beauty
soothes Libra's soul, not mine
autumn's Sunset only makes me feel more lonely

although California seemed, to me
almost a foreign land

I guess I believed, or hoped — or prayed
the seaside sights, like white capped waves
. . and salty smells
the sound of foaming breakers
lapping against rocks and sand
would calm my troubled spirit
and I would find it all, somehow . . inspiring

instead, my first few strolls along the water's edge
were merely desolate . . and soul tiring

as I thought . .

not even the ocean is peaceful anymore
while I walked and walked
along the trash and bottle littered shore

it seems to be forever lashing and churning, the sea
or is it but a reflection
of what crashes and churns . . . inside of me ?

why am I here ? I wondered
what am I supposed to be learning
from the ocean's angry crashing and churning

. . the sea gulls' graceful, soaring flights

> *. . and those distant ships out there*
> *lithographed in steely grey*
> *on the far away and hazy blue horizon ?*

what truth can I gain . . what peace
from watching the sandpipers
hobnobbing . . and bobbing their tiny heads
staggering, tipsy-like

>   around the pier

> *. . why am I here ?*

I discovered soon enough the answer
on a cool and breezy afternoon . . it was . . <u>November</u> <u>the</u> <u>Eleventh</u>

>   the reason I was lured by longing
>   to this deserted stretch of beach — was not
>   to catch the falling star of my lost faith
>   but to experience a series of nightmares . . . encores
>   to the stranger's mesmerizing act in Colorado

the first one
came upon me, unexpected

>   for who connects a nightmare
>   with a bright and cheerful daytime Sun
>   even when it hides its face behind a cloud
>   momentarily, in shadow ?

>   all clouds have silver linings
>   do they not ?

or are the linings of some clouds
shaded only by a ghostly, ghastly grey ?

those which briefly hid the Sun that day
were shaded so for me

>   on impulse, I had, with a sharp razor blade
>   just cut short and feathered my mouse-colored hair
>   and it was hanging, forlorn and limp
>   from the salt spray in the air

>   I was sitting alone on the beach
>   that quiet, nearing Sunset hour . . no one was near

tracing butterfly feathers
in the
    damp sand

with my hand

> *. . your hair smells like raindrops . . and*
> *it feels . . like butterfly feathers*
> *oh, how funny, how funny ! to imagine*
> *a butterfly with feathers . .*

. . . lost somewhere within the sound
pouring out around me, drowning . .

. . in the tape cassetted crescendos of poor Butterfly
singing the soaring *Un Bel Di* aria of hope and faith
                                        . . in Lt. Pinkerton's return
oh ! one can drown in music
as in cool, green water . .

. . trying to translate the Italian lyrics
more with my heart than with my unlinguistic mind

misty translation of predestined sorrow
on a fine tomorrow, meant never to come . . for some
like Butterfly . . and me

I struggled with the words . .

> "oh, un bel di ! one fine day
> I shall come upon the shore . . and see
> his ship appear on the horizon
>   yes, un bel di
> I shall surely see his ship
> that one fine day . . and he . . will cry
> poor Butterfly !
>   dear-little-baby-wife of mine
> dear orange blossom
> and I shall hide a bit to tease him . . yes !
>   one fine day
> he'll come to me . . oh, un bel di !
> and I shall know
>   he loves me so . . . that one
> bel di . . fine day . . "

as Puccini's chords of *Un Bel Di* . . from my small tape recorder
rolled and thundered out to sea
                on waves of music, I could see
a larger ship against the skyline

> *a far-off ship*
>   *on the horizon*
like Butterfly . .
        and I wept

yes, uncontrollably, I wept

    staring at a distant ship
that somehow foreboding hour

      watching the smaller birds dip into the deep
  . . to take their salty shower
          in tiny bubbles of white foam

              . . bubbles of white foam
    remembering . .

      those other white, foamy bubbles
      of his Seaforth shaving lather
         and watching him shave

   while the Sun made lacy patterns
across the white heirloom spread . . .
      those loving-loping mornings in St. Mary's

and wondered why . . . .

      why this memory, so dear . . so near
      so unaccountably clear and vivid
      should bring with it such icy dread

when it should bring only
the chords of lost, but tender sweetness

    poor Butterfly . . I thought

poor Butterfly, once his orange blossom
dear-little-baby-wife
      poor Butterfly
Lieutenant Pinkerton was a Gemini — like him
a restless, seeking Gemini

    poor Butterfly . . he will not return

so why do you wait ?
he is gone, gone, gone !
I heard myself cry

        and then the pain . . oh, God, the pain !
        sudden, sharp and stabbing

quickly, protectively, I put my hand to my head
the waves of agony blending with the rolling, rhythmic
beat of music from my tape cassette . . pounding, pounding

    but the pain was not in my head

the aching throb
was in my tooth . . I thought it bled

    pounding and pulsing
    and throbbing with the sound around me
    growing worse . . and worse
                    terrible pain
        in my tooth

it throbbed . . and pulsed . . and pounded

            until I remembered
            an ugly, ugly, buried thing
                        a ride in his car . . his car
            speeding speeding speeding
                    my mouth
bleeding bleeding bleeding

speeding in his car . . speeding-speeding
my mouth bleeding bleeding
                from a broken front tooth
broken, when my head accidently
                    struck the car door
trying to open it . .
        trying to get out of the car

                    and heard him shout . . drowning in his
                ocean . . drowning in his churning vodka ocean
                        "don't try to get out !
                    stay where you are !
                        we're going to speed, and race a star !
                a little lost star . .
                        and see if we can catch her somewhere
                                        out there
                        STAY IN THE CAR !"

it was . . one week
after we buried Anne, with an 'e'

SPEEDING !

    BLEEDING !

    I tried to stop the car . . to find the ignition . . oh ! I tried
    to stop the car, as my tooth bled
                    and struck my head . . again
    but I couldn't stop the speeding speeding car
                        . . out of control
    for he was drowning drowning drowning
    in a churning vodka ocean . . where are the brakes ?

I don't know how to drive
         . . where are the brakes, where are they ?
and we speeded speeded speeded
            speeding speeding, my tooth bleeding
    bleeding bleeding

        "don't get out !" I heard him shout . . . *"stay where you are !*

          we're going to speed . . and race a star !
     a tiny star . . who fell
            out there . . somewhere"

an ugly, ugly buried thing
      . . . deeply buried memory
the only, only un-marvelous moment we ever knew
except for the three grassy . . . graves
and the time of . . . her
        the cool, sure one

    the only really nightmare time of hate and fear
      . . except for those . .
we ever knew, in all our shining beauty days

         it was . . in our last drowning year
and after that, we spent
the next ten drowning years apart
    until he died
separated by a country, coast-to-coast

      me . . back east
         and him . . back here
      drowning somewhere along this very beach
            . . Laguna

     in his vodka ocean

it was far better left deep-buried
this painful memory fragment

    why did I come to this forlorn beach
    and allow it to be uncovered in these alien sands ?

    alien to me . . but not to him
    for he had once walked along this very shore
    maybe even sunned himself on this very spot
    where I now sat . . remembering

I placed my hand, still trembling, against my pulsing cheek
to hold back the hurt of my throbbing front tooth
long since extracted . . but aching, just the same
with nearly unbearable, sharp stabs of pain

then placed my other hand against my breast
to hold back the same hurt, throbbing there
and cried out a useless, unheard prayer . .

oh, darling ! I forgive you !
wherever you are — know that I do
know that I forgive the pain and ugliness
for the fault was mine
                              . . yes, mine

then, staring at a distant ship out there on the horizon
as the music of poor Butterfly's lost hope soared across the water

    I remembered . . *as I was staring at that ship*

            how he had said, after it was over

            "if God would allow me . . I would take
            the pain from your tooth into my own
            and bear the hurt for you
            I really would — if only I could
                              do you believe me ?"

yes . . I believe you . . now

        I doubted you then
        but I believe

            you now . .

the reality of that ugly moment, long ago
lasted less than half an hour . . as a sharp memory
of childhood's tooth fairie swept through my mind
until he stopped the car, sobbed out his sorrow
                              . . and I forgave
then the Sun, forgiving too
came out from behind the clouds
to brush our faces with gentle pink-gold once more

yes, twenty minutes or so, it had lasted
that only ugly time in all our shining beauty
except for her — and the three trips down a grassy hill

    except for those memories . . .
    our only nightmare time of hate and fear

and yet, somehow . . out here
    the unexpected memory of it . . seemed to last for an eternity

and I thought of a poet named Lynch, Eileen

. . some lines of hers I had once read
leaping back, now, into my head . . and ringing
like a long-forgotten chapel bell

> *"there is a strange foreboding in the sea*
> *it crashes hard upon our hearts*
> > *and wakens memories of shipwrecked dreams . . . "*

after awhile the throbbing in my tooth — stopped
and, as before, the Sun came bursting forth again
from behind the dark grey, shrouded clouds
melting the memory of terror, slowly making it fade

                    . . and none too soon

had I guessed this haunting of <u>November Eleventh</u> was not the last
I would have surely gone away
and decided not to stay another single day
                    on Laguna's lonely beach

  but Life . . and death
  had more lessons they must teach
  and the next one . . was the following afternoon

<u>Beaches and Boulevards — Wednesday</u>

when I awoke next morning, it was not yet light outside
also not light . . inside my room
nor yet within my mind, still faintly tinged with gloom

    the glowing hands
    on the clock beside my bed . . still set on East Coast time
    pointed to seven, straight up . . four a.m. out here

I lay there quietly, not moving
listening to the rhythmic pounding of the surf
just beyond my window

. . boom splash . . boom splash . . boom splash . . boom splash . .

. . . .

splash boom . . boom splash . . splash boom . . boom splash . . splash

        . . . boom

a sound with no beginning . . and no end
the alpha and omega of the surf . .
eternal music of the ocean, never ceasing
releasing waves and tides of surging water
 to crash against the shore . . . .
wearing down even rock itself
                . . . . . over centuries of time
        steadily . . . .

 . . . astrology teaches that water is the strongest
of all the elements . . because water does not resist
it opens up . . receives . . then closes over obstacles . . and flows on
                . . undisturbed . . unchanging

        . . . . . . water, unresisting, eternally unconquered
                by stronger-seeming elements
                                        . . water
                extinguising the flames of fire
                        . . moistening earth
                absorbing air . .

    Jesus said
    resist ye *not* evil

        . . . .   water, un-resisting

splash boom . . boom splash . .   boom . . . .
                . . splash boom
                        . . . . splash
 . . . .
        resist ye not evil . .

        what did the stranger say to me, that dreary grey
        and wintry day . . in Colorado
                        . . what did he say ?
                . . about . . water . . ?

                        . . is it the shape and design
                                of the clay pitcher
                        that cools the thirst
                                . . or the water within ?

            . .
    . . .   .
        . .
        . .   . .
I lay there, floating between two worlds
    . .   . .

reaching for consciousness, yet still half-clinging
to some fragmented dream, slipping away
      and praying, hoping
that no memories of sharp sorrow would return today
                  to haunt and hurt
only loping memories I could recall
more softly, with gentler tears . . and no chilling fears

      why would this icy clutch
      of death and desolation . . not release me ?

is it wrong to mourn this long ?
there must be some way I can snap myself
back into the world of living . . or at least existing

    Gibran was right, when he wrote . .

   "ever has it been . . that love knows not
   its own depth
                until the hour of parting"

      . .   . .
        . .   . .
          . . .
      . . .   .

    then the misting, fading fragments of my dream
    focused vividly . . in one last brilliant flash

    lifting for one second only
    the veil . . between sleeping . . and waking

the veil

      between the wakefulness of sleep
      and the sleep of wakefulness

. . and I remembered
    oh ! I remembered . .

        " . . darling, St. Paul said . . .
           the only way to measure
        devotion . . is to know
           that love lasts . . and so
        I guess there's nothing
        we can do or try . . .
           you and I . . .
        but trust each other
           till we die . . . "

and even longer, darling
even longer . . . even after that
even now . . I love you
not just until . . we die

       but . . even longer
           must we . . trust

then came the memory of my response to his words

     " . . *now there's a cop out to end all cop outs !*
        I guess I'm supposed
            to hang around until
     I'm on my death bed
          and then, if you should just happen
  . . *to still be there*
          I can close my eyes
    in peace . . and go
        . . because I'll know"

OH ! why do people speak such thoughtless words
of self pity to a loved one, never guessing
how they may someday strike
a knife into the heart . . . when the one
to whom they were addressed
         is . . no more ?

how could I have uttered such cruel, unthinking words !
it was not I who "hung around" till I was on my death bed . . . to see
    no, it was he
and he could not even close his eyes in peace . . and go
             and know
    because I was not there with him

I did not "just happen . . to still be there"

cruel words I spoke, partly as a joke
partly selfish, wounded pride . . not realizing
it would be he who would die alone
          not me
why didn't I see ?
why didn't I try harder to see
that it might be *he* . . that *he* might be
the one to die, not me ?

     why did I always think only of myself
     of my own personal hurt ?

no, I could not bear more sorrowful memories
       of my love-blindness
and so . . the second day, I tried the beach at Sunrise

not at sunset

        would this time of day, perhaps, be kinder
       and make me, mercifully, blinder
            to my former sightlessness ?

at first, it was

      yes, at first, the Sunrise was, somehow . . kinder
      I could not feel it robbing me of calmness
      through the throbbing of remembered pain

walking along the shore again this second morning . . .
after strolling for an hour or so beside the foaming surf
and flirting back with the promiscuous sandpipers
doing their funny morning imitation
              of a teeny-tiny penguin walk

. .

     I felt some drops of rain . . . .

    and a mist began to fall, a drizzle
    promising to fizzle out before too long

but, in case I might be wrong
I ducked into the all night coffee shop
across the cobblestones
between my hotel lobby . . and the building
              just next door
to have some orange juice and toast

      then someone . . dropped a quarter into the juke box
      and played Van Cliburn's recording
          of *Rachmaninoff's Rhapsody*
the one he played
so often . . and the one we listened to together
so many, many times before, mentioned in his letter
about skiing in the Swiss Alps
and expanding into the Universe . . oh !

      I felt another stab of hurt — not in my tooth
      but throughout my lonely, empty body
      sitting there, in that tulip-decaled booth
           and could not finish my late breakfast

so I paid my check, and left a tip
then walked back outside, to see the thing
Californians say can never be true

       it was raining . . hard

blindly, not having even a vague idea
of a destination . . just urgently needing
to erase this newest memory sensation . . mindlessly

> I hailed a taxi

I told the driver to take me to the center of town
and when we were there, discovered that most stores
were not open until later . . . and so
I instructed him to simply drive me around . . and around

> and around . .

a twenty dollar cab ride
with a five dollar tip
which made him happy

> and made me calmer
> if more numb

after leaving the taxi, I entered a small hotel breakfast shop
to escape the downpour . . and ordered . . I don't know why . . a cup
> of peppermint tea

> the waitresses were dressed
> in bodices and vests . . to match the Swiss decor

then his words . . rushed back once more
skiing, in the Swiss Alps
> soaring . . like a bird
into the Universe . .

> was there no escape ?

I sat there, staring into nothing
stirring the spoon around and around in the tea
until it grew ice cold . . not even sipping

> then . . slipping two dollars under the saucer
> for my long rental of the table
> > . . it was now past two
> I paid the check, and left

noticing that the rain was now reduced
to a misty haze of dew

> . . not knowing what else to do
> I walked again . . along the beach

and then . . I walked and walked
up and down the streets

until my head was damp . . . I walked
my wispy hair hanging in short, limp
Medusa strands
looking like a half-drowned mouse

then glanced up, and saw I stood before a theatre
this day, offering a matinee
the marquee announcing, in tall, black letters
the featured film now playing there

ironic title
in this weather
On a Clear Day

I had heard, or read somewhere, that this movie
starring Barbra Streisand and Yves Montand
about a girl named Daisy
(crazy daisy ?) Gamble . . and her psychiatrist
was about reincarnation
and about . . seeing forever
on a clear day

seeing forever

I had heard the sound track album many times
. . the lyrics
. . were haunting

and so

wanting . . to kill time
which I was beginning to believe
deserved nothing short of murder

in self defense
I decided to kill it

time, that is . .

memories, like cats, have nine lives
and are not so easily murdered

since the cashier said the Early Bird Feature
was just commencing, I bought a ticket . . . .
handed the stub to the dozing doorman
walked down the aisle, into the gloom

blinking raindrops from my lashes

and seated myself in the orchestra section
my favorite location in a theatre . . . dead center

noticing that I was one of maybe only a dozen or so others
in what seemed to be a strangely silent audience
waiting, like me, for the sound and images to transport them
away from reality . . momentarily, at least

soon, after having blinked away the raindrops
two teardrops stung, then fell . . and I wiped them away
hardly knowing the difference between the two kinds of rain

                except . . for the pain

finally, the picture started
and began to unfold its story

        but . . just as I was feeling a stirring of interest
        in the scenes before me

              the sound stopped

  no sound at all

                silent film . . no sound

     actors mouthing
     unspoken lines

then a few half-hearted stomps and whistles
from the impatient audience

              HEY ! TURN ON THE SOUND !

       but still . . no sound

a silent screen

       I, too, was growing restless and impatient, although not as vocal
       wondering what dialogue or piece of plot
       which might fit my own Life-Death puzzle . . I was missing
       inwardly urging the man behind the silent scene
       to repair the sound track swiftly

but . .

           still no sound

     I looked around

                noting the annoyed expressions
                on the unfamiliar faces nearest me
      silence

no sound

                actors speaking, but unspoken
                grotesquely mouthing unheard words
                        Good Grief !
                was that a *dog* speaking on the screen ?
                                a dog . . conversing with Streisand ?

        a dog speaking ?
up there, before me

        silence . . .

                                as the catcalls, stomps and whistles
                                grew angrier and louder
        suddenly

the lights went out

                        the screen went blank — no picture

for a seemingly endless time

                there was . .
                no sound . . no picture
                the screen went blank . . in the silence

                no house lights either
                it was . . pitch dark
                as dark, as black
                                as pitch

shouts rose of . .

HEY ! WHAT HAPPENED TO THE LIGHTS ?

dark theatre

                silence

no sound

                        pitch blackness

        then, in that eternal
        soundless, silent, black velvet moment

        I felt a light tap on my shoulder
        from somewhere behind me
        and a voice . . whispered in my ear . . so near

so near . . I felt his breath against my cheek

                        as he softly murmured

                        "darling ! thank God I found you !
                oh ! why didn't you wait for me ?
                I told you I would be back
                you should have known I would be back

                now you can't hear — or see
                and it serves you right for coming here
                                        without me
                you should have waited . . .
                so we could see this film together"

this was no ghost . . no ghost
the whisper was real
so real . . I could actually feel
his warm breath

                        as again he murmured
                        into my ear . . so near, so near

                        "it serves you right, for coming here
                        without me . . for not waiting . . "

I felt myself
                . . fainting, growing dizzy, losing consciousness

                        "you should have waited
                        so we could see this film together
                        but it's allright now . . I've found you
                        darling, don't be angry . . please
                                I was only teasing
                        I'm glad you're here . . I wanted so
                        for us to see this together
                                        why didn't you
                                                wait for me ?"

HEY ! COME ON UP THERE !

        WHAT'S GOING ON ?

    LET'S HAVE SOME LIGHTS !

then suddenly . . .

        as suddenly as the sound and lights
        had disappeared — they both returned

                the lights went on again

and the sound . . came crashing

in a burst of startling, now high pitched volume
Yves Montand was singing . . screaming . . to a pounding drum beat

"COME BACK TO ME ! COME BACK TO ME ! COME BACK !"

then Daisy's high, shrill shriek

"WILL YOU STOP BOTHERING ME ?"

and, as the sound and light
returned to the screen

I whirled around in my seat . . to meet

a pair of strange eyes

I faced a total stranger
and saw an instant shock upon his face
as though reflected from my own

. . he mumbled a flurry, then
of apologetic words

"oh, my god ! it isn't you . . I mean
it isn't her . . I mean, excuse me, Miss
you looked like . . . I thought . . well
you see
I thought that you were she . .
my girl . . she was supposed to meet me
in front of the theatre . . this afternoon
but the thing is
we had a fight last night — and . . I'm sorry
look, Miss, I'm sorry . . I made a mistake
it was so dark in here . . so dark
there was no light . . . and we had this quarrel
and I was late for our date . . and she
well, I missed her, I guess
or else . . she didn't come at all . . and
well . . I'm very sorry . . "

without answering, or even nodding in polite recognition
of his courteous, embarrassed apology, I left my seat
and ran up the aisle of that theatre
as though demons were chasing me . . I ran
my body fueled by a surge of desperate adrenalin

escape ! escape ! forget the rest of the film !
forget polite manners . . just escape . . get out of here !

then stopped — stopped dead
in the lobby

remembering something
                    unbidden

remembering *his* voice . . somewhere, sometime
long ago . . . . . disembodied voice
                    of my husband
            my love
                        asking me gently, curiously

                        "why are people so frightened
                                        of each other ?
                        always afraid to speak . . or smile
                        or be kind to strangers ?

                        did you ever notice people jammed together
                                closely, in an elevator ?
                        they just stand there, and stare
                        so numb . . at the floor numbers lighting up
                        above their heads, one-by-one
                        as if they had all been struck dumb
                                        not even smiling
                        frightened of one another
                        not even exchanging a smile of kindness
                        you'd think they were all waiting
                        for a time bomb to explode . . so very
                        frightened of another human being"

and I remembered . . when I first heard him
speak those words
I had feared them to be a gesture leading to promiscuity
only later understanding that he meant them simply as . . .
an endorsement of a gesture of kindness
toward a fellow human being . . not the first step
toward a casual sexual encounter or a romantic liaison

        although, it had been
        difficult for me to accept those words
        as he had meant them — a painful lesson to learn
        which might still burn
        if he were to, somehow, magically return
                            and repeat them today

still hard for me to believe that casual sexual encounters
could be separated from open kindness
                            between strangers
depending, of course, upon the motive
and the intent . . of each

but . . had I learned that lesson — even yet ?
a lesson only truly mastered
when complete trust in the one you love
who also loves you

                    . . has finally been mastered too

complete faith and trust in the one you love
who also loves only you
for perfect love casteth out all fear

        could I learn that lesson now
        would I trust him now
        if he . . if he were still here ?

    oh, hard, hard lesson — trust in love
    the most difficult and soul searching one
    all lovers must master, by far

                and does anyone, really — ever ?

lovers should remember that the prized gift of trusting
may be given without pain, only when the recipient of such trust
makes loyalty and love constantly plain — to be seen and heard
                    by tender glance, and loving word
for, constant reassurance of affection and devotion
is a necessary foundation of trust . . . . . and it must !
yes, it must be given freely
            before the need ever arises . . to ask

        faithfulness . . fidelity . . must not be *requested,* but *given*

        would — or could — Romeo or Juliet ever be mistrustful ?
        which one would ever dream to doubt the other
        with each lover offering such constant declaration . . and
        lacking this, then trust must tarnish with the rust
        of jealously and suspicion
                which are only lonely synonyms for fear

yet, a rust so easily removed — by love
in word and deed and glance made clear

        for, neither Time nor tide nor sea
        can keep my own away from me
                    . . as the poet wrote

nor *take* my own away from me, he might have added
if 'my own' declares repeatedly that he is, indeed, my own
or if she declares, as the case may be, to him — the same

    I felt a flush of shame

rush to my cheeks — then turned

. . . walked back down the aisle to where he sat
the unhappy fellow human being
whose sincere apology for his mistaken identity intrusion
I had so rudely ignored

while walking, wondering . .

could I believe my own kindness motive
would also be true of the one I loved, should he be here
and trying to cheer . . a strange woman ?

and knew I could not attribute my own innocence of intent
to him . . unless I had strong cause to know
that he loved only me
and could not be tempted by any other — ever

no, never . . . tempted
by any other — ever

then unexpectedly thought of her — the cool, sure one
becoming suddenly dizzy and ill, almost turning back
from my errand of mercy
at the agonizing recollection of that breach-of-trust
he claimed was caused by me
                    NO ! NO ! NO !
I still do not see
how that was caused by me !

NO ! it was not caused by me !

I forced myself to continue moving down the aisle, slower now
toward the disappointed man, from whom I ran so unkindly before
still uncertain, unsure of what to say

when I reached his seat, I noticed that he was not a man
but only a boy — of seventeen, or maybe eighteen

and, leaning down near him
saw that he'd been quietly sobbing
for, as he looked up in quick surprise
there were tears in his eyes
                    and streaked across his face

I hurriedly whispered, then
just these few words — I don't know why

"please don't cry . . I'm sure you'll find her, or she'll find you
just try to *believe* it's true, and expect . . . expect a miracle"

then walked back up the aisle, feeling strangely lighter
nearly floating . . on the memory of the fleeting flash of sudden hope
I had seen, for one brief second, pass across his face, and fill his eyes

    and my own eyes filled too, with tears
    for the first time in weeks, not for myself
            but for someone else
    whose sadness was as deep to him, as mine was to me
    at least for the moment, causing him comparable aching and longing

    and I prayed that those un-planned miracle words
    might, through some power of their own, ease the pain in his heart

when I walked outside
the rain had stopped

        the Sun was shining

I'll see the movie later
I murmured to myself, and hailed a taxi

    gave the driver the address of my small oceanside hotel
    leaned back in my seat, closed my eyes . . and thought of . . nothing

still lighter, floating . . gentler
softer . . . with my former tenseness gone
and somehow . . yes even the now familiar dread
                   was lifting
    easing slightly, it seemed

after I paid the driver, I walked to the Dolphin
past the parking lot, around the pink hibiscus and striped
                    tiger lillies
      . . the longer way
avoiding the lobby

    only because the mental hop scotch I'd been playing all day
    had depleted me, leaving no vitality
    to offer strangers . . in casual conversation

the fatigue a part, I suppose, of my floating lightness sensation
    brought on by the momentary elation
                on the boy's sad face
when I told him to expect
a miracle . .

maybe, just by expecting it, and by thinking this stranger
who was I . . . possessed some secret wisdom . . maybe faith alone
would reunite them . . simply by giving him more courage
                  to try
for, did not Jesus say often

when he performed miracles of healing
                              body, mind and soul

       Let it be done to you
          according to your faith ?

and had he not also said that . .

          whatsoever things ye desire
             pray as if ye had already received them
             and ye shall surely have them ?

but there was no way it would ever be
that whatsoever thing I desired . . could come to me
not even through faith as strong as the Rock of Gibralter

                    . . or as teeny-tiny as a mustard seed ?
like the faith of a child ?

the faith of a child — in the impossible ?

       did I have faith — or only hope
       of finding the answer ?

faith and hope

       the two are widely different
       weak hope . . and vibrant, unquestioning faith . . which is *knowing*
       different in both motive and results . . this I knew
       from everything spiritual I had learned was true
       through moments of joy . . and pain

when I reached my door, I unlocked it with the key
then locked it again, with the inside chain
walked to the bed, and threw myself across its virginal whiteness

       oh, I needed so to sleep !
       it seemed I had never been so tired, so craving sleep
       I closed my eyes . . and slept straight through
                              till the following morning

       . . . as I fell into the blankness
warm and quiet and soft

       I heard . . or remembered . . scattered pieces of the lyric
       from the theme of the movie I had partly seen . . a haunting refrain

       the words faded . . skimming in and out, through my brain
as the last dot-dashes of consciousness
                              before I slowly fell down below
                                     the trap door of sleep

but first I heard the crashing sound
of a strange, yet familiar chord . . in my inner ear
        strange . . yet so familiar
so well known
            CRASHING ! CRASHING !

 and saw . . . a rainbow
of brilliantly spectrumed colors, like an auric light
over the head of one . . with no features on his face

        blank face

all these impressions
        blending with the fading in-and-out
lyrical snowflakes . . falling
                    cool . .
                    and pure

    . . and white
            and clear . .

on a clear day
    rise and look around you

    . . and you'll see who you are !

            . . on a clear day . . . how it will astound you !

    when the glow . . of your being

outshines every star !

            you'll feel part of . . every mountain
            sea . . and shore

        you will hear
. . from far and near

                    . . a world you've never heard before !
        . . and on a clear day
on that clear day . .

        you can see forever . . and ever

and ever . . more

        then saw a blinding white light flash !
        from behind my closed eyes . . . against black velvet
        and heard the Colorado stranger saying . .

        "you must try to see the auric colors

of his individual spectrum . . . listen to the sound
of his harmonic . . chord vibration
his own . . . chord alone . . no other . . "

and fell into the deep
of sleep
. . . . hearing music

Beaches and Boulevards — Thursday

it was the morning of the third day
since I had checked into the small, beach front hotel
near a wishing well — on Tuesday last

feeling the Present fleeing too fast
I was trying to build a tower of truth for the Future
from the sand castle memories of the Past
tossing pennies of prayers
into the deeper wishing wells of my mind
still hoping to find . . a miracle

now I sat a quieter, less shivering Shiva
on this Pacific beach, which had drawn and pulled me
to its secrets

like the polarity of a magnetic Amulet
worn by some powerful High Priest of Atlantis
now lying buried beneath the floor of the opposite ocean

and was all Life, then, a polarity ?
all mystery contained, somehow, in this ?
even the mystery of the Eden Snake hiSS
which held the bleSSing of Adam
and the curSe of Eve ?

or was it the other way around
that the truth could be found ?

I sat on this lonely Laguna spot of Earth
watching the green-foamed, white bubbled surf
kissing the shore, her lover
. . still damp from her
now gentle, caressing him tenderly
subdued . . after the violence of her crashing against his rocky strength

last night
and he . . forgiving, as always

Canto Thirteen ☆ 371

the two inseparables, the surf and the shore
microcosm lovers
caught up in the passionate ebb and flow
of Nature's eternal periodicity

. . Nature's everchanging, yet consistent pattern
of conquering and submitting . . . . . of taking and giving

and then to rest again, each
in the warm beauty of the macrocosmic Sun
who permits the gentler Moon to rule the tides
for a greater purpose
not turning over to her his own bright command
but delegating a midnight authority to her Lunar control
with constant evolutionary wisdom

. . as the lover shore
to the moody surf . .

and as I sat there, I listened once more to tape cassetted music
this time, Puccini and Tchaikovsky replaced by Lerner, Alan Jay
not wanting to hear the lost chords
of the songs of longing, sung by yesterday

I had left back in Colorado
the cassette of the original musical score
from the film I'd seen the previous afternoon, only in part
but had found a new one in a nearby record store

now, as Streisand sang out the clarity of a clear day
in her belting, rock-it-to-me, sock-it-to-me way
urging me to rise, and look around me
for something both she and the composer promised
would absolutely astound me

I wondered . .

what did Barbra Streisand and Alan Jay Lerner know
that I did not ? or were they, like me
merely guessing . . and experimenting with truth ?

as I listened to the lyric
pouring its spring melody
into November's cold cup

I was desperately trying to see Forever. with my imperishable wish
to penetrate the curtain between my twin soul and myself
separating the Then of his reality and physical being
from the Now of his disappearance into . . . . . nothingness

no, Mr. Lerner — you do not have all the answers

your hopeful message is enlightening, but too ethereal for me
too ethereal to make me actually see
                              . . Forever
in any tangible, touching way
that matters . . .
neither you nor Puccini have successfully explained it

        but I thank you for trying
to raise the curtain of ignorance about living and dying
and your instinctive intuition may yet lead me . . somewhere
toward some prayer I have not yet learned to pray
some miracle mantra I have not yet been taught to say
which will open up a practical Heaven-on-Earth
with the key of Death and Birth
                if I can only find which lock it fits
    One Fine Day

                . . someway

I had come out on the beach this Thursday
on a foggy, somewhat soggy morning
trying to see Forever on a clear day . . but this one
was tinged with a fog of bluish-grey
                    that showed no signs of lifting soon

        I had come out to meditate on the shore, once more
        on this morning of the third day
                              . . shortly before noon
now, it was nearing Sunset again
where had the time gone ?

        Sunset . . my sadness hour, containing the fading twilight of hope
        and holding — or hiding — some inner fear . . oh !
        whatever the place, the month or the year
                        Sunset always frightened me

        . . . the morning of the third day ?

what memory trigger did that phrase pull
threatening a blast of truth . . . . . another bullet
from the repeating rifle of confusion ?

        . . it sounded so familiar

then I remembered — it was from the Bible
about the resurrection

        . . and on the morning of the third day . . he arose

I dug my bare toes

deeper into the sand

frowning at the innocent sandpipers, as I tried to understand
my inexplicable anxiety about the approaching Sunset

beginning by changing subjects in my mind, as quickly as I could
for this one had an eerie ring . . *on the third day*
he arose from the dead
and from the tomb

I had no room, now, for desolation
for dwelling on ghosts and such
for I had been immersing myself lately, entirely too much

in the subject of death

I needed to meditate upon the practical side of resurrection
not the intangible aspects or deceptive church dogmas
containing no shred of proof
no sensible explanation of how each person could rise
from the grave, as he did . . if he really did rise

which I doubted

the incident of the previous day, in the darkened, silent theatre
was sticking in my mind, like glue
refusing to come unstuck, or to be lifted
until properly analyzed and sifted, fancy from fact

the tear-streaked boy clearly possessed little tact
that was plain, from the words he whispered to me
when he imagined I was she — his girl
in the dimness of the theatre — and
even had I been the girl he was seeking
his remarks were blunt and chiding, as if he believed
the theatre management had conspired to shut off the light and sound
simply because she didn't wait till he came around
to make up their fight — and be forgiven

I smiled, thinking of his egocentricity
and wondering if his girl would have been pleased or annoyed
that he considered their personal quarrels
important enough for a mass universal conspiracy of silence
and lack of light
to punish her
for not waiting for him, after their fight

. . and hoping it was allright with the two of them by now
that they had finally found each other . . and the miracle of love

but as I pondered it, I realized

he may have been more correct than he guessed
about the involuntary meddling of the theatre management
in his romantic affairs

                  yes . . he may have been unconsciously right

for, his attitude of relating these apparently unrelated events
reflected a strange Universal Law I'd read about in esoteric texts

    the law of Synchronization of the Universe

or the Harmonics of the Universe

        it is taught, in metaphysics, according to ancient writings . .
        also according to modern mystics, including the respected Carl Jung
        that everything in the Universe, at any given moment of Time
            is synchronized to everything else
      all working together, all interlocked and interdependent
            all related, inseparable
        astrology itself being a demonstration of this law

because . .

              each human being upon this Earth
             is a living, walking Moment of Time

        each person . . the solidification-into-flesh
        of that exact instant of Time when he or she was born
        reflecting the pattern of planetary vibrations
            of whatever harmony and discord
        existed in the Universe . . at the moment of the first breath

representing literally, not just symbolically
the relationships of each planet to the other

    . . the natal positions of the Sun and Moon revealing even the attitudes
    of the infant's father to its mother

and also representing the relationships of all stars
moving and fixed . . to all other solar systems and galaxies

    so that, for example, a person born on March 7th, 1948
              at three fifteen P.M.
    is actually . . that Moment of Time
    represented at the geographical location of birth

almost as though, when people are meeting and mingling
it is really Moments of Time which meet and mingle
adding more comprehension to Einsteinic theories of Time's relativity
and making it easier to see how Time is single — is all One

    Past, Present and Future . . the same

not a separate plurality

still . .
     and I meditated deeper
  as I drew pictures in the sand
with a small stick . .

     . . of what use is this proven law of Synchronicity
  to me . . right now ? of what practical use to me
                   the Harmonics of the Universe ?

  . . . . supposedly, when something impresses itself upon the mind
with enough intensity to be considered a part of Beingness itself
     not minor worries . . petty problems
      nor trifles of fretting
but something of serious and real concern

     the solution to that problem is there for us to learn . . .
       the answer to that question lies
in the Universal Mind . . . infallibly there, to be plucked from the air
imbedded into the ethers, requiring only that one looks
                and listens . . for it
for, at the same time the question arises
to its greatest pitch of anxiety in the human heart
     since all is inter-related

when something is seriously wrong
and one honestly seeks guidance in the matter

   it may be found . . threaded through the ribbons
of the lyric of a song
       buried in the reporting of the five o'clock News
to arise unexpectedly at the turning of a dial

    . . . perhaps hiding within a chance remark
heard while one is moving through the rushing people traffic
walking along . . or crossing . . a street

    . . . voices discussing an unrelated subject
floating into the ear, in a familiar restaurant . . from customers
                   conversing
in a nearby booth
bearing for the aware — and for the truly listening
         some unsuspected truth

    sometimes, words dropped by a clerk
   a waiter, a waitress — occasionally a friend
     a relative . . an enemy
. . or a stranger

   these having no idea they are playing a cosmic part

in the Synchronicity drama, never guessing they're being employed
as channels for a message, symbolically relayed

messages which, if no one is there, or sufficiently aware
                                        to receive them
remain as pieces of themselves, in the larger puzzle

  let those who have eyes — see
    and let those who have ears — hear

            if one opens the eyes, to truly see
            and opens the ears, to truly hear
                        the messages coming through
            will be startlingly clear

yes, the boy was unconsciously right, to connect the lack of light
and the blackout of sound — with his own romance
for the personal message to his girl, had she cared to know
unlike its message to any other person present
was that — unless they reconciled their quarrel — all would be darkness

her message, yes — if she had been sitting there, instead of me
in some nearby seat, alone
through her unforgiveness and impatience with him
with no one to hold her hand . . no one to care or understand

      and then, with her boy friend's reappearance
the lights and music would have been restored again for her
had she been truly looking and listening

        but . . what was *my own* message in the theatre ?

there was surely no doubt
      when the sound and light had gone out
that my desperation and intensity
were deep — and needing, seeking answers

    the theatre was as black as a grave . . or a tomb

allright, the blackness, the darkness — the lack of light
I could understand and see its symbolism
yes, the message of *sight* I could comprehend
it meant that night . . is not the end
it lasts but for a little while, and then the dawn
                        for morning . . always comes
but what of the message of *sound* ?
the words he thought were whispered to another
were also meant for me, symbolically

    spoken by him — to her
    yet intended by Universal Synchronicity

for me — for me alone

the meaning I was supposed to hear was not clear
no more than this waning day is clear, I thought crossly
with its blue-grey mist . .

what were the words murmured into my ear ?

something about . . *you should have waited . . I said I would be back*
now you can't see . . can't hear . . why didn't you wait for me ?
I wanted us to share this film together . . . it serves you right . .

   no, I could not translate those words
   into any cryptic light . . of truth

I could not comprehend how those words could mean . .

         . . those words
            I wanted you to wait
               so we could see this film together

   . . . . what could they mean ?

then, looking up from the pictures I was drawing in the sand
the bent twig I was using as a pencil, fell from my trembling hand

     trembling because . . an icy shudder
         shook me unaware
     as I gazed out there . . across the water

        . . . . *the distant ships against the far horizon*
         were curtained from sight, invisible now . . . .

and I felt an unreasonable fright
for I saw that Sunset had come

       creeping up behind me, unexpected
       without warning

the Sunset hour I dreaded, feared
with illogical panic

       a Sunset hour without a Sun
       lacking even a rosy glow to dilute its sadness
                      and foreboding
the Sun was hiding
afraid, like me

for . . the harmless morning mist
  had grown into a shapeless, giant fog
    coming in across the strangely calm and quiet water

inching, inching, inching forward almost imperceptibly
deceptive, crawling . . as the tide
but steadily, surely . . gaining ground . . and inching

where had the birds flown ?

I was alone

yes, the giant, shapeless fog . . was gaining ground

I looked around

glanced up and down the beach
but could not see a distance of even twenty yards
ahead . . or behind

the fog was hanging thickly over the shore
and moving toward me . . silently

like some voiceless, blue-grey living thing
corpse-colored, slowly approaching

I leaped up from where I sat
and once more stared at the shrouded shoreline
seeing nothing but emptiness

. . as that familiar chill of dread began to spread
inside me
why had I not seen this coming ?
immersed in such intense and frowning meditation
drawing nothing in the sand . . . I had planned
to leave the beach before the twilight time

my heart pounding, I walked quickly
in the direction of safety . . to the entrance
leading up the back steps of my hotel

. . but where was it . . the entrance . . where ?

it was lost in fog and mist . . invisible

oh ! where is that landmark rock ?
I asked myself, with mounting fear
I must not be such a fool as to get lost out here

why had I lingered so long
to be caught by this gloomy land's end blending
of Sunset sadness and damp, grey fog ?

Canto Thirteen ☆ 379

then my thumb accidently pressed
the volume dial on the tape cassette I carried

    sending music to boom into the nothingness
    as Streisand's Daisy Gamble voice now rose and fell
    seeming to toll some kind of warning knell . . with each word

      . . . I heard
her sing

      . . *my dearest love, who existed in a dream*
        till this evening, when a wave came
          and swept me out to sea . .

did I hear, then
a distant sea gull scream

      . . or was it me ?

I turned off the sound
and walked faster . . faster

    looking anxiously for the landmark rock
    that marked the entrance of the steps up to the lobby
    to safety, lights . . and warmth

    but the fog grew
    thicker, like a shroud

damper

      greyer

          and I was cold and chilled

why hadn't I the sense to have avoided
this inclement weather
by remaining indoors, and trying to write
my Happiness poem inside my room ?

    walking briskly, then, I defied the gloom
    and nervously hummed the melody of *On a Clear Day*

incongruous song, to accompany me along
          this darkening beach
yet helping me to reach
a note of sanity and steadiness . . normalcy

    oh ! *where* is that rock ?

I seemed . .

     to have

          . . somehow

lost my way

      and then it happened

    what I had feared and dreaded on that dreary grey
    and unexpected wintry day . . in Colorado

      had become a reality

somewhere within my tortured brain, a thread of reason
some cord . . had snapped
and I had one instant thought of terror, like a flash of blue light

     they would give the cause of insanity as — grief

yes, I had surely gone mad

        for there before me . . but a few yards away
        surrounded by a mist, yet visible
        in a clearing pocket, opening in the fog
        walking directly toward me
            kicking aside a driftwood log
                with his foot
was . . . him

      he, who had died

    after years of silent threats and warnings
Sunset had, at last, kept its eldritch promise
        . . a promise I had always known
must be fulfilled
        and I was chilled

    chilled to the very marrow of the bone
    not by the dampness of the air alone
    but by the icy, dawning truth
    that this resurrection was of flesh and blood

yes, blood and flesh
not made of mist or fog

    no mere spirit would so roughly kick aside

a driftwood log . . nor imitate the solid sight
of that well remembered walk I knew

no conjured vision could adopt
that slightly-dropping-to-one-side pose of head
long arms dangling . . long legs striding, like a crane

seen just so, a hundred times

walking on the sands of other shores and beaches
where we had sunned ourselves, like lazy turtles of contentment
in past summer loving-times

and, since such a thing
simply *cannot* be . .

then I was . . I *must* be seeing this

with the wild, dilated eyes of sheer madness

the rising panic of my thoughts
took but an instant to pass
as though this moment had stopped — dead

to be photographed by Eternity

allowing Time itself to roll the film
to gauge the light and distance — before the shutter snapped
and the flash . . exploded

it was, to me, a scene of horror
unmatched by any tale of Poe
or song of woe . . or the graveyard scream
of any half-remembered nightmare dream
I ever knew

what does one do ?

where run, where hide
when such terror spreads inside ?

what words are fit to tell, or accurately describe
a sight one's eyes and brain both know
to be emphatically real — and no hallucination

no words, none

it must suffice to simply say
believe me, it was he

oh ! *believe* me, it was truly *he*

no spirit essence, ethereal ghost
or mirage formed from the thirst of longing . . no mere vision
composed of ethers, decomposed
           taking form and shape again

nor was this but the marked resemblance of a stranger — **NO !**
could I not, with normal physical sight
identify my own husband ? with my own eyes ?

    my heart swelled suddenly to bursting size
pounding in my breast a drumming beat

            and I grew faint and dizzy
            spinning in the thinning mist
            weaving now around me

    as he steadily approached
        deliberately, it seemed
relentlessly bearing down
        on me

                his eyes fixed directly on mine

closer, closer . .

    nearer, nearer

        oh, dear God, dear God
        what shall I do . . or say ?

the hairline, lock of hair hanging forward
yes . . . his alone

    large, soft brown, deep-set eyes
        with a glint of silvery-ocean-green spots
like tiny fish, swimming

            yes . . his eyes, just so

    the pronounced, unusually long lower lashes
spikey — always visible, even at a distance — especially
when wet . . from a shower or a swim
            or tears
which had earned for him
the nickname of "Eyes", in school

his lashes, yes

his ears too, protruding slightly
from his head . . long lobes

the Cherokee high cheekbones, tanned skin
his mouth . . oh, God ! yes . . his mouth

      and nose — nose exact
      but why not ?

why should I marvel that my own features
seen in a mirror were my own ?
or marvel, now that *his* nose should be so exactly
                           like *itself* ?

   no need to marvel
   that a nose looked like itself

does not the sand look like the sand ?
and my own hand like my own hand ?

      and as all things look . . however they look
      being but themselves
      as he was himself, *himself* . . none other

oh, this cannot, cannot be !
and yet — it is

          closer . . closer

   bearing down

      ten feet away . . still walking

nearer . . near

            now — here

and as those dear, familiar eyes
stared deeply into mine, I moaned, half audibly

      then . . his kissed-a-thousand-times-by-me mouth
      grinned its old remembered crooked grin

      as, passing me, and brushing my arm
      accidently ? I heard him say

        "hello ! isn't it a lovely day ?"

even his slight sarcasm
his old sardonic sense of humor
twinkling . . and . . . oh !

his voice, his voice, his voice
oh, God, you *know* it is his voice !

Jesus, help me . .

he walked on by
walked past me . . slowly
and the moistured wind
bore back to me . . the unmistakable scent
of Seaforth soap or shaving lotion

oh, Jesus, can you hear me ? God will not listen
but you know, Jesus, that it is he
oh, you can surely, surely see
that it is truly he
Jesus, help me, please !

his walk, his body . . his features, his voice
were heart-wrenching enough . . but this scent
this well remembered scent of Seaforth

slammed memory into me so hard
such vivid memory of loving mornings
loping back into bed
for only "one moment more"
a foamy kiss . . . and morning Oneness bliss

the kiss always demanding
an intimate encore of the passion shared
the night before

struck with such a sharp slap of remembrance
I abruptly turned, helpless to control my urge

. . whirled around
and sharply called his name . . *"Bill !"*

"come back ! come back !"

but . . . . . .   the beach was deserted

save for birds . . heard, not seen

caw ! caw ! caw !

crying into the silence of the fog
piercing the damp air

Canto Thirteen ☆ 385

one screaming
at a distance . . shrill
    caw !
                                    deserted beach
    no one there

    empty of all life
    except the unseen birds . . and I

my own voice
    echoed back
on the wind . . to taunt me

    my call, unheard
    by human ears

        had I, then, been hallucinating, after all ?
        instant relief ! I was *not* insane, driven so by grief

I had only seen a ghost, not flesh — no
simply a vision of the past
so real . . a shattering experience, but not new
as even calmer minds may sometimes do

        yes, even gifted scholars lose the way
        for brief moments — even those
        whose brains and minds are immune to illusion
                                    and self-deception
I have heard . .
they do

            another bird

    CAW ! CAW ! CAW !

    then screamed
or was it me ?

                    the beach was empty, but . . .

was he only a ghost
    now disappeared into thin air

or . .

            had the flesh and blood form gone, instead
            around the corner of the edge of the landmark rock
            I could now, at last, see just before me ?

around the corner of that rock, were the wooden steps
leading up the embankment to the back door of the hotel's lobby

had he done this

in the instant before I turned, and called to him
the waves drowning out the sound of my voice . . so he
could not hear me . . . and therefore, didn't answer
                                        or turn back ?

    it had grown darker, with approaching dusk
    and I could no longer see the water
    or the shoreline . . the fog was even thicker than before

suddenly, I had to know

    I had to know !

immediately . . hurry, hurry, hurry !

                                    run, run !

    heart thundering
    like a pounding hammer

I ran around the edge of the rock

        but . .

                        no one was there

    he was . .
            nowhere
in sight

            I felt a chill of fright

then leaped . . loped . . leaped !
two-at-a-time, up the decaying wooden steps

            and burst through the door
            into a lobby . . as silent as the beach

    empty

                        except for the clerk
                            half-dozing at the switchboard
                        behind the desk

        empty, silent lobby

gone

        gone

                        he was gone

or had never
been real at all ?

                        a ghost, a spirit only
        then . .

                in the growing, grey-violet dusk . . suddenly
                the lights automatically clicked on
                flooding the lobby with a warm, golden glow
                reality returned . . yet I still shivered

he had seemed so . . had looked so
like flesh and blood . . so solid appearing
he nearly *had* to be real

        but . .

the silent lobby
empty . . said no

                he was but a ghost, now gone
                no more to haunt me

I stood there, wondering
undecided what to do

                but knew . . I must accept this actuality
                whoever and whatever he had been — he was gone
                back into the mists from whence he came
                disappearing, perhaps, the instant I had called his name
                as though the sudden sharpness of my cry
                had broken the spell of his . . . ethereal . . . ? . . . manifestation

still depressed, even if no longer chased and haunted
I sighed . . and moved woodenly, with heavy steps
toward the desk
                to check my messages and mail

but . . what mail or messages could be here for me ?

        I had no reason to expect a friend
        to keep in touch, or try to reach me
        in this unannounced and out-of-season oceanside retreat
        where I had fled — or thought to flee
        from the nameless dread I named anyway . . and called
        the coming winter of happiness
                        the poverty of all emotion
        for, who would now
        communicate with me — and how ?

none, save wandering astral visitors

      wistful spirits, seeking company, ever-lonely
      and having little choice, being chained to some level of awareness
      not conducive to conviviality shared with those
                living in a world of three dimensions only

      traveling in etheric realms
      unreachable by those who might want to pass
      the time of day . . or night . . with them

such souls are spiritual beggars
who certainly cannot be choosers — and
was the one I saw along the shore just now
                such a beggar, then ?

      oh, darling, no !

please, God — not that
don't let him be so lonely

      better that it had been hallucination
      than the thought of him — an astral beggar
      I could not bear to image him a lonely spirit, lost

wandering on the wind out there . . and breathed a prayer

      . . oh ! let there be some other explanation
      anything but that he's so lonely
              anything but that . . my own madness even
and . .
      other than such astral entities
      who else would leave a message for me here ?

      no one . . except perhaps the Holy Ghost Himself — or Herself
      still pursuing the hopeless quest
      of redeeming one so conspicuously lost to former faith

but even so . .

      even should this Holy visitor . . friend or enemy ?
      be more successful in tracking down the quarry here
      than in my pachyderm-burial-ground in Colorado

. . and whether this persistent fraction
of the Trinity be . . he . . or she

      sex regardless, spirits do not write or phone
      or telegram, unless through 'Eastern Union' wire

      sometimes . . tapping out their soundless code of esp

more ancient, yet more swift and sure than Morse
to the initiated listener . . but this not I

initiated — me ?

no, I was far from being an Initiate
what mystery of death — or Life — had I yet solved ?

none — not one

I clung to but a single rock of hard-earned wisdom
that rock being — oh ! without equivocation
the necessity of fully penetrating the secrets of the former
before Heaven sends a single ray of light
to shine upon the meaning of the latter . . . yes
this I knew, if nothing more

the riddle of death must first be solved
its puzzle fitted, piece-by-piece together

before the game of Life may be understood
for, otherwise, what rules are there to follow ?

not even any way of determining if the game is worth winning
let alone playing — unless to kill Time
which might, after all, be the real secret of winning Life's game
and solving death's riddle too — the missing link between them

yes, Time . . the unknown quantity

the quality of it unknown too
and variable

Time — the fourth dimension

and science only barely able
to grasp the fundamentals of three . . let alone four . . or more
so obsessed by their 1-2-3 rules
that they insist on chopping Time into neatly packaged thirds
labeled Past — Present — and Future

ignoring the surprise package — the gift
still unopened . . of a believable and Eternal Now

although Einstein, with the curiosity of genius
and the naivete of a child
maybe peeked inside the wrappings of Eternity

oh ! the gift of a truly believable Now !
where he would always be . . as he was then

I may have penetrated the fourth dimension
along the shore, in the fog, briefly perhaps

    but if I should claim always to see him
    as I did . . oh, yes ! I *did* . . on the beach

if I clung to such a momentary vision
               of fourth dimensional comprehension
I would be judged unstable by all those
                   still stubbornly insisting upon existing
    in their cramped, three-sided boxes of Time

no wonder I've tended to turn away
from the benefits of prolonged meditation

    after all, where can it lead you ?
    either back from whence you started
    or into becoming a pariah
    for trying to live with a foot in two worlds

simultaneously

    neither choice is attractive — or comforting
    no . . neither result of such concentrated meditation
    is worth the effort . . or the brain fatigue

fine choice !

    around the circle of material ignorance . . and back again
    or Bellevue, if you should make a breakthrough
    like deciding which you prefer — death by boredom
                    or by ridicule
    but in any case, eventual death

        of deeper truth

and so, lacking now, even the dubious excitement
of the fourth dimensional mirage on the beach
                   . . if such, indeed, it was

    I walked un-expectant
    to the desk

        across a lobby oddly haunted by omission

haunted by the lack of haunting . .
by the absence of those ethers I had seen

    a non sequitur, yet true

        I stood there at the counter . . weary

with dreary and defeated posture
thinking how unkind it was of me . . to awaken
the dozing clerk
with such a futile inquiry concerning messages or mail
I knew would not be waiting

in my name

still, so much needing to perform
a mundane, ordinary function of this sort
    which could slide me back
without a jolt, or astral twitch, or jerk
into the world of stability

                or rather . . back into the insanity
                we have been taught to call reality

                        mistakenly

I waited for the groggy hotel manager, with the unlikely name of Kit Carson
awakened from his semi-sleep into his usual cheerful alertness
by the intrusion of my voice
to give his usual negative response

                " . . no mail, no calls
                    no messages in your box today, Miss"

also waiting for the thin satisfaction
of the "Miss" I normally heard, instead of "Madame"
possibly implying I was not yet showing . .
                    . . despite my aged-by-centuries despair
my inner chronological calendar
which gave my date of birth as long enough ago
to make me one hundred and three, going on one hundred and four

    the Miss instead of Madame brought . . small comfort
    yet, still a comfort
    in the knowing that I projected spring outside

        and winter inside only

but . . for how long ?

        then forgot this minor feminine vanity
        the instant I heard him say

                "just one letter here today
                        for you, Miss
                sorry it's been opened, but you see . . "

oh, God !
    oh, Jesus !

no, no, no !
             it can't be true !

NO ! his writing . . **HIS WRITING** . . on the envelope

how could it be from *him ?*
yet, I knew that script . . oh, how well I knew
that familiar writing
          scribbled, as dwarfs or druids write

          was this a fourth-dimensional breakthrough ?

if so, I dared not feel the wild elation of the psychic pioneer
since I knew well the synonym for such a Columbus-like discovery
into the world of Time, not flat — but round and circular
would be . . oh, I could take my choice of

                    crackers, nutty-as-a-fruit-cake, off-the-wall
                    schizophrenic, paranoic, batty, dotty
                    pixilated, flaky — or plain old-fashioned cukoo

my heart truly trembled, as did my hand
each of them shocked by seeing the letter, on their own
without the direction of my mind
for did they not also, my heart and hand — have cause to tremble
have reason to remember too — and miss him ?

     . . as the man behind the desk gave me the letter
which I accepted numbly, simply staring
               he also handed me some other papers
newspaper clippings, and some cards
                         all mine

          . . and continued explaining

while this new jolt, or lightning bolt
of mixed terror and miracle hope
gradually subsided, as the others had before
into grey depression and futility
and the quiet desperation of the certainty
that there was no magical place of Time and Space
called . . an eternal Now

               " . . . because, you see . . the letter"

               he went on

               " . . it was among the things you dropped
               in the coffee shop next door
                              yesterday morning
               when you were having breakfast

Canto Thirteen ☆ 393

or possibly . . as you were paying your check
but you disappeared before the girl
                              could catch you
so she brought them here, for us to hold . . and
since your name was on the cards
although the surname on the letter's envelope
was different . . we assumed

                    that all the items belonged to you
                              but I assure you . . .
                    we did not intend . . that is, you see
                    as you will notice, the letter
                    has already been opened . . and we
                    did not open it ourselves . . I hope you . . "

as his apologetic voice
trailed away
I hurried to end his anxiety

"yes, it was already opened . . see ?
perhaps you didn't look at the postmark
but the date is some years back . . from Germany

I do thank you for keeping
all these papers I carelessly lost
and . . may I . . give you something
for your trouble ?"

                    but he waved away my offer
                    and returned to the switchboard
                    now blazing with impatient callers

                         mumbling . . "oh, it was
                         no trouble at all . . glad to be
                                   of help, Miss"

        of help ?

nice man, but
this was no help

            no help to feel my heart
            leap so, with hope . . and soar

. . and wing

        and sing . .

        to fill with terror, yes
        but terror only of the unknown
        to leap toward a mad-miracle prayer

of maybe, maybe, oh, just maybe . .

     then to crash

into the discovery of this letter, returned
to torture me again
made even more painful by the newspaper clipping
of his obituary . . among the other papers

  of what help is this ?

I should have known that there is no Eternal Now
in which the dead can write
                  from above, or from below
for . . when they go
the dead are forever gone
how well I know — but I forgot

  I forgot, in hoping for the mad miracle of maybe

and I leaned upon the counter, for support
my legs no longer willing to take the risk themselves
of holding me up

    feeling a wave of consuming sadness sweep over me
    oh ! who can force words to describe desolation ?

it is a mood of emptiness and hopelessness
impossible to comprehend — unless felt

    and once experienced, leaves scars
    which may fade, with time . . but which never disappear

desolation is a barren landscape
offering no relief from thirst, save for the mockery of mirage

    why do I still hope — why ?

    when people die, they die

    why, oh, why can't I realize that ?
    I believe it — I know it
    but why can't I . . . . *realize* it ?

. . and I glanced once more at the contents of his letter
eyes skimming the words . . . wondering if, by various mischiefy of fate
it was destined to thus plague me periodically

    long ago written words . . flying through my consciousness
like winging birds of memory . . . . rustling leaves of yesterday

. . do you love some image of myself, or me ?

so worried about this test
             . . the later it gets . .

. . but don't worry
                    . . I know we're going to pass it

       if we can just remember to . .

baby wife, spunky mouse-spouse

                    . . sorry I was so unkind
                            . . so blind
    so blind . .

                it is such a hard test we are taking
                                . . you and I
    . . if I grew a beard

       or if my skin should turn green
                        . . nose reversed
whatever mutation . .

                a monster, maybe — but still me

       would you love me then ?

. . and if my hair

            . . this test of separation

            as the words leaped up from the page
            then faded again, crazily tumbled and jumbled
            tears stung my eyes bitterly
                and I silently cried out to him

would I know you ? yes, yes, of course I would !
and never mind a change of hair — oh !
and never mind a beard — or clean-shaven
you should never have feared
that I would not know you . . anywhere . . on Earth
    in Heaven . . or in hell

did I not recognize you
on the beach, at Sunset, just now
in whatever form you took ?

    did I not know you instantly . . even though
    there was no reason to anticipate you there — by all the rigid rules

of death and Life ?
                        yet, I knew . . I *knew* that it was you !
      I knew . .

why did you disappear so quickly from my sight
leaving me only the parting comfort of one brief greeting

        . . so few words ?

I had no cause to expect you to appear, but I knew, I knew . . . .
      you were not merely a ghost
and I knew it was no stranger, spelling danger
                        no, it was not a stranger

        oh ! why didn't I return your greeting
            speak back to you ?
        is there some special mystical alchemy that decrees
            I must first show — that I know
        before you can remain . .
                        and allow me to touch you, hear you
        see you more closely . . hear your voice
                            speak longer ?
yes, I should have replied to you
when you first spoke
why didn't I speak back ?

        and as I questioned myself silently
        with these imponderables . .

            I saw there
                resting on the counter

      his hand

                the one on which I slipped the gold ring
                so cold and still, in the coffin
                        so cold . . but still dear
                familiar hand

I would know his hand
from one hundred million others

        it was his hand, even to the long, slender fingers
        and the odd-shaped half moon on the thumb nail
        smashed that day, closing the car door
                    . . the day I had recalled
        this past Tuesday, sitting on the shore
                    . . as Butterfly cried

        it was

Canto Thirteen ☆ 397

his hand

could that hand be attached
to the same flesh . . or etheric ? body
I had seen pass by me, on the beach

and which had spoken to me
with his voice . . calling this afternoon of fog-drenched haunting
sarcastically . . . a lovely day ?

I hardly dared look
but forced my head to turn
my eyes to see
       . . and

  it was he

      it was he, the same

       standing there, so tall
       towering above me, looking down
       and smiling . . eyes gazing into mine

   eyes gazing down
his eyes . . spikey lower lashes . . his eyes

dark, deep brown

   but now . . oddly . . wearing glasses

which he never wore . . .
he wore no glasses by the water, did he ?

  and the hair . .
the hair was brushed back more smoothly
than before, along the shore

  not falling over his high forehead in the careless way
he used to wear it . . and as the breeze had blown it . . no
it was brushed back now, revealing the same prominent temples
   more severely . . . than he had ever worn his hair
      . . yet still the same known
   chestnut brown and gold streaked color

I won't be fooled by trivial things
like glasses, and a way of wearing the hair

  he is so tall . . so tall
  exactly the same height . . . six foot two . . . and easily measured
  by how high I must raise my eyes to meet his
      . . as I used to do

and all the other features too
are there . . high Indian cheekbones

    ears . . nose . . coloring . . and mouth
        oh ! mouth . . mouth that I have kissed
    and missed . . and missed

        then noticed . . even the front teeth were protruding
          slightly, like before

    and saw his mouth once more . . gently twist itself
into that old remembered crooked grin, as on the beach

        and heard him say . .

oh ! I was right
        about the voice
it is . . *his*

            and heard him say

            "it's still a lovely day, don't you think ?"

I must have stared at him, then
like some wild creature of the woods
caught unaware, by a hunter
for that is how I felt, exactly . . hunted, caught

and saw him hesitate a second only
when I did not — could not — answer

          then repeat . . "it's still a lovely day
          if you like fog as thick as pea soup

           . . I meant to stop, when we passed on
                the beach
          and tell you I enjoyed your music
          which I heard clearly
              from where I was lying in the sand
          behind some rocks nearby
              I don't believe . .
          you noticed me there . . . "

the crooked grin stretched wider
until I felt almost as though my very heart reached out
              toward him
did he notice ?
is such a thing as a heart reaching out . . visible ?

        he went on

        "I meant to tell you that I enjoyed the music

and I wanted to ask you . . . but . . well
you seemed in some way
to be meditating on something . .
                                        far away
and I felt I might be intruding
if I spoke to you further then, but . . . "

      he paused

" . . so I showered and changed in my room
and stopped in the lobby
      hoping I might see you again
to ask you . . . well, you see
I'm here on business and leaving
in the morning, so I thought perhaps . . . "

then once more
I was aware of the strong scent of *Seaforth*
      from him
   and I was overcome
by this sharp, insistent tug of memory

   scents are powerful movers of the subconscious
so overcome was I . . . that my first words
were ridiculously illogical . . . personal, inappropriate
to exchange with a stranger

      but, no, not a stranger
      it was my husband

I blushed as I spoke, unable to control my words
as I was unable to hide my shock
and heard my own voice asking, as though it came
from far away . .

  "do you . . I mean, are you wearing . . ?"

      he smiled a deeper smile

      "*Seaforth* — it's called
I've used it for many years . . I guess
it reminds me of the ocean
      and of someone . . a girl
who gave it to me for Christmas
      a very long time ago"

an uncontrollable tremble
accompanied by a sharp pain
swept through me . .

      he flushed slightly

> "maybe it's too strong . . I hope
>   it doesn't offend you"

next, he tried to switch his own
discomforture to me — how well I knew that trick !
that clever Gemini sleight-of-tongue
with words . . that Mercury glibness of speech
and wondered how to find a tactful way
                       to ask his Sun Sign

> "does it offend you ?" he repeated
> I'm sorry if it does . . but I didn't notice
>   because of your perfume
> it was quite striking, though pleasant
> even on the beach . . in all that foggy air
> do you wear . . . *Je Reviens* ? or perhaps *Chanel* ?
> I have quite a nose for women's colognes"

"from your experiences
with . . so many women ?"

I asked with shocking bitterness

> he looked surprised
> but did not reply

I owed him an apology
but, did I ? if so, why ?

of course, *he* would know I wore either *Chanel*
or *Je Reviens* . . .

so I spoke quickly

"yes, *Je Reviens* — I'm sorry I asked
such a personal question — forgive my rudeness
it doesn't offend me at all
it's only that . . you see . . well, I once
knew someone, and he . . . "

and could not finish

> recovered, now
> from his momentary embarrassment
> he smiled again, remarking smoothly

> "well, it's good to know
> we like each other's choice of scents
> and that can be a very personal thing
> like food or drink . . . music or art
>   do you think perhaps it means

Canto Thirteen ☆ 401

we might be compatible enough
                              to share . . . something cool ?
                    there's a restaurant next door
                    and we wouldn't have to swim through
                                        the fog again . . "

"something cool ?"
I repeated after him, like a parrot

                    "something cool and refreshing . . yes
                    I've heard the natives around here
                    produce a superb ice cold coconut milk
                    from ordinary cows . . "

I smiled politely at his intended cleverness
or thought I did

                    "but . . something cool can also mean
                    an icy glass of orange crush . . . or, for a lush
                    I suppose something cool
                    can mean an entire lost-week-end
                    it depends on the interpretation
                                        and . . personal desire
                    something cool can just as well be
                    as innocent as a breath of fresh air on a muggy day

                    you're like that, you know
                    or . . *do* you know
                              how very much like a spring breeze you are ?
                    you reminded me of a druid on the beach"

my thoughts scattered through my brain
like frightened swallows
oh, he had not lost an ounce of his charm
and social ease . . . smoothness of manner
adroitness with words
          . . quick, clever . . persuading

no, he had not lost . . . . . . but, who *was* he ?
who was he
          . . . . and *what* was he ?

and . . how did he know
the magic password — *druid* ?

          had I not discarded the Saturn-Seven-cycle
          soul change possibility
          of his return to me, in another body Temple ?

          yes, discarded it as illogical
          that rainy, sleepless night in New York

because of the memories of childhood

yet . . maybe

     there might be some metaphysical rule
     about the mind's memory I had not yet learned
     something . . I didn't know
     which would account for the remaining memories of childhood
     and make such a soul transference
                    feasible and logical after all

if so . . perhaps

     maybe his soul had entered *this* Body Temple, and . .

no . . this could be no *new* Temple
          now inhabited by the him-of-him

where could he have found a Temple
          which was such an exact duplicate of the former ?

this was — this had to be the *same* Temple, the same flesh body
not merely one of similar appearance
                         . . the same . . exact
          identical

and therefore, it was truly and totally, completely — him
somehow resurrected . . but in what manner ?

     not resurrected soul alone
     but resurrected Body Temple too

and this could not, could not be true — unless
I was hallucinating . . observing some mad mirage of grief
or had perhaps stumbled on the key
to existing momentarily in an eternal and believable Now

     but, if this were so
     then why did he not recognize me too
     and wonder at this miracle
          of time-displacement ?

          he had given no real sign that he . . . recognized me . . as *me*

whatever the answer might be
I could only discover it
          by accepting his invitation
to share something cool
          . . though, as a rule
I would not have made a date on such a casual pretext
with a stranger of the opposite sex

I have been friendly with strangers, yes
even given gifts to them . . such as books . . and time
and conversation
     but . . this sort of date was a different situation
still, I replied . .

"yes, I'd like something cool — it does sound
somehow, refreshing . . . after
     such a dreary, grey and foggy day"

               his reaction to my somewhat numb acceptance
               was immediate, grinning . . bright

                    "great ! I *knew* you would say yes !"

something was — not quite right
I sensed a sort of broken karmic rhythm here
a chord of music, indistinct . . unclear

I was ultra sensitive, I guess — but
     I wished he hadn't said
that he *knew* I would . . . say yes

     he would have known
          that it was more like me to say — no
although
     perhaps he only meant that he thought
     I might say yes — this one time

the scene simply would not rhyme
                              not in any way
this haunted day . . had been against all rhyme and reason
logic . . and common sense

     I tried to fence . . and countered with

"I can only join you for a few minutes or so"

               he smiled

                    "then, shall we go ?
                    if we have only such a few minutes
                    we don't want to waste even one"

still wavering inwardly, see-sawing with indecision
in the face of this unexpected memory collision
I followed him through the door, in the obedient haze
of one following an usher into the semi-darkness of a theatre

          unsure of the way — uncertain, even
          of wanting to see the play — fearing its denouement

but it was too late
to turn back from this drama of Fate

the curtain was already rising on the stage set by Time
the dialogue written by Destiny, even now being spoken

by the soul's precognitive pantomime

the eyes . .

have rightly been called the windows of the soul
for the soul hides behind them
as an actor in the wings, wearing the disguise required
by the role played, in each incarnation

and so . . I searched carefully his eyes
for some flash of recognition of the soul I knew as my twin, within
surely easy to identify, if I were willing to try

was the actor lurking there really *he* . . .
truly the other half of me ?
or was that twin of my own self not risen to confront me
with this mad miracle of re-joining, here on Earth
but waiting, instead, for reunion in some far off Heaven ?

the lights were not bright enough to mirror such reflection
as we sat facing one another in the booth of the restaurant — bar
or nightclub . . it seemed to be all three
serving a trinity of purposes

as I tried to compose my features
hiding my uneasiness beneath a coolness and calm
I didn't feel

he spoke

"you are so quiet . . as you were
on the beach
is this your usual way with strangers ?"

then he charmed me
with his painfully remembered
little-boy crooked grin once more
or attempted to do so

"my way with strangers"
I replied stiffly

"is not to share a rendezvous for something cool
just because we happened to say hello . . .

I don't even know your name
        . . nor do you know mine"

                    "that's fine ! makes it like a game . .
                    let's don't tell each other right away
                    it will keep everything more mysterious
                                        between us"

"what an odd thing to say !"
I exclaimed

            then immediately realized
            how rigid-frigid I must sound

            he was merely trying to be light and amusing
            yet succeeding only in confusing
            and I felt . . so defensive
            nevertheless, I tried again, and said . . . .

"I'm not normally shy with strangers
        or with anyone
my astrological Sun Sign is Aries — and Rams
are not noted for timidity
or for social frigidity . . belonging to the element of Fire"

if I seem quiet, it's because recently, I . .
but first — what is your Sun Sign ?
I was wondering if perhaps, you might be a Gemini . . "

                    "that's quite clever of you, really !
                    I'm not so expert at guessing such things
                    yes, I am the Twins — or a Gemini
                    two-people-in-one
                            isn't that what they say ?"

I knew it, I knew it !
            I thought
but replied simply

"yes . . that's what they say"

    strange remark for him to make
        'two-people-in-one'
    especially in view of his teasing refusal
    to give me his name . . or ask for mine

then, from out of nowhere, came the waiter
to take our order . . and I said

"a lemonade with lime, please
and crushed ice"

and heard him say . .

"I'll have a double scotch on the rocks
with no fog
                    . . only a light mist of soda"

scotch, not vodka ?
I wondered

                    he interrupted my private musing
                    swiftly with . .

                    "I usually drink vodka
                    but everything is so . . . unusual today
                    it seems to fit right in with the scene
                    not to order in the ordinary way
                                        . . don't you think ?"

I was struck silent by his apparent reading of my mind
and what appeared to be the deliberate symbolism of his remark
unable to utter a word in reply, I stared intently
        as though admiring the decor
at a cluster of coconuts and a stuffed mohair monkey
hanging above the door, directly behind him
feeling again that slow spreading dread of the unknown

                    he repeated his question

                    "a most unusual day, don't you agree ?"

I answered, hesitating
my voice halting only slightly

"yes, it has been . . unusual . . for me
in many ways, I suppose
first, so foggy on the beach, I nearly lost my way
then after that, well . . "

                    and heard him say

                    "it can be frightening to be lost
                    but you've been found now
                                . . so don't look so sad"

oh ! why did every word he spoke
seem to contain secret pebbles of twin meanings
that struck ripples of response
from the bubbling brook of hope within me ?
was he merely flirting ? were these
but typical Gemini gems of charming repartee
springing from a quick and clever Mercurial brain ?

.... or were they coded words of mystery and love
welling up from some deeper knowing of his spirit . . and growing
from an inner recognition, as yet unspoken between us ?
were we reading each other's minds — or was I alone reading
an imaginary story on a blank page ?
             sometimes, his eyes did seem blank
     but at other times . .

I was relieved to see the waiter return
dutifully playing the second entrance of his walk-on part
                  in this unfinished Drama
giving me more time to search my heart for answers
                          and his eyes . . for clues

blessed man, bringing our order
and thereby saving me from the necessity of comment
on his last observation — that I had been lost
                       but now was found

                    "say, garcon !
                    the next time you're back around
                    you'd better bring me a second double Scotch
                    to save yourself another trip"

oh, God, don't let it be . . .
don't let him still be drowning in an alcoholic sea
         was he still drowning ?
I felt myself frowning

             "and you, Miss ?
             what about you ?"

for a wild and weaving moment, I thought some Master had inquired
if I, too, might be drowning in my own kind of ocean
of recrimination, unforgiveness and bitterness
an example of Universal synchronization
perhaps a self accusation, not consciously suspected
but channeled back to me, through the waiter

             "and you, Miss ?"

"I beg your pardon ?
no . . nothing more for me, thank you"

     he had noticed my frown, and smiled an abashed smile
        gently curving the lips I had so often kissed
lips which had whispered so many secret love words
into my ear . . then lifted his glass, and said . .

                    "Cheers ! one drink may not be enough
                    to steady my nerves

this has been, not only an unusual
                   but a tiring day
         exhausting for me in more than one way
         first, some unanticipated business snarls
         then, of course, the unexpected
         and very pleasant surprise . . of you"

I wanted to reply, in imitation of his airy glibness
with some remark, such as: oh, yes ! it must indeed be tiring
requiring, I imagine, great amounts of etheric energy
to pull off complicated ghost maneuvers like this

but I said nothing, continuing to stare
at the glassy-eyed monkey, clutching coconuts on the bamboo branch
tearing a paper napkin to shreds beneath the table
where he couldn't see my nervous hands

         inwardly, I cried out . . please !
oh, please don't tease me so — stop this cruel game
and tell me your real name, who you really are
have we truly found and touched a star ?
a star of Time . . . have we discovered our own Eternal Now ?

         your eyes, your hair, your mouth . . somehow
         yes, and your cheek and ears
         even your hands and nails . . your voice and laugh
         are so alike . . so like his . . identical

your speech patterns, words, light sarcasm
sardonic wit, twinkling tenderness
so like him, so like him ! or . . if you *are* he
then . . so like *you*

I simply must know what is true — and what is false
              oh, tell me soon !
tell me if perhaps I died on the beach this afternoon
then joined you somewhere on another awareness plane

         . . or if you have returned from the world of the dead
to the world of the living, where I still remain
                   to join me instead

my thoughts ran wild and uncontrolled
I felt as though I'd been cursed, as the gypsies say
by having heard the mad call, the crazy cry of a loon
and thought . . if only I were near enough to pick up the scent
of his skin and hair perfume . . they would tell me . . yes

the voice and features could be an accident, sheer coincidence only
and even all the other things . . perhaps imagined
because I've been so very, very lonely

but not your individual scent of skin and hair
                        the smell of you, I thought

            the scent transferred somehow, I know
from Temple to Temple . . brought in some mystical way
by the soul itself, to echo its inner essence
                        to the perceptive
        the smell of you
that always told me I was home, when I was in your arms
could not be conjured or imagined

        I mused upon all this
        yet dared not lean near enough to try love's test

then suddenly, I noticed
beneath his chin
a jagged, faded pink, triangular shaped scar
                        oh, God !
the very same as his — as *his*
from a dog bite
            when he was three or four
by a neighbor's dog, one summer

        I could bear no more — and, forgetting all pretense of manners
        poise, or social grace
        I stared at his familiar face, looked deeply into his eyes
        still veiled with the soul's disguise
        and fired a direct question, point blank

"whoever you are, now look here — I don't mean to be rude
but you remind me so . . . you remind me so
of someone I used to know
and I . . well, do you mind if I ask some personal questions
just to be sure I haven't taken leave of all my senses ?
I'm certain I must be wrong about what I'm thinking
but you . . oh, you *do* remind me of that someone so . . .
and I simply have to know"

                    he gazed at me with . . was it
                    mild surprise — or comprehending patience ?
                    tender tolerance — or amusement ?
                    I could not tell

        then, swallowing the last drops in his glass
        and reaching for the second, he said

                    "yes, I rather thought I did . . and you
                    well, you've been reminding me
                                of someone too
                    so, go ahead, ask anything you like
                    it's quite allright, even if . . "

he smiled

" . . even if the discovery of the reason
for our familiarity . . takes all night"

I disliked the implication inherent in his words
but decided, for the present at least, to ignore it
then asked him bluntly

"the scar beneath your chin
how did you get it — and when ?"

unconsciously
he touched it lightly with his fingers

"when ? this scar ? let's see . .
I guess when I was about nine or ten
a neighbor's dog got loose
it had, I think, distemper . . and I was
playing in the yard . . I remember
that the tetanus shot was . . "

"please, I . . I'd rather not
hear the whole story"
                    I interrupted rudely
"I don't mean to sound unkind, but . . "

                    "not at all . . I understand"

"and your line of business ?"

                    "I'm with a beverage firm, based in Canada
                    I am their representative in the States"

"did you — did you ever
want to become a doctor ?"

                    he grinned, and seemed
                    honestly surprised
                    or was he simply teasing ?

                    "you really must read minds ! why, yes
                    as a matter of fact, I was in Med school
                    two of them, actually . . . . "

oh, God . . oh, God !

                    "but I didn't stay, you see . . because
                    most of the pre-med students I knew
                    were in it for the financial rewards
                    not all, of course, but many, and I . . . . "

Canto Thirteen ☆ 411

I waited for him to tell me
that was why he left medical school
because it hurt him so to know
how many doctors have no real wish to heal
but choose their profession because . . .

           " . . I discovered that physicians don't earn
           as much as some people believe
           my annual income with this Canadian firm
           tops that of most established surgeons
           and without all that brain-busting study"

    the crooked grin again
    yet now, not so reminiscent of a small boy
    some innocence gone . . .

"I see . . then that's why
you didn't become a doctor . . well . . "

  my heart still reached stubbornly for a star
  disregarding the discordant warning notes
  and the swiftly emerging broken rhythm pattern

"well, then — perhaps you thought instead
that you might heal with music, or art
or through writing . . I mean
you said you enjoyed my music on the beach . . "

  oh, why did I still strain for some familiar chord ?

           a look of genuine puzzlement
           passed over his features

           "did you say heal — with music or art
           or through writing ?

           I'm afraid I don't understand exactly
           what you mean
           is that some occult trick, like witchcraft ?
           how can one heal in such a way ?
           surely a composer can't set a broken bone
           nor can an artist or a painter
                       operate upon the spine
           you must be joking
           what would Da Vinci or Tchaikovsky do
           at Johns Hopkins — or any hospital ?
           paint murals ? install a stereo ?"

my soul was sinking fast, into a black sea of despair
numbed by awful waves of ice cold water
but there was one word — a life raft

and I grabbed it quickly, groping
in the dim and smoky air

"Tchaikovsky ? you like his music then ?"
I asked, my pulse pounding an off-key melody

           "I wouldn't say I particularly *dis*like him
           but he wouldn't be my first choice
           on a romantic evening like this . . .
           Tchaikovsky as a background
           for such an unusual twilight of reality
           as we seem to be swimming through together ?
                  I think not . .
           that classical, long hair music
           doesn't really turn me on, you know ?
           but *you* do . . *you* turn me on

           I was just about to ask
           if you have some more modern tapes to play
           than those you were listening to today
           and yesterday . . and the other afternoon
           that opera
                with the soprano yelling in Italian
           well, that turned me off too . . .

           oh, I've noticed you before this sunset
           sitting there alone on the beach
           and somehow, intuitively I knew
           I'd find some way to break through to you
           so we could get to know each other better
                  before I had to leave

           as for music, I like the beat of rock
           it calls to something primitive in me . .
           and the cooler folk albums
                and some country western too
           but — how about you ?
           what do you really like
           when you're not listening to the classics ?
           we could stop at the music store
           down the street . . . pick up some tapes
           and stroll along the shore tonight
                don't worry
           I promise you won't get lost this time
           or if you do, we'll get lost together
                what's wrong ?
           you've become quiet again
           did I say something to disturb you ?"

I was fighting the drowning

fighting, fighting — insisting on knighting this stranger
and finding my Holy Grail
    blindly groping, still reaching . . I asked
"do you . . like to ski ?"

                        "waiter ! another double here !
                        make that two — another lemonade for you ?"

"no, no — nothing for me"

                        "yes, I love to ski — mad about it
                        is there anything you don't know
                        about my personal life and habits ?"

"does it make you feel . . as if you
were . . expanding into the Universe ?"

                        "it makes me feel like expanding into
                        . . a deeper knowing of you
                        say, could you steal a weekend away ?
                        there's this terrific ski lodge I know
                        where they always have snow
                                in November . . and we . . "

"I'm sorry . . I merely asked if you like to ski
I don't mean to pry, it's just that I . . . "

          he grew quieter, less certain
          sensing now, that the Carousel was spinning
          too fast . . and retreated
          into a slower tempo . . a softer beat

                        "forgive me, I guess I got carried away
                        by the unusual experience of today
                        I didn't mean to say . . that is
                        this man . . who looks so much like me
                        you must love him very much
                                  are you divorced — or separated ?
                        or is he — was he — a lover ?
                        I'm sorry too, for being so personal . . but
                        as long as we've gone this far . . . "

          he was right, of course
          it was too late for shy reticence
          we had, indeed, already gone too far

with my casual acceptance of his invitation for something cool
breaking every social etiquette rule
and . . with my own probing inquiries setting the mood
how could I brood, and accuse him, now — of insulting me
in blushing maidenly modesty

.. or claim an invasion of privacy ?

"he was .. my husband
and like the Bill from *Carousel*
        he was always reaching for a star
we were divorced, yes
but now he is .. "

                I spoke so low, he had to bend his head toward me
                        to hear my words
                and I trembled, lest he lean .. too near

" .. he is dead"

                        "I'm sorry to hear that"
                                he said

yes, I thought
he is dead, dead, *dead*

                        "I lost my wife too
                        the one who looked like you — I mean
                        you remind me of her so
                                but that was .. a long time ago"

he also lost his wife ? Oh ! maybe ..
maybe, maybe .. through some twisted turn of Fate
it might not be too late !

my brain was spinning, spinning
maybe there was still some way of winning
        this game with death
I took a deep breath — made one last, desperate attempt
to match a falling snowflake
                .. and asked one more question

"did you .. do you have
any children ?"

                        "we lost three"

oh, symphony, symphony, symphony !

        then, a jarring note
like a cymbal crashing
in the middle of a violin solo

                        "we lost three — but it was years ago
                        and life is too short
                        to mourn the dead forever, you know ?

how about seeing a movie tonight ?
maybe that would cheer you up
                    . . remove your frown
there are two films playing
in this god-forsaken small town
one is some musical drag
about reincarnation — and the time lag
I believe it's called *On a Clear Day*
or something equally corny
anyway, I'm sure it would bore us

but there's a Swedish import playing
at the other theatre
an erotic film — I heard it won an award
at the Cannes Festival last summer

I can't remember the name — but
it's about the Living Game
about men and women loving — not dying
maybe that's an attitude
                    you should be trying
you seem to be so . . forgive me
but you appear to be so up-tight
I can check to see what time the feature
begins tonight, and we could . . "

"no, thank you — please don't bother
I really must be going now"

        he saw how bluntness sometimes offends
    and quickly, with typical Gemini adroitness
                    tried to make amends . .

"don't tell me this is how a faerie tale ends !
look, if you don't want to stroll along
                    the beach
or see a film together . .
maybe we could go to my room
or to yours — have some drinks
and just talk, you know ?
you were so correct about the events
in my life
and you remind me so . . of my wife
do you, by chance
happen to know something about astrology ?
and if I gave you my complete birth data
could you perhaps tell me even more ?"

his complete birth data ?
oh, why hadn't I thought of that before !

my hands and heart and voice — all three shaking
I asked quickly
                    "when were you born — exactly ?"

                            "I'm not sure of the exact time — but
                            I was born in Ohio, on June 19th, 19 — "

             as his voice faded . . . .
                    the room began to whirl
                    like a speeding Carousel

his birthday — *his !* the very same *day* and *month* and *year !*
now it was painfully clear

          an *astral twin,* I thought — of course !

an astral twin — one of those born so near the other by clock time
on the same month, day and year — as to have the same
                                        Ascendent or Rising Sign
as well as all the same planetary positions
causing the physical appearance to often be as close
as that of blood line or genetic identical twins

so alike in appearance
that astral twins have been known to completely fool
even one another's parents . . siblings . . and
                              mates
the same, yet different in some ways
with the individuality of the souls veering, one right — one left
occasionally, in different directions
and the time of similar events in the lives also varying slightly

yet, the life events so synchronized, the physical features so identically matched
it was frequently uncanny

why hadn't I thought to ask him his birthday before ?
I had spent much time studying the fascinating subject
                              of astral twins

and had been amazed over the discovery
                    that the phenomenon had been proven to be valid
by scientific testing and research
and the additional discovery that nearly all American Presidents
and even Vice Presidents, like Nelson Rockefeller
were frequently, for security reasons
                    impersonated by their own astral twins
and that certain government agencies
also utilized astral twins as agents . . for obvious reasons
this practice having started as far back as World War I

          and I remembered . .

that sometimes, even the members of the families of astral twins
bear also a strikingly similar appearance
or are the same general type of people

oh ! why hadn't I thought of this earlier ?

now I knew, with chilling dread
at least I knew there was no further hope

he was dead

and I had been gazing at — had been knocking upon the door
of a Body Temple designed from the same blueprint as his
by the Master Architect, using a specific formula of clay
made from the same month, year and day
but a Temple lived in — owned — by a stranger

then suddenly came, from out of nowhere
a cold and clammy memory

a year or so after our divorce, passing through St. Mary's
with some friends in a car, one sunny afternoon
overcome by a surging of sentiment
I had asked them to stop in front of our first home

. . the house where we had rented
our lovely antique honeymoon room

. . and the awful black feeling of frightened emptiness
when a strange man answered my knock on the door — disgruntled
unfriendly, refusing me nostalgic entrance
to walk through the house
grumbling that I had disturbed his nap

after he closed the door, I stood there on the front porch
unbelieving
it was, somehow, unreal . . impossible

that this step, this bannister . . . this screen door
opened by our hands on so many summer evenings
. . that this very hole in the green and white awning
darned by *him* on a long ago August morning
. . that this happy doorbell he rang so often
the same door bell he rang

to tease me
that time when he was pretending he was the Valentine man
though it was April, not February . . as he knew Dadoo used to do
bringing me candy surprises . . from the Land of Love

Can this possibly be mere coincidence ? These "astrological or astral twins" (non related little girls) were born in the same hospital in White Plains, New York, within five minutes of each other on February 20, 1947. They are Jean Henderson and Joyce Ritter (or vice versa !) There are photos of other astral twins in existence.

Photo by C. Bernstein from Black Star

it was somehow unreal . . that this place could be
                    inhabited by another

    oh ! how could it possibly be inhabited by another ?

when it was very . . so agonizingly . . *familiar*

    I remembered my overwhelming sense of sadness and disbelief
and above all . . the feeling of unreality

then, immediately following that hurting, depressing memory
 came another . . happier

        . . the first day the Carousel Bill
had taken me to his home, to meet his mother

    I had never been inside it before — it was a strange house
        a completely strange house
    yet, from the first moment I had entered

it became familiar

    warm, friendly safe — a loving place
    a place I knew and knew and knew
                        oh, yes, a warm and loving place
        I knew and knew

because . . simply because *he* lived there
and I felt welcome, at home too . . because *he* lived there, that's all

    and, after an hour or so, talking with his mother
    in the kitchen . . I felt I had always known and loved
                    this house — his home

and . . was it thus, I wondered . . with other houses ?
was it thus with the Body Temples of the soul ?

was it the same with the Temples housing loved ones
                    residing there . . or having moved away ?

if so, then the stranger who now resides
in the exact replica of *his* Temple . .

                    he interrupted my reverie . .

                    "you seem upset . . I hope my mother
                    didn't choose an unfortunate birthday for me
                    or is it, perhaps a birthday
                    you have some reason to remember ?

I'll tell you what — if you promise to smile
I'll make believe I was really born
on a snowy December day !
oh, come now — don't look so glum
things just can't be that bad
have I said something to make you sad ?"

"no, you didn't say anything
it's just that . . . it's just that I . . "

then my voice broke completely
and I began to cry — not silently this time, but openly
            tears flowing profusely
tears I was powerless to stop

            he was acutely embarrassed
            and offered me his handkerchief

but I refused it — and took a napkin instead
suddenly, inexplicably
unwilling to touch — or be touched by
anything that close to him — to this stranger

            "you really shouldn't cry like this
            you're too beautiful to cry . . "

but the Gemini charm had no more magic
            his glibness now seemed only shabby and . . cheap

I tried my best to explain
through the throbbing pain in my head . . and heart

"if I had . . if I had a photo of him, a picture
you would see . . you are astral twins
and someday you must read about them . . in astrology
they are often so identical that . .
well . . I'm sorry I don't have a photograph of him
with me, to show you . . they are all in my room
but I thought that you and he
well, you see . . I saw you in the lobby, and I thought . . "

            impulsively . . he reached out for my hand
            and instinctively . . I pulled it away

oh ! unkind reaction to his expression of sympathy !
I grasped for something — anything
to ease the rejection I knew he must be feeling — as a man
then reached into my pocketbook
and pulled out her picture — our Anne

    and with it, the note — those last words he wrote

> *the night grows kind*
> *the wind blows soft . .*

and, swallowing the lump in my throat
held them out toward him

"this is . . this is our baby
and this note he wrote, the night he . . "

> he glanced at the note and her photograph
> with the politeness of a stranger
>   not really seeing them . . not even
> accepting them into his hands
> murmuring casually — three words only

>   "cute baby picture"

> then, obviously uncomfortable, he asked
> "how old is she now ?
> is she here with you — in California ?"

slowly I replaced the rejected picture
and crumpled note
inside my pocketbook, and answered dully

"no, she's not here — she was not quite a year . .
not quite a year old when she . . died
we lost three babies too, like you
            she was the oldest of the three
and I thought you might like to see . . "

then felt a pang of regret for my blindness

"I'm sorry — I'm afraid I've been thoughtless
perhaps her picture brought back memories for you
of your three . . please forgive me"

>   but he replied swiftly, smoothly

>   "no, nothing like that at all . . . you see
>   they weren't full term infants
>   just three unfortunate accidents . . and
>   I guess it's just as well
>   that we didn't raise a family
>   as you already know
>   not all, but most Gemini Twins — like me
>   need to be free
>   to chase the wind out there
>   and search for a star somewhere"

"yes, that's true"

"but I am very sorry for you
that is, I'm sorry about your own loss
I truly am — sincerely"

and he *was* genuinely sorry
I could see that he was, in his fashion
honestly sorry, bewildered man
trying, yes truly trying to understand my passion

well intentioned, charming, handsome Gemini man !
confused by me — and by my clinging memory
bearing lightly the burden of his own obsession
        a yearning to breathe free
and answer the Mercurial call of his constantly present Twin

      poor stranger
          not intending any danger
  poor man

      lost verse I tried so hard to scan
      and force into rhyme
      cruel trick of Fate — and Time
      lost chord of music
           gone now forevermore

deceptive Destiny, to place before me such an identical Temple
such an exact duplication of face and body — even voice
ironically answering my desperate plea
and granting my insistent demands for the physical
for the tangible . . for the *touching things*

forcing me to see that this was not what I longed for after all
no, not this . . not this alone, without its essence

    then, unbidden . . the quiet, kindly face
    of the gentle stranger . . on that dreary grey and unexpected
    wintry day . . in Colorado

flashed before me

    and his voice
low, clear, patient
    . . explaining

          " . . *physiognomy of feature and body
          can be elusive and misleading . . but yes
          I do see that you need this proof*"

those words he had spoken
and programmed into my mind

those words which then seemed so kind
and full of promise
now took the shape of a hurting test
one from which he had, perhaps, tried his best to shield me
to save me from enduring — but I had insisted
    yes . . I had insisted

  . . . where are the eyes . . and the nose and ears
the voice, the hands . . where are the touching things ?

> " . . and you must listen
> for his mass chord vibration . . his music
> you must look for his individual
>   color spectrum
> . . . his auric light"

oh, Guru, your lesson is well learned
whoever and whatever you were . . . . . you were right
and I have learned my lesson painfully this night
    I have memorized it well

the Body Temple is dear, familiar, precious
sacred even — yet the Temple is but an empty, haunted shell
when the one you love does not live there

      what means a scar on the chin — if the loved one is not within ?
what good the same texture and color hair
        what solace the same ears, nose — or hands
if the one who gazes out at you
from the windows of identical eyes is not the one
                  who remembers too, with you
  the one who understands ?

what comfort is any well-recognized, oft-visited Body Temple
house or home — when the one you love
no longer lives — or never did live — there ?

what comfort ? when the loved one has moved out
or moved on . . into some other Temple, leaving you alone
to ring the bell, or knock on a a familiar door
only to be answered by a soul unknown — a stranger ?

        "I am . . sincerely sorry"
            repeated the stranger

        "truly, I am . . is there
        something I can do ?"

  I rose
trying to speak kindly
"no, nothing really . . nothing"

it was I — I thought — who knocked
upon *your* door, uninvited

it was I, not you, who came to re-visit a Temple
a home, where I believed someone lived . . . someone
I once knew . . I was at fault, not you

    and spoke again

"no, nothing really . . . nothing you can do
I was the rude one, not you
to so burden you with my personal grief — and I thank you
for sharing something cool
    even though I don't as a rule . . .

that is, I mean to say . . .
I did enjoy your company
and I'm sorry, but
    I really must leave now"

        his face fell, and he looked suddenly tired
        older . . lonely . . no longer so much like Peter Pan

        "oh, must you go ?
        please stay a little longer"

"I really can't — because
well, you see . . I came here to write a Happiness poem
a poem about being happy
and I haven't yet even written the first line"

        "a Happiness poem ?
        but why try to write about happiness ?
        it keeps you so confined — besides
        perhaps there is no such thing
                as happiness
        and anyway . .
        it's more fun to search for it
                than to write about it
        see ? like me !
        and then, even if you never find it
        you've lived — and felt — and learned
        and experienced life
                . . not just memories"

poor, lost Peter Pan
still trying to sell himself on the magic of freedom
even as he outwardly seemd to be . . . . selling it to me

    Poor Gemini

and for a moment, I almost . . . . . . almost said
let's fly ! let's fly away together, you and I
to Never-Never land . . and catch a brand new star !

    as I glanced once more at the well remembered grin
    the familiar scar beneath the chin . . my heart turned over
    those cheekbones . . the mouth . . brave mouth, yet vulnerable

the way he tossed his head when he laughed
so achingly, achingly . . . *known*

handsome face, charming, charming man
who could never — no, who could never understand
why my soul trembled
at the sight of his familiar hand

and . . as I allowed his voice once more
to sink into my being . . those known, and well remembered warm tones
my heart sighed . . and tore a little — oh
I felt it rip inside
        and cried more silent tears
as something deep within me
reached out toward him, sensing his hurt
                his private fears
his feeling of rejection
and I wanted so to give him . . to give him what ?
        more of me ?
to ease the loneliness I saw behind his eyes

        eyes so like his . . so like his

but I had nothing to give this man
however lonely he was . . and also lost, like me
      I had nothing to give him
for I was empty, robbed by both death and Life
of completeness . . and my once shining wholeness

    robbed of Oneness, along with my faith
    yes, and my old dreams . . even my belief in miracles

I was too poor
to give him a single gift

    except perhaps a wish, a prayer . . a blessing

I spoke gently . .
with a tenderness I truly felt
deeper than I could express in words

    "you may be right about searching
    that may be the best way to find happiness . . at least . . .

well . . but it is late

and there are some phone calls I really must make . . back East
I would love to stay and talk longer
                              but please understand . . "
and I lightly
touched his hand

                    oh, God, *his* hand, *his* hand !

"please understand
I need to be alone . . just now"

                              he grinned bravely
                              and sang his whistling-in-the-dark song
                              saying, with pseudo-cheerfulness

                              "of course, you run along !
                              I do know how it is
                              sometimes one needs . . to be alone"

                    then he shrugged his familiar shoulders
                    in a gesture achingly remembered

        oh !
so achingly remembered

                              he shrugged, and said
                              "well, I'm glad you passed my way
                              and I still believe it's been a lovely day
                              even if somewhat haunted
                                                  because . . "
                              he paused

                              "because we met . . and said hello
                              and now, I'll let you go
                              I may phone you later, just in case
                              you might change your mind
                                          about seeing a show
                              good luck ! with your Happiness poem"

there was something so lost, so defeated
so lonely . . about his brave smile . . and proud posture
I felt a misty rain fall softly, in my heart
but he could not read my mind . . or hear me silently calling him

he could not sense my sudden yearning and compassion
for his soul was not known to mine

and so . . I said goodbye, and left
pausing to look back just once

to see him staring at the drink before him
stirring the ice cubes
                              unsmiling

then ran ran ran !
away from this strange, lost man
                    tears flooding my eyes
my heart screaming silent cries

      ran . . through the lobby . . past the desk
                                        to my room
entered . . slammed the door
threw myself on the white, sterile bed

      and wept and sobbed
      as I had not wept and sobbed
            since I placed the wreath of lilacs on his grave

never in my life
had I felt so completely all alone

            and as I wept, it rang — the telephone

R-RING !

                        R-R-RING !

I knew it was him — the desk clerk had given my number
I knew it was — oh ! I knew

      calling, Gemini-like, to make certain
      just to see if I might change my mind
      about seeing a show   **R-RING !**
RING !   my choice of films now, I knew that too
                  no more suggestions of Swedish eroticism
                  I could choose this time
                  he knew me better now . . and I could choose

RING !
            he was so lonely . .
                        R-R-RING !
. . and I was so all alone

                        RING !
R-RING
                              R-R-R-RING !
insistent telephone

      he is worried about me
      and sincerely wanting to offer sympathy
      needing human warmth as much as I . .

R-RING !

           RING !

he is kind . . charming
and intelligent
    and he looks like you   **RING !**
oh ! how he looks like you !

                  R-R-RING !
   RING !

        . . and his voice

his voice . . filled my heart
with memories
    just hearing his voice   **R-RING !**
your voice

RING !   maybe never again will I ever hear a voice
           so much like yours . . to fill my heart
           with memories . . maybe never again . . never again

                  R-RING !

    oh ! I *need* to hear it once more
            his voice . . . your voice

I need . . I need
        R-R-RING !

but he isn't you
he has your *voice* . . but he isn't *you*

                R-RING !

   still, his voice
          could warm me once more
   and fill the room
          fill the night with memories

R-RING !

            what if I never — ever

what if I never see
a Temple so like yours . . ever again   **RING !**
never hear a voice like yours

. . ever again ?
      R-R-RING !

but he isn't you

. . if I answer the phone
just to hear your voice once more . .
just to hear your voice . .

RING !

oh, no, no, no ! he isn't you !

OH ! STOP ! STOP ! STOP !

I heard myself cry
STOP RINGING !

R-RING !

RING ! no, he isn't you . . but he is
my last chance to . . memorize you

my last chance to memorize your mouth
to memorize your eyes . .

. . but he isn't you !

suddenly, I knew what I must do

immediately . . leave   **RING !**

leave this place
leave the hurting haunting memory
of his lonely, familiar face   **R-R-RING !**

get out of here !
the sooner, the better

blindly, I began to throw clothing, in a tangle
jerking open dresser drawers and closets
pulling hangers loose
tossing everything into suitcases

not packing . . not caring
toss everything in, any way at all
get out of here, get out of here
any way at all !
oh, he was so tall, so tall   **ring !**
and his voice . . . .
ring !

then it stopped

the telephone

it stopped
and again, I was
all alone

how silent was that room . . . without the ringing phone

what if he might be . . coming to my door ?
approaching, even now
coming here, to my door . . and I could
hear his voice once more
to fill this room with memories
and warmth

hurry ! hurry !   get out of here !
hurry !

if we went for a stroll along the beach
I could hear his voice once more
touch his familiar hand

HURRY ! HURRY !

get out of here !

silent telephone

the phone was still silent
was he coming to the door ?

I hurried hurried hurried
grabbing toothbrush, bathing suit, papers, letters
determined to flee
as quickly as I could pay my bill
check out at the desk
have the bellman take my bags
call a cab . . . .

hurry ! hurry !

the silence was maddening, now
in this room
the gloom
relieved only by the rolling surf

BOOM-CRASH ! BOOM-CRASH ! BOOM-CRASH !

. . . outside my window
drapes blowing wildly in the wind
a small glass vase

crashed to the floor

> damp air floating in
> fog creeping in . . through the window

hurry ! hurry !

HURRY ! HURRY !

> as I zipped up my skirt, buttoned my blouse
brushed my teeth . . washed my face

> I turned on the tape cassette recorder
> to drown out the crashing of the surf . . to drown out the surf

and fill the silence

> the Clear Day musical score tape
> was still inside . . I pressed the start button
> and turned the volume
> > as high as it would go
> on Streisand's voice . . oh ! let her sing

> > > loudly, loudly !
> to drown out the crashing surf

let the lyric of whatever song it is
fill this awful silence . . drown out the surf

> then the music filled the room, full volumed — loud
> but, as she began to sing

R-R-RING !
the phone began to ring — again

> the phone . . once more . . began to ring

R*I*N*G

> **R*I*N*G**
> oh, Barbra, sing — please sing !
> so I can't hear the telephone ring !

R*I*N*G !

MUSIC LOUDER ! MUSIC LOUDER !

get dressed . . leave here . . hurry
I can send the bellman for the luggage !

> **R*I*N*G !**

then Barbra's voice   **Ring !**
rose . . and fell . . and filled the room

filling the silence
drowning the surf
                              Ring !

              making the rings softer . . softer

Ring !

                    Ring !
the music, lyrics falling
like snowflakes . .

            . . *how could I be this at ease with him ?*

       pour out my heart as I please with him ?

                              . . . . . . *he isn't you*

please sing
     Oh, sing !   . . *he isn't you !*
drown out the insistent ring of him

              when will I feel so in bloom again ?
                   when will a voice warm the room again ?

he isn't you
       . . *he isn't you !*   **Ring !**

Ring !   *memories may fade*
                   in the shadows behind me . . . .

               . . . . *but there'll be the dream*
                        that will always remind me   ♪

   a dream
        I'll forever   **Ring**
             be comparing him to . .

OH ! love me, he may . . even die for me

     drown out his ring !   . . *sweep every cloud*
  oh, please, sing !   *from the sky for me* . .

       Ring ! Ring !
              he may be king . .
              but he'll never be you

     he'll never . . be you

the music stopped .
so did the phone .

         once again, the room was silent

and I was alone

I glanced at the window
of the Dolphin suite
        drapes blowing in the wind
damp fog misting in . .

                dark outside
                        the surf . . **BOOM-CRASH !**
    empty room
                        gloom . . gloom   **CRASH-BOOM !**
silent room

            . . damp fog misting

quickly, I phoned the bellman
to come up to my Dolphin Suite
        and get my bags

I walked out the door

            ran to the lobby . . ran ran ran !

            paid my bill, with a rising panic
            looking over my shoulder at the door
            to the restaurant

        but . .

                . . no one was there

                    no crooked grin
                            no scar beneath the chin
                    no one . . was there

            no voice to warm the room . . .

        soon the bellman came down
with my luggage

                    he had already called a limousine
                    so I tipped him, in tears . . . said goodbye

                    "I'm sorry to see you go, Miss
                    please don't cry . . . "

        then I climbed inside
        the waiting limousine . . . and said to the driver

"Los Angeles, please
the Hollywood Roosevelt Hotel
it doesn't have . . . . a wishing well"

                    "what's that Madame ?"

Madame ? I must have turned
one hundred and ninety eight today

                    he asked again . . "what did you say ?"

"nothing . .
    I was talking to myself"
            then wearily repeated to him the address

Beaches and Boulevards — Friday

            so I went to a crowded hotel, on Hollywood Boulevard
            crowded with people, not memories

            where there was smog . . but no fog

where traffic was not as dangerous
as the crashing Laguna surf — nor as loud to my inner ear

and here . .

            in a bright, cheerful, 12th floor room
            filled with the delicate, fresh perfume
            of the flowers I bought the morning after I arrived
            and placed on the table, near the open window
                            as a surprise to me . . from me

here, I thought
        my pain will cease
and I'll write my Happiness poem

        and rest . .

yes, this is best

            my long walks now, were down a busy Hollywood Boulevard
                    not along a lonely shore
            and it lifted my spirit far more . . . these nights
            to see bright lights
                            and Life !

life, at least being lived with color and courage
not dull grey ghosts . . running into clouds of shrouds

yes, it was more peaceful here
than beside the churning ocean
and my solitude was easier to bear

      I was even beginning to enjoy it, my solitude
      and it's a strange and lovely thing — to enjoy solitude

            at least it was for me

I was almost growing accustomed to the garish
            lime green and orange Christmas tree
dusted with sparkles of pink snow
in the window of a shop near the corner news stand
where I bought the evening paper
            in front of Lee Drugs

      and I was drifting . .

            into a kind of soft and soothing lifting . . . of my soul
            through my quiet solitude on Hollywood Boulevard

people-watching every night
the human sandpipers
         skipping across an asphalt beach

trying to reach . . a star

         like me

Part Three

THUNDERBOLT   PATH

CANTO FOURTEEN

Heart of my heart, I know you from afar:
There is a measure of such recognition.
There is a sign that is all intuition:
In your strange eyes I see my rising star.

Did blue-green musky moth-wings waft you down
To bear me tidings from the skies of night
And, softly glowing in my soul's own light,
To wash me in your tresses softly blown ?

It all seems long since gone as in a dream
That came and vanished centuries ago
Whose fireless shapes can only feebly glow
And feed the currents of a nostalgic stream
Whose phosphor images before me flow
To seas of final thought, so timeless slow.

* * *

If you should ever dream my love grown cold
Or wasting slowly with the pace of time,
Or deem my kisses are but leaden gold,
And that my love lives only in my rhyme.

If such grey thoughts in sunless days you cherish,
Believe, beloved one, it is not so, —
How could be slain, what slain makes life to perish,
And how deny my love whence I do grow ?

You are the sweetness of a springtime promise
You are like shining dawn when night is gone —
In you there glows mysterious surmise,
Your eyes bestow the peace of heavens won.

All is still yours when all of this is dust,
For Love was my pen, and my pen's word your
                                        trust

Kyril Demys (Musaios)
Prismatic Voices

439

And the Angel Said: "Fear Not"

you intruded upon my December solitude
like some uninvited visitor in the silent night

O ! holy night

how did you get past the watch dogs at the gate
and the sign that plainly said **KEEP OUT ?**

I had run in off the darkened, teeming streets
of Los Angeles, City of Angels . . . fallen
to escape the recorded Ave Marias, pouring from public holiday speakers
blended with the steady tolling of Salvation Army bells

" . . . . Sister, can you spare a quarter or a dime ?"

accompanied by a clear soprano reminder
of another lonely, waiting street, in another darkened time

*. . . . O ! little town of Bethlehem, how still we see thee lie
above thy deep and dreamless sleep, the silent stars go by
yet in thy dark streets shineth . . . an everlasting Light
the hopes and fear of all the years . . . are met in thee tonight*

blinking back the unexpected tears
that rose up from some inner well of sorrow . . seeking haven
I rushed blindly through the nearest open doorway

and suddenly . . you were standing there

a tall, Wise Man

sending me a gentle smile, across the narrow, crowded aisle
of Pickwick Bookstore, on Hollywood Blvd . . . . now called B. Dalton
unlikely cradle for a miracle

why not the Madonna Inn, where we went months later and

were told they had
no room ?

for a spinning moment
I thought you had materialized from another planet or star

a familiar stranger
gazing calmly through the stained glass windows of my eyes
stained with memories of recent grief . . and the gathered dust
of old mistrust

I returned your smile, uncertain . . . .

while with some mystical permission, surely not from me
you rang the bells of my heart, long stilled
knocked on the door of my mind, till it opened

then reverently, as monks walk
you entered the dark and lonely temple of my soul

                    to light a candle

Stranger Rhymes With Danger

I had just bought a book about the ancient laws of Karma
when you gave me that knowing look across the crowd
and it startled me so, I dropped the book . .
instantly, then, in some way I still half believe was magic
your hand caught it in mid-air
                    you really weren't that near — did you fly ?
and you gave it back to me, still smiling that same shy
yet somehow knowing smile — knowing what ?

I murmured briefly, "thank you" . . smiling back at you
with what I hoped was cool reserve, my eyes lifting nearly a foot higher
to meet your own — you were so tall

        but as I turned away, I heard you softly say

        "that's the kind of book I came here to look for too
        does it tell about the deeper knowing-things ?
                        is it a good book ?"

obviously a Uranus-type remark, I thought
fraught with subtle shades of nuance
were you an Aquarian, I wondered — a New Age thinker ?

I wasn't sure what you meant by 'the deeper knowing-things'
and felt oddly reluctant to pursue it
though it evoked some answering echo from the vaults of my mind
            even you, who had phrased the question
        instinctively pulled down an invisible blind across your face
or did I only imagine your instant regret
that you had used those words with a total stranger
in such an unlikely place as Pickwick Bookstore ?
            were you some kind of a Guru ?
and if we spoke longer, could you tell me more ?

                    but . . . more of what ?

I didn't answer about the book right away
taken as I was, by surprise — and in that moment of contemplation
noted your calm, clear, quiet ocean-green eyes
your honey colored hair and beard . . . your tallness
                          and some indescribable brightness around you

        like a light

yet, not like a light — elusive, difficult to define
perhaps it was only a glow of health, for you were tanned
and smooth skinned, with that squeaky-clean look
often described as one looking as if he had just stepped out of a shower
rain-washed, somehow . . although it was not raining outside

            there was . . a strange manner about you
            was it simply your stillness ?
            or the way the store lights made your hair shine and gleam ?
            I felt lost in an old childhood dream . . .
            was it the compelling clearness and steadiness of your gaze
            or your dignity of bearing ?
            you stood so straight, like an Indian
                          I thought of deep-deep-cool-green-woods

was it the wells of compassion so visible in your eyes
or your air of ancient wise ?
I thought of the peace that passes all understanding
            yet, there was a conflicting impression of arrogance
perhaps humility lessons to be learned — but no
            your humbleness of manner was almost a tangible thing
how can a man be both humble and arrogant ?
                          were you a walking non sequitur ?

you possessed a cat-like-grace . . a waiting look

        a quiet poise

totally ignoring the chaotic holiday crush — the rush, the noise
with the serene tranquility of the sage
combined with the confident composure of royalty . . a Leo ?
were you a Lion ?

if so, you were clearly born free, too proud for a cage
it seemed impossible to guess your age, like Peter Pan
were you, then, an eternally youthful, yet also eternally immature
double-identitied Gemini — like him, the Carousel Bill ?
you looked nothing like him, your features
                bore not the slightest resemblance to his
nevertheless, might you not also be a Gemini
forever searching the canyons of your mind
for something you'd never find — hovering somewhere
                          between sainthood and sin ?

that Sun Sign the gods both bless and curse
no, not a Gemini, surely — not a mercurial Twin
eyes too steady — and yet, an undeniable mental quickness
you might even be my equal at playing mental chess . . and
maybe you might even win

the total impression was overwhelming
bordering on the hypnotic . . . a Scorpio ?

oh, no, I thought, my senses taut — that would be ironic
for they say that Scorpio *knows*

. . . . knows *what ?*

well, if he's a Scorpio, I continued musing
there's some danger that his intentions aren't purely platonic

sometimes, an eternity can pass in two or three seconds by the clock
how long did we both stand there
your unanswered question suspended in air ?

" . . *does it tell about the deeper knowing-things ?*
is it a good book ?"

for those few brief seconds, perhaps three or four
which seemed like an hour at least — or more
neither of us seemed able to speak a single word
except in a mystical language only our souls heard
on a higher level of awareness

it was suddenly and inexplicably silent between us
though not awkward or uncomfortable in any way
    just a strange oasis of silence
in a shimmering bubble of reality illusion
formed from the Babylon sounds of people confusion

and we stood in the dead center of this bubble
where it was still . . and calm and soundless
like standing in the vortex of a tornado
                why did I think of a tornado ?
portending some intense energy and unleashed power
unseen, unheard . . but felt

or like standing motionless at the haunted midnight hour
in the whispering shadow of the Great Pyramid of Giza
                why did I think of the Pyramid ?
finally, I found my voice
and replied . . "yes, I'm *sure* this book
contains such knowledge — or I *hope* it does"

after that nervous use of the contradictory 'sure' and 'hope'
I smiled politely, turned away from you and left . . but
after charging the book at the desk, I abruptly stopped
then slowly turned back around — like a puppet, feeling a strong tug
                                    on an invisible string
I really can't say what called me
did I hear your sigh ? I simply cannot explain it
I'll never know exactly why — yet I returned, as though mesmerized
helplessly drawn back to where you stood in that glowing brightness
                            did I hear you praying ?
and placed the book I'd just bought in your waiting hands
only dimly aware of what I was saying . . . .

            "here, take it — it's yours
            a gift — for Christmas"

at first you didn't answer — or thank me — or even smile

you simply accepted the book, and looked deeper into my eyes
so intensely . . as if you were searching for something of great value
                                    you had lost
            then after a moment
            you asked, quietly

            "why should you give a gift to a stranger — *why* ?"

having been about to walk away again, I paused
blushing in sudden embarrassment, as I groped for some reply
and wondered — why are people so rocked and shocked
by a friendly gesture, like a smile — or a gift from a stranger ?
this was no offer intimating the kind of danger
inherent in sharing something cool, as in Laguna Beach

I had offered you, not myself — not even the slightest hint
that I would accept a casual date
I had offered you only the gift of a book, as I often do
to friends and strangers alike, expecting nothing in return

when will I learn ? must I show a driver's license for identification
to identify myself as one with no desire
except to spread the light of truth, through written words ?
I've given such gifts impulsively, for no specific reason
not to quicken either love or friendship's season
but as an ordinary token of good will, to male or female, young or old
yet every single one of them has wondered "*why ?*"
either verbally, or through surprised expression — awaiting
                            what confession ?
I never had an answer
for those who asked "why ?" when I created this impression
but I did now . . yes, oddly, for the first time I did now

"why *not* ?" I asked, in reply

and heard you murmur
softly with a touching wonder . . "wow . . oh, wow !"

"I beg your pardon ?"

and you continued

"well you see, that just happens to be

exactly how I feel myself, about giving
and strangers — most people don't, you know

did you ever notice a bunch of humanity
huddled closely together, on an elevator ?
they stand there, too frightened to speak
        or even squeak hello
or peek out of their shells, to smile
not caring, just staring at the floor numbers
lighting up above their heads
as though they were watching the countdown
for the final nuclear blast-off . . . . "

I felt as though I were listening to a tape of yesterday
played at a different speed — through him — or you ?
yes, a different speed, yet expressing the same need
        to understand — and be understood
faint feedback to the memory, hauntingly lonely

but I answered only . . "yes, I've noticed that too"
happily feeling taller and taller, not foolishly smaller and smaller
as I usually did when people persisted in asking me "why ?"
not even feeling shy, as was my usual reaction
when my motives were misconstrued, as they were with the nameless man
who walked out of the fog . . . was it less than a month ago ?

yes, it was warm and right and good
to be so well understood
to have my good sense unquestioned
my ethics so simply accepted — not doubted
as all those many times before, too many to tell
when I had been asked

"why did you give that blind man
a flower ? he can't see"

"well, he can smell . . . . "

""why did you give that woman your money
because she told you she'd lost her billfold ?

how do you know she wasn't lying ?"

"I know she was crying . . . . . . "

    "why give all your cash to that man on the sidewalk ?
    just because he sits there, and begs ?
    how do you know he doesn't live in a home
                    better than your own ?"
"I know he has no legs . . . . . . "

    "why-why-why do you give ? why not just live-and-let-live ?
    charity begins at home, or with close friends
    why give that gift, that book, that cash — your time
                        to a stranger
when such an act could so easily spell danger ?"

truisms, so trite — but you somehow made my giving seem right
oh, yes-yes-yes ! I suddenly felt taller, not smaller
                    though not as tall as you

        "well, I'm glad to know you !"
        you grinned, with your mouth and your eyes

and I saw, with surprise, your air of aged wisdom
magically transformed and replaced
with a new, shiny-faced and small boy exuberance
but small-boy-sure, not wistful Pan
a fine line, perhaps, but drawn quite clearly

    like watching one try on different masks, at Halloween
    with no intent to deceive
    indicating only versatility of viewpoint, mood and outlook
    the ancient one still hiding . . calmly waiting
    somewhere behind your eyes . . . and how many others there too ?

yes, at least one planet in Gemini, but well aspected at birth
by some powerful vibration
its chameleon qualities not abused or mis-used, I thought
and discovered I was right, a few hours later that enchanted night

                still grinning, you spoke again
                "thanks for the book ! and say . . you know
                I really wish you'd stay and talk with me
                would you like to join me somewhere nearby
                for a cup of peppermint tea ?"

"oh, no, I don't have the time, you see
I'm trying to complete a poem I'm writing, and I couldn't possibly
take the time . . . " I began, then trailed off lamely

            "a poem ? about what ?"

446 ☆ Canto Fourteen

                                you asked with genuine interest
"about . . happiness"

I answered cautiously
afraid of ridicule again
as from the stranger in Laguna

                "happiness ? that's a great subject !
                why, you could cover the whole Universe
                and never run out of material
                if you held fast to the theme of happiness
                and how — and where — to find it

                it's an important thing to write about
                an exciting thing to teach
                a state of mind everyone is trying to reach
                and so much nearer . . easier to find
                than most of them ever believe . . look
                do you really have to leave ?
                                please don't go"

ignoring your question about leaving
I started to say . . no
it's a phony subject — happiness
like the resurrection of the dead

but something in your eyes made me say, instead
"yes, it's an exciting subject — happiness
an important thing to teach
and to try to teach . . . what is your name ?"

                and you told me

two names, leaving such conflicting impressions
each mirroring, then reflecting back such different images
as I heard you speak them

the first one was a common, Norman Rockwell kind of name
recalling sledding in the snow . . apple trees and summer rains
the same as Big Potato's . . did it also rhyme with secret sob ?
a name reminiscent of front porch swings
                . . . . and other, warm, nostalgic things
like the Scout camp scent of pine and spruce
and an Indiana memory . . . of someone surnamed Bruce

                it was a name familiar
I trusted and knew . . . borne also by the Scottish poet, Burns
                . . . and by Browning too
as for your surname . . . . oh !
it brought an ominous chord to pound within my memory
I had never heard it spoken before

                Canto Fourteen ☆ 447

but I had seen it written before . . . and now, here it was
once more . . this time, spoken aloud

    . . through some ironic twist of Fate, it was . . . .
  it was . . . .
the same six letter name as the doctor in Virginia
who kindly did not write that the cause of death was . . . drowning
a name to unexpectedly remind me of . . a phone call
        made too late

unwilling for you to notice me frowning
I took a deep breath
and tried to set my features in blankness
but could not prevent my thoughts from expressing their own features
          of fear
like creatures of unfathomed waters
swimming too near . . oh, much too near !

for your surname rhymed with a three-dimensional viewer
who might see into my secret self, so long hidden
it rhymed with true . . and truer
but I prayed it did not also rhyme with the intimate inquisition
of some spiritual interviewer
who might delve into . . might penetrate the deeper wells of me
as that other stranger had, on that dreary grey
and unexpected wintry day . . in Colorado

. . . your eyes were as calm and as quiet as his
yes, also as wise

    yet somehow . . in some way . . different

still trying to disguise
my uneasiness and flash of remembered pain
I searched my mind for a way to learn more about you
then choked back a sigh, and asked . .

"your surname . . is it English, Scotch or Irish ?"

     "the ethnic derivation of my surname ?
     I've never thought much about it
     English, I suppose — I really don't know"

   and your smile dimmed slightly, almost as though
   you sensed my silent memory tug
   but how could you ? then you added . . *"I'm sorry"*
   spoken very, very low
      . . did I really hear it ?
and I thought . . sorry for what ?
does he have x-ray vision ?
did he *see* my heart skip a beat ?

you were staring at me

and unconsciously, I trembled
"do you . . happen to have any relatives
in Virginia . . who are doctors ?"

> "no, none — no relatives at all in Virginia
> and very few here in California
> my mother and father
> two brothers and a sister
> there are no doctors in the family
> of the medical kind

> I have a B.A. from Cal Poly . . . but
> it's in marine biology
> > I'm not a physician"
you paused . . . .

> "why are you so sorrowful . . . . so sad ?"

the same question asked by the lonely Laguna stranger
now acutely sensing approaching danger
I replied, too callously — "I don't know what you mean by sad
that is, well . . I had . . recently I had a loss, a death
but I don't cry about it anymore — see ? no tears . . . . . .
and now I really must get back to my hotel
I hope you enjoy reading the book"

> you gave me a deep, inquisitive look

and immediately, I regretted my seemingly unfeeling tone and words
oh ! he must think me so insensitive, I thought — yet could see no way
to retract what I had said . . . about the dead

> "do you have a car ?"

"a car ? no, I . . . . you see, I don't drive
besides, the Hollywood Roosevelt Hotel isn't far
just a few blocks from here"

then waited, cringing inside, for the inevitable shock
> "you don't *drive ?*"

> but all you said was, "I'll drive you then"

"no thanks — I'd rather walk"
I answered firmly

and then you laughed — a perfectly marvelous laugh !
so exactly like a rippling brook — it took me by surprise
because it contained such lovely chords of deep-green-cool pine woods

snowflakes .. stars .. elves .. sunrise
                              yes, a rippling brook, your laugh
I asked
"is something amusing ?"

                    and you spoke gently . . . .
                    "only that I knew you would say no"

you knew I would say no ? you *knew* ?
be still, my foolish, leaping heart
any man could play this part, or say the same — and his name
his surname is only a coincidence, I told myself, feeling my pulses pound
a coincidence, that's all — nothing more
      then heard a small bell chime
      as you glanced around, and remarked

                    "I believe that means the store
                    is closing . . . . . . "

      again, the small bell chimed
      in the back of the store, like a warning

on sudden impulse — to soften my refusal of your offer to drive me
I blurted out — "I wasn't going directly to my hotel
that is, well, there's a coffee shop next door, called the Bonanza
and I thought I might stop there first"

                    "Bonanza ? that sounds like a town of deserted gold mines
                    in a place like Arizona or Colorado
                    but since you're going there first
                    if you don't mind, I'd like to go with you
                    and quench my thirst
                    for more knowledge of the deeper things in books
                    like this one you just gave me"

I knew there was nothing now that could save me
from extending the invitation to talk we both were wanting
and there seemed to be nothing amiss in this
nothing like my lonely Laguna twilight haunting
following that sinister sunset, in the fog

      your voice was even and steady

                    "as I told you, my profession is marine biology
                              but for some time now
                    I've been wanting to learn more about astrology
                    also reincarnation, spiritual theology . . . numerology
                              and other metaphysical subjects
                    to see if there might be . . . perhaps, some link . . "

some link ? I wondered, surprised

what does he mean — some link ?
how can there be a link between astrology
and marine biology ?

you barely hesitated, then went on
as though you could read my thoughts

"I think — that is, I nearly believe
that all things on Earth are unalterably related
and in many ways, science is still blind
so may I join you next door ?
I know we've never met one another before
but it's possible that my mind
may have touched yours somewhere
at some time, out there . . reaching for the stars"

by the way, I've been trying to guess . . . . . .
are you ruled by Mars ?"

you were taking unfair advantage
appealing to my love of teaching, of making things clear
to someone who truly wants to know — yet, even so
was I — or were you the Teacher ? who played the role of student here ?
then heard myself cheerfully, trustingly exclaim

"oh, yes ! please do — please join me for a cup of tea
you were right — I am ruled by Mars !
and I do possess some knowledge of astrology and the stars
unlike my ignorance about shifting gears, and driving cars"

I smiled . . and you smiled too

and somehow, we materialized together in the coffee shop next door
to discover a few more things we shared and cared about . . . .
you were making my mind unwind its long-tied knots
and I was uneasy about what might happen, if we explored
much further
but how does the consciousness rehearse
for such a drama, played in reverse — without a script ?
I was relying on you for every cue
had we been cast by the gods in a comedy or a tragedy ?
and was this Act One or Act Two ?
why did I feel so unreal — as if I were only acting a part
  if I felt unreal — were you, then, acting too ?

and what about the final curtain . . . . who wrote this passion play ?

we sat facing each other, happily reaching and teaching and learning
for nearly two hours, in a booth in the Bonanza

. . . . the name has since been changed to Dai Shogun

Canto Fourteen ☆ 451

> but the faint, faded letters of *Bonanza*
> are still visible on the building
> > high above the door . . . . . .

later, as we were preparing to leave
and talking of walking back to my hotel, not needing to drive
the few short blocks . . . I correctly guessed that you were a Lion
with Aquarius rising on the eastern horizon
Leo Sun sign, Aquarian Ascendent — indisputably astrologically opposed

and wondered wildly to myself . .

> is the frightening polarity of this Aquarian Age
> which has so confused and bemused me these past years
> at last taking schizophrenic shape and form
> to symbolize my own hidden fears ?
> materializing into a human Frankenstein monster
> of half roaring Lion — half Aquarian Water Bearer of truth ?
> and I suppose, to top it off, his Moon is in Scorpio
> > the sign of hidden knowledge
>
> it was

but what came next, by no pretext could be defined
as merely an odd astrological combination . . no, what came next
with the impact of thunder crashing
was like the sudden, unexpected lashing of a maniac's whip
for, as we left the Bonanza coffee shop
you began to tell me about your recent trip . . . . and a ship

> the incredible incongruity of our mutual cosmic acuity
> had been thus far disguised behind your unfamiliar features
> your honey colored apostle beard
> reminding me of some sun-splashed painting of long ago
> I had no memories of — no close friends with a beard
> > or with green eyes, crystal clear
> so how could I have anticipated an earthquake of remembrance
> or guessed a lightning bolt so near ?

you said you had just returned from Mexico, a few weeks or so ago
on a ship called the *Atlantis* . . . . the Atlantis ?

> I heard a faint, far-away warning note
> strike a minor key of danger in my inner ear
> as you began your innocent discussion of a ship
> > and . . . . Mexico

oh, no ! I thought . . . . oh, no !

> I'd always shuddered when anyone mentioned Mexico
> though I could never explain my involuntary sensation
> and half believed it sprang from subconscious recall

of some evil done to me — or by me — either in Peru
or in some long forgotten, Mayan or Incan incarnation

        strange . . . . . . the word incarnation
        contains the word *Incan*

as likewise does the synonym for mantra . . . incantation

where had I heard — or read
that the word Incan means . . The Lost Ones ?
and why did that make me indescribably sad ?

        your voice halted my reverie . . . . . .

        "you see, I drove down there
        with some friends, by way of Baja — but
        when they left, I stayed alone
                for a short while
        then hitch-hiked back here by boat
        it was a perfectly marvelous float
                on the ocean, and . . . . . . "
a perfectly marvelous float ?
I thought . . he's using druid language
and asked abruptly, "what did you say ?"

        but you ignored my interruption
        does anyone ever successfully interrupt
                a Lion
        in the middle of a speech ?
        and went on . . . .

        ". . . . a really fantastic trip
        and the Captain of the ship knew all about
        Atlantis, because he and some others
        recently found what they believe to be
        the ruins of that lost continent
        on the ocean floor — a great stone wall
        and he gave me some chips of rock
                from there
        remind me later — I'll give you one"

so confident of there being a 'later' for us, you were
so sure . . and I agreed, as certain as you
as though we were friends of many years, not just for an hour or two

"yes, I'll remind you later — I'd love to have it," I replied
both of us accepting this future 'later'
by unspoken agreement, quite naturally, it seemed

        "there was just one negative aspect

about the trip on the Atlantis ship . . "

"and what was that ?" I asked
all unprepared for the blow I was about to receive

        "there was only one minor annoyance
        in all that time — just one
        I was lying on the deck, asleep in the Sun
        during the last lap of the trip
        as we passed a place called Laguna Beach . . "

first lash of the whip !

        ". . . . and suddenly, I felt a sharp pain
        in my tooth — I almost thought it bled, and . . . . "

CRACK ! another maniacal lash
of memory's flogging

        ". . . . and you see, I never have a toothache
        really, never — and I was shocked"

some dam within unlocked
as waves of crashing surf pounded in my ears
boom-crash ! boom-crash ! boom-crash !

        ". . . . and it grew worse and worse
        this terrible pain in my tooth, throbbing
        and aching — and then the fog came up . . . . "

another lash !

        ". . . . it finally became so unbearable
        I knew I had to see a dentist when we landed
        but it was so strange, because . . . . . .
        he found nothing wrong with my tooth
        it was healthy, he said — and strong
        and he could find nothing wrong . . . . "

whiplash !

        "I thought it was . . maybe something
        in my horoscope, or birth chart
        and I wondered if you could — oh, here
        you dropped your shawl . . well, anyway
        it seemed so odd
        that there was nothing wrong with my tooth
        despite the pain . . . nothing at all"

        you know, I like your Laura Ashley dress — I guess

somehow, it makes me feel . . . .
as though I'm slipping off the time track"

what we are doing, both of us, I thought
is slipping away from sanity, into a weird world of the unreal
not slipping off the time track
but, stunned as I was, I managed to ask you
                    "when was this ?"

                              "you mean, the pain in my tooth
                              when my ship passed Laguna Beach ?"

oh, my god ! must he repeat it ?
I anguished within

                              " . . . . I believe it was a week or so, no more
                              a week or two before Thanksgiving Day
                              it was . . yes, I remember now
                                        it was *November the Eleventh*"

was this a dream ? I prayed you wouldn't ask me
why I questioned you about the exact date of that strange day
wondering at the same time if it was too late to pray
            you heard my prayer
as if we were connected by an invisible astral telephone
and did not ask . . except with your eyes
        I turned my glance quickly away
unwilling to answer the question in them just yet
                    thinking . . this has to be a dream !

for awhile, then, we walked along Hollywood Boulevard in silence
past Eleanor Boardman's star, imbedded in the sidewalk
I had been struck dumb, and my mind was reeling, numb
but when I could find my voice again, I spoke firmly and clearly
with no sign, I hoped, of having uttered a silent scream
yes, this has to be, I thought . . .
some sort of precognitive dream

        all the way to the door of my hotel
        I kept up a running verbal stream — a dialogue of nonsense
        anything to keep you from speaking
        and playing more tricks with my brain, bringing on such pain
        but not in my tooth — no, this time, in my heart

Born Free

now, when I recall that haunted December, I blush with shame
even today, I still wonder what you thought of my fevered commentary
that night — or if you knew the name of the game was: Fear
as I tried desperately to hide my gradual knowing-growing that a mystery
I preferred not to solve was here . . . and much too near

     I chattered on about unrelated subjects in a pixilated way
     and had my say . . . on everything from cabbages to Kings
     I even made it clear how I felt about chauvinistic mates
     who trap a spouse in the house, like a mouse
     oh ! I must have sounded like a revved-up Lucy
                          spinning her wheels, with Charlie Brown
     as I told you, with emphasis . . . . . .

"my own personal view, if it's of any interest to you
concerning the battle of the sexes
is that I have no intention of allowing this Women's Lib intervention
to seduce me into relinquishing my female privileges and prerogatives
just to prove to the world that I'm equal to men
when I already know I'm superior"

     in my attempt not to appear foolish and inferior
     what consummate ignorance I was projecting
     then I thought — he really must like me !
     because you didn't even symbolically strike me
             with your mighty Lion's paw
     when I tested you so aggressively with my rudeness

     instead, as we reached the lobby door of my hotel
     you just gave me another wise, gentle smile
                   and said

             "please don't go in yet — let's talk awhile
             it's not too late"

     so we did

and those watch dogs at the gate of my heart
who had guarded me so long and faithfully

against being hurt again — against the need to weep

 relaxed . . . .
       grew drowsy

 and finally fell asleep

Shall we Grok around the Block ?

it was good to talk and walk together
good to watch you wisely considering, and carefully weighing
the deep personal convictions I was so earnestly, intensely conveying
about the beliefs we both seemed to hold
wondering if there were others, yet unspoken, that we shared
like making it snow . . with magical mantras, or by just wishing it so . . . . . .
there were so many things we were separately thinking
not saying, but needing so to know
     in the middle of a discussion about space ships and distant planets
     you asked me, with a searching, cryptic smile

       "and what do you believe, or disbelieve
      about Robert Heinlein's fictional Martian, Michael
                         Valentine
      who was a stranger, in a strange land ?"

"I'm glad you asked," I replied, in freezing tones
delivering, then, what I suppose was a rather scathing monologue
not knowing for certain where you personally stood
and afraid of hoping you would or could . . . . . . believe as I did
                         about that book
I threw you an icy, disapproving look
my voice clearly frigid, and somewhat rigid, as I went on

"well, although I certainly grok the occult powers
of Michael Valentine's inter-planetary tricks

like making baddies disappear, with a few magical flicks
of his super-charged wrist . . and breathing underwater for hours
I most emphatically do not grok — and am determined to fight
the gospel this Mars-hatched stranger spread in every bed
while supposedly visiting our grokky planet, so fast losing light

I do not grok the '23rd psalm' of this Martian and his part-time girl
nor the pseudo-religious ecstasy of their 'New Testament' group sex whirl
somehow, I can't picture the Almighty
joining Martian Valentine, his friends and his partner, Jill
in a swinging flesh orgy — or grokking a multiple sensual thrill
although I do believe, with all my heart
in His omnipotent presence between two people who honestly love
does that make me sound like a naive child ?"

      you didn't answer — you only smiled

---

*   Robert Heinlein's book, Stranger in a Strange Land, uses the word
     GROK as a substitute for any and all verbs.

and so I continued . . . . . .

    "I hear that the fictional Martian's fans, here in Los Angeles
the city of angels — fallen
are spreading this false teacher's apostle's creed

            . . . . which may not have been author Heinlein's
               original intent, but nevertheless . . . .
spreading this creed
to thousands of groktized, but unbaptized swingers
in this very strange California land of yours — not mine
by using his book as their missal
and holding periodic, erotic and unholy masses on water beds
with the dubious blessing of wine
and charging plenty of bread to reserve a front pew seat
so . . . . . . if you happen to be one of those who grok that scene
don't come grokking around, telling me that "thou art God"
                     and all that rot
because I'm not — I'm only a strange Gooober
in an anti-Gooober land
I have to be sure I love someone . . and certain that he truly loves me
before I even sit in the movies and hold his hand
        let alone anything more intimate — Good Grief !"

then, my soap box oration not quite finished, I added . . . .

    "having been given a quadruple nine vibration at birth
I receive my own telepathic beam from Mars — and I know this much
about the metaphysics of human electrical energy, here on this Earth
    mixing up auras, with indiscriminate sexual abandon
never mind the hypocritical "share-love-with-one-another" intent
can really short circuit your soul — grok ?"

          you knew what I meant, and replied

          "check, baby — grok !"

    your eyes held a soft, tender glow
that told me all I needed to know about *what* you were
although . . I was still wondering *who* you were
        and which one of us was stronger

then I glanced at a clock on the corner — and saw
that we'd been grokking for less than a half hour
yet it seemed I had known you for centuries
              . . or longer

after that lengthy speech of mine, you probed and explored and felt
with searching fingers of questions
the private confusions I was unsure of myself
                    kept hidden away on a dusty back shelf of my mind
secrets I preferred not to expose to the light
with a total stranger . . . . on a strange and unexpected December night

                    "if you feel so strongly
                    about promiscuous grokking around . . . . "
                    you grinned at me disarmingly

                    "then you must believe in ideal unions
                    like the blending of twin souls
                    once the lost half has been found"

                    then waited for my answer
                    with a curious knowing showing in your eyes

oh ! why does he mention twin souls, I thought
when all we're discussing is mutual goals ?
and I considered my reply carefully

"no, I don't . . . . I don't believe in permanent unions"
                    and I paused again
"at least, I don't believe it's an ideal one can ever realize
in a world where everything born — sooner or later — only dies"

            I could tell nothing from the quiet expression
            in your watchful eyes, as you asked . . . . . .

                    "what *do* you believe in then ?"

"I believe in myself !
in nothing less certain than that"

                    "in yourself ? allright . . . . . . but who *are* you ?"

oh god ! were you going to ask me
to identify myself with a driver's license ? I wondered
"who am I ? Well, I don't know — I guess I'm a loner
that is — who do *you* think I am ?"
I countered, with sudden resistance

                    but you pursued your question
                    with relentless persistence

                    "who do you *think* you are ?"

Canto Fourteen ☆ 459

I am being asked for identification
panic panic panic panic
"who would *you* say I am ?"
            I stubbornly repeated

        then you answered gently . . . .

        "you're Cinderella, looking for the glass slipper
        she lost at the ball . . and that's not all

            you're also Snow White
            waiting for her Prince to find and awaken her
            so the world can be the same as it was
            when she fell asleep"

the same as it was ?
what does he mean, the same . . ?

            "and a few others I could name
            like Alice — and Mary"

oh, what's the use of pretending ? I thought
he knows, he knows — it shows
what's the use !
then asked him . . "who's Mary ?"

            "Mary ? She's Mary, Mary, Quite Contrary
            from Mother Goose"

how far will this go ?
what else does he understand ?

"and . . who is Alice ?"

            "Alice is the astrally oriented girl
            who orbited all around Wonderland"

"I've heard about them," I admitted
unwilling to lose this game of mental chess
"but that was when I was much younger, and still half asleep
now I'm much older and wiser, and have no faith
in words like 'forever' and 'always'
or promises that people make, and never intend to keep"

            you sighed, and replied
            with yet another probing question
            "can't you even try
                  to trust in tomorrow ?"

"why should I try ? when tomorrow will only bring me sorrow"

"don't you remember all the happy endings
in the faerie tales you read, as a child ?"

"**NO !** I've grown up since then, and I'm no longer beguiled
by leprechauns and druids . . and magic wishing rings
or living-happily-ever-after, and all those other naive things . . . . . .
the Holy Grail is only an illusionary cup"

suddenly, you looked up
and pointed toward the sky

"look ! a falling star !"

"where ?"

"oh, hurry ! make a wish before it falls !" I cried

but you tricked me — you lied
there was no falling star
and when I asked you, reproachfully

"why did you lie ? that wasn't fair"

you said quietly . .

"only to show you, Little Girl Lost
that all your old dreams are still there"

Slipping Off the Time Track

as we strolled several times around the block
on the way to the Roosevelt that murmuring night
after you had lied to me — oh, yes ! it was a lie
there was no falling star, streaking through the sky . . . . . .
we shared the strangest conversation
on two levels — or was it three ?
no one else was near, as far as I could see
there was only you . . . . only me

"it's going to snow tonight
I can feel it in the air"

do you see how white the Pyramid gleams
by moonlight over there ?

"I thought it never snowed in California"

the music of the Nile is crashing
in my ear . . do you not hear ?

"It doesn't very often
            but I believe it will this year
maybe we could make some snowflakes fall
if we concentrated hard"

bringing in the logs, for the long, cold winter
promises of later . . far away

"you mean, if we pray ?"

"yes . . miracles can happen
if you really want them to"

silver ships and rolling thunder
déjà vu . . oh, déjà vu !

"well, I don't know . . "

"you mean you've never made it snow
just by wishing it so ?"

"that sort of magic is only possible in a dream"

beating tom-toms, smoky camp fires
wild bird's scream

"I'll prove it to you !
then we'll make some snow ice cream
it's healthier than the kind that's made with sugar"

"yes, I guess that's true"

and then you came . . and you knew

"say, do you read Charlie Brown ?
do you believe in astral projection . . and
are you against the A.M.A ?"

"oh, yes, I do ! I mean
oh, yes, I am ! also the F.D.A."

. . . . . . *even pharaohs turn to clay* . . . . . .

"wow ! now I *know* I'm right
it *will* snow tonight !"

"yes, I suppose it might

if we really pray . . . . . . "

Written in the Stars

      strange, strange enchanted light . . silent night
      holy night . . of shining light

at the elevator, in the lobby, after I'd told you goodbye
I pressed the button for the 12th floor quickly, wanting the car to fly !
so I could reach my room, with its fresh flower perfume
open my Ephemeris, and calculate your horoscope
to see if there might be something the planets told, at the time
                         of your birth
which could instruct me and enlighten me
about whether our meeting should intrigue me — or frighten me
    or be casually disregarded

oh ! but how could I disregard the fact of the ship I'd seen
on that November 11th afternoon in Laguna, etched against the horizon ?
your ship, I realized now — yes, your ship
          returning from your Mexico trip

how could I disregard the lashing of that memory whip
and the obvious truth of the pain in your tooth
              at the same time I felt mine ?
staring at you, out there, though unaware . . . on your ship the *Atlantis,*
            lithographed against the skyline

    and then . . . . biology and physics, his subjects too
    perhaps it was just coincidence
            and yet . . . .

I sat in the small dinette, of my large, two room apartment
at the Hollywood Roosevelt Hotel — Suite 1217
where I could see, through my open window, the small white cross
planted on a far hill . . behind Grauman's Chinese Theatre
          now called Mann's Chinese — but
            what's in a name ? it's all the same . . . .
I sat there, and I wondered . . .
if you were there with me, would you notice that cross ?
and would you think it as inexplicably moving a sight as I ?
for I had begun to, somehow, feel it to be
         an omen . . of something veiled in secrecy

    I thought of your last question

        "may I phone you tomorrow or the next day ?"

and my answer . .

"yes, why don't you call me ?
meanwhile, I'll calculate your natal chart
and see if the stars have anything exciting to say
about your Past — and Present"

then your comment . .
"I'm more interested in the Future
although it really doesn't matter
since all three are one
and only appear to be separate
but I guess that's something you already know"

and my reply, just before we said goodnight

"yes, that's something I already know
but it's good to talk with someone who knows it too
all life is that way, though most people don't see it's true

because of blindfolded scientists
who are always trying to divide everything into three"

and your final remark, smiling at me

"that's right, nothing is what it appears to be
so we must be aware of all moments . . . . . . on all levels"

I sat there in the sea green chair, near the window
staring at your birth chart, mentally comparing it to my own

the inter-locking planetary compatibility
between our two life paths
was almost unbelievably positive and smooth
your Sun trine my Venus, with Mars harmonious to it too

your Sun also conjoined my Neptune — exactly
the Leo Sun that caused you to be born free
explaining our uncanny esp
and flashes of mutual mental telepathy
nearly all your planets
conjunct, sextile or trine to all of mine
like a well marked line of roads once walked along together
and to be walked along . . once more ?

I tried to ignore the clear indication
of the magnetic physical attraction between us
so strongly predestined
by several planetary aspects between our nativities
with unpredictable Uranus also there in the act

because . . even if we should see each other again
this could grow into nothing but friendship
                        as far as I was concerned

oh ! I believed this truly, forgetting everything I had ever learned
from observing the inevitable results
                        of such powerful cosmic configurations

never had I looked upon a pair of natal charts so perfectly matched
and I had studied hundreds, comparing them to each other
but never, never any two — as harmoniously linked as the horoscopes
        belonging to me — and to you

yet, a couple of astrological revelations disturbed me

one was your Saturn

        the wise, stern, mature and stable planet — Saturn
        both its sign and house position . . . Cancer . . . 5th house
        showing your attitude toward romance to be serious
        also in several haunting aspects when you were born
        trining your Scorpio Moon
                        and conjuncting your natal Venus
        at the moment of your first breath

I knew what your Saturn clearly revealed
Saturn being the planet of karmic debts due
as well as being the planet of spiritual wisdom
patience . . and secrets sealed

        your Saturn implied a soul so evolved beyond this level
        that it had returned to Earth by choice
                        . . . . as a few periodically do
        not by karmic requirement or demand
        but here only on the holiest of missions . . . yes
        obviously, you were not a young soul
        such souls are not so aware of the illusion of Time
        no, a new soul surely could not make Life rhyme
        as musically as you seemed to do

        then it could only be true that you were an old soul
        with an ancient, wise heart
        here for some reason I could not guess, or read from your chart
        for . . often, these matters are hidden from the astrologer
        when the interpretation might be ill-timed
        later, sometimes clicking naturally into place . . . .
        a necessary protection from the Guardian Masters
        when Truth is veiled for some greater purpose
                        like an inner secret of outer space

and . . . the Jupiter-Neptune conjunction in your 8th house

                    also revealed the undeniable presence
                                of an enlightened Avatar

but what troubled me most about your Saturn was its square to my Sun
the single adverse aspect between the planets in our nativities
no, not adverse — I dislike that word
a square is actually an aspect creating tension
                                for the purpose of energizing
. . . . . . I knew but too well what that square had to tell
astrologically, how it must eventually reach me
it meant, infallibly, that you had some great lesson to teach me
for, when Saturn squares the Sun between two charts
and in our case, the square was exact

            it means there are lessons to be taught
                        and the Teacher is not
            the one whose natal Sun is squared
            no, the Teacher is the one, whose Saturn squares the other's Sun
            and therefore, in charge of the Truth to be passed between them

            so, you were the Teacher, and I — the student
            even though I was the astrologer, not you
            but, to teach me what ? and were you even aware of this ?

another starry phase vibrating its promise
that made me imagine I heard a Serpent hiSS
was your Venus conjoined my Pluto
        an exact conjunction

            this was a mutual aspect between two horoscopes
            which had fascinated me for years
            and though I'd looked for it in the charts of many couples
            I had never come across it — until now

there it was . .

            my Pluto — by hour, minute and second
                    tightly conjoined with your Venus

            Venus . . the planet of Peace and Love
                Pluto . . the planet of Death
                        of Mystery and Reincarnation

the implication alarmed me, because I knew its meaning by heart

when these two planets are so situated together
in the nativities — not of relative or good friends — but of lovers
providing certain other mutual aspects are also found . . . .
there is astrologically no doubt what the relationship is all about

        according to the Chaldean texts

                    466 ☆ Canto Fourteen

"these are two, who have lived many incarnations together
                so powerfully linked and synchronized
that, when not in one another's physical presence
they feel a nearly unbearable longing

                and the two, once joined

except for occasional, temporary intervals
associated with karmic learning
may never be Earth-separated — except through
                                the force of death

and even then . .
inseparable in Heaven

                what God hath joined together, let no man put asunder
                applies to such as these, not to every bride and groom"

I grasped at a straw of comfort . . . .

                but we were not lovers, nor would we ever be
                        surely not you and me
                besides, the writings state
                that the two may not be separated, *once joined*
                and we were not joined
                except, perhaps, with our eyes

much later, in bed, as I fell restlessly asleep
my mind wandering . . . I rhymed the word 'lover' with 'cover'
and slowly losing consciousness in fragmented dreams
mistily wondered . . what is it the word 'cover' means ?

                hearing a faint whisper in my ear . . . Comforter

                        drawing, then, my blanket near
                        I entered other worlds . . . and slept

Good Grief, Charlie Brown !

the next morning, I awoke with the certain feeling that I wasn't alone
although I was, of course

                did I hear a robin sing ?
                no, surely not, in December

                and I stared at the phone
                somehow expecting it to ring

it did

but it was only Room Service, returning my night before Breakfast Call
and re-checking my morning order

> "grapefruit, whole wheat toast
> and tea — will that be all ?"

"yes . . I mean, no
I'd like a morning paper, please"

> *you* called later . . .

as I was reading Peanuts in the comics . . . . . . and I marveled at the way
my heart skipped a beat, at what Lucy was wistfully suggesting
> to Schroeder that day   ➡

we said very little on the telephone, though your voice was warm
and mine uncertain . .
I promised to meet you in the lobby, around six thirty

> later, on the way down, in the elevator
> as the recorded robot voice echoed its usual "Floor please !"
> I mused to myself — Lucy is a Gooober
> then idly wondered if you might have read the comics too
> that morning . . . a fleeting thought, nothing more

but when we met in the lobby, I forgot to ask
with you so near . . it was all I could do to remember my own name
and the confusing game of Who's Who you had started

> was I Alice or Mary — Brown Owl or Contrary ?
> Cinderella, Snow White, or druid ?
> was I Little Girl Lost or Maizie — or crazy Daisy . . . . Gamble

> Lerner's heroine of *On a Clear Day* ?

and who were *you* ?

a Merlin of miracles — a viewer of Life — or a Brewer of magic
who thought I looked tragic, and therefore
decided to do a good deed for the day, like a grown-up Boy Scout ?

what was this all about ?

> we agreed to see a film together
> and bought a paper at the corner newsstand by Lee Drug Store
> where I'd picked up the late edition so many nights . . . alone

turning swiftly, smoothly, with Leonine grace
to the Entertainment section, you held the paper open
there on the street
while I read aloud the names of the feature films playing,
                                    so we could decide

    my heart executed a barely perceptible flip-flop inside
    when I came to *On A Clear Day*
    and as I spoke the words of the title, my voice catching slightly

        I heard you say — "that sounds interesting
        have you seen it ? would you like to go ?"

"well, yes and no . . I mean, I don't know"

I hesitated only a fraction of a second

"it's probably a good show, that is . . . . . .
I saw a small part of it recently, out of town
but something happened to the sound — and I didn't stay
I decided to wait, and see it later
    yes, I guess I would like to see *On A Clear Day*
would you like to see it too ?"

        "yes, I would — but let's go right now
        or we'll miss the next feature
        it's playing at a theatre all the way across town"

    you glanced at the paper again
    and I saw you frown

        "we'll have to hurry . . . . so
        you go inside the drug store here . . . . . .
        phone the theatre, and ask what time it starts
        there's a typo in the ad where the hour is listed
        it looks like 7:30, but it could be 7:00
        so you'd better check to be sure . . . .
        I'll get my car from the hotel lot — drive once
        around the block, and meet you
        back on this corner — don't take too much time
        here's a dime — now be out here, like I said
        in this traffic, I can't park or wait
            . . . . so don't be late"

Period. I thought, to myself
well, Period. I felt like a Private, in the army
should I, perhaps, salute, and answer "Yes *Sir* ?"

    although your grin somewhat softened and hazed

your Leo take-charge-and-give-orders mien I knew so well
from having been raised by another Royal King of the Jungle . . .

nevertheless, I knew you were softly, but surely, taking the lead
telling me what to do — giving the orders, making it clear
                 just who was in charge here
with courteous consideration, and not offensive at all
yet annoyingly *so sure* — so irritatingly confident and sure

but — why did I like it ? why did my eyes suddenly, shyly fall ?
and why did I feel my cheeks flush ?
usually, I felt resentment stir, in an impulsive rush
when my wishes and opinions were not consulted
or when people spoke to me curtly and briefly
saying, however gently — now you do this, or you do that
                                      right away

obviously expecting me to jump and obey
especially men

          why did I feel so . . *warm* about it then ?

finally, I answered, mentally saluting
"don't worry, I won't be late
I'll only take a minute to phone
then I'll be right here on the corner, waiting"

I spoke with an unaccustomed docility that inwardly exasperated me
why was I so weak and meek ?
who were you to tell me where to be — and when
with such crisp manner and authority ?

          you winked a friendly wink, and said

          "just be sure you are"

well, Period.
I thought to myself again

          then you repeated, still politely, but firmly

          "be sure you are — I don't want to drive
          around the block twice, in this tangled traffic
          or miss the beginning of the show — and so
          I'll see you in five minutes"

you flashed a quick smile, and I watched you go
as I wondered — were you getting even with me, perhaps
for my speech about Women's Lib and chauvinistic males
when we first met ? were you retaliating for my independent airs
and my Mars-ruled, dominant star of defiance ?

Canto Fourteen ☆ 471

showing me that, although you permitted it once
                    "watch out, girl — not too far
                    with your Aries self reliance ?"

yet, even your last curt command
given in a tone clearly expecting compliance
didn't annoy me as much as it should have — *why* ?

I dialed the wrong number several times, from sheer, nervous tension
before I finally reached the theatre, losing three dimes

but . . . .

I was there, the December wind tangling my mind and my hair
oh, yes, I was there on the corner, waiting, ahead of time
one of the few occasions in my life I was early, rather than late
as I normally am, for any kind of date
                    whether business or social — *why* ?

I climbed into your car, a dusty blue Bug
and confirmed that the film would begin promptly at seven
then sat back in my seat, watching you drive . . . effortlessly
and after a moment, you casually mentioned a girl you'd once known
whose first name rhymed with pill
and with Jack and Jill went up the hill — and thrill ?
you said she knew something about metaphysics and astrology
        not as much as I, you smiled — but a little
and she had first "excited your interest" in these matters . . . . . .
some time ago, you said, she had "aroused you"

                    excited your interest ?   aroused you ?

to the same degree, or more . . I wondered . . as the Scorpio girl
you'd mentioned the night before ?
the cool, sure one, who had gone with you to Pickwick Bookstore
then left you alone, browsing, for me to find
while she went on her way ?
her last initial was 'H', her first one 'K' — and she rhymed
                                    with curtain
but not with uncertain — oh, no !
a cool, sure Scorpio, slender and tall with light blue eyes
and curly, long hair . . could never rhyme with . . uncertain

I'd nearly forgotten, your mention of her had been so brief
you had said only something about how close she was to your family
how well she got along with your mother — and still does
even though you seldom see each other any more
I wondered, then — why did she go with you to Pickwick Bookstore
then leave you alone ? was she really only a friend now . . or . . . . . .

        and . . the girl named Jill, who rhymed with Pill

was she a romance ?   Past-tense . . or Present ?
did *she* rhyme with thrill ? for you ?

I felt a faint, familiar stab of pain, a quick flash of fiery sparks
then felt a flame of fear flare and burn — why ?
was it any of my concern ?
no, it was not — it was none of my concern at all
                              not in the least

then shocked, heard my voice asking

"were you — are you in love with either of them ?
I mean, the Scorpio — or the one who first aroused you
that is, who excited your interest in the occult ?"

why in God's name, I anguished
did I ask you that ?

                    you stared straight ahead
                    at the moving stream of traffic
                    and replied quietly . . too quietly ?

I tried to judge by your profiled face
but it was absolutely blank — stone face, expressionless
Moon-in-Scorpio poker face
I thought. . who cares ! but listened carefully

                    to your reply

                    "no, not real love — one was just a girl
                    I knew during a lonely spring and summer
                    a wandering soul, who hears
                                   a different drummer
                    I guess we helped each other along the way
                    but our acquaintance was quite brief
                    so neither of us felt any grief
                                   when she moved away
                    as for the other
                    the one who's so close to my mother
                    we shared a tentative romance
                                   for more than a year
                    but it also finally came to an end
                    and now she's only a very good friend

                    romance is searching — love is an eternal thing
                    so, neither relationship could have been love
                    because both of them are past
                    and I've always believed that, *if it's love* . . . .
                                   . . . . *it will last*"

I felt the fiery sparks
and tiny flame of remembered pain . . . . disappear

as the crash of the Laguna surf sounded in my ear

only seconds later, you turned your head
              at a Stop Light — Red
smiled directly into my suddenly shy eyes, and said

                    "I'm glad you didn't see the film before
                    it's good that you waited
                                so we could see it together"

thunder pounded in my very brain
where had I heard those words ?   somewhere
walking in a misty fog . . or rain ? . . . echo from a voice in Laguna's
                                darkened silent theatre ?

"I beg your pardon ?"

                    "I'm glad we can see this film together now"
                    you repeated patiently, once more

                    *"I'm glad you waited before
                                and didn't see the show"*

        then you turned away
        and the light was Green, for Go
                    against your hair and cheek

I didn't answer you for the simple reason that I couldn't speak
I only sighed — but you didn't seem to notice that I hadn't replied
with even a smile or a nod, to your comment
almost as if you'd made a required observation,
                                and that was that

        of course, you couldn't have known
        what memory bells your words rang within me

        yet, the way you spoke them, as though on cue
        not even curious about my silence
        when normally, I should have replied, politely
              "I'm glad I waited too"

              it . . puzzled me

we arrived at the theatre, just as the feature began to unwind
              you led our way down the darkened aisle
and I followed, a few steps behind . . . . the seats you chose
were too far back to suit my taste, on the left hand side
I prefer the center orchestra section, I thought to myself
but said nothing, only followed you meekly — *why* ?

somewhere in Time, during the unfolding of the feature — or the Future ?
maybe when Yves Montand was singing *Come Back To Me* to Daisy
                              crazy Daisy Gamble
the floodgates of my heart burst open
releasing rushing torrents of memory

          you had gone to the lobby for a moment
          and when you returned, you had a surprise, as you said
          with a funny druid twinkle in your ocean-green eyes

                    "here's something for us to munch
                    I had a hunch you'd like these"

          then you . . . . Oh !   he — or you ?
          handed me a box of Goober's chocolate covered peanuts

I couldn't speak, my knees were weak
I couldn't utter a single word, and my eyes were blurred
          with tears

                    as you whispered into my ear
                    like a private druid secret . . . .
                    "this chocolate is no good, you know
                    maybe someday, we can convince Goobers, Inc.
                    to cover them with carob instead
                              . . . . what do you think ?"

and I whispered back, inanely
"yes, they would be healthier that way
maybe we can do that someday"

          then you reached for my hand
          almost . . not quite . . like a test
          and I knew that if you had taken it into your own
          I would not have pulled it away

          because I felt baby robins quiver in my breast
          when you reached for my hand
          almost . . not quite . . then stopped

but strangely, my hand felt as thought you held it in your own
all through the show — our hands were all alone
still, they somehow touched — or seemed as if they did
and I wondered then, as now — did you know ?

          when the film was over, and the house lights went on
          we sat silently for a long . . long moment
          while people were moving, talking all around us
                              walking up the aisle
          we just sat there

Canto Fourteen ☆ 475

not speaking or moving . . silent

then, as we rose to leave, our eyes met — and locked
for one flashing second only
but in that second, I nearly saw Forever
as clearly as on that evening, so many years ago
watching another show
holding hands and eating Goober's Peanuts in Carousel . . oh ! Carousel

.... *if I loved you*
If I loved you . . . .

when we . . . . as we
were leaving the theatre
for no reason at all
you turned to me, and asked

"did you see the film, *Carousel ?*
the part I liked best, was when Bill
. . . . the carnival barker

stole a star from Heaven, to bring back to Earth
and give to his daughter . . . . after he died"

OH !

Oh !

oh !

then I saw forever-forever-forever

and more

I saw three little lost stars fall through the dark
of the wide night sky . . . . making a glow around your head

until my soul wrenched and swelled
and leaped inside my beingness
as my heart said — No ! he is dead — he is dead

but I made a silent wish
on the teeniest-tiniest star, shining there above you

it was almost as if

almost . . as if

I loved you

we used the yogurt

we were both uncertain, unsure enough to need an excuse
to make it allright — so, we used the yogurt
as an obviously logical reason for you to come up to my room
after the glimpse of Forever we caught that night
                              watching a Clear Day

I told you I had some blueberry yogurt in the refrigerator
of my small kitchenette — you said the plain kind was better
without all that white sugar to clog the system
I agreed, so we stopped in a small grocery store, near the hotel
to pick up some fresh yogurt — plain
feeling very smug, healthy and wise — then walked through the lobby
on little puffs of Indian smoke, and as the elevator started to rise
                              pressed the button for the 12th floor
                                        together
although it was an accidental thing
it made me notice your hand — why did it seem so familiar ?
but it's only a hand, I argued silently with myself
and it isn't . . it couldn't be . . because I still remember the Brownies
the boats at camp and the socks in my sweater — and so
the Saturn-Seven-cycle can't be true
if I'm not still the old me, why would I remember so clearly
                              all those things from my own childhood ?

then I noticed something else about your hand
the absence of a wedding band

        funny, I hadn't thought to ask about that before
        after all, it is the Aquarian Age of anything goes
        whichever way the desire wind blows
        with no shouldn't, just should — with wrong called right
                              and bad called good
        maybe the beliefs I thought we shared
        about the ground rules of Life and Love were only skin deep with you
        and even without a wedding band, how could I be sure ?
        what does the absence of a ring mean today
                when the cat is asleep, and the mouse wants to play ?
            I'd better ask

so, while we were mooning our yogurt with runcible spoons
talking of wheat germ and honey
wrapped up in a five pound note . . the book you almost wrote
about the difference between a Ram and a Lion . . Pyramids
and Atlantis . . druids and ships and **UFO** trips
                I slipped in the marital question

Canto Fourteen ☆ 477

"no, I'm not married — I've been waiting"
                              you answered

something in the way you said it
made me rush for words
to fill the quivering air around us . . any words at all

"are there lots of things
you never told about, while you were waiting ?"

                    you smiled straight into my eyes

                    "oh, yes, there are ! multitudes of things
                    I never told to anyone
                    whole snow-covered mountains of secrets
                              which reminds me
                    do you know that mountains can fly ?"

"no, I don't — I mean, it's impossible
for a mountain to fly" I murmured, in a state of genuine shock
why do I lie ? he knows, he knows . . . . . .

                    you rose from your chair as I spoke
                    walked over to the window, then
          and stood for a moment, looking out on the small, white cross
          planted on Mt. Olympus, on the far hill, behind Grauman's
                                                  Chinese Theatre
          and when you turned back to face me
          your eyes were full of twinkle and druid-dust shiny

                    "speaking of snow covered mountains
                    one of the things I never told
                              while I was waiting
                    is that the most perfectly marvelous challenge
                    would be to ski down a hill — just lope
                    down a snowy slope, high in the Swiss Alps
                    because, you see, if you ski
                              at an altitude that high . . . . . . "

"it would be easy to learn the magic of making mountains fly"
"it would be easy to learn the magic of making mountains fly"

                    we said together, in exact unison
                    grokking like two interlocking, tick-tocking clocks
                              with the hands set on Forever

then, overcome with memories of letters bearing German postmarks
I murmured, almost inaudibly
" . . to ski down a snowy slope — to lope
down a Swiss Alp, and make it really fly . . . . how would that
make you feel ?"

and you answered

"it would make me feel — oh, I don't know
I guess it would make me feel
as if I were swelling and expanding
                              into the Universe"

"would you like some tea ?"
I interrupted, turning my head
so you wouldn't notice the sudden mist
that filmed my eyes

                    "tea sounds great ! do you have peppermint ?"

"I'll see," I said

          then I paused, and my eyes met yours
          mist and all, like two bar magnets

"do you . . do you like music ?"

                    "oh, yes, I do ! I love Tchaikovsky"

please don't — please stop
I cried inside

                    but you went on . . . .

                    "I really think the music of the masters . . . . "

          an almost imperceptible
          pause after "masters" . . . .

                    "I believe the music of the masters heals the soul
                    as I believe that natural nutrition heals the body
                    and a good writer of happiness and truth
                                        can heal the mind
                    I would like to find . . . . . . no
                              I am *going* to find a way
                    to do one of the three someday
                    it doesn't matter which one . . . . . . just so I can heal"

I pulled down the blinds of my eyelids
so you couldn't see into the me-of-me
and almost ran to the kitchen sink
to draw water for our tea

          when I came back into the room
          you were standing by the window again
          as down below, in the street . . . . . .

Canto Fourteen ☆ 479

a winding serpent line of pig-tailed Hare Krishna disciples
was snaking its nightly way up Hollywood Boulevard
chanting mantras of Heaven, in Saturn voices . . ringing silvery bells
                              and there were seven

I stood beside you, but not too close
and for a time, we watched together the silvery-serpent line
winding and snaking across the street

slithering-serpent-of-seven
            snaking its way through traffic, in yellow robes
                        chanting mantras of Heaven
                              in a slow, sing-song
                        O ! hear the silvery bells
                              ring ding-dong, ding-dong

      ding-dong . . . . ding-dong !
      slow Saturnine sing-song
      silvery mantras of Heaven
            slithering serpent of seven

      it startled me, when you suddenly turned and spoke aloud

. . . . and I jumped back

                        but you didn't notice — your eyes were far away —
                              and your voice was quiet

                        "you said, that first night . . . . . .
                        didn't you say you had a loss ?"

I couldn't answer you for a moment
the chanted mantras floating through the window
the ringing bells . . the incense burning in the room
creating a faint, musty perfume
all combining, blending . . made me feel as if I were spinning in a tomb
and trying to escape

                        and then, you spoke again . . . .
                        "you're not wearing a ring, and I was wondering
                        are you . . were you . . . . . . ?"

"no, I'm not . . . . I was
I mean, yes, I've had a loss . . . . "
and my voice would not continue

            you made no comment at all — you glanced once more
            at the small white cross on the far hill
            then, sighing softly, turned around
                  walked over to the dresser . . . . picked up her picture
            the one of the three, small druid . . . . Anne with an 'e'

and held it in your hands
you said nothing, not a word — nor asked a single question
neither with your lips or your eyes
you just looked at the photograph — stared at it
for a long, long moment
then replaced it, setting it down very gently
. . . . . . so very gently

I spoke quickly — too quickly
"no, not her — that is, she was a long time ago"

                    and you answered, very low . . . . . . "yes, I know"

know ? how could you know ?
for a moment, I thought I'd only imagined
hearing you speak those three words — but
I could see a mist film your eyes
the same as mine — sudden and unexpected

        yes, tears sprang into your eyes, then — but why ?
        why should you cry — for her ?
        do tears just go naturally with a tender heart
        a compassionate spirit, and an intuitive mind ?
        that must be it, I thought
        just normal sympathy, not anything deep
        sympathy such as any friendly, sensitive stranger might offer

but . . so many others had gazed on her face, without a trace of tears
others with more memory reasons to weep
                    and they didn't cry . . then why . . did you ?

        as though you missed her as much as I
        and wished she hadn't been sacrificed to die
        upon the scarlet altar of the sin of pride

oh, God ! was our selfish pride
the reason she died ?

        I glanced back at you, but you said nothing
                        . . . . eyes cast down

                    you only sighed

When the Student is Ready

oh, those brilliant northern lights
of our blinding, cosmic aurora borealis !

      we heard silvery bells ringing, as our minds and thoughts
      went winging — and our spirits were soaring and singing
      flying across the room, and bouncing off the ceiling
      yet, each still uncertain
      what our hearts were doing . . and feeling

from somewhere, during that enchanted night . . from somewhere
maybe from the bottom of our tea cups
or from our mutual silence about . . . . my loss

           we both had the same idea
             at the same time

not surprisingly, since our extra-sensory attunement was so synchronized
we had ceased to be surprised at anything between us
                of a telepathic nature

      I told you that this was caused, in part
      by your Sun's exact conjunction with my Neptune
      although I did not tell you of the Venus-Pluto aspect . . . . . .

instantaneous thought had now become the rule
not the exception taught in school, that supposedly proves it

no, this was not "the exception that proves the rule"
          but rather . . . .
we seemed to own and have created the rule itself, and were somehow blessed
or were we not blessed by any rule
        but rather, possessed by some ancient druidic spell ?
    might we merely be obsessed ?

      even worse, what if we were cursed by some lower astral entities
      playing tricks upon our subconscious
             on a sidereal, ethereal lark ?

I turned on more lights, not trusting these sensations in the dark
but left the incense burning

      and so, not really knowing — yet feeling something growing
      we decided to try together, a basic and simple
      occult test of learning

anything, I thought . . anything as a brief respite
              from this verbal shocking
and cosmic grokking — with our eyes constantly locking

and you knocking-knocking-knocking on the door of my mind
                    or was it my heart ?
that was the part, the piece of this puzzle I was so afraid to find
please, let it only be that he is knocking on the door
                                        of my mind
not ringing the bells of spring
in my heart . . where are my watch dogs, where ?

        why did I wonder ? I knew
        that my watch dogs were no longer there
        and the sign that said **KEEP OUT**
        now read **BEWARE** !

        we placed our right hands, palms facing
        one above the other, an inch apart
        to test the occult theory that, after a few minutes or so
        each person should feel an unmistakable energy flow
        from one hand to the other
        proving the existence of the unseen vibrations of the human aura
        unseen only because we *believe* we cannot see it

        'sensitives' can see it clearly, as anyone can, who really
        not nearly, but *really* believes and knows it's there

before this night of our cosmic borealis light
sending out its own auric vibrations into the ethers around us
neither of us had ever seen — or felt — a human aura

although I fully expected to — someday, sooner or later
and had made the affirmation many times

        "no, not yet — but I *will* see the human aura soon"

I would always say
when asked

        we were sitting across from each other, near the kitchenette
        and you pulled your chair closer, till we were physically nearer
        than we had been so far . . our palms facing
                            yours above, mine below
        waiting to feel the auric energy grow

then I noticed you were wearing Jerusalem sandals
I don't know why I noticed that
and saw you look oddly at the small gold cross
on a chain, around my neck

                    and so . . we waited

        oh ! the nearness . . . the nearness of you
        was such a cool, tranquil peace

Canto Fourteen ☆ 483

> like the deep-deep-green of woods
and filled the thirsty parts of me
with fresh, clear water

> the experiment worked

we both knew it, after a few seconds — but still we didn't speak
we only sat there, gazing at each other's hands
and allowing the energy to flow, that made us know . . so much
we felt its flowing, but kept the knowing inside ourselves
wanting to make the communion last longer, as the flow
> > became stronger

I was feeling the heat from your hand
burning throughout my being
feeling so strongly the flow from your stillness
that I somehow knew . . you were feeling my flow too
> inside of you
and you were, because finally you said

> "this is . . hard to control"

and drew your hand away

when you looked at me then, your eyes were calm and quiet
as calm as a crystal-green sea
with the strangest . . oh, what was that light in your eyes ?
that strange glow ? it was so . . silvery-wise

"what is hard to control ?"
I asked

> when you answered
your voice was measured and steady

> "the knowing," you said

"the knowing ?" I was finding it
difficult to speak
my knees felt weak, and my mouth was dry
the way a dental anesthetic feels

"the knowing ?"

> "yes, the knowing-things you somehow know
and yet, may not speak . . . . "

"but why . . . . " I paused, thinking to myself
what an odd thing to call them !

"why shouldn't these knowing-things
be spoken ?"

"that's one of the knowing-things
I don't know yet myself
I only know that it's so
some knowing-things may be spoken

and some may not . . . until . . . . . . "

"until what ?"

oh, deep deep deep in my soul
I knew what you meant
by the knowing-things . . yes

the *knowing*-things
are something like the *growing*-things

yet, somehow . . in some way . . . different

it's easy to talk about the growing-things
memories we all share, however individual . . like recalling
scout camp, birthday parties
                    some hurt — or joy — in childhood
the first day of school . . graduation
one's own marriage
                    the birth of children
and their own growing days . . all memories of yesterday
whether a few — or many — years ago

but — the *knowing*-things are not the same at all
and I have been full of these strange fragments
since I was very small

and could not ever speak of them to anyone
although I could never say why
                    and so . . I knew what you meant, in part
but my question still lingered

"until what ?"
            I asked again

            you didn't answer, and I saw you were staring at me
            staring staring staring
                        as if in a trance

            your body absolutely still
                        as if you were not even breathing

I shuddered inwardly
but could not look away

        I was mesmerized by the silvery-wise

of those burning, glowing eyes
                        like a mongoose
I felt myself swaying
                    somewhere deep inside
as if to the rhyme of far away music . . as though
I could hear, in an inner ear
chords I had never heard before
                    no, I had never heard this music anywhere
this faint melody to which I felt my heart
                                        keeping time

or had I ? some melody I remembered . . yet *didn't* remember
I couldn't recall the name of it or the lyrics
                        if I had ever known them

                    still you didn't speak
                        nor did I

then, as I felt myself fading away
my eyes stinging and burning, yet oddly refusing
to close for relief, even for an instant
staring, like you . . staring . . staring . . staring
just as I was about to lose consciousness

                    you spoke

                    and began to question me
                    as your eyes continued to burn and glow

            not as though you sought or needed answers — no
            you asked, as a teacher queries in a classroom
            to test the knowledge or progress of a student
            and as you spoke each careful word
        your eyes never left mine
        staring, glowing, burning like coals
        like two incredible embers of green fire

or like . . a cat's eyes in the dark
but the room was lit by several lamps
                    and was not, therefore, dark
there even seemed to be
a light around your head, shimmering and sparkling
against the pale yellow wall
yet I could not be sure of anything I felt . . . or heard . . . or saw
        there was a sense of unreality
                    as I had always known reality
about this moment

for I heard myself answering you
with a knowledge I did not consciously possess
I swear I did not know all the things you asked

486 ☆ Canto Fourteen

only a few of them . . although
I answered them all in a quiet and low . . and
measured tone, exactly like your own

no . . these were not my words
although they were passing through my lips
and I was compelled to allow them to pass
fascinated by this inescapable compulsion
but also frightened

or was it awe . . not fear ?
you spoke the first question
"what is the symbol of Eternity ?"

and you waited patiently
each time — for each answer

a few heart beats passed
but I could not seem to speak

then heard you repeat
"what is the symbol of Eternity ?"

"the serpent . . the serpent
eating its own tail" I answered dutifully
yes, I knew that first answer consciously
but the rest . . . .

"what does it mean ?"

"what does it mean ?
I don't . . . ."

"the serpent eating its own tail . . . .
what does it mean ?"

"energy — it symbolizes energy"

"what kind of energy ?"

"a kind of energy unknown
or as yet unchanneled . . or not yet suspected
by any of our Earth scientists today"

"in what way
does the serpent eating its own tail
symbolize this energy — in what way ?"

a vagrant thought intruded itself
upon my own conscious level
Good Grief ! I grumbled silently

he's worse than the Little Prince, who — as it's said
would never, never — not *ever* — let go of a question
                                        once asked
until he got an answer

and yet, he already knows the answer
oh, yes, I knew — that you knew
the answers, all of them — and I could see
that you were transmitting them to me
although I did not comprehend how
and by then, I didn't care
it was enough for my mind to bear
that the answers were there, for us to share

                        then you repeated
                        with dogged persistence

                        "in what way ?"

"the tail . . the serpent's tail
is feeding a Positive energy flow . . . . "

I waited — the words came

" . . . . into the serpent's mouth
and the mouth is feeding a Negative energy flow
into the serpent's tail . . at the same time
that is, simultaneously . . . and . . . . . . "

                        "and ?"
                        then you waited

" . . . . and neutralizing each other
the Positive energy flowing into the Negative
and vice versa
allows them to neutralize each other — and . . . . . . "

                        "and what ? this neutralizing
                        is then creating what ?"

"a transformation of energy
            . . . . an energy transformation
a releasing pressure
with . . with an explosive effect"

                        "but this neutralization
                        is creating — *exactly* what ?"

I paused again
until the words flowed forth in a stream
from some long forgotten dream . . of knowing

" . . . . creating a third kind of energy
which is neither Positive nor Negative, and . . . . . . "

"and what ?"

" . . . . . this third energy
is the source of power for space craft
and for human telepathy — the source of all power
                similar to the eye of a hurricane"

                and I thought I saw you smile
                when you said
                        "no, that is not completely correct"

"I meant — also similar to the vortex
of a tornado, and . . . . "
                I faltered

" . . . . the vortex of a tornado and the eye of the hurricane, where something
yes, where something — a flow of energy ?
is traveling, as with the serpent
clockwise and counter clockwise simultaneously
creating a vacuum in the dead center, which has . . . . . . "

                "which has ?" you pressed

" . . . . which has the incredible combination
of power and delicacy
sufficient to uproot and move a building
and settle it several blocks away
without so much as disturbing the furniture within"

                "and this is . . . . . . ?" you questioned

"this is — in some way I cannot explain
in some way, this is like unto . . . . "

why did I use such an unfamiliar, archaic phrase
as 'like unto' ?

" . . . . this is like unto — this neutralizing
energy flow, symbolized by the serpent
eating its own tail — is like unto God
in some way I cannot seem to fully explain . . . . . . "

                outside, suddenly, it began to rain
                soft sprinkles of silver . . and a breeze
                blew in from the open window
                sweet-smelling, like wet grass . . and I didn't finish

what strange power my eyes have

                        I thought
not to blink all this time

                and you — also unblinking
                continued to ask more unanswerable — to me — questions
                but evidently not unanswerable
                to some unfamiliar part of the me-of-me

                                ignoring my incomplete previous answer
                                you asked abruptly
                                "what is the body — the human body ?"

oh ! I knew this answer only too well
on a conscious level
had it not been torturing my restless sleep
for weeks ?

"the body is the Temple of the soul
it is like . . . . "

                                then you used the archaic phrase
                                I had used before, to ask

                                "what is it like unto ?"

"it is like unto a house
a Body Temple is like a house
in which someone lives, but . . . . "

I was becoming uneasy, disturbed by questions
which seemed to be leading down the same blind alley
I had followed these last months . . confused and distressed

"but, you see . . . . "

                                you ignored my restless vibration
                                and asked
                                    " . . . . and may the soul, then
                                move in and out of this house
                                        . . . . this Temple called the body ?"

"well, yes — no

I mean, I don't think so — that is
it *may*, but you see . . . . "

                                again you ignored
                                my confusion, and asked

                                "may the soul move in and out
                                of the Body Temple — only at birth and death ?"

                        490 ☆ Canto Fourteen

"there is . . there is a possibility that . . . . "

my conscious doubts
were intruding upon the flow of words
and I hesitated, then went on
                          against my own will

"there is a possibility that the soul may move
from one Temple into another . . into
the Temple of a sister or a brother . . . . "

              and somehow knew that I did not mean kin
              by brother and sister

" . . . . every seven years or so
sometimes by choice, sometimes not by choice
but I don't believe . . that if the soul . . . . "

                          again you ignored
                          the doubts intruding upon
                                    my automatic answers
                          and pursued the positive

              "and what astrological vibratory influences
              govern the time of this seven year cycle ?"

I hesitated for an eternal moment
my spirit churning, troubled . . . then replied

"the vibratory influences of the planet Saturn
Saturn . . when aspecting by conjunction
                          square or opposition only
its own position at birth

but the Body Temple has not changed
at the time of these Saturn-to-Saturn aspects
and I don't see how . . . . "

                    " the Body Temple has not changed ?"

"well, yes — I suppose it *has* changed
there is, so to speak, a new body — or a new Temple
approximately every seven years, because . . . . "

because why ?
          I wondered

                  "explain this please"
                            you insisted

Canto Fourteen ☆ 491

then the words flowed once more
not of my own volition . . . .

" . . . . at approximately that interval of Time
called seven years, as measured here . . . . "

as measured here ?
what did I mean, as measured *here* ?

" . . . . at that approximate interval of Time
as measured here, on this planet — in this Solar System
approximately every seven years
throughout an Earthling's life span
this new body — this new Temple is accomplished by . . . . . . "

Earthling ?
was I not also
an Earthling ?

"accomplished by what ?"

"accomplished through the body's
own regenerative process . . through the constant
regeneration of cells

such as one's hair and nails — and skin and blood
and tissues . . and . . the cells of all body organs
create a new Body Temple approximately every seven years
but not always a superior body, because . . "

I hesitated

"I mean, one's hair and nails and skin and blood
even the tissues of the body organs
are not the same at any time — as they were seven years previously — but
the regenerated seven-year-cycle body
is not always superior because . . . . . . "

and I hesitated again

"these body cells
which form the design and structure
and condition of the Temple
they are created and re-generated
by what — and how ?"

"the new Temple is created by . . . and
the body cells are regenerated through . . . .
the food one eats — through food and through thought
both together
yes, through food and thought

this is how body cells are regenerated
to form the new Temple — every approximate seven years"

　　　　　　　　　　"and what type of soul
　　　　　　　　　　may or may not enter the Temple
　　　　　　　　　　or the body
　　　　　　　　　　at these seven year Saturn periods
　　　　　　　　　　　　　　of transformation
　　　　　　　　　　not *caused* by — but *sychronized to*
　　　　　　　　　　　　　　Saturn's movements ?"

"yes, not *caused by*, but *synchronized to*
Saturn's movements and aspects"
I repeated, realizing
the vital astrological import of his words

　　　　　　　　　　"what type of soul ?"

"the type of soul
moving into a Temple or a body at this time
depends upon . . the condition of the Temple
it depends upon the condition of the Body Temple
through food and thought
partaken of during each approximate seven year period
of cell regeneration . . . . . . "

　　　　and I went on, somehow feeling
　　　　this deserved repeating, or re-phrasing

" . . . . depending upon the care given the body
through food and thought . . since what you eat creates what you think
and what you think creates what you are
then either a lower or higher evolved soul may enter
a lower or higher . . spiritually evolved soul . . although
this does not mean . . . . "
　　　　　　　　I hesitated

"there are times when a Body Temple
is diseased . . and this does not always mean . . . . "

　　　　I could not find the words

" . . . . that is, sometimes — not always, but sometimes
a high soul may enter an ill body
for a higher karmic purpose . . sometimes, not always"

　　　　　　　　　　"a soul . . from where ?"

"a soul from the same level of awareness
　　　　from this existence — from a Body Temple
which has also reached the seven year Saturn cycle

and wants to change or trade . . . . . .
or a soul from . . . some other level of awareness
such as . . from another galaxy
or a recently deceased Earth-bound soul
if pulled back into a Body Temple by the grief
of the bereaved, or . . . . . . "

       my mind was growing numb

"or . . any other soul entering the body
during the Saturn indicated seven year cycle change"
          I finished hastily

then looked at you
with a new and frightened awareness
but saw nothing in your eyes
       except the same burning embers
of silvery-wise
now deepened by some strange inner light and glow

        "in order to build a finer Temple
        so as to magnetize or attract
              a higher soul
        at each seven year cycle period
        how is this accomplished ?
           repeat this please"

"through food and thought"

       "which are responsible for ?"

"which are responsible
for both one's actions and the type of regeneration
of one's body cells
and each cell in the body is regenerated
by this process, until . . . . . . "

       you interrupted my stream of words

       "that is not correct"
          you said sadly, and softly

    oh, why so softly
      so gently — and so sadly ?

"what is not correct ?"

       "each cell in the body — each organ
       does not have the power to regenerate . . .
       which cells making up which organ

of the body — do *not* contain this power
of regeneration ?"

I waited quietly for the answer to come
waited for the words
and found comfort in your eyes
                    while I waited

how much time passed, while I waited for the words
to flow from my lips ?
one minute — an hour — an eternity ?
yet, as I waited, I found such comfort — in your eyes

            and then . . the answer came

"the human brain . . the cells of the brain
do not . . regenerate themselves"

                        you seemed to be deeply pleased
                        with my answer — although
                        your expression did not change

                        "that is correct — and this
                        would indicate, then — what ?"

"it would indicate that alcohol
that . . among other things . . alcohol . . . . "

        an ocean of vodka
        oh ! an ocean of vodka !

" . . . . it indicates that drugs and alcohol
destroy the tissues and the cells of the brain
tissues and cells which cannot be regenerated
and is not . . should never be . . . . . . "

        and could not finish

                        but you spoke gently, with compassion
                        just the same as if I had finished

                            "that is correct"

                        then after a moment's pause . . . .
                        "the brain itself — what does it do ?
                        what is its true function ?"

"it does many things, but the brain . . . . . .
essentially . . the brain is . . like unto a computer
and it stores . .
        the brain stores . . . . "

a great white light seemed to be slowly
suffusing my mind, as the meaning of my own words
dawned upon my consciousness

"it stores all the memories
of the activities of a Body Temple
in its present existence
the memories of the body's words and actions
                              dictated throughout the Life span of the body
by the various souls
which have resided in it
during a particular Temple's beingness on Earth
the brain . . records and retains these memories somehow
like unto a present day computer
and it also acts as a generator, the brain . . a generator for . . . . . . "

                    like broken fragments
                    the words tumbled out

" . . . . yes, as a generator also
in addition to storing the memories or the *growing* things
                    of the body's actions
dictated by the souls which have resided in it
during its Life span
in addition, the brain is a generator — or a transformer ?
which transfers — how I do not know
but which impresses upon the mind
fragments which are . . which are *déjà vu* memories

from the soul's experiences in *other* Body Temples
yes, memories of each new soul which enters at the Saturn Seven cycle
and the brain acts as a transformer for these subconscious memories
                    sometimes called *déjà vu*
allowing them to occasionally surface when . . "

                    faster faster faster !
                    my words were halting, broken
                    because my lips could not allow them to be spoken
                    as quickly as they were flowing
                    from within my inner being

"these fragmented memories, contained in the subconscious
or subjective mind — which are brought into the Body Temple
at the Saturn-Seven-cycle

. . . these memories, or subconscious fragments . . .
they are . . I believe they are . . .

" . . the lesser *knowing*-things"

you completed for me

"not the ones of which we cannot
                                    yet speak
                but still, *knowing*-things"
                                        you added

"yes ! the *knowing* things of which we may speak
when the brain, acting as generator
                helps us to recall them
these fragmented memories
brought by the soul from other Temples or bodies
are stored in the subconscious of each Body Temple chosen
when the new soul moves in
to be later generated by the brain, through the Mind
into a conscious awareness . . during meditation
or whenever . . that is, I believe that, during . . . "

                "that is — sufficiently correct
                not in its entirety — but
                for the moment . . . sufficient"

                you chose your words
                carefully

        my unspoken thoughts were soaring now
        with a new lightness
        and the excitement of discovery

so *that's* why I remember the *growing*-things
all the people, places and events of my past !
that's why I remember the Brownies
                and all I ever did !
even though . . even though I may not still be
the same me-of-me as before

        I was overcome with the beautiful simplicity
        of the answer to my former doubts

so *that's* why I remember !
even though the new me-of-me in this Body Temple
did not experience the things the brain itself recalls
yes, of course I can recall these *growing*-things
more easily than I can recall the *knowing*-things

for each new soul, like the present one which is part of me
as it entered this present Body Temple
brought with it these fragments of *knowing*-things
and the brain remembers them for me, acting as a generator

just as the brain retains, records and plays back for me
also the *growing*-things — or the actions of my Body Temple
as it was directed by *all* souls residing in it
                          during its life span

now I truly understand the me-of-me !

but what about *him* ? I wonder. could he . . perhaps
could he . . then the Easter gladness
and the lost keys . . oh ! if only the Truth could be that perhaps . . . . "

        I hesitated, then asked you

"does this mean that, if one . .
does it mean that, when a person dies . . . "

                          and you interrupted

                          "yes, it does . .
                          depending on many things
                          we may not discuss now"

but I had yet another question
one which would not have concerned me
on any other night than this
but it seemed urgent
                so I asked you

"is it possible . . for more than one soul
to exist in a Body Temple at the same time ?
is it possible for an Earth-bound soul
to reside in the same Temple at the same moment
that a soul from another level of awareness resides there ?
a soul from another galaxy or . . . "

                          suddenly, you closed your eyes
                          and your face was full of pain

        the rain
outside the window
fell harder
and splashed on the sill

"are you ill ?"

                          "no . . I seem to have a pain
                          between my eyes . . "

                as you spoke these words
                you opened your eyes again
                          and the glow in them was gone

                498 ☆ Canto Fourteen

                    the silvery-wise remained — still there
                    but the burning green embers
                                    were gone

and the trance-like state
we had each fallen into faded
as consciousness and awareness of reality
returned like a rubber band — **SNAP !**

the dreamy mist dissolved . . the lights grew brighter
in the room . . and my own head was throbbing
with a faint, not extreme — dull ache

"can I get you . . ?"

                            "no — it will go quickly"

                    then you smiled

                    "I never have headaches
                    this is unusual
                    very . . unususal . . for me"

I spoke slowly, unsure
if I should speak at all
and asked very quietly

"the things you questioned me about
and the words I spoke in reply
how did you — or — how did I . . . . ?"

                    "I cannot answer you — I'm sorry
                    these particular knowing-things
                    are — well, I never spoke of them
                                before this night
                    yet they are . . *ordinary* knowing-things
                    not like the *other* knowing-things
                    which may not be spoken between us yet
                    I'm sorry, I can't answer you
                    I just don't know — that is the truth
                    truly, I do not know . . . "

and I knew you spoke the truth
you did not know, any more than I
from whence our words had sprung — or why
although you possessed a certain indefinable sureness
I did not feel myself — which caused you to say to me
        that we must not speak about certain of these things
any further now . . . until . . .

        until what ?

but I did not ask
your eyes forbade me

and I wondered, as I cleared away our tea cups
why are your eyes so familiar ? they are ocean green
and his were . . . dark brown
but why is something *behind* your eyes — so familiar ?

your features are not familiar at all — at least, not yet
they are still the features of a stranger I've known
                                        only a short time
but the eyes . . are so familiar

            standing in the kitchen, rinsing out the cups
            I glanced at a calendar on the wall
                        today — tonight — was December 7th
Pearl Harbor Day ?
                        yes, but . . something else

December 7th . . something

            . . . yes, now I remember
            the clerk's mistake — the clerk at the morgue

the clerk's mistake about Bill's date of birth
on the death certificate . . . listing it, in error, as December 7th

            outside, from a distance
            I heard twelve chimes — midnight

            somewhere, I thought . . . .

                        . . . . somewhere, a clock is timing us

Miracle at Midnight

yes . .
            yes, the *eyes* were hauntingly familiar
            but the *features* were strange

                    so we decided to arrange
                    a confrontation with Truth

we darkened the room, turning out all the lights
then sat on the bed — across from each other
legs crossed in the yoga position

yet I had no fear that this would become an awkward situation
for we had both sublimated our magnetic physical chemistry
        to stronger spiritual passions
as we sought intently to solve the mystery of our attunement
with nothing more than enlightenment
                anticipated or desired by either

compelled to follow the unfolding of some nameless secret
we knew we shared, but could not quite identify . . . .
we lit a candle between us . . placing it on a book . . . the flame, nose-high

        to try an ancient Egyptian meditation discipline
        which sometimes causes strange illusionary — or real ? — images
        to appear upon and transform the features
        supposedly into those of former incarnations
                when each was known to the other

and we stared into each other's Third Eye
that powerful point of wisdom exactly between the brows
obeying this particular discipline's rule of *avoiding the eyes themselves*
we stared in the blackness, across the single, flickering candle flame
with a knowing akin to, but not the same . . as the earlier knowing
related, but somehow different, not as forbidden

            . . never dreaming with what excitement
              whole galaxies of stars were watching . .

        as we waited for a sign

        then after a long while, both saw an infant's face
        emerging slowly, dimly
        in the wavering, gentle candleglow
        then appeared two more . .

            . . Ave Maria Maria Maria
                oh, no . . don't go !

    something growing
  reaching out . .

            . . musty stables, shepherd's shout !
                bleating lambs . . incense and straw
        quiet streets and lonely rooms . . . ocean shores
                crowded temples . . empty tombs
        far away and long ago
            oh, no ! don't go . . don't go !

how could we know
into what bottomless wells of longing and needing

our mutual confessions would soon be leading ?

        you whispered intimate questions
        too sensitive for me to answer — but I did
        I whispered intimate questions
        too personal for you to answer — but you did

then both of us hid
behind twin masks of new-felt fear
pretending not to hear
      each other's unspoken cries

and finally synchronized, done with all pretending

          "who *are* you ?"   "who *are* you ?"

our two voices blending
in exact unison
like some rehearsed duet

        now our features — noses, cheeks, lips
        ears and brows and scents of skin
        all were remembered, intimate . . known

the Jerusalem sandals you wore
      the glittering gold cross around my neck
had we seen them there before . . somewhere ?

        our senses were acutely aware
        of each nuance, each sigh . . each *why*

a gust of air from the open window stirred our hair

        nearly extinguishing the candle's flame
      then . . as you reached out to curve your fingers
    in a sheltering circle around it
            I saw it clear

a warm, strong, dear . . familiar hand

          and had no more questions

      these moments cannot be told or explained
      no words have been invented
      to define the certain, flashing knowledge of heart and soul
      when Eternity is suspended . . in one instant of Time
      and the curtain is torn asunder
          long enough to see . . Forever

      no, there are no words . . .
      nor are they needed now

it was *his* hand — that is enough
             it was his hand, I don't know how
yet it was but a fleeting sign
and did not remain for long . . it was the eyes

no, more than the eyes
it was . . all the memories which spoke to me
from *behind* the eyes . . the pain

             then, frightened still — and unsure, uncertain
             I thought of a child's game I used to play
             in moments of intense need to know — a game
             timed to the pulse of the Universe
             although I didn't think of it that way in childhood . . .
             and made up a word
             an ordinary, everyday, conversational word
             thinking to myself — if he says that word
                          within a minute or two
             then all this is true
             and before the thought was even completed in my mind
             you spoke the word: "wonder"

                   "I wonder if . . . "

as I heard from afar a rolling thunder
but said nothing to you

             I had my answer from the Universe, pulsing
             but did I dare accept — believe in
             the credibility of a Universe perhaps also gone mad, like me ?

             as for you . . you knew

oh, yes, you knew . . you knew it all
but not from me, from where ?

             was some invisible spirit there
and murmuring in your ear
that you should know so much
             and feel such pain with me ?

you spoke of infants . .
                   "were there three ? and when did I . .
                   I mean, when did he . . die ?"

     you simply knew
not how — and not from where — or why

             you only knew that you knew . . and I
             yes, I knew too

Canto Fourteen ☆ 503

then other images moved across
             the shimmering screen of our reflected dream
suspended between us . . like a silvery-white cord
                              of pure white light

                    . . towering pyramids, ebony slaves
                              dusty desert . . sandy graves
                    swelling music . . azure skies

I saw distinctly a pale golden halo rise
around your head and shoulders . . an auric light
you saw the same mist around mine

             as we lost all consciousness of Time and Space

             and the illusion we had called reality

from somewhere, deep inside my soul
I heard a church bell chime
             . . a baby robin sing

             then, as you held out to me your strong, steady hand
             I placed on your finger a gold serpent ring
                              with ruby eyes
             I had found in a store in Colorado
and kept . . yet not worn . . just treasured
not knowing why, until now
until this moment of calm, holy still

                    you said only . . "thank you"

             but I felt my own eyes fill
             as I saw a single tear . . like a tiny raindrop
             streak down your cheek
                    and then one more

for a breathless, timeless awareness
we sat in the stillness . . apart
our physical senses reeling . . each feeling
our auras blending into an ecstasy of Oneness
             each sustaining an overwhelming need to fulfill and feed
                    body . . mind . . and soul
             into the spiritual trinity of complete consummation

             the knowledge between us grew unbearable
             until, at last, you spoke
             and your voice was low and clear

                    "what are we going to do about it
                         . . *now* and *here* ?"

                    504   ☆   Canto Fourteen

for one throbbing moment

       silence

dead silence . . in the vortex of the tornado swirling around us
we were suspended in the center of an echoing tomb

      then a streak of cosmic lightning
             flashed across the room

    we touched . . and trembled

      someway . . somehow . . I was in your shaking arms

    our bodies fused together

         as the whole sky exploded with shooting stars

    and from somewhere within the depths
      of a wordless prayer

            we knew that God had been there

Home Again, Oh ! Home Again

all night long

      all through that deep blue velvet night of peace
      we exploded with the stars, sang back to them
      and affirmed our wonder
      with ecstasies of intimacy and touching

sharing half-remembered fragments
without a need for words . . we spoke silently, each to the other

yes, this singing body of mine
that lies here beside you, entwined and clinging fast
has known and belonged to the you-of-you
when it resided in his Temple, as now in yours
the pronouns blend together . . his and yours

for he, my love, my only love — he and you are simply
              you
and the me-of-me
    how many earthly heavens
has it visited with the you-of-you ? across how many forgotten beaches

have we walked along together
weaving in and out of this present existence
                        through our Saturn Seven cycles
while the golden Serpent hiSSed its secret to us
as we remained still blind and unaware ?

        Oh ! we shall never again leave our Body Temples — these
without each other, playing karmic hide and seek
no, one shall wait longer and linger — the other will hasten
                                and not be late
and we shall stay, leaving only by pre-arranged Saturnine appointment
moving into ever cooler, grander alabaster Temples . . never parted

                our Saturn Seven cycles are close together in Earth time
                by planetary movement
                thank God for that karmic blessing
                and bless the pain that earned it for us

                throughout . . how many incarnations ?

oh, darling, when you went away . . before I could forgive you — *her*
you should have left a note to tell me into which Temple you moved

        you chose another painted horse to ride
        so I could not find you for the longest, longest time

and . . I almost fell off the Carousel

                I really nearly did . .

Merry Christmas Everyone — and God Bless Tiny Tim !

our first morning of waking together
is lithographed on my heart
like a fine steel engraving of a Currier and Ives print

I awoke . . to see the pale December solar rays
painting pastel splashes of sunlight rainbows on the carpet

                in the town of 'saints' — Saint Mary's ?
                        or in the city of 'angels' — Los Angeles ?

no matter . . I was back inside the sleepy-warm, protective circle
                                of your arms again
watching the ribbons of light streaming across the bed
bathing our faces in gentle pink-gold
and coaxing our eyelids to blink open . . as I snuggled near you

in a surge of delicious contentment
curling my toes . . and tracing the delicate sun-laced patterns
on your strong, tan arm with my fingertips

                    I had to squeeze my eyes tightly
             to keep the glad-tears back

a great welling up of thanksgiving spread joyously within me
and nearly burst open . . then you stirred
I smelled your cheek, you sniffed my ear . . and oh ! the dear
familiar scents of each other's skin and hair
that formed an almost unbearable lump of tenderness in our throats !

yes, you . . oh, you remembered too !
but you recalled our past loving-times
with the fainter *knowing*-things of the you-of-you

        and I recalled with the more vivid recollection
        of the recent *growing*-things
        more easily called forth from the brain's memory bank
        added to the deeper knowing-things of the me-of-me

                    "good morning, darling"

"darling, good morning"

        . . my Comforter has returned

        my eyes began to fill again
at the sound of your voice, newly remembered . . so long ago learned
and I sobbed softly, as you whispered

        . . how could you know the words ?

            "shhh ! *be still, my love, be still*
                    . . I'm here"

we smiled at each other in a deep, deep knowing
then felt the hunger growing, until your hand, full of fever
lightly touched my breast
pressed harder, and lingered . . crumpling my knees to tissue paper
yes ! I have been here before, I know the breeze
beyond the window . . the cool of the air . . the musty scent of your hair
                  the sounds outside the door
you have been mine before

unexpectedly, I trembled, remembering the intimacies
the shared private words and touches no one knew but you
        we had murmured and exchanged
                in the deep blue velvet night behind us

. . you pulled me closer
and we kissed
a long, hard kiss of morning wanting

as your heart pounded in your chest a violent demand I could feel
in the sudden strength and tightening of your arms
making me grow faint and still
with an urgent hollow of aching only you could fill

then you sighed . . with a throb of needing only I could fill
as I did before, when our violet spring was new
but not so intensely then, not understanding the meaning of total surrender
afraid, then, to allow its honey-richness to envelop me
but I am afraid no more
there is so much, now, to give . . frigidly, rigidly held back before

you moaned . . "deep"

I whispered, "yes, I know"

then we began the slow
and steady rhythm of our music

O ! we loved, we loved . . . like soaring sea gulls !
move together, back and forth . . sway together, forth and back
wet eyes shining, catching sunbeams
complete unfolding, burning with crescendos of desire . . faster, faster
chords of glory . . explode in fire !
. . cool, green water

ecstatic pain . . cool, clear rain

then fell from there . . from the dizzy height of other galaxies
through immeasurable miles of space
floating back down, love drenched . . returning
into each other's arms again
and afterwards . .

our cheeks glistened with tears
from the intensity of our passion

and from our deep-felt gratitude . . for the quiet peace
of its fulfillment in each other

though it was still December, a faint perfume
a fresh, lavender-lilac scented breeze of spring haunted the room
wafting a mist around us — and from that day forward
spring meant more than just a season of the year — it became our code word

for this deeper kind of loving between us

it is our season, Spring . . and contains our Easter gladness

I'm glad you awakened the overflowing wells of my love
        that December morning
for the very first time
              . . in the sunlight

so I could see your smile of joy and pride
and you could see the tremor of my wonder at this unsuspected secret
I never knew that I contained within my waiting body
waiting lonely . . only for your touch . . to trust you
                  with all my mysteries of being woman
now I feel like a stream . . yes
I know how a stream feels, rushing out to meet the river
that draws it on . . and on and on . . into the ocean
then into final Oneness with the Universe

      yes, I gave you cause before, I gave you cause
      frigidly guarding my flowing secret of being woman
      and holding back its wonder, but no more
                  we forgive each other now
      and flow together into our ocean of Oneness
      through the deeper rivers of our souls
      which now hear chords of music they did not hear
                in former Body Temples
yes, I'm glad glad glad
that it was you, who *knew* — and released my mystery

    my flowing love . . in the sunlight

                       later . .

when you were sudsing yourself with lathers of happiness
and I was brushing my hair with happy too
making it snap and crackle with sparks . . I was standing
at the bathroom door
    you stuck your soapy head around the shower curtain
           looked deeply into my eyes — and smiled

    that's all — just smiled

then I loped over to the window
and looked out on the small, white cross, planted on Mount Olympus
on the far hill, behind Grauman's Chinese Theatre
remembering your half-teasing whisper, after our "spring"

              "darling, we love like this
              because we are a god and goddess
              from the Oober galaxy of stars
                not from Mars
              and we love all Earthlings

. . as I began to croon
a tangled up Mother Goose tune

> *this is the day they give miracles away*
> *with half a pound of peppermint tea* !

but I never got to tell you what I was singing
        there were too many little hurry-bells ringing !
we had to get dressed and fly outside
to see the world for the very first time . . all clean and fresh
                     and bright and shining

      oh ! Merry Christmas everyone !

      God bless Tiny Tim
      Anne with an 'e'
      all baby druids everywhere
      and lonely Scrooges too

and all that day — we ran up and down that holly-berry town
        giving miracles away

     then we stopped in C. C. Brown's, for some peppermint tea
     served by a jolly lady, with snow white hair
     wearing crinkles and twinkles and holiday smiles . . .
     who was obviously Ms. Santa Claus
             just helping out in the rush hour . . .

     and beaming little splashes of joy on us
     as we floated there in our cherry wood booth
     gazing on each other like delighted children
     dizzied and dazzled by a glittering Christmas tree

with a wondrous star
at the very tip top . . the Star of Truth
our love had opened up for us to see
for we had learned that the more miracles of happiness
we gave away to others . . the more we had left for you and me

Knowing

the knowing-things we shared that first night, when we stared
          we never spoke again
though we discussed related things — like space travel, serpent circles
quarks and angstrom units
the body and the brain . . Life and death and birth
and other matters of Heaven and Earth

but not the staring and staring . . of our sharing
the flowing energy, the glowing eyes . . and the surprise
of our trancelike speech, so silvery wise

> from that night forward
> each time the staring and the knowing-growing returned
> through that pulsing force, that burned

we were silent

> transfixed, it seemed, by some unspoken galactic agreement
> in the vortex
> of our mutual tornado of unexpected knowingness

somehow, never again needing to speak
the eyes-into-eyes, like burning embers, were enough
we did not again need words
when those entranced and pyramidic moments came and went
always suddenly . . for no reason
> in the middle of a sentence
we stopped — and stared

> and *knew* . . in silence

and then continued talking, after the moment had passed
as if nothing had interrupted us at all
until I began to call these moments — secretly, to myself
the times . . when you come and go

> and now and then, I would wonder
> when will he come . . and go . . again ?

> never thinking to ask myself why I expressed it so
> in my private reflections
> it was enough to simply know
> > that you would come . . and go
> gradually, it became, in my own mind
> a coming and a going thing — an unspeakable knowing thing
> a time when I learned so much . . so much
> yet could not consciously recall a single word
> > that had passed silently between us
> nor any exchanged wisdom
> when it was over . . like waking from a dream

> I wanted to ask if you remembered
> but your eyes somehow forbade me to speak of it
> so the questions remained inside me in the night
> > lying beside you
> the silent knowing-thing between us

Canto Fourteen ☆ 511

like a deeper spring . . remembered . . yet forgotten

Albert Had a Theory

since you and I turned into Us
      I can't say why — or how — or when
but I know our Now was also Then

how many times have we felt this need ?
the Present is but a memory we're moving through
           at a different rate of speed
the beautiful simplicity
of Einstein's Relativity is finally clear
        for . . Yesterday will soon return
and Tomorrow has already been here

    now we shall never need to draw . . a final earthbound breath
    because there is no Life, until you love
        and then there is no death

Telepathic Telegrams from our Easter Union

isn't it strange, the way we read each other's minds
and the many other kinds
of uncanny anticipation we've discovered between us ?

when we call each other
we answer the phone before it rings
and since you touched me
I hear the song of a bird before it sings

    last night you whispered

        "darling, I knew why you cried
           before you told me
        in the same way that I tremble inside
        before you hold me"

"oh, yes, it's true !" I whispered back
    "I tremble inside when you hold me too
and I always know you will . . just before you do
it's like being one beat ahead of the pulse of the Universe
now that we've learned that a Little Prince

can love one rose — and mountains can truly fly !"

        " . . . and that druids are real people
        who can laugh and cry
        and we have a whole shining lifetime together
        to teach each other why

        the miracle of Us . . . is not easily defined
        because, all we really know . . . "

" . . . is that it was planned
many eons ago . . . "

        "yes . . before you were born, I was yours
        and before I was born . . you were mine"

CANTO FIFTEEN

Your words are lovely,
Your love is still more beautiful,
With strong steps your gentleness has borne me
Beyond all mountains.
You have taught me to stand
Astride the vortex of all winds,
Thus to be steadfast *because* of them.

This is our language —
You have bestowed myself upon me
In granting me this heart-speech.

Your words are lovely . . .

We shall be called
To always-wanted vastnesses,
Tread upward-curving sky-paths
As those who always knew
The Way.

> Your kisses saviours are by what they grant,
> Your hands' light touch bestows an inward grace
> Upon me that does fix a covenant
> Transcending good or ill, or time or place.
> Do men still speak of pow'r, or boast their stores,
> And seek to slay that they themselves may live ?
>
> You are my love, and I am surely yours,
> Does aught remain to boast, to take or give ?
> For love is sovereign, in itself complete,
> (Though sleeping glories must be born through pain)
>
> And only those who cannot love compete
> Where there is only one, can two remain ?
>
> Here lies the art of our infinity:
> *To love mid death till death no more can be.*

Kyril Demys (Musaios)
Prismatic Voices

Dear Charles Schulz — When Was Snoopy Born ?

while you went out to get the Sunday papers
one squeaky-clean morning
after a pitter-patter of silvery nothing-is-the-matter rain
on the birthday of Us — one week old !

    I was lying across the love rumpled bed, half dreaming
    and rapping with an old friend

"Good Grief, Charlie Brown, you silly clown !"
                         I said
"Good Grief, Charlie Brown
you've sure been around, to know about "good" grief
all along, you've understood that grief is good

yes, grief is good — it makes you grow
                  and makes you know . . the *knowing* things
not just the *growing* things

    but I'll bet you don't know what I know, Charlie Brown
    I'll bet you don't know that grief can also make you grow
    to discover that a lover . . is a blanket

      that's right ! "thy Comforter shall come"

and I'll bet you don't know that love is not an old thing
or a then thing — or a new thing
              or a maybe thing — or even a **WOW !** thing

      love is . . a **NOW** thing

an eternally eternal **NOW** thing
oh, yes, love is indisputably a **NOW** thing

if anyone scurries and scrambles and rambles
through your druid town, where Lucy is obviously the Brown Owl
if anyone there is aware — and hip
to that silvery-Serpent-Saturn-Seven-Heaven secret trip

        it would be Snoopy

good old dippy, loopy Snoopy
that perfectly marvelous Aquarian dog, who gets high on Life
and chases the Red Baron, wearing a scarf and goggles
then slips on his dark shades, when he's making like Joe Cool

    oh ! Snoopy is nobody's fool
    and if anyone who scurries and scrambles
    and rambles through your druid town

knows the seven-come-Heaven Golden Rule
about love being a **NOW** thing
                        it's Snoopy

        then you came in, with the morning papers
        interrupted my serious rap with Charlie
                kissed me on the nose, and teased

                "you have funny looking toes
                for a special, unique rose — but you know
                they're starting to grow on me . . .
                let's get spaced-out on carrot juice
                snuggle up together in bed
                and read the funnies, mouse-spouse"

then I asked . .
"listen, blanket, I was wondering . . "

                and you said . . "what ?"

and I giggled, and said
"I meant, listen, darling — I was wondering
what do you think Snoopy's Sun Sign is ?"

                "why, Goob, don't you know ?
                Snoop is clearly an Aquarian dog !
                good old sloopy, dippy Snoop
                has all the canine scoop
                        on the new Uranus vibrations
                Snoopy is a Gooober too
                and I'll bet he's even in love, like you
                          . . . and me
                with a twin soul of his own"

"then where is his blanket ? that is, his Comforter
I mean, his girl friend . . his only love ?"

                "oh, he probably keeps his true love
                              a secret
                so that liberated Lucy wench
                won't nag his ear off about it . . "

"you male chauvinist pig !" I murmured
as I smelled your cheek
don't put Lucy down — she's just like me"

                "she is ? hmmm . . well, then
                I guess she's a rather wonderful wench
                and I love her madly"

"you do ? oh, Gooober, you really do ?"

"I love her madly"

"even if she's a little pushy
and aggressive and outspoken
      . . and independent, and . . "

            you repeated

            "whether Lucy is a timid little mouse
            or an independent, liberated female
            if she's like you — I love her madly
            now, come here, spunky wench
            and stop stealing the pillow . . remember
            you're a willow
            who has learned how to bend . . "

    then we spaced-out
    on a healthy, smoochy, carrot juice kiss
    and read the comics together

        Lucy wasn't in them that morning

           Snoopy was   **⟶**

Thought Transference
‾‾‾‾‾‾‾‾‾‾‾‾‾‾‾‾‾‾

    our kooky, beautiful esp
            that transmutes us into Us
    instead of only ordinary you and me

      started so soon

    the seeds of it planted, perhaps
    that first night in the Hollywood Roosevelt
    to later grow into a startled knowing between us

on that first night of *spring* — our miracle at midnight
I was stricken with shame when I realized the secret
             I could no longer hide from your eyes
must be disclosed

    my long chestnut hair, that gleamed in the candlelight
    and fell around my shoulders in a veil of feminine mystery

        was not my own

I had to tell you . . . .   how could I wear that artifice

as we fulfilled our passion ?
    oh ! what if it should slip off
                        and just lie there on the pillow
for you to see, and laugh at me
or worse — turn away in a shiver of disappointment ?

    no, I could not risk such a bizarre intrusion on our love
            and so, I removed my "fall"
    confessing to you that I had feathered my hair short
    with a razor . . in Laguna Beach

" . . and until it grows out long and shining . . "

    I said that twice
    " . . and until it grows out
    long and shining . . like before . . "

    then I said it once more . . to reassure you
    that Mother Nature wouldn't let you down — or me

" . . and until it grows out again
well, you see . . I wear this fall, that's all

I don't know why I cut it
I'm sorry I did, and . . I wish
well, I wish I hadn't cut it so short
but . .
        but it will grow out again
                honestly-*honestly* — it will"

then watched your face, for the slightest trace
of sudden coolness or distaste
my heart skipping and tripping a staccato of possible rejection
so desperately needing a sign of affection
as I stood before you, shorn of my shining crown of glory
my own un-even locks a mousey shade of ash blonde
so short and frizzled from the razor's ruthless strokes

    I stood there, a quaking, shaking mouse
    struggling in oceans of fear
    which nearly drowned my earlier desire

        but your eyes burned with no less intense a fire

            as you said . . "your hair is lovely
            it is soft, silky, baby druid hair
            we will stuff you with carrots every day
                    and brush it every night
            and soon it will grow as long and strong
            as that wench's who used her hair
            as a ladder for her lover to climb up to her

oh, Goob . . your hair is lovely
. . just right for a druid"

then we kissed, and our mouths clung together
fused in flame again
and once more the thunder pounded in us everywhere
as you whispered . .

"hurry . . hurry back to me"

and your fingers trembled, as they stroked my hair

"oh, darling . . hurry, hurry"

then I slipped out of your shaking-again-arms
and left the room, still fearing that, when I returned
my hair might not be the only hurting-thing

I was not prepared for love . . and you

I owned no whispering folds of silk and satin
which only half conceal the breasts
and outline every intimate curve and body secret
with seductive enticement

nor did I dare to face you
in unashamed nakedness of giving
unsure as I was
of such a consummation of consuming need
for so long forgotten
through lonely living

. . . you told me later
as your eyes misted, and you swallowed hard
that you felt a sudden, unaccustomed tenderness
at the initial sight of your sensual Temptress
seducing you in the comical "bridal gown" I finally chose

but . . as memory returned more vividly and clearly
you laughed and wrinkled your nose
yes, while you described the scene later, you laughed
reminding me of how I had walked into your waiting arms
dressed in the old white night shirt
I wear when I wash my hair
several sizes too large . . big enough, you said
for both of us to hide in

the sleeves rolled up above the elbow
like an Irish wash woman, you said . . preparing to strip a bed
and do the Monday laundry

white, virginal cotton

Canto Fifteen ☆ 521

enveloping my so long unseen and untouched body
in tent-like folds of modesty
my bare ankles and feet protruding from the bottom
like some awkward child, making her debut in dancing school
and overcome with stage fright

it crushed me . .

when you described my shame with such amusement
and I gazed at you with wounded eyes

"you're making fun of me — that's not very kind
                    I'm not blind
I know I didn't look like a Playboy Bunny centerfold
        I saw myself in the bathroom mirror
and I'm aware that I more resembled Mahatma Ghandi
preparing to kneel on a prayer cloth, and fast
than a woman preparing to plunge into passion

        but . .

and my voice broke

"but I wanted so . . . oh ! I wanted so
to be beautiful for you our very first time together
and I was only . . I was only ludicrous"

        then you took me into your arms, to comfort me with soothing
        and your voice was gentle, tender
        as you told me I was magic . . that our love
        had transformed my white night shirt
        into a perfectly marvelous bridal gown for you

so I dried my tears . . but not my fears
no, not my deep-seated fears of personal inadequacy

        they remained

buried even deeper than ever before

        were you comparing my seduction with others before me
comparing me, perhaps, with *her*

        whom I'd briefly met with you, accidently, on the street
        on our second night
        before our "spring" — and after our meeting in Pickwick Bookstore ?

comparing me with her, the cool, sure Scorpio
with whom you "shared a relationship", you said
before we found each other ?

                    the cool, sure one
with the poise of Pluto and the nubile appeal
of one and twenty ?

eventually, I permitted you to make a private joke between us
of my foolish, wedding night raiment
                              . . or pretended to permit it
and in your tumbled-backwards Oober language
you began, teasingly, to refer to my white night shirt
as my Night-White-Shirt

                    "oh, no ! you're not going to wear
                    that awful Night-White-Shirt again, I hope"

                    you teased the next day
                    after I'd washed my love-limp hair
                                        with Ivory soap
                    because the shampoo bottle was empty

the following week, after I had flown away and left you
tearing both our hearts in two
back to Fun City, Manhattan — metropolis of black lace bras
and G-strings . . or no bras at all
I felt once more that small growing pain of rejection
at the thought of the clumsy image I must have presented to you
on that special night of our winter springtime

        so I impulsively dashed off a letter
        with only six words on the page — six words of hurt
                        for you to see

            Dear Gooober . .
                you hate my white night shirt . . .

                    Me

and sealed it — and addressed it — stamped it First Class
drew on the envelope a small daisy and forget-me-not
took it outside to the corner mailbox
                    and dropped it angrily in the slot

when I returned, just minutes later
my morning mail was waiting for me at the door
and there was a letter from you
        with only six words on the page
six rainbow words for me to see

            Dear Gooober . .
                I love your Night White Shirt !

                    Me

Canto Fifteen ☆ 523

then I cried inside . .
oh, Goob ! thank you, thank you for loving me !
and for feeling my frightened insecurities
even before I sense them myself

      receiving my letter
      and realizing it had crossed yours, in the mail
                      you wrote back

           darling . . I forgot to mail the second page
           of my letter — and send it now to you

           . . when you came to me on that starry night
           all dressed in flowing white
                you looked like . .
           you were to me . . an Atlantean goddess
           standing there in the moonlight
           you were lovelier by a thousand years
           than all our yesterdays will be

           and the next morning, in the sunlight
           you were more beautiful
                than all our tomorrows were

           how can anyone be more beautiful than that ?

           I do love your Night White Shirt, I do, I do !
           and if I were there this minute
           which I actually am, you know . . because
              Yesterday is the Present
                and the Future is also Now . .
           I would climb inside it, with you
           and show you how much you are loved
                eternally . . . by

                Me

and as I read your words of reassurance
faintly familiar, I thought . .

oh, Gooober — you say it better every time
in each new Temple — the Forever Thing

then suddenly remembered
how I laughed at the funny, awkward, clumsy way
you cut your own hair, with big shears
shaping it into a toadstool . . but beautiful

and how I can never hold back my giggles of amusement
over the weird, dwarf way you clutch a pen or pencil
with your thumb curved around it — almost upside down

learned, somehow, backwards in kindergarten
when you were a tiny, left-handed Lion cub

I recalled the look on your face, the wounded frown
those unthinking times I laughed and teased
oh, Goob, I'm sorry . . so sorry . . I never thought . .

and hurried to write and tell you
how tall and golden-god-like you were that night
on Mount Olympus — and will always be — to me
and about the soft marshmallows that melt in my heart
when I watch you cutting your hair . . or when I touch it

    and how slowly reciting the Lord's prayer together
as we do, after spring, nearly every time, before we go to sleep
makes my soul weep . . with happiness and pure peace

        and how I always get tender mump-lumps behind my ears
        when I watch you hold a pen, and write like an elf
        and how, every single day and night
        I worship the beauty of the new Temple you chose
        what perfectly marvelous toes
        you have . . and other personal, private things between us

realizing then, I believe, for the first time
your inner need to know . . too
and promised myself never-ever again to forget
your own hurts — no less than mine
though hidden inside your wells of Leonine pride
and unexpressed in spoken words
                only in words my heart hears

    oh, darling, I see your unshed tears
    and feel all your silent fears . . as you do mine
    and so, I wrote — and tried to tell you

        but I didn't tell you, in my letter, the secret things
        so hard to express — like the way your strong brown arms
        make me quiver into jelly, make me weak and dizzy
        when you're just filling the gas tank, at the service station
        because the attendant is busy

        . . how that makes me feel like I'm a girl mouse
        watching her man, moving around, not making a sound
        just a tiny girl mouse, who wishes her spouse
        would be less vain and arrogant and bossy . . but who secretly
                        enjoys
        playing girl mouse — to her man
        a man who can do anything . . oh ! anything
        she'll ever need — who can make her happy forever-after
        if he'd only stop insisting that she always follow

and now and then, allow *her* to lead

and I didn't tell you . .
               because I couldn't quite find the words

                    . . about the baby birds
                    who flutter their wings inside my breast
                    when you hold my head
                                   and let it rest
                    against your heart

or how your hands
          on the steering wheel . . steady
so confident . . so sure and wise
sometimes cause glad tears to lope into my eyes

               just seeing your hands
                              on the steering wheel of the car
          just because they are . . so sure
                              of what they are doing

                    only that

or . . how I smile with warm loving, deep inside
when you're wearing your old hiking hat
no matter how I sometimes tease you
I always want to hug you tightly
               when you're wearing that funny hat
why can't I find a way of telling you that ?

          and did you know

I like to watch
the muscles ripple in your thighs
when you step on the brake — suddenly — in traffic

               . . and that the way your hair grows
               at the nape of your neck

               overwhelms me ?

all those things
     I can't seem to tell you . .

and yet, our silent thoughts reach out to each other
in a constantly flowing stream
as though we were connected by a telepathic beam
of steady light — day and night
every hour — every second — in every way

          just the other morning

your letter in the mail
had this to say . .

"Dear spunky Lucy-wench . .
how would you like to play house
with a vain and arrogant
but adoring and devoted spouse
who may sometimes make you feel
like a teeny tiny girl mouse
but who loves you with all his heart ?"

oh, Gooober . .
there's no way I can keep secrets from you !
you're still reading my mind, as you always do

but . .
I still wonder if you know

. . that the way your hair grows
at the nape of your neck

overwhelms me

A Matter of Vibrations

once you wrote to me an astral formula
and began the letter
in your wonderful pineapple-upside-down-cake-way

. . as if you were not accustomed
to the typewriters on this planet

Gear Dooober . . .

I've rust jeturned from a spin in a saucer
with some Master Oobers
and have learned the higher mathematics of love
as calculated in the Oober galaxy

one Goob + one Goob — apart
= two lonely Goobers

or

one you and one me — apart
equals an empty Universe

and if you don't hurry back out here
                to me soon
I'm going to rocket to Manhattan
by way of the New Moon

or socket there
on a telepathic beam of light
        some night
or catch the very next astral flight
        or fly in my dusty blue Bug
or walk in a Greyhound bus . . to you
because I am missing . . Us

and I wrote back, to explain
that the plural of Gooober must be spelled with a 'z' — as in "Gooberz"
because of the ancient
Chaldean numerological vibrations

                then you wrote . .

                "I always knew you were a witch"

        so I wrote . .

"oh, be still !
        I am a good witch, not a mournful Medusa
I only use white magic
        to turn sorrow and sadness
into joy and gladness
        to try to make unhappiness go"

                and you wrote back . .

                "I know, darling . . I know"

A little Professional Advice

listen, Goob, you're always telling me how you want to heal
through one of the sciences or arts
and how discouraged you are with all the false starts
that have prevented your daydreams from becoming real

you're always saying how much you admire people
who compose symphonies . . or write poetry . . and teach
well, I don't know about the symphonies
        but poetry is certainly within your reach

along with all forms of creative writing
if only you could declare peace
     on this loneliness of spirit you keep fighting

God knows you think in measured meter. sometimes too much so
as for expressing yourself, you write . . you speak
with words like colored beads
     strung together on a glittering chain of imagery
using them as uniquely, as individualistically
               as an artist mixes oils
your letters are all unpublished poems
needing only to be placed on the page in stanza form
for the words to spread their wings, and fly free
like this verbatim quote from a letter you sent to me
              . . . and there are dozens more

     "I'm happy to be back in this part of the country"
          you wrote from Pismo Beach, not long ago

     "I've missed the ocean so much . . the hills and trees and sky
and I've missed this feeling I always get
when I see a flock of wild ducks, winging south
or a lone golden eagle, hovering miles above my head
     even the fog seems alive and beautiful here
when it creeps and flows down into the valleys
         and across the meadows . . .
it's good to see the seals again
flapping their flippers
     and basking on the rocks in Pirate's Cove"

in one of your recent letters, between two paragraphs
all by itself, for no apparent reason at all . . . you wrote

          "zoo is a funny word"

oh, Gooober, don't you see ?

     that's the way becoming a poet begins — having loopy thoughts
with no particular reason, or rule
never mind what they tried to teach in English class, at school

and Zoo *is* a funny word !

     once you wrote to me about trying to convince
your skeptical relatives
of the validity of the Pyramid's healing energy
and the first line of your letter was . .

       "well, I shot a few bullets of truth
      across the cranberries
         and the pumpkin pie today"

Canto Fifteen ☆ 529

maybe we should write a book together
you could cover the subjects
of seals and dolphins . . and Martians . . and fog

and I could cover carousels, humans and smog

       but we'd better collaborate soon
       or I'll be tempted to publish all your letters

Exploring the Deep

one mystery about you intrigued me when we met
and puzzles me still

     from the beginning you told me
     how disillusioned you were by the few and uninspiring opportunities
     open to you, as a marine biologist
        in today's chaotic, competitive world

you tried working for several large corporations
    in this country, Canada and England
until you realized their motives were less than idealistic
then, because you didn't want to become part of such negative
                        experimentation
with the inevitable result of further wounding
our already long-suffering Earth
and despairing of any one ever recognizing your worth

     you resigned each position, one by one
     until there were three behind you

and when we met
you were working on what you called a "special assignment"
for a private individual, based in Alaska

     it was to be brief, you told me — in Hawaii
     just some scattered research and testing, here and there
     not a permanent thing . .

but . . . sometimes you mentioned the possibility
of another "special assignment" you expected to materialize soon
              on the island of Truk
and when I asked what it might involve
you merely laughed, in your teasing way, and said you would be
part of a classroom, in a school of fish . . actually, dolphins
     . . . something you'd always wanted to do

I thought that a most unusual wish
to be part of a classroom in a school of dolphins and fish
and decided you must be joking with me

   but you said, quite seriously

    "I'm not joking at all
    dolphins are wiser than most people surmise"

"I'm not 'most people'
there are things you may not suspect that I realize
I already know, you see
that dolphins can probably be taught
to speak with you or me
or at least — to communicate well enough
to be sent on spooky, secret missions

is that what your next assignment is all about ?
are you, perhaps, going to try to teach dolphins to talk ?"

   you looked straight into my eyes
   when you replied

    "if I ever became friends with a dolphin
    I would never presume to try to teach a creature
    more evolved than most humans could ever be
    on the contrary, I would try to *learn*
    whatever a dolphin might be kind enough
        to share with *me*

    train dolphins for secret missions ?
    I'd prefer to train them how to remain free
    that is . . if I were ever to meet one
    and the two of us
    should happen to share a cup of tea"

  then you smiled
  and changed the subject

as I marveled at the strange universal synchronicity
which had guided me, in Lonely Laguna, to a suite
       called *The Dolphin*

Whiplash

when I flew back out to California
to lope into your waiting arms

> you met my plane, with rain in your hair
> and a mist in your eyes
> rushed me outside to your dusty blue VW Bug
> gave me a giant bear hug
> > your cheeks smelling like fresh air

made me look up first
to wish on a star . .
> then pulled me inside, with a shy kind of pride
> in your double surprise waiting there

> two gifts — from you to me

> . . the soaring sound of Puccini's *Un Bel Di*
> One Fine Day — pouring from your tape deck

and a small pot
of African violets

> then kissed me gently
> > to the sound of music
> the scent of flowers
> > and damp earth

> . . the violets of forget-me-not

and as you kissed me
to the rising chords of Butterfly's sad song
> > . . you whispered

> "thank you for returning . . it's been so long
> and I've been so lonely since you left
> have you missed me, darling
> > as much as I've missed you ?"

> déjà vu   déjà vu !

how could you possibly have known that the Los Angeles airport
was the very last time I ever saw the him-of-you
> . . the Carousel Bill
and his farewell gift . . was a bunch of wilted violets
because of the ones we long ago planted on three small grassy hills
it was raining hard that night too
when I flew away because he had chosen to stay
and drown himself in an ocean of vodka . . and I . . oh !

I nearly drowned myself
after I told him goodbye, in his car — like yours — a dusty blue Bug
standing alone, where he left me
                              weeping a rushing waterfall of tears
and missed my plane

        all these years, it's been buried deep inside me . . the pain
        of those wilted violets, in the rain
                I never mentioned it to you

        and now . . oh, déjà vu !

                I never told you that
                but you knew, you knew . . .

                        you knew

It Will Never Sell

in the beginning, I wondered about many things
but I kept them inside, and pondered them in my heart
sharing my deepest doubts and fears
only during our moments of staring into each other's eyes

                yes, so many questions troubled me
                        and I wanted so . . oh ! I wanted so
                to find the answers without asking
                so I could be as wise as you . . all by myself

one night, I spoke to you for hours, as you slept
and I wept . . wondering if you could hear me
communicating with you astrally . . you stirred slightly
and the circle of your arms closed around me more tightly
                                        holding me nearer
as I lay awake, speaking with you silently
but other than that, you gave no sign
                        that you heard . . . . a single word
        listen, darling . .

if it's true, as he insisted so often, on the lonely shores of Galilee
that to err is human — to forgive Divine
then how difficult are the requirements of divinity
                        for most mortals, like me
yet how effortless you make it appear to be
I marvel at the way in which you manifest humility
                        yet never seem weak
no, turning the other cheek

only makes you seem stronger . . much stronger than I

but, even if it's true — what good does it do ?

what good is there in knowing that the greatest strength
                                        is gentleness
and that meekness holds infinitely more power
                        than violence ?

            what does one gain by proving this ?
                more power, more strength . . by whose definition ?

I mean, just look how hard *he* tried . . how many bitter tears he cried
alone in the Garden of Gethsemane, deserted by everyone
                                        even his closest friends
who couldn't manage to stay awake
and watch one hour with him . . and what was his reward ?

            he was crucified

no one really believed his resurrection promise
        except, perhaps . . her . . . the Magdalene Mary
and I'm not at all sure that she actually saw him on Easter morning
outside the empty tomb, at Sunrise
she may have been simply hallucinating
                a common relief of unbearable grief

and is death, then, the only result of trying ?
that's madness ! I see no glory in dying !

            I've known since I was twelve years old
            that the Easter story is a lie
            that when people die — they really die
                any child knows
            that gladness cannot possibly rhyme with sadness

how can I complete my Happiness poem I've decided to title *Gooberz*
or make any sense from reincarnation
        even through experiencing the miracle of Us
when it's so painfully clear
that the masochistic lesson of Calvary
hasn't kept humanity from rhyming with insanity ?

to allow yourself to die . . well, just how weak can one **BE** ?
        Mike Todd himself
couldn't sell such a dreary, desolate idea
not even if he promoted it Around the World, for Eighty
                                plus a thousand days
with a ticker tape parade
hundreds of marching bands, pounding drums
                and a million pink balloons

Gooober, don't you see ?
the Oober catechism will never set imprisoned souls free
humans will always cry "what's in it for **ME ?**"

if they follow his teachings — if they really, truly try
to be meek — and turn the other cheek — they need to understand

WHY THEY HAVE TO DIE !

. . . and so do I

suddenly, you awoke beside me, in the bed
kissed me slowly, interrupting my silent reverie

and softly said

"I thought I heard you crying
did you have a bad dream ?"

"no . . no
I'm sorry if I disturbed your sleep"

you drew me nearer
as you whispered . . "deep"

then we loved

and death seemed far away

Bunnies and Seaweed and Tombs

it was one of our golden Sunday mornings
after an angry grey Saturday night
in Pismo Beach
when you hid that zonky Easter rabbit
inside the refrigerator door
so it would surprise me when I opened it
to get your grapefruit

I laughed — and I think it hurt you

but I didn't laugh because his fur
was such a freaky shade of seaweed green
that we named him Algae

I laughed in joy, because . . I thought you'd forgotten the resurrection
and its special, personal, Carousel meaning for us

Canto Fifteen ☆ 535

but you remembered, you remembered !

you even bought some colored dye
        so we could make pink and purple eggs
and roll them across the lawn . . that ended in a sheer drop
        over the cliffs, into the ocean
where the fog padded in that morning . . on quiet little bunny feet

and when I blurted out
"my god ! that's the ugliest rabbit
I ever saw in my life !"
I really meant
to say . . "he's beautiful"

      oh, Gooober, he was, he was !

        and you were beautiful — and the ocean was beautiful
          and the world was beautiful
             spinning rightside up again
        and I was beautiful too
          because I knew you loved me

and because I knew . .

        you hadn't forgotten our personal Easter after all
        like that other glad-golden morning
        when Mary Magdalene called out . . . to him
        thinking it was the gardener

           "where is he ? oh ! where have you taken him ?"

   and he told her

           I am risen

Petals

the next day you brought me a daisy
a daisy-for-forgiveness, you said

        "I should have given you — not Algae
        but a huge fat pink and white bunny
        with long silky ears"
               you sighed

"oh, no !" I cried

"I love Algae so . . oh !
I do, I do love him so"

and felt a sharp loving-pain
for Algae and you

        after that, every time we quarreled
        you brought me a daisy
        a crazy daisy . . for forgiveness

    why do I remember the flower
    but so few of the reasons behind our winter seasons ?
    I guess because . . most of the time
    there was really nothing that memorable to forgive

    just moments when you made me cry
    and neither of us knew exactly why . . oh, Gooober

      most of the time

    there was nothing . . . to forgive

Teach Me, Reach Me

our lovemaking . .

      was like a flaming volcano of mysterious origin
      lightning flashes at its summit
              and quaking at its base
      rain falling in its hollow
            with hot lava pouring over us
      in an uncontrollable avalanche of violence
      which could then swirl into baby rivers of tenderness
                    and gentle

an alternating stream, anew each time
and new and new
      that flowed into
and calmed and steadied . . our spirits

      our words of love
    contained more mystery . . words we taught each other
    to say for us alone
    and those sacred whispers of our need

      created sea serpents of desire
        sliding slippery sensual
      through every sleeping curve and hollow

                              of our rediscovered bodies
from the beginning . .
                we named things

                yes, we named things . . feelings, needs and desires
                and other parts of each other, as lovers do
                        you named some — I, others
                with tumble twisted verbs and vowels
                        and the words became our secret language
                containing the deep mystery
                of the nearing moment when the you-of-you
                                              and the me-of-me
                exploded into the me-of-you
                and the you-of-me

locked in our timeless Oneness, no longer separate entities
but one body, mind and soul . . indivisible and whole

it was a language no one knew — no one but me, no one but you
a language no one else could ever share or feel
or transmute from its soft, symbolic shyness into
                                    the starkly naked real

we used weeping willow words of want
humming-coming-drumming-pounding-sounding words
some as old and tried and true as love itself
                        some original at dawn or dusk
woven of the mystery-musk of our abandoned, private passion

words all our own that no one knows — or ever will
but us . . words that sent a trembling thrill
shaking and snaking through our quaking bodies
when we murmured them beneath our sighs

        and sometimes . . the words alone themselves, sans touching even
                cooled our fever with misty rain . . and our eyes
        reflected such surprise
        that "spring" could reach across the room its hypnotic perfume
        to drench both of us in its beauty
                        and often, all it took
                was a whispered word . . and one deep look
        to feel and know the familiar chords
        of our humming-coming-drumming-pounding-sounding
                                    symphony of love

some words cracked memory whips, without conscious intent
when they slipped past your lips . . memory whips
of him — or rather, of the him-of-you
                original words, which left no doubt
words impossible for anyone else to invent
        words and names of things that turned me inside out

when I first heard you whisper them softly . . . slow . . . and low

      oh, they turned me inside-out and outside-in
with memories of the you-of-him
for they were words and names which were carved
                      in marble memory
having been tw-ice born
and also tw-ice conceived . . and left you shaken too
with the awe and wonder
        of such proof of knowing

understanding, but not remembering
from which wells of yesterday they sprang
      at first believing you had made them up yourself
you grew still beside me

        . . then when you realized, once more we melted
        into an intense embrace of Oneness
            even more complete than the blending of before
        when there were freedoms of speech and action
        nuances of passion . . I had not released to you
                in that other Temple

some speak of bird's nests . . snow and sleet
and fields of goldenrod and wheat
as Nature's wonders, not as private codes
and secret symbols

      yes, others would be mystified to hear our tangled gibberish
      of letters of the alphabet . . linked in combinations
      which could make no sense to anyone but Us

others could never comprehend our mysteries
though they might be intrigued into searching for a clue
as people do . . when they try to untie
        a tangled knot of string or rope

      yes, a tangled knot of rope
      another secret code . . for me, one of hope
      that you would see and understand, when I touched your hand
      oh, not the knot that sailors tie
      or Scouts . . still, a knot . . or knots demanding loosening
      perhaps to be untied inside a cool green wood

and afterwards, you would always ask
to be sure you were really an expert sailor or Scout
and wait for me to answer yes
      and I always wondered why you weren't able to guess
the answer, from my stillness
        or from my toes, no longer twisting
but as motionless as a statue's . . or from the gentle pink-gold shade

of tranquility and peace within my aura
                    . . which was always there for you to see
as your own auric light was always visible to me

but the most erotic words you ever spoke or whispered
ever-ever-ever . . and I never told you
were those you once combined in a paragraph of sentences
which whirled us into a frenzy of feeling
one night, in Pismo Beach, in our magic cottage
when the sound of someone knocking on the door . . reached us
as we were standing near the fireplace, embracing
lost in some far off heaven or galaxy
our bodies were tracing . . as we stood facing, clinging

        . . . . we didn't know if it might be the landlady
        a friend — a stranger
        or the paper boy, collecting on his route
                            this time, after sundown
we decided not to answer
the friendly knocking sound
                so we tip-toed around
turned off the lamps
            closed the bedroom door
and loped into bed
hiding beneath the blankets
like guilty kittens or puppies, being called
and pretending not to be there

        it seemed to me, somehow, as if we had no right
        to pretend we were not there

            and then you whispered . . so low and slow
            deeply deeply . . velvety and husky
                        into my ear, and said . .

oh ! it was such a plain and simple thing you said
lying warm and close beside me in the gentle-soft bed
but it suddenly made me burn and glow
with the knowingness of what it really means
        to be man and woman
belonging to each other, sharing secrets no one else can fathom

        yes, those words you murmured, like some ancient mantra
        we once knew . . . had the magical power
        to make me understand all that, and more — evoking in me
            strange and new sensations I had never felt before

            . . until I was filled with a brilliant, bursting awareness
                    like a wave, sweeping me out to sea
            not just through my mind and body . . but throughout my soul
                    of what it means to be truly whole

. . and I misted into a deep blue heaven
then melted into the Universe . . and you

as your whisper, slowly . . lowly
like velvet . . husky . . intimately clear
crept inside my ear

"darling, we have every right
to pretend we are not here
when we turn the room to darkness
and lie in bed together
then we can do . . and be . . to each other
whatever we need that brings us
near to understanding
the deepest mysteries of *Spring*
for, when we close our bedroom door
against all outside intrusion
we leave this world of reality illusion
and escape together
. . to our own galaxy"

that night . . we spoke our language of Oneness
whispered our tumble-twisted words, both ancient and new
again and again and again
as we loved . . over and over, how many times ?

for we had closed our bedroom door on the Earth and all its Earthlings
and slipped away to play
among the starry shamrocks of a lost, remembered Eden

exploring love's oldest, silent secrets through our "deep"
until we fell, exhausted, into a cosmic-coma sleep
that lasted through a thousand dreams
and slept till noon the following day, under comforters of peace

when we awoke, our mouths were pressed together
then you sent a darting humming-bird word — "again ?"
and I answered with a darting humming-bird-word — "yes"

"darling, good morning" . . .

. . . "good morning, darling"

The Little Prince Knows About a Rose

sometimes, when lovers — or even just ordinary mortals
become temporarily annoyed with one another

    they shout . . or mumble . . or grumble

or say, in an unkind way

        "oh, go get lost !"

        "go sit on a tack !"

you said it differently, in your funny, upside-down
but rightside-up Oober language
in Pismo Beach . . . one troubled day

    when I was grumbling angry thunder in my voice
    flashing lightning from my eyes
    and churning storm warnings of wounded pride

you took my hand, like a wise and knowing monk or sage
and pulled me firmly out the kitchen door
to the rose bush in the yard, drenched with Nature's dew

        then pressed my quivering nose of rage
        into the dew-splashed petals
        of its largest, most fragrant deep-pink bloom

        a rose of full-blown beauty

        and regally commanded — "now smell !"
        "no, don't just sniff
            you sassy wench
        inhale it deeply, deeply . .

        you heard me, spunky !
        inhale it deeply, deeply . . "

OH !
      Oh !
          oh !

and somehow . . someway
the fragrance of that full-blown pink rose
was such a heavenly essence of mystical perfume
it erased every trace of stormy gloom within my being that morning

    it made me fairly ooze with warm
    and bubbles of fresh

                    . . . like spring snow

it smelled — yes !
it smelled of miracles being born !

        and I hugged you tightly
and whispered, "thank you, Goob . .

that was a truly beautiful thing for you to do
a splendid magical trick of ancient alchemy you taught me
oh, you are a wise and profound teacher of Life !
to use a rose . . and a nose
as your textbooks for lessons in happy"

                        then you kissed me lightly
                        on the cheek

                    "why, everyone knows . . . "
                    you smiled, with silvery-wise eyes

                    "everyone knows that a rose
                    is very, very magical
                    and don't be afraid of its thorns
                    they're no more dangerous
                    than a girl Ram's make-believe
                                        paper horns"

and always, after that, when I stormed or thundered
over a hurt from some dim yesterday — I feared might return
to haunt me tomorrow — or when I sobbed softly
against your shoulder, with some indefinable sorrow

        . . or when I was inclined to brood
and twist my toes . .
                        you either murmured tenderly
                        or shouted at me, depending on my mood

        "oh, Goob — **go smell a rose !**"

        and I did

until my anger — or sadness
suddenly, miraculously turned into gladness

        oh ! you are, you are ! a perfectly marvelous teacher
        you always stop the rain in my heart
        and you know just when to make Life rhyme

but I wonder . .

        did the alchemy magic come from the growing part of you

                    Canto Fifteen   ☆   543

or from the deeper wells
of the him-of-you, who *knows* ?

. . like long ago, in dancing school
when you left me with only a lonely rose
and a song I still can't remember
that comes . . then goes

Abracadabra — Oh, Heck !

you crazy, wonderful, outrageous nut
you're stuck in some kind of a mystical rut !

running around town like an overgrown druid
trying so hard to be teeny tiny and magical

. . . . that's not easy to do
when you're six-foot-two

and thinking you can make miracles
as effortlessly and swiftly as an elf at the North Pole
makes a red and white striped, peppermint candy cane

today, you even tried to stop the rain

it was pouring cats and dogs outside

and you said . . .

"I'll bet I can bring out the Sun for you
and stop the rain . . just watch !"

then you squeezed your eyes shut tightly
and concentrated tightly too
squeezing your mind
and you prayed and prayed
and you waited and waited
and you believed and believed

murmuring . . "abracadabra . . magic !"

oh, you were so grieved
it hurt you so, I know
when the rain wouldn't stop

you just stood there forlornly
in your sloshy Jerusalem sandals

your toes all squishy-squashy wet
with tiny raindrops sparkling on your lashes

and I watched your yellow-gold aura
grow dimmer around your head
. . as you said
softly, so sadly

"well, I guess I lost my bet"

no, you didn't stop the cloudburst — you failed
but you tried, you tried !
that's what was so perfectly marvelous . . you tried !

oh ! Gooober, did you know how it made me ache inside
and how deeply I understood ?

it gave me a sharp loving-pain
when you tried so hard to stop the rain

and believed so hard that you could

Mouse Cookies and Candy Kisses

we had little half-hearted spats, in the beginning
every time we went to the market together
because you would not allow me to load our basket
with gooey-rich-sugary, lovely-whipped-creamy-cookies

"they are bad for you
and for the small druid
who may come to live with us someday"
you'd always say

every time I tried to sneak a package of crunchy brownies
or delicious, chocolate cream Oreos
into our shopping cart, when you weren't looking
. . or so I thought
I was caught . . red handed

and you would sternly
admonish me, then, and say

"I love Oreos myself
they're my favorite cookies — but
they're loaded with white sugar
unhealthy preservatives and additives

Canto Fifteen ☆ 545

and I know what they do to my body"
"well, yes, but . . "
        I would feebly respond

                then you would interrupt
                "I don't know about you, but my soul
                does not choose to spend this incarnation
                in a shabby, run-down
                        wrinkling, withering Temple
                and so . . even though
                I love Oreos madly myself
                I am strong enough to resist temptation"

so I would be shamed and guilty
            and return the cookies to the grocery shelf
feeling chastised, like a naughty elf

            but one sunny February afternoon in Pismo Beach
            I wept angry tears of pure frustration
            when you caught me again
                    tucking a package of Oreos in our cart
            under a fat loaf of whole wheat bread

and said . .
"you are an impossible, arrogant Food Snob, so there !"

            and didn't even care
            about the snickers from the clerk
            who was adding up our groceries on the register

                until finally, with an air
                of gentle resignation, you said . .

                    "allright, we'll get them this time
                    just this once, you spunky mouse
                        for you to munch
                    when you're good . . in the house"

and I promised you later, driving home
that I would only munch or crunch on one
every week or so — just as a special treat

"I won't make a pig of myself, I promise
honest — druid honor !"

                and you twinkled at me
                "okay, wench, now don't break your vow"

            as if you knew I would, somehow
            so I decided to show you that I had more will-power
            not to mention won't-power . . than you

to prove that a Ram is stronger than a Lion
and to prove that I have real, not paper horns

I didn't go near the cookie jar for several days
then, one misty-foggy morning, when you weren't there
. . you had gone for a walk, along the ocean
to breathe in some healthy air . .
my will grew weak
and I decided to sneak . . just one Oreo

but when I lifted the lid of the cookie jar that usually contained
the delicious, nutritious peanut butter balls
you made yourself, with honey and wheat germ and such

I saw that there were only four, no more
of the full package of Oreos left inside
and I had not eaten a single one of them so far

so, when you returned from your ocean walk
bringing back some melt-in-your-mouth, spinach-like leaves
you liked to pick by the shore, and cook with butter

I accused you

and you denied the theft of Oreos
with innocent, outraged indignation

"I did not eat a single Oreo !"
you claimed, wounded
"it wasn't me — what a sneaky way
to hide your own guilt
oh, wow ! just look ! I see a new wrinkle
near your left eyebrow — I've told you
you can't eat cookies and junk food
without showing it on your face
just look at that new wrinkle !"

but . . did I see your eyes twinkle ?

I was slightly furious, and also curious
so, the next afternoon, I went into town alone
and bought two teeny-tiny toy mice at the dime store
all soft and furry, with long, skinny tails
then tucked them inside the cookie jar
to catch the Cat, who was stealing the Oreos

and sure enough . .

that very same evening, near dusk
while I was pondering the rhyme and meter of my Happiness Poem
at the typewriter . . you yawned, rose from your chair

Canto Fifteen ☆ 547

and said ·

"I think I'll have a glass of carrot juice"

then walked casually, gracefully
like a slinking, Leonine Cat, into the kitchen

while I followed you stealthily, on tip toe
and peeked around the door
to see you lifting the lid of the cookie jar

suddenly, you uttered a medium sized Tarzan yell
of shock and surprise, turning your face to me
with little-boy guilt in your eyes . . . as your hand touched
the furry mice

and I cried — "you were caught in my mouse trap
you sneaky Monster Cat !"

then I ran into your arms, and we hugged each other
and laughed till the funny tears came

"well, at least I know
what's right and wrong — and I am
essentially strong . . "
you said

"I told you cookies do not belong
in this house
you tricky mouse-spouse
no matter if I do become
occasionally weak
now you can't squeak
and call me a Food Snob anymore"

"no, you are not a Food Snob
or any other kind of snob"
I murmured, against your cheek

"you are a dear, funny Monster Cat
but now that I've proven who was wrong
and who was right . . may I have just one bite ?"

and you answered . . "don't quibble
you may have only one nibble"

it was after that
we began calling all bad things to eat
mouse cookies

"stop eating those mouse cookies !"

you'd playfully say
when you caught me sneaking a Milky Way
in the car, while you were
                      filling the gas tank
and I was trying to hide the wrapper
under the seat, or beneath my feet

. . we took our two teeny tiny toy mice with us
every time we moved into a different, magic house
later they had a baby
                      . . I bought another one
so there were three

        and you used to play with them
        making them do funny Oober things
        that caused me to laugh

one lazy March afternoon, when I was puffed up with anger
like a balloon — or like a pathetic clown
because you had remarked that you thought my hair
would look better parted in the middle, and hanging straight down

        I told you that you might just as well say
        you hated it the other way —
        the way I'd been wearing it before

then suddenly felt ugly — and ran into the bathroom
slamming the door

        but as I stood there, nursing my wounded vanity
        I noticed the two toy mice
        you had arranged for me to see

the smaller Girl toy mouse was sitting up, vainly and proudly
looking at herself in the mirror of my compact, preening her tail

and the other one . .

        the larger, Boy toy mouse . . was crying
        with his teeny tiny hands placed over his eyes
        his soft, furry grey tail all skinny and wet
        with the tears you had sprinkled on it
                              from the water faucet

        just lying there — face down
                              trying to drown . . in sadness
        his tail no longer proud
        looking as if he was hurting

. . and I cried

you taught me so many unexpected lessons
that made me laugh and cry
with the funny Oober knowing-things
you did with our teeny tiny toy mice

arranging them here and there . . and everywhere
        playing games . . that reflected us

Our Colorado Secret

one early miracled morning, all faerie-fresh and dew kissed
driving in your dusty blue Bug
we both saw . . each of us saw . . suspended in a strange, golden mist

            a huge rainbow

spectrum bright, and shaped exactly like the Great Pyramid of Giza
through some rare combination of haze and light
or atmospheric condition over the mountains that day . . in Colorado

        would anyone believe us
        if we told them that we stopped the car
        and trembled in awe
        because we really, truly saw . . a huge rainbow
        shaped exactly like the Great Pyramid ?

            I guess not

that's why we never told anyone
and kept it in our hearts
a secret . . between you and me . . and the Earth
                            and the sky
                                and God

Ring the Bells and Tell the People

        oh, the miracle of Us !

at last, we found a mountain who could fly

        a mountain who could soar across the sky
        and flap its wings of feathered peaks
                like some giant snow bird, dipping

in and out of clouds

when you and I were watching it together
holding hands, and touching hearts
rubbing noses, making magic, then . . oh, how it flew !
showing off the acrobatics it had learned to do
all through the centuries of waiting for our faith

yes, we found, at last
a mountain who could fly

Pike's Peak, in Colorado

sometimes it wore, our mountain
shimmering streaks of silver starlight
in its hair, at dusk
          or at sunset, trailing rosy ribbons

          sometimes the pale and lemon sliced New Moon
          painted it with whispers of lavender, at dawn

          then, not to be outdone
          the yellow-round-balloon Full Moon
          would brush it with a deeper violet hue

and, jealous of the softer Moon
the brilliant-red-orange-Sun, at noon
colored it with blazing pink-gold splashes
and drenched its snow-capped peaks
                    with dazzling white

          there were never shadows cast upon it
          day or night
                    . . by either Luminary

          for shadowed mountains only cry
          and cannot fly

          how could shadows ever fall on such a flying mountain ?
          it was too wild and beautiful, looming there so proud and high
          against the robin-egg-blue sky
                              and smiling down
          upon the teeny tiny, cobweb
          gold mining, ghost-filled town I had found and loved
          when I was lost and lonely, just before
                         we found each other once again
where could there
be shadows now ?

          so we bought a funny crooked house

on a little crooked street
in that happy, teeny-tiny cobweb
slipping-off-the-time-track town
                snuggled safely in the loving arms
of our flying mountain
who cradled it tenderly for us . . and sang to it each night
a haunting lullaby of déjà vu . . without a name

until we came . .

                one brand-new, bright and golden-sunny August day
in a perfectly marvelous magical way
                            like pixilated druids
and flew unto
                our happiness

    we flew in your dusty blue Bug
                winging through puffs of fluffy-snowball clouds
and laughing skies . . to the sound of musical butterflies
                                down winding roads
past the deep-cool green
of murmuring pine and aspen woods
                slowing down and bending low, to flow
beneath the Tunnel of Time

and passing through it, both could see

Forever . . clearly
looming just ahead of us

                then made a perfect three point landing
in Cripple Creek . . as a tumbling crowd of friendly puppies
out on a lark, gave us a joyful bark of greeting

and two shaggy, velvet-eared burros, called 'mountain canaries'
threw back their heads
                to sing us their morning song
with lyrics that said
                . . we've been waiting for you !
                what took you so long ?

    then we ran into our little, red brick crooked house
that stood there, holding its arms out wide
                and floated inside, smiling and sighing
laughing and crying . . and bear-hugged
                and elf-danced around to the tinkling sound
of the far-away music of long ago
                from the old Edison in the corner

    you whispered to me
    and I whispered to you

552   ☆   Canto Fifteen

"oh, I do — yes, I do
I do love you so !"

as we unpacked our hearts — and our souls and our minds
then raised all the blinds, to let the rainbows in

you said . . .

"the very first thing we're going to do
is adopt two kitties — a boy for me
and a girl for you
and we'll name them Love and Peace"

and I answered . .
"oh, yes Gooober, let's do !
let's adopt a kitty or two
and name them Peace and Love"

still reading each other's minds
we exchanged one small snowflake kiss
of gigantic, swelling, sun-bursting bliss

as our eyes reflected
a promise of . . soon

then we smiled a springtime knowing smile
that said . . we'll wait, just a little while

and our hearts rushed in to say
yes, sometimes it's deeper that way
when we wait . . for awhile

so we sat there together, on the fainting couch
near the old spinning wheel in the parlor
for a long, long time
making Life rhyme
in that suspended moment of homecoming
spinning dreams
of steeples chiming wedding bells
wishes tossed in penny wells
fragile-strong dreams of white and blue, Forever-true
a soon-to-be-legally-united you and me
trimming our very first Christmas tree
delicate dreams of baby druids
oh ! and maybe . . kitties and a frog pond
yes, and someday dreams of ducks and chickens
and our own horses to ride
snuggled outside . . in a stable you would build
as we slowly filled with happy . . except

except . . that I absolutely refused

to agree to a snake

ABSOLUTELY NOT !

a slippery, slimy, slithering snake in our basement ?
you must be joking, darling
but you were not

you told me I should learn
not to fear them . . but I changed the subject

. . not interested in hearing about the snake
you kept as a pet, when you were a boy

turning the old fashioned spinning wheel
we spun the circle of our remembered Past
and happy Present . . into a living-happily-ever-after Future

for we had found, at last, you and I
Gooober and Gooober
a mountain who could truly fly !

then you whispered into my ear

"listen, mouse-spouse
I believe our 'soon' is here"

it was time to love . . . .
so we loped upstairs . . into the Indian room

and made a miracle

My Sixth Sense is You

sometimes, like now . .
I close my eyes, and let myself sink softly
into warm-scented pillows of contentment
drinking in the sounds and smells
when you are somewhere nearby

doing fresh and bright and sunny daytime things

I hear you and I smell you . .
brushing your teeth with foaming, creamy mint
splashing in the bath tub, sending out clean soap aromas
scratching matches across the grate to light a crackling fire
that fills the house with the fragrance of wood smoke
and Christmas pine

making cheerful symphonies of tinkling music
when you stir the orange juice
and strike the spoon against the glass

or bringing in the morning paper
            your cheeks smelling like wet snow
and trailing little whiffs of ozone as you walk

my favorite sounds . .

        are the wild, piercing Tarzan yells you scream in the woods
        when you're bursting with the joy of just being alive . . .
        the funny, froggy sounds you make, in bed
                when you're slowly struggling up from sleep
        the trembling tenderness in your voice
                        when you whisper . . . "deep"
        our private word
        for a sudden, aching hunger
        and urgent need . . that will not wait

my favorite smell . .

        is your hair in the Sun . . sweet
                                damp
                                        and musty
        . . like a bird's nest

darling, let's have our toast and orange juice later

        "deep"

Yearning — Burning — Learning

strange, that I should have been guided
to the enlightened texts . . . only after Life — and you
had taught me first, the Saturn-Serpent-seven secret

        and now, having studied the illuminated words
        of the mystics, not advertised . . or seeking converts

        but waiting to be discovered
        by those earnest, sincerely seeking souls
        who have paid their debt, first with the coins of faith
        then, with the gold of *knowing* . . not weak hope
        I know our miracle does not happen
        every time — to every soul
        for the great, heavy stone of death that seals the Easter cave

may only be rolled away by the greater Angel
                              of the Higher Self
    when grief is deep enough
    to be unbearable

unbearable, unbearable bereavement — and then
the intensity of the suffering, being a powerfully magnetic energy
becomes a pulsing, vibrating cosmic cord
that tugs upon the departed soul, and urges it
to return soon — if that be the true Free Will choice of each
in the pattern of karmic lace that must trace itself
upon this present existence

            yes, urges it to choose another adult Body Temple quickly
another painted horse to ride on Life's Carousel — near to the bereaved
in some way I have not yet learned — but *will*
for a time, holding back the truth from the blindly grieved
deep behind the eyes . . which are truly the windows of the soul

    and if the one crushed with such an unbearable weight
    will but look and listen, with the spirit's sensitive awareness

                        and be ready
the proof will soon be seen . . and heard
sufficient signs will be gradually given . . the familiar words
the recognition . . the secrets no one else could know or remember
a laugh . . a manner of speaking . . a walk . . a shrug
or a turn of the head, just so . .

        and then — oh, then ! the heart will know
                            the re-kindled ember
        yes, yes — the heart will know !

ask, and you shall receive
knock, and it shall be opened unto you

for whatsoever thing you should desire
pray as if you had already received it
and you shall surely have it . .

                    pray as if . . you had
                    already received it
yes, strong faith
        not weak hope
not hoping, but *knowing* is all that's required
not praying with "please" — but with "thank you !"
for a miracle already granted before it's requested
to the one who believes and *knows*
and no force upon Earth can change this cosmic law

it seems so simple, such easily attainable magic and power

ah ! but not so, not so !
how many can guard their knowing
from the contamination of a sliver of weak hope
a silent, subconscious "maybe" ?

      like building, carefully, a Pyramid of tiny grains
      of sparkling white sand
      then allowing the teeniest-tiniest speck of negative grey doubt
      to creep in . . entering unobserved
      and all the tiny grains of sparkling white sand
                            disappear, de-materialize
      so that the Pyramid of Knowing
      must be built all over again, from its very foundation

no, it is never easy to acquire the knack of *knowing*
only a few manage to "master" it
and to completely comprehend the deeper meaning
of the biblical counsel

      . . . for whatsoever thing you should desire
          pray as if you had already received it
        and you shall surely have it

and even after one has learned to master this awesome power
by achieving contact — tuning in — to the Higher Angel of the Self
one can forget . . and fall
             and thus face the sad task
of beginning again

          . . Jesus wept

for each soul
yes, wept — for you and for me

      for all those who remain stubbornly blind
      and refuse to see

oh, Earthlings ! look — feel — behold !
comprehend the power of your own sacred me-of-me
in whatever Body Temple of the moment

      this each soul must probe and ponder for himself — herself
      if the great and heavy Saturn stone of death
      is to be rolled away from the Easter cave of grief and loss

each soul . . must be crucified with longing on the cross
of unbearable sorrow — if the one recently departed
                  from the Body Temple
is to be strong enough to find the way
to feel the tug on the silvery-blue cord that still connects
and understand — then reach out a once more *living* hand

turning back, to return into a bright tomorrow
                              which is also yesterday

    while others, who bow beneath a more bearable burden of sorrow
    who possess the inner strength and calm and knowing — to wait
        saddened, but uncrucified by agony
    will also meet the one departed and missed . . again
    to blend together once more in the higher levels of awareness
                  of other heavens
    or in some future earthly incarnation
    just as surely — when the time has come for this to be
    in their own *slower* karmic pattern
                of the path to eventual reunion

the Easter miracle
need not be experienced in the same way
for those who can bear to wait

    but those who cannot bear bereavement's burden
    and who have called upon the Higher Angel of the Self
    to roll away the heavy Saturn stone from the cave of grief
    must never forget . . to forgive

do not forget — oh ! never forget

      to forgive

        to forgive each hurt of yesterday
        or else it will be multiplied a thousand fold
        in the remembered tomorrow
            of the return of the departed

    yes, it will be magnified a hundred-thousand fold
    each hurt and past aggrievement still unforgiven then

    do not forget that forgiveness is Divine
    while un-forgiveness leads to the unrelenting torture
    of multiplied, magnified sorrow — repeated
    remember well . . one path flows to heavens of happiness
    but the other winds its slow and grinding route
              to the hell of reflected miseries
    until the way back to grace
    through tangles of karmic lace — is once more found
    spinning round and round the ever-turning Carousel of Life

the number of the beast — and man — and woman
is 666 — when added to 18 makes nine
the three-times-three of the Holy Trinity

      of the you-of-you
      and the me-of-me

nine — the vibration of the Universe
ruling electrical and magnetic energy, as well as human life
upon the planet Earth
      still struggling in its third dimensional awareness
as nine also represents, to metaphysicians
the Red Dragon of ancient alchemy 666 999
the numbers inverted . . all equal nine

. . a fragment of nine's secret also hidden
in the subconscious minds of those who bore the name
of the sacred scarab of Egypt — the Beetle . . . or "Beatles"

    when they channelled the strange recorded mantra
        on their best selling album
of Revolution Nine — 9 — 9 — 9 — 9

    Revolution Nine — containing the secret
    of the evolution of the soul

and those missing golden keys . . . .
they are not lost . . they are only mislaid

    for the Keys of the Kingdom are teeny-tiny, reflecting the Sun
    like druids . . or small children
    who *believe* on faith alone — and who know

                yes, *know* it shall be done
                   unto them

the Keys of the Kingdom
      are not ancient and rusty
but cast of pure, bright gold . . . the gold of *knowing*
not the common brass of hoping

    but the gold of knowing and believing
    that it shall be done unto you

there are seven . . on the shining Serpent Ring of Heaven
      and the larger key
the one which unlocks the heavier door . . is the stone of grief

             Saturn

    mark well, mark well, in the here and now
    where Saturn spread his starry lessons — and how
    he laid his stern, wise hand of discipline
            and why

    upon the soul, at birth

now I know that the Holy Trinity of the three-times-three

of each you-of-you and each me-of-me

                              is

              Us . . united
              Forgiveness
              and Truth

          which equal Eternity

when I told you what I had learned
you smiled, then . . and misted at me
through your silvery-wise eyes

              and gave a joyous Tarzan yell

              "that's it, Goob ! we're home free !
              don't you see ?
              that's the beginning catechism
                            of the Oober Galaxy !
              the cosmic Serpent circle
              where one into one equals three
              each 'one' remaining itself — yet, when blended
              creating a third, creating . . . magic !
                              yes, that's the word !"

. . . whoops ! whee ! we're all home free !
let's get back on, and try it again !
          . . the Keys to the Kingdom are teeny-tiny

              then you said, with your eyes
          so innocent-wise shiny

              " . . and the Red Dragon secret of alchemy
                        the mystical nine
              which can, when one learns its deep mystery
                        transmute metal into gold
              cannot be comprehended, until the alchemist
              has mastered complete knowledge of the 6 and 9
              for 6 is Venus — woman
                              and 9 is Mars — man
              together equaling Love
              and the six and nine when reversed
              or turned upside down 6 . . 9 and 9 . . 6
                        equal each other
              one of the deepest mysteries of all Universes
              for, only those who understand every facet
              of the six-nine secret . . are able to vibrate
              on a high enough angstrom unit frequency wave
              to discover the ancient alchemy formula

              560 ☆ Canto Fifteen

of turning metal into gold
through the mystical Red Dragon of Nine

as you've already learned yourself . .
one must be able to transform
the brass of hope into the gold of faith . .
before one can become a true alchemist"

"but . . is it a good thing or a bad thing
to turn material metal into gold ?
has it to do with the motive — whether that be
greed . . or . . "

"someday . . " you answered, twinkling

"someday, I'll slip away
on an Oober space craft — a flying saucer
with some Master Oobers
            who are Higher and wiser than we
to learn lots more
                        about coming home free

meanwhile . . darling, I love you so
                        I do . . I do"

    I snuggled my head
on your shoulder
                and said

"oh, Gooober you funny and perfectly marvelous druid

. . . . . . I love you too"

druid Talk

do you know what it is about us
that brings my gentlest peace . . and my strongest faith
my most trembling "springs"
and the clearest rings of the silver bells deep inside me ?

            it's that small, funny druid thing
            we do with each other
            when I'm baking biscuits or taking a bath

            changing a typewriter ribbon . . or brushing my hair

            while you're reading the comics . . scraping cucumbers

                    making fat Gooober candles
                    or standing on your head near the dining room chair

and our eyes meet . . to lock
in a deep, deep knowing

                    then we fly together

                        touch noses

            and whisper . . *magic* !

Drinking Raindrops

        one day, in August . . I walked into our antique kitchen
        from a scented oil, Egyptian type bath
        feeling like one of the Pharaoh's favorites

and found you hiding something
in the kitchen drawer

"what are you doing ?"

                    you blushed, and handed me
                    a scrap of paper
                    you had been trying to slip in
                    between the dish towels and the Brillo

        it said simply

            "I love you, spunky"

            we bear hugged, and then
                        you told me

                    "I thought it would be nice
                    if you'd find my note some morning
                    when you were washing
                        and drying the breakfast dishes
                    and I was at the Post Office
                            getting the mail . .

                    say, have you seen
                    my blue cashmere sweater ?
                    I thought I left it on the dining room chair"

"I sent it to the cleaners"

> then you poured us both
> some grape juice, in our ruby colored glasses

> > "drinking grape juice and raindrops
> > tastes better than fermented beverages
> > don't you agree ?"

"is your dislike . . for alcohol
a growing thing, Goob
or is it a knowing thing ?"

> > and you smiled . . "I guess
> > it's more of a *knowing* thing
> > than a *growing* thing
> > perhaps a fragment from another Temple"

> yes, fragments . . . .
> > . . . . fragments

Slowly, Slowly . . Oh !

sometimes, we enter our bed
> with an unspoken promise dawning
then hurtle downward, through the yawning
> > trap doors of our minds

as a heavy weight pulls down the blinds
across our closing eyes

> forgetting need and vow, somehow
> too overcome with unexpected drowsiness to even kiss
> > goodnight
> with more than just a brush of lips
> as unconsciousness, uninvited, slips . . oh, softly
> in between us, warm, to swaddle us in down
> and smother us in billowing sleep feathers . . so to drown
> > desire
> . . and fall into
> a dreamless slumber

until, as through some mystical clue
we awaken to a purple throbbing darkness . . and lie so still
> so silent, listening
to the memorized first movement
of our symphony of passion
as it progresses slowly, on a sliding scale of half and whole notes
from mellow to allegro, conducted as composed

in free flow form

like the libretto of some past Master
of the soul's lost chords

a song of longing, without beginning lyric, or a verse
too well remembered to rehearse
with practiced gestures . . as we feel a slowly-growing-knowing ache

      not reaching out at first, to cling — but waiting
      for this ache, not unlike pain, to bring its sudden sting
                     of tears
      as it begins, a loving-lump of aching
            inside our throats . . behind our ears

no, not reaching out, at first — to touch
but lying very still . . . so still . . so silent
and thus allow the ache to grow
so it may lead us, step by step, to the secret-heaven-place we know
                     of Oneness

oh ! it says so clearly, this nearly-hurting-aching
loving-lump inside our throats, behind
our ears . . bringing its wonted sudden sting of tears
                 it says that this need, now being
born again . . because it must

was not conceived from the mating of sensual with lust
but from the gentle innocence
      of childhood's shining faith and trust

      made of Christmas-morning, baby-birds, first snowflake
fat-puppy-tummy, funny-froggy lumps of loving
      made of sweet-hay-barns, cool-rain-woods and country roads
chiming-church-bell lumps of loving

      rising from some quiet well of goodness
      where our love lies buried deep

and then, as we slowly, slowly, oh ! awaken from our still half-sleep
our almost-hurting-with-it-sweetness ache
                grows stronger
. . . grows slowly stronger
      until we cannot any longer
pretend we do not know
      where it is leading us to go
               . . and why
and so . . we sigh

      when it moves to rest inside your chest
      and fills my breast with slowly, slowly, oh ! the sound
              of music

then crashing cymbals

as our pounding-sounding heartbeats synchronize
to add the heavier drumming beat of pulsing desire percussion
       until the snowflake tender-sweet
and Christmas morning chords . . . deepen into a fuller sound

      spreading slower, moving lower, down into wells
of pure sensation . . stirring feelings more intense
                 to gradually increase
the slowly, slowly, oh ! release . . of love's incense
dew-drenched, remembered lilacs
          dyed the purple shades of passion

then the ache begins to roll into pounding waves
of such insistence that we groan aloud, and tremble
        reaching out, at last . . to touch

first touching fingers, tenderly
then warm., moist lips . . . . . your hands hold soft my face
as if it were a fragile daisy, easily bruised
      oh ! when your strong familiar hands
so gently cup and hold my face
and your fingers slowly trace its features, outline my nose
I can never find the words to tell you
that this is my most holy moment of communion
within our concert hour

      reminding me, each time, of the sunny April morning
I pretended I was a flower — when I was almost ten
in Aunt Maud's cool-green garden

but you might laugh at me, as I was laughed at then
so I cannot speak of it — and say, instead, a private prayer
that you will know of this
as I kiss your cheek, drinking in the scent of your skin
         uniquely you

   yes, you-you-you . . who are also me
      the Us . . that equals our own trinity . . with God

while you bury your nose in my tangled hair
         so sure of finding there
a sweet, and well known musk
and drinking it in . . as I am drinking in your hair and skin
with my nose . . and thinking
      the only scent more dizzy-ing than this
is the fragrance of a rose
you taught me to inhale when I am mad — or sad

   and doing this together

where is what the rigid call sin ?
it is cemented within their own sterile images

                for this sniffing of me . . of you . . of each other
is very like unto . . small, mewing kittens
                        as they burrow and smother into furry warm
instinctively seeking the trusted
                        not caring where . . or separating
right from wrong . . driven by Nature's strong and primal confidence
in the known, familiar and familial scents of love

protected by Nature's warning of danger
in the scent of a stranger

                                . . yes, like mewing kittens
                        seeking trusted warmth

        . . or like a hungry man will wander through
the smells of Christmas tangerines . . and fresh-baked bread
guided by the nose of memory
                        to recall a childhood kitchen
        warm, familiar, cozy
                                sweet . . and safe

by now, the ache is everywhere — from head to toe we feel the burn
of purely flaming passion, making honey
                                as slowly, slowly, oh ! we twist and turn
every single nerve and sinew
singing carols of clinging and mounting desire
                each swelling hollow on fire, impatiently awaiting

        the fulfillment of mating

our minds and hearts
meekly accept the sudden, fierce possession of our bodies
filled only with the wild obsession
                                of forcing us to blend
and end the need they feel . . to complete this song of longing

                our singing bodies clearly
asserting an intelligence and powerful purpose of their own
demanding that we now leave them alone
        to urgently pursue
                the thing they know so surely we must do

        this conquering of me . . by you

and so, our weakening, once-strong wills
fade into pale submission, experiencing the repeated thrills
of surrendering to the always unexpected strength
                                of body over mind

making us blind to all save sensuality
as we allow our hands and lips . . our arms and thighs
to control the faster movements
                of the crashing climax of our symphony

sighing sighs . . mingling little moans
                of the loving lumps of pleasure
finally . . relinquishing everything to the senses . . . .
to touch — and feel — and instinct
abandoning all
        . . . . to the invisible conductor of this concert hour

        yes, willingly . . we abandon ourselves
to a wiser, stronger, older power
holding the ancient secret we, ourselves, once knew

                        but have forgotten
the awesome mystery
of the miracle of giving and receiving love

        O ! cry out ! for there is no one to see — no one to hear
or judge our blissful, bursting blending
as we feel it thrusting, sending
into our very beings . . ever-higher streams of light
yet also sending us into ever-deeper depths
                        on this purple throbbing night
yes ! this is right . . to fill our cup of love
with brimming stars, and with rich, overflowing wine

        as I become completely yours . . and you become completely mine

then slowly, slowly, oh ! once again we come together even closer
singing, winging, springing . . and soaring up into
                        the final chord of music
in the symphony of the Me-of-You
becoming Us, in Oneness
                becoming whole . . and true

        somehow, through a mystical clue
of calling out silently, in the night . . each to each
as we were both sinking out of reach, in sleep

        we have once more fulfilled that promise in our eyes
    first made under now forgotten skies of brighter blue
in another time . . another place
                    when together, we then knew
how to make Giving and Living rhyme — with Love

        when we once knew . . . . oh, déjà vu . . déjà vu !

    in which far away and long ago

Canto Fifteen ☆ 567

when I was yours, and you were mine
did we know ?

in that other time, of dreamless sleep
when we made Life rhyme
and lay us down, our souls to keep

     . . did we both die before we could wake
     then pray to the Sun god, our Twin Selves to take
        and guide us back together
     through some no longer remembered mantra or prayer ?

the answer is there . .

     where our love lies buried in wells of goodness
     and in the fragments we sometimes recall
        when the Eternity ember burns and glows
     during our sharing-of-the-staring into each other's eyes

              . . . but then forget

     and yet . . remember again, at the fleeting moment
     of the final chord of music in our symphony of Oneness

and lose . . .

        as we drift back into sleep

     only to discover once more, in dreams
     flowing into silent streams
        . . . of ever-deeper "deep"

CANTO SIXTEEN

Defend me from this rage of deadening sorrow,
Defend me with your arms and kisses bold —
Make haste, dear love, before another morrow
Dawns with its kindless loneliness and cold.

O sweet, these are the days of fleet forgetting,
Love's triumphs are but small when wars make spawn
Instead of children in begetting,
And marriages are stifled with a yawn.

These are the days that bode but ill to living,
Love struggles to be heard above the screech;
Men mock their loveless lives, and unforgiving
Dance hate's dances on a livid beach.

But that lies far below us, love : our path
Of trembling brightness is
                              God's Sword of Wrath !

Kyril Demys (Musaios)
Prismatic Voices

somewhere deep within the unfathomed depths
of our burning-growing-knowing moments . . of staring
and staring
and staring
I knew a vague — a dim and misty secret
of the Serpent

difficult to fully comprehend
for, with mind and heart, I could only grasp a part
not all of its wisdom
yet, it was burning and growing in — and memorized by
my soul
relating to the profound mystery
of Yang and Yin and Original Sin

buried within the noisy din of battle between the sexes
and also between all other haves and have-nots, as well as in
the eternal polarity of Heaven and hell . . of Positive and Negative

the polarities
of rich and poor
of youth and age
of black and white
of dark and light
of day and night
and male and female

and the deepest, most mysterious and urgent
positive-negative polarity of them all
I was beginning to believe
is that between man and woman

with the Eden-snake hiSSing the secret
of the fall of Adam and Eve

each blindly schizophrenic polarity motivated and urged
by hidden fears and jealousies
into repeated attempts to destroy the other
each driven to annihilate its opposite
into temporary or permanent extinction

like the midnight-dawn conflict of the weaker Moon — and stronger Sun
yet, the Serpent Circle mystery contains the Eden secret
of neutralizing each — by blending two separate polarities into one
thereby creating a new and powerful energy
able to power space craft, to channel telepathy — or conceive
human life
an energy . . like unto God

or like . . unto our *Co*-Creators

for there are two
yes, Heaven reflects, of necessity
the same Positive-Negative principle of polarity . . . and
of Perfect Harmony — as Earth

but though my soul had memorized the Eden-snake secret of blending
of feeding into, and not destroying, my mind and heart
                                        comprehended it not
and then one August morning
humid and sticky-hot . . the earthly, human you-of-you
playing your Master Teacher role
taught the earthy, human me-of-me a primitive lesson

one I almost, but not quite, memorized with my mind
as I had memorized the Serpent Circle mystery with my soul
                almost . . but not quite
I was sitting on the bed, my temper flaring
over some improbable, imaginary hurt — having just rocketed
a fiery blast of words at your non-committal back
as you were leaving the room
                . . when you turned, and answered me

                        softly, quietly
                        with your wonted purring patience

but I thought I noticed a spark
in your tilted-at-the-corners green cat eyes
they seemed to glitter with a primal dark and sensual wise
with some hint of animal evolution, not quite forgotten
some savage convolution, not yet completed . . still in-bred
as you stretched your splendid Leonine muscles
and glided . . . with cat-like grace . . . toward the bed

                you draped yourself beside me . . very, very near
                then whispered smoothly, with silken voice . . . into my ear

                        and the breath of your words
                        was hot and musty . . like jungle grass

                        "darling . . " you murmured
                        very slowly . . . and very surely

                        "darling, I love you deeply
                        but please don't forget
                            who and what I am
                        remember that I am a Lion
                        and you are only a paper Ram"

"*only* ? what do you mean, *only* ?"

I bristled indignantly

> then I felt, rather than heard your voice
> grow even smoother and silkier . . when you replied

> > "well, did you ever see a paper Ram
> > play with a Lion ?
> > I'll tell you what happens . . . . . . "

and I listened, hardly breathing
strangely silent . . unwilling to interrupt
as you continued watching me carefully
out of the tilted corners of your cat's eyes

> > "at first . . " you said . . "when the Ram
> > butts its horns against the Lion
> > the Lion just yawns a huge yawn . . stretches
> > rolls over . . and goes back to sleep in the Sun

> > the second time
> > > the Ram butts its horns against him
> > the Lion opens his enormous mouth
> > shows his sharp teeth, and roars loudly . . like this"

> and you roared, like the MGM Lion . . "Grr-roar ! **GRR-RROAR**"

> > instinctively, I drew back
> > an inch or so
> > losing all my steely Martian poise
> so startled was I
at the unexpected savagery of the noise

> > your next words were measured, oddly controlled
> > like the deceptively soft footsteps
> > > of a wild beast, stalking prey

> > "and the third time
> > > the Ram butts its paper horns
> > against the proud and noble Lion, he lifts his
> > > > > mighty paw
> > then, with all his great strength
> > he smashes the Ram's horns into splinters
> > > > > . . . . like this"

> and you brought your mighty paw — I mean, your fist
> down against the pillow — hard
> > and smashed it shockingly
> as I raised my hand protectively . . . to my head
> in an unconscious, but automatic gesture of defense
> but you went on, relentlessly

"now, if the paper Ram
continues to butt the Lion after that
with its impotent paper horns
.... do you know what happens ?"

"no — what happens ?"
I asked, in a teeny-tiny voice
outwardly amused, yet inwardly, inexplicably frightened
and watched you shake your mighty Lion's mane of wheat colored hair
narrow your green-tilted eyes
assume the controlled crouch of a powerful animal, about to leap

as you spoke in a low growl

"then the Regal Lion, Royal King of all the beasts
the undisputed Lord and Ruler of the jungle .... "

"oh, stop it !   what happens ?"

"he devours the weaker Ram — **GULP !**
he ravages her in one bite . . like this !"

then suddenly, you pounced !

kissed me long and violently

and I had . . absolutely nothing to say
as we loved in a new and primal, untamed way

the familiar melody of our spring had been changed
by unspoken sensual agreement between us . . into a different rhythm

now abandoned to jungle passion

first . .
trembling, silent waiting
then . .
sudden, fierce lunging

over and over . . and over and over . . wild and demanding, even menacing
yet, totally fulfilling the primitive instinct for consuming union
through the need of Woman to surrender to Man
and for Man to conquer his mate

proving the inseparable Serpent Circle entwining of loving and hating
as we blended in the ecstasy of absolute mating

and I knew, within

that Man must first surrender to Woman
in a subtle, more intricate submission

before she allows him to completely conquer her . .
the same being true of all polarities

the ancient mystery
of Yang and Yin

yes, we loved silently . . violently
in an insistent, primordial way
and I almost, but not quite . . memorized the lesson

that our deep
was the deepest of all our deeps

that day

You Won That Round

one night, in our funny, crooked house
I made to you what I believe to be
a fine, dramatic and eloquent speech
. . . which I guess I may do
too often

although I'm truly trying to avoid over-doing it
so I won't lose too many points in Behavior
with the grading system
you've been using lately
when you make out my Love report cards

I carefully explained with a certain perverse pride
that I simply cannot keep my emotions chained, or bottled up inside
when anger strikes me suddenly, making me desire
to release the ball of fire . . . flaming in my volatile solar plexus

"at times like that" . . I told you

"which can occur once a month or once a week
or once a day — it depends
I **MUST** violently break — or bust — or crash
or smash something, anything that's near
just so it makes a loud **BIG BANG** noise I can *hear* !

it's absolutely the only thing huge enough to do
to loose the surging energy I feel
when my adrenalin churns and burns . . and needs
to be drained
sometimes, you see, it's not enough to just scream and shout

then, immediately afterwards, I become calm and cool
because the fire has been put out !
but I must have that **BIG BANG,** don't you see ?
and the louder, the better — to set my boiling anger free
or I would burn my emotions to a cinder from the heat
        do you understand ?
the explosive noise makes everything complete
                    somewhere within

then, when it's all over
I can be sweet and sensible . . and rational again
my **BIG BANG** reaction is much healthier, I believe
than locking up my feelings inside of me
           . . . Gooober, don't you agree ?"

      you made no answering comment at all
         you just looked at me for a long moment
in total silence . . with your silvery-wise eyes
raised your eyebrow a fraction of an inch
and gave one of your quiet sighs
             . . I believe you even yawned

    then you rose from the couch, lazily stretched
and gazed into my eyes

        but all you said

      was . . "it's late . . let's go to bed"

later, lying in the darkness beside you
your arms wrapped tightly around me
I pretended to be asleep when you kissed me goodnight
and you turned away then — slowly, but surely
withdrawing the warm circle of your arms

as I thought . . it serves him right — he started this fight
by ignoring me completely, before, downstairs
now I suppose he'll pout all day tomorrow
oh, well — who cares ? I'm not going to lose sleep over it

    but I did . . and, my dreams were troubled

when I awoke the next morning, I felt a moment of panic
your pillow was empty — you weren't there
you were already in the kitchen . . . making orange juice
    and after awhile . . you called to me

        "breakfast is ready . . .
        come on down and smell the fresh air !"

that afternoon, I was in the kitchen pantry
happily humming . . and sweeping the floor

> while you were replacing a bulb
> in our fat china lamp, in the den . . then

suddenly

> I heard an ear-splitting, thunderous **BOOM** !
> like a shot from a cannon — accompanied by a **CRASH** !

so I dropped my broom, ran into the room — and there you were
poor, comic Oober Valentine
> standing abashed, flushed and barefoot
amid thousands of tiny slivers of glass everywhere
some of them even sprinkled in your hair . . like stardust

the lamp had been smashed in a dozen pieces
beyond all hope of repair . . **OH** !
our beautiful, fat, china, handpainted antique lamp . . broken

> I rushed over to you, then — smiling
> where you were standing near the old rocking chair
> to give you a bear hug
> > and to tell you that I didn't care
> but before I could speak, to let you know I'd forgiven you
> you thought of a way to save face
> > > . . and put me in my place
> > beneath you

> > "I should have let *you* screw in the bulb"

> > you remarked, in your casual
> > subtle, low-key way

> > "just think, darling . .
> > it could have been your **BIG BANG**
> > > for the day
> > and saved us the trouble
> > > of another fight"

instantly hurt, I didn't answer
I pretended I hadn't heard
> but I thought to myself . .

. . . you and your damned Moon-in-Scorpio last word
must you *always* be right ? who *started* this fight ?

> it was you — not I ! !

sometimes, I think I hate you — yes, I really do

you seem to enjoy making me cry
and I'm **NOT** a rebel without cause ! you just don't try to understand
the underlying fears behind my angry tears
I never fight without a good reason
and it's **YOU** who always brings on our winter season
with your Leonine arrogance and Saturnine gloom

> then I went into the kitchen, returned
> and handed you the broom

saying . .
"sweep it up yourself
it's *your* mess, not *mine*"

> when you didn't speak, I angrily turned away
> but . . I did allow the lamp you broke
> to be our only **BIG BANG** for *that* day. . . . . .

If I'm Bonnie — Where's Clyde ?

do you know what turns me into a cringing coward
> crumbles my Aries courage
and causes my Ram's horns to quiver and shake ?

> it's not the threat of an earthquake — a nuclear blast
> murderous muggers — the abominable snowman
> > evil Hobbits, like Gollum
> Frankenstein — Dracula — or the Wolf Man

> > or even wild, roaring Lions like you
after all, I'm a Fire Sign too . .

it's the icy stares I get
when I'm trying to cash a check
and they ask me for identification

> "could I see your driver's license, please ?"

and I answer, in a teeny-tiny voice
stripped of my identify

"I don't have one . . I don't drive"

> ### "YOU DON'T DRIVE ? MY GOD !
> ### YOU DON'T HAVE A DRIVER'S LICENSE ?"

suddenly, I'm suspect — in a bank, a hotel

a department store, or at an airport
never mind my library card or telephone credit card

I don't have a driver's license

obviously, there's every possibility
I might be the moll of a hold-up gang, waiting curbside
in an ominous black car
with tommy guns and Warren Beatty . . (no such luck)
perhaps the bag woman for a shoplifting ring
. . or at the very least

a bomb-carrying
hi-jacker
. . maybe it's my ticking temper *they* hear !

then inevitably, the curious question
"but how do you get around if you don't drive ?"

"oh, I manage, I manage . . somehow, I survive
I was born with two feet, for walking
and two arms, for hailing taxis . . see ?"

I finally figured out a way to shake those credit conformists
a friend who works for Avis, where they try harder
got me one of those VIP rental cards
to prove I'm a Very Important Person — on the move !
and when I flash that, they bow and scrape

"but Madame, naturally then . .
you must have a driver's license ?"

like a broken record, stuck in a groove

"of course not !" I reply, with a look of haughty shock
"I never drive myself
now will you please hurry, and cash my check ?
my chauffeur is driving around the block
I'm late for an appointment at Vidal Sassoon's
and my hair is simply a wreck !"

sometimes it works . .
when I'm wearing my Tiffany ring

but I was wondering . . . if that's the wrong way to speak to you
when you've forced me to admit it's true
that love doesn't give me a license to rage — or to lock up a Lion
inside a cage

should I answer you instead
in my teeny-tiny check cashing voice

when you sternly demand an excuse

for my impulsive behavior and angry abuse

and say meekly . .

"I'm sorry . . I don't have one
will you forgive me ?"

Ghost Writing

it was shortly after one of our minor squabbles
of querulous quibbling . . that you remarked, tenderly

> "darling, mouse-spouse
> spunky Lucy-wench, whom I love madly
>
> shall I help you write your Happiness poem
> with some timely tips and happy hints
>   from the secret, very illuminated text
> of the Oober Galaxy
>   Galactic Rhyming Dictionary ?
>
> in that ancient rhyming book
> of metered scanning and happiness planning
> if you'll look closely in the Index
>   you will see
>
> that Forever rhymes with You and Me
>   also with Eternally
>
> and Emotional Security
> rhymes with Emotional Maturity
>
> but Emotional In-security
> rhymes with Spiritual Impurity
>
> and Jealously rhymes with Misery
> also with Imaginary and Unnecessary"

then I whispered low

"no . . jealously rhymes with fear"

> but you were playing with Love and Peace
> and tickling their tummies

as I repeated, silently

Gooober, did you hear ?
I said Jealousy rhymes with Fear

I Remember-I Remember-I Remember

"I'll go with you to the Post Office
to get the mail"
I would say, 'most every day
                . . and usually

                    you would answer — "oh, good !
                    let's go together — then take a walk
                    in the woods
                        and call coyotes under a tree
                    would you like to call coyotes with me ?"

        or answer . .

                    "oh, good ! I'll only be gone
                    five minutes or so — but
                    since I miss you when I'm away
                    only half that long
                    come on, darling — let's go !"

        then once you said . .

                    "do you think you should ?"

                    instead of . . "oh, good !"

and I asked — "why not ?
have I been bad ?"

                    and you replied, with a smile so sad
                    "Goob, you should know by now
                    that I read your every thought — and
                    it is obviously not to be near me
                    that's not the reason
                    you want to come along
                            to pick up the mail"

I tried to bluff
and cried — "hey, that's enough !
come on, stop teasing me"

                    but you persisted, with quiet eyes

"let's not have even any little white lies
of omission between us

you wonder if I receive any letters
                                    from *her*
and then hide them
so you won't see — after I've read them — in the car
that's the real reason
you like to pick up the mail with me
and I've told you, over and over
I will not lie to you
so you need never be afraid
of that kind of hurt — ever again
how many times must I tell you ?
you don't have to be afraid
of *his* lies . . . ever again . . from *me*"

so I stayed in the house that morning
like a good mouse-spouse
while you went to get the mail alone

but . . before you returned
you called me on the phone . . just two or three minutes
                                    after you left

to affectionately say . .

"hey, Lucy-wench ! it's starting to snow
and I'm lonesome for you already
            I'll be right home
then we can play Post Office together, okay ?"

oh Gooober . . do you know
how much I loved and trusted you that day ?

A Problem in Abstract Math

I was reading a critic's review today, in the Times
of a book written about Albert Einstein — by his sister
telling how the sibling of a genius sometimes feels

she said that Al was a "holy-terror-on-wheels"
as a child, and even later
with a wild, explosive **BIG BANG** temper

and he used to frequently bang her over the head
with a book or a rock — a sock — or a tinker toy

anything that happened to be handy
          when the mood streaked across his mind

and he was only a relatively gentle Pisces
somewhat shy — not ruled by Mars
               as I . . am ruled

isn't that surprising ?
maybe the Moon was in Aries
or the sign of the Ram was on his Acsendent
when he was born

          anyway, I was just wondering . .
          since you insist that I be so severely schooled
          in the lessons of Living you keep giving

          I was wondering, that is . . I mean
          well, there's one thing, at least, I know for sure
          you *do* respect Einstein, don't you ?
                    and so . . was *he* emotionally immature ?
like me . . ?

          you see . . I've also read or heard somewhere
          that Abstract Al never learned to drive
          of course, it may be only a rumor — but I'll check it out
          when I get the book — and let you know

               OH !

          WOULDN'T IT BE PERFECTLY, PERFECTLY MARVELOUS
          if Albert Einstein didn't have a driver's license ?

A Dolphin to Play With You

the new race of Atlanteans, according to Edgar Cayce
as a race, is still in its youth
but the souls are as old as Time itself

old souls being simply those who have chosen
to live many more times in Earth incarnations . . than others
                              have chosen to do

the other day, I was reading a book of prophecy
about the New Race . . and the New Age thinkers

          how they are destined to try to prevent
the Earth changes and cataclysms predicted by geologists

                                        and metaphysicians
the text pointed out that, if compassion
is increased — toward both those from the human
                                    and the animal kingdoms
    . . . . and the spread of vegetarianism
is a beginning . . . .

then the vast and awful Earth changes may be avoided
and we need not endure
the terrible inundation experienced by Atlantis

    . . if we remember to love one another
and remember that we are our brothers' keepers
                                    including our animal brothers
        and our sisters' keepers too

and if we don't forget, as the book warned
the message of the Nazarene, that . .

                    "verily, the little child of the spirit
                    in the new time (new age) shall be ruler"

    the prophecies also said that . .

    " . . you can recognize these very old Atlantean souls
by their childlike quality, their naivete
        their high level of emotional intensity
                    and lack of worldly sophistication"

    "such as . . . . " the text continued

" . . such as the man, who sometimes acts so much like a little boy
and the woman, who sometimes acts so much like a little girl
for only those innocent ones — so old in soul
yet so young of heart and appearance . . and behavior
contain within themselves the alchemy for working miracles
of healing the crippled . . returning sight to the blind"

                how comforting ! I thought
                that the druids may have been right !

perhaps the secret of magic
is truly to remain a child — and not be ashamed
in today's snide and sarcastic society
to be considered foolishly immature . . perhaps

    this is the way to magic !

as I meditated on the words I'd been reading, I laid down the book
some memory bell . . . was chiming carols
                    in the back of my mind

this past Christmas, when I was in New York
and you were in our little crooked house, out west . . alone
when we could communicate only by letter or phone
you wrote to tell me . . that the only thing you really wanted
                                    from Santa

was a duck — a dolphin — and a fleet of sailboats
                        to play with you in the bathtub

so I rushed over to F.A.O. Schwartz
in a slushy mush, through the holiday crush — and bought them
and wrapped them with faith, all shiny-new
            and tied them tenderly, with ribbons of love
then mailed them to you . . in Colorado

            . . and on Christmas morning, in New York
            watching the lonely, falling snow . . feathering
                                    past my window
            when I opened your gift to me
                        it was exactly what I wanted too !

a gift Santa had somehow forgotten
one sad childhood Noel . . of long ago

            oh ! Goob ! I never-ever told you . . so
            how did you know ?

it was . .

            a happy-bright, smiling Raggedy Ann
            with shiny-black-button eyes
            and a red heart that said — *I Love You*
            hidden beneath her calico dress

once, when I was impatient with you
        I shouted

"how can a grown man splash in the water for hours
with a toy duck, dolphin . . and sailboats ?
you're emotionally immature !"

            and only last week . .

when I flew back here to say I was sorry
for something I'd said on the phone — but mostly
for leaving you alone, on Christmas
we quarreled again . . as usual, neither of us sure just why
and as I sat on the couch, in the den, clutching Raggy
determined not to let you see me cry
                        you shouted at *me*, impatiently

                584 ☆ Canto Sixteen

"how can a grown woman
sit there hugging a silly rag doll ?
you're emotionally immature !"

I wonder if we wounded each other
that deeply in Atlantis too ?
and how many other "old souls" are doing the same
to one another . . every day ?

maybe you should stop hurting me, Gooober
and I should stop hurting you
there's so little Time left . . to spread Light on Earth
and so much healing to do

Did I Ever Tell You I'm Glad of You ?

you're lying on the couch in the den again, sleeping
and I'm sitting in the dark, near the fire
rocking and weeping
softly, lest I disturb your nap, your royal Highness

but I'm also thinking . .

. . and wondering why it is
that we've stopped telling each other
the way we really feel inside

sometimes the Oober things you say and do
make my heart swell up with love, like a balloon
until it nearly bursts with tenderness

like the time you decided it wasn't at all proper
for our two kittens, Love and Peace
to mix socially with the other cats around town
and have to explain that they didn't have a surname
since you and I were not married yet

"poor little Peace . . " you sighed
with a frown
"those gossipy neighborhood felines
will put her down . . and
she'll never get a husband that way"

so you re-christened them
Blueberry Love — and Pumpkin Peace

and the time you took poor Bones, our outside cat, who only visits

to the Vet in the Springs
after first trying to heal him yourself, with tender, loving care
the reason he got better, Goob
wasn't the goo the Vet smeared on his paw
or the shot he gave him that day
                             it was you . . your love
somehow, I never got around
to telling you that . . but it's true

          yes, it's true . . and Bones knew !
          he told me so himself
          just before he ran away last week
          probably to share spring with his own twin soul
          who lives somewhere over in Victor

and I remember . . tonight, I remember

          your Christmas tree, this past bleak December
          when I couldn't stay, but had to fly away to New York
          and leave you here alone
          in our funny, crooked, slipping-off-the-time-track house
          to celebrate the miracle of Christmas all by yourself

I found it later . .

          after I returned — your Christmas tree — on the pantry shelf
          it was . . a sprig of Scotch pine, only two inches high
          too tiny for even a druid or an elf
          stuck in a pot, you had painted gold and red

at first, I started to laugh — then surprised myself
and swallowed hard instead
because I felt a pain . . a growing mump-lump of love
                             behind my ears
          sharp and unexpected

afterwards, when I asked you about it, my eyes filled with tears
twin-tears, to match your own
as you told me you just didn't have the heart
to trim a big, showy tree with colored lights and tinsel;
when we were separated by so many miles
          . . and when half the world is hungry

          "besides . . " you added sadly . . "to murder a tree
          then decorate it, like a corpse in the parlor
          doesn't seem to me . . to be . . . . the right way
                             to celebrate
          Peace on Earth
          to all of God's creatures . . oh ! Gooober
                             don't you see ?"

I saw

and, as I was cleaning out the desk drawers, just now
I found two clippings you had carefully cut out of the paper

one is a picture of the First Family — smiling
lighting a huge tree on the White House lawn
with a detailed description of the gala festivities
planned in Washington, for the holidays

the other is dated a few days earlier
a big, black headline

PRESIDENT ESCALATES BOMBING OF VIET NAM

they were taped together . .

darling, your teeny tiny druid Christmas tree
was just the right size for our shining Star of Truth
and your concern for the unhappiness of others
is just the right size too
immeasurable

. . and I'm thinking about

the times you decide to drop all inhibition
and go on an ice cream binge
to prove to yourself that you're not a Food Snob
just because you preach health and the proper nutrition

gulping down great gobs, all in one night — of Raspberry Ripple
and Peanut Delight — Caramel Fudge — Rocky Road and Cherry Chew
or Strawberry Crunch and Butterscotch goo
then become predictably ill — and punish yourself by fasting
for three whole days
convinced, like Francesco di Bernadone, of Assisi
that you will never win the eternal war between your Higher Self
and the seductive whims of Brother Body

you always like to have me do the same
to binge right along with you, and share half the blame
but I can never keep up — you eat circles around me every time
especially when its Rocky Road . . or Oreos

and . . those bubbly moments of bittersweet
when a tapped out stranger stops us on the street
to ask you for a dime or a quarter

a fellow Earthling, who's lost his way for awhile
you always smile, then hand him five or ten — or twenty
even when you're broke yourself

and it's your very last five or ten — or twenty

and when the Taker looks shocked, as they often do
you call back to him, over your shoulder . .

"listen, if you need any more
                          just give half of that away
          don't save it for a rainy day
          rain rhymes with pain — Give rhymes with Live !"

and when he answers . .
"right on, man ! I dig, I dig !"

we smile at each other, then squeeze hands tightly
because we're spreading the Jerusalem magic
of the small boy's loaves — bread cast in Life's river
to one new convert
and maybe turned him into an apostle . . a Giver

you always say . .

"the planet is so over-populated
with Takers . . . and so empty of Givers
but just wait until all those people
we've touched with Oober Galaxy love
discover the rocket-socket Truth
that they will get more — they really will !
much more, almost immediately
if they give half of what they have away
and get in tune
with the harmony of the Universe !"

sometimes, we bump into them again, on a sunny day
and they remember — then they tell us about the miracles they found
by letting go, and spreading whatever they have around
how they discovered the spiritual gold
of seeing what they gave returned — sometimes three or four-fold
because we *are* our brother's keepers
and our sister's too
each of us channel for Love to flow through

    . . . and the way you take the time, between your bath tub floats
playing with your yellow duck . . dolphin and boats
to dash off enthusiastic thank-you notes
when you read in a newspaper or magazine about someone
who's pleading the cause for saving plankton — or baby seals
whales — New Hamshire foxes
                          or even one tree

  someone who's published an article about the evils of hunting
the courage of the Indians at Wounded Knee

or attacking the hypocrisy of the AMA and the FDA

. . how you rush to the typewriter
to let them know they're not alone . . to congratulate them
for caring enough to speak out

and the time you gave a Tarzan shout

as you wrote to me, in a letter . .

"I'm a huge atomic mushroom — unleashed !
booming Pyramid rainbows of Love and Peace
into the world
striking Positive harmony into Negative hateful
I feel myself growing and expanding
into the Universe !"

. . while you were standing on your head
in your usual way . . with Tchaikovsky playing in the background

so "high" on Life . . so much in love with all you survey
no wonder you're puzzled by people
who need alcohol or drugs to see Nature's beauty
and hear her symphonies of glory
come crashing through the constellations
in clamorous crescendos . . yet gentle enough to awaken a violet
from winter's sleep

oh ! Gooober, here it is !

I thought I had lost it, but found it
at the very bottom of the top drawer in the dining room buffet
stuffed under your library card

the letter you wrote this past December
after you had opened your Christmas gifts from me
all alone . . sitting beneath your tiny pine sprig tree

yes, sitting *beneath* it — it was a *tall* tree !

. . and the postscript you tucked inside
just right for the Cosmopolitan nude, male center-fold

a picture of you

in the bath tub

THANK YOU FOR MY DUCK, DOLPHINS, FISH AND BOATS.

.. why do I sit here in this rocking chair, weeping
when I should be so happy, so full of peace
just to know you're lying in the den — mine, and sleeping
so warm, so near and dear ?

what would I do without you ?
O ! what would I do if you ever grew weary of waiting
for me to show that I care about you
                              weary of waiting for me to understand
and I reached out some midnight
                              for your familiar hand
but you weren't there
and I touched empty air ?

        what would I do if someday, you happened to leave
                                        .. to go away ?
the room is dark
                it has suddenly grown colder

        the fire is dying . .

            I know what I'll do ! before we're one minute older
            I'll go in and wake you . . but not by crying
            as I did when I woke you from your nap last week

            no, I'll tiptoe quietly into the den
                              and awaken you slowly, tenderly
            with a tiny snowflake kiss on your cheek
            to let you know
                        . . how glad I am of you

            yes ! that's what I'll do !

            I'll wake you softly, gently
            then tell you how much I need you and love you

                and thank you for loving me, too

February 12th

Lincoln's birthday, yes

        but also her anniversary — the other Raggedy Ann
        the one spelled Anne with an 'e'
        not the anniversary of her arrival — the anniversary
                                        of her departure
    you were not there

you'd gone to the grocery store
when I was suddenly overcome with memory . . and ran upstairs
closed the bedroom door, to grieve alone

and wept

softly, quietly sobbing
as I silently whispered his name . . the Carousel Bill

then felt a warm, strong, dear familiar hand on mine
and looked up, startled
to see you standing there

"I was driving down the hill
when I thought I heard you calling
and I came back
oh, don't cry so, Gooober . . be still
my love, be still

darling . . . did you call me ?"

One Divided By Two — Equals Lonely Again For Both

. . when I was born

the druids must have pasted on the shadow of my memory hastily
backwards . . upside-down and wrong-side out

because the things I promised you I would forget
I keep remembering — and yet
the things I vowed always to remember
I seem to keep forgetting

O ! Oobers . .

twinkling your teeny-tiny stars
to guide us through our Earth-lived night
as we spin within your galaxy of Truth and Light

. . calling it, blindly, the Milky Way

why do you not offer
to your forgetful fallen angels
a Memory Course for the soul ?
. . how to keep the Oober faith ?

keep the faith, baby

yes, keep the faith, children
keep the faith !

    telling them, at Sunrise, the ancient sunset story
                    of each soul's lost Power
and birthright of Glory
teaching your Saturn-Serpent-seven lessons
              perhaps through elephants, at the circus
with carob-covered peanuts
          as a reward for memorization

yes, those Great Remembering Beasts
could better help the children re-learn
the miracle mantras they once knew
that magically made two — eternally equal one

    Saturn is too strict a teacher
    to hold the student's attention

        the square of Gooober's Saturn to my once-bright Sun
        is too silent, stern and cold
        teaching me only . . lessons in lonely
        and the catechism of growing old

The Meek Shall Inherit the Earth — And You

G-o-o-o-b-e-r, are you listening ?

    i was wondering if **YOU'D** like to see a movie tonight ?
    i really don't care which one
    i know my wishes don't really matter . . so, as usual
    i will try to enjoy the film **YOU** choose, Dear

    i won't take time to change clothes — it's after eight, and
    i don't want to risk upsetting **YOU,** since **YOU'RE** such a crab when
    i unintentionally make **YOU** late — and
    i know how **YOU** hate to sit and wait

    i don't believe i'll need a coat, do **YOU ?**
    i was outside, burning the trash in the yard — because, well
    i didn't want to disturb **YOUR** nap by asking **YOU** to burn it . . and
    i noticed the air is soft and warm, like spring

        YOU'D rather stay home tonight ?
            but . . what about me ?

    i need to get out of this mouse-trap of a house for awhile
    i haven't been anywhere for over two weeks, almost three — and

i get bored, just watching **YOU** sleep on the couch
                                    every night, after dinner

i won't be more than a minute — go ahead and warm up the car
i guess i'd better open a can of tuna for Love and Peace
                        since **YOU** forgot to feed them

i don't understand . . Gooober, why are **YOU**
                                looking at me like this ?

i didn't say anything wrong, did i ?
i can't imagine what it might have been . . oh, **Wow !**
i give up — what terrible sin am i guilty of **Now ?**

            YOU see what always happens ?

i try to show **YOU** how willing i am to submit to **YOUR** commands

i try to be docile and weak and meek — and
i try to let **YOU** be the Man — and me, the mouse-woman
i try to subdue my own nature, in deference to **YOU**

        and **YOU** don't even bother to *listen* !

    YOU don't even *hear* me !

HOW CAN I SPEAK IN A LOWER CASE i ?

i mean . . how can i *speak* in a lower case i ?

        are **YOU** angry because i
        begin all my sentences with i ?
                    is that why ?

allright, okay . .

        from now on, every single thing i do or say
        will begin with **YOU** — a capital **YOU**

            and *end* with a lower case i

    YOU-YOU-YOU-YOU-YOU and i-i-i-i-i

        do **YOU** think i'm improving ?

you don't ? I see . . . .
    well, damn it, I *do* !
with a lower case you — and a capital I for **ME**

it is a matter of great consequence to a rose
once unique in all the world
to be considered weak and foolish
because of her sharp-prickly thorns

which do not, after all, protect her
but only make her . . . untouchable

didn't you know how it made my anger flame and burn
to have my thorns so ridiculed ?
to be icily ignored — after I'd been adored
simply because you wanted me to learn your eternal lesson
of the grace of tranquility ?

oh ! didn't you know, all those times you made me weep
that a proud Ram, turned into a sheep
by the Lion's more graceful agility of action and speech
cannot rest or sleep ? especially when exiled out of reach
. . and touch
didn't you guess that a Ram
bent unwillingly into the shape of a sheep — is dangerous ?
and that a sheep can eat a rose ?

every Little Prince knows . . that a sheep can eat a rose
and is that not a matter of great consequence
a matter of great concern ?
as great as the matter of a proud Lion
bent into the shape of a mouse
and no longer King — no longer Lord and Ruler
in his own house
yes, these were matters of great concern
warnings of deep karmic lessons we both had yet to learn

it seemed . . a miracle was needed

but what miracle could mend the broken link
in the chain that binds our souls . . this weak link
growing weaker every hour
. . before it breaks ?
perhaps . .

perhaps . .

perhaps, with the keys I possess
which unlock the secret wisdom of the planetary cycles
perhaps I might . . when the time is exactly right
make a miracle

a miracle of three-times-three
the miracle of a small druid, to visit you and me
not imaginary, but real . . a new Anne with an 'e'

O ! Gooober . . . I thought . . a small druid !
would that not surely be
a splendid, magical and healing mystery
for you and me ?

if one — just one of the lost three, could return, to help us learn
to teach us how we might mend this broken link
and help us re-discover our dazzling Christmas tree
                with the Star of Truth at the very tip top
would that not be . . a joyous thing ?

and so, I gathered all the planetary wisdom I knew
to make a small druid miracle for you
and stirred the imaginary potion with shreds of secret hope

I brewed, not the rich nourishment of Knowing
that feeds a hungry heart — and makes any kind of dream come true
but a weaker witch's brew, of thin promise — my magic concocted
from the fearful and diluted faith, called hope

hope and Knowing . . how fine a line between the two !

and I could not tell the difference between them
as I murmured incantations over my cursed witch's brew
which was only — as I knew
        ordinary magic

then the scheming, plotting me-of-me
beckoned to the faithful, trusting you-of-you
and smiled into your eyes
until you trembled with desire, and thundered in your loins
with the knowing-things of passion between us

. . until you stroked my hair with gentle
in the black velvet night
                . . and tenderly whispered

"I love you, little druid sprite
in spite of all the hurting things you do

"I love you with all my heart
you are still my tamed, unique rose"

. . as you loped into the mystery bed beside me
kissed my nose . . and smelled my ear
but did not hear the Full Moon laughing overhead
rustling the clouds

so deafened were you by the crashing chords
                              or our deeper symphony
O ! you exploded love within me at the very hour
the wiser planets — not the unreliable rhythm of the calendar
had decreed for planting magic seed
                    and never heard the Full Moon's secret glee

                because you trusted me

and when I knew for certain that the Morning Star
had carried back to Heaven her message of joy
streaming through the sky
I told you . . and I also told you why

        oh, Goob, I *tried* to tell you why

but you gazed on me with hurt, suspicious eyes
like some wounded animal — and you sternly judged me
by the Saturn coldness in your heart
not because of the planned return of one of the three
                        you said . . oh, no !

but because I had not
        permitted you to know

you glared at me in righteous anger, like some red-eyed Isaiah
and judged me icily
for daring to experience the awe and wonder of that magical mist
                                        alone
just me . . without your knowledge
of the Morning Star
when you had so long waited, you said — when you had so long
believed and prayed that holy moment
would someday be dared — and shared — by both of us, together

                    your voice was cold
                    when you spoke . .
                    and your eyes were green ice

            Oh ! your voice was so very, very cold
                        when you spoke

                    "that's quite a clever joke
                    you played on me . . . you lied to me
                    a sin, not of commission
                            but a sin of omission
                    you stole from me

                    you stole a star from me . . oh !
                    how could you lie to me ?
                            you . . . . lie to *me* ?

Canto Sixteen   ☆   597

how could you steal from me ?
you ? steal from *me* ?

when we have always freely given
                              to each other
why should you
                    ever steal from me
when all I have is yours ?

                why ?   why ?

you should never, never
need to lie — or to steal — from me

          you stole a star from me !"

. . and as we were leaving
the theatre, for no reason at all
you asked me . . did you see Carousel ?
the part I liked best
was when Bill . . stole a star from Heaven
to give to his daughter
              after he died . .

          "you lied ! you lied ! you lied to me !"

I wept, then . .
with a sorrow unknown to me before
in any Temple — for, at last I understood

yes, I understood what I had done to steal from you
to rob you of your chance to watch the Morning Star together
the moment you had waited so long to know — and to share with me
throughout so many ordinary times of "spring"

          and I returned to you my ring
          the one on which you'd had engraved
                Love is Eternal
          for I was not worthy to wear it anymore

                only minutes later
          you took me into your arms
          near the back porch kitchen door

                placed the ring back on my finger
                and said slowly . . sadly

                "I forgive you, I forgive you, darling
                and I know why you thought you had to lie
                it was not you, this time
                who lost points

in the grading of our love — no, it was I
because I caused you to be so afraid
to share that miracle with me
I should not have been so cold
                              that you believed
even for one moment
that I did not also yearn
for the someday return of one of the three
to help us learn

I guess I only thought . .
well, I thought we ought to first be done
with doubt, mistrust — and quarreling
and the rust of old memories, better buried
before we . . and before she . .

but now I see
        I should not have been so cold
that you believed I did not yearn
for a small star to return, and help us re-learn
all we both once knew — and yes
what we both know *still* . . . is true

it's not too late . . "

and you touched
my face

        " . . it's not too late, sad druid
because I love you — oh, I do, I do !
please don't cry
I understand now — and I know why
you excluded me from the Morning Star
                                moment
Goob, this time
it was I who was to blame — not you

come outside with me now
and see where I'm going to plant a lilac bush
in the front yard
and build a frog pond nearby . .
        and all kinds of perfectly marvelous
things . . you'll see !
come ! run outside, now, with me
and let me show you
            all the happy things I've planned
darling, believe me — I do understand
how many times must I explain

that I always understand

                                    . . everything you do ?

                        this time, I lost points — not you"

oh ! that was not true !
it was not you, it was I who was to blame for the shame
of cooking up a witch's brew
and of having so little faith in you, my Comforter
it was I who was to blame . . but just the same

                thank you for loving me
                dear, gentle Gooober
                especially . . when I don't deserve it

Do Not Open Until . . . . . .

it was not Christmas — or Easter — or Groundhog's Day
but I brought you a gift anyway
                            in a small, white box from Saks

        yes, I brought you a gift — a gift from me — for Us
        and handed it to you with uncertain hands
        for, inside was a happy affirmation . . of faith in her
        she, who would help us lope back into three again

a gift . .

        there were forget-me-nots
        stitched on the tiny collar of the smocked white dress

                and a yellow flower for her to hold
                to play with
                kissed by a dizzy, dazzled bumblebee

                        you looked at me
                                when I handed you my gift
                        of happy affirmation

                        and said gently

                        "thank you for loving me, Goob
                        I know I don't always deserve it"

                then we touched noses
                        and whispered . . . *magic* !

and all that night, your arms were wrapped around me
with ribbons of love and tenderness

                    600   ☆   Canto Sixteen

that tied us tightly back together, as before
                    as a gift . . to each other

        later, when we awoke, with our secret signal, near dawn

             just before you whispered "deep"

                    you said . . "sweetheart, you must try
                    to get plenty of rest
                    and be sure to take your vitamins
                            every single day
                    and not allow yourself to become upset
                    over nothing . . these next nine months . . or eight
                    no smashing emotions . . did you
                    take them today, your vitamins . . did you ?

"yes, Gooober, I did
and I promise, druid honor, not to forget
I won't allow unimportant things to make me upset
or make me weep . . "

                    then you murmured "deep"
                    and we loved, like before

no, not like before
we loved with a strangely woven blend of gentleness
mingled with urgent passion — and a new longing
that made our familiar, intimate rhythm
more intense than ever before
more flowing desire . . more exploding fire
                            . . and more flooding peace
just before you fell asleep
after we had made soft-whispered, fragmented plans
to arrange a perfectly legal bunch of violets
all those necessary things . . . you murmured once again, drowsily

                    "you must stop eating mouse cookies now, for sure
                    it's bad for her
                    and not do so much flying around . . no silly crying
                    bringing on our winter season, for no reason
                    and get your rest, and take your vita .
                                                          .
                                                            .
                                                             .
                                                              .
                                                               .

"goodnight, Little Prince, sweet Prince"
I hush-a-byed into your left Gooober ear

"a rose is so lucky to be tamed
and be, therefore, unique in all the world . . "

for a long, starry while
I cradled your head against my breast, as you slept
I was awake, yet dreaming too — with you

>   and when I dropped a single snowflake tear
>   on your slumbering cheek

your hand unconsciously reached out
to brush it away

>   but . . you brushed *my* cheek
>   *my* cheek you touched

when the wetness you had felt
which had stirred you to reach out
>   . . was on your own

oh, I love you !

I love you . .

>   and I even forgive you for saying
>   when I first tried to tell you about the Morning Star's
>   new baby druid

>   "don't interrupt me
>   I'm watching Star Trek"

Southern Cross of Northern Borealis Lights

not long after I told you about the small druid
I was called back to New York, unavoidably
leaving you alone again

>   back in our little crooked house
>   writing letters . . to someone
>   about the chance you'd been offered
>   relating to oceans . . dolphins . . and marine biology

>   an offer which meant you might soon have to leave
>   for just a little while, you said

possessing, as I do, the keys to astrology
I knew that this was true
>   . . that you would very soon begin
some new and challenging goal
>   connected with your profession

you would be involved, you said — for only a few months
in something which required top security
but would someday, you smiled — possibly make both of us proud
although you would not be allowed to discuss it
with friends or family . . or me . . until after you returned

                all I knew . .
was that your work would be done in the Pacific
during the approaching time of our . . brief separation
not for a government agency
                            . . or so you said
but instead

                        for an intelligent, sensitive
                        and powerful person . . in the Arctic
                        who evidently liked to keep secrets
                                    . . nearly as well as you

sometimes, we made small, unsure jokes

"when will you be climbing aboard
your flying saucer ?" I would teasingly ask

                        and you would cryptically reply

                        "perhaps some exciting, explosive Fourth of July
                        when the Master Oobers notify me
                                        that it's time . . "

"do they live in Washington, D.C.
these Master Oobers ?" I asked tentatively

                        "oh, no . . they are strange creatures
                        who are accustomed to cold weather

                        and might, perhaps, from time to time
                        land their saucers in Alaska
                        since it's mysteriously near the
                                            North Pole"

"oh, so that's it !" I would say

"Oobers are actually from the Inner Earth
and they leave and enter
                through the North and South Poles
well . . you'd better buy yourself
some gloves and wool scarves . . and ear muffs"

        I told myself I would worry about it later
        for it was not yet a definite plan

                   but . . it troubled me

You Were — You Are a Poet

           sitting here alone in Manhattan
having just spoken with you
                across impotent telephone wires

        I am trying to recall . . I don't quite know why
        but I am trying to remember a verse he wrote
            the him-of-him

                        when the you-of-he
                        also the three-times-three
                        of you and me
                                    lived in that other Temple
        built, I thought, in St. Mary's
        of fine marble and alabaster

                        what were the purple-shadowed words
                        the he-of-you wrote that night ?   was it . . . .

. . . into the dream you came
and across the soft carpet of my reverie
you walked . . . with hobnail boots

                    no, not that verse
                    not that one, written so long ago
                    to the me-of-me
                                by the you-of-he

        I need to recall
        the other one about . . . . . .

                        yes, now I remember it
                        I remember it now . . .

            he . . you
                    wrote . .

                . . the lone child cried
                            its cries filled the womb
                    cries of fear, foreseeing its doom

                    with fist tightly curled
                                it cried out its fear
                    as little words of hate

                604 ☆ *Canto Sixteen*

crept into its ear

then the World gazed upon it
with a Great Loving Eye
but its fist remained curled
and its first word was . .

why ?

Blow Softly, Winter Winds

tiny stars . .

do not ride their painted ponies
with such dogged persistence

as do the grown up riders
on Life's whirling Carousel

they know how
to leap off

more quickly

not before their rides are over
as determined by the Carousel Owner

but . . more quickly
and she . .

fell off the Carousel

she tumbled over in the grass, in her dreams
reaching for a clover . . or a violet
before she even had a chance
to ride the painted pony she had chosen

and I stayed on, still spinning
my tears splashing
on the empty, riderless pony
she had been holding out her tiny hand to grasp
when she fell . . and tumbled over in the grass

it happened . . so suddenly
when I returned from a long day of shopping
and unexpectedly . . felt the familiar iron band of pain

I had walked home twenty blocks, in the rain

oh ! why did the Carousel Owner allow her to fall ?
she was so small, so dear . . so new

.. and you didn't even see her fall

or hear me call

to you

Star Trek

sadly, wearily . . sadly, sadly

I returned to Colorado
from New York

I returned to our little crooked house
where we were still playing the game
of woman — man — and mouse

. . came home to let you count the score
of the points I had gained or lost
. . while I had been away

with you not knowing, at first
that something more precious than a point

had been lost

yes . . I came home to see you still reaching for a star
you didn't know was no longer there

and yet, as you sat quietly, that first night
of my homecoming
staring at me, in the rocking chair . . in the den
there was a light you missed
you said
when we had kissed . . hello again

you were strangely silent, then
as you sat there, in the rocking chair
and stared at me
with an indescribable sadness

you asked
"is something wrong ?"

with those glowing embers burning
in your silvery-wise eyes

I looked away
and answered . . . lying

"no, nothing is wrong"

before I told you . . I was trying, trying
trying to find some way
something I might say to make restitution
for this terrible and unretractable retribution
of Destiny

. . and so, three nights later
I came in to you, to tell you of our tragic loss
hoping the way to ease its pain
was to admit to you the awful guilt I somehow . . felt
for some . . reason

and ask you to forgive me

you were sitting on the couch, in the den
with Love and Peace curled around your shoulders

and I spoke

"Gooober, I have something . . . to tell you . . "

and you replied
as you had once before

"I'm watching Star Trek
. . can it wait ?"

I felt a sudden storm of anger
sweep through my empty body, consuming me
with rage . . then reached out silently — to God
and asked for deep-blue-velvet peace

my prayer was answered

as I thought . . how could you know ?
of course you can't
or you would hold out your hand . . and understand

and felt a swift stab of anguish
for the pain I was about to give you

as you turned
and gazed expectantly at me

I trembled
when I answered

"no, it cannot wait
it has waited, already . . too long

    . . when I was in New York last month
    and you were, I suppose
    skiing down some snowy trail . . in Vail
    as you do most weekends when I'm not here

    . . one little star fell through the sky
    did you not look up — in Vail
          and see a falling star ?"

             you answered quietly
             "I was not in Vail while you were gone"

. . oh, hurry ! make a wish
before it falls !
*   . . that wasn't fair*
why did you trick me ?

        . . only to show you
    Little Girl Lost . . that all your old dreams

                  . . are still there

        then you asked — slowly

        "what are you saying ?"

      I was lost
for a moment . .

"I'm sorry . . I was making a wish
I mean I was remembering . . something . . "

. . oh, hurry !
make a wish before it falls !

    . . that wasn't fair
why did you trick me ?
        look ! a falling star . .
Little Girl Lost
    . . all your dreams are still there
hurry ! make a wish . .

then, gathering strength from some dark and secret
and hitherto unknown part of the me-of-me
some dark secret part . .

I spoke clearly

"this is I you see here before you
                    only I
no longer part of three — just me . .

          . . oh, God !

. . oh, God !

          " . . Gooober, she was so new, so small
          and could not stand against our winter winds
          so she . . tumbled over in the grass . . she fell"

                         and your silvery-wise eyes
                         reflected back to me, then — my own grief

          but crucified a thousand times
                    on the cross
          of some strange knowing-thing within you

                    oh ! your eyes reflected such pain, such hurt
                    that I forgot my own sorrow
                    forgot the pity I was trying to borrow
                    and ran into your arms . . . to comfort you

          . . not to seek comfort
                         . . but to give it

               we wept and clung together
               that whole sad night

neither of us caring which one was wrong — which one was right
and felt our love grow deeper, stronger
because we truly cared no longer — who was wrong
                                   and who was right
and my soul was still
as the icy trails carved in my heart
throughout our recent winter season . . melted

          for you comforted me, my Comforter
          and I comforted you, in return
          enclosed within the warm and understanding
          circle of your arms

                    each of us believed this pain to be a rain
                    which had to fall

          . . yes, each believed
          but in a different way . .

each thought this was a lesson
needed to be learned . . . one which burned
into the *knowing*-parts of the you-of-you
and stabbed into the *growing*-parts of the me-of-me

after a long while
you murmured into my ear

       "she was so small
            so new
               so dear

yet had to leave before she even
said hello to us . . before she took one breath
for, she couldn't stand against
our winter storm . . she was such a tiny prayer"

and wept once more with me

after a time, night turned to day
the rain stopped in our hearts

the cold winds ceased . . the Sun came out to shine through a rainbow
as always, after our storms have blown over
the world was fresh and green again — and spring was violet-new
for you loved me, and I loved you — just like before

and we were once more . . Us

we were still magic

through the miracle

of forgiveness

Before the World's Awake

maybe Raphael's and Botticelli's jeweled colors
Rembrandt's and Da Vinci's too . . were real
    not just painted

the way Life looks
through crystals of tenderness

        you smiled at me tonight
           at the bottom of the stairs
        with so much love in your eyes

swimming in a mist of almost-tears

all you said was . .

"let's go for a walk, in the woods
tomorrow, at dawn
                just you and me . . alone
before the world's awake

I'll show you how we can make a deer
                            come near
by remaining very, very still
                . . . projecting kindness"

and all I said was . .

"I'll set the alarm for five"

                but we were stained glass
                ruby red and azure blue . . . . and the choir was singing

Will Someone Please Start an Oober Sunday School ?

. . . the memory of the soul
within its Body Temple, born of flesh
                is unpredictable, and fleeting . .

small souls are taught, in Sunday school
            the Golden Rule
and also learn . . . it's wrong to take a life

                then grow up, and learn to believe it's right
                to kill for a thrill . . called patriotism

    and why not ? this is what their rulers
    decree is just and good
    both the rulers of their countries
                    and the rulers of their churches

"go forth, sons of Assisi !"
                shouted the Catholic Bishop
"war is beautiful !"

        yes, small souls
        grow up to learn
                that any sort of Crusade is beautiful

even when it involves murdering strangers
forgetting the lessons of Sunday School
and the Golden Rule . . of childhood

the memory of my soul, also
is unreliable and brief

refusing to memorize karmic lessons
so hard-earned, through grief

and during years of lonely tears
down through countless Ages

yes, after we had taught one another
the awesome Power and infinite Glory

of Forgiveness

written in blazing letters
on the illuminated pages of the innocent Oober Faith

the things I promised you
I would forget — I too often remembered

and the things I promised to remember
I forgot — too soon

O ! where out there
among the stars
do they teach Memory
to the soul ?

east of the Sun — or west of the Moon ?
I've lost my way back home

what if . . oh ! what if the miracle of Us
was but a dream

and there's no such place as the Oober Galaxy at all ?

to which Star, then
must I return

to learn what makes a fallen angel . . fall ?

Wrong Number

do you suppose Ma Bell will grant me a refund
on my next long distance phone bill — for today's call
from me, in New York — to you, out west ?

no, I guess I won't be given a refund for a test I didn't pass
I'll just be demoted again, to the rear of the class
and more points lost, Dear Teacher
how will I dare bring home my next failing Love report card ?

        I was glad — not sad
        glad about it — not mad about it

. . about your picture being taken for a magazine cover
publishing your helpful, healing words of fasting and nutrition
and clearly stating your position of the power of mind over matter
oh, I tried to communicate only cheerful chatter !

    I swear, I was trying to sound simply . . happy
    not flippant or angry or snappy . . and surely not malicious
    what reason could I possibly have to be suspicious
    that you might be . . disloyal to me ?
                . . unless

        unless you count that time of the you-of-him
        so many years ago . . with *her*

the time I promised you I'd forget
and you know I never break a promise — ever

I was only joking, not strangling and choking
when I remarked to you on the phone
that three hours together alone . . seemed an awfully long time
for a girl photographer to do a simple thing
                like snapping her shutter
or did it take longer
to flutter her lashes . . before she caught just the right pose ?

            then heard you begin to mutter
            something under your breath

so I made my voice as smooth as butter
and lightly repeated . .

"I mean, well anyone knows it can't take three hours
to snap a shutter . . or even to flutter . . . "

        suddenly, the receiver went **CLICK** !

so I called back

> and when you said . . "hello
> look, darling, you surely must know
> there was really nothing to . . . "

then I hung up on *you*

> score tied

>> are you satisfied ?

Vail-Vail-Vail

> no, I had not decreased the distance between us
> by hanging up the telephone
> I had only lost a few points more . .
> not evened the score

oh ! what is this stern test you're giving
in the difficult subject of Living
requiring the constant study and memorization
of Faith — Trust — and Forgiveness ?

> why do you teach that I must, I must
> have Faith and Trust — and be eternally Forgiving
> then seem sometimes so cold
>> and unforgiving yourself ?

> yes ! so cold and unforgiving

are you sure you are properly qualified
to teach the subject of Living ?

> as I stared at the ominously silent telephone
> I felt suddenly and dreadfully . . alone

then had a dream — no, it was not a dream, but a nightmare
for what it warned was unspeakable, unthinkable
>> and eternally unforgivable
making a mockery of Faith and Trust

> I thought I even screamed . . . as I dreamed
>> oh, this — yes, this — this Judas kiss
> is unforgivable — forever unforgivable !

and so, I flew back to Colorado, to run into your arms
and silence the shrieking fire alarms of my dream
                    still sounding shrill sirens of warning in my heart

            . . .   .

but it was quiet and empty
        in our little crooked house
            in our slipping-off-the-time-track house
you were not there

            you had gone, said your note, skiing in Vail
            you were loping down a snowy slope
            somewhere — in Vail — you were not there

later . . when you called New York
and there was no answer
you called me, then, at our funny crooked house
from your snowy slope in Vail

                    and said . . "darling
                    tomorrow is Thanksgiving Day
                    shall I come home ?
                    and will you bake a hot mince pie
                    while I'm building a snowman
                    in the back yard ?"

"you have been skiing
down some mountain trail, in Vail
and didn't bother
to tell me you were going ?"

                    "well, it was snowing . .
                    and I thought . . . ."

"you didn't tell me you were going ?
and I flew out here, un-knowing
to tell you I was sorry about hanging up the phone ?
why did you go
without letting me know ?"

                    "I wanted to walk in the snow
                    to be alone — to think — and to ski
                    and to try to see
                    if I could understand
                    what is happening to you and me"

"I'll tell you what is happening !
I am weary, sick and tired
of losing points with you, for everything I do

I am tired of playing this game
of Monster Cat and chastised mouse
and I will not be caught
in a trap — by remaining in this house
and baking a pie
while you are out somewhere alone
making mountains fly . . and didn't even ask me
     to come along
oh ! this time I am right
and you are wrong — wrong — wrong !"

      "Goob, when you hung up the phone
      from New York that morning
      and didn't want to talk — I thought . . . ."
outraged, I interrupted

"that's not true ! that is simply not true !
it was you ! it was *you* who refused to talk to *me* !
oh, what's the use ?
   it doesn't matter anymore . .

I am weary of trying to write a Happiness poem called *Gooberz*
and of trying to make Spouse rhyme with Slave
they do not rhyme, those two words
and if you were really a poet, you would know it
you would know that Spouse should rhyme with Rose
a special, unique rose
     . . but you

oh ! **YOU** make Gladness rhyme with Sadness

and they . . **DO NOT RHYME — THOSE WORDS !**
DO YOU HEAR ? YOU ARE NOT A POET !

I am not going to stay in this trap of a house
playing the role of a chastised mouse
writing an empty poem about happiness
while you are out skiing down snowy slopes
and making mountains fly, without me !

not even . . not even caring about me
how could you go to Vail — and make mountains fly
without me . . not even caring about me ?"

      "yes, I am here without you . .
      so how can I — with only half a heart
      be making mountains fly ?
      they don't fly for me, when we're apart
      and I do care about you
      sometimes I realize that most of all
      when I'm alone . . and for a while

                                   without you
               sometimes, my aloneness
               causes me to be aware of how I've hurt you
               and helps me try to understand
               what I might do to heal the wounds

               . . sometimes . . when I'm alone
               I can think more clearly
               about what I need to say — or do
               to make you smile again, and trust me

                   why are you so upset ?
                   can't you see I've given you
                   no real reason to feel this way ?"

"no real reason ? I have every reason !
it is never I — no, it is always you
who brings on our winter storms
don't try to justify yourself
by cleverly trying to place the blame on me"

                   then you repeated, firmly

                   "shall I . . *may* I come home
                   for Thanksgiving ?"

"come home ? so we can give thanks ?
give thanks for what ?
why should you leave Vail, and come back here ?
so I can lose more points, I suppose
for some thoughtless, unintentional smashing
while you are pouting and splashing
with your boats and dolphins in the bath tub
and you call ME emotionally immature ?
oh ! what have we to be thankful for . . anymore ?"

                   then suddenly

             we were disconnected — cut off

             from any further emotional disaster
             by the telephone company ?

. . or the unseen hand
of some Master from the Oober Galaxy ?

                                   or by God ?

we spent the day of giving thanks — apart
separated by more than the miles between us

we spent Thanksgiving — each alone
because of a dis-connected telephone

or was it our own telepathic wires
which were crossed ?

was I a stiff Puritan — and were you a warpath Indian ?

or was it the reverse ?
back and forth — and forth and back
I tried the labels
first on you — then on me

but . . whichever one was to blame
that Thanksgiving Day was ominous with warning
a snow storm warning
and in my misty, recurring dream . . I wanted to scream
but did not know why

and I wanted to pray — yet, had no words to say
Pike's Peak was a lonely Plymouth Rock
on that quiet, empty Thanksgiving Day

if you really love me, I thought — then why do you shove me
into flaming anger . . with your freezing ice ?

and if I really love you . . then why do I shove you
into such coldness . . with my fiery words ?

what is this lesson of Forgiving
in the subject of Living
you demand that I learn — and why ?

I shivered there
in our once cozy, rosy house of warm
I trembled there . . imprisoned in a pit — yes !

imprisoned in a damp and slimy pit
of crawling serpents of suspicion . . strangling me
with coils of dreaded treachery
and mocking me, with quick-darting forked tongues
to hiSS at me
Beware !   Beware !

listening to the mournful mewings of Love and Peace

who seemed to also sense with me — some impending shock
that would rock our little crooked house
and transmute the shining gold of love and trust
into the grey ashes of betrayal
through the negative alchemy of pride . . both yours and mine

. . and was not to suspect
for what seemed like endless years hence
that the betrayal was not seeded in either you nor me
but in our being caught up into . . a larger karma
the karma of those who do not hesitate
to cruelly attempt to control the personal fate . . of others

  a spiritually dangerous practice
  if they but knew . .

     still, there was also some cause in me
     and in you . . through our mutual pride

     for, without it, those others could not
     have so easily controlled our fate

we Earthlings have no "luck" — either good or bad
which is not brought upon us by our former actions in previous lives
under the karmic law of Cause and Effect
as we unconsciously elect . . . to teach ourselves much needed lessons
  and those who appear to be controlling us
are merely — and unsuspectingly — channels for our karma
used expediently by the Masters . . for a greater purpose

  so, we share the blame
with those others, within whose larger karma we became entangled

    and with ourselves

  . . a few days later
you called

    and made a confession
    as though you were a sinner
    and I was a Priest

YES ! you were the sinner
and if I was not the Priest — then, at least
I was the one sinned against
and more pure than you, I thought . . as I listened
to the reality of the fulfillment of my nightmare dream

  and screamed a silent scream
while I absorbed, painfully, the treacherous serpent poison

of your calmly confessed version
of a Judas kiss of betrayal

echoing the throbbing wounds of yesterday
but she . . she was not my best friend . . not even a casual friend to you
and your voice seemed far away
oh ! did I really hear you say
you kissed a *stranger* ?

this was no dream
this was oozing from the bubble
of reality illusion — and people confusion

oh, God ! let dreams be the only reality !
the true awareness for the human soul — not nightmares — not this
not this unbearably hurting Judas-kiss

like a relentless ticking clock
your measured words tocked on . . .

" . . on Thanksgiving night . . in a pharmacy
while I was eating . . not your hot mince pie
but cold, burned toast
I met her, at the counter — she was alone too
and we talked for an hour or so
then I drove her home to where she lived
kissed her goodnight, in the car . . and that's all"

in the car ? in our magic, dusty blue Bug ?
oh, God ! please let this be only a nightmare

or let it be . . whichever one
dream or Life . . whichever one is *un*-reality
do not let this be real !

why did your voice
sound so zombie-numb ?

so numb . . as you told me
this unspeakable unspeakable unforgivable thing

this Judas kiss . . this kiss of serpents
with forked tongues . . snaking and coiling
around my soul . . oh ! this forked-tongue Judas kiss
of betrayal

yes, serpents
coiled and snaked within me

until tears streaked down

O ! couldn't you see the tears

streaking across the cheeks of my soul ?

                              " . . that's all it was . . one kiss

forked tongue Judas kiss !

                         . . and then I thought of Us
                         and turned my head away
                         walked beside her to the door
                              . . said goodnight
                         and drove back to my hotel room
                         it meant nothing . . absolutely nothing"

          your voice faded in and out
          coiling around my heart your rattlesnake words
          so you thought your voice was whispering gently
          softly . . of your Judas kissing

        IT WAS HISSING, HISSING, DO YOU HEAR ?

    IT WAS HISSING !

          like a cobra

                         "it meant nothing — it was nothing
                         just one kiss, that's all"

   "that's ALL ?"

                         "I promised you that I would not allow
                         the smallest lie — to ever stand
                                                between us
                         and I have kept my promise
                         I told you the truth
                         it meant nothing . . nothing
                         but I promised you truth — and
                         I will not lie to you"

   then I cried
   "oh, why, why, why ?"

                    you sounded like some pompous sage
                    when you answered

                         "oh, Gooober, just listen to the terrible rage
                         and the powerful hate in your voice
                         you ask me why ?
                                you have no right to be so furious
                         but I'll tell you why — I was curious"

   "I have no right to be furious ?

you were **CURIOUS ?**"

"yes, curious to see — in this unholy game
between you and me
of which one is the mouse in our house
and which one is the man . .
I was curious to see — to discover
if I might, perhaps, be under . . . . "

from outside
came a crashing roll of thunder
or was it not from outside
but from inside . . myself
that booming crash of thunder ?

"to find out if I have been under
some witch's spell — some eternal curse

not from Heaven — but from hell
some cursed witch's spell
which can turn a Prince into a frog
or a man into a mouse

and now I know — I am a man
don't you see ?
I had to know — and now I do
now I know I'm not the mouse in our house

and you ?
have you been wondering too
if you are, perhaps, not a woman
but also a mouse ?
I can tell you — you are a woman
and I'm sorry if anything I've ever said
or done . . has made you feel
that you are not
because you are, you are — a woman !
the only one I'll ever want
will you forgive me
for trying to turn you into a mouse
as *I've* already forgiven *you* ?"

"oh ! why did I ever believe
the things you promised me ?
everything you told me about faithfulness
was untrue !"

"I did not lie to you — it was nothing
but I told you anyway
knowing the pain it would bring
to both of us

because . . I will not lie to you"

you repeated, wearily

then asked, in an even quieter tone

"since the holidays can be any day
                    we choose them to be
shall I come home now
so we can celebrate Thanksgiving . . . late
as if nothing had ever happened to us ?"

"AS IF NOTHING HAD EVER HAPPENED ?"
I heard myself scream

"yes . . as if nothing hurtful had happened
because literally, it did not
as I've said . . it was nothing . . and even
your angry words today
                    have not been real
remember what I once told you ?

if it was negative . . it never happened
except in the world of illusion
for in the *real* world
                    there is only happiness . . .
cruel, evil events of pain
occur only in the world of illusion
          the reflecting mirror of the true world
and in which of these two worlds
shall we choose to live ?
                    the true, positive world
or the negative, reflected mirror world ?
now, may I come home ? I need you"

my words snaked with venom

"don't preach to me
with more of your deceptive philosophy
and do not return to this house !
you are, truly, a weak and despicable mouse
      an unfaithful, ugly, warty frog
                    no ! do not return !

this is the last lesson
I shall ever need to learn — from you
      I hate you !"

. . oh, what could I say
that would hurt you enough . . that would
hurt you as much as you had hurt me ?

Canto Sixteen ☆ 623

" . . I even hate your old hiking hat
do you hear that ?
I have **ALWAYS** hated your old hiking hat !"

I hardly knew what I was saying

      and still don't know
      if it was myself — or you
      who hung up the phone

           or if we were once again dis-connected

                by the Oober Masters

. . or by God

      whose side is God on anyway ?
      the side of the Puritans — or the Indians ?

            . . and which one of these are you
            which one am I ?

      how can I celebrate a late Thanksgiving now
      and give thanks to God . . . for wanting to die ?

Interview For a Mating

regardless of my angry refusal
of your request to return
finally, you came home from Vail

      after having carved another icy trail
      of unforgiveness in my heart

yes, you returned, to see what new lessons I had learned
in your arrogant School of Living and Loving
you came back to satisfy your curiosity
about who was woman — man — or mouse — in our house
you came home to once more count the score
                    of points I had gained or lost
in your absence

      for a time, we called a neutral truce
to our undefined troubles
yet, despite our mutual attempt to pretend
that everything was allright — it was not
and a grey cloud of foreboding seemed to hang over our house

sometimes, now . . when I look back
I understand how Judas felt
after all, how could Jesus have become a Super Star
without his destined betrayal ?

and how could you fulfill your destiny of leaving
for whatever reason . . .
without me as your karmic channel ?

how could you become a Super Star with your nameless dolphins
and your mysterious goals
without my help . . in giving you an excuse to leave ?

or am I merely searching
for justification for my actions ?
and what if I am ?

isn't the seeking of justified motives
the only way to genuinely search one's self
and discover the truth ?

it was *not* my fault ! it could *not* have been my fault
because it was touched off by such a minor incident

minor then
. . major now

a letter you had received from your sister-in-law, in California
where your parents, brothers and younger Aries sister also lived

you even read it aloud to me, before you burned it in the fireplace
your solicitous female relative
writing to you about *her* . . telling you that *she* still asked about you

. . the cool Scorpio
sending you her new telephone number
and address . . just in case you might want to "get in touch again"
the letter said

no matter that the information was unsolicited by you
no matter that you insisted
the letter writer had misrepresented the facts

no matter how you earnestly
assured and re-assured me . . saying

"she and I are only friends now — and even before
it was never deep, like us
never real or forever . . like us
darling, please be sensible and logical
what does all this have to do

Canto Sixteen ☆ 625

oh ! why couldn't you understand ?
if you had, just once, tenderly touched my hand
and said 'Goob, I do understand
you are a stranger, lost in a strange land
fearing shadows of fears . .'

" . . . . . . someday, I shall make a doll," I told you
in the exact image of Heinlein, Robert — Bob
and jab it with just one small needle
     just one tiny stab of pain
to even the score with a strange, however talented man
who has made my life rhyme with sob
and the lives of how many others
who have followed faithfully, as a new religion
his fictional Michael Valentine's group sex whirls ?
according to a multitude
of east and west coast booksellers

and never mind the other excellent prose
this popular author has undeniably given the public
he has also planted seeds of harm
with his talent to use words to charm

     then you repeated . .
        " . . what does all this have to do with *us* ?"

  with us ? nothing, I suppose
I don't know . . I thought

     I just can't say

then asked myself . . and what has all this
to do with *her* ? nothing I guess, except that she just got in the way

    . . nothing I can say for sure
except that I sometimes feel as far removed
from the moral codes and ethics today
as the Atlantic is from the Pacific
        . . even though I know
this has nothing specific . . to do with her

    yes, fearing the shadows of fears

I feared the mores of this strange New Age, couldn't you see ?
I still believed that stranger rhymed with danger
but that purity no longer rhymed with maturity
or with emotional security — to anyone out there . . but me

    must one always have a sane and sensible reason
    for a sudden winter season ?

does anyone truly know just when — or why — it will snow
in the human heart ?

what does all this have to do with her ?
you might as well ask what it has to do with Vail
and a forked tongue serpent kiSS

         as for her, the Scorpio . . . I continued musing
                while you stared at me

as for her . . oh, Gooober, could you not see ?
like all the rest of the world today . .

    she was so . . *different* from me

so tolerant, so permissive, so . . bra-less
she was so cool and calm and poised
so self-possessed, yet so un-possessive and sure
        so unlike me

outwardly sure, at least — what did I know of her inwardly ?
but you knew her . . inwardly . . . yes, *you* knew her inwardly
                    . . . and *intimately*

    she was so unafraid, so un-teared
    oh, why couldn't you see what I really feared ?

wasn't it enough reason to cause strife
just to know that, according to the letter you'd received
there was someone from your past
still anxious to be interviewed for the position of your wife ?

      and are you hiring this year
      or firing maybe — and firing who ?

        her ? or me ?

whatever my secret, subconscious reason
perhaps as much a mystery to me
as it was to you . . I panicked

and told you, with alternating Fire and Ice
that I did not choose to throw the dice — and gamble
on winning the chance to be your mate

and I gave you such sharp-edged, exaggerated reasons
which wounded you so, I know
but my unspoken, deeper reasons . . hurt me more

they cut sharply into my heart like a knife
as I told you all the reasons I didn't feel qualified

to be your wife

oh ! why did you not guess
my anguished torment ?

 it was a monologue of outrage, delivered with biting sarcasm
 and no motivation behind it, other than fear — inexplicable

why did it happen just when we had nearly untangled
all the hurting-others snarls that seemed fated to keep us
     from being mated ?

just days before this cataclysm between us, earth-quaked by me
    we had been making plans

so that my magic Love is Eternal gold ring you'd given me,
      in Pismo Beach

would become my really-truly wedding band

 so why did I pretend I was being interviewed for a mating ?
 but it happened — a crisis touched off by my fear
     of the shadows of old fears

I knew I had already been accepted for this position as your wife
you had given me no real reason
to feel I was being interviewed for a mating
and yet, I felt this fear . . oh ! why didn't you

  . . just touch my hand
    and say, 'Gooober, I understand' . . ?

I was caustic
as I told you

"I noticed the Classified Ad in your eyes, Sir
and thought I would answer it
but before I commit myself — to full time employment
     in your service
may I ask a few questions
about your requirements for the position ?

 I want to be absolutely certain
 that I am properly qualified for this job
 I'm not interested, you see, in the financial compensation
 nor in any fringe benefits
 I just need to know what type it is you're looking for, Sir
 perhaps a cool, poised Scorpio — like *her* ?

yes . . what type are you looking for ?

do you want a woman who will smother you in peace and quiet
who will never start a riot, over being ignored
and who will you call you her Lord — and Master
              as she genuflects to your will ?"

then my words
        tumbled out faster . .
and my tone went higher and more bitter

"do you want a woman who will allow you to run off and ski
who will build for you, with devoted heart, near sand and sea
a house of total freedom for your whims ?
who will allow you passion for stranger or friend
permit you to travel to Mexico or Bombay
            with anyone you choose, for company on your cruise ?
and who will allow you to stay as long as you like
to peruse your latest mystery, whether it be poking around
in the Pyramids — rummaging through ancient Roman history

or slipping around in the desert
looking for an encounter of the Third Kind ?

      are you seeking a woman who will never impatiently bristle
      while you sit for hours, in the woods
      calling coyotes, with a silly bird whistle — leaving her at home ?"

oh, how unfair of me . . I thought . . . even as I shouted it
that's so wrong — he always asked me to go along
when he went to the woods to call coyotes
yet, I couldn't seem to stop, so I continued
oh, why-why-why
didn't you touch my hand
and say . . . Gooober, I understand ?

why didn't you stop me — why couldn't you guess
that it was this Permissive Aquarian Age I was fighting — not you
not even her — why couldn't you see
that my rage had absolutely nothing to do . . with you
               or with me ?
it was incited by so many things
not a part of us in any way

        . . . things like television commercials

     for perfume and . . nearly anyone's jeans
showing two half nude men — and one woman

     or two half nude women — and one man
their arms interlocked

giving one another seductive glances
while a sensual voice in the background intones

        with velvety, implicit meaning . .

        " . . . *for the way you love*"

implying . . strongly
enthusiastic approval for kinkiness
insinuating that every love affair on Earth . . is a ménage à trois

deliberately making the viewers feel
that this is where it's at, baby !

      if you're involved in just a plain old one-two affair
      you're out of it completely

get with it ! try a ménage à trois ! after all, doesn't *everyone* ?

      so transparent . . such commercials and magazine ads
      stating the case for promiscuity
      so strongly it can't be missed . . by anyone in love
                      even . . children
what did all this
have to do with you . . or with us ?

     nothing

nevertheless, I went on, determinedly continuing to fight
facing your silence and stoney face
and my fears grew larger . . my tone more angry
as my exaggerations exploded in a volcano of fright

      seeking a denial from you . . needing so desperately a denial
            . . but receiving only
                  your cold and stoney silence

"do you want a woman who will agree that wrong is right
and what is dark is light
if Masters and Johnson, Helen Gurley Brown and Hugh Hefner
           all say so ?
do you want a permissive dove
who will help you celebrate the rejection of love
by joining you in drinking the heady wine
of a modern 'open marriage' ?

      do you want a female who's humble and meek
      who will turn the other cheek, and never-ever shriek
      when you find fault with everything she says and does
      who will part her hair the way you tell her to
      with every feeling locked, and every action clocked — by you ?

is the ideal wife to share your life — a homecoming type, who . . "

    . . oh, I was thinking of *her* then
yes, this was where *she* came in . .

" . . a homemaking type
who sews all her own clothes

      and loves to trade recipes with your sister and mother
      while you're running around with another

      who smiles when you flirt
who won't scream
        when she's hurt

      who is never jealous, suspicious or mad
or furious or curious — or lonely or sad ?

      do you want a woman who will never ask questions
      about the girls in your past
      who will simply shrug her shoulders, if love doesn't last
      and who won't grieve when you leave
      but merely wish you 'better luck next time !'
      so you can still be friends, when the faerie tale ends ?

WELL ?

    I see — I mean, I hear — no denial

look, Sir — if you don't mind my making a suggestion
I really think you ought to re-hire
the girl you fired last year . . you know ?
the one who's so friendly with your family — and who
knows how to cook and sew

      she's in your waiting room right now
      and she has all the right qualifications

I don't believe I'm exactly
what you're looking for

      I'm sorry I took up so much of your time
      I thought the Classified Ad said . .

          no experience necessary

can you direct me
to the Emotional Welfare office ?"

almost immediately, I could see
that I had wounded you less by my anger
than by my lack of trust

       less by my exaggerations, unfair and untrue
       than by my failure to "keep the faith, baby" — in Us

   yes, almost immediately, I knew

       and I tried to think of a way to atone
       oh, I tried to think of a way !
       but before I could exorcise my hasty words
       you had gone upstairs
              and left me alone
. . after first handing me
a book of Shakespeare, from the shelf
opened to a page, where you had marked the words
     "much ado about nothing"

YOU AND YOUR MOON-IN-SCORPIO LAST WORD !

Gooober, what is this tearing thing we do to each other ?
and who really starts it — and why ?
                     you — or I ?
   I will not — no, I will not
   follow you
   and force a reconciliation or apology
   from whom — to whom ?

       I will just sit here in the den
       with Love and Peace purring in my restless lap
       yes, all furry-and-purry in my restless lap

       I will sit here, and try to think what I did wrong
       which one of us is weak — which one is strong

I don't really believe your bird whistle is silly
and I love to call coyotes with you
even when you make me sit where it's rocky and hilly
and cold and damp
         . . and I didn't say a word
         that morning you broke our fat china lamp
         not a single word, did I ?

   well, **DID I ?**

       NO, I DID NOT !

Chord Progressions

in which forgotten lifetime
did we forge this cursed link

this one weak link in the chain
that binds our happiness ?

and how long will it take us to weld it together
. . to complete our karmic circle ?
oh ! let it be soon

sometimes . . I think you know
yes, sometimes I believe you know
and have been forbidden by some Deity
to speak of it . . until I remember it too

when you stare at me — and stare and stare
with that strange light in your eyes, of silvery-wise
as if you were trying-trying-trying

to express some truth too deep for words

. . as if your own Supra-conscious
is telling you . .
. . let her see for herself
look deeply into her eyes
just touch her hand
she'll understand . . . soon

I know . . . this weak link began . . long ago
did it begin with the him-of-you ?

and now, you and I are the ones left
to heal the break

. . . what did the Colorado stranger
say to me ?
. . you will be with one
whose spiritual name is *Al*tar

Prelude

our souls are inseparable
forever fused in some long-forgotten heaven

the electrical impulses of our auras
formed through misty eons of Time . . pulse in rhythm
and create such light
that all who see us say . . what brightness there is around them !

do they love ?

yes, we love

in each pride and each passion, we are the same
there is but one difference between us

only one difference . .

after an un-intended hurt from one of us to the other
I must, I must cry out !
for pain infuses me with a deep, intense urge to talk
and pain fills you
with a deep, intense need to walk
in silent gloom
or meditate alone, inside your room

so close we are . . and yet so far apart in this

of what stern stuff is it made
the high, forbidding wall that separates us now ?

is it made from the heavy blocks of ice
of your protective, emotion-locked poise ?

or from the rougher bricks of my jarring noise
and screaming indignation ?

no matter

each block of your ice — each brick of my anger
is sealed with the cement of our mutual, hidden fear
that we are not really, completely loved
each, by the other
even in our fear
we are alike

you interpret my deficiency of faith
in your steady present — and loyal future devotion
as a lack of love for you
while I interpret your deficiency of patience
with my more impulsive nature — as a lack of love for me

no . . . you have been patient, you have
and you are still patient, except . . . well
you don't shout at me

but walking away and leaving me alone
                    . . is that patience ?

        to me, it is not

is it I, then
who have perhaps, been impatient with *you* ?

oh ! what does it matter which one of us is to blame ?
what does it matter, when only last night

                    . . we awoke, and touched noses

                as you whispered . .

                    "thank you for loving me, Gooober"

        and your eyes were wet
        when they met mine
        then you used your funny-froggy voice

                to say "deep" — again

shall I go to you ?
shall I go to you now — and thank you too ?

            yes ! I shall run upstairs
            lope into the bed beside you
                    and say thank you for loving me too !

    but . .

            it is so still in this room . . so still . . so dark
            could you be asleep ?

            could you be sleeping
            while I am here weeping ?

how can you **SLEEP** while I **WEEP ?**

            it is so still in our room — the Indian Meditation room
            the room where we loved so deeply last night
            before our fight
                    why should I knock
                        on this door you have closed ?
why should I knock ?
it is *our* room — not *your* room
no ! I will not knock !

                    my god ! have you actually

Canto Sixteen   ☆   635

turned the lock ?
what an arrogant thing to do !

this is not — just your room
it is my room too !

this is MY room !
it doesn't belong to you !

how dare you lock me out
of MY room ?

Unfinished Verse

you are frowning at me

you are frowning sternly
because I have stormed into your monk-like sanctuary
driven by the panic of rejection that clutched at me with claws
when you locked me out — until I demanded entrance
and would not respond to the rushing torrent
of my angry words — nor even, later
to my fumbling words of expiation
you do not speak

your features are set in the harsh lines of contempt
oh ! you are contemptuous and contemptible !
frozen as a marble statue
where is my tall and gentle one, who covered me
with blankets of tenderness — where are you ?

I dare not even call you
by the Gooober name we use for love
you would sneer
I look deep into your face
searching for my own reflected there
and see a terrible blankness
who is this haughty, arrogant stranger in our bed ?

this stranger . . in our bed

this total stranger — with hard, suspicious eyes
gazing at me like some wounded forest thing
have I done this to you ?
oh, you are ugly-ugly-ugly !

and I am ugly-ugly too

with large and staring Bette Davis eyes
                              you said
my face contorted
by some curious paralysis

          my lips curled and twisted by the quinine bitter taste
          of the words you will not allow me to speak

you told me I was beautiful . . .

          . . . you told me I was beautiful

          but the mirror of your eyes, where I once saw confirmation
          is frosted over with the film of studied boredom
                                        and detachment
          I see my image there, distorted now
          reflecting back a creature naked, rejected and ugly

oh ! look at me ! I am defenseless
vulnerable — and ugly
in the mirror of the eyes I used to trust

          eyes that told me all the things I could not ever be — I was
          seeing me through druid dust
          because they loved me, draping me with rainbows

          now you have torn off all my rainbows
          and I am vulnerable, pathetic
          so . . how can I be beautiful anymore ?

                    . . without my rainbows

     without my trust
          that I am loved

               no rainbows . . no rain bows

               only bows of rain

arched with pain, and shooting boomeranging arrows, poison-dipped
from the quiver of my heart, back into myself — with deadly aim

          for, I remember, once you said
          when *you* had wounded *me*

                    "darling, how can hurting you
                    do anything but hurt me too ?"

yes, it's true, it's true

          when you are hungry, I am empty

Canto Sixteen ☆ 637

                    when I cry, your own tears flow
          when you are cut, I bleed
                    when I am thirsty, you crave water
          when you reach out in loneliness
                              I ache with need
          as lonely, then, as you

          we cannot destroy our Oneness
          even as we tear ourselves apart like this
                              . . our souls still kiss
                    ignoring us

the room is dark

                              I cannot see

          I am blinded by the blackness of your disapproval
          and I cannot see — there is no light

yet, even blind, in darkness, I would leap over this wall
I would leap, as lizards leap — or kangaroos, when danger threatens
but multiplied a thousand times . . to reach you on the other side

          NO ! . . I will not leap over this wall, — I am too afraid
                    what if I should fall, on the cutting edge of your ice ?
          OH ! . . I am so afraid of falling, with your arms
                                        not there to catch me
they are folded across your chest
                your arms
in firm, unyielding resolution
                              your arms, your arms

          your arms . .
that held me tightly, just last night

                . . last night, last night

when we were sleeping, back to back — but touching
and suddenly awoke, in the waiting, knowing darkness
to feel an uncontrollable longing
                              aching in our throats . . spreading
like thick honey
          through our sleep-warm bodies
                    flowing down into our trembling thighs
instinctively, we turned
and pressed together . . whispering secret sensualities
                              slowly giving and taking

brimming kisses
          from our open, hungry mouths
. . as we clung, and murmured

urgent, intimate words
          moving together in half-conscious
remembered rhythm . . you moaned

                    I drew you nearer, nearer
                    deeper . . . deeper . . . deeper

until you exploded love inside me, again and again
while a thousand colored flames burst open
          streaked, comet-like across the ceiling
touching our eyelids, foreheads . . and hair
filling the room with dazzling light
                    . . and filled us, too
the me-of-me, and the you-of-you
          with the blinding, unbearable ecstasy of love

          . . then faded into soft-blue-velvet-peace

     as we floated
          floated
               floated
               floated
                    down to Earth
                    from Heaven
                         like gauzy butterfly feathers . .

and fell into the still
that follows our passion

     wrapped around each other
as baby rabbits snuggle . .
          sniffing the warm, familiar smells
our swollen, love-bruised lips
     exchanging little snowflake kisses . .

I was . . nestled on your shoulder
                    my nose pressed against
     the throbbing hollow of your neck
your hand . . half sleeping, found my breast
               and your touch was tenderly possessive . . sure

     then I gently stroked your cheek
                    and tangled hair
still damp from love . . . .

returning to the coldness of the present
I whispered . . .

      "listen !

          hear the snow fall ?

Gooober . .
      can't you hear the snow falling ?

                      look out the window ! see ?

  we were going to make a snowman

                  the first snow

you said . .

          . . . you promised me

                you promised, last night
Gooober . .
      look ! it's snowing " !

      I am silent now
        I am spent with anger
and biting words

            I am silent

but I am calling you

        my love, my only love . .
        reach out to me
            give me your hand
        just touch my face
          or kiss me with your eyes

across this darkened room

Overdrawn

not long ago, I was going through a box of letters
     photographs . . and other memories my mother saved

. . and left to me
    after she . . died

and I found the strangest thing inside — it was a check
printed with the name of her bank
a check — made out for one thousand kisses — to my father

      signed by her
      with a small red heart beside her name

and I noticed that he had endorsed it, on the back
           . . . and his handwriting
was very trembly and shaky
when he endorsed the check, so he could . . cash it

    it gave me a sharp stab somewhere
    in a half-forgotten corner of my heart

    . . and I thought
how strange . . . how very strange

    the way they often fought
    I never dreamed they loved that much
         . . I never dreamed
    maybe . .

yes ! I shall make out a check to you
a Valentine's Day check — for one thousand kisses
         and sign my name
    that's what I'll do !
    I'll write a check to you

Roses Are Red And Today Is Blue

most people mail out lacy-red hearts
on February 14th
      I wore mine on my sleeve

I never thought you'd break it
on Saint Valentine's Eve

we celebrate holidays in the most unusual way
scaring each other on Halloween
                              crying on New Year's
exploding in anger on the 4th of July

now we're celebrating this one
                          by saying goodbye
        the cupid card
I made for you last night . . said

                        Dear Valentine
                        I love you so . . don't go

and I enclosed the check

CatandMouseCatandMouseCatandMouse

                you ignored my Valentine
                you tore my lacey-red heart

and I made it myself
I made it myself . . for you

                with glue and ribbons and lace
                and inside I drew . . a Happy Face

                    you didn't even look inside

                    to see my Happy Face
you said I verbally lash you   you didn't even look . . .
you said I always doubt you
you said I always smash you
you said I always berate you

        always ?

                what about the times I loved you ?
                have I always shoved you away ?

                do I *always* berate you ?

                        oh, I **HATE** you !

you didn't even . . want my check for a thousand kisses
you didn't even endorse it . . . to collect my love

Poise Does Not Rhyme With Noise

so you are going to leave
unless I do something — do *what* ?

say what ? I'm sorry ?

if I say that
you'll only say — 'you're always sorry'

that's what you'll say, isn't it ?
well, I won't give you the chance !

what about the times you tell *me* you're sorry
when *you're* to blame ?

I always forgive *you* — I always do

DO I NOT ?

shall I be silent, then — and play your silly pouting game
just watching you sulk around the house
chilling me into shivers of fear . . . for how long ?

how long will it take this time
for you to see we've both been wrong

for you to condescend, and unbend
your stiff Leonine pride . . . and forgive ?

how long ? how long ?

I cannot wait
I am not that strong . . to wait

I am weary of it all — weary
you are not tall anymore

you are a pigmy, a dwarf . . you even hold your pencil like a dwarf

you are a pigmy, a dwarf
yes, a dwarf like Grumpy, in Snow White
not tall at all — with no strength to forgive

don't you know it takes strength to forgive ?

Canto Sixteen ☆ 643

you, who believe yourself to be so tall, so wise, so strong
and never, never wrong — don't you know it takes strength
                              to forgive ?

         where is your great strength, strong Lion-hearted, where ?
         you and your insufferable, arrogant pride

WHERE IS YOUR STRENGTH, KING OF THE JUNGLE, PROUD BEAST ?
IT TAKES STRENGTH TO FORGIVE !

         "I THOUGHT YOU WERE STRONG — AND TALL !"

     I cried . .

                  you frowned . . and your features froze
                  then you shouted at me . . *shouted* at me

                       "OH, GO SMELL A ROSE !"

FireAndIceFireAndIceFireAndIce

         I am weary, weary, weary
         weary, do you hear ?

         weary of keeping score
         and losing points.
                         .
                         .
                         .
             for sneezing
                        .
                         .   . . you should have taken your Vitamin C
                         .   three points lost . . for carelessness !

             or freezing   you should have closed the window
                        .   before you came to bed, like I said
                         . six points lost — for laziness !
                         .
                         .
         I am like a porcupine in shock
         with all its quills jerked cruelly out

no points left to give up to you

         I am a stark-naked porcupine
                  with holes
         where my protective quills
                  used to be

                  no more quills left . . to give up to you

                  644   ☆   Canto Sixteen

the Little Prince understood how it was
with the thorns of his rose
no matter how she bragged, he knew
yes, he knew that her thorns were no real protection

why can't *you* understand that ?
why can't you understand about porcupine quills
                    and Ram's horns
as the Little Prince understood and knew
about the vulnerable thorns of his special, unique rose ?

oh ! her thorns were fake . . and a Ram's horns can break
and a porcupine is naked and helpless
without its points — its quills

                a porcupine chills . . without its quills

        is a Ram really clever ? will the Cat catch the mouse ?
        will the sheep eat the rose ?
        will you always and forever be stomping on the toes
        of all my hidden anxieties . . convinced that I'll never learn ?

are not all these things matters of great concern ?
matters of great consequence ?

        I'm weary of being kept locked up in a child's play-pen
        weary of sleeping in the den, in exile . . . your Majesty

so leave ! I won't grieve ! I'll never even miss you !

        I'm tired of this eternal Fire and Ice
        sick of this game played with crooked dice
        I don't care who's to blame
        I only know nothing's the same anymore . . as it was

but don't hang around, making a dramatic Leonine exit
you Monster Cat — do you hear that ?

OH !
        Oh !
            oh !
                        you dare to smile ?

    you dare to smile, while I stand in this imaginary play-pen
    where you keep me, so I can't get at your pride ?
    you dare to smile, while I clutch this freak antique doll
    you bought and gave to me — and we named Emilie ?

        you dare to smile at me ?

    that's all . . that does it . . get out !

                Canto Sixteen   ☆   645

AND GET OUT NOW !

it's what you mean to do anyhow
sooner or later
so let's make it sooner — let's make it **NOW** !

oh ! I can still read your mind
I know your kind — I know exactly what you plan
arrogant chauvinist man
I know all the tricks you hide up your sleeve
you plan to leave — as soon as you finish this last round
of cat and mouse torture
and have the pleasure of hearing the sound
of my last, pitiful, small mouse squeak

oh ! you **REEK** of arrogance
and unforgiveness

you've packed all your rags
in your traveling bags — so **GO** !

GET OUT !

I'm not a pitiful, squeaking mouse
GET OUT OF MY HOUSE ! I'm not a mouse, I'm a ma . . . .
I mean, I'm a . . woman

I won't be a child, kept in a play-pen
and I won't be a slave, your Majesty, Monster Cat
I won't be a meek little mouse, caught in your clever trap

here ! don't forget your colored map
of Mexico
or is it Alaska ? who cares ?
just go
get out . .

you walked slowly
toward the back porch kitchen door
that eclipsed morning
after my anger was spent
and neither of us had spoken a word
for over an hour

you were leaving

but as you reached the door, you turned
looked at me hard
then asked the craziest, most insane thing

                    "Gooober, can you name
                        the Seven Dwarfs ?"

"can I . . name . . what ?"

my face and heart both tear-streaked
your question caught me by surprise
and dumbly . . numbly
automatically and haltingly . . I replied

"Sneezy . . Dopey . . Doc . . Sleepy
and let's see . . Bashful . . and Grumpy"

                        "that's only six of them"
                                you said quietly
                        "what about the seventh ?"

"I don't know the seventh one"
I answered dully
"is this your idea of a joke ?
            if so, it's not at all amusing"

                        "no, it's not a joke
                        it matters . . very much"

"well, it may matter very much to you
but it doesn't matter in the slightest to me
please stop playing your childish games
and leave me in peace . . just go"

            I dropped my eyes to the floor
            for I could not bear to look at you anymore

            and when I next raised them
            you were gone from the house . . . gone

                        you were . . . opening the car door
                        to climb inside your dusty blue Bug
                            parked out back, by the shed

I glanced in the kitchen mirror
and thought desperately
oh ! I look like something a cat dragged in
a drowned mouse . .

            then I ran to the door
                    and cried out to you, in honest anguish

"Gooober, come back !
please, come back for just one minute
there's something . . something I want to say"

you stopped beside the car
hesitated for a moment . . and slowly

came back

as you stood there by the kitchen door
looking at me, saying nothing
my heart pounded wildly . . and I waited
until I was calmer, to speak

"I guess . . all I wanted to say
was that I look so . . awful . . so ugly"

I choked back a sob

"and I wanted so . . oh ! I wanted so
to be beautiful for you . . when we said goodbye"

you looked at me strangely, then
for one split second
and the corner of your mouth trembled
ever so slightly
your eyes misted over . . and your voice
was oddly tender, very low

as you said

"that doesn't matter — don't you know ?
it doesn't matter how you look
don't you know that by now ?
to me, you always look . . . beautiful"

and my heart reached out to your heart
across the kitchen
while my naked lips formed the word softly
very softly . . unsure
. . uncertain

"*magic* ?"

then once more . .
"*magic* ?"

I saw your eyelids crumble
then squeeze shut
as if struck by some blinding pain

the muscles in your throat
contracted in a sudden spasm
and you swallowed — hard

then you stared at the kitchen floor
where I had, earlier that morning — angrily smashed
your gift of Emilie . . the antique doll
you bought me, just after we met

. . stared at her head on the floor
broken now, into hundreds
    of splintered pieces

you waited . .
    for a long, still moment

finally, you looked up
your eyes veiled, and full of sadness
gazing somewhere beyond me . .
then you spoke so low
    I could barely hear you
as if you were lost in a dream . .

"what does it mean ?
   what does it all mean ?

I'll come back when you can glue
    Emilie's head back together"

I turned away, and walked into the den
overcome with a sudden flooding of emotion
your words echoing behind me . . . *what does it all mean* ?
somehow, I knew you had to leave
and there was nothing either of us could do about it now
I also knew . . your heart was breaking too

    as I heard the car pull away
    I remembered . .

. . . I remembered the name
of the seventh Dwarf

   it was . . Sneezy . . Sleepy . . Doc . . Dopey

  Bashful . . Grumpy

    and . . . . Happy

Haste Makes Waste

       when you drove away this morning
without a single backward glance

              or even a Howard Hughes rain-check
    for tomorrow

you left behind . .

       your hiking boots . . your Peter Pan clock
                 your old grey Christmas sock
       your red and yellow candles
          your blue cashmere sweater from Saks
       the forms for your income tax
           your stuffed beast, with the mane of curly hair
     your two winter coats . . your dolphin that floats
         your library card . . some old dreams
            your electric saw . . your Vitamin E . . and C
     one unshed tear . . your Ivory soap
     the torn shred of rainbow you wore under your left ear
         your autographed book
            and our last, long look

     although you remembered to take with you
                your serpent ring
   my own gold band
           and the front door key

   Gooober . . please come back

        you forgot something . . . . . me

The Art of Falling

     I am falling falling falling
     oh ! I am falling off the Carousel

I am falling . . . .

            NO !

I am glued upon this grinning, painted horse — why fall ?

     I learned my lesson well, in the deep-deep-green-cool woods
     someone always comes

like the Girl Scout Counselor, with flashlights
and the Sheriff
yes . . someone always comes

and then you lose all your credits
for the merit badges you have worked so hard to earn

I will not fall

I will not lose the karmic credits for the knowledge
I've worked so hard to earn . . and to learn

I will not fall

Shell Shock

you would never leave me, you said — never, never, never
you were mine forever, you said
forever-and-ever-and-ever
love is eternal, you said
and had it engraved in my ring, last spring
my magic gold druid ring . . of love

well, how long is eternal ?   six months — two years ?
how long is forever in the Oober Solar system ?

HOW LONG ?
forever . .

you said you would stay and love me at least as long as forever
and maybe even longer . . for a million billion forevers
you said
oh, you did, you did ! you promised that
I still remember the night you promised
a million billion forevers — well, how long is that, you Monster Cat ?

the Great White Knight
has tarnished his armor with falsehood
and your horse . . is a splotchy grey burro

you broke your forever promise, and left me all alone
I was a willow, and you taught me how to bend

I was trying so hard . .
then you said it was the end
just when I was learning how to bend

never mind ! I will not droop and bow my head
like a lonely weeping willow — I shall be strong
I'll show you how strong a Ram can be !

 and I'll . . . . what is this here on your pillow ?

on your bed — our bed — all neatly made
the bed where we used to lie — oh, Gooober, why-why-why ?
why did you go ? **NO !** I will not cry
I promise myself I won't cry anymore — not a single tear

 but . . what is this and what is it doing here ?

it's a folded piece of today's paper
 . . the Classified section of Lost and Found ?
well, you've lost **ME** forever !
and don't expect you can come sneaking back around
saying you're sorry, and all that rot — because you're not !
I don't care if you **NEVER** return from your trip

 now I see . . it's the Peanuts comic strip
 you probably left it here for me to find

as a phony apology plea
or is it just a clever reminder
of just how much you secretly hated me ?
 ALLRIGHT !
I'll read your silent message . . .
or the message of the Universe

 to discover the coded Great Truth
 of why you broke your promise, and went away
 what did Porcupine Lucy do
 to lose her points today ?

 ⟶

Moment of Truth — or Folly ?

I never knew how to interpret that biblical warning

 "pride goeth before a fall"

does it mean
that hanging on to false pride
is what trips you up, and makes you fall ?

or does it mean
that when you lose your proudness, it won't be long

till you're flat on your face
so hang on to your pride for dear life !

        which one ?

      I chose the latter — why not ?
      it has been my choice in every crisis
      since I was born — naked and bald

yes, I chose the latter, no matter that Pisces Ruth, who rhymes with Truth
and who goeth with me, whither-soever I goeth
believes the former — and thinks I should decide to remain
to nurse my pain, and wait here
for what she is certain will be your eventual return

      she does not know how I burn !

she is of the Water element
and I am Fire
         and whither-soever I now goeth, with my pride
         I am alone, and on my own — this time, when I depart
         Ruth cannot follow, with her gentle heart
         no, she cannot wrap me
         in the soft cocoon of her Neptune compassion
                  in California
where my pride will either cause
or prevent my fall
         when I confront the one
         I believed was tall

yes, I shall interpret the Scriptures by choosing the latter
no matter that Mars will soon oppose my natal Uranus

indicating erratic action, deeply regretted

      I am Fire ! Fire ! Fire ! and all that doesn't matter

      my natal Mars will not permit defeat !
      I choose confrontation — I will not retreat !

Dress Rehearsal

a week or so after you left, I flew to Los Angeles
I flew through the sky on a **TWA** Broomstick, First Class

      I am not an ordinary witch
      when I set out to stir a potion of eye of newt

and toe of frog — with wool of bat — and tongue of dog

 my name is listed on the passenger log
 as **VIW** — and Very Important Witches travel
 by First Class Broomstick only !

I am not a tourist — my business in the dizzy-Disney land
of shrunken oranges and withering palms — is not sightseeing
no, I am neither an ordinary tourist, nor an ordinary witch

  I am a unique rose, turned **MACBETH** !

I am not a loser, no — anyone can see I am a **VIP**
or rather, a **VIW,** with pride, pride, pride !
I am not a loser, nor a beggar — I am a **CHOOSER** !

 choosing my own fate — I do not wait
 for astrology to give me its starry permission
 to do what I must do — and say what I must say
 before another day is past . . to you

let Mars oppose Uranus !
yes, let Saturn also square my Mercury !

let all planets in the heavens oppose my Venus and Sun
I will oppose them too
    one-by-one-by-one !

 Mars is my ruler
 and fights on my side — to win !
 we never lose, Mars and I

so I will fly . . but take no daisies with me

 once before, I flew to you in Colorado
 on wings of love, a gentle dove — to make amends
 after one of our last quarrels
 how long ago ? a fortnight or so ?
  I brought you happy daisies then
    and placed them on the table
 near your chair
    . . you didn't even notice they were there

Gooober, you never even *mentioned* them
my forgiveness daisies

 oh, no ! no forgiveness daisies this time
 my Lord and Master, my monarch in exile — my ex-teacher
 of the arrogant point system of fouls and defaults
 and three-strikes-you're-out, baby

I am not a bright faced Daisy, named Gamble
this is no Clear Day — and there is no way — to see Forever now

> I am a rose, un-tamed
> a fallen angel, still un-named
> I am a druid, un-magical
> a flower, no longer special or unique

but I am the captain of a ship that will not sink !
the Master of my own Destiny — the ruler of my own soul

> and the boss of my own goal

I may be only half, no longer whole — for, I no longer belong to you
but I am still true — to myself
                                        I AM WHAT I AM — A RAM !
> and Rams do not fear Lions

so . . I took no daisies on this flight
no happy-faced daisies to whine and beg and plead my plight

> no sunny daisies, to be coldly ignored
> by a cruel King, now bored
> who seeks the variety of new Queens
>   and thinks to relegate me to the role
> of mere pawn

I AM NO PAWN OF FATE !

> neither am I the pawn of an arrogant King
> born under the royal star of the Lion
> why should I present an offering of daisies
> to his Majesty's golden throne ?

> daisies are forgiveness

and it will require at least a thousand centuries
at least a million Earth incarnations — for me to forgive all this
O ! especially that forked-tongue-serpent-kiss
                                        in Vail Vail Vail

> never mind what *you* have to forgive *me*
> no, never mind all that
>   you Monster Cat !

how can I ever forgive you — for breaking your promise of Forever ?
for darkening the light between us
                and making every truth false . . . even *spring*
for refusing to return my *Love is Eternal* ring
                                you had engraved for me
        in Pismo Beach

it's **MY** ring, isn't it ? **MY** ring, not yours !
Indian giver, Indian giver !

> no, Indians can be trusted
> they are proud and honorable — and tall
> you are not honorable at all
> > you broke your treaty with me
> so you are not an Indian giver
> you are a hiSSing Eden-Snake giver !

how can I ever forgive you
for making the magical baby druids, who hid in the shed
and came out to play with us at night — a lie ?

> for making me cry
> in my soul again

oh, Gooober . . . .
> how could you make me cry in my soul again ?

Act One

> no . .

> no daisies this time — all I took with me
> on that last frantic, furious flight
> was my raveled pride, hanging about me in tatters

and for countless solitary confinement hours
I sat in our old miracle room at the Hollywood Roosevelt

> the hotel where you waited for me in the lobby
> one night, after our very first fight
> for hours and hours and hours
> and told me you would still have been there . . mummified
> > years later
> if I hadn't forgiven you
> when I did

> oh, liar, liar !

I shouted the ugly, untrue words
into the shocked room — twice

LIAR ! LIAR !

I was born under Fire

and you were born already-frozen-in-a-cake-of-ice

then I sat alone, in the gloom, with the drapes drawn severely
across the windows overlooking Hollywood Boulevard
to shut out the light — and the painful sight of the small, white cross
planted on the far hill, behind Grauman's Chinese Theatre

                              . . planted on Mt. Olympus

I washed my pride, and pressed it
to iron out all the wrinkles
and darned it, and mended and patched it
till it was nearly like new

              finally, I gathered it around me
              like the Red Queen's robe

                  wiped away
              every single hurt tear

then called you at your parents' house
to say . .
              "hello — I'm here"

Patience is a Virtue

your voice was still warm with memory on the phone
still, somehow faintly caressing
despite your statement that you would not come to my room
                              and be smashed again

              I knew that was what you would say
                  I also knew . . that you would come
              no matter what you said . . . eventually

and so I waited
      . . an eternity or so
                              inside that haunted room

              it was the waiting . . yes, the waiting
              that finally un-did us
                        that broke the link
              and untied the knot between our hearts

we could have, somehow, made it through
this dark Gethsemane of our spirits
if you had come to me when I first called

but the waiting . . oh ! that is what finally did it

> with your pride keeping you away
> and my pride keeping me from calling you again

I had too much time, those days and nights
too much time to think — and there were too many memories
pointing fingers of ridicule at me
from every corner of the room . . our magic room

> no longer magic . . only tragic

it is not logical
for magic to rhyme with tragic . . is it ?

Poetry is the Creative Alchemy of Genius

while I wait for you to phone this room
I have made good use of my quiet, lonely tomb
to write for you, a poem
a squashed bug poem, of sensitive alchemy —
not creative genius
> first verse:

the biggest lie was told, in the Colorado mountains
where they used to dig for gold — not in the West Virginia hills
who cannot fly, and never-never could
but in the Colorado mountains, who can lie
> I should have known they would

. . I take poetic license with my pronouns, Sir
oh, I may not own a driver's license
but I have a poet's license
and it is mountains *who* can fly — and lie

> second verse:

> a Monster Cat is curious, and thereby hangs the tale of Vail
> in the mountains of Colorado
> who can no longer fly, but who can lie
> oh ! curiosity killed the cat, they say
> and curiosity killed a Monster Cat — in Vail
> > on Thanksgiving Day

third verse:

> yes, killed the cat — how do you like that ?
> it blew the lid, it did, right off the pail in Vail

as far as I was concerned
the cat's curiosity that burned in Vail a trail of no return

last verse:

you can't rely on Gemini
and, whether he's King of Siam or Rio — don't trust Leo
you never know with Scorpio
but it's easy to lie to Aries
because they believe foolishly in magic and faeries

THE END

do you think I'll get the Pulitzer prize
from your silvery-wise eyes, stained with muddy lies
for my poem ?

I tell you, it is the "creative artistry of genius", my poem
and I demand the proper respect
for the alchemy of my bleeding, sensitive soul
oh ! I have every right to expect a Pulitzer prize
from your lie-stained eyes
for my literary masterpiece of artistic, creative suffering

never mind the rhyme and meter

FunniesFunniesFunnies

I think I'll read the comics . . I used to call them "funnies"

strange word, funnies
rhyming with the legal term of monies
and gentle-soft Easter bunnies

in Lexigram form, mysteriously containing
the words Fun — and Sun
also the letters that form the word Nun

Sun . . and Nun

why should those words strike haunting chords of sorrow ?
they seem to echo some promise broken
surely not by me — I never break a promise

'funnies' even hides within itself the letters spelling 'nine'
that powerful, vital number of energy and life . . and sudden pain
why am I playing with comics ?

next, I'll be cutting out paper dolls in an endless chain

perhaps the twinkling Oober Galaxy is channeling a message
to my Higher Self — about how to make you know
                              it's time to "come home free"
but . . should I shout
Red Light ! or Green Light ! which one ?

            the sky is so dark — what's happened to the Sun ?
            it's only noon
                    a storm must be brewing

what is this insistent melody, this fragile, fragmented tune
I keep hearing in my head, from a summer long ago ?
why does it come, then go . . and what were the lyrics
                              . . did I ever know them ?
I can't seem to . . remember

            Gooober, please tell me — which it is, which one ?
            help me remember — I've forgotten how to play

            is it Red Light ! or Green Light ! I'm supposed to say
            so you'll know it's time to "come home free" ?

I've tried to do everything you taught me to do
I've almost stopped crying — and I'm really, truly trying
to understand the reason for our barren winter season
that began with your cold decision
to leave me alone in the frozen grasp of nameless dread
caught in the withering clutch of too much need
so long avoided in this life, and through countless centuries past

            how long will it last — this unaccustomed, naked need ?

NO ! I will not plead
and give you the smug satisfaction of seeing my soul weep

            you didn't allow us nearly enough time to make our love rhyme
            only a little more than a year — that's not enough time
                    to make **ANYTHING** rhyme !
            not even long enough for your Majesty to learn
            that my jealous rages flare and burn
                    because they rhyme with secret fear
            so, how could you expect me to complete
            my Happiness poem . . in only a little more than a year ?

Gooober, do you hear ? that's not enough time
                        to make **ANYTHING** rhyme !
you're as silent as the small white cross
planted behind Grauman's Chinese Theatre
still staring at me, from Mt. Olympus

Canto Sixteen ☆ 661

on the far, far hill

                              . . be still, my love
                      my lonely love . . . be still

maybe there's a clue to the tragedy
of Us — in the Peanuts comic strip today
that will help me solve this maddening Oriental puzzle
of Yin and Yang . . some secret, coded clue to what it is
                                    I fear in you
and what it is you fear in me
that makes you continue to stay away

            what impending, earth-quaking, soul-shaking Apocalypse
                  or as yet un-christened crisis

            what do you telepathically sense, or mystically see
                                    between you and me
            that forbids you
            to come here, to our magic-miracle room
            and chase away these shapeless purple shadows
            of deepening gloom . . . with the sunlight of your smile ?

what is it you fear from me that keeps you away from this door ?
am I the one who is wrong ? and if so, — how ?
how could I have said or done anything so wrong
to keep you away this long ?

            I really believe that cartoonist Charles Schulz, even now
            has our hearts bugged, our souls tapped
            he always manages to come up with a Lucy-scene
            that fits all your unjust descriptions of me
            your cutting accusations, so unfair . . . and untrue
            how did you manage to persuade him to conspire with you
            in your cruel game of mental chess ?
            who charted the rules for your cat and mouse tricks ?
            are our liberated Lucy messages
            sent by the Universe to curse or bless ?

oh, Goob, what's it all about ?

where's the morning paper ? did the maid throw it out ?
I'll make myself a promise
whatever I read in Peanuts, I'll behave in the opposite way
when you finally come to me, here in this room
no matter what you do or say — I swear I'll do the opposite
of whatever I happen to see that Lucy is doing in the comics today

            this time, I will — I promise me

and I'll foil your sneaky plans

you and clever cartoonist Schulz

> now, where's the paper ?   oh, here it is, in the wastebasket
> where I must have tossed it myself, and forgotten
> is my memory failing ?
> I can't even remember how soon you told me
> you would be sailing . . on your ship of Destiny
> so far-far-far away from me

will this morning's funnies perhaps tell me when ?
can I learn both why and when . . from a sly cartoonist's pen ?
maybe I should just leave the newspaper in the trash
and sit here in this empty chair
while your Destiny ships beckons to you in the fog out there
and stop trying to analyze the comics of Life and Love

why must I always lose, while you go right on winning ?
my painted horse grown stiff with fears, all streaked with tears . . . .
. . . . your proud, victorious mount so strong
so bright and arrogant . . . . enigmatically grinning

> why did I think you were tall ?

O ! Carousel, stop spinning, stop spinning !

> Lucy and I . . . . are about to fall

I'm Sorry

I remember the lesson you taught me in unselfish praying
it was after our first serious quarrel
as you sat here in the lobby of this hotel, where I was then staying

       for hours . . and hours . . and hours

by yourself, all alone
when I refused to answer your knocks on my door
or your urgent calls on the house phone
telling myself there was no possible way that even you
                        could make a miracle now
no, not after wounds
I falsely imagined were so cruel
and mistakenly believed had left scars so deep

       but I was restless, unable to sleep . .

and when I finally decided, in lonely midnight desperation
to go for a walk down Hollywood Boulevard
        and search for the peace of my former solitude there
wondering which one of us had caused this winter season . . . of hating
the first thing I saw, as I stepped out of the elevator

       was you . . . in the lobby . . waiting

       just sitting there, in a large yellow chair
       as motionless and still as a statue
       with such sadness and sorrow etched on your face
       yet, bathed in the almost visible grace
       of the gentle patience that colors your aura

you didn't speak

       all you did was stare — and stare — and stare
       I tried to ignore you, but found that I could not
       it was like trying to ignore a forest fire, blazing

       the back of my neck felt burning hot
       in the spot where I knew you were steadily gazing
       attempting to pierce my very soul

with a surging flood of adrenalin, sudden and intense
. . an instinctive psychic self-defense . . .
I rejected your powerfully projected plea
     with a silent scream you surely must have heard
indignation flaring in every word

       . . oh, leave me alone !

why do you hang on, when you know I'm through ?
can't you see I want nothing to do with you ?
                                    . . get out of my life !

then I whirled furiously around, and laser-beamed you back
with a magnetic Mars glare, as cutting as a knife

                    but you only sat there, in that yellow chair
                    meeting my fiery blast with an even deeper compassion
                    mutely asking my forgiveness
                                    . . and continued to stare

            until, at last

your love reached out and touched me
across the turbulent miles of my wounded pride
calming my storm of anger, deep inside — and when it was stilled
I did what you had so persistently, telepathically willed

                    I went over to you and smiled
                    that's all — just smiled

your eyes filled with tears, then, as you returned my smile
and my heart turned over, as I heard myself say

"oh, Gooober, let's stop hurting each other this way
what does it matter who's to blame ?
I'm lost without you . . and I need you so"

                    very slowly, you rose from your chair
                    while the returning fire of desire swept through us
                    bringing its familiar ache
                    and our hands found each other . . and locked

                            as you answered

                            "I've been lost and lonely
                                        and needing you too
                            let's go upstairs . . . "

for a suspended time, we stood there, trembling
then we walked to the elevator together
still holding hands tightly . . . touching hearts
and pressed the button for the 12th floor
our bodies crying . . hurry ! O ! hurry-hurry-hurry
so we can blend once more, and heal the wounds of separation

                    later . . after we had become Us again
                    and you were lying beside me, so near and dear
                    blessed by the cool peace of our newborn Oneness
                    I murmured a half-teasing question

into your warm, sleepy ear

"darling, suppose I hadn't come to you tonight
to make up our fight
but had decided, instead, to never forgive you till I died . . .
how long would you have waited for me there
in that yellow chair ?"

     and you sighed

     "for a million, billion Forevers
       . . until I mummified"

  I laughed
 and snuggled closer

"mummified ? oh, Goob, how very funny !
to imagine you as an Egyptian mummy
like some ancient Pharaoh
guarding the secrets of the Great Pyramid of Gizeh
and the mystery of the Sphinx
druid honor, would you really have waited so long
for my forgiveness ?
I'm afraid I could never be that strong
how long is that ? a million, billion Forevers ?
longer than an eon ?"

    but you were silent

  then suddenly, I noticed you were shaking with fatigue

I felt your hand tremble on my breast
and your face . . was a greyish color, like lead

when I asked you why
again I heard you sigh, as your words came slowly

    "it took so much vital energy
    to just sit there and wait
    projecting strong, positive vibrations
       of love
    to cancel
    the powerful negative vibrations of hate
    you were sending into me
    through rage and fear
    such an intense concentration
       of needing and pleading
    that you cruelly refused to hear

    I feel as though . . . my soul is bleeding
    so if I'm shaking now
      . . I guess that's why"

I started to cry

      then you held my head against your chest
      kissing away my sorrow
      burying your nose in my tangled hair . . . soothing my tears
      as I whispered a tender prayer

. . thank you for loving me, dear gentle Gooober
especially when I don't deserve it
and please know . . I didn't mean to hurt you so . .

      unable to speak the words aloud

            but you heard me anyway, and murmured
            "don't cry, sad druid
            I always understand — everything you do
            and thank you for loving me too"

Final Curtain

and so, finally you came to the room
unexpectedly, as is your wont

      like the negative of a photograph
      where white areas show up as black or grey
      the scene was printed by Destiny — or the Masters
            in reverse

now it was the *faces*
      which were hauntingly familiar
but the *eyes* were strange

during this final
confrontation with Truth

      every thought and feeling was reversed
      in the development of our negative vibration
      every word and action — carefully studied and rehearsed
      no spontaneous elation
         or tender surprise, as before

our features were not softened, now
by gentle, wavering candleglow
they were cruelly outlined by the harsher light of naked bulbs
in dreary hotel lamps

nor were our senses sweetly drugged by incense . . no
our noses were offended by the stale smell
of my forbidden-by-you and defiance-from-me cigarettes

      there were no whole galaxies of stars
      watching us with excitement
      on this bleak and purple shadowed midnight

the stars scurried through the firmament like frightened children
hiding from the dark hour of our souls
behind the clouds of some higher heaven
                           unconcerned with us

as we are unconcerned with the agony of ants
crushed beneath a heavy, god-like boot

     stars . . . . fair weather friends

                   and where was he ?
            oh ! where was he ?

                   who said . . *suffer the little ones*
                   to come to me ?

was he . .
a fair weather friend too ?

      we played our cursed parts on the darkened stage
      of our once shining miracle-room
      turned now into a raging battlefield, presaging doom
      for both sides — defeat — with victory for neither
      for who is ever the winner in any war ?

      and shot great cannonballs of hurt at one another
      across the puzzled, waiting, snow-white bed
                   where we first loved
      dressed for this tragic melodrama
      with one hidden, tear-soaked pillow
      I was too proud to let you see
      and virgin, sterile sheets, unwrinkled, smooth
      no longer stained with the pure spring rain of love

it was like some nightmarish movie, made of old, odd bits of celluloid
from *Macbeth* . . *Hamlet* . . *King Kong* . . the *Hunchback of Notre Dame*
Rosemary's Baby . . and the *Bride of Frankenstein*
                       starring Bette Davis eyes
spliced together crazily
by some lunatic Hollywood film cutter
suddenly gone mad
in the land of shrunken oranges and fallen angels

brown-withered grass, and heavy, smoggy air

oh ! this was the room where we loved, where we loved . . . .
the room filled with the fresh perfume
of flowers and mystical incense . . the same, warm bed
within   where you once said

"I love you, spunky Lucy wench
funny druid, Gooober-girl, I love you — oh, I do !"

the room where we were spiritually wed
the very same bed . . where you asked
in a voice so low and clear

"what are we going to do about it
now — and *here* ?

how could you, could I, could we
so desecrate this magic room ?
how could we so blaspheme this sacred place
where you first touched me intimately
and tenderly cupped my trusting face
in your warm, strong, dear familiar hands
. . where I first smelled your cheek
how could we ?
oh ! how could we ?

but we did

even when you entered, unexpectedly at midnight
not in answer to my silent, pleading, telepathic call
but driven by some beastly need to see me bleed
in heart and mind and soul

. . even then, there was no rushing home
into the safety of each other's protecting, understanding arms

only pre-calculated moves of chess
where you held all the Kings
and check-mated every desperate attempt I made
to end the game

that is, precalculated moves by you
I didn't know the rules — or even why we played
and therefore, could not plan ahead
holding in my empty hand . . only memories
I hoped that you might share

when the doorbell of the suite jangled harshly, and I cried out — who is there ?
you answered "Western Union" — in a voice so tight
so strange and strained

670 ☆ Canto Sixteen

I honestly expected
to see the bellman's face, not yours, when I lifted the chain and lock
     I felt shock — when I saw you
for, somehow you looked . . literally . . not as tall as I remembered
closer to six feet . . . than to your towering six-foot-two

you walked inside our magic-tragic miracle room
without a single word of greeting
as you brushed by me, barely touching my arm

       casting a distorted Quasimodo shadow
       against the pale yellow wall
       where we had first seen each other's auras

hunched over

       your hands clenched into fists of anger
       jammed into your pockets, bulging with the strain
       and glaring — not staring — at me

the windbreaker you wore was a gift of love from me
in our flower covered cottage on the beach, in Pismo
where we played house . .

       . . when you tried it on that day
       you stood straight and tall
          . . and cast no shadows

the memory of your entrance
torments me, even now . . why did you say "Western Union" ?

       why should you have needed
       such a thin, pathetic, weak disguise ?

surely not because you were staging some playful Gooober prank
or mouse-joke — there was no humor in your eyes

            this was no comedy we were acting out

   were you . .

       could you have been — afraid ?
       afraid I might not unlock my heart, and open the door
       if I knew who it really was . . who stood outside in the hall ?

. . . but, who was it
if it wasn't you ? and why should you fear my knowing it was you ?

       oh, surely, surely
       you could not have been afraid

it would be more than I could bear
to know you doubted and feared me that night
as I doubted and feared you
more than I could bear, to realize it now — too late

yes, I was mortally terrified of you, my blanket — my Comforter
my very spirit cowering, trembling
under what I read as the hatred — or even worse
                          the bored disinterest
                              on your set features
surely you were not as terrified of me ?
all I sent to you was love . . and needing

      or was my love — my need — invisible to you
      by the strange process
      of the negative-reverse development and printing
      of everything we looked upon and heard ?

and if so . .

      was what I saw upon your face that night
      also love and need
      mirrored into its negative polarity of arrogant independence
      only through the reversed interpretation of my mind
      as you were similarly blind — to my own love and needing
      neither heeding the other's silent pleading ?

then the ironies of Fate
are too fearful, too cruel to even contemplate

I summoned all my courage, drew my Robe of Pride close around me
sat up straight and tall — as straight and tall as I could
                              on the bed
cool, calm and poised . . I thought
forgetting that I was clutching Raggy
giving myself away

      but maybe making up for that vulnerable gesture
      of sentimentality — with the bored disinterest
      reflected — I hoped — in my eyes

I told you all I had wanted when I called you on the phone
      the only thing I desired from you
was the chance to say goodbye with dignity and grace
then fly away from this dreary place

  . . as I tried to keep my face
a total blank . . oh ! were you blind ?

      you asked me where I planned to find
      such calm and peaceful emotions

for the purpose of farewell
when I had already smashed all reason
within your heart — and my own

the first words spit out of your mouth
were solid stones of sneering — drenched in venom
   dripping with bitter accusation and recrimination

                   later, taking on
                       even more grotesque and twisted form

oh, Gooober
all I really wanted that night was . .

     . . I wanted you to cash a check for me — a check of apology
     a cancelled check, to cancel out the satire I had staged
     by trying to do multiple division
                with her — and you — and me

by trying to divide one into three . . or two into one . . the One of Us
   I was never any good at fractions

I wanted to say to you, I'm sorry, darling — I'm sorry
I know now — I swear I do
that she means nothing-nothing-nothing to you
I should never have tried to divide
               two into one
when I know that you and I
are indivisible figures
when I know that we can never be divided by
or divide into . . anyone else

     I was choked by the dust of my old mis-trust
     forgive me . . oh ! and ask me to forgive you too
     for all this hurt between us
            just ask me — I'll forgive you !

  but I could not speak

     how could I find the voice to speak those words
     while I was watching, in horrified fascination
        lizards and toads and snakes
             pouring out of your mouth ?
I covered my ears
with my hands

     to shut out the sound — but not the sight
             of your words
     for I could still see
     the lizards, forming unthinkable threats

"I am going far away" — you said
"and when I return, you won't know me
you won't even want to know me
for the things I'll do while I am gone
will wound you so
you'll be glad to see me go . . "

lizards . . lizard words . . snakes . . toads

electric shock eel words

how could all those toads and snakes
come tumbling from the lips that kissed me tenderly

. . like the re-play of an old horror faerie tale
when diamonds and daisies and violets
                                   and bits of gold sparkle
used to pour
              like a shining waterfall of truth
from your lips . . when you spoke ?

your mouth . . oh !
      your mouth that once was full of foamy-mint kisses
and fresh orange juice kisses . . rainy-ozone kisses
pine needle kisses . . . sweet and clean and cool

              tender-violent kisses of passion
                   and gentle little snowflake kisses . .

is this a dream ?

      and your lips . . oh !
the toady-snake, rough-scaly words

      you spat out at me, from across the room
      me on the bed — you in the chair
      distorted them, your lips
              into a disdainful curl of contempt

      your ugly-warted words
that once spilled out in a sparkling stream
of such rainbows of changing colors and shapes

         . . . baby rabbit words, soft-kitten-ear words
      robin-egg-blue and satin-ribbon words
              velvety words of lilting crescendos
         whole symphonies of words of lost chords and beauty

              your voice was scratchy sandpaper
              abrasively informing me

that I had lost all chance for a dignified farewell
when I smashed Cynthia's head
on the kitchen floor, back at the house

Cynthia ?

       Cynthia ?

"I don't understand . . what do you mean
I smashed Cynthia's head ?"

            you looked genuinely puzzled
            honestly confused . .

            "the doll — the doll"

                   you said

"do you mean . . Emilie ?"
my heart was pounding with a quickening fear
of the unknown — as I wondered
how could he have forgotten Emilie so soon ?

            "yes, I mean Emilie"
              you answered, clearly relieved

            "don't look so surprised — that doll
            was never important enough to me
            to be bothered with remembering her name
            you just thought she was, that's all"

oh, God, oh God !

    Emilie, Emilie, Emilie
our chronological freak and antique doll
nearly ninety years old, yet still an infant

Emilie, Emilie . . .
who contained our secret hope
and secret sorrow too
she was . . she was a gift from you
so how could you say you didn't care about her ?
when you'd affectionately teased
so many times . . and even held make believe
conversations with her . . .
what was happening on this Halloweenish night of fright
here in this unholy, haunted room ?
what can I do ?   have I gone mad — or is it you
who have taken leave of all your senses ?

"but, Gooober . . you named her yourself . .
and you said you thought . . "

"what difference does all that make now ?
the point is — you smashed her head"

"yes, allright ! I smashed her head !
in Cripple Creek, when you were leaving
on the kitchen floor, near the back porch door
another **BIG BANG** for me — another point for you
chalk one up for your side !
and what's the score at this moment, my love ?
nothing-to-nothing, with no one ahead
and only seconds left to play — a tie ?"

somewhere . . I thought

somewhere a clock is timing us
and a Master Referee is keeping score
. . not you or I

then your sandpaper voice
told me all my credit was used up
no chance to cash a check of apology

"I don't know you anymore"
I said

"I swear, I don't know you
who are you ? surely not the man
I once loved . . "

"who am I ?" you laughed

"I'm the one who should be
asking that question of *you*
who are **YOU ?**
as far as I'm concerned
you're a total stranger . . I don't know you
at all anymore — so who are *you* ?"

you were asking me
to identify myself . . oh ! panic-panic-panic

"who are you ?" you repeated
"you can't even reverse gears in a car
who are you ?
I don't know you"

regal Lion, like my father
placing a deadly weapon in the hands of a maniac
insinuations that I do not have enough poise
to handle a car — or life — or love

then I shouted at you
with an impassive face

      "do you know who **YOU** are ?
      well, who are you ? and the hell with your car !
      do you know who you are ?
      you . . who used to quest for a star with me"

my anger was rising swiftly
outraged indignation mixing with awful fear
pouring through my veins . . thundering in my head

"the way you speak . . the words of a stranger
and the way you look
you don't even *look* like yourself anymore !
you're not even tall . . . "

      I had used the tallness as a symbolic thing
      privately, when I sobbed to myself
      that you were 'tall' no longer

and yet . . it did truly seem on this night . . .
it seemed that you were actually, literally not as tall as you were

"you're not even tall anymore !"
I shouted again

                but you remained silent

"and your eyes are not your eyes
they are strange . . because they are
             stained with lies !
yes ! stained with lies
and muddy, no longer ocean-green, your eyes
you're no longer six-foot-two
and your eyes are not silvery-wise
         they're milky, deceptive blue !

oh ! how could I have believed
your eyes were green ?"
            then suddenly
            you lowered them, your eyes
            staring at the floor

     I waited

            finally, you raised your milky-blue eyes
            and looked at me coldly

            "you are wrong, you know" you said
            "I have never been six-foot-two

Canto Sixteen ☆ 677

that was only because you imagined me
                    to be so tall
I was never any of the things at all
that you pretended to yourself I was
I'm actually only six feet tall
and my eyes have been blue since I was born

                    . . perhaps you imagined them to be
                    as you say, in your poetic way
                                        ocean-green
                    and silvery-wise
                    because of your tendency to idealize
                    anything you see
                                into what you wish it to be"

was this true ? was this true ?
had I only idealized you ?
were you but a dream . . a dream conceived
by loneliness and grief ?

urgently, desperately, my thoughts
darted to and fro within my brain, like butterflies
sorting fragments, trying to remember
            trying to . . *know*

was it possible that you were right ?
had I woven such a fantasy around the him-of-you
that I had never even noticed
your eyes were not ocean-green
                    but merely ordinary blue
. . that you were only six feet tall
and never a towering six-foot-two — like him — ? could it be
that I made a mere fantasy appear to be real ?

            is it possible ?

yes, anything is possible . . anything at all . . I suppose
but, if this be true . . . I thought
if I have caused a fantasy to appear to be real
then how can I ever again be sure of anything I believe or feel ?
if this is true . . then there was never any me-of-me
                                or you-of-you
        even the Saturn-Serpent-Seven
                        cycle is a lie
and so . . is Easter

            determined that you would not see me cry
            I blinked my eyes rapidly
            took several deep breaths . . remaining, for a time
            as silent, watching and waiting — as you

I gathered together my feathered thoughts
into some semblance of stability
as I sat there on the bed, with Raggy
waiting for my pulse to stop pounding, so I could
                        trust my voice not to tremble
                when I next spoke
I thought . .
            with a consuming weariness of soul and spirit

no . . you do not know me anymore
and I do not know you
you are ugly-ugly-ugly, strong handsome Brave
and favorite of the Sun god — you are ugly

and I am ugly-ugly-ugly once more too
I am also tired
                . . so very, very tired

finally, I asked quietly

"when are you leaving ?
where will you go ?   what will you do ?"

                        "I am leaving in a few days
                        out of the country — maybe even
                                off the planet
                        to find myself, heal myself
                        and end this bad dream we shared"

                        you paused

                        "you want a dignified farewell ?
                        then let's have it, and be done with it
                        it's getting late . . "

I thought . . oh, Gooober
don't you see how late it really is ?

            . . . somewhere
                a clock is
timing us . . .

                        "well, go on — save your sacred dignity
                        if you have anything to say — say it"

for a moment, I could not speak
save my dignity ?   I thought wildly

the patches in my Robe of Pride
have all burst open at the seams — what dignity ?
I sit here clutching a sorrow-stained rag doll

Canto Sixteen   ☆   679

. . oh, Raggy, Raggy
you gave her to me yourself

        . . Emilie . . Rosemary's cursed baby
    Raggedy Ann . . or Anne
                        . . oh, tiny wreath
        of violets

I spoke to you silently
            could you not read my thoughts ?

dignity ? I sit here, stripped of all confidence
in my own judgement
with cream on my nose . . and hair washed
                            just before your surprise visit
            hanging around my witch's face
in limp, snake strands
                    like a mournful Medusa

hair all sticky and gummy with the shampoo
I had no time to rinse out before Western Union knocked on my door
I am the Bride of Frankenstein
                    Monster ! see your blushing bride ?
I have no dignity — I have no pride

        . . you used to watch the sunbeams dance
    in my hair, when you brushed it for me
                gently, carefully, so as not to split the ends

    dignity ?

then I spoke aloud, and said

"forget about my dignity . . you can go now
just look at me ! what dignity ? my hair is a mess, and . . "

        suddenly, my poise crumbled

and involuntarily
I cried out, in honest anguish
as I had before . .

"oh, Gooober . . it would have been nice
if I could have looked . .
I mean, I wasn't expecting you, and I was
washing my hair . . and

oh, I wanted so . . to look beautiful
this very last time we saw each other"

and I swallowed hard, so you wouldn't

see me cry

                    you looked at me steadily
                    and spoke just one word . . . . . . "why ?"

I had no answer

          then I saw that you were writing some words
          on a piece of paper
          and my heart tugged within me
                    you were . . holding your pen
          clutched in your fist, like a dwarf
                         in the old, familiar way
          but . . . something was not . .

               something was . . you were writing the words
               with your right hand

your right hand ?
but, Gooober, I thought . . you are
yes, I *know* you are left handed
we talked about it so often, and . . a hundred times
I've seen you write with your left hand

                    "here — take this" you said

                    "it's the address of a friend of mine . . .
                    my parents are leaving for a long vacation
                    in Switzerland — and he's accepting
                                        my mail for me
                    while they're gone

                    if you don't mind . . well
                    it would be kind of you to send
                    all the things I left behind in Colorado
                    to this address . . "

I hardly heard your words
concentrating as I was . . on your hand

"you were . . you were writing just now
with your right hand . . I don't understand
you are left handed, are you not ?"

                    "no," you replied firmly "I am not
                              left handed
                    I have always been right-handed . . too
                    haven't you ever heard of anyone
                    who can use both hands ?
                    it's called being ambidextrous"

Canto Sixteen ☆ 681

"oh, I see . . "

I fumbled for words

"but I was sure, so certain . . I guess
my mind has been confused for a long time
perhaps since . . you . . he died

I'm sorry . . but
oh ! Goob, I am truly so confused . . "

                    your eyes filled, then, with a gentle glow
                    and your features softened
                              with a trace of compassion
                    as you said
                          . . softly
                                    "I understand"

"you do ?"

          and I reached out once more
          with the same aching need as before
          trying, trying so hard . . to expect a miracle

as I whispered, gazing deeply into your eyes
                          . . just one word

          "magic ?"

                    you turned away . . walked to the window
                    and stood there, facing the small white cross
                    planted on the far hill . .

          it was very still

                    after a moment . . you turned around
                    your eyes expressionless
                                    blank

                    then you tied your Halloween mask
                    back on your face . . said coldly

                    "there's no more magic"

          and left

Be Still, My Love, Be Still

I am unbelievable
even to myself, I am unbelievable

      facing the irrevocable fact
      that I had cause to mistrust my own senses
        that my imagination had possibly
            led me far astray

      and facing the equally irrevocable fact
      of the weakened link in the chain
           that bound us together
I would not believe
that chain could ever be broken

      some hard-tied knot inside of me
      a stubborn knot of Faith and profound Knowing
         all snarled and tangled
      yet still a hard-tied knot

      kept me trusting in the me-of-you
      tugged hard on me, tightening my will
      and seemed to say
           be still, be still
      truth will return

      how long will I be haunted
by that ghastly, nightmarish week
in California ?

the first night I arrived
before I phoned you from the room
        pulled by some powerful cosmic magnet
I had walked down Hollywood Boulevard
toward Pickwick Bookstore
          . . unlikely cradle for our Christmas miracle
        and even more unlikely for one now . .

. . . yet was pulled and drawn to enter
and move slowly, magnetized
to that sacred spot where I first saw

      your smile

         "is it a good book ?
               does it contain the knowing-things ?"

      did I see light
      still shining there ?

some fading light of Love and Truth
impressed, somehow, upon the ethers . . and
lingering in the shape
of the swirling vortex of our tornado

did I see light misting over the heads
of strangers streaming past ?
unknowing and unseeing strangers
walking oblivious . . through the ghosts
of Us

. . I could not tell

and then, at some moment

during that night of horror and unreality
while you were there — yet not there — with me
in our miracle room

I mentioned that I had gone to Pickwick Bookstore
and you seemed to flinch when I said that
momentarily startled

"you went there . . to Pickwick ?
oh, that is strange . . so very strange"

you murmured, then
as if to yourself

"why is it strange ?"
I had asked

but your Halloween mask
was securely tied back on
when you answered . .

"only strange because . . well
well, it's just strange, that's all"

then shifted in your chair restlessly
avoiding my questioning eyes

and I wondered . . if this is . . . somehow . . *not* truly *you*

then did the *real* you, perhaps go there too ?
and see the light still lingering
and the oblivious strangers
walking through the ghosts of Us ?

but I could not tell — I swear, I could not tell
if you had gone there too

that ghastly week, all dimensions lied
perception had been dulled
gone haywire

and there was only a crackling static
where once had been a smooth flow of energy between us
creating instant intuition

as if some Higher Masters were manipulating the elastic strings
attached to the helpless puppets of you and me
jerking our words and actions . . in a crazy, frantic dance
for some unguessed Galactic purpose

. . as if the Higher Angels of ourselves
had attached an etheric scrambling device
like on the President's telephone
to the silvery-blue cord of light that pulsed between us

no, I could not tell
if you had also been magnetized, as had I
to Pickwick Bookstore on Hollywood Boulevard

. . now called B. Dalton Bookstore
yet still . . warm and familiar

and even if you had gone there
then why was it that I did not know when ?

and why did you not know the very moment
I was standing on that sacred spot ?

even if you had gone there — yes, even so
why did neither of us know ?

some inner voice . . would have guided both of us
to synchronize our steps on such a pilgrimage
at any other time . . not left us to reach toward each other
clutching only empty air
not left us

to reach toward each other, clutching only emptiness
not left us to the lonely sorrow of watching strangers . . uncaring

walking through the ghosts of Us

oh ! we were desperately
seeking Us . . . and finding only shadows

. . . caught up in a pre-destined cosmic crisis
pre-destined by the you-of-you and the me-of-me
on some other Star, perhaps

as a testing of our souls for worthiness and strength

but . . for what mission ?

we had arrived
at the dangerous crossroads
of cross-purposes

our telepathic connection cruelly short circuited
and suddenly, with no warning
. . or had there been a warning ?

we were running
in emotional Serpent circles
tripping over our astral selves

both of us

but Destiny must have her way, and so I waited
growing stormier and more unforgiving
by the minute . . every day
and yet, that hard-tied knot of Faith and Knowing
kept tugging on me, telling me
. . *be still, my love, be still*

why did I not listen ?

Tomb Rhymes with Womb

. . then does Death rhyme with Birth ?

I am a lively corpse
the habit of existing dies hard

I am a quaking ghost, haunting this hotel room
waiting for you to ring my sepulcher
and tell me we only dreamed this separation

. . that it cannot be real

I am not yet embalmed

I am waiting here in the morgue
to be identified
but I have no identification

no driver's license . . no way, no way

                    to identify myself, to prove . . who I am
                                        even to you

how long, then
must I wait for burial ?

            I shall not wait any longer
            let me bury myself in peace, now
            naked, without my transparent Robe of Pride
            sans all dignity and poise
            leave me alone, Gooober, just leave me alone

I am dead ! do you hear ?

at least, the part of me that loved you
is dead . . and what other part can be left ?

            but . . before I left that haunted room
            determined to leave without a further scene
                            or a single more tear

I wrote a farewell note to you
a silent cry, to say goodbye

                        oh ! the me-of-me is dead !
                        so why am I still breathing . . why ?

            yes, I wrote a farewell note across my heart
            and wondered if you could read it . . or even see it

could such cold, blank, expressionless eyes, stained dull blue with lies
read my note . . without glasses, to magnify the teeny tiny print ?

my note said . . . .

            when you drove away that morning . . . down the alley
            behind our little crooked house . . in your dusty blue Bug

            I almost fell off the Carousel
            I really-nearly did

oh, Gooober !
            didn't you care at all
that I really-nearly did ?

CANTO SEVENTEEN

My faults have cried aloud for their redress,
My weaknesses have wept in silent choirs;
No former holy power does now possess
Me, as in those flaming days of high desires,

      When at the touch a lily petal gave
Almost sweet madness, and a soft black musk
(As sights to smells translate) shook in the boughs
Of spruces leaning nearly to the dusk
On the horizon's gilt-edged wings, like vows

      When they brush across stained windows in a nave
Of purple vastness. Luminous achievements !
They are ceased . . .

      And silently this siege
Upon me cried in my deeds these strange bereavements . . . . .

Kyril Demys (Musaios)
Prismatic Voices

the Rosicrucian Adeptus
disguised Tibetan monk
Master or Avatar

who came a-knocking
on my closed-to-strangers door
that dreary grey
and unexpected wintry day
in Colorado

whoever and whatever he may have been
and still may be — or from where
from Egypt or the Far East . . or from Outer Space

. . . . although I cannot deny that he was clever
there is certainly no doubt that he was spaced-out

whether Inner — or Outer Space
is the place he calls home base

he was

spaced-out

beyond any doubt

oh ! far-far out was he
when he said that I would someday be
with one whose spiritual name, is . . *Al*tar

I mean, just how far-out can an Avatar be
to tell a whopper like that to me ?

or was it, perhaps
just an honest, well meaning mistake ?
nonsense !

a visiting angel simply does not make a careless mistake

no way

although an angel can fall, I guess — oh, yes !
an angel can fall, and lose the way — and forget how to pray

there are surely lots of those around
in this city named for the heavenly hosts — Los Angeles
City of Lost Angels
Los Angeles . . haunted by ghosts

ghosts from where ?
Poesida . . . . . Atlantis ?

what is that occult teaching about Atlantis and California ?
something about . . yes, about the High Priests and Priestesses
of that materially blessed, astrally tuned-in
and metaphysically spaced-out fair land,
                              now beneath the Atlantic Ocean floor
                              the polarity of the Pacific shore

                  those wiser ones
who knew before the others of the approaching floods and cataclysms
soon to come and turn day into night . . a long, long night
based on the principle of the ancient law of Dark attracting Light
and the other way around, as well
                              . . of Light attracting darkness
no rarity, but a simple fact
of the ever-present polarity

                  of Heaven in opposition to hell
                  and vice versa

. . . those High Priests and Priestesses, who knew of the shadows to come
yet failed to warn the people of Atlantis — in time

and also failed to explain
how they might join together, to stop the reign . . of greed and lust
of selfishness and gain
failing too . . in warning them of the danger of nourishing
                              the fast-growing baobab seeds
  . . those Enlightened Ones
              who did not enlighten
their fellow Atlanteans

                  to the method of reversing the polarities

of Heaven and hell and dark and light
like . . . the black and white negative reversal
                    . . of our magic room that night ?

        . . . those who neglected to show the way
to shut out the inferior light of sexual promiscuity and material greed
which was swiftly multiplying the negative vibrations of Earth

    . . who neglected to demonstrate how to expose the false glitter
of greed and lust — and failed to explain
that the people must brighten the dying flame
                  of Faith and Love and Trust
      to stop the rain . . and the reign . . . of evil

those who did not share what they knew, according to legend

Canto Seventeen ☆ 691

and according to each occult sage — have been reincarnated
in the present, dawning Aquarian Age

and have been given another chance — to warn the people

yes, to warn them of the once more approaching
                                        darkening of the Sun
on the planet Earth

and to explain how we, like the citizens of Atlantis
can, if we try — stop the rain
of greed and lust and selfish gain . . in time
                                        . . this time
and also according to the legend
these reincarnated Atlantean High Priests and Priestesses
are being born in — or irresistibly drawn to
                                        for one reason or another
the once fair land of California

to be given a second karmic chance
to warn those who walk upon the uneasy ground
where San Andreas lies at fault
                    . . but blameless

driven near to breaking by something more than Nature
bombarding every inch of earth around its bed

            to warn . . of evil yet un-fed

and to warn of baobab trees — those not yet watered
into fast-growing giants . . by the rain
                            of greed and lust
                                and selfish gain

well, it's not an illogical legend, I suppose
for, as everyone knows — and as it's clear to see
this is a land of gods and goddesses

                        . . oh ! I was once one . . . and he
                        standing in this very room
                                    yet secretly on Mt. Olympus
                        he told me . .

yes, a land . . of gods and goddesses

            their golden stars engraved in the asphalt beach
            of Hollywood Boulevard's sidewalks
            their hands and footprints embedded in the cement
            of the Far Eastern Chinese theatre . . across the street

imprints of the hands and feet . . of fallen angels

once gods and goddesses of love and light
beneath the mute and patient gaze of the mysterious white cross
                    planted on the far hill behind

          oh, yes !

this is indisputably the land of occult seers
and my own astrological peers . . sprinkled generously
among the withering palms and shrunken oranges

             the land of those stuck-in-their-sexual-ruts
             and dangerous nuts, who practice voodoo and black witchcraft
             the home of Martian Valentine's orgiastic religion
             and other freakish cults
                         such as politics and polygamy
called fruit and nut land
by some . . the golden land of miracles, by others
so, I guess it could be that the legend contains some veracity

             but . . what is all this to me ?

sitting here alone, beside a silent phone, in this darkened room of gloom
my soul torn and wracked by spiritual, emotional and mental confusion
sitting here amid a pouring profusion of memories . . of glory
which were merely part of a make believe story

only make believe, like Cinderella and Alice
Snow White and all those other fictional phonies

             . . sitting here in the land of racing ponies
             Disney carousels and Hare Krishna bells
                         . . Seabiscuit defrocked

my faith in love — and you — mocked
my heart locked once more
lonely lonely lonely as I was before
with no Far Eastern messenger from our Eastern Union
knocking on my California door, to give me answers

there is nothing I know for sure and certain
behind this dark curtain of fear . . in this room
where nothing seems real anymore . . where nothing is true
not even your eyes I thought were ocean-green
and silvery-wise . . but are, and were, only dull, milky blue
and your shortened height of six feet
when I imaged and idealized you . . into being six-foot-two
             like him, the Carousel Bill
oh ! grief affects the judgement
of the mind . . and makes one blind to reality

             damn it all, damn it !

Canto Seventeen ☆ 693

why don't you knock on our magic door ?
why don't you come, and speak to me
low and clear
" . . *what are we going to do about it*
now . . and here ?"

why don't you come, Gooober — and end this trembling fear ?
have I locked you out ?

my Guru friend was grossly mistaken
although well-intentioned, no doubt . . when he said
I would be with one
who would teach me about birth and death
and the re-birth of love

both the kind known above
and the kind known below . . and many other
enchanted things, we mortals call Fate

HA !
he should have said that my Comforter would come
to teach me hate — yes — to teach me how to hate

after what he has done, it is too late
for him to teach me love . . of the kind known above
or even of the kind known down here below

my Rosicrucian friend
Master Adeptus . . Avatar . . or whatever you are

hate is all he taught me
my spiritual guide you said would come
my Comforter
hail ! the great Al-tar !

the all-star god of hate

if that, indeed, is who you really are
your Majesty, Sir — if that is who you were
or will be . . ?

" . . *we may not speak*
of the knowing-things, until . . . "
until what ?

until what ? **WHAT ?**

who do you think you are ?
the Chief Brown Owl of Heaven, with seven lives ?
boys are not allowed to be Brown Owls

only girls can be Brown Owls

EVERYBODY KNOWS THAT ! GOOD GRIEF !

and you should certainly know it — you, of all people
Al-tar, the great all-star quarterback for Heaven
who calls all the shots, and plans the sneaky, serpent strategy
of this eternal, infernal game we're playing
refusing to give me a single rule of how to win

                              Monster Cat !
            Al-tar, the great all-star

no . .

            no, if there ever was such an entity
            with whom I made an astral appointment
                  with whom I made such a destined date of fate
            if there was ever such a one under God's Sun
            who made a dare with me on some other planet or star
            to share with me the agony and anguish
            of returning to this waning Earth
                        to spread the Truth of growing-things
            and the Light of knowing-things

            if there ever was such a Twin Self
            who traveled with the me-of-me for that long, that far
            then agreed to volunteer for National Guard duty down here
            it was certainly not the you-of-you
                  whose Body Temple plays host to *Al*tar, the all-star

that spirit essence, whoever and whatever he is
who comes and goes in your Temple, as a guest

            who comes and goes
                        and stares at me
                  through your eyes
            I believed to be silvery-wise

oh ! . . and ocean green

            I know him no better than you
            and he is a guest, from time to time
            in your Temple, not mine
                        or . . do you see him come and go too
                        through *my* eyes ?

I never thought of that
when we stare and stare . . are *my* eyes
to *you* . . silvery-wise ?

                  my eyes . . silvery-wise ?
      well, anyway

if it was *Al*tar, if it was truly he
with whom I made such an astral date
he was not *you* — that much I know
for certain is true

he was not — is not — you
and he *surely* is not *me*

do either of us know him ?
or will we ever ?

who are you ?

who am I ?

and who is *Al*tar ?

will I always be alone ?
OH ! I HATE THE TELEPHONE !

silent, silent

never ringing
not once a ding-a-linging

there is no more joy
winging through this room
it is full of gloom

and I will not answer the phone before it rings !
because . . I no longer hear a robin . . before he sings

no ! I will not answer
before it rings . .

not even if I die from the silence
and neither will I cry, for I have shed all my tears
and am left with only these lonely and somehow
unearthly fears

I wonder if Altar hears
whoever and whatever and why-ever he is

I wonder if Altar hears my unearthly fears ?
if he does, then why doesn't he ring my phone
knowing I'm so scared and all alone
and need so much to speak with him ?

. . or ring some bell in my mind, if he's really-truly kind
whoever and whatever . . and wherever and why-ever
he is

the entire, unholy mess

is probably a case of mistaken identity

> this entity . . known as Gooober . . this phony entity
> calling himself
>
> > . . well, at least leading me to believe
>
> that he was *Al*tar
>
> is a pure and simple case of mistaken identity

show me your identification, Al-tar, the all-star from Heaven !
no, a driver's license just won't do — not for you, my lad
it's too bad, but a driver's license just won't make it
NO ! I refuse to take it . . . as your identification

> I don't care if you *do* drive a car
> that does not prove to *me* who you are !

can you identify yourself, then, as a Brown Owl ?
NO ! only girls can be Brown Owls — as you should already know
not men or boys — not even Peter Pan himself !

> whoever and whatever you are, my ex-love
> you were surely hatched on a very strange star
> wherever and why-ever you are
> your spiritual name is more likely to be
> Willie Sutton, Don Juan or Casanova
> or Bossy-Nova . . or even Clyde
>
> > . . than Altar
>
> yes, Clyde . .
>
> > surname, Casanova-Bossy-Nova

or maybe Eden-Snake is a more likely spiritual name for you
for an Avatar who cannot be true to a promise faithfully made
yes, Eden-Snake or Casanova Clyde is the name of the Serpent-Spirit
inside your desecrated Temple

> > . . the spirit inside

lurking and sneaking and snaking
around in your Temple . . and peeking out at me
through muddy, milky blue eyes, all strained out with broken promises

> > > and lies
>
> not Altar, who rhymes with all-star
>
> > . . not *Al*tar

> you've even caused me to lose my faith in astrology
> and that's really hitting below the belt
> since I've always felt that astrology holds all of the answers
> or most of them . . the important ones
>
> how could you smash me like this ?
> by causing me to lose my faith in astrology

along with my faith in love

and goodness

and you

your Venus conjuncts my Pluto
by exact degree — then where *are* you ?
why aren't you here ?

shall I read again your Natal chart — or the astrological texts
I know by heart, and can repeat blindfolded ?
                                    those eternal words

            . . in the nativities of lovers
when Venus in one chart conjuncts Pluto in the other
these are karmic relations in love
                        . . a configuration indicating
many lives spent together on this Earth
                        and in other galaxies
. . and the two . . will meet involuntarily
                and never be separated . . never . . except
through death

                it's not true ! it's not true !
                we are separated now by a million miles
                and we are not lucky enough to be dead

if those words are true . . then where *are* you ?

three different mystics told us that we were Essenes together
        also husband and wife in Egypt . . and Atlantis . . and Greece
OH ! they are metaphysical con artists
                like Gemini St. Paul . . and like . . yes
                        like my Guru friend too

            what do I do when astrology stops working
            astrology — the Truth of the Universe ?

what do I do, when phychic readings
turn out to be an illusion . . nothing but delusion ?
what, then, should I — or anyone — do ?

            consult I Ching, the Book of Changes ?

no, scratch the I Ching
all those Orientals ever tell you is that "perseverance furthers"
and I can't even prove they're wrong
because I've never had enough of the stuff to check it out

but even so, assuming they're right — furthers what ?
your ability to bear your solitude ?
is that what "perseverance furthers", I Ching ?

maybe the Essenes knew the answer
but if I really was an Essene with you
then why can't I remember any of the ancient wisdom
we used to teach to others . . together ?

shall I read the Tarot cards . . or investigate witchcraft and voodoo
and make a small creature, who looks like you
                              . . looks like you *now* . . . or *then* ?
and stick long hatpins into its heart ?

                              oh, no !

        I wouldn't want you to bear sudden pain
        when I'm not there beside you, to make it go
        as you healed all my hurts so . . miraculously
        by the simple laying-on-of-your-hand
                              . . as we heal
                                    each other
if not astrology or physic readings
or palmistry, Theosophy, Scientology . . I Ching or Tarot
witchcraft or voodoo, then
                    oh, **CHRIST** !
what would *you* do ?

                    pray ? in what way ?

Christ, look — level with me now
I wrote a poem about you once, on Easter
when I was in Protestant Sunday school
I know it was a little corny, but I was only twelve
and I hadn't sopped up much alchemy yet . . you know ?

    although . . . goodness-mercy-knows I was sensitive enough

            oh ! was I ever sensitive !

but the thing is, you see, I'm trying to write a poem about happiness
I've been trying for the longest, longest time
and I can't seem to get past the part about sadness — and gladness
about — why those two words should rhyme
and then too, there's the Easter story and the resurrection being a lie

once I thought I had it all figured out
then I discovered I couldn't even trust my own judgement
about the height and the eye color of the man I love
        my very own Twin Self
so, how can I have faith in what I once believed I knew
            in Sunday School . . . about Easter . . . and you ?

that's what I want you to level with me about
so you can help me lose all this fear and doubt

      you can tell by my poem
      the one I wrote when I was twelve
           that I like you

I mean, I love you
whether you are ordinary or magic, you see ?

            yes, ordinary — or magic
            you are, somehow, very special to me

so you can tell it to me like it is
not as Christ — but as Jesus, the man

        it won't make any difference in the way I feel about you
      whatever you tell me — even if you confess that Easter was never real
        it won't make any difference in the way I feel
because love is trust, and . . oh ! love is understanding
and forgiving someone's faults and mistakes
                        when they hurt or disappoint you
                           with clumsy clay feet
you said so yourself . .

      about forgiving people with clumsy clay feet

that's why I feel so safe with you
because you know and understand all my Lucy traits
and you love me anyway

      but I have to know the Truth
      right this minute, Jesus — the Truth about you
      so I can decide what I must do
      about continuing to hang around down here
      on this perfectly *un*-marvelous planet . . oh, Christ !

I mean . . Jesus

      please level with me
            please tell me like it is

druid honor, now

did you learn the mystical secrets of what Life really means
when you camped out in the mountains with those spooky Essenes ?

did you really pull off that multiplication miracle
with the loaves of bread . . heal all those lepers . . walk on the water

      and rise from the dead

                    like all those bearded and barefoot
                    apostles said ?

and Mary, the Magdalene

          the one you taught how to pray
          did you really-truly forgive her scarlet sins
          and love her anyway ?

is it true what they say
that you changed water into wine ? whatever for ?
and that you turned the other cheek
for Judas to kiss . . and found the purest joy and bliss
                              in children ?

and, oh, *why* did you trust Peter with those Keys to the Kingdom
when you *knew* he was an Aries, who loses things ?
sometimes I forget things myself
and I can't remember what I'm supposed to do

because, you see, I'm a Ram too, like Peter

     no, not like him

I would never-ever, as he did, deny you three times
before the rooster crowed at dawn

          I would never-never-never . . I mean
          I may be an Aries, and all that
          but I'm no coward, and I would never deny
          anyone I loved, through fear

                    I would never deny anyone I lo . . . .
through fe . . . .
                         that is . . .

well scratch that for now
we'll talk about Peter another time

                    Jesus, I trust you

but I simply must know
was the whole Super-Spectacular New Testament show
only an ancient magician's trick ?

     I simply must know !

          just tell me, please tell me
     I promise I'll believe you . . oh !
          I'll believe whatever you say
     I swear it ! **OH !** I will . . **I WILL, I WILL !**

did someone speak ?

    Jesus — oh, **CHRIST !** why don't you answer me ?
    I need to **SHRIEK !** I need to **SMASH** the already broken toys
    in the cluttered attic of my mind

why do I clutch this tear stained rag doll ?
    why do I still play with toys ?

toys are for little boys . . and little girls
not men and women — but he gave me Raggy himself
he did, he did, and he told me to sleep with her
every night — when he wasn't there
to hold me in his arms . . . and he also told me . .

O ! toys, toys, toys !

    I need a **BIG BANG** noise ! to bear this agony
    I must hear the sound of a **SMASH !**
    as I feel the lash of the whip of memory
    cutting this deep gash
                across the back of my soul
    I want to **SHRIEK !**

        CHRIST ! SPEAK !

THUNDER ! THUNDER !

    oh, wow !

        there it is now ! just what I needed !
        thank you, Jesus — thank you, Christ

    A BIG BANG NOISE ! THUNDER ! POW !

it has started to rain

    . . it has started to rain outside

yes, rain will ease the pain
rain, rain . . . the blessed relief of Nature

    when the bursting clouds release
    their agony of gathered moisture — rain

    splashing silver needles on my upturned face
                from Heaven
heal me, silver rain !

as I lean far, far out the window of the 12th floor
of this Dracula castle . . . in the maniac's tower room
where he came — oh ! not to kneel with me and pray
but came only to cruelly accuse me

and throw me some stale crumbs on visiting day

rain, rain . . splash your blessed relief on my face
and in the open, bleeding cuts of the wounds across the back
of my soul

beat silver needles down on my bowed head
as I try to keep from falling . . falling off the Carousel

rain, rain

why do I still cry, like you ?
blending my weeping with God's own tears
called raindrops

I strongly suspect
that the Sea Scrolls are dead

and therefore, appropriately named
and I wonder . . oh ! how I wonder . . . **POW !**

ANOTHER CRASH OF THUNDER !

why is there such darkness within me, and dread
as this rain pounds down, beating Judas-silver on my head ?

the Judas-silver
of whose betrayal — whose ?

are the Sea Scrolls of the Essenes really dead ?

are they dead too
like me — like you — like Us ?

if they are not dead, the Essenic Sea Scrolls
then why is there such a dearth — of Truth and Light
on this spinning, grinning Earth ?

and what is the goal of my soul ? if, indeed, my soul
still lives . . it seems expired
no longer fired . . by love
or inspired from above

please, Jesus . . not Christ
but Jesus, the man
oh, please, please tell me !

if we were truly Essenes, he and I
then why couldn't he stop the rain that day ?

and why can't I make this rain go away ?

why can't either of us . . remember how ?
if we were really-truly once Essenes

oh, Jesus !

why doesn't Gooober hear me call him

now ?

Account Still Overdrawn — Balance Zero

you didn't call
and neither did I . . call you

so, after three days in the tomb of my haunted 1217 room
I flew back home . . that is, I flew back to New York

but before I left, I mailed a check
to you . . from the airport
a check made out
for one thousand miracles

not kisses, this time
one thousand miracles

and at the bottom
where I signed my name
"Gooober"

I printed: *magic* !

Night Letter

tonight, I sent you a telegram

not by Western Union — they're on strike
I sent my telegram by Eastern Union — or by our own
Far-Easter Union of souls
. . our telepathic union of knowing

and I felt my aura glowing
as I sent my message through
the strong and silver-blue astral cord

still connecting us

        did you feel the tug, as you slept ?

        did you feel the pain, as I wept ?

        did you wake . . and know ?

the message was brief
    two words

           Gooober . .

                don't go

this trip is star-crossed with danger
oh, darling
       please don't go

When in Doubt, Punt

      my mind must have been sleeping
      what is the matter with me ?
      you don't win ball games by weeping

not baseball, not football, not tennis
no . . not even stick ball
like the kids in Brooklyn play in the street

      I am ruled by Mars
      and Mars does not know defeat

Mars always wins

      should I phone you, long distance
      and end this other awful distance between us ?
      you said you were going away to find yourself
      but *you're* not lost — *I'm* the lost one !

      if you go that far away
where I cannot reach you by letter or phone
and leave me back here, all alone . . I'll . . . .

      yes, I'd better write a letter right now
      before it's too late
      and I'll be happy and cheerful
      all bright and sunny and funny, like we used to be

as if . .

     . . as if nothing had ever happened

Don't forget Your Passport and Your Typhoid Shots

    hey, Funny Face !

would you like to fly a kite with me . . or climb a watermelon hill ?

    pitch some Lincoln pennies . . buy a castle in Spain
    hide in a haystack . . expect a miracle . . or walk in the rain ?

slide up a rainbow, slip down a drain . . jump on a space ship
catch a running brook . . . read a symphony
                      or listen to a book ?

would you like to ride a whale to Vail
        sprinkle salt on a coyote's tail
count each other's freckles
    jingle holly on a trolley . . or tumble in the snow ?

no . .

    I guess you'd rather sail off to Mexico
    like a snooty Owl, in a beautiful pea-green boat
    with a pink pussycat . . a jar of wheat germ and honey
                 and sing to a small guitar
      Bon Voyage !

I wish you a montage . . of every good thing
will you be returning home before spring ?

    that's the loveliest time of the year, back here
    you really wouldn't enjoy it across the border
    those Mexican springs are rainy-to-freezing

    and who's going to be there, to take care of you
    when you're lonely and cold
               . . and sneezing ?

Maybe-Maybe-Maybe

                a letter, a letter, a letter !

the postman is a messenger from the gods ! yes !
a messenger from the gods on Mt. Olympus

                    winged Mercury . . bearing love from you to me

your familiar handwriting
            your dear funny left-handed dwarf scrawl
was on the envelope
                        maybe I only dreamed you wrote, that night
                                    with your right hand

my heart skipped a beat
            and glad-tears sprang into my eyes
when I opened it, your letter

            but . . all there was inside
            was my Gooober check for one thousand miracles
            that's all there was

            only my Gooober check — spurned
            un-endorsed on the back, simply returned
            with no message . . . not a single word

            I won't mail the letter I wrote to you last night

    you were right
                    there's no more magic
            *
    magic
    magic

        magi
        magi

            mag

                ma

                m
                 a
                  g
                   i
                    c
                m
              a
            g
              i
            c   Canto Seventeen ☆ 707

Unanswered Question

why do I remember now
the very last words you spoke

    the very last thing you said

the really very last thing

    before you climbed into your car, and closed the door
        switched on the ignition — and backed up, by the shed
    then turned your Bug down the alley
    behind our funny crooked house . . and drove away ?

the really very last thing
was a question . . asked more of yourself
or of the silent Universe
        than of me

a question you seemed to ask
of some entity unseen
        you asked . .

        "what does it mean ?
          what does it all mean ?"

    then gave me a look . . so deep
    one last, long look of knowing
    and closed the door . .

    "Gooober, look !
it's snowing . . .

        oh, dark and thunderous February day
        that I watched you drive away . .

CANTO EIGHTEEN

When you despair of Spirit's master plan,
When naught looks firm and the future's rim is dark,
When all seems fallen from what once began
In greater joy, when nothing hits the mark —

Then is the time to know that all is well
Despite that all's not known, nor yet surmised.

Then is the hour, beloved one, to feel the swell
Of silent tides grow full, their sands surprised
By rising beachheads and advancing shoals,
The waves of your soul's future, O but see,
Carving a nearer path to long-sought goals.

Instead of self-bound lakes you'll have the sea —
Before you Love's Ocean, pure and deep and vast,
To carry you to joy beyond all past !

Kyril Demys (Musaios)
Prismatic Voices

he does not wish to write . . or call

he does not wish to write
a Happiness poem with me
not now — not ever

                              he is on a ship, a ship

          he has sailed away One Fine Day
          oh, Un Bel Di, Un Bel Di !
                    Lt. Pinkerton is gone
          he has sailed away to sea

cry, Butterfly, cry . . . , little orange blossom, once his special rose
cry, Butterfly, cry . . . , little orange blossom
                              who never wore orange blossoms
          or a white veil, in a church
          who was only a bride once
          through the mercy of a Justice of the Peace
          no, only the bride of Justice
                              there is no Peace
cry, Butterfly, cry
          cry, small baby-wife of his . . oh, baby-wife
dear little baby-wife-of-mine, he said

          that's what Lt. Pinkerton said . . and lied

cry, dear-little-baby-wife . . who never wore orange blossoms
oh ! cry as that other poor Butterfly cried

                    just before she died

                    just before she stabbed a knife
                    into her heart — and died
                              because he lied
cry, Butterfly, cry !
for it will do no good now . . to sing your *Un Bel Di*
useless, futile to sing the hopeful lyric
that you will "hide a bit to tease him" . . when he returns

cry, poor Butterfly, cry !
your dreams are all behind you
                         and it will do no good
                              to hide a bit to tease him
          you no longer please him

poor Butterfly, little-no-orange-blossom
ex-dear-little-baby-wife of his

cry, Butterfly, on this shadowed Un Bel Di

    Lt. Pinkerton has set your heart free
    and has sailed away to sea
    he has sailed beyond the point of no return . . oh !
    far, far beyond the point of no return

and his ship . . is not called the *Abraham Lincoln*
as was the ship of the original, peripatetic Pinkerton
who made the other Butterfly cry

                nor is it called the *Atlantis*
                as once before

    as just before he found you
    deep in a dream, on an astral trip
    no, not the *Atlantis* Ship
    on which he had such a perfectly marvelous float
                   on the ocean
      except . . for the pain
      in his tooth
          and the lump in his throat

which throbbed for him, and for you
as the *Atlantis* sailed past the shore, where you sat in the sand
so sad and blue . . and felt his pain . . as he felt yours

  what cruel star were you trying to reach
on that Un Bel Di in Laguna Beach
          . . you and your Pinkerton sailor, poor Butterfly ?

are you certain that he, too, is not a Gemini ?
did you ask to see his birth certificate ?
          as he asked to see your driver's license ?

you do not know for sure that he is not a Gemini
cry, Butterfly, cry — at least you know

    he once lived within the Temple of Gemini
    poor, foolish, trusting Butterfly

but you do not know if his present name
is Altar — Casanova Clyde — or Eden-Snake

    nor do you know the name of his ship
    the name of the ship on which he sails today

    the ship on which he is the Master
    of his new Destiny

NO !   the name of his ship is not . . the *Abraham Lincoln*
        on which that other perfidious Pinkerton sailed

        nor is it — this time — the *Atlantis*

not the *Abraham Lincoln*
nor the *Atlantis*

        he is searching for a new star, this phony Altar
        while you pursue your own Star Quest of Truth
        nor does he any longer feel a pain in his tooth
            he feels no regret
        for his desertion . . for his broken promise

    you don't know the name — or even the true and hidden *purpose*
    of his present Ship of Destiny

    you do not know where he sails
                to which far distant shore
cry, Butterfly, cry !

your midnight-miracle-dream-of-spring . . is dead
you will see this perfidious Pinkerton no more
he is already loving another dear-little-baby-wife
on some unknown distant shore
                and you will see him
                no more . . no more

oh ! un bel di
you will not see
him return

        don't cry, rejected butterfly
            dear little-no-orange-blossom
don't cry

        burn, baby-wife, burn

YES ! BURN, BABY, BURN !

do not be a fool, and cry
poor trusting Butterfly, burn with anger — **YES, BURN**
and **KNOW** he will never return

        Fire is your element — Fire !
        not the weak water of tears

        no, Water is not your element
        Fire is your element — **FIRE !**

        the Fire of both Heaven and hell

                    the knife ?
                    dear-little-no-blossom-baby-wife
                    the knife ?

NO . . . BURN BABY BURN !

    and live to tell

        he will not return . . he'll never return
              burn, baby burn !
      there is no Justice — there is no Peace

where is your pride ? you were never his bride
never a bride, in a church with a veil . . white veil

        remember Vail, Remember Vail

         remember your pride !

you don't even know the name of the ship
on which he is questing for a star
nor do you know its destination . . or its purpose
you only know that he sails on it as the Master
                  of his own goal
      but not the Master of your soul !

  don't cry, poor trusting Butterfly
burn, baby, burn . . .
         and live to tell

yes, live to tell

        no, I will not burn or flame

I shall not burn or flame
with uncontrolled hysteria

      I will remain cool and sure and calm and steady

        he was never an Essene
        neither of us were ever Essenes
        none of those mystical dreams
          were real
this is real !
right now — *this* is real

    oh ! Life is real . . . . and Life is earnest
    and the grave is its only goal

      he may be the Captain — he may be the Master
      of the ship of Destiny, on which he quests for a star

but he is not — never was — and never shall be

the Master of **MY** soul !

and the poet, who wrote those lines . . claiming that the grave is *not*
the goal of the soul . . he lied, he lied !

the grave is the *only* goal !
and *no one* is Master of *my* soul !

DO YOU HEAR THAT, JESUS ?
OR ARE YOU DEAF ?

is that why you never
hear my prayers ?

DO YOU HEAR THAT, JESUS ?

no, forget it, Jesus . . just forget it
this is a case for the Highest Judge of all

this is a case to be heard and judged
by the Father, not the son

yes, God — oh ! God is the only one
to judge this case

God, just see what he has done !
he has sailed away, and left me all alone
my Comforter has sailed away to sea
in a beautiful, pea-green boat
without even a post card or a daisy- note

to have a perfectly marvelous float
on the ocean
. . without me

oh, God, just see what he has done ! he has sailed far away

oh, black black day !   he has sailed away . . to sea

Un Bel Di !

Lt. Pinkerton, God . . has gone off again . . to sea
he is out there sailing

on a ship called Perfidy
on a ship called Deception
on a ship called Danger
on a ship called Stranger

on a ship called . . Endless Quest
on a ship called . . Falling Star

on a ship called . . Orange Blossoms

AND HE DOESN'T EVEN HAVE A LICENSE TO PILOT A SHIP !

do you know that, God ?

HE HAS NO LICENSE
TO PILOT HIS SHIP OF DESTINY !

he has only a license to drive a car
and to drive me mad
but he has no license to pilot a ship

    from where did he get his license
    to pilot his perfidious ship of Destiny away from me ?
    did John, the Baptist — or the Heavenly Hosts
                                or maybe Peter
    give him such a treacherous license ?

perhaps You — yes, You, God ! or maybe your son
or your mutual friend, the Holy Ghost
gave him license to pilot his ship of Destiny

        not Headless John or Butterfingers Peter

yes, where else, God — where else could he get such license
except from Your own sneak-flunky — the Holy Ghost
the one up there in your Heaven crowd I've always mistrusted
                             the most
Jesus wouldn't have done it
    no, Jesus would never give anyone license to hurt
so Jesus didn't give him license to pilot that perfidious ship

to which one, then
should I drink a toast

    to celebrate the blessing of being set free
    by Lt. Pinkerton, who is off to sea

    to which one shall I drink a vodka toast ?

    to the Father
        to the son
            or to the Holy Ghost ?

is that blasphemy ?
    is it ?

have I committed a cardinal sin ?
am I a blasphemous Ram ?
do You intend to slam . . the Gates of Hell

                    on my soul ?

ah ! but you forget, God
I am at home in Fire and Flame
Fire is my element !

and when that Heaven-Snob, Saint Peter
asks me for my name
before he sends me down below — I want You to know
yes, I want You to know
that I'll ask Peter for *his* identification

                    show me
                    your driver's license
                    Peter, old chap !

do you have a driver's license, Peter ?
what license did you have to lose those keys ?
what license did you have to deny him — three times ?

          you ask my name ?

               you want my identification ?
               the identity of the me-of-me ?

I'LL TELL YOU MY NAME !

I do not fear Hell's flame
I can identify myself

               my name is . .
     . . my name is

          my name is Alice-Mary

yes, that's what he told me
that first night
when he promised to make it snow
just by wishing it so
     . . your name is Alice-Mary, he said
and a few more I could mention

          my name is Alice-Mary . . Mary-Odd . . Alice Todd
          Mary-Smith . . Alice-Jones . . Mary-Very-Odd
          Alice Brown . . Alice Small . . Mary-Tall
          Allie, like Nanoo
          Mary-Marble . . Mary-Green . . Mary-Grass
               Alice-Through-The-Looking-Glass

716 ☆ Canto Eighteen

Alice-Berry . . Mary-Peters . . Alice-Terry
Marilyn Odd . . Alice-Todd . . Mary-Jean
Norma-Jean . . Mary-Baker . . . Alice-Eddy
Mary-Mary-Quite-Contrary

Alice-Seeking . . Mary-Sleeping . . Alice-Odd
Mary-Fallen-From-The-Hand-Of-God

yes, Mary-Mary-Quite-Contrary
or any other Mary
you may find in a rhyming dictionary
Alice-Gold . . Mary-Brass
Marilyn-Through-The-Looking-Glass
Alice-Lost-And-Very-Odd
Mary-Fallen-From-The-Hand-Of
God

my name is Alice-Mary

and I am a Brown Owl

ask Giant-Druid-Gooober Mike Todd !
he can identify
a super star destined to play a role
on the stage of Dante's roaring Inferno

and is it not odd, God — and Peter
is it not odd, when you consider the rhyme and meter
that Alice lexigrams into ice ?

and Mary, spelled backwards, is **YRAM ?**
just remove the **Y** — for You, God
and is it not odd, that what is left is **RAM ?**

a ram with bent horns
a rose with broken thorns
a porcupine without a single quill

BUT I STILL HAVE MY WILL !

yes, I can identify myself to You God
my name is Alice-Mary
Alice-Ice and Mary Yram

and without the **Y** for You
my name is **RAM** spelled backwards — **MAR**
but I am not a lost star
wandering through the skies
my name is **MAR**
and I am not foolish — I am wise
can You not see . . I am a Brown Owl in disguise ?

I do not fear Butterfingers Peter
who lost the Keys to the Kingdom
no ! I will not fall on my knees before Peter
in quaking fear

          and I'm not afraid of Old Man Saturn either
          who thinks he's so tough
          just because he rules all the Capricorn Goats
          and the Hebrews — and Wisdom — and Maturity

why should I, a strong Ram
be afraid of a stern old man called Saturn
who rules Howard Hughes — and all the other billygoats ?

and who up there, in your Seven-Serpent-Heaven
yes, who up there in your ghost town
          or in your Heavenly Host town
wears the official
nightgown
      long white robe
    or ludicrous night-white-shirt of hurt ?

which one up there rules perfidious boats
and an imaginary butterfly feather that floats
             floats
             floats

WHO RULES DANGEROUS PINKERTON BOATS ?

if Peter is in charge of Lost and Found Keys — mostly lost
and Old Man Saturn rules the Hebrews, Hughes and the Goats
then who rules this single butterfly feather
that floats and floats and floats . . and threatens to destroy me ?

who rules perfidious boats
and anything at all that floats . . away

Neptune ?
        Neptune ? I do not fear the sneaky ruler of Pisces
        with sea-weed in his hair
        with algae-green seaweed coiled in his serpenty curls

I face the Highest Judge of all
with **MARS** as my bodyguard — yes, **MARS** !
my quadruple ruler

do You think, with **MARS** beside me
that I fear the retribution of hell ?

MARS !   the vital thrust
      the searing energy

the sharp sword
the Undefeated Warrior . . **MARS** !

he is . . .
Mars is my friend
yes, Mars is my only loyal friend

I will face all your planets — all your galaxies and solar systems
I will face all your pale and trembling stars
with the flaming sword of **MARS** !
MARS ! who has my own
fierce pride and courage

and together, Mars and I shall win a Victory
over both Heaven and hell
Mars ! Mars ! Mars ! is the strongest of all your stars !

like the Bill from Carousel
I say to You, God — the Almighty

I reckon my sins are good **BIG BANG** ! sins
and the punishment won't be small
so take me before the Highest Throne
and let me be judged by the Highest Judge of all

MARS will save me !

and one last thing, God
one last thing . .

there will never be another April
I mean . . spring . . will never come again

and my *Love is Eternal* ring, like spring
is gone forever
no, not gone . . neither of them were ever real
both were only brass
. . he does not wish to write
a Happiness poem with me
he sailed away, oh ! *Un Bel Di*
and is sharing the beauty of spring
with another Butterfly . . somewhere

on a shore unknown to me
he is loving another . . on some distant shore

OH, GOD !
I do not believe in u anymore

I do not believe in u

Lucifer Is Not Unlisted

I wait here
for the erotic thrill
of Satan's embrace
to obsess me

                for the fiery chill of hell
                to possess me

for the mad miracle
of insanity to claim me

                to Satan, I pray

    I am not afraid

    I am not alone

                the Devil, they say
                takes care of his own

Hell Has a Telephone, Unlike Heaven

the Carousel is spinning dizzily
round and round and round
faster and faster and faster and faster

when I pray to my new god, Satan, he hears — and answers instantly
no unlisted, unpublished telephone numbers for Satan-Seth-Set
                         and his impish crew
I telephoned the Devil this morning
I dialed Satan-Set, fighting for my very survival

    struggling, for some reason, to find the strength not to die
    but why ? oblivion would be far more peaceful

yes, the blessing of death . . but with my final breath
                     I called the Devil
praying cursed incantations
and he heard me
oh ! Set-Satan answered on the very first ring !

he promised, swearing on Dado's fire and brimstone
that from this day forward, my eyes would be dry
for I would have no need to cry — ever again

he whispered sensually into my ear
I need no longer be tortured by unrewarded faith and loyalty

for I was finally free !

and I knew, then, he was there
my new god, Satan — watching over me

oh ! what beautiful poetry Hades creates !
perhaps not making Life rhyme
but at least giving scanning and meter to death

I have discarded Easter as my favorite time
and now I play . . on my new, adopted holiday
enjoying pure gladness, unmixed with sadness — on Halloween !

Halloween even rhymes with Essene
no more the celebration of a false resurrection
my new holiday does not symbolize a silent tomb
it's filled with the friendly sounds
of screeching Black Cats . . . who do my bidding

not with the pitiful, weak mewing
of impotent puff-ball kittens, like Love and Peace
my Black Cats can release
any kind of magic I wish
and my new friends
. . the Halloween goblins

are infinitely more powerful than the frail Holy Ghost
whether she-he be a masculine or a feminine freak
no, my goblins are not weak
they are all virile males, with strength to haunt
not trembling wraiths, who pale and faint in a crisis
and teach the heart only un-answered want

with Satan-Set, there are no unanswered prayers
each plea is answered immediately
with a new diabolical scheme, that makes me scream
with laughter and sardonic amusement

Hell rhymes with a Wishing Well !
where imps hide in murky waters, hearing every penny splash
greedily gobbling coins of wishes
making them come true

as long as I do not wish for . . you
the only, only wish they refuse to grant

but who cares ! the whole sweet world, decaying, they've promised me
if I will but turn my futile, impotent Happiness poem, called *Gooberz*

into an Ode to Satan-Set — and tell everything I have learned
                    on my Star Quest
while being so cruelly scarred and burned

Hell also rhymes with **TELL** . . tell the truth, the truth, the truth !
you lied about the pain in your tooth ! you lied, you lied !
and now you're sharing spring with another, on some far away shore

        but I need not grieve anymore
                    for I am free

FREE ! FREE ! FREE !

        free of all my former misplaced faith in you
        come join me, faithless, cold and cruel lover !
            let us drown together in this Devil's Wishing Well
        come ! join me in Hell
                    and let us drown together . . together

Satan has lovingly warned me to be careful
so that nevermore . . oh ! nevermore, quoth this Raven to me
will I be ripped and torn and crushed . . by a forked-tongue Judas kiss
the kiss of a hiSSing traitor . . to our vows of eternal faithfulness

yes, Satan has kindly warned me . . wisely
to hesitate, before it's too late
don't trust, don't trust — never, never, never believe
count to ten before you give your heart away

then the Devil, Satan-Set
whispered more sensual, unthinkable evil into my inner ear
with the hiSSing of a Serpent, he told me what to do

        "take a sharp knife" . . he said

and I did

        I did exactly as my new god commanded
                    I took my foolish, childish gifts from you
        Algae, ugly-ugly rabbit . . sickening shade of seaweed green
        and Raggy . . Raggedy Ann without the 'e'
        staring, with button-brown eyes, a forgiving smile at me

as I slashed them coldly into a total of 14 pieces
obeying each word my new god said

        and my own heart ripped and bled
        with each cruel slash of the knife

I amputated first Raggy's arms and legs
but could not scar or touch her smiling, forgiving face

finally, Algae . .

I sliced off his funny-bunny ears, his floppy feet
split open his plump chest . .

                             and saw no heart there
        only cotton padding

when I gazed upon my handiwork, I saw . . . . . O ! I saw
on Raggy's breast, the bright red heart
with the words I Love You printed on it

                             . . *I love you*

and hot, scalding tears pounded in my ears
damned up there . . damned damned damned tears
refusing to fall from my eyes, dry as desert sands, my eyes
but burning, stinging . . from the unshed tears

then I looked once more upon this terrible thing I had done
still with dry eyes . . for Satan whispered . . . now you are free !
        and be warned to guard your heart

lest you make it vulnerable to physic attack again
from a hiSSing Eden-snake, named Altar
by wearing it openly and trustingly on your sleeve

kind, compassionate, wise and understanding Satan
murmurs silken truth into my inner ear
                        and says to me, so low and clear

                        Believe rhymes with Grieve !

    AMEN !

Glory be to Je — -

    Glory be to the Devil !

Big Potato had it right
he just got a little mixed up with the name — that's all

    a case of mistaken identity again

yes, mistaken identity . . suddenly
I had a new and urgent request to make of the Devil
and surely he could help !

my mind has so long been tortured by the doubting
                        of its own judgement
by the frightening fact
that I had been so entranced with . . and tranced by

this entity I once called Gooober
that I was blind to the actual color of his eyes . . . and his height
not to mention my inability
                              to tell his left hand from his right

and Satan answered my prayer swiftly, as usual
assisting me to locate someone long experienced in such matters
as snooping and sleuthing . . and spying on others
                              for a fee
and this calm, cool and efficient professional
was able to obtain for me . . all the papers I requested

        a copy of your driver's license
        the one in California — and the one in England
        the records of your enlistment in the National Guard

also . . the pertinent records pertaining to
                              your college years at Cal Poly
oh, thank you, Satan
              thank you-thank you !

for returning, unharmed, to me — my sanity
and self respect
I was not wrong, I was not wrong !

        I am so joyous over this, I may even write a song
        called *I Was Right ! I Was Not Wrong* !

for, every single record I obtained, with the Devil's aid
bore the very information I had so long prayed
                              would return my faith — in me

after your name . . . on each document of record
were listed various vital statistics . . . and other data

and . . each and every one of these
unmistakably gave your eye color as green
                              your height as six-foot-two
and noted also, that you had
                    always been left-handed

no, not ambidextrous, for the space with those words printed
had not been checked on any of the forms
although the observation of your being left-handed
was clearly marked on all of them

        oh, it's true, it's true ! it's true !
        the man I knew — as you
        is left-handed, with green eyes — and is six-foot-two

not right-handed, or ambidextrous

with eyes of milky blue . . and only six feet tall

    I was so elated with this discovery
    of the certain and official proof of my powers of observation
    so blessed with the knowledge
    that I had not hallucinated, nor idealized you
    as you so cruelly insinuated on that night
                    in our haunted miracle room

so elated . . . that I nearly believed
this blessing had been sent by the Higher Angels of ourselves
                          or by God
no . . there is no God
this prayer had been answered by the Devil

    . . or at the very least
he was the one responsible for the methods of obtaining it
and as the Catholic Church does teach . . the end
                    justifies the means
oh ! how cruel of you
to accuse me of idealizing what I wished you to be
that frightening night in California . .

                  but . . how could it
                      have been *you*
                that night ?

did my eyes deceive me ? **NO !**
I now have proof that my eyes and heart and mind
are fully intact — and do not easily fall into error

    I know the answer to this mystery
    Presto ! the Devil has told me the solution !

yes, Presto ! the Devil has told me so !

you were maliciously playing a game of mental chess
to break my spirit and confuse my mind
thinking you could make me blind . . blind enough, temporarily
to believe that you possessed blue eyes — and were a shorter man
                      than I remembered
so you could piece together your diabolical scheme
to make me feel like a squeaking mouse
    you were capable of such hypnotic trickery
this I knew from the way you stared at me

                were you, perhaps, a hypnotist
                or a student of black magic ?

that's even worse than having been faithless and untrue
O ! how could I ever have believed in or loved one such as you ?

who so cruelly played with my mind
when I only flew to you . . to say goodbye with dignity

disguising yourself as a messenger from Western Union
to set the deceptive mood for the cruel game
                                    of mental chess you planned to play
I remember how I wondered
what it was you feared in me . . that night

what fear it was which kept you so long away
and caused you to say . . at the door . . Western Union
now I know what it was you feared
you feared that I might not be as willing a victim as you hoped

of course, that's the obvious answer
your eyes were just as green that night as they had always been
and you were just as tall — as you really are
but from some dark depths, from the other side of midnight
using some cursed black-magic-alchemy — and hypnosis
you managed to cause yourself to *appear* differently to me
to lay the foundation for your attempt
                                    to cause me to doubt my own eyes

perhaps you thought this would be
an easier way to make certain we would never see each other again
if you were able to humiliate me
and make me ashamed of having idealized you
                                    into what I wished you to be
            as for your hand . .

I was so crushed and numb that night
that I hardly noticed the writing on the piece of paper
and even now, have no idea where the note you wrote . . might be

            oh, you must have practiced for days
            so that you would look natural, and appear to be at ease
            when writing with the right — but wrong — hand
            while I watched . . while I could see

if I had the note you wrote, with your friend's address
it might tell me something, but . . .
                                    now I remember
I impulsively tore it up
before I left to fly back to New York
                                    and threw away the pieces

            why did I not save it ?

you see ? Satan-Set sensually whispered into my inner ear . . . .
this man you knew as Gooober . . was more evil

a more negative and unevolved Earthling than you

ever dared to fear

capable of the darkest of deceptions
you are well rid of him . .

he was not worth a single tear
you shed for him

yes, yes, I am well rid of you, Eden-Snake
how could you have done this to me ?

never mind, now , at last, I am free
free of you — and free of love

I lift mine eyes, oh ! not above
no, I cast mine eyes far, far below

and know

as I watch the silent telephone
that the Devil takes care of his own

do you hear that, Jesus ?

you, with the unlisted telephone

my new god, Satan, is loyal — true

and unlike you

the devil takes care of his own

Don't Go — Oh, No — Don't Go

hear me squeak
in agony

hear me, all you singing saints
who praise the Holy Spirit, the Father and the Son
the mystery Trinity of Three-in-One

look at me

all you rainbow choirs of Heavenly Hosts
praising Him from Whom all blessings flow
don't ring down the curtain yet

on the Final Act of my Big Bang farewell — don't go
please stay — at least till the end of the show

look at me, all you saints and mystical hosts

    look at me, possessed by ethereal astral ghosts
    possessed, I tell you, possessed !
                        and Mars-obsessed
    obsessed by mighty, fiery Mars
    no longer blessed by the gentle touch of Oober stars

        no longer blessed, I am possessed
             I am obsessed

bleSSed ?
      poSSeSSed ?
            obSeSSed ?

hiSS ! hiSS ! what is this hiSSing Serpent I hear in my inner ear ?

    the hiSSing of a Serpent . . yes, the Serpent 'S'

oh, how ridiculously insane, how positively inane
for both hiSS and kiSS to contain . . . a double Serpent S

does the Same Eden Snake, then . . coil itSelf around the meaning
             of all theSe wordS ?
is a Serpent hiSSing, while loverS are kiSSing ?
and iS Satan, then, obSeSSing . . while God is bleSSing ?

    there is no double Serpent S . . in Heaven

and I dreamed one night, so clearly
that I nearly believed it not to be a dream

    . . I dreamt that those entities we Earthlings call Martians
    who live, it's said, upon the planet we call Mars

              . . call their home
                  their proud, red Planet
Massar
      MaSSar ?   it rhymes with Star

does the eternal coil of that Eden Snake Serpent
even Slither itSelf around MarS — MaSSar
the proud, red Star — MaSSar — who is my only really-truly friend ?

is this final winter season . . the end of all sanity and reason ?
is this Serpent-HiSSing the end of even MarS — MaSSar

the proud, red Star — my only really-truly friend ?

double SS coiling Serpent, Stop hiSSing in my inner ear
and trying to Snake yourSelf around my Sacred Third Eye
don't try . . to coil and snake yourSelf
                              around my Third Eye
I refuSe to liSten
to your inSiStent hiSSing !

        look at me, all you Saints . . look at me !

I am an angel, but from me no bleSSingS flow . . oh !

        do not praise me, only raise me
        so I can grow — and know

                                I am a Fallen Angel

        no . . lower case, don't try to save face

            I am an angel, fallen

lost somewhere out there, among the stars
of a distant, silent, half-forgotten galaxy

            oh, look at me !

Mary-Through-The-Looking-Glass
Alice-Mary-Quite-Contrary-And-Very-Odd

        fallen from the hand of God

Et Tu — You Too ?

first the Father, then the son — and the Holy Ghost
one-by-one-by-one
like the tiny druid three . . have all deserted me
                              and gone
then Satan himself — and even Mars-Massar
my only really-truly friend

        all have forsaken me now, at the end
        during the last Act
        of my Super-Spectacular Big Bang show
        with me as the Super Star

oh ! even my only-when-I'm-scared-and-lonely
my really-truly best and only-when-I'm-lonely friend

       Mars — Massar

did not stay to see me play the starring role
in the final Act of my Big Bang show
every planet and star . . yes, they have all forsaken me
                    at the end
      and you Al-tar ?

et tu ?

      you too . . Brutus ?

et tu, my Comforter ?
oh, please, Goob, not you too — not you
you were so good and kind and gentle
          so silvery-wise

NO ! you were not kind and good, my clawing Lion
you were only a fake cigar store Indian
not carved from the deep-green-cool of forest pine
you were made from cheap, second-hand wood
            you were not kind and good

you were never really my Oober Valentine
never really — not even nearly — mine

      you had only a supporting role to play
          you possessed no magical druid art
     only the cruelty to play a cosmic part
                . . a Comforter's part
    an Al-tar all-star's part
           to smash my heart

yes, you had only a small cosmic role to play
and you had the unkindness to pretend you would stay
to promise me you would always, always stay
        to help me find the way . . and even pray with me
but after we prayed . . . and
after you played your part in the Second Act
you left me all alone
beside a silent telephone . . and left no understudy

    you are not of the theatre
    and do not believe that the show must go on
      you played your part
    then went away and broke my heart

                do you know you broke my heart ?
                you broke more than my heart, you broke my spirit
                                                    my pride

and left me so dreadfully lonely
so Halloween-scary-empty-inside

                and I have died

I tell you, I have died
only I have just not laid myself yet, down to rest
Gooober-Gooober-Gooober
you have broken my heart, my spirit and my pride

                and I have died

        because you've left me with only the cold grave as my goal
        you have . . . destroyed my soul

to break my heart and pride and spirit — to destroy my soul
was this your goal ? your mission of Love and Peace on Earth ?
then your mission has been accomplished
and you may return to whatever galaxy or star you call home

                oh, Goob . .

                        I thought your home
                        was here in my arms

is that not so ?
did you not say to me . . that night in Pismo Beach
when you were so late coming home

                                "darling . . my only love
                                my druid sprite — Lucy wench
                                spunky mouse-spouse
                                please don't be frightened
                                if I ever leave our house again
                                and forget to tell you
                                                when I will return

                        when will you learn ?
                                        do you not know
                                that the circle of your arms
                                is the home I cannot ever leave
                                however far away I go ?"

oh, Gooober !
                is that not so ?

        remember ?

                        Canto Eighteen ☆ 731

Quiet, Quiet — Shhh !

       shhh !

shhh !

       Satan is sleeping

            he is asleep . . I can hear him snoring

if he is fast asleep
perhaps ignoring . . my thoughts

      then, maybe I might play that old game
      that silly, foolish, childish game
      with the pulsing of the Universe . . one more time

          . . . just one more time

shhh !
      don't wake Satan
          I am taking a brief respite from hell
    shh !

             I am squeezing my eyes tightly shut
          and asking the Universe for a sign
                    from you

     shh !
    if Satan awakens
       he will be angry

Sh . . S-Serpent-Saturn ?
         Shhh ?

    Shhh !

I am asking someone . . someone
higher above me than I am now able to see
to give a sign to me

of what you are thinking
what you are doing
at this moment

       some message
       from you to me
              from wherever you are
              right now . . . . . .

some sign . . . . . .

some Valentine . . of contact . . of communication
between our souls

                    so torn and bleeding

mine . . so needing

            and yours ?

no words came from my lips, but my heart tried hard to pray
then I heard a noise outside my door . . in the hallway

        someone has left . . something at my door . . ?
        with my shaking hand on the lock

                    I opened it, in mild shock
                    and surprise

            it was not the Valentine man
        from the Land of Love

Dadoo disguised
        from my innocent eyes
as in childhood

                        who left something outside my door
                        . . . just the nice, but ordinary mailman

        and he had left no message of love
        at my door . . no letter . . no post card

not even . . a daisy note
        from you

            I cried . .
                inside

and walked back into my lonely room
clutching my comic Valentine . . that could not make love rhyme

a comic Valentine

        the mailman's weekly delivery
        of a magazine called
                        TIME

a magazine called **TIME**
dated July 24th, 1972

        with a photo on the cover, of two men making wishes
        two men — one named McGovern

his smiling running mate . . unknown to me

who cares what madmen
drive this waning planet further into destruction ?
with either evil — or good — intent

bad men . . good men
stupid men . . or wise men
        who cares ?

                they cannot halt
                the cataclysm coming to the world
                        and to my soul

yes, both geological and political cataclysms
are surely coming . . possibly too late to be prevented
by the magical power of Oober love
                        but . . what care I ?

        I am not running
        for office . . or away from the end

I face the facts
and no longer pretend

                that you and I, together
                might make a miracle for the planet Earth
                a miracle fashioned of love . . to give

                        a miracle rhyming with . . forgive

I am the Devil's disciple now
a realist . . yes, a realist

                these political figures
                can give me no sign to make Life rhyme

                then I glanced once more
                at the brightly colored cover of . . **TIME**

        and saw an old rhyme
from long, long ago

                stretched across the magazine's cover
                in a yellow ribbon banner . . . the words were printed

                In Quest of a Second Miracle

Look To the Rainbow

in quest of a second miracle ?
when there are no such things as miracles ?
oh, no, no, no, no, no, !

                        numb, I was . . numb

then suddenly struck
with a stab of pain impossible to describe
it seared my beingness with a more consuming flame
than the receding fires of hell itself

      a flame too scorching, an agony too torturous to tell
      and I shouted, dry-eyed still, into Heaven's silent skies

don't send me more lies ! don't send me more lies !

      don't send me on a quest for a second miracle

then I stared for one thousand years — from the Pisces Age
                                 to the Aquarian
I stared across one thousand years
at my comic Valentine . . called **TIME**

        with its half-forgotten rhyme
streaming across the cover in a yellow ribbon of promise

until finally . .

      some power higher than Satan . . . higher, higher
      at last released my damned-up tears
      and they flowed down in a cleansing stream across my face

    then . . .

        . . we are climbing
              Jacob's ladder, ladder . . we are
Grace Carpenter's voice
sang softly into my inner ear

♪ *we are climbing . . higher, higher . . soldiers . . of the cross*

I was in the Carpenter kitchen
    freezing-cold outside . . warm, cozy fire

hot chocolate simmering, fragrant
                    . . Grace singing
toasting my toes . .
                Good Morning, Little Potato !
here's a kiss . .
        for the tip of your nose . .
for my special rose . .
                    we are climbing . . higher . . higher

        the sound of Grace's voice
fell lower . . then rose
                sweet and clear . . into my ear

        . . *swing low, sweet chariot*
                    . . *comin' for to carry me home*
            I look over Jordan, and what do I see ?

                nobody knows the trouble I've seen
nobody knows . .
            but Jesus
                        nobody knows . . but Jesus . . .

. . . and Grace's song
            her gentle voice
then changed into tones
        of fading organ chords
                    . . as I heard Dado's voice
                        smelled his greasy garage
felt the touch of his work-worn hands
on my tear-stained cheek

                . . *don't cry, Yellow Wax, don't cry*

        . . *I come to the garden alone*
while the dew
            . . *is still on the roses*

                and the voice I hear, falling in my ear
. . . *the son of God*
            dis-clo-o-ses
                    . . *and he walks with me*

. . . *and he talks with me*
            and he tells me

. . I am his own

see the pretty tree, Yellow Wax ?
*   ***

*   see the snow ?   *   catch a falling snowflake !*
*   *
*   . . the first snow*   *
*   *   *
*   *
*   *   we'll make a snowman !*
he died for you and me, Yellow Wax   *   *
see the pretty Christmas tree ?   *   *
*   *   *
*   *
*   *
then St. Raphael's burst upon my heart   *
like a streaming rosary of midnight sun   *

      . . . these beads are for you, little one

so you will never lose
    your love for Jesus . . .

O ! little town of Bethlehem

* . . how still we see thee lie . . as in*

thy deep and dreamless sleep
the silent stars go by
*   . . yet in thy dark streets shineth*
*   an everlasting light*
   freezing cold outside

falling snowflakes . .

     Good Morning, Little Potato !
      . . a kiss on the tip of your nose

  . . oh, darling, you are my special, unique rose

     Goob, stop twisting your toes !
go smell a rose !

   . . may I have this first dance
with you ?
     hail, Mary ! full of grace . . .
Mary, full of grace . .

   soft, creamy-tan face
     framed in Irish lace
and her hands
   always busy . . with needle and thread
     and the fire in the kitchen
. . . to bake tomorrow's bread

. . . oh ! I love that man so

    I guess I loved him
      . . before I was born

and I'll go on loving him after I die . . .

      I love that woman so
        . . it makes me want to cry
   but don't tell her   oh, me . . oh, my !
      Little Potato . .

don't tell her, do you hear ?

        don't tell, Little Potato . .

   . . . don't tell

      and I felt it receding far away . . hell

. . we are climbing
higher, higher . .

      . . I come to the garden alone
      while the dew . . . is still on the roses

   . . . he died for you and for me, Yellow Wax
see the pretty Christmas tree ?

   I rose from the altar of the cedar chest
   a great peace flooding in my breast
   and I searched, till I found a needle and thread

      then gently gently gently

I lifted the torn parts and pieces of Raggy and Algae
from the casket box where I had placed them
to be mailed to you
      . . for you to bury

    tenderly, I placed them on my knees
and kissed each one softly . . a gentle snowflake kiss
to make all the pain go away

     and whispered into their warm ears

    "love is an anesthetic
  shhh !
    don't cry . . it won't hurt"

and I sewed, with needle and thread
teeny-tiny stitches of love and healing

and put them back together again
stronger then new

                oh ! much stronger than new

in the healing, becoming much stronger
as Gooober told me broken bones always do

       then, kneeling
           with Raggy and Algae both smiling at me,
    forgiving

I prayed . . forgiving too

       dear Jesus . . please guide us
       on our quest for a second miracle

Part   Four

THE KEYS TO THE KINGDOM

CANTO NINETEEN

Yesterday, late afternoon, I saw your faith
Burning rose and golden
In the clouds of heaven.
Today I know your sure avowal
In the glowing victory
Of ancient hero-wanderings, —

Your heart sings magic,
I listen, waiting — to act . . for us — out there.
Tomorrow is no dream-promise of the sun sinking,
Tomorrow is a sword that I hold in my hand today :
Weeping lives lie waiting in the past-time,
To be fashioned anew by a sword-kiss.

$$* * *$$

No bread for me
And put the wine back on the shelf,
For this night brought great things
That took me from myself . . .
A cloud rose high
And burst apart in light,
And on my ears a voice of music swept,
And on me shone the light of radiant eyes:
"Beloved, I shall ever wait for you — throughout all
    darkness there below, until you walk to Me."
"I too shall never rest till You are found !" — and there I
       was alone,
Speaking to the night,
Forgetting all but that real . . I knew

O no, not wine tonight,
For I am drunk with love,
And fed with a cup of light !

Kyril Demys (Musaios)
Prismatic Voices

if you sing before breakfast
you'll cry before supper . . they say

all my life, that old warning has kept me from waking like a lark
even when we awoke together, in each other's arms

. . darling, good morning
good morning, darling . .

. . . and I felt lyrical at dawn, with the music of you beside me
I was still terrified to sing to the Sun
from being brainwashed by a platitude

so I never sing before breakfast
but I cry before supper, just the same
every evening since you left . . and especially at bedtime

I've always heard that *absence makes the heart grow fonder*
and it seemed to contradict the warning of

out of sight — out of mind

not anymore
now I know they're both true . . .
your absence has made my heart grow fonder
and since you've been out of sight
I've been out of my mind — and body — astrally
trying to communicate with you

I guess I could fall back on that great catch-all
it's an ill wind that blows no good

but it doesn't comfort me the way it should
what possible good
could come . .
from all this loneliness between us ?

oh, begone, ill wind ! be gone today
the only real love I ever knew . . you blew away

A Promise for Tomorrow

how do I regain my soul, now lost
call back the spring to melt this winter frost
that blankets my heart in ice ?

surely not by lingering in the twilight of our glory
recalling the beginning of our enchanted story

or by holding a lonely wake
over the cold remains of the shining mornings
when we both believed we were once Essenes
who knew the way
to make miracles to give away to others
keeping some for us

surely not by sitting in sorrowful silence
and sifting through the grey ashes
of the faded hopes and rainbows of your old letters

no, I shall burn them all, your letters
and disconnect the telephone
so I cannot answer it before it rings
for no robin sings
outside the door of my heart anymore

if I burn your letters of love, perhaps . . .
like the legendary Phoenix of Scorpio
in some future life, they will rise
and live again

oh, twin soul ! where was our mission, what was our goal ?
I need so to understand
how did we fall ? by which Master's hand . . or by our own ?
when did I lose my way along the starry trail I walked with you ?
the trail of secrets we once shared, and wisdom we both knew . .

I wonder . . .

should these written words of the testament of our passion
reincarnate into life again, as the language spoken between us
in some finer alabaster Body Temples of tomorrow
shall we, do you believe, feel a dim and misty sorrow ?

if these words , like the Phoenix, should rise
will we then look deeply into each other's wiser eyes
. . . and know ?

will you gaze upon my face
and remember when the eternity ember burned for us that night
telescoping time, and making Life rhyme . .
and will we perhaps recall . . only a part, not all
of the knowledge so hard earned . . the lonely tears we cried
the hurt we hid inside . . and the karmic lessons we learned
only to forget again, through pride ?

but somehow . . .

   I cannot burn this letter

  no, not this special one you wrote to me
  it seems to possess some blazing fire of its own
some glowing spark of knowing
      that will not be consumed by a lesser fire
  and my hand will not release it
no, not this letter . . .

  as I stare at it, it stares back at me
  and will not leave my fingers
  to be thrown into the fireplace and destroyed
  nor will the memory of the peace I knew
       when I received it
    ever leave me

I had been troubled one day, as everyone is
at some point along the way . . about the March of Time and Age
and their inevitable companion — Death

  and when I expressed my fears to you, in a letter
  feeling my spirit was about to smother
  you wrote back the loveliest words I ever read
  in this world . . . or in any other

  "darling, listen

    when you and I are ready to make a transition
    out of this plane of Time and Space
    we will have the knowledge and the power
    to do so in any manner we wish

  I don't believe you are fully aware of who you are
  or who I am . . . or who we are

when the day comes that our tasks are completed here
    leaving, for us
will be like stepping into the elevator at the Roosevelt
holding hands . . and pressing the button for the 12th floor
it will be as natural as that

there is nothing scary or lonely . . dark
unknown . . painful . . or even uncomfortable
that will happen when we leave
a thousand centuries from now, if even then
for, as you are already aware, we have the Free Will choice
to control our Body Temples' destiny . . of Immortality

and what are these numbers you keep bringing up ?
65 — 73 — 80 — 92 — 110 years ?
they are such foolish fears
there is no clock of illusionary Time
    nailed in my head — or in my body

earth years don't apply to us
they apply only to those humans
who allow the negative energy forces to manifest
in their physical and astral bodies
     you know that
so why do you keep forgetting it
  from time to time ?

dear girl, when we leave this dimension
it will be because we *want* to — not because we *have* to
and that makes all the difference in the Universe

 but that trip is too far away to think about now

we have lots of mundane trips to plan before then, down here
not to mention all the work we have to do
    the light we have to spread

so stop daydreaming about what you will wear and stuff
when we finish up on this planet, and head for home
don't worry, darling . . it will be a great trip

     we've made it many times

as for your chronological tempest in a teapot
you're right — age is a terrible barrier between us
because, the thing is, you see — you're much too young for me
I am one hundred and ninety eight
and you range somewhere from six down to three

    everytime I see you
I expect you to start skipping rope
but don't add any years, darling — or take any away
you are exactly right, just as you are
we match perfectly . . . . . and we always will

  now, to return to those trips in the present
  when are you coming back out here to California, Goob ?
  my arms are aching again
  and I have a giant lump in my throat . . oh, I miss you !

    hurry . .
     Me

P.S. you know the sad expression

on the Lion bank you gave me ?
that's just how I feel now . . the way he looks"

no . . I cannot burn this letter

Mother Goose Reminded Me

Mary-Mary-Quite-Contrary

     how does your garden grow ?

with Easter bells and old clam shells, and sunny daisies, all in a row
but it's full of lonely weeds, just now
                    and I suppose it serves me right

I never come upon a field of daisies that I don't see
in their innocent faces of gold and white
through a blurred blue mist
a vivid image of each unnecessary fight . . . each quarrel we endured
and the pain in your patient eyes
so long inured to my senseless anger, when I shouted

     "get out ! why do you stay here
     where you don't belong ?"

oh, Gooober, I was wrong, so wrong !
it was you who were strong — and I who was weak
you shouldn't have turned the other cheek, when I hurt you
you should have given me, as the Gaelic say
                  the back of your hand
for behaving that way

       . . . but you only gave me daisies

     you gave me daisies-for-forgiveness
except for a few special days, when you gave me
violets-for-remembrance
to fill the bleak and empty hole grief carved in my heart
                so long ago
once, after we'd hurt each other deeply
in our magic cottage, in Pismo Beach
         you brought me a single, Giant Paper Daisy
that filled the room with its gentle perfume . . . of reconciled love

I've never told you, but I keep that daisy above my bed
and last night, during an electrical storm

while I was aching in the dark
for your hands to hold my face, like they did before
my Giant Daisy fell to the floor

then a torrent of rain beat down on the window
and a streak of lightning flashed from somewhere
as a roll of thunder shook the air
and the light on the desk snapped on — then off — three times

     do you know ? did you hear ? were you there ?

last August, after a quarrel, you sent me a card
with a note inside, that said
               " . . if I were a daisy
                      you would like me all the time"
    it broke my heart

and I ran back into your arms, to say
"darling, I'm sorry, I'm sorry"
               and you said . . . . .
                "I'm sorry too"

another time . . when a full week
of the cross country silence between us
had frozen a great lump of fear in my throat I couldn't swallow
I decided to swallow my pride instead — and flew back to you
with a bunch of our daisies for forgiveness

I put them in your carrot juice pitcher
on the dining room table, near your typewriter

     you never even noticed

I guess the daisy magic just works from you to me
not from me to you
              my flowers only made you go

    how far ?

Where is the Pumpkin Peace of our Blueberry Love ?

      I cannot complete my Happiness poem in New York
there isn't enough of it here to study and analyze

there's more of it back there, in our little crooked house
on our little crooked street
in our little crooked, slipping-off-the-time-track town

maybe if I walk around our house
and get to know Blueberry Love and Pumpkin Peace better
. . you always played with them more than I did . .
I may find some old memory, over-looked before
                        that will help me write my Happiness poem

I'll take two small squeaky toys to Love and Peace
                        and surprise them
they must be lonely
          with both of us gone

the two little boys next door
promised-on-their-honor they would pet them . . . and feed them
but it's not the same as being loved by us
                        . . by their own family

          oh, yes, they must be lonely
          poor little Love and Peace

I'll leave today . .

The skcolC Are Running Backwards

our funny crooked house on the little crooked street
in our little crooked town, where the world turns upside down
for happy people . . . the slipping-off-the-time-track house
we found and bought and loved together — is so very, very empty

without you here . . . repairing the 1825 spinning wheel
when the kittens break the spools
heating sweet-scented bayberry wax in the kitchen
to make us fat Gooober candles

chopping logs in the shed . . for the long, cold winter
cleaning out the chimney of the old Franklin stove
carving out chunks of walls
to find the gold you were so sure had been hidden there
somewhere . . . sometime . . long ago

winding up the grandfather clock at night
and making me tremble, later . . . under cozy grandma quilts
sleeping with your arm around me . . and your nose in my ear
keeping me warm in the frosty room

          oh ! who's going to chop the wood
and sweep the chimney . . and shovel the snow
dig for buried treasure

        keep me warm all night, and love me
in our funny crooked house
on the little crooked street . . in our
                              slipping-off-the-time-track town
        now ?

Homesick, Inside-Out

I just cranked up the arm of the old Edison
and put on my favorite record . . *I'll Take You Home Again, Kathleen*

to keep me company, while I look out the window
and watch the falling star flakes
trim the Christmas pine in the yard with white sparkles

I could never understand why that song always made me so wistful
but I think I know why now

I guess because it's about a man who loves a woman so much
that he knows, without being told . . how she feels
what makes her hurt and ache inside

he notices the tear in her eye
and he sees how the roses all have left her cheeks
so he tells her tenderly he's going to fix it
he's going to take her home . . to where her heart has ever been
since she was first his bonny bride

        yes, he's going to take her home
to where her heart will feel no pain
he's going to turn the world rightside up for her again
for she belongs to him . . and like the Little Prince, he knows
that a man is forever responsible
for the flower he has tamed . . his special rose
different from all the others, and unique . . only because
she is his . . he has tamed her

                        Before Us

I cried over the words
because it was so lovely, so beautiful
to think about being warmly loved and protected like that
just to imagine such cozy, crazy-quilt devotion

        After Us

I wept when I played the record

because it made me so happy to realize
that I was loved as Kathleen was loved . . at last

and I weep as I listen to it now
because I'm no longer your bonny bride
the roses all have left my cheeks
and you don't even notice . . or care

      also because . . we won't be goin' to Ireland together after all
to pick starry shamrocks and kiss the Blarney Stone
make friends with the leprechauns . . and run into each other's arms
through green meadows and misty rains
                    Acapulco and Anchorage
                    are a million miles from
                      from County Cork

I suppose it also makes me sad

      to think that Kathleen, bein' Irish
      must have had a terror of a temper, at times

sure, and she was after bein' a bit of a pixilated dreamer
and probably didn't even have a driver's license
but it never made any difference to *him*

      . . he loved her anyway

Loving Hours

      I'm curled up
      on your side of the couch
      here in the den

did we actually used to fight
over which side of the couch was whose ? my god !
oh, Gooober, what a waste of loving hours . .

Blueberry Love and Pumpkin Peace are playing peek-a-boo with me
from the wooden buckets on the book shelves
              where you taught them to hide
  . . and I'm remembering

how you used to search for Love and Peace
after we had a quarrel — yes, after each hurtful fight
when I was wrong, and you were right — you searched for Love and Peace

you would call them . . "babies, babies !

                    . . come on now, you kids
                    stop playing hide-and-seek
                    it's time to come inside"

I remember how you would hold them in your lap
and tickle their ears, and rub their tummies — and cut their toe nails

they held so still for you — Love and Peace

sometimes you would wad up little pieces of Kleenex
to toss under the dining room table
so they could bounce after the paper balls
and carry them happily back to you . . Love's tail
                              so tall and proud
Love was quicker
Peace always seemed a little confused

but I would complain, in a voice unnecessarily angry
about the mess of paper — or Kleenex — on the rug
while the tenseness between us grew
                    because I was being ignored for the moment

        . . in which class in school did I learn the brass rule
that being temporarily ignored is a synonym for rejection ?
then you would sigh softly . . scratch Love's chin
gently stroke Peace . . and always say
                        "kitties are the only good things"

I can't count the times you said it
"kitties are the only good things"

you were right, darling
kitties are Gooberz — and very, very dear
Peace misses you scratching her tummy
and Love misses you too, when you're not here
to cut his toe nails . . and tickle his ear

        oh, yes

            kitties are the only good things

                    left

Reflections

the Mad Hatter was timing me

    with his counter-clockwise gold pocket watch
    and muttering . . "it's late, it's late, it's late !"

when I tried Alice's experiment this morning

you know . . when she stared through the looking glass
and saw a reversed room, with everything backwards
then stepped inside . . . and ran straight into Wonderland !

I stared, like Alice, into the mirror
of the old-fashioned hat rack and umbrella stand
in the front room downstairs, near the beveled glass door
where your funny old hiking hat used to hang
near my funny old granny sunbonnet
                hanging there now . . forlorn, alone

and I thought that maybe . . just maybe
like Alice, I might see, through the mirror
the beautifully crazy and backwards world of yesterday

            then step inside . . and run into your arms
                back into the Wonderland of Us

I remembered what you taught me
about the negative world being only a reflection
of the real world of positive faith and happiness
and thought it might be reversed . . . perhaps
    the so-called real world of our empty house
was but a negative reflection of the *true* real world . . in the mirror
of our happy, positive yesterday

and . . if I could only manage to become magical, like Alice . . . and
step into the mirror, back into the Wonderland of Us
we could have a peppermint tea party, with mouse cookies and carrots
and the nine of us . . you and I

        and Algae and Raggy and Emilie

and the Red Queen and the White Queen

and our two toy mice, with the long, skinny tails
could all munch on miracles, sprinkled with wheat germ
and float around the table, doing an Elf dance
while Kathleen whirled on the old Edison, in the corner

but all I saw through the Looking Glass

was a reflection of the large hole in the wall you dug out
when you were looking for gold
             and when I tried to break through
          to the other side of the mirror
to see if you might be there . . . . . just out of sight
in the reversed back yard, getting a big box
                     to scoop up the mess you made all over the floor

        I bumped my nose . . hard . . on solid glass

no one said

    magic !

the room was silent

             and I thought I heard the Mad Hatter laugh

The Circle of Your Arms

          dreams ! dreams ! dreams !

why will my dreams not release me ?
each night you come to torture me, in your astral body
bending closer, closer . . until I can feel and smell
                     your sweet, musty, jungle-grass breath
        whispering . .
                     "darling, tomb rhymes with womb
                     so birth rhymes with death
                     and far-away rhymes with home-to-stay"

        your astral words are lies !

they are all senseless non sequiturs, do you hear ?
no matter how real you seem, in each vivid dream
you're not here . . you're not *really* here
I am beginning to fear
to lay me down to sleep each night . . afraid to turn out the light
and be left alone in the dark with your ghost

        last night I fell asleep
        after tucking your note under my pillow
        the one you wrote when you left the house
                     that black February day
             you drove away
in your dusty blue Bug

the note you left, along with the Peanuts cartoon
you had clipped from the newspaper for me to read

and in your note, you wrote . . .

        "love is not always
            doing what brings pleasure
        love is also doing what is good for someone
        whatever the cost at the moment
        sometimes . . it's leaving . . for awhile
        and the love is shown then
                in the pain given
        because pain is a lesson
        best learned from the one who loves you the most"

maybe it was your note beneath my pillow
that caused my dreams to be so real, so vivid

    this morning you came to me again, at dawn
    and murmured gently, so gently . . .

        "Gooober, sad druid . . why is it you do not know
        that the circle of your arms
        is the home I cannot ever leave
            however far away I go ?"

you told me that in Pismo Beach !
I cried . . and you lied !

    the sound of my own cry woke me suddenly
    . . . this time, you had left a misty astral blessing
    an indefinable feeling of peace
    a half-slumbering knowing . . slowly growing within

but after awhile . . . it faded into futility again

Prisms

the salesman at the lighting store in Colorado Springs
believed we had gone bananas that day
when we told him we wanted to buy
sixty or seventy of his finest and largest Austrian crystal prisms

he must have thought we were going to re-create Versailles
and build our own chandelier for the ball

then we hurried back home . . and tied a string

across the window in the upstairs hall
where we could see the magic the first thing each morning
from the Indian room, when we awoke . . together

and hung the prisms on the string
　so they could make happy, dancing rainbows
splashing and crashing colors all over the walls and floor
with the infinite multiplication of the spectrum

　　　　then hung the rest across the dining room windows downstairs
　　　　so we could have rainbows for breakfast

　　　　　　　　. . they're still here

just now, the kittens are trying to catch them

　　　　　　　　　　with their paws

they never manage to quite do it
the colors always slip away . . rainbows are like that
but Love and Peace keep right on trying
oh ! kitties are the only good things . . . .

Maybe in Guffy

Emilie is sitting so quietly
in her old handmade antique Indian cradle
Love and Peace leap up into her lap
and rock the cradle . . swing it back and forth

　　　but she doesn't say a word
　　　she doesn't even cry

I've washed and ironed her long, lacy-white dress
and polished her tiny gold locket . . but she doesn't say a word

　　　　　she can't

　　　　　　　, she doesn't have a head

I tried to glue all the pieces
back together
after I smashed her head on the floor
　　　　　that angry day
remembering your frown when I heard you say
"I'll come back after you've put Emilie's head together"

I spent the days trying . . but
they simply would not fit
and finally, I had to throw them away

but I kept her long, shining chestnut hair
just in case, someday . . maybe in the antique shop, in Guffy
I might find another head for her
with the same strange, sad brown eyes . . the same pink mouth

and the same inscrutable smile

A Small White Box

do you remember the small, white box from Saks
with the hurting-things in it
the affirmation things that didn't work out ?

a small gold bracelet . . . a delicate white dress
. . . there were tiny blue forget-me-nots
and a bumble bee kissing a flower . . stitched on the collar

I can't find it

I've looked literally everywhere . . inside every closet
in every drawer . . under each bed . . behind the fainting couch
down in the basement . . out in the shed
and it simply is not here
as you once said
"we've lost something very dear"

through your carelessness . . or mine ?

it has gone, just disappeared
do you suppose the lady-who-came-to-clean-on-Saturdays
found it . . and didn't look to see
if there was something very precious inside
and thought it was just an ordinary box, like any other box
and decided to just . . throw it away ?

we were going to teach the small druid

while she was young enough to understand
the bumblebee magic

about the fact that the bumblebee
by all the inflexible laws of physics and aero-dynamics
cannot possibly fly

because of the wing span, in relation to the body weight

but no one ever told the bumblebee that
so he just goes right ahead and flies anyway

maybe the rules of physics don't apply
when you're unaware of them . .

                    yes . . teaching

you tried so hard to teach me the things you believed were important
·and necessary for me to learn . . I remember you taught me

                    " . . it's not what people say
                        that matters
                            it's what people do . . "

I guess you put the small, white box
away someplace, before you left . . with my *Love is Eternal* ring
so they would be safe
                    for tomorrow

Oh ! . . . .

in those moments of longing, when I awaken in the night
damp . . from tears shed in dreams of Us
                    aching with the need of you

        I know the difference
        between lust and love

                        there is a difference

oh ! there is an unmistakable difference
and the poets are right . . . not the pornographers

when you hold my hand in the movies . . . or in the car
or on the couch . . and my knees grow weak

        when your mouth is suddenly fused on mine
        in the middle of the night
        and I tremble in the dark, then melt into honey

                when we are loving "deep" . . or loving
            any way at all . .

and the floods of passion
. . rise and fall in me

it is never what you are doing
that brings on my weakness, my trembling
my melting into the waves of ecstasy
that ebb and flow, within me
then stream out to meet your flood of love

no . .

it is not *what* you are doing to me
but that it is *you* who is doing it

. . that these are *your* hands
these are *your* lips
this is *your* body, pressing against mine

my passion comes . .

is all-consuming

and is fulfilled, not from the intimate touching — oh, no
not from the touching, but from the blinding eroticism
of the thought that it is *you* who touches me !

so . . how can we ever find *spring* alone
or anywhere . . with anyone . . in any way
but through each other ?

tonight, I remember
when you once murmured, against my lips

and moaned . . "oh, darling
you have taught me that *spring*
is nothing . . without love
that *deep* is empty
. . without you"

yes, tonight I remember
the wonder of your words

do you remember too ?

Winged Messenger of Our Easter Union ?

a strange thing just happened
                    a strange thing . . . .

remember the time I flew to you — to the airport in Los Angeles
when you gave me the violets and the Butterfly music . . in the Bug
after you made me look up, and wish on a star ?

before I left the house in New York that glad morning
to catch the plane . . there was a letter from you
but I didn't have time to read it . . I was late, as usual

            and I didn't want to miss my flight . . to you
            so I tucked the letter, unopened
            in the bottom of my pocketbook . . and thought
                            I would read it on the plane
then was so excited
flying through the clouds, to you
I forgot all about it

            and all this time . . . all this time
            that letter has been there
            mixed with cancelled airline tickets
            scribbled with numbers
                . . movie ticket stubs from On a Clear Day

            and all other
                    odds and ends clutter

this morning . .

I suddenly decided to clean out all the trash
for my fresh, new page of Life . . . and empty
all the collected odds and ends
from my pocketbook — and my mind and heart
for my quiet start

        down this unfamiliar, but somehow peaceful road
        to an unknown destination
        with maybe no one waiting at the end

but a wiser me-of-me

        with nothing waiting at the end
        but the same loneliness of the beginning

and . . I found it
your letter, still unopened

it was as though . . oh, don't you see ?
as though you were sending a message to me

I know you wrote it a long time ago . . but it was as though
somehow, you knew . . how dreadfully much I was missing you

                    and managed to break through

    my hands shook
        and my heart tremored
    as I opened it

then my eyes blurred with tears, as I read your words
in your funny left-handed Dwarf scrawl
oh ! I'm so glad you didn't type it, darling . . I'm so glad
you wrote this letter by hand
so I could feel the you-of-you come through the green ink
                                    on the yellow paper
    your words . . written
                so long ago
did you know ?

did you know . . somehow . . when you wrote those words
that I would be reading them . . now ?

                    "baby-wife, spunky mouse-spouse
                    I'm sorry if I was mean and crabby and cold
                    when we spoke on the phone this morning

                    I was so worried about this test
                    this test we are taking, you and I
                    it's such a hard test . .

                    I know I shouldn't be worried about it
                    but I am — and the later it gets
                    the more I worry if we're going to pass it

                    the minute we hung up, I knew . .
                    I realized I had hurt you again
                    without meaning to

                    I wanted to call you back . . and tell you
                    how sorry I was that I'd hurt you
                    but before I could call
                    you called me back — to tell me, you said
                    that you thought it would be better
                    if you flew out here — not now
                    but next month, when the weather
                                would be . . warmer

                    and I knew that wasn't why you called

it wasn't to tell me that
        no, it was only to try and see
what was wrong with me

I'm so insensitive sometimes
                so wrong and blind
sweetheart, I'm sorry
I had to hurt you again . . and seem unkind
it was only because . . well
I'm so worried about the test we're taking

will you forgive me ? I miss you so
and I'm so lonely out here without you
please try to fly out soon
        . . as soon as you possibly can

oh, I miss you, I miss you . . miss you !
and I'm so lonely
                I love you . . ."

                Gooober

    I ran upstairs
with your letter

    and compared it with one the you-of-him
    wrote so very long ago
    it wasn't exact, word for word
    but so nearly . . so nearly . . it was . . unreal

almost . . un-earthly

    then I loped into our bed . . . hugged your pillow
    and I cried . . I cried so hard

and I whispered . . "oh, Goob, I *have* forgiven
I have, I have, I have !
please come back home . . so I can ask you
to forgive me too
we *have* passed our test . . don't you see ?
    come back to me
            come back to your home
here in my arms . . . "

    and saw then your aura slowly appear . . against the wall
    next to the Indian Chief and Squaw painted figures there

did you hear
    . . my prayer ?

        were you there ?

        Canto Nineteen ☆ 763

It Is April

       it is April
       and you are gone

but tonight I remember
the spring of December
      when the ember of Eternity
glowed until dawn

wherever you are . . look up at our star
on the very tip-top of our miracle Christmas tree
and remember with me . . that other midnight

      when we celebrated Christmas
      and the resurrection
      with the hyacinths of memory

      and the gift of love

It's Spring in Colorado

the two little boys who live next door
to our funny crooked house, in Colorado
the ones who look like Tom Sawyer
and Huckleberry Finn . . . Steve and Marvin Cook

     called me in New York today
     to tell me about Bones, our outside cat

remember how you always called him
the toughest Tom Cat in the Rockies ?

     well, it seems that, while the boys
     were in the kitchen this morning, feeding Love and Peace
     they heard a noise in the laundry room

and when they opened the door, to look inside

        there was Bones

        blinking at them
        with glittering green eyes of pride
        and meowing excitedly

        "behold ! this miracle that I have made . . "

darling . .

        the "toughest Tom Cat in the Rockies"
        has just given birth to a litter of three kittens

            Bones is a mama

I told the boys
to get him some sardines, as a special treat
and to give him lots of milk, for the babies
        I mean . . her

        my other news is half-glad, and half-sad
        you don't have to worry about Pumpkin Peace
        getting a husband now

I guess she and Blueberry Love decided to get married
because . . a few days ago
            Peace also became a mama

she had two babies
but . . . one died

        I kept thinking that maybe if you had known
        she was in the family way
        you would have stuffed her with vitamins and good things
        and maybe . . oh, poor little gentle Peace !

        no one was there with her when her babies were born
        she was . . all alone
        and you know how scared she always got
        when Love became romantic, and chased her under the beds

I hope she wasn't afraid or lonely
and I hope she understands . . and will forgive us someday
for leaving her . . all by herself

        of course, she had Steve and Marvin every day . . .
                and Love
but he was probably just as frightened as Peace

for all his long tail and superior ways of a male
        he's really quite unworldly and un-sophisticated

they both needed us

          well, that's the sad part

now, the glad part is
. . . we have four new kittens
        to chase rainbows

but then, the other sad part of the news
is that you aren't here to help me choose
happy names for them
        I thought I might name one of them *Please*
          and one of them *Hurry*
            and one of them *Home*
        and one of them *Soon*
    what do you think ?

Please Bones . . Hurry Bones
and Home Bones
      . . and Soon Peace

or should it be Soon Love ?
I guess it would be best
to name the baby after its father

    anyway, I was just thinking it would be kind of daffy
    to call them in, from outside
    I could stand there on the front porch, and call out . .

Please ! Hurry ! Home ! Soon ! Love ! Peace !

      . . no need to call Bones
    you know how tom cats are . . .
        always out somewhere
        prowling and catting around

Oh, Well, Why Not ?

    I was unfaithful to you last night

        will you ever forgive me
    for breaking our solemn vow to each other ?
    I know it was wrong
        . . but it's been so long

and I thought by now . . surely
you would write . . or call

        he was tall

                though not quite so tall as you . .
                  his eyes were sparkling brown
              not ocean-green, like a crystal sea

but he had an irresistible power over me
and I was as helpless as a marionette, under his steady gaze

his voice . . was low and clear
and he sounded so sincere
when he murmured . .

          "it's wrong for you to have to wait this long"

and, Goob, it has been
too long . . that I have waited

        I didn't want to be untrue !
          I swear I tried to keep my vow to you
but when he gently repeated . .

          "I'm sorry you've had to wait so long"

I melted . . .
and decided to see it through

          then he smiled at me . . his eyes so kind
          his arms . . so tanned and strong
          and asked softly . . "is there something
                    I can do for you ?"
standing there, so tall and strange
giving a little boy his change, over the counter

I told him . . yes

    "I'll have a quart of Rocky Road . . .
and two pints of Caramel Fudge"

and came home

          and ate it all in one night — that quick !
          then became dreadfully, lumpy sick
               which serves me right

and I've been fasting for three whole days

      oh, I miss you !

So You Will Know

Gooober, darling, funny Lion-face
sailing all alone out there

just so you will know, if I should ever have to go
I have written for you, not a poem . . . but a prayer

I will hide it softly, like a secret
here in our little, crooked, slipping-off-the-time-track-house
so maybe someday, you will find it
and understand, then, the way I love you
                            how deep . . and why
I hope it doesn't make you cry
for perhaps we'll never have to say goodbye
but will leave this Earth together
like you promised . . that time in your letter

        until then . .

when I lay me lonesome down to sleep
I say this Oober prayer

                God bless the silent planet Saturn in you
                with its rays of silvery-wise
                that shine out tiny stars to guide me
                from the windows of my soul . . your eyes

                God bless the baby in you
                            the small boy, hiking
                the man of passion, who gentles me and trembles me
                        and the other, holy one

God bless each and every you, within your Temple, living there
each other half of every me
                        all those I know . . and knew
which, when joined together
become the always and eternal Us . . the Forever Me-of-You
that makes your heart reach out to mine
and mine to yours . . across an ocean or a room
                        to pull us back into each other

        even when we've torn ourselves so far apart
        that you look up to wish for me . . upon the mid-day Sun
        at the same time I look up to wish for you
                        upon the midnight Moon

God bless your skin and hair perfume, so well remembered, memorized
from centuries of touching, trusting you
                        my own twin

that tells me you are home
within the circle of my arms . . complete
with all your scattered pieces whole

    so when I lay me down to sleep
    I pray to you my soul to keep
    asking you to keep it safe
    all through our Earth-lived night

but . .

    if I should die before I wake
    I'll pray to our Mother and Father Who art in Heaven
    my soul to take

    while I'm all alone and frightened . . lost
    till I find my way back home to you
    and hear your chord of music
                calling me through Time and Space
    then smell your cheek, and touch your face
    and tumble back inside your arms
               once again . . Forevermore

Last Flight

it's so empty here in Cripple Creek
with all the skcolc running backwards

    Kathleen keening on Edison in the corner

. . and Emilie not speaking a word

    your Lion, with the mane of curly hair
    sitting so still and silent . . on your bed

and the hole in the wall I dug deeper
thinking maybe I could find the gold hidden there
               and surprise you
. . but there was only soot
and grey ashes from the old chimney

    it is time to leave

Love and Peace won't miss me — not really — no more than you do
the two little boys next door will love them and feed them
play with them . . . and the new kittens

and who is loving you, I wonder ?

who . . is loving you ?

>this time, I bought a one-way ticket
>to New York — coach, in the tourist section
>I no longer fly First class, VIP
>>I am no longer a Very Important Person

. . only a lonesome druid

Fig Newtons

there is much I have learned
yet, much I still seek to fathom

>in some silent depths I feel mysteriously compelled to probe
>for lost Essenic pearls of Truth
>>which first appear, then disappear
>. . in swirls of deep green water

water . . the sea
     the sea . . and you and me
and the spirit

>   . . the sea and you and me
water . . and the *spirit*

>what are these fragments . . floating in my mind ?
>floating like butterfly feathers in my brain . .

I desperately need some kind of guidance
for I have lost my way . . and my soul seems to have been struck
by the blight of a forfeited inner sight

my mind is not yet fully awake . . I need more study and thought
to make the fragments fit any pattern
my comprehension is still too muddy and unformed
to piece together each small bit of shredded, colored confetti
from Heaven's distant Mardi Gras

.. each splintered shaving of stardust
each pastel snowflake
* no two alike

.. no two alike *
*

* * oh, the fragments *
the fragments *
*

* * the fragments

wisps of love .. hazes of fear *
sometimes distorted .. sometimes clear *

Serpent hiSSing in my inner ear
blinking off and on .. and flashing, in my Third Eye

the seat of deeper wisdom ..
and always the question
WHY ?

words .. words .. words
fluttering winged birds .. of truth

oh, the plight
of my soul
now half
once whole
oh ! the night
of my soul
without the light
of its twin

where do I come from
... and where am I going ?

and always the cry of .. why ?
sometimes accompanied by songs of the sea
and the recurring sensation of discordant
music
heard in rooms and tombs ..
from Palestine to Paris
.. from Rome to London
.. and back again to Galilee
by way of Scotland
small attic rooms ... in Normandy

and beyond that ..

moments of grace, near violet hills
with a strangely familiar face . . blurred and indistinct
yet, still perhaps a link
                to my present need for compassion
from sea-green crystal eyes
                                . . of silvery-wise

what is this tugging pull
on my mind ?

        what is it urging me to find ? is it simply a need I feel
        to pursue the truth, with compulsive Aries persistence
        of the reason for humanity's continued existence ?

No, I fear it is something more . . long lost on a forgotten shore
and calling me on and on . . to explore . . . the ancient laws
                            of Karma

I sit here numbly, listening to the wild March winds outside
and feeling them
        . . as they blow through the open window
                    the frangrance of cool-sweet-clean air
the fresh-grassy-rainy
scent of approaching spring

        they are singing me a lonesome song, the March winds
        on-why-oh-why isn't Gooober here ?
        yes, why aren't you here with me — where you belong ?

. . listening to the March winds
singing me a lonesome song

        . . drinking a glass of grape juice
and munching on forbidden mouse cookies . . Fig Newtons

        Fig Newtons

they recall a misty, floating fragment of memory
seemingly unrelated to my present sadness

why do I remember our unexpected meeting in Beverly Hills
that December you found me . . an unexpected meeting

        why do I remember such an odd thing
                as our meeting with a Fig Newton
on that Oriental Far Eastern night ?

there was a man we met, a stranger
introduced to us by a friend, a metaphysician
named Ralph Bergstresser, who was . . . and still is

deeply involved in the mystical

. . . a stranger
or did you already know him, in some way ?
the two of you stared and stared and stared at one another
all through dinner . . well, maybe not

> mostly, I guess . . yes, mostly *he* stared at *you*
> his eyes burning and glowing — but why ?
> all through dinner that strange night . . . .
> in a Japanese restaurant . . served by a kimona-clad Butterfly
> our table . . was near a burning fireplace

he was incredibly handsome — strong, and tan and wise
with the strangest . . silvery-wise, glowing-knowing eyes
yes, I guess . . very much like your own

and his skin, sun-browned, was crinkly, like tissue paper
but one hardly noticed that
because of his burning-glowing-knowing . . . and piercing eyes

> his name was Newton . . Dr. Newton
> like these Fig mouse cookies I munch tonight

> yes . . Newton

and he was some sort of a scientist — or was it a geologist ?
who was fond of morning glories — his favorite flower, he said
and he was, he told us, deeply involved . . officially
in the government's investigation of fake flying saucer stories

> he had so many curious things to say
> about space . . and planets . . the way energy works
> > and the laws . . of gravity

I can never forget
the strange, glowing embers in his eyes . . also in yours
as he stared at you — and you at him
while he was telling all those fascinating Martian tales

> I was suddenly chilled
a chill unexpectedly overcame me
and I visibly shook
> > then saw him look
> at you . .
> > > . . and you
> > back at him . .

and . . what did he say, then ?
> > he said . . "when an astral entity
> > from any level of awareness . . whether it be

the astral of a recently departed person
. . or a space traveler
or merely the astral
of someone who is somewhere . . asleep"

" . . . anyone out of the body
when such an entity, in whatever form
from whatever dimension
approaches . . comes near the vicinity of a human

that entity is vibrating at such a higher rate
of angstrom units per second
than the vibratory frequency of earth-bound humans

. . it causes a marked drop in the nearby temperature

the air currents are suddenly cooled
and the change is so sharp and unexpected
that one might . . shall we say . . feel a draft ?"

everyone laughed

then you whispered
"darling, did you see a ghost ?"

and offered me your sweater

it's all so dim and vague
. . my impression of the scene that night
by the roaring fireplace . . with Dr. Newton
but I recall more clearly . . the smaller things

like . . how he told me the way to spell Essene
and before that night, I had been spelling it wrong
with only one Serpent S, instead of two

and I remember, too . . that his first name was Silas . . and also

that he told me . . or did he tell you ? that he was
working on a theory, which would disprove the Law of Gravity
as we now believe it to be . . . or would expand it
something about the temperature of the air
being the key to gravity

and I recall asking him . . . .
"was it originally Galileo
I mean, with the apple and gravity . . and all ?"

then immediately corrected myself . . "oh, no — how dense of me !
of course it was Isaac Newton, who discovered the Law of Gravity
I always confuse the two of them, for some reason !"

and I still remember my embarrassment . . when everyone smiled

at some time
during that Oriental Far Eastern night
I asked him for his birth date
that strange, tissue-paper handsome man
asking, of course, for the purpose of astrology

then felt like making an apology
right away, when I heard him say

> "I make it a rule never to discuss
> chronological age and I really
> don't know
> > . . how old I am"

"were you adopted ?"
I couldn't help asking

> and he answered, faintly smiling

> "something like that . . I've never been able
> to locate my birth certificate"

I was suddenly ashamed
because it seemed I had asked too personal a question
about his parentage or past
then you came to my rescue, and changed the subject

later . . back in our room, at the Roosevelt
you and I both remarked that it was curious
the way he so closely resembled Rembrandt's painting
> of the Polish Rider

and we both decided that, after all
since Rembrandt would never reveal the name of the subject
of that painting . . we must have met a Martian
> or a druid of old
we were only joking, but still . .

was it a mystical chill I felt that night ?
it was so strange, to find myself shaking uncontrollably
with such an icy chill . . when I was sitting less than three feet
> from a roaring fireplace

but I guess it was not an ethereal thrill
nothing supernatural . . for later, I sneezed and sneezed
and you teased, reminding me of the occult saying
that, when a person sneezes, it indicates an astral entity
is temporarily visiting . . or possessing one's Temple
> for a moment . . for some purpose

"oh, don't be spooky !" I answered
"I have simply caught a cold, that's all"

     why do I remember all of this tonight ?
     when the important thing is *now* — the emptiness inside me

as though I have lost more than I ever dreamed or guessed
in losing Us — as though I had also lost
all the wisdom and beingness I ever knew . . along with losing you

I don't even know to which church I would go
if I could find my faith again . . and I need so . . oh !
I need so to *believe* once more

Returned, With Postage Due

     I wrote you a letter today . . from New York
                  where I've been living . . . no, just existing

Dear Gooober

       since you've been gone, my hair has grown so long
       my hair is long and strong, and silky-smooth
       just like you said it would be — oh ! you should see
       how long and silky my hair is now
       and you would brush it for me, and be so proud

       my hair has grown so long
            just the way you wanted it . .

but I couldn't mail it
where should I mail it ?

should I address it simply in care of:

       You, the tall one
       Somewhere in Mexico or Alaska
       Zip Code: Nowhere
       and use extra postage

or should I just mail it in the hollow of an oak tree
at midnight . . and trust the druids to address and mail it for me ?

ah, yes !

  sniwt fo dlrow suoiruc eht . . Alice-through-the-Looking-Glass
  double-double, toil and trouble
  reflected through the mirror of Mary-Mary-Quite Contrary

     Life grows curiouser and curiouser . .

sometimes, these strange
Aquarian Age . . fragments
scramble and ramble
    . . through my mind

like the pieces of a jig-saw puzzle
scattered . . falling here and there

      until . . a picture emerges

eavesdropping is a nasty, naughty
extremely rude thing to do . . Nana used to caution me

  nice children do not listen to conversations
they are not meant to hear . .

     but . . Nana

what if . . one was *meant* to hear ?

  if one was meant to overhear by the synchronization
  or harmonics of the Universe . . by being at a certain place
  at a certain time . . when the mind is stumbling
  the heart fumbling in darkness . . is it not
    then permissible to listen . . and thus be instructed ?

yes, I listened . . and did not feel naughty or rude
not at first, no . . at first the words I overheard
were boring
   and my only effort was ignoring
   or trying to ignore . . a conversation
      in which I had not the slightest interest
  at first . . but then . .

this morning, having breakfast in a small coffee shop on Madison Avenue
I couldn't help but overhear . . floating in and out of my ear
fragments of a conversation between two businessmen types sitting
      in the booth behind me

it must be admitted that they were making no attempt

to keep their discussion ultra-private in any way
their voices rising and falling . . in the tones one uses
when discussing education or inflation . . or politics of the day

the two men were obviously scientific types, judging from their jargon
their professional field, equally as obvious — computer programming

but with technical equipment
. . not the same as the technique
the stranger used . . to program my own mind
like a computer . . on that dreary grey
and unexpected wintry day
. . in Colorado

yes, at first, I was truly bored by their scientific shop talk
and politely turned my head away
not really desiring to hear anything they might say

until . .

one of them made a remark
that caught my attention . . like a shot

"yes, I've heard of astral twins . . . "

astral twins ?

OH !
OH !
oh . .

I'm sorry, Nana . . I whispered to myself
but this time, I must listen . . I'm sorry, but I *must*

and I turned my head, then
leaning closer to the back of the booth
straining, now — to hear each word spoken

their exchanged syllables and sentences bounced back and forth
forth and back . . over the net between us . . and I caught
nearly every one

. . .   . .
. . .   .

"I just read a book called *Astrology, the Space Age Science*
by someone named Joe Goodavage . . and there was a chapter in it
about astral twins . . I had just finished another book
on the subject of twins, called, I believe, *The Curious World of Twins*
by Vincent and Margaret Gaddis, published by Hawthorn Books
although it covers identical and fraternal twins
born of the same parents . . it also includes a section on astral twins

. . . unfortunately, it's out of print
I found my copy in a used bookstore . . but the Goodavage book, you know
in the chapter I mentioned about astral twins . . . . . held my
interest . . . the author, in fact, approaches the entire
field of metaphysics . . . from a clearly scientific point of view
with none of this magical nonsense . . . "

        "astral twins . . . yes, I've heard of them
        my wife's brother is an astrologer
        and we were discussing it at dinner last week
                you know . . . I was thinking
        now that birth data can be programmed into a computer

        it would be an intriguing experiment
                to use the programming . . in such
        a way . . that we might each locate our own astral twins

        and . . . it would certainly . . . . be fascinating
        to come across an exact . . or nearly exact replica
        of one's own self . . don't you think ?"

"yes, but you see, a person may have a double or a look-alike
who is *not* an astral twin . . in other words . . who was not born
at the same time . . . there can be doubles also
who are several years apart in age . . perhaps not quite so identical
as astral twins — but able to fool most people

"you are aware, of course . . that all this double business
is becoming more prevelant . . doubles have been used
for security reasons . . for several of our Presidents
and now . . there's all this talk
of Lee Harvey Oswald being a double for another agent
and the book my wife just bought
published, I believe, by Harper & Row . . is about
Rudolph Hess being a double too"

        "really ? is that true ? I mean, what you just said
        about people who are doubles, who look enough alike
        to be twins . . yet are not *astral* twins
        that is, strongly resembling each other
        even though they are several years apart . . in age ?
        that seems impossible to me . . you see
        I could understand the planetary
        or astrological basis, if you will . . of astral twins
        that theory makes some sense to me, but this . . . . . ."

"in this speeded-up Age we're living in
anything is possible . . don't you see the scientific logic of it ?

with over five billion people on Earth
as there are today

there are surely only a limited number
of mathematically possible arrangements of two eyes
a nose, a mouth . . a chin, a forehead
a couple of ears . . arms, legs and so forth"

> "well, yes . . statistically, I suppose
> looking at it from a mathematical point of view
> I agree with you . . there would quite probably be
> a finite number of individual arrangements
> of body structures and facial features
> > . . as you say"

. . and their voices faded then, for a moment
> . . as another voice overshadowed
their words

> . . . *a Maker of clay images, like unto clay pitchers*

> *the Architect . . of the Temples of the soul . . may he not*
> > *create these clay images in duplicate*
> *if he should choose . . . and many times over ? . . .*

. . then the remembered echoes of the stranger
> on that dreary grey . . and unexpected
> wintry day . . . faded once more
into the words of the strangers . . in the next booth
> . .   . .   . .

> . . . .

"my college room mate, Clark Johnson
is with one of those Think Tanks for the Government
and he told me this really incredible thing . .
he says it's not generally known . . but somewhere
near Langley, Virginia . . and I believe he said
also somewhere in Alaska . . a group of people . .
he didn't say whether or not it was a government agency
but I assume various government agencies utilize it
from time to time . . . anyway . . there is this computer
programmed for locating doubles . . . for multiple reasons
if you'll pardon the pun . . . "

> "a computer . . to locate doubles ?
> did Clark say who developed the programming ?"

"not exactly . . he insinuated it was some powerful
and wealthy group of men
funded by several major universities . . and the computer
has been programmed with photographical input . . that is
millions of photos have been fed into it . . photos

according to Clark . . of high school and college
graduates . . prostitutes and others who have been arrested
and therefore photographed . . actors and actresses . . .
nurses . . members of the armed services . . and so on

. . . and, let's say someone wanted to find a double for you
or maybe even . . several look-alikes for you . .
all they need do . . . is to feed your photograph into the computer
which would then reduce your features to *micro dots*
and these would then be the comparative catalyst
for the computer to . . search and locate . . . other photos
which corresponded as closely as possible . . with
the arrangement of micro dots forming your face, in a mathematical sense

in effect . . . producing as many 'twins' or doubles
as the computer might contain . . of yourself"

        "yes . . a series of micro dots . . elementary, really
        that's been done for some time . . but not . .
        not for such a purpose . . . . I can see
        how the matching up of a complex network of
        micro dots, comprising the features
        of a photograph . . could then allow a computer
        to read out . . matching . . . faces . . my God !
        that's . . well, it somehow makes me feel . . uneasy"

"I agree . . Clark says it's uncanny
he's seen it in action . . he was invited to watch
a demonstration of it, with a group from his Think Tank
and he said . . . well, much the same as you
he told me that it gave him nightmares . . . especially
when the damned thing located twelve photos
of guys who were dead ringers for him"

        "listen . . do you think a computer could be
        programmed . . for the mathematical statistics
        of how many probable doubles each of us would have

        . . based on statistical assumption ?"

"how could a computer do such a thing ?
there's no input possible concerning such a probability
when you consider that . . perhaps, out of five billion people
one billion look like the other four . . or would it be
on a basis of every ninth factor . . or would there be
       some of the five billion
who were unique, individual and distinct . . ? who knows ?
only God, I guess . . . and I don't believe in a Deity
so maybe . . only Mother Nature knows . . but I just thought
about that old truism . . you know the one ?

they threw away the mold when they made you, baby ?"

        "I believe the word is pattern — not mold"

"either way, same thing . . semantics
my friend, semantics . . right ?"

        "well . . I don't know about God or Mother Nature

        but maybe my brother-in-law, the astrologer
        could calculate the probability statistics
        by the planetary movements and all that junk"

"don't laugh . . Clark says these people
also have astrologers working with them, timing events
or some such thing . . . for what purpose, I have no idea
nor does Clark . . . but I do believe it's logical
to assume that the computer is, on occasion, used by various
government agencies, in agent work, and the like"

        "I feel foolish admitting it . . but
        this conversation has set my nerves on edge
        how about getting out of here . .
        and walking over to the Shamrock for a double scotch ?"

"you're on ! I find the whole business
more than a little creepy myself . .
I'll get the check . . . waiter ! check please !

    they left

        for a long time, I remained in the booth
        not moving . . not even thinking

I simply sat there, in a daze . . . wondering

what Thunderbolt Path of Accelerated Karma
has the Higher Angel of Myself . . . imposed on me
that I should have been so earthquaked
by such shattering experiences as being soul tested
by *his* astral twin — and perhaps also, by *your* double ?
why have I been so painfully submitted
to *both* tests . . . . . . astral twins *and* doubles ?
one on a spiritual level — the other, clearly
                on an Earth level of deception
    but why ?
finally, I got up, and walked to the cash register
                paid my check
    walked out . . .

and someway . . . somehow
found my way back home to my apartment

> I walked over to the window, in the bedroom
> pulled up a chair . . and sat there
> staring out at the twinkling stars
> for several hours . . remembering
> > from childhood

. . . *twinkle, twinkle, little star . . how I wonder*
> > *. . what you are . . .*
how I wonder . . . *who* you are . . .

Back Through the Looking Glass

there is something buried . . yes, something buried in Colorado
some missing fragment I must find
> hidden somewhere in the back of my mind

> hidden, perhaps . . somewhere in our little crooked house
where you were so sure, so certain
> > something *was* buried

> > when you used to dig for gold
> > within the walls . . gold you were positive
> > > so positive and sure

was hidden . . buried there . . long, long ago

but what if the gold you were seeking
was a different kind of gold . . than the indestructible metal
others try to mine from beneath the Earth ?

> > what if you were seeking some finer gold of wisdom

> > related to the soul's memory
> > buried there . . somewhere . . and hidden

in the walls . . or beneath the basement floor
of our little crooked, slipping-off-the-time-track house

> > in Colorado ?

yes, there is still something . . I must find
and it is not here, in New York

it is back in Colorado . . awaiting my discovery
so I shall fly back there

this very afternoon

and begin my search . . .

Call John

tonight, in our little crooked house, I'm thinking of that morning in Pismo Beach
when I watched you dive down into the green waves . . . from the shore
over and over . . . and over again . . you dove into the sea
like a frolicking dolphin, in your wet suit

. . while I watched

then we walked along the beach together
while you gathered what you called sea-spinach
growing near the rocks and the sand

later, you cooked it for us, with butter
and as we were eating . .

I remarked . . "this is delicious"

you smiled, then
. . deep into my eyes

and said . . "no, delicious is not the word
this sea spinach is . . delectable"

and I thought to myself
as you stared at me, silently
delectable . . delectable . .

a small silver bell chimed . . in the back of my mind
and yet, I did not know what it was that I remembered

. . something about . . food
and the sea . . something about the word . .
delectable

then I recalled the fragment
and realized what it was I was remembering
it was a verse . . yes, a verse the you-of-he
had scribbled on the back of the small piece of paper
containing also those last words

he expressed the night . . he died

and I left the table suddenly
to go and look inside
the small box . . where I kept his things

and I found the note with his-your words
that said . .
>   *the wind blows soft*
>   *the night grows kind*
>   *sleep's not far off*
>   *peace fills my mind* . .

and turned the paper over . . to read the words
the him-of-you, or the you-of-him
had scribbled on the *back* of the paper
seeming so unimportant at the time I first read them
just a silly little verse, with no special meaning

a verse I had previously dismissed
as absolutely meaningless . . and it still was

the words were still too cryptic for me to decipher
those words written by the Carousel Bill
the him-of-you

except . . for the skip of a heartbeat I felt
at just one of the words . . the word you had just spoken

delectable

when I showed you the verse
you only sighed
and we both felt a sudden chill
still unidentified . .
but we stared into each other's eyes
again . . for a long time
as always . . silently

I hold the verse in my hand now
and stare at it . . . and wonder how I could have imagined it to be
any sort of secret message from the him-of-you
of the you-of-him . . . to me

although it is about the sea
what else does it say . . from the him-of-you
to the me-of-me ?

such a strange ramble . . of words
such an Ogden Nash scramble . . of fluttering birds
of words

just three lines, written in light pencil
on the back of the paper containing the verse . . the wind blows soft

just three lines

           " . . the sea is full of secrets
         which make delectable dishes
             . . if that is what your wish is"

strange scanning . . odd planning
of words . . peculiar meter . . and rhyme

    and why did you say . . that day
    "this sea-spinach is more that delicious
    it is . . . *delectable*" ?

        perhaps it's like one of those Chinese puzzles
        or an ancient anagram . . and I am

    somehow compelled . . to fit the words together
    to see if there is a hidden meaning . . or message

perhaps if I take the first words of one verse
and the last words of the other . . and put them together ?

      the first words of one verse . . *the wind blows soft*

and the last words of the other . . *if that is what your wish is*

    the wind blows soft
    if that is what your wish is . .

the wind blows . .
    . . your wish is
        the wind blows . . your wishes ?

    the wind blows
    wherever it wishes ?

is there some hidden meaning there ?

    it is such a small scrap of paper, torn in half nearly
    torn down the center . . and now I see

      I see . . written very, very lightly
      in pencil . . a name and a telephone number

so pale and light it is
in contrast to the dark blue ink
of the words of the 'wind blows' verse . .

      call John McGuire
      345-8436

that's what it says
when I fit the torn paper
neatly together

      I do not know this man . . . this John McGuire
      he was, I suppose . . one of the faces
      in one of the places . . somewhere
      during our last drowning years . . of being apart

  but . .

          the paper is torn down the center
          and the only writing on the piece about the wishes

           and delectable dishes
                    . . the only writing

    on this torn piece
    is just half of the name and telephone number

just half the name
and number . .
      it just says . .
      on this one torn piece

      call John
        345-8

and on the other side
of this torn paper — the other side of this half
is the verse which begins . . *the wind blows*

      the wind blows . . your wish is
      the wind blows your wishes . .
      the wind blows . . . wherever it wishes ?

       call John
         345-8

Call John ? the Bible ?
the Book of John ?

    what will I find if I should turn
    to the Book of John ? in the
                 Bible ?

the Book of John . . . Chapter 3
and Verses 4 — 5
    and 8 ?

      the verses could be simply meaningless words

with no special meaning for me
                              nevertheless, I shall look

              yes, I shall look
       in the book
                of John

                     Chapter 3
                Verses 4 — 5 and 8

here it is, in the New Testament
the Book of John — Third Chapter

              verse 4 says . . . "how can a grown man be born again ?"
                     Nicodemus asked
                     "he certainly cannot enter
                     his mother's womb . . and be born
                                        a second time"
verse 5 says . . "I tell you the truth"
                replied Jesus
                "that no one can enter the Kingdom of God
                unless he is born again
                         of water . . and the spirit"

and verse 8 says . .
                     . . *the wind blows*
                     wherever it wishes

                     the wind blows wherever it wishes ?

OH ! Oh ! oh !
how strange . . how very, very strange

              I wonder what it all could mean ?

and the end of verse 8
the last words of that sentence are . . .

                     "but you do not know where it comes from
                     or where it is going . . "

that's true . . yes, that is so true
I do not know . . where I am going
or where I came from either
what does it mean ?
can these verses be only . . coincidence ?

       I know the Baptists believe one must be baptized
       in the water . . something to do with the spirit
       although . . most Baptists do not also know . . why John

the Baptist

not gentle John, the apostle
but fiery John, the Baptist

   why he was so successful in the sacred rite of baptism
   because . . in the Egyptian initiation, in the Great Pyramid
   one was allowed to 'die' . . the spirit left the Body Temple
   and returned . . with full memory . . while the Priests
   guarded the flesh body during this sacred flight of the spirit
   and the purpose was to teach each Initiate the first steps
                          in Ascension
   by proving that the spirit could leave
   . . . then return . . and was independent of the body

   John, the Baptist possessed the delicate skill
   of holding each pilgrim under the water . . precisely long enough

   for the spirit to briefly leave the body
   but not long enough to 'die'
   not long enough for the silver cord to be broken

   so that, when the spirit returned
   there was a feeling of inexpressible joy and exhilaration
   within the heart of the one thus baptized

of course . . this ritual has since been diluted by other sects
into a sprinkling of water over the head . . as in my Trinity ceremony
because it became too dangerous to correctly baptize
as fiery John did . . and there was no point in nearly drowning
if one was not going to come out of the experience . . truly exalted

as did occur when fiery John was baptizing
and as also did occur . . in the Pyramid, when the Priests
                 were performing their Ascension training

              of Egyptian Initiates
and there is also
the persistent and oft-told tale . . of drowning survivors
that, just as one is about to drown
before being rescued . . one's entire Life is projected
as on a movie screen . . the images flashing
across the mind . . in but a few fleeting seconds
the images . . of the experiences of an entire lifetime

   but . . what does it *mean* ?

water . . and the spirit
spirit . . and the water
            fiery John . . gentle John

fiery John ?

what has the element of Fire
to do with the element of Water ?

> and what has Spirit to do
> with either . . or both ?

Fire . . Water . . Spirit

> oh, what does it mean ?
> what does it all mean ?

was fiery John
like John, the apostle
also an Essene ?

> I must not have been one myself
> for, if I had really been an Essene
> I would know what it might mean

> I could surely solve the mystery
> if I had ever been one of the Essenes

> but I am only me

> and I cannot see . . what any of it means

I Will Fear No Evil

where is my Bible ?

> no, not the revised, King James version
> of watered-down, one-sided preaching
> based on changes in the New Testament teaching

I need both the New and the Old
> Testaments

I need all Testaments ever written — for my highly unlikely
and unsolicited by Heaven or hell re-conversion
to a renewed faith in my own common sense and sanity
along with my former faith in the decency and goodness
of the masses of Earthling humanity

yes, all Testaments I need — each tiny mustard seed
of Truth and lie ever testified to
by Reformed — Orthodox — or Hasidic Jew

Catholic and Protestant — or any other form of Gentile   N
                                                          E
      if I am to make my own Testament   V
      and sock it or rocket it through   A
                                  E
        up Jacob's ladder to   H

      or down Satan's snake pit to   H
                              E
with no wild, growing-knowing rose to smell   L
in a grassy-green, ocean backyard   L
to tell me the difference between upstairs and downstairs
or to suggest that each may be the self-perpetuating illusion
of a Tower of Babel, built from the babbling language
                           of religious confusion
I seek the truthful Testament
of pessimistic atheist and searching agnostic
whether it be bland and sugar-coated, or cynical and caustic
I need the enlightenment of Buddha
                        the wisdom of Hatha Yoga
the guidance of every Guru
    who meditates in turban or toga

I want each Tibetan monk and disciple of Zen
with their silent, wise language of Oriental nods
to tell me precisely where and when
I shall be led to the secrets of all the ancient gods
buried in Pyramids and worshipped under stars
                     either Lunar or Solar

I must hear the conviction of every polygamous Mormon
and the speaking-with-tongues diction
                of each ecstatic Holy Roller
I demand the Gospel Truth
from each bachelor Jesuit Priest and wedded-to-Christ Nun
about the Trinity of the Holy Ghost, the Father and the son

I need an eyewitness report
from every Jewish Rabbi and Protestant Pastor
also from Mahatma Gandhi, the tough-ascetic faster
who starved himself and carved himself a name
in the peaceful, non-resistance Religious Hall of Fame

    and I particularly need to comprehend

the motivation of Mohammed
who also had trouble with mountains who refused to move or fly
can Mohammed explain why a mountain can't fly . . .
             but a Gooober can lie ?

I must know the honest goal and secret fears

behind Martin Luther's table talks
what personal charisma incites all those wild cheers
during Billy Graham's TV cable walks
for God and Christ . . . at every singing outdoor rally

give me the inspirational story behind the good old 'Sally'
that Army of Soul Salvation, featuring street corner oration
and spreading the joyful elation of being saved
knowing so well that hell is paved
                              with good intentions

LORD ! LORD !

send me Blavatsky's esoteric Theosophy
          Rudolph Steiner's spritual inventions
and the evangelical intentions . . of Billy Sunday

the preachings and teachings of Seventh Day Adventists
and those who pray only on Thursday or Monday

reach me, oh, reach me ! with the Faith, eternally steady
born of the ever-glowing Light of Mary Baker Eddy
who taught her followers the astounding miracles of self-reliance
and laid the firm cornerstone of the controversial Christian Science
by shoving drugs and surgery back on the shelf
with the sensible and biblically defensible . . .
                    . . . Physician, heal thy*self* !

I MUST KNOW !

I want a three-ring, Star spangled show
of all those swaying and trapezing religious acts
before the final curtain of my own failing faith

I desperately need the Testament of Moses . . . Holy Moses !
and the Little Prince's Testament of tamed, unique roses
the New Testaments of Matthew, Luke, Mark . . . . and James
and most especially . . oh ! especially
                    the Revelations of gentle John

I demand and command the Testament of the Rosicrucions
all those White Lodge Elder Brothers, with the Upper-Hierarchy names
like the Count de St. Germain
one of most distinguished of all the Elder Brothers
who was also Shakespeare . . Isaac Newton . . Francis Bacon
and only God — and he — know how many others

     yes, St. Germain

now there is a quick-change artist of Light, who hides and confuses !
a true Master Alchemist and Adeptus of the Muses

who flew in and out of the Body Temples of Guru and Sage
and still does, for all I know
every six hundred years or so, when he's starting to show his age

O ! St. Germain — whatever may presently be his earthly name
it's very plain, whether he resides in New York
Beverly Hills . . . Santa Barbara . . Switzerland or Spain
is truly an inter-planetary All-Star
like that other strange alchemist and magician called *Al*-tar
not the same entity — this I know for sure and certain
                                        although equally as sneaky

now that I've read that the true identity
of Rembrandt's Painting of the Polish Rider
is . . . St. Germain
I remember more vividly our strange meeting
with a Fig Newton . . . Dr. Silas Newton

but St. Germain cannot help me on this yearning night
to find the Light — or make me see
for he never materializes for ordinary mortals, like me

                I need . . oh ! I plead
                for the deep, wise counsel of St. Germain
                to teach me some way to alchemitize this dreary rain
                into at least a pastel rainbow

but . . beggars can't be choosers
so I'll take any old Guru, who's hanging around idle
if he's on the team of the winners, not the losers

I'll accept the wisdom of any duly and truly
licensed-by-Heaven Avatar
who can teach me to pilot my own astral course
as I ride this bucking, painted horse
on Life's spinning Carousel . . . yes !
I'll take any accredited Avatar, who can teach me to drive a car
without stripping the gears
and who can quiet my Fire and Brimstone fears

send me anyone who will lead me or creed me
to my own personal me-of-me identity
who can preach me, and teach me the rules
of the Soul Salvation game
            by any strange or familiar name

                because the rules are never the same !

the signals change
when the cataclysm whistle blows
at every millennium half-time

I need now

all the magic tricks of each genie who hides in a bottle
the flight secrets of every extraterrestrial who soars in a spacecraft
I call on all ordained Ministers of every secret or sacred theology

except astrology

the stars and planets will not come to my assistance
when my mind offers such stubborn resistance
                              to all things mystical
I thirst for the tangible
not the in-tangible

                    I hunger for the physical
                              not the meta-physical

there is no druid mantra . . or long ago memorized ancient Incan rite
that comes to me on this dark night, when wrong seems right
and emptiness yawns in the fading starlight

I recall no long ago incantations . .

              . . incantations, incantations ? as I noticed once before
          I wonder why the word incantations
                    contains within it . . the word Incan ?

but, however-be-it . . I remember no long ago incantations
murmured as I glided through forgotten caverns in former incarnations
neither black nor white magic do I recall, from any or all
of those bygone Temples of Truth

              even though a mystic once told me
              that I had, in one past lifetime
              been sacrificed to the gods as a virgin
              then added
                    " . . it doesn't pay to be one"

it doesn't pay to be a virgin ?
caviar comes, I've heard, from a virgin sturgeon
and that's why caviar's a very rare dish

      I'm not so sure I agree that it doesn't pay to be a virgin
      since it seems to me . . . that may very well be
      a perfect example of one of the times
      when what you don't know — can't hurt you

I mean, longing for "deep" can't rob you of sleep
if you never have cause to know . . just how deep . . deep can go

yes, it may pay to be one — if you're not a fish

but . .

whether I was ever a Vestal Virgin or an Essenic spook
                    the me-of-me, that is
whether I was an ordinary apostle, or a disciple of St. Luke
I have this psychic fluke, just now — this mystical hang-up
and I cannot remember a single curse or chant
to stop the agonizing pain of this reign of hell and Satan
                                                over my soul

I cannot end the rain of the reign of hell
or banish my apathy for life and love
with this never-ending silence from above
                    or by a half-forgotten ancient spell

I NEED THE TRUTH !

from Solomon or David — Moses, Buddha or Krishna
Rebecca or Ruth . . who followed, was it her mother-in-law ?
whither and wherever she went

I NEED THE TRUTH !

why can I not recall
the Oober catechism of faith and trust ?
have I been ex-communicated by some distant galaxy
or is it but a merciful blotting-out-of-the-mind
because you are an Oober
now cold and cruel — when I once thought you were gentle and kind ?

        I didn't even make notes . . . let's see
        the Oober Faith you brought to me
        was it one divided by two — makes three ?
        or was it two into three makes one ?
        did it say you should pray to the Moon or the Sun ?

                    or was it Mars ?

was it Massàr ? or did the Oobers allow you
to just take your pick of any star ?

                    dibs on Venus !

I shall not look, ever again, to Mars for help
no, not to Mars — to any star but angry red Massàr

I'm sorry, but — look, Mars
I was true as long as you — no more

Canto Nineteen ☆ 795

no more, Mars, no more

you are not quite the vibration I am searching for
you do not always win . . . and as you should well know
to me — not to win is a cardinal sin

    I am no longer interested in matters mystic
    only in facts I can label as realistic

but . . perhaps if I try to meditate
                    . . on *why*

yes, I shall sit here in the quiet candleglow
and see if I might create an enlightened mood

    I shall light the incense beside me, and perhaps
    perhaps . . an errant salamander spirit might somehow
                        . . drift through
    perchance to guide me . . to whisper
                  this is false
                      and this is true

    . . don't you know that you still need him
and he will always need you ?

NO ! NO ! NO !

oh ! how did that pixilated salamander spirit get in here
to buzz such a big lie into my ear ? I asked for Truth ! . . not more lies

extinquish the candle !
    snuff out the incense !

        I will not trust the words
        I heard that sly salamander spirit say

          it was probably only
          a frisky poltergeist, wanting to play

I was never much for long periods of meditation anyway

    electricity is safer than candlelight
    and much easier on the inner ear . .

the candle flame only makes me hallucinate
a voice . . . so low and clear
            "what are we going to do about it
            now . . and here ?"

OH, STOP ! STOP ! STOP !

quickly, quickly, quickly !

open the Bible, any page will do . . any page at all
never mind false and true
don't let your heart play this cruel trick on your mind

hurry ! hurry ! find a verse, a verse
any verse to read . . just so it doesn't contain the word *need*

. . . oh, Gooober, my God, my God !
I need you, need you, need you so . . . .

hurry ! hurry ! just close your eyes tightly
turn the pages . . and place your finger on a verse
anywhere your Higher Self guides you
. . then open your eyes and read
whatever it says to you

. . and you must listen
for his individual chord of music . .

OH ! STOP ! STOP !

read the Bible, read the Bible — Old Testament or New
don't allow this explosion to break through !

read read read read read

oh ! need need need need need

I read like a mad woman, flipping pages, skipping lines
back and forth, forth and back
. . explode in fire !
then cool, green water . .

BE STILL ! BE STILL !

read read read
find a verse . . . any verse

read read read

close your eyes . . place your finger on the page
any page, any verse . . find a verse

" *. . is it a good book ?*
does it contain the knowing things ?"

OH, GOD ! OH, STOP !

here's a verse, here's a verse !

about a winter wind . . which blows

      oh, God ! I lost my place
please ! give me grace !
where is that line about a winter wind
which blows . . . . ?

              "hey, spunky ! you have funny toes
            for a special, unique rose
                . . . but they're growing on me"

DAMNED SALAMANDER SPIRIT !
DAMNED INCENSE AND CANDLE !

    STOP !

oh, Christ ! I beg you

    see ? I am kneeling to you
    I am on my knees — oh, please, please
    make his voice go away . . until I'm stronger
    Christ ! please
    I cannot bear it any longer . . I so need the Truth

OH !
    OH !
        OH !
            I remember . . .
      . . the Sun rises over the hilltops
      oh, beautiful One, way up above
          . . on that first Easter morning
      when Jesus arose . . .

    no . . .
I can't remember
I can't remember

    help me, Christ — not Jesus, the man, but Christ !
    oh, please help me

. . on that first Easter morning
        when Jesus arose . . all the Earth
was glad . . and a poem of Happiness
ought not be . . . NO ! should not be . . sad
no beautiful line of poetry . . or prose
Should make anyone sad . .

        "darling, darling . . don't be so
               churning and burning
        darling, I love you so . .
        please don't twist your toes
        . . go smell a rose !

I love you so, I do, I do
my special flower, my druid sprite . . in spite
of all the things you do . . to make me blue"

oh ! I will go insane
from the pain of hearing his voice

     dear Christ . . see my heart bleed ? please
     stop his voice
     I need, I plead for your comfort — where is my solace ?
     please send me solace, Lord
     and guide my shaking finger on these pages
     to some verse of solace from the Ages

OH, CHRIST !

PLEASE ! I AM ON MY KNEES !

       . . I will lift up mine eyes . . .

yes ! yes ! tell me, tell me
tell me where I should cast my eyes — and look
guide my finger in this Holy book
oh ! where, where shall I lift up mine eyes ?

OH, NO !

     please, please don't let me see
the pale shimmer of his aura over there . . oh, see ?

       over there . . against the wall ?

CHRIST ! I tell you
he is at this very moment . . here . . in this very room !

       don't you see him ?

OH, CHRIST ! see the pale shimmer of his aura
over there, against the wall ?

where may I lift up mine eyes
so I do not see that pale auric light
that shines over there . . oh, Christ **WHERE ? WHERE ?**

       . . I will lift up mine eyes
         unto the hills
      from whence comes . . . my help

help ? from the hills ?
NO ! I cannot lift up mine eyes unto the hills
from whence my help once came

I cannot lift up mine eyes unto my magical druid mountains
for I know — now — there are no hills
                    or mountains who can fly
I need Truth !
I cannot, I will not cling to that old lie
about making mountains fly
please ! guide me to some words of Truth !
I need . . some word . . some word

> *. . and the word was made flesh*
> *and dwelled among us . .*

    fragments, fragments
skimming pages . . Rock of Ages

> *. . . upon this rock, I will build my church*

    skimming pages . . songs of Solomon . . psalms of David
Matthew, Mark . . Luke and John . . and all the sages

    Old Testament . . New Testament

Moses, Moses . . David and Goliath . . David

  . . watch out for Bathsheba !

Moses, Moses . . . Ruth . . . Rebecca . . . Ruth
                    Mary Magdalene . .

    oh ! I have cast no stone
    why am I alone ?

fragments, fragments . . skimming pages . . Rock of Ages
psalms of David . . songs of Solomon

Christ, did I ever tell you ?
if Emilie . . I mean, if she
if she had been a boy . . we had chosen David
      David and Emilie
Emilie and David . .   David . . psalms of David

    fragments, fragments
skimming pages . . . songs of sages
    Rock of Ages
          psalms . . psalms

> *. . from the strife of tongues . .*

> *. . my punishment is unbearable . .*

YES ! TRUE ! TRUE !

. . I have been young
and now am old . .

YES ! THAT IS ALSO TRUTH !
I am one hundred and ninety eight
give or take fifty years . . either way

. . a broken and contrite heart . .

Oh ! I am finding Truth !

. . I am forgotten . . as a dead man
out of mind . . I am a broken vessel

but . . I have not forgotten Gooober
what does that mean ?

. . lead me to the rock
that is higher than I . .

oh ! take me to your leader . .

. . deep calleth unto deep . .

CHRIST, NO ! NO ! NOT THAT ONE !

. . deep calleth
. . unto deep

find another line
. . another verse . . quickly quickly !
close your eyes . . . find another verse

. . . . I am fearfully and wonderfully made . .

is that true ?
fearfully made, yes
but wonderfully made, no

. . can one go upon coals
and his feet not be burned ?

well, I don't know . .
Gooober was studying about some mystic
who could . . but we are not mystics . . nor do either of us
know the disciplines of Hatha Yoga

. . for the lips of a strange woman
drop as a honeycomb . . and her mouth . . is smoother
than oil

STOP ! NO !

FORKED-TONGUE SERPENT WORDS !
HISSING-HISSING-KISSING NO ! NO ! NO !

> *. . but her end is bitter wormwood*

bitter . . bitter

> *. . a wounded spirit*
> *who can bear . . ?*

true ! true !
my spirit has been wounded
and I cannot bear it . .

I CANNOT BEAR IT !

> *. . if thou faint in the day of adversity*
> *thy strength is small . .*

what . . were those words . . again ?

> *. . if thou faint*
> *in the day of adversity . . thy strength*
> *is small . .*

> *. . I am fearfully*
> *and wonderfully made . .*

oh, no, no !
I am not, I am not — no !
only fearfully made

> not wonderfully made

at all

> *. . how shall we sing the Lord's song*
> *in a strange land ?*

> oh, that is true true true !

how can I sing Silent Night
or remember the melody to that forgotten song
I keep hearing . . then losing

> . . and how can Gooober ever be true to me
in this strange Age . . and this strange land of grokking ?

> *. . let he who is without sin*
> *cast the first stone . .*

I cast no stones !
>   oh, I cast no stones !

> *. . . . where is he ?*
> *oh ! where have you taken him ?*

NOT THAT ONE ! NO !

> *. . . . where have you taken him ?*

NO ! NO !

> *. . he that repeateth a matter*
> *separateth very friends . .*

> *. . and the woman said*
> *the serpent beguiled me . .*
>> *. . the serpent . .*

PLEASE ! NO SNAKES !
NO EDEN SNAKES !

> *. . now the Serpent is more subtle*
> *than any beast . .*

oh, yes ! a serpent is subtle
and a serpent is sneaky . . sneaky sneaky

he wanted to keep a pet snake
did you know that, Christ ? can you believe that ?
I SWEAR ! he asked me . . in Colorado
he used to keep them as pets . . when he was a child

> *. . now a serpent is more subtle*
>> *than any beast . .*

SLIMY CREATURES !

> *. . and your eyes shall be opened*
> *and ye shall be as gods . .*

I don't . . understand

> *. . and your eyes shall be opened*
>> *and ye shall be as gods*

yes, once . . eons ago . . I know
all men and women were
      once . . long ago . . gods
and goddesses
            but I don't quite . . . understand
      I don't understand

Genesis . . Exodus . . Genesis . . Exodus
            Old Testament . . New
New Testament . . Old
            new and old . . . silver and gold
skimming pages . . . Rock of Ages
            words of sages . . give me **TRUTH !**

                    . . I have been a stranger
                        in a strange land . .

what ?   what was that ?

                . . I have been a stranger in a strange land . .

that's in the Bible ?
          Heinlein got it from the **BIBLE ?**
my God !
                        . . I have played the fool . .
true !   true !

                    . . the Morning Stars sang together . .

     QUICK !   QUICKLY !
ANOTHER VERSE !
          FIND ANOTHER VERSE !

                            . . seeing the root of the matter
                        is found in me . .

          . . seeing the root
of the matter
          is found in me . . ?

                        . . seeing the root of the matter
                            is found in me . .

                            . . I am brother to dragons
                        and a companion to owls . .

     oh, that is truth, that is truth !
how strange . . that I should have placed my finger on those words

     yes, I am a Brown Owl, did you know that, Christ ?

I am a Brown Owl . . I think

                        . . behold ! this dreamer cometh !
                        and hath taken away thy blessing . .
what ?   what ?
                        . . be sure your sin
                            will find you out . .
                    . . be sure
                        your sin
                    will find
                        you out . .

these pages . . the pages
          the pages are . . stuck together

be sure . .

> *. . your sin*

> *. . will find you out*

THE PAGES ARE STUCK TOGETHER !

> *be sure . . your sin*

> > *. . a three-fold cord*
> > *is not quickly broken . .*

what ? what was that ?

> > *. . a three-fold cord is not quickly broken*

I don't see . . I don't
understand

> > *. . a time to keep silence*
> > *and a time to speak*

> > *. . be sure your sin will find you out . .*

the pages are stuck together, **I SWEAR** they are !

> > *. . a three-fold cord is not quickly broken*

> > *. . a time for silence*

> *and a time to speak . .*

> > > *. . though your sins be as scarlet*
> > > *they shall be as white as snow . .*

as snow . . as snow . . oh !
that is lovely . . so lovely
as red as Mars, as red as blood
scarlet red . . yet made white as snow

> sparkling white . . like snow . . oh, the glow !
> the burning glow when his aura glistened . . oh !
> it glittered, his aura . . like snow diamonds
> > like diamonds . . in the snow
> snow diamonds

> > *. . by night on my bed, I sought him*
> > *whom my soul loveth, but found him not . .*

CHRIST ! THAT IS ENOUGH TRUTH
ENOUGH, I TELL YOU !

.. *by night, on my bed*

I sought him whom my soul loveth

.. *but found him*
not ..

please, Christ, please
no more truth — I can take no more truth this night
are there no words of comfort ?
please help me find words of solace and comfort
I have closed my eyes once more
and am turning pages .. Rock of Ages
please, Christ .. let me place my finger now
on words of solace and comfort .. somehow meant for me

    guide me .. to the words
meant .. just now .. only for me

        .. hide thyself, as it were
for a little moment
        until the indignation
        be over past ..

    .. hide thyself, for a little moment
until the indignation be over past ..

    .. sorrow and sighing
      shall flee away
        .. sorrow and sighing
    shall flee away

    .. Rachel, weeping
    for her children ..

PLEASE ! OH, PLEASE !
    oh, no
      no
      no

    .. Rachel, weeping for her children

      .. and would not
        be comforted ..

please .. oh, no !
no no no .. please, another verse

    .. oh, thou of little faith !

    oh, thou ..
      of little faith !

. . wherefore didst thou doubt ?

it is I . . be not afraid

. . it is I . . be not afraid . .

. . and the angel said: Fear Not !

and I will give thee the keys of Heaven . .

no, Christ — no, not that one !
it has a sad ending

I do not want to hear again
of Butterfingers Peter

but I forgive him — yes, I do
because I am careless too
I am careless . . and I lose things

*. . my little daughter
lies at the point of death . .*

OH, STOP ! STOP ! STOP !

*. . my little daughter
lies at the point of death . .*

STOP ! PLEASE . . . . . . STOP !

. . oh, thou of little faith !

. . oh, thou of little faith ! wherefore didst thou doubt ? . .

. . what manner of man is this ? . .

yes, yes !
what manner of man was Gooober
what kind of man . . to hurt me so

. . what manner of man is this ?

*. . with what measure ye mete
it shall be measured to you . .*

*. . to what purpose is this waste ?
to what purpose is this waste ?*

*. . there was a man
sent from God . .*

Canto Nineteen ☆ 807

.. there was
a man
sent
from God ..

.. and the Light
shineth in the darkness
and the darkness comprehendeth it not

.. and the Light
shineth in the darkness

.. and the darkness
comprehended it not

we may not speak
of the knowing-things
until . . .
until . .
until ?
until ?
.. nothing is secret
that shall not be manifest

oh, please, Christ — please
I am so afraid .. he has gone away
and he may never return .. I am so afraid
I may never see him again

.. there is no fear in love

perfect love casteth out all fear . . .

.. the Day Star arises in your hearts

.. perfect love
casteth out fear

.. if his understanding fail
have patience with him ..

.. have patience with him ..

.. and the Day Star arises
in your hearts ..

oh, Eternity ember
glow and burn
glow and burn

ask and learn . . .

oh, silvery-wise eyes
glow and burn
help me, help me learn

. . ask and

learn . .

. . there was a man sent by God

. . many are called
but few are chosen . .
nothing is secret
that shall not be made manifest

. . be not forgetful to entertain strangers
for thereby some have entertained
angels unaware . .
. . and your eyes shall be opened
and ye shall be as gods . .
. . look to the rainbow !

. . ask and learn

and if his understanding fail

. . be patient with him

. . be patient with him

. . look
upon
the rainbow
. . the Day Star arises . . . in your hearts

. . and the Light
shineth in the darkness

. . there was
a man sent from God

. . what manner of man
is this ?

. . and I shall light a candle
which shall not be put out !

then reverently, as monks walk
you entered the dark and lonely
Temple of my soul
        . . to light a candle

. . and I shall light a candle
which shall not be put out . .

the knowing-things
oh, the knowing-things !

.. *weeping may endure for a night*
but joy cometh in the morning ..

.. *weeping may endure*
for a night
but JOY ! cometh
in the morning ..

.. BUT JOY COMETH !

.. *unless ye become*
as little children
ye cannot enter the Kingdom ..

.. the keys to the Kingdom
are teeny tiny ..

and your eyes shall be opened
and ye shall be as gods ..

oh, let me hear your own words !
your own words .. your own
I need your words as Jesus, the man
not as the Christ
tell me your words as Jesus, the man

.. *Jesus wept*
.. *Jesus wept*

.. *my God, my God !*
why hast Thou forsaken me ?
.. *why hast thou*
forsaken me ?

.. *the Lord is my Light*
who, then, shall I fear ?

.. *and I shall light a candle*
which shall not be put out ..

thank you, Christ
now I remember my mission with Gooober
I remember my goal

.. *for whatsoever things ye should desire*
pray as if ye had already received these
and ye shall surely have them ..

thank you, Jesus
you have restored my soul

While the Soul Slumbers

oh, words divine !
    oh, words sublime !
oh, holy holy words !

                    a picture is worth ten thousand words
                    so the Oriental sages say

            and therefore is the higher . . nay ! nay !
            shame ! shame !
            for it takes words to tell
            even of that ancient claim, does it not ?

yes, the glory of every story shines in words words words !
the glory of the Easter gladness overcoming death's final sadness
is told in words words words !

words have wings like birds
that fly through the sky of the mind

                . . be ye wise as a serpent
                        but harmless as a dove

doves, blessed birds . . spreading their wings of words
of peace and love
flying down from above to comfort me

        wise serpent words poSSeSSing and obseSSing
        for the purpoSe of bleSSing

be ye wiSe aS a Serpent
but aS harmleSS aS a dove

        oh, words ! words ! words ! of holy knowing and growing
        words ! those perfectly marvelous scribbles on a page
        containing the wisdom of every Age
                    the experience and teaching of every sage

sending rays of light into the darkness, with knowing sounds
as the Universe pounds
            a strong pulse, with each ray of light
words . . falling on my heart

oh ! the beautiful rhyming of the proper timing of words
powerful, powerful words . . words that ring with Truth !
words that sing, forsooth ! words that sing — words that ring

        words of spring . . and every good thing

like kitties . . .

words hurt — oh, yes, words hurt — 'truth' contains the letters of 'hurt'
and 'sword' is 'words' — each is the other, with the letters transposed
but words teach, and they also reach the human soul
words make me remember our glowing-burning-knowing ember
and words remind me that I must always . . as you taught me

                    Expect a Miracle

and now I notice, for the first time
that the Chaldean numerical value of each letter of those druid words
                    Expect a Miracle
when added together, total to the single number 5
and on the Double Number Tree — they add to thirty two — 32
which has the same vibration as the powerful 23

twenty three ! the double number
called by the astrologers and wise men of Babylonia and Chaldea

            The Royal Star of the Lion

23 ! a number which, the wise men say
promises . . and even guarantees . . success, through help from superiors
and protection from those in 'high places'

        help from the Masters ? protection from Heaven ?
        then, if I do as you always taught me, and . . expect a miracle
        the spiritual chords are truly lyrical !

for, when I do not merely *hope for* but **EXPECT** a miracle
I can also expect
a mystical smile from the holy faces of all the saints
and the helpful protection of wise Avatars in high places above
who know the magic of the miracle of peace
                    that comes from love

and now I wonder . .

        about the night my soul . . . was nearly torn
        I seek the meaning of another number
        calling to me in my wakeful slumber — and I must know
        if it was tragic, and not the rhyming magic we once knew
        that night, in our haunted California room
                    when you said "there's no more magic"
        not for us, not for me, not for you
                    were your words that night false . . or true ?

for, did not the Egyptian Adepti teach . .

                    "put the mysteries of wisdom into practice

and all evil will flee from you" ?

yes . . put wisdom . . into practice
and evil will flee

where are my torn and tattered, but trusted books
of ancient number symbolism, containing the numerical Chaldean alphabet ?
I must look up the occult numerological interpretation
of our haunted room, on that Halloween-scary night

. . . numerological contains the word 'logical'
but of course !
the science of numbers is wise because of its logic
as Abstract Al knew
in the Wonderland world of the higher mathematics
of his Relativity
numbers hold all the deepest mysteries
of the truth of this and all other solar systems
galaxies and Universes
everything in Heaven and on Earth
is arranged according to numerical disciple
and the laws of meta-physics . . meaning *beyond* physics
are as inflexible . . and as reliable
as those laws governing the ordinary physics of material matters

like words, numbers are not dead — no, ciphers live !
and they give to the mind that seeks a knowing
in the dawning light of growing

. . answers

while the soul slumbers
God speaks to us through numbers

that's worth repeating to myself — repeating to my elf ? to my S-elf ?
while the soul slumbers
God speaks to me . . through numbers . . speaks to my elf ?

allright, God, I'll listen !

I'll open my sleepy Third eye
remove the cotton from my inner ear . . and listen !

the number of our Alpha and Omega room
of the Beginning and the End of Us — in California

is room 1217   which adds to 11

eleven, according to the wise Adepti of metaphysics
is a Master number

11 is . . a Master number ? the number of Masters ?

and also, in a deeper and more intricate interpretation
according to the ancients, the number 11 symbolizes

> a clenched fist . . and a Lion muzzled

muzzled by whom ? kept from speaking by yourself — or me ?
or by the Masters, who overshadowed that strange
> > and Master numbered room ?

> were Masters from another galaxy, then
directing our helpless actions in that haunted room
from the Beginning to the End . . planning the doom . . of Us ?

no no — not that ! I must remember to expect a miracle !
yes, I must seek all the complex numerological vibrations
as the Kabalah teaches one to do
so . . what is the total vibration of the room — plus me, plus you
the trinity of three
> > our magic room . . plus you . . plus me ?

the occult values of each letter making up your name
using the shortened form of your first name, that rhymes with "sob" add to 6

and those making up my own name add to nine — 9

what magic number tricks can I do, when I add the six of you
to the nine of me — plus the eleven of our room of destiny ?

since 11 is a Master number, in most cases, it is taught
that it may not be reduced to a single number, through addition
> > such as . . . 1 plus 1 = 2

only under rare and privileged circumstances
is the Master number 11 permitted to be reduced, so the ancients tell

only when there is a sufficiently great cosmic cause and concern
to seek the latent, or the underlying complexities
> > of a microcosm situation, person or event
is it considered proper
to reduce the Master number 11
through adding its digits

and so, if I wish to gain the Macrocosm — not the microcosm
point of view . . concerning you
> > myself . . and Room 1217

I must begin by adding the 11 of our room
as a Master number, unreduced by being added to its single number 2

> 11   for the room
> 6   for you

$$\frac{9}{26} \quad \text{for me}$$

26 ? twenty six ? what is the Chaldean-Babylonian symbolism
                                        of that number ?
within myself, I seem to feel
a faint remembered thunder . . of warning

      yes, the Chaldeans instruct that 26 is a number
      full of the gravest warnings for the future
      26 foreshadows, they say, thunderous and stormy events to come
      often triggered or incited by — bad counsel
      deception and lack of sympathy

      with the primal cause of such disasters being Saturn
             Saturn, the planet of Karma
      because Saturn vibrates to . . and is represented by
             the single number 8

which is also the number achieved
by adding the number 2 and the 6 of 26   2 plus 6 = 8

      therefore, say the texts . . the dangers so foretold
      may eventually be lightened or dissolved
      only when all the karmic lessons thus meant to be imposed
      have been accepted as one's due fate or destiny
           and paid in full

      for Saturn, the disciplinarian, demands
      the completion of the karmic circle — and sternly commands
           the fulfillment of past obligations
      before the sweet rewards of wisdom are bestowed

then, are we heading toward even greater disasters — separately
than those we have already endured — together ?

NO NO NO — I must keep remembering the magical number 5
of our druid mantra . . Expect a Miracle
and its meaning on the Double Number Tree — of 23

          twenty three . . The Royal Star of the Lion

yes, 23

      which promises — even guarantees — help and assistance
      and protection too — from those in higher places
             the White Lodge Elder Brothers
    the Masters themselves

and also from . . the Higher Angels of our *own* s-elves

and so now . . . . . as allowed in rare and privileged circumstances
since there is a sufficiently great cosmic cause and concern . .

                    . . at least, there is within the cosmic Universe
                              of the me-of-me
for we are all — each of us
gods and goddesses, who rule over
the individual Universes
              of ourselves

and so . . I will seek the latent, or underlying complexities
                        of the *microcosmic* situation
by reducing the Master number 11
of our haunted Room 1217
to its single number vibration, by adding it
                                    1 plus 1 = 2
and achieving
its single number value of 2

              then I will add it to myself . . and you
meditating on the happiness of our miracle at midnight in that room

when our eternity ember burned
and we learned . . so much

    2   our room
    9   for me
    6   for you
   17

                              seventeen ?   17
                              seventeen ?   17
              1 plus 7 = 8   8 again

oh, will I never escape
from the Karmic fate
        of Saturn's solemn and eternal 8 ?

but . . wait !

26 equals 8   twenty six and seventeen both add to eight
17 equals 8   that's true — but there is a *difference* between the two !

seventeen, say the ancient laws of numbers . . .

        17 is a highly spiritual number
        and is expressed in Essenic symbolism
        as the 8 pointed Star of Venus
                        . . a symbol of Peace and Love !
Peace and Love ?
    Love and Peace !
oh, kitties are the only good things !

the 8 pointed Star of Venus !

the Star of Truth
at the very tip top of our Christmas tree !

being 8 pointed, through the celestial 17
it cancels out the karmic fate of the number 8
through the scary number 26

oh, how perfectly marvelous !

what glorious druidic magic !

the 8 pointed Star of Venus has the power
to *neutralize* the karmic Saturn 8 — of Destiny or Fate
which held our magical 17 room in its icy clutch of the number 26
on that Halloween-scary night

. . and also represents, secretly, to you and me
our own Star of Truth
at the very tip top of our miracle Christmas tree !

our Star of Truth
Goob, you're almost home free !

you're getting closer and closer
to coming home to me !

what else can I find, growing on the Double Number Tree
to enlighten my mind . . about seventeen ?

the number 17, according to all esoteric sages, is also called
the Star of the Magi
Astrologer Kepler's Stella Octangula

also the Star of the trinity of astrologers
the three Wise Men . . the Magi
who followed its brilliant light
to the stable, on that holy night, silent night
. . smelling sweetly of hay
and further . . say the texts

17 expresses that the person or event it represents
has risen . . superior to all trials, tests and difficulties
of the past
and is also the Number of Immortality
which signifies that the person, entity or event 17 represents . .

will live on, after supposed Earth-death
deliberately arranged through the Saturn mystery of 8

Canto Nineteen ☆ 817

for secret cosmic reasons
and will never die, but shall become immortal

oh, Gooober ! Oobers are eternal !

not nearly, but *really* eternal !

and the mystery lies within Saturn's karmic 8
which is, actually — a double Serpent Eternity circle
a double symbol of the Serpent, eating its own tail
so the Serpent-Saturn-Seven-cycle of reincarnation
is merely profound Saturn, using subtle Neptune's number 7
to hide his deepest mystery from those not yet ready to receive it
as hidden in the Stella Octangula 17 !

. . . and such a difference there is, in the 8 contained within 26
and the 8 contained within 17

seventeen ! seventeen ! seventeen !

what else can I learn from the language of numbers
spoken to me by our co-Creators, our Father and Mother
Who art in Heaven
while my soul slumbers ?

in the ancient Mystery Schools, it is taught in the secret doctrines
that the more advanced or enlightened student
when seeking further wisdom from the profound celestial language
of numbers
may properly and correctly
add to the total number of a person or an event — in the microcosm
any Macrocosmically related number
which the mind may discover through attunement
or arrive at through the sacred process of intuition

in-tuition meaning, literally — to be taught from within
so I shall meditate, using my in-tuition
and wait for the too long ignored Higher Angel of my own s-elf
to guide me
for this is the deeper way
to use numerology as a tool for understanding all profundities
as it has been told by every sage of old
only the initiated pilgrim may see all the mysteries of numbers unfold
in their complete and fourth dimensional, deeper-layered revelation

am I, then an initiate ? I do not know
but I am certain, in both my heart and mind
that I've survived the beginning agonies of spirit
of an initiation to . . at least some fragment . . of Truth

and I call on . . I demand ! at least that fragment . . now !

I will, therefore, imitate Abstract Al, of the Relativity equations
and delve into the fourth dimensional mysteries of numerology
according to accepted esoteric formula
                        by way of the *third* dimension

making to myself no hypocritical excuse, or self effacing apology
but listening carefully only to the still, small voice within
which is the Higher Angel of the me-of-me

                        and my in-tuition whispers . . three !
        three . . the Trinity

            also, the three-times-three of you-and-me

I will properly and correctly, then — esoterically appropriately
add the three of the Trinity

        I shall add the 3 of the Macrocosm Holy Trinity
        or the 3 of the microcosm trinity
                        of you . . and me . . and our room
        2   our room of destiny
        9   the vibration of me
        6   the vibration of you . . making our microcosmic trinity
        3   the Macrocosmic Trinity
       ───
        20

                                    twenty
                                    twenty
                                    twenty
so our haunted room
        added to you and me
plus the three of the Trinity
                    . . vibrates to the single number 2
                        2 plus 0 = 2
2 symbolizes dreams
        . . dreams of the Essenes ?

and the double number 20, according to all the wisest seers
is the number of hidden, secret fears
but the final occult evaluation of the vibration of the number 20
        is spiritual uplifting — and salvation

                    twenty

twenty is pictured
by the Chaldeans as The Awakening

it is also called The Judgement

and is symbolized, state all the mystical writings
by the figure of a winged Angel, sounding a trumpet
while from below . .

                    a man, woman and child are seen
rising from a tomb
their hands clasped in prayer

* and . . the deeper occult interpretation of this, says my book . . oh !
Gooober, look ! just look what it says in my book !

          . . the deeper-layered meaning of the number 20
     is the awakening of new purpose — of new plans

     of new goals . . . an inspired mission on Earth
     the call to action for some great cause

     so our haunted room was not a tomb !
     it was not a room of doom . . but a room of eventual joyful destiny !

     it was — and still is — a room watched over by the Masters
     a Master numbered room, not a room of gloom or doom

     oh ! and not a tomb ! . . no !
     but a room of Easter hyacinth perfume

                         where a small white cross
                         planted on a far hill . . on Mt. Olympus
                         looks down upon the figure
                         of a winged Angel, here on Earth

for tomb rhymes with womb !
and death rhymes with birth !

          a winged Angel, sounding a trumpet, while from below
          a man, woman and child are seen . . . rising from a tomb

               with their hands clasped in prayer

yes, in prayer
               and there . .

          in that haunted room of our miracle at midnight
     where you stood as a god . . so tall
               where we saw each other's auras
     against the pale yellow wall . . there, in that room, was pulsing
     the secret vibration of a holy purpose

* The reader wishing to learn more of the
  Chaldean method of calculating and interpreting
  numbers are referred to Chapter 5 in <u>Linda Goodman's Star Signs</u>

a silent, unspoken call to action . . the awakening
of an inspired mission on Earth
an inspired mission

to make death rhyme with birth !

but . . some of the older texts relate a symbolism
we know, Goob . . to be part deception
for they say that the number twenty is inter-twined, symbolically

to the terrible Judgement of Osiris
Osiris, the god — the judge of the quick and the dead

Osiris, the god of the dead

they say that the pictured Awakening, with the trumpeting Angel
and the man, woman and child rising from a tomb

symbolizes Osiris, Isis and their child Horus

only partly true, only partly
do you remember when we channeled those strange truths
on that silent night of our knowing . . . about the god Osiris ?
not the first night of our Eternity ember's glowing
but months later . . during another midnight of burning, unexpected
knowing
I had forgotten it, until now
until the numbers awakened my memory

we channeled many truths
about this god and goddess . . one of these being
that the Twin Selves called Isis and Osiris

. . . the letters of her name, **Isis,** eternally held
within the letters of his name, **Osiris**
forever inseparable . . .

that these two created, through their love
not one child — but three ?
Horus was their son . . . and Isis gave birth also to twins
who were named Mercury and Vulcan
Vulcan, the goddess — not the god — of Thunder
for Vulcan is a female planet

then later, I promised myself
that I would someday sort out the tangled webs of false mythology

only half seriously, and more than a little sadly, because
there were other truths I channeled after you left
related to Greece, Mt. Olympus . . the Great Pyramid of Gizeh
Egyptian secrets of Initiation

and . . yes, of Atlantis too . . and the buried records

and I couldn't see how such revelations could ever be told
without ridicule from the Egyptologists . . and Bible Fundamentalists
for I had no proof that all these things were true
as they were channeled

no proof . . unless

unless someday, together, you and I
might in some way . . find the proof which would deny

each and every ancient lie

by discovering
the secret hiding place
of the buried records of Atlantis

and uncovering Truth . . by calling on a certain mantra
a sound . . a phrase of music . . a forgotten fragment of melody
which would, within its chromatic scale

have the unsuspected power
to roll away the heavy stones of sealed memory
where the records lie, even now

awaiting . . discovery

was that, too . . but a dream ?   and yet . .

what if it was ?   what if it was but a dream
a dream of some brilliant tomorrow, born from a bereaved yesterday
under a golden Sun and robin's-egg-blue skies
discovering the records which will shine the light of Truth
on all the ancient lies . . down through the Ages

with the help of those in number seventeen's "high places"
perhaps even the saddened god and goddess themselves
who have, for so many eons, been searching for someone, somewhere
to channel the Truth of their teachings
weary of hearing them maligned and distorted
longing for someone to be their medium of expression . . .

. . . . with the help of the mathematical chords
of some forgotten music . . some melodic sound of Abracadabra !
or Open Sesame !

yes, what if it was but a dream ?
are not dreams the true reality ?   oh, they are, they are !
and someday, together, you and I . . perhaps along with others
shall heed the pleas of this sad god and goddess

calling within our inner ears
and expose each Serpent lie — of life and death and love
coiling and snaking around today's mythological illusions

                                and delusions
through the remembered truth and music

           . . of the soul's lost chords

and the records of Atlantis
also contain other recorded truths of Egypt
such as the building of the Great Pyramid

      its magical purpose . . and the true identity of its architect
                    who was not Cheops

yes, someday, some way, we shall do this
even though we are not, either of us, great scientists
no famed Egyptologists, nor renown archeologists

        but simply . . you and me

fallen angels . . along with how many millions of others ?
only another fallen god and goddess . . who will someday, once more
be bleSSed with the lost, forgotten powerS

           all of us poSSeSSed of yore

for . . the Serpent is a Subtle beaSt
and our eyeS Shall be opened . . aS Shall be alSo theirS

           all the other loSt and fallen oneS

we shall, you and I
give the world a Christmas gift
the gift . . of our Star of Truth !

      lovely words !

what perfectly marvelous words of gladness, to end my cosmic sadness
and transmute the Earth's despair into our birthright of **JOY !**

    and how very, very strange
    the manner in which the truth also rains . . upon our names

    what celestial tricks the numbers and stars play upon us
    that my numerological vibration should be Nine, for Mars
    and yours should be Six, for Venus

    how strange, that I should vibrate to 9
    the number of war and courage, through Mars
    and you should vibrate to 6

the number of peace and love, through Venus

as though, through the essence of our togetherness
we create, like all men and women, a fearful and wonderful polarity
between the planets and the stars

your Venus conjuncts my Pluto — and we cannot be Earth-separated
nor Heaven nor hell separated either
no treacherous ship of destiny
no bitter tear or hidden fear can hide the starry truth . .
                              I have been blind !

and now I must find . . those winged words of the holy scriptures
those ancient winged and flying birds of words
                              which relate to astrology

yes, here they are ! in the Book of Ecclesiastes
the words that lead the heart
        to wish on and follow a star

"to every thing, there is a season . . and a time
                    to every purpose under Heaven
a time to be born . . . and a time to die"

              no ! no more shall there be a time to die !
              for, as John wrote, in Revelations . .

              God shall wipe away all tears from their eyes . . .
              neither shall there be any more death . .

              no more death ! through the starry
              Saturn-Seven-Serpent secret of the soul's cycle
              and through cell regeneration

"a time to plant . . and a time to pick up
        that which has been planted . . . a time to kill"

no ! no more killing . . . no time to kill
for war shall be no more in the new and golden Age of Aquarius
when the Serpent, who is more subtle than any beast
shall open the eyes of all the fallen angels
                              and they shall be as gods
        and goddesses

a time to heal . . . a time to break down . . and a time to build up
        a time to weep . . and a time to laugh
a time to mourn . . . and a time to dance . . . a time to cast away stones
        and a time to gather stones together
a time to embrace . . . and a time to refrain from embracing
        a time to get . . . and a time to lose
a time to keep . . . and a time to . . . cast away

a time to rend . . . and a time to sew"

> yes ! as there was a time to sew
> Raggy and Algae back together again

"a time to grow
. . a time to know

a time to keep silence . . . and a time to speak
a time to love, and a time to hate
a time of war . . . and a time of peace

> and . . . a time to cast away . . . "

A Time to Cast Away

yes, it is time . . .

> it is time for love
> it is time for peace
> it is time to heal

> a time to renew my forgotten goal
> a time to have faith in my own twin soul
> a time to believe, and a time to know
> that we will soon be reunited . . and together
> we shall strike the powerful positive
>> into the terror
> of the hateful negative on Earth

>> . . those beautiful, peaceful love-dove
>> flying words of yours
>>> in your letter . . .

and it is time . .

> that I must cast away the heavy burden
> of unforgettable, unforgivable memories
> which has weighed so heavily
> oh, so wearily on my heart . . and which
> has kept my soul from soaring into the light

> it is time

and so . . I have taken all these unforgivable memories
of unforgivable words and unforgettable scenes of unforgivable people
in unforgettable places . . all the unforgivable memories
> of yesterday, today and tomorrow

and tossed them together
　　　　　scrambled them
and mixed them up

　　　then tied them securely
　　　inside a strong canvas bag

　　　　　　　　shaped like a balloon

. . Star Trek . . . .
. . trail . . don't interrupt . .
. . e when I'm watching Star Tr . .
. oshster . . Vail . . unopened sur .
. e in a closet . . two lies . . Jack and .
. ga · Circle . . torn Valentine . . you didn .
. Icox hurt . . telephone operator from Low .
. ican Villa and telephone operator from Lowa .
. Mexican Villa . . unopened surprise in a close .
. namen . . her . . Vail Vail . . icy trail of unforg .
. rn Valentine . . you lost two more points, baby .
. ore magic . . there's no more magic . . it's not go .
. Cynthia ? smashed her head ? Cynthia ? you .
. ashed her head ? . . you mean Emilie ? Doberm .
. ig Bang . . it's not good to see you again forge .
. ga Circle . . forked tongue serpent kiss . Ro .
. ster . . Vail Vail . . serpent kiss . . lies .wh .
. hmes with pill . . Jack and Jill . . Rocheste .
. namen . . you can't rely on Gemini . . an .
. ow with Scorpio . . Newport Beach to s .
. lied . . why did you say . . . Karen .
. ent's kiss . . with the Newport .
. Wilcox . . well . . you lose two .
. re points, baby . . and .
. ee you again . . bab . .

and marveled at the weight
of this heavy burden

which had, for so long, crushed my heart
and curved the spine of my soul

and tonight . .

with Jack and Jill and Mary-Mary-Quite-Contrary
nearly squeezing out of the bag

                                . . though I quickly stuffed them
                                right back in again . .

                I stood on the front porch
                        in the cool
                with Love and Peace mewing
                        beside me
                looking down over Bennett Avenue

with Mars twinkling Red at me   and Venus twinkling Green at me
        from the left   from the right

            and threw the heavy burden of that bag
            with all my might . . far. far out into the night
                        way out of sight . . . .

                and watched it fly
            on a broomstick, through the sky

            to orbit around some insignificant fixed star
            a billion trillion light years away

                        Forever
                        and Ever
                        and Ever

                        Amen . . Awomen

Peace

    I slept last night the whole night through
    for the first time . . since the last time I saw you

                this morning
                        the rainbows splash
                in the upstairs hall
                    somehow . . brighter than before

and Love and Peace
           seem to come closer
to catching them
                 in their paws

                              not quite, but . . almost

Love

        you knew about my shaggy, Old English sheep dog
        I loved with all my heart, and christened
                                    Heathcliffe
        because I thought
        it would be a wild and weird
                     and wonderful thing
        to call him
             out on the street
        and hear his name echo through the tangled canyons
        of Manhattan skyscrapers . .

                     turning the crowded city
                          into Bronte moors

        and you knew too
how much it hurt me

when Heath grew too large for my New York apartment
and peeked out at me
                    with his beady eyes
                    of wistful, restless lonely

till I understood
and gave him to some friends
with a farm in the country

                    where he's happier now
                    flopping his funny mop feet
                    and chasing butterflies
                         through real moors

or at least a better imitation of them
than West End Avenue

        you told me it was kind of like that with Buckwheat, your cat
        when you had to go away from the beach one summer
        and leave him behind, grieving for you
                              with friends

because the traffic
in front of your home, in Hollywood
would have killed him, sooner or later

yes, you knew how it was about loving things . . and losing them
because you love them too much to hurt them anymore

> I guess that's why you surprised me
> one tender spring twilight, in Pismo Beach
> when I had been sad all day, and couldn't explain why

I was wandering out in the back yard
smelling a rose . .
> feeling the green grass
tickling my toes . . and you had gone to the store
> > for something
> when you returned
> > you called me in from the yard

> > > "hey, Goob !" you cried
> > > all twinkling
> > > "come on in here
> > > and see who has come to visit us !"

I ran inside . . . and there on the bed

> in the room with the fireplace
> sitting up proudly, on our heirloom spread

was a huge, life-size, shaggy Old English sheep dog

made out of paper mache
> with a pink cardboard tongue hanging out
and a perfectly marvelous
> round black-button nose
looking for all the world like a real-live-panting
trusting and lovable . . best friend

> Heathcliffe, the Younger

> > and you said . . . . "Heathcliff is a Gooober, like us
> > and each time you look at him
> > > I want you to remember
> > that you will never be lonely again
> > because you belong to me now
> > > like I belong to you
> > and it's Us together . . . Forever-and-ever
> > against the cold-hearted traffic
> > > of the world"

I wanted to reply . . "my cup runneth over"
but the words wouldn't come
so I smiled, instead, with my heart — and you knew

        Gooober, is it still true ?
        is it still "Us together . . Forever-and-ever
        against the cold-hearted traffic of the world ?"

Heathcliff, the Younger
is back in New York now . . where I took him
after we both left our magic cottage in Pismo Beach

    so maybe I'll fly back to Manhattan again
    and visit with Heathcliff . . . maybe, since you're gone
    he will talk with me, and tell me how I can avoid being so hurt
    by the world's cold-hearted traffic . . and by
                a Gooober who can lie

I'll leave for the airport this very weekend

Changing Numbers

    before flying to New York
I decided to stop for a day in L.A. . . . to pay a brief visit
to our magic room . . **1217** . . at the Hollywood Roosevelt Hotel
thinking that perhaps the room's vibrations of **Us**
might return, for a moment
the enchantment of our "miracle at midnight"

    but the hotel, I found
has since been taken over by new owners
who have changed the room numbers on all the floors
the new **1217** is now a small and ordinary room
and our old room **1217,** where we first shared "spring"
has been re-numbered to **1221**

the new manager is Alix Baptiste, an intuitive Aquarian
he understood my wanting to spend a few minutes
alone in our old room . . . and gave me the key
though he couldn't possibly have known why

the magic is still there, as powerful as before
but the truly miraculous thing is the new number . . **1221**

remember when we discussed the ancient Chaldean meaning
of our room's old number . . **1217** . . adding to the Number **11**
an unreducible **Master Number** of painful karmic soul testing

and adding my number **9** made it a **20** . . **"The Awakening"**
meaning a "call to a great mission" ?
then adding the Number **4** for you, made it a **24,** adding to **6**
        the number of Venus . . . and Love

NOW the new **1221** adds to a **6** all by itself
no more Master 11 . . . we've passed our karmic test !
and adding my Number **9** is **15** . . adding again to **6** for **Love**
with the double Number **15** being the Chaldean Number
        of **Magic and Mystery**

if you are ever in the new **1221** room with me, adding your **4**
you and I and the room would add to **19** . . adding to **10**
which the ancients call the Number of **Isis and Osiris**
Oh, Gooober, what does it mean ? what does it all . . . **mean ?**

Rings-Around-Saturn-From-the-Falling-Dust-of-Maldek

the misty Sunrise season of gentle pink-gold spring is here again
and I am lost and lonely
walking down a West End Avenue you have never walked along with me

    where are you, this soft May twilight ?

I guess you're somewhere tramping through uncharted woods
exposing the genius quotient of your multi-faceted mind
to the intricacies of ferns and spider webs
and the reproductive responses of moss, mushrooms and toadstools

    or sailing through uncharted seas
    exposing frolicking, rolicking pink dolphins to color film
    knowing they will lose a tone or two of magic in the development

. . . maybe arguing with the blind orthodoxy
of some dogmatic medical or physics tome you're reading

   . . or gathering splintered shavings of stardust
from the dome of an Oober saucer
        floating toward a distant galaxy
   . . speeding silently past the Milky Way

    you are smelling fresh, clean winds . . or cool, green pine trees
tangy splashes of salt water
      or the musty-sweet pages of an ancient book

and not even curious, not even wondering how this spring breeze

smells back here to me
                    I'll tell you anyway
        sweet peas

it smells like sweet peas . . and it smells like lilacs and rain
green grass . . . sadness and gladness inter-twined

but mostly, it smells of Us . . . our magic days
our violet-misty-loping days of wishing
when the world was bright and fresh and new . . and we knew
that miracles are real . . and dreams come true
and nothing is too wonderful to happen . . if you really want it to

that's how it smells to me, back here
how does spring smell out there to you ? oh ! I wish I knew
which uncharted woods you walk
                    or which uncharted seas you're sailing through

and how this first spring we've been apart
feels . . and smells . . to you

        a six year old, with rosy cheeks and pigtails tied with yellow yarn
        is skipping rope in front of me — she plays each day I walk
        like a sign of teeny-tiny to remind me to believe
        oh ! she expects a miracle, every hour or so . . and finds it
        sometimes it's a perfectly marvelous new flower
                            being kissed by a bumblebee
        or a lady bug who has landed gently on her knee
        and who must be set free . . with the magical mantra

        "lady bug, lady bug, fly away home !"

so she won't forget where she lives . . and lose her way

yesterday, she found the green miracle of a grasshopper
and watched it hop over the cracks in the sidewalk, for hours
then tried to coax it to hop back into the grass in the park
a block away . . before it, too, was lost

            I think it was she
            who did that . . or maybe it was me

when I'm pretending I'm small enough
to talk with bugs and birds and things . . and believe
in shiny gold wishing rings, that are lost — then found
and to hear the song of a robin, before he sings

the spring breeze is playing follow the leader with my mind
already I've walked two streets out of my way
and if I don't hurry, the health food store will close
before I can buy a loaf of bread — but this is the twilight hour

of hyacinths for the soul
                              and bread cannot feed my hunger
not even whole wheat bread

perhaps I'll stop at the corner apothecary, and buy instead
the largest bottle of Je Reviens they have — or should I buy Chanel ?
no — Je Reviens, because it means "I shall return"

        . . and splash it all over my hair and skin . . then let the spring air
        transmute its scent into a miracle of myriad memories
                                        of happier twilights

you don't approve of perfume, as I recall so well
you class it with other forms of fraudulent subterfuge
like painted faces, plastic Christmas trees
        the synthetic boost of pills . . and caffeine and nicotine

still, I think I'll risk your ghostly displeasure
and drown myself in perfume anyway

        I have been entirely too Pollyanna-perfect lately
munching healthy lettuce, drinking carrot juice
        not wearing much make-up . . no false lashes anymore
taking my vitamins every day, and doing Yoga head stands
no Excedrin or coffee . . or cigarettes
not even slamming a door . . no Big Bangs at all

        the Earth vibrates these days, they say
        to such a negative frequency
        that one who is ultra-sensitive in any way
        must adopt a vice or two
        to keep one's molecules from flying apart
                        . . exploding into space

and I wouldn't want that to happen
because I wouldn't know in which direction to fly . . to find you

I'm sorry you're not around this spring twilight
so we could have a good, healthy fight
that make-believe tenseness lovers often manufacture
to mask their total empathy . . lest it become too boring

        yes, if you were here, I guess I would affectionately
        pick a teasing quarrel now
        by attacking your disapproval of fraudulent subterfuge

then afterwards, we could kiss and make up
and turn the calendar spring into the breathless wonder
of our own private *spring*
                              our own miracle of deep

I would begin by asking you
if your scrupulously honest heart grows cold
at the sight of the flashy red and gold smeared across October leaves
a pathetic attempt to make you remember their April freshness
                                        . . just before they die

as a woman past her teens wears brighter rouge
to remind you of her springtime

how you must hate the contrived strategy of December
cleverly using ice and snow
to transform ugly skyscrapers into counterfeit faerie castles

      consider the gaudy, pretentious Sun
      bleaching your toadstool-cut hair . . . for shame !
      into various shades of gold
      on Pismo Beach that last spring and early summer
      and turning your skin a coffee tan color
      not common to its natural pigment . .
                  oh, Nature is a subtle cosmetician !

then, of course, we could discuss the ultimate deception . . . .
those phony purple shades painted by the frightened Moon
on Pike's Peak, in Colorado — at midnight
to seduce the Great Pretenders, who wore the artifice of anger

           to hide an honest, naked need for love

      even the gentle, white dove . . of Peace
      is an elusive, eternal myth
      masquerading as an attainable reality
      on this hypocritical planet, called Earth

              as for planets in general . .

Mars is blinking crimson at me right now
from high up in the sky
thrusting through the curtains of drifting twilight clouds
above my head . . and tonight I remember
                that you once said

      "it's misleading to call it red
      that's just an optical illusion . . caused
      by the large amounts
      of radio-strontium oxides on its surface"

or did it originally obtain its reddish hue
from the falling dust of the fated planet, Maldek
another Earth of fallen angels . . in a far-off solar system ?

you didn't think I remembered that, after all these millenniums did you, my love ? my wandering twin soul . .

well, since the game we're still playing, even while apart
is, as usual — Truth versus lie

. . Truth !

back to where we started that rose-drenched December
full circle . . . full Serpent Circle

. . the real truth is . .

I suppose you could claim it's part of the issue
that I said I would never miss you
in your darkened monastery room, on that purple-shadowed night

and that's not true . . because

now there's no one to fight . . no hurt to forgive
since you've returned to Mars, where you obviously live

if you were really-truly from the Oober galaxy
you would hear me call

and I've heard nothing from you — nothing at all
except the faint echo of your rippling brook laugh
and the occasional light touch of an astral hand

you are a Martian, not a Gooober . . and have left me
still a stranger
in this strange and lonely land

Missing

I have decided that it's easier . . missing you in New York
since you've never been here with me

somehow, we never got around to exploring Manhattan
in all the ways that really matter

we've never watched the hailstones splatter
along Fifth Avenue, at noon . . or bought a red balloon
from the clown who wanders around town
and dances across the street
like a ballerina, dodging cars, on his tip toes
and bobbing his huge red nose
at the delighted children

we've never stood, hand in hand
with the other little girls and boys . . and stared
wide-eyed, at the incredible toys in the windows of FAO Schwartz
where I bought your duck and dolphin and boats
                                        to play with you in the bathtub

we've never mingled in a reality-illusion-dream, with the human stream
flowing past Brentano's . . Saks . . Bergdorf Goodman's
                                        and St. Patrick's
or heard the church bells chime
                        exactly at five

                blending with the taxi cab horns and rushing people traffic
                in a symphony of the excitement of just being alive

        we've never wandered through the wonderland of the Village
                                        at midnight
        or watched the sunrise
        from the George Washington Bridge . . or visited the Cloisters
        and strolled along its quiet stone paths
        where monks once reverently walked . . and prayed

        there are so many things
        we never found the time to come here together and do . . .
        we've never had a sunny breakfast of apples and pears
                at the Central Park Zoo . . and whispered to the Lions
                                        and monkey and bears

                how sorry we are they feel so blue
                because they're caged . . when they were born to be free

or drifted through . .

                the Metropolitan museum, to see the ancient Egyptian jewels
                perhaps once worn by you and me
                                we've never sipped peppermint tea
                beside the streaming fountains of cool green water
                                and the statues of gods and goddesses
                lounging there . . and tried to remember the sandals and robes
                                        we used to wear . . long ago

we've never been invited, by television
to say hello . . to our "friend"
at Chase Manhattan Bank

we've never given away any miracles
to the lost ones, in the Bowery
                        who have no friend to thank
at Chase, or any other bank
        and no one to love . . and nowhere to go

                    we've never watched it snow . . . in Times Square
                    on George M. Cohan's statue

we've never seen a Broadway show
or gazed at the golden glow
        of Oriental lanterns, in Chinatown

                    we've never bought hot bagels on the street
                    or a red balloon from that funny clown . .

        . . or watched it snow
        walking from a Broadway show
or shared the glow . . oh, no !
                            it isn't true

        it's not easier missing you

    in New York

            it's not easier at all
            even here . . you're always there
            I hear you and see you . . and smell you in the air

like today . .

    I walked by a store window, near Times Square
    with a triple window display of Castro-convertible beds

            just that . .

    just all kinds of beds
            with blue and green and white quilted spreads
    and I remembered . .

        how you used to say
    you were going to stay awake all night, till dawn
    and study some book about nutrition or healing . . or physics
    or biology . . or medical astrology
                        . . and after an hour or so
you would crawl into bed
and snuggle up against me
            with your head on my shoulder
and I would ask you . .

"darling, shall I turn out the light ?
are you tired . . do you want to go to sleep ?"

                    and you would answer

                    "oh, no, don't turn out the light . .
                    I'm going to stay up and read all night

I'm just resting my eyes
just resting my eyes . . . that's all . . "

and in less than a minute
you would fall fast asleep . . in my arms
all warm and dear
. . and near

just now, as I walked past Rockefeller Center
and stopped to watch the colored flags of all nations
fluttering in the breeze
. . I heard your rippling brook laugh

did I ever tell you that you laugh
like a rippling brook ?
. . and did I ever tell you . .

how very much like a guilty small boy
you would always look
when you dropped your book
and snuggled your head against my shoulder
in bed and lied
and said you were only
just resting your eyes ?

. . and do you know
I just cried
when I saw a bird's nest
because it reminded me
of your hair ?

yes, even here . .
where you never were
you're always there
I see you and hear you
and feel you and smell you
in the air . .

oh, why did I never tell you
that the way your hair grows
at the nape of your neck
. . overwhelms me ?

why did I never tell you
all those secret, special
loving, mump-lump things ?

Echos From on Earthquaked Temenos

darling . . I have been dreaming such a lot
since you've been gone . . and strangely

> I've been remembering my dreams when I awake
> in the morning . . and I've seldom done that before

last night, I dreamt I heard a voice

> a voice of terrible beauty . . awful anger . . and crashing glory
> sending thunderous syllables of passionate pronouncement
> echoing down the caverns of Time
> and the words remained within my conscious memory
> when I awoke . . my spirit trembling

down, down, down . .

> intoned the voice of terrible grandeur

down down down down down . .

> down through countless centuries of tortured time
> beginning ages before the oblivion of Poesida

Satan-Set has seeded spiritual slanders
seething with sinister and serpentine intent . . to mesmerize
the subconscious minds of students, engrossed in the perusal
of the muddy, murky myths of Egyptology . . and Greek mythology

> and so . .

these blinded hieroglyphic hierophants, thus innocently corrupted
these learned men and women of fleeting worldly fame
having been seduced by the subtle Prince of Death and Darkness

> . . to teach unsuspecting Earthlings that the ancient legends claim
> the fair young Horus did swear a cold revenge
> upon the murder of his father — a vile oath to return
> > evil for evil
> therefore, engaging his uncle — Set
> in hideous battle
> urged on by his bereaved and bitter mother — Isis
> goaded in troubled, restless dreams
> by the angry astral of his brave sire — Osiris

can you not hear the outraged cries of Cassotis and Cassandra
from the broken rocks and ruins of a million adyta ?

> neither trust the jeweled and perfumed wench — Nephthys

till she repents — swears atonement
and begs forgiveness from all humankind today

for her sisterly devotion, falsely pictured in Egyptian drawings
engraved in blue-gazed stone and ruby studded idols
                    is but a grinning mask
hiding deeds horrible beyond all earthly pleasure

she, who first mated with animals for sensual pleasure
her womb the beastly terrarium
of the half-jackal child of Hades — called Anubis

O ! gullible sheep
the Truth is not as misguided seers have repeatedly and falsely told

it happened thus . .

            while young Horus fell into a trance-like sleep
            during secret rites in a Temple of old, at the age of twelve
            Set, cleverly disguised as a Coptic Priest
            did hypnotically induce in the kind and compassionate lad
            a thirst for bloody revenge
            as part of a heinous, hellish plan to dis-grace the grace
                                of Isis and Osiris

his purpose to gradually discredit
the memory of Love's Wisdom
taught and demonstrated by these two
who multiplied themselves
at the command of Ra . . into other gods and goddesses
who possessed great powers
and whose mission was to channel the gentle, healing rays

of Pax et Bonum
            to Earth

true . . Isis wept bitter tears
in her inconsolable grief
at the awful dismemberment of her beloved mate — cut into 14 pieces
by his jealousy-driven, greed-crazed brother
                    Set

    yet, she knew no hate
    and did not drive her son to kill

lies ! lies !   for she was then — and she is still
                    as she shall be eternally

                    a vessel for Love and Forgiveness

nor was Osiris a retaliatory god

of barbaric custom
destined to rule those icy nether regions
as Judge of the quick and the dead

for he was then — and he is still
as he shall be eternally

a vessel for Mercy Everlasting

RA ! RAH ! AH ! MEN !
AH ! WOMEN !
Amen . . Awomen . . Amen

. . and Gooober, as my dream faded
although the crashing chords of words
lingered on as remembered music . .

I thought of something . . .

the time I noticed the great ebony statues of Anubis
guarding the entrance of the Egyptian Theatre
on one of my walks down Hollywood Boulevard
and recognized in that long-featured visage of Anubis
a similar appearance to the dogs today called Dobermans
which caused a violent chill to shake me

. . and I am shaken now . . by a different and tender trembling
for I recall the time we discussed these unfortunate dogs

we spoke on the phone . . of the hideous practice
of those who in-breed Dobermans

deliberately training them, as well as breeding them
to possess the killer instinct — and to "go for the throat"
eventually causing them to even turn against their own masters

and breeding this carefully into . . . their small
puppies

fat-tummy puppies

you told me this need not be so
for you once owned a Doberman yourself

a Doberman ? . . a snake ?

and you said you trained your Doberman
to be gentle and loving to smaller creatures
really . . to all creatures . . including humans

when I doubted this, you mailed me a polaroid photograph
of your Doberman . . a picture you took yourself

seated on his head were two pet pigeons
        doves of peace
who were his best friends . . timid birds

        sitting trustingly on the head

of a "vicious" Doberman
                  . . and tears stung in my eyes
              when I looked at the photograph you sent
    for I knew . .

        you were trying to teach me
        that anything — or anyone — like Anubis-Dobermans
           can learn to love

if anything or anyone
    is forgiven
              even Set   even Satan

              even all of us
              on Earth

THE OPENING OF THE THIRD EYE

Reproduced from an oil painting by the well-known artist
Mikron K. Sarailian, Copyright, 1962, by Manly P. Hall

NOTE: For a large, full color reproduction of this painting to compare with the color codes described on the following page, see inside of back cover.

The Opening of the Third Eye

The painting of the head of Minerva on the inside cover shows, in part
the activities of the pineal gland and the pituitary body at the time of the
phenomenon commonly termed "the opening of the Third Eye". The Kundalini
fire is seen rising upward through the spinal canal into the pons of the medulla
oblongata. The golden light radiating from the base of the brain, at the back,
gradually increases in size and intensity until it forms the nimbus, etheric
or "halo" of the "saint" or one who has been illuminated.

The pituitary body is here shown surrounded by an elliptic rose aura.
The pineal gland — the Third Eye of the Mysteries — is here depicted
as blue in color, and surrounded by a radiating blue aura. In reality,
this aura includes within itself all the colors of the spectrum, but blue
decidedly predominates. The tiny vibrating finger on the pineal gland
points directly toward the pituitary body. This finger, vibrating at a very
high rate of speed — or angstrom units per second — is the
actual cause of true spiritual illumination.   *Manly P. Hall*   *

The bright blue triangle above the eye represents the pathway to the
pineal gland, and is located above the nose and between the eyebrows
in the human head. The pineal gland can be reached and stimulated
at this point, which is why, when there is a sharp accidental blow on
this spot, the Third Eye is partially activated, and the person becomes
"psychic" to some degree. The serpent seen at the top of the head of
the painting represents the Kundalini, the etheric serpent coiled at the
base of the spine, which must be released through the top of the head
before complete illumination is realized. The origin and meaning of the
Kundalini will be given in the sequel to this book, with the working title
of *Twelfth Night Secrets* .

Symbolically, the vibrating finger on the pineal gland signifies a Macrocosm
consummation or "marriage" — a union between the pineal gland and the
pituitary body, comparable to the true spiritual mating between Twin Selves,
on a microcosm level, which likewise causes ecstasy, making the man and woman
temporarily "one with God", the supreme Creators — as evidenced by the
creation of a Spirit into flesh, through the conception of a human infant which
can result. Mating between two who are not Twin Selves, of course, may
also create human life, although the illuminating ecstasy of the union is far
less intense.
As to the level of evolvement of the human life thus created, it depends upon
the intention of the hearts of the man and woman during mating, which can be

*   My sincere gratitude to noted metaphysician, Manly P. Hall, for his
      kind permission to reproduce the Minerva painting on the inside
      cover, and his description of the opening of the Third Eye contained
      in the first two paragraphs above.

pure, even though in error. This is why an infant born from the physical union between true Twin Selves is called "a love child".

Many humans mate with at least the sincere intent of love, mistaken or not, and under the Universal Law, motive is always to be considered.

Know this.
Myráhi is
The Bird of the Wondrous Power
The realizer of miracles
for those of clean heart only;
Whose resting place
is in the mighty tree
which is five trees in one —
banyan, oak and cypress, pine,
palm of coconut and date —
the secret sacred towering tree
of the double Rose of Shiraz
guarded by the man-lion
great creature called the sphinx
whose other name in anagram is
RaHram

Whose lips say *Sh-h*
Whose right eye pierces with S-s
Whose left eye burns with Z-z
and on whose forehead
stands the sign of the mirrored **R**:

    Gem of the Fan and keystone
    of the arch whose span
    is opaque time and all the manifest.

If any, curious, wander
into his domain
RaHram asks
What is my name ?
And the name beyond my name ?

If the wondering wanderer cannot answer
then the flowering **R** falls
into the lion's mouth
and *Sh-h* rises to the forehead
in a horrid lightning hiss
The mane of the noble head disappears
and remains now only the devouring Lioness
Kali
Roars.

The doors
of the great jaws open
to the furnace of the flame
The unclean-hearted fool
is slain by the guardian fire
beyond the roaring doors —
for his impurity
has killed him outright
Or if less impure
he stumbles back into the world
of men
a frothing imbecile
until his day of death
a living warning to the wise
a joke for fools.

But the clean of heart
pronounce the name
and the Name beyond the Name
go past the tree that grows
beyond the doorway-whirlpool's rose . . .
Myráhi's wings
fly to the Land !

Kyril Demys (Musaios)
Wings of Myráhi

Our Dreams Are Made of Sterner Stuff

Question: how long is 6 years
Answer: 6 years is a million-billion Forevers

the sixth spring since you left has come and gone
with its empty, unfullfilled promises
so has autumn . . the season I never trusted anyway
yes, the sixth autumn has come and gone, without a single
                                        backward glance
leaving me no chance to catch the brass ring
on the Carousel . . . and transmute it into shining gold
leaving me forlorn and naked, rejected and old
at least several thousand years older than yesterday

          six times four seasons have come and gone

and I'm still here alone, beside a strange telephone . . in New York
that rings unexpectedly, at odd hours
and when I answer, and say "hello . . hello . . hello ?"
I hear only a heavy silence there
a gentle breathing for one or two minutes
                              this morning, for three or four
     then a hang-up click — and silence once more

Gooober, is it you ?

are you trying to communicate something
you can't yet express in words ?

          is some unknown authority — or Deity
          forbidding you to speak, until . . .

                         until *what ?* until *when ?*
why should you be forbidden
     to speak ?

OH ! THIS SILENCE, THIS WAITING, THIS EMPTINESS IS SO BLEAK !

do you feel me, sometimes . . in the night
when I kiss your ear . . . and smell your cheek ?

               it is . . so very quiet here

Christmas and New Year's have also come and gone . .
you've left me alone for six Christmases
as I left you alone that holly-berry time, to make the season rhyme
back in our little crooked house . . while I was in New York

and you've left me alone each New Year's Eve too

Canto Twenty ☆ 849

without a single message from you
oh, Gooober, didn't you know how deeply I'd grieve
to be left all alone every New Year's Eve
the time, you once said . . . . . of new beginnings ?

      legend claims that the person you're with on New Year's Eve
      is the one you'll be with all year — and who might that be — myself ?
      like all those lonely years before we found each other again

   but . .

today is February 14th . . also the eighth one since you went away
and you didn't forget — at least not astrally
                      to remember me on St. Valentine's Day

I was searching for something this morning, in the desk drawer
and my hand touched a piece of paper, stuck in the back
so I pulled it out, wondering what it might be

      it was . . a message from you to me

how do you always know when I hurt the most
and send your gentle astral ghost
to guide me, with some words of yours from the past
some fragments of wise teaching and reminding ?

      a long time ago, I sent you a poem I had written
      long before Us I wrote it
      when I was lonely, yet still whistling in the dark
      trying to be a brave Ram, unashamed of my strength
                  and proud of what I am
        the poem said . .

you see ? I am still me
the secret place inside, where my dreams will always hide
from the withering clutch of too much need — has not been reached

      I remain myself . . with courage still to face the Sun
      it's not a hollow victory I've won — to still be me
      why should I grieve ? my dreams are made of sterner stuff
      and spring will be here, soon enough

and I mailed, along with that poem I had written
another verse for you to see
a very brief one, about Aries people — to instruct you astrologically

      "Mars is the ruler of Aries"
        "*nothing* rules Aries"
     "Mars is the ruler of the First House"
      "*that's* better !"

as I unfolded the wrinkled paper
jammed in the very back of the desk drawer
I saw that it was a letter from you

mailed to me in New York, from Colorado
that Christmas, when you were all alone back there
without me

how did it get stuck in the desk drawer ?
all wrinkled . . . . . by my own impulsive haste
and carelessness ?
it was not a long letter

you wrote to show me how you had transposed the two poems I had sent
into new words, with new meanings — new lessons
and as I stared at your written words
I remembered that your Saturn squares my Sun
and that the teacher is never the one — whose Sun is squared
the teacher is the one whose Saturn, squaring
is in charge of the lessons both must learn
no matter how fiercely those lessons may burn

at the top of the page you had re-written
transposed my second brief verse — the one about astrology, to read:

"Mars is the ruler of Aries"
"*nothing* rules Aries"
"Leo rules Aries — the Lion rules the Ram"
"*that's* better !"

then you wrote, transposing the pronouns in my first poem
from the singular to the plural

"you see ? we are still us . . . the secret place inside,
where our dreams will always hide
from the withering clutch of separation . . . has not been reached
we remain Us — with courage still to face the Sun
it's not a hollow victory we've won . . . . . to still be Us
why should we grieve ? our dreams are made of sterner stuff
and spring will be here, soon enough"

then you closed your Christmas letter
by writing a final message of growing-knowing, loving words

"oh, darling . . I love reading your poetry
especially these two verses you sent
they make me feel so much closer to you
I love you more than I'm able to express, in words
but soon, I'll be able to show you again
meanwhile, here's a line from another poet, Gibran
with a special meaning for now . . and later

trust your dreams of spring
for in them is hidden the secret of Eternity

all my love forever"

Me

why did you send me
this special letter . . that Christmas . . along with Raggedy Ann ?
did you know the way those words would reach me this year
          the year of my awful fear ?
was it a precognitive letter — did you sense somehow
that your words would bring us together faster
after the cataclysm of our mutual pride had torn us apart ?

  oh, darling, is it true — is it still so ?
      are my arms the home you cannot ever leave
  however far you go ?

          and is it also true . . that we do remain Us
          with courage still to face the Sun
          or is this but a hollow victory I've won
          to find your letter on this Valentine's Day ?

      then I knelt down, and tried hard to pray
      but without you beside me, the words were empty
                          and made of brass

      have I lost more points, teacher ?
      will I be demoted again to the rear of the class
      because I am still failing the subject of Living ?

HAVE I NOT PASSED THIS ETERNAL TEST OF FORGIVING ?

Midnight Vortex

      he is sitting here in the corner tonight
          Heathcliffe, the Younger

and peeking out at me through his wiggley strands of paper hair
with little beady eyes of wistful, restless lonely

      it's almost as if . . as if he were speaking
and asking me what I'm still seeking

      as I ask myself

....

there is something
that still beckons to me . . something
just behind a veil
and sometimes I think it lies behind a veil . . of Vail

I have thrown away all those old memories of hurt
yet something still lingers . .

    where is the teacher — or the book of knowledge
    to tell me the things I need to know . . to quiet these questions
    still demanding answers — and why do the answers
    seem to forever lie . . . just out of reach ?

I read whatever and whenever I can
between the spurts of taking and giving, called living
and I dream . . yes, I dream

        but always, I seem . . to hunger and thirst for more
        more echoes of some pain . . or peace
                I knew somewhere . . before
or both ?

I thirst for complete memory, not mere fragments
I need the esoteric initiation of total recall
where . . and when . . and most of all, *why* . . did I fall ?

    yes, fall . . for I sense that I fell from an ecstasy
    I can only guess today . . and feel so strongly the spell
    of a haunting song of longing, when I pray

a faint, sweet melody
that seems to say . . *I have not gone away*
        but . . who ?

yes, you, Gooober
but who . . are you ?
and who am I ? and most of all
why . . are *we* ?

    oh, Heath, just look at you ! your little beady eyes
    of wistful restless wise . . are mesmerizing me

tranquilizing and hypnotizing
    drawing me . . . into a vortex of unconsciousess

    I feel I am sinking
    into a trance . .

your little beady eyes are silvery-wise, and they are glowing with knowing as I am growing . . nearer the edge . . of a swirling, whirling vortex

                    of cool green water

          so cool, so still

and so much stronger than the current of my will
Heathcliffe, Heathcliffe, how can a make-believe sheepdog
possess such hypnotic power
                    to send me into this trance-like state ?

      it must be the hour
            for it has grown very late

b ! b ! b ! b ! b ! b ! b ! b ! b ! b ! b ! b !
  o * o * o * o * o * o * o * o * o * o * o * o *
  n * n * n * n * n * n * n * n * n * n * n *
  g * g * g * g * g * g * g * g * g * g * g * g *
    ! * ! * ! * ! * ! * ! * ! * ! * ! * ! * ! *
      *   *   *   *   *   *   *   *   *

bong ! bong ! bong ! bong ! bong ! bong ! bong !
                bong ! bong ! bong ! bong ! bong !

          did the clock strike twelve ?

twelve . . the magic-mystery-hour
the magic clock-strikes-midnight-age I once wanted so to be

          twelve !

twelve midnight . . the hour of our first growing-knowing-burning
in our miracle room, when the Eternity ember burned
                    as we learned . . that December
      midnight . .

      Heathcliffe, you seem to glow
      with the strangest light . . I seem to be falling
      into a trance

                    it is . . so late

I am yawning

    and it is dawning
    on me

the importance of sleep

    sleep is necessary for the repair of the body
    the Temple of the soul . . and the mind
                    . . sleep
sleep is also necessary
for the instruction of the soul

    for God's Universal Wisdom speaks to us
    in dreams . . and through the vibration of numbers
    while the soul slumbers

                    I am so very sleepy, Heathcliffe
        . . so very, very sleepy

sleep . . rest
my Temple needs sleep
      needs rest

    all those times you slept, Gooober
                  were you wiser than I ?

      when you slept, as I wept . . were you wiser ?

to sleep, to sleep
    not to weep, not to weep
to sleep . . to sleep

            . . . . oh, I cannot stop yawning

what was it I used to believe
about sleep ?

    I believed that sleep was when the druids
    made mountains fly . . and performed their magic rites
    at the foot of the old oak tree
                while I was . . asleep
to sleep, perchance
      . . to dream

yes, to sleep, perchance to glean . .

who said that . . wrote that . . an Essene ? no, it was Hamlet
yes . . no, Shakespeare, who wrote . . to sleep, perchance . .
to dream . . perhaps to glean . . some light

was the Bard, then . . an Essene ? to sleep, perchance . . to dream . . and
to drift . . I am drifting into a stream . . of unconsciousness . . perchance
to dream . . I see a beam . . a brilliant beam of white . . I see a Light

was it Hamlet . . or the three blind mice . . who wrote those words
. . to sleep . . at night, perchance . . . or was it Francis Bacon
        . . or St. Germain . . no it was Hamlet . . or Shakespeare, Will
my will is fading, Will . . . perchance to dream . . my will is weakening

was it a cookie . . . a mouse cookie . . . three toy mice . . did an Oreo
cookie write those words . . to sleep, to sleep . . perchance to . . or perhaps
it was a fig . . . a Fig Leaf . . or a Serpent . . from the Garden of Eden
Eden Snake . . . . hissing serpent . . . a Fig Newton cookie wrote those . .
words, to sleep . . . or an Oreo . . perchance to dream . . a mouse cookie
or a Fig Newton . . Fig Leaf . . . Eden-Newton . . . Isaac wrote . . .

        Sir Bacon . . . Isaac Bacon . . Francis Newton . . Bacon
Shakespeare . . Germain Newton . . St. Shakespeare . . the Count . .
of Oreo wrote the Count of Bacon . . with scrambled eggs
yes . . that's it . . Bacon and eggs . . Fig Newton . . Oreos and Adam . . Eve

three toy mice . . . say it over, say it twice . . three blind Fig Leafs . .
to sleep, perchance . . .

        . . gravity . . . the reversed gravity of sleep . . reversal . . into
levitating Oreos . . . the Law of Gravity discovered by a Fig Newton
mouse cookie . . gravity discovered by an Oreo . . from a falling
apple . . gravity . . . Eve's apple . . apple of Newton . . . falling tree

was it Hamlet who said . . to sleep ? no, Will . . it was the Bard . . he
said to sleep . . who was an Essene . . and was Will, then, an Essene ?
was Shakespeare a spooky Essene ? . . . is that how Will learned
and was burned . . into knowing . . that sleep can dream . . my will is
fading, Will . . to sleep

        is that how Shakespeare learned . . . why he burned . . to make
Life rhyme ? . . in verse . . Shakespeare made curSe rhyme with
bleSSing . . did Will know the Eden-Snake . . and the Leaf of Fig
Newton . . or Adam Bacon . . on the Eve of the beginning of the End . . of
Eden . . the end of Eden . . . . Shakespeare made Life rhyme . . is there
a Light . . is that a Light I see around the bend ? . . shining there . .

        it is time . . . it is time that I must . . sleep

I am sleepy, as I was sleepy . . in childhood
in my father's house

. . what did he say about his father's house ?
. . mansions . . many . . sleep
mouse ? Fig Newton
mouse . . his father's house

Adam snake . . . Eden-snake . . . Eve of the End . . a snake . . and sleep

I cannot seem to stay awake
Eden-Snake
. . to sleep . . to sleep

perchance to dream

to sleep . . . perchance

to

dr

ea

m

Many Mansions

Gooober, were you there . . at midnight
when I slept, sitting up in the chair . . under Heathcliffe's
hypnotic stare ?
I dozed, trance-like, and dreamed
the strangest dream

and thought I saw a beam of bright white Light
and felt . . you near

then heard you whisper

*"darling, go to sleep — it's allright
Heathcliffe and I are here . . . "*

I dreamed I was a stranger in a strange land
where humans were silent . . . and animals were wise
with little beady eyes of wistful knowing
yes, I dreamed that animals were kind . . to their human pets
and not so blind as man and woman
to the linking of God's creatures . . and the Oneness of All

and in my dream . .

as I felt unconsciousness begin to unwind around my mind
I believed I heard Heathcliffe bark
and thought — what an unexpected lark !
what funny druid magic — a Guru who can bark — a Master Teacher
in the form of a sheepdog, who wants to play astral leap frog !
what a peculiar sleep fog I must be drifting through . .

      then heard you laugh . . your rippling brook laugh
      and agree with me . . that this was
            a perfectly marvelous thing to do
to sleep . . instead of weep

      we spoke together
      my canine Guru and I

of many fearful and wonderful things . . like Fig Newtons and Kings

      and Pyramids and tombs and golden serpent rings
      secret subjects, from Eden-Snakes to Noah's Ark . . O !

      it was truly a fantastic lark !

to learn so much
from a Master-Avatar-Guru
who can bark

"Heathcliffe . . " I asked, in my dream

"can you tell me about both Then and Now ?
and can you tell me how
      I can understand Gooober better ?

oh, Heath, he has not sent me a single letter . . not even a daisy note
while he's been having such a marvelous float on a boat
          a boat — without even a name

can you tell me the rules of this game of love ?
can you help me see deeper and more . . about the me-of-me
      and the him-of-him
and all those Temples we visited together before ?

there's so much I don't know about false and true
I still can't make the verses scan . . in my Happiness poem
and lots of the words don't quite rhyme
well, sometimes they do . . but not all of the time

      and I can't tell the difference
      between a Forward and Reverse gear
      or which star to follow and wish on . .

        sometimes nothing at all seems clear
like the truth about the bodies — which are the Temples
                    of the soul

and what is my goal . . and why should I be
so deeply stirred, when I hear thunder roll ?
is it better to keep one's emotions locked up inside ?

        then . . why did I feel especially tender
                    every time Gooober cried ?"

        but Heathcliffe did not answer my flow of questions

        he just sat there, staring at me, with a glowing-knowing
        in his little beady eyes of wistful lonely
                    almost imperceptibly . . . changing into eyes of silvery wise

and so, I repeated

"is Gooober far away . . or is he still near ?
        Heathcliffe, can you hear ?
do you understand . . and can you make it clear ?"

                    then Heath barked loudly, quite proudly too
                              ARF ! ARF !

                    and somehow . . magically
                    his barking changed into spoken words
                    like fluttering birds . . as he said

                    "tell me which things are still not clear
                              just ask — and I will answer"

"yes ! I shall ask and learn . . "

                    "when the student is ready
                              the teacher will appear"

"tell me first about the bodies
which are the Temples of the soul"

                    "as in a literal house, more than one soul
                    may live in a Temple at the same time"

"more than one soul ? more than the me-of-me ?
I'm afraid I don't quite see . . . . "

                    "even during each seven-year-Saturn-cycle of change
                    there is but one you-of-you
                    the Spirit . . or the Higher Angel of the Self

                    Canto Twenty ☆ 859

which is the Owner of the Body Temple
and responsible for the lease
to the Landlord . . God, if you will

however, may not one entertain visitors
in one's home . . at times ?"

"yes, of course . . one may certainly
entertain visitors in one's home, at times
so I suppose, on occasion, a Body Temple could also be . . crowded"

"in the ancient writings, it is so taught
that sometimes, the visitors are friends
and at other times
                    . . strangers may be entertained"

"strangers ? you mean strangers who are . .
that is, may one entertain angels, unaware ?"

"yes, angels may visit the Body Temple
sometimes, angels who are . . . "

" . . . like unto an Adeptus
          . . or a Master Avatar ?"

"they may be called as such — or gods
or goddesses — or celestials
whatever term you happen to choose or prefer"

"but, for what purpose do these visits occur ?
why do they visit, these celestials or gods . . . or goddesses
whom we entertain . . unaware ?"

"for many reasons, these visiting angels come"

"well, can you give me just one ?"

"there are mutiple motives, as I have stated
but first, you must understand
that these are often highly evolved souls
who exist on other levels of awareness
above and beyond the Third Dimension of Earth's plane"

"above our Third Dimension ?
you mean the fourth . . or even the fifth ?"

" . . and even higher . . Saturn, as an example
is an Eighth Dimensional planet
and Saturn's surroundings rings hold great mystery"

"from eight dimensional levels of awareness, then ?

and even higher-higher-higher
             . . like unto Jacob's ladder ?"

                    "this is not vital for you to presently know
                    but . . higher and higher even, yes . . this is so
                    and from other galaxies, solar systems
                                        and Universes too"

"I've always, somehow, felt that was true
and some, perhaps . . from Mars ?"

                    ". . . there are no beings who live upon the stars
                    not literally or physically
                    although there are beings who do control and guide
                    the cosmic, electromagnetic forces and influences
                    emanating from these stars and planets . . . .
                    and although it is not yet time for you to know why
                    the Fixed Star Arcturus . . is known as the Port of Call"

"I am suddenly reminded of astrology"

                    "astrology may be symbolized as God's Computer
                    to make certain karmic patterns more clear
                    serving the necessary and useful purpose here
                    of holding Earthlings and their Karma
                    reliably and sensibly, in some order of efficiency
                                        so to speak"

"you mean, while one's own Free Will is still weak ?
before one fully comprehends how to rise above one's Karma
or how to become immune to planetary influences
and control one's *own* Life . . is this right ?"

                    "until one sees the true Light . . this is correct"

"isn't it sad that science is so blind
to the enlightening truth and synchronicity of astrology ?
and isn't it also discouraging
the way the average man and woman still fear it ?"

                    "little wonder that they fear and shun
                    the art and science of astrology
                    they quite naturally think of it as a frightful
                                        and dreary burden
                    since they are taught by misguided astrologers themselves
                    that their future Destiny
                    is entirely governed by the stars alone
                    therefore, if they can change nothing
                                        why fight against the tides of predestination ?

                    they truly believe what they are taught by false prophets

Canto Twenty ☆ 861

that Nature's fate, and the animals' . . and humanity's
are fixed by the far-away and unreachable stars
and so they can't see
what possible advantage there can be
for them to learn of how it works — or why the patterns
                                        do exist
they feel this is a useless knowledge
as well as an eternally futile and disappointing inquiry
for what use are the starry displays
of the planetary configurations
        if all present and future events
are already determined — by their apparent movement
                                        in the skies ?
        all is in vain, they believe
                        if the planetary aspects
cannot hasten by even so much as one timeless second
the Light of true illumination

this concept of astrology
causes Earthlings to feel they are mere puppets of Fate
that they are simply playthings of the stars"

"yes, I know . . for I have felt so myself
when I cast horoscopes . . and see the amazing accuracy
with which one can predict certain events and behavior in a human life"

        "behavior may be analyzed accurately, yes . . by astrology
        and this — the reading of *potential* character
                        and personality traits
        is the true and helpful nucleus of this ancient
                                        art and science

        but as for the *predictive* portion of astrological study
        it is, even yet, sadly misunderstood by humans
        simply because it has been so grossly misinterpreted

        they forget that the Higher Angel of the Self
        about which you will learn much, as we continue speaking
                they forget that this Higher Angel
        is no part of Nature — or of the material world
        all else upon your Earth — even the Sun which lights it
        is a part of Nature — but the Higher Self is *not* — and
        if man and woman would learn to allow these Angels
        to govern the animal-human nature in them
        then each man and woman would be the powerful Master
        of his or her own Fate and Desitny

        for the Higher Self is not subject
                        to the influence of the stars"

"then why do human events so reliably manifest

under the influence of the planetary aspects ?"

      "they do so because the instinctive
      or the animal-human nature
      is subject to the stars, by long-ago ordination
      for excellent cause . . as you will learn
      at the allotted time for this lesson

      but as soon as the animal-human Earthling
      learns to obey the Higher Angel of the Self
      and the Third Eye thus opens
      then man and woman will feel the movements
                     of the stars and planets
      simply as inclinations
      and no longer as compulsions, you see
      for it is written . .
          that the stars were *designed and destined*
      to *incline* . . but *not* to *compel*"

"are these the reasons why it is true
that the less a person believes in esoteric astrology
the more that person's horoscope fits like a glove — and accurately reflects
past and future events in that person's environment ?
and is this also the meaning of the ancient counsel that . .
the horoscope of a saint is impossible to interpret ?"

      "what you have just surmised is correct
          the physical Body Temple
      will always feel the influence of the stars
      until one finally achieves true Free Will choice
      by channeling or tuning in to one's Higher Self
      then one is released from all planetary influence

      . . as the Nazarene taught . . 'seek the Truth
      for the Truth shall surely set you free'

      and you should always keep in mind
      a further fragment of wisdom, which is this . . .

      although astrology is a sacred and valuable servant
      it can become a subtle and dangerous master
      however, the belief of today's science
      that astrology is merely a parlor game of some sort
          is equally dangerous
      for such disbelief never has — and never will
      keep astrology from being a true
      and totally reliable measurement, in wise hands
      any more than disbelieving
      in such an equation of, say, one plus one equals . . two
      would affect the laws of mathematics in the slightest"

"yes, I've observed
that not believing in astrology doesn't keep it from working . . .
now, may we return to those entities of unknown identities
who visit Body Temples, from time to time ?
do they come . . for a variety of purposes or reasons ?"

        "men and women, like unto the Earth they live upon
        are subject to many astrological seasons
        and these celestials may visit earthly Temples
        for various periods of time
                as indicated by planetary movement
        to help make Life rhyme . . on your planet"

"to try to keep us from destroying ourselves ?"

        "yes, and in the process of this
        through a chain reaction — also destroying Life
                elsewhere
        in other galaxies, solar systems and Universes
        which in no way have brought harm to Earthlings"

"then these angels visit our Body Temples
on what one might call a mission of prevention ?"

        "this is frequently the prime intention
        but whatever the true purpose
        they always come on a mission of Peace and Love"

"I see . . . celestials from somewhere above
    our own awareness level
on a gentle mission of Peace and Love
one should, then, of course
    make every effort to make them feel welcome
is this not true ?"

        "of course one should make them welcome
        if — and when — one is aware . . that they are there"

"angels unaware . .
does this mean that these visitors themselves
are unaware of who they are . . or
does it mean that we, who entertain them
are unaware of their identities ?"

        "it means both . . or either
           and sometimes neither"

"both — or either ? and sometimes neither ?
I'm afraid I don't understand"

"you need not comprehend this fully at present"

"but, I don't see how . . . "

      "as has been stated, you need not
      understand all of this in its entirety just now"

"so we entertain, in our own Body Temples
on occasion . . . strangers
who could be angels . . sometimes aware
that they are there
      and sometimes not
but, you see . . I have always thought . . "

      " . . and sometimes the visitors are enemies"

"yes, I've heard of that . .
a Temple possessed by an unwelcome entity
possessed temporarily . . such as in epilepsy
or sometimes for longer periods
such as insanity . . but how are we to know
which visitor is friendly . . and which might be an enemy ?"

      "both friendly and unfriendly strangers
      may visit — some are gentle, some are bold
      and are not easy to recognize
      as a child cannot tell brass from gold
      but there is a safeguard one may choose
                      to use"

"a spiritual safeguard one may choose ?
do you mean, a sort of psychic self-defense ?"

      "one always needs a psychic self-defense
      against various forms of pretense
      for, there are always those who pretend to be
         what they are not
      in both spiritual and temporal or material matters

      you will learn more of these specifics later
      but you might consider an analogous example

      there is currently a widespread fear
                   of the use and abuse
         of tape recorders
      utilized to eavesdrop in one's own office or home
      or one's own car — or even when walking on the street
      by way of a directional microphone
                 aimed from a distance

      but this present obsession with being overheard

is only a dress rehearsal for humankind
of the day approaching sooner than suspected
when tape recorders will be but toys

because one's thoughts may be clearly read
through the growing awareness of mental telepathy

and quite obviously — if the logical defense
against the 'microcosm' of tape recorder eavesdropping
is simply, not to speak anything
                    one would not want others to hear
unless one is certain of being truly alone

then the logical defense
against the 'Macrocosm' eavesdropping of telepathy
is the same, except for changing 'speak' — to 'think'
and this is why what is called the 'bugging' fear
of today — is properly called a dress rehearsal
to prepare humans for a swiftly approaching future
when evil will be unable to hide behind veils of pretense
                    when there will be no defense
against exposure of negative thought and action
except for their removal from the mind"

"that sounds more welcome and desirable than fearful
for, evil would then be forced to gradually flee
from sound and sight — is that not right ?"

                    "that is correct — negative deeds
depend upon darkness for their manifestation
and cannot succesfully function in the Light"

"but . . what of these details or specifics of psychic self-defense
you said I would later learn ?"

                    "as stated, you will learn at the proper time
                         because such specific safeguards
                    for what you have called psychic self-defense
                    are only necessary as emergency measures

                    now, to return to your question
                    of how one is to deduce or surmise if a visiting entity
                    is a friendly or an unfriendly 'stranger' . .

                    this depends entirely upon two matters
                    which you completely control yourself — as all do
                         it depends, quite simply
                    upon both the condition of the Body Temple
                    and the hospitality inclinations of its Owner"

"I'm not sure I know what you mean

866   ☆   Canto Twenty

by the condition of the Body Temple
. . will you explain ?"

"is the Temple a shack — a house badly in need of repair
or a fine alabaster mansion ?
is the soul of the Temple
of such aim and disposition
to attract higher — or lower — entities to visit ?

these are the questions one must ask one's self
if one is to truly see the Light"

"then Gooober was right . . .

as the Temple of the soul, the body must be maintained
with constant care — I fear my own is badly in need of repair
I was wrong to eat all those gooey-sugary mouse cookies
and Rocky Road ice cream . . and tobacco
but I'm doing much better, really-truly, I am trying . . "

"when one's heart is loving and compassionate
and if the genuine goal of one's soul — is Truth
a small leak in the roof
or a house in need of minor electrical re-wiring
does not necessarily cause a Temple
to be uninhabitable for desirable visitors
and as you say . . you are truly trying

but one should, nevertheless, always strive
to improve one's 'home'
if one aspires to entertaining angels . .

and sometimes . . one may entertain
or invite to remain
one's own self
. . or another piece of one's self"

"myself ? how can the me-of-me
entertain, or invite to remain in my Body Temple
a piece of my own self ? I am completely confused"

"on occasion, the Body Temple's Owner
or the Higher Angel of the Self — the Spirit
might choose to send split pieces of its Soul
to enter several Temples during one Time period
or one level of awareness
in order to gain a variety of Earth experiences
more swiftly, you see
and this is frequently the decision made
near a time of possible approaching cataclysm
when much experience must be gained quickly

Canto Twenty ☆ 867

it is called, by the Adepti or the Masters
the Thunderbolt Path of Accelerated Karma"

"the Thunderbolt Path of Accelerated Karma ?
that's an interesting term . . . I've heard it before"

"yes, interesting, of course, to you
for it relates to your response to electrical storms
lightning and thunder
which were present, even, at your birth
upon this suffering planet, Earth"

"so now I see that my odd empathy . . with thunder
is symbolic of the Thunderbolt Path of Accelerated Karma
I seem to have chosen in this present existence
but I still don't yet completely understand
the mystery of all those split pieces of the me-of-me"

"I shall attempt to make you see . . how this can be

*'let those who have ears, hear
and let those who have eyes . . see
the others . . who do not heed
are not yet ready to learn
what they so desperately need . . to know'*

is it not logical . . indeed, even to be expected
that a Body Temple's Higher Self
which has decided to send out its split Soul pieces
for the reasons previously given
might, through Free Will option — then choose
at the various periods of that Body Temple's
                                    Saturn-Seven-cycle
to recall . . each time
one or more of those pieces 'back home', so to speak
bringing with it — or them — all the multiple experience
                                    thus gained ?

and is it not logical for such a Temple Owner
to repeat this pattern of choice, at each Saturn-Seven-cycle
until all these pieces of its Soul
have finally returned, much wiser, to their origin

rather than to move from the Temple-House
at the Saturn-Seven choice cycle — to a different Temple
while another Owner takes over the 'house' left behind
            as some Body Temple Owners
each seven years or so . . . may choose to do . . unless
the choice is to remain in control of the same Temple
which is also often chosen — is all this not logical ?"

"let me see if I comprehend what you seem to be saying . .
you appear to be implying that not all Body Temple Higher Angels
choose to periodically exchange their Soul pieces — but instead

either choose to remain as Owner of the same Temple
which was selected at its birth — retaining all the original soul pieces

or if not that, then choose to become the Owner
of a different 'house' or Body Temple . . every seven years or so

these being different choices than that made by the Temple Owners
who choose to send out their Soul pieces
    for the reasons you explained
then gradually call those lost and scattered pieces back home
into the Temple the Owner of such pieces directs and controls
    at approximate seven year intervals
until all have joined together in the same Temple once more
with far more wisdom than was possessed before
when the split pieces were first sent forth for experience"

                    "that is correct . . and stated with unusual clarity
                    you have summarized *the only three choices*
                    granted to any Owner of a flesh Body Temple
                    at the time of the Saturn-Seven-cycle
                    first — to remain in control of the Temple selected at birth
                    second — to trade 'houses' with another Owner
                    and *third* — to send forth the soul pieces
                    in order to gain simultaneous experience
                    within several Body Temples — then recall them

                    there are other complexities
                    relating to all this, which will make it more clear
                            and which you must also learn as we speak further
                    but at this moment, I sense that your attention
                    has slipped away . . back to a statement I made earlier
                    which you presently ponder . . is this not true ?"

"it is . . you have evidently read my mind"

                    "that is no extraordinary accomplishment
                    but merely an ability possessed by all humans
                    if they would but recognize their own powers of telepathy"

"I beg your pardon
I consider telepathy to be an extraordinary accomplishment

and certainly a most unusual ability
for a sheepdog Guru to possess and demonstrate"

                    "ARF ! ARF ! ARF ! one must agree"

"there are other matters which also trouble me
and which I need to have explained in much more detail
but I do wish you would attempt to do so
by speaking properly — and not by barking — if you don't mind

we are, after all, discussing topics of serious import
and this sense of the ridiculous you insist upon projecting
is causing all these matters of great consequence
to appear to be foolish and trivial
which is the very last thing one should consider them to be"

       "a sense of humor, my dear Pilgrim
       is a precious gift indeed — for it is synonymous
       with a tuned-in intellect, and a highly evolved mind
       as well as with spiritual profundity

       know that there can be no wisdom where there is no humor
       and, while all those with humor do not contain wisdom
               they possess the initial sparks
       conversely, all those with wisdom do possess humor

       for, there can be no wisdom where there is no humor
               and no healing laughter
       a sense of the ridiculous is a necessity for enlightenment
            which is why Buddha chuckles

       it would behoove you to always keep in mind
       to beware of a man or a woman
       who is unable to laugh at himself — or at herself
       or at the entire Universal pattern of existence
       for humor, you see, has as its foundation
            a true and deep perception
       of both the human and the galactic condition
       revealing the person who possesses it
       to also possess infinite compassion
       and above all — a sense of perfect balance"

"I stand chastised — besides, I was only teasing"

       "I am aware that you were"

"oh, stop it ! you're beginning to sound
as arrogant as Gooober himself

but actually . . you have reminded me of something
pertaining to the cartoonist, Charles Schulz
who keeps tuning in to Goob and me
and eavesdropping on our very deepest feelings
    thoughts and emotions

for there was a Charlie Brown and Peanuts cartoon

I read recently — in which Charlie and Lucy
were arguing about this same topic — jokes and humor
and Charlie said to Lucy
                    quite properly, as I now see

that no one would have been invited to dinner
as often as Jesus was — unless he was interesting
and had a good sense of humor"

                    "Charlie won that argument with Lucy
                    for, it's true — Jesus did, indeed, possess
                    that rich sense of humor
                    which runs through the veins of all humans
                    but especially those descended from the Hebrew race

                        this truth was removed from your Scriptures
                    by those who feared that a 'Divine God'
                    who possessed the ability to laugh
                    would not inspire the necessary fear and awe
                    in the hearts and minds of those masses
                    they felt needed to be controlled
                        . . . but let us now return to your former question
                    concerning the possible approaching cataclysms"

"since you say these may be prevented, under certain conditions
I need to ask if you mean the intervention of celestial visitors
on a mission of prevention, as we discussed earlier"

                    "in part, I do mean this — and relative to such missions
                    you may want to ponder the lines
                    of one of your more profound poets, Kyril Demys, who wrote
                              in his perceptive verse . . called *Realities*

                              the ageless melody
                              unheard, heals
                              the healing vision
                              unseen, leads
                              the true leaders, unknown
                              rescue . . "

"strangely, those words
cause me to remember, somehow . . a melody
a fragment of music I have forgotten
and as you spoke them
I almost . . not quite, but almost
heard some of its chords again . . then it faded"

                    "it will return, your forgotten melody . .
                    but the approaching cataclysms
                    which all sensible scientists and geologists
                    and all perceptive astrologers

know full well are already casting
                    their shadows
may also be prevented
by Earthlings themselves — as well as
                        by those unknown Leaders
if the danger is realized by enough souls
and if both the metaphysical
                    and the geophysical signs
are recognized in time — this time

and to make all Earthlings aware of this
is the purpose of particular visits
to certain Body Temples . . by celestials
at this dawning of the New Aquarian Age"

"is there . . a time already cosmically fixed
for such possible Earth changes
    as the reversal of the North and South Poles
earthquakes, floods . . the inundation of both coasts
and the flaming volcano created
by the unimaginable horror of the A.E.C.'s cobalt, H and A-bombs
unexpectedly exploding, and igniting the very air around us ?

is the time for these possible disasters
already . . cosmically ordained ?"

                "do you truly seek the answer
                to such a fearful question
                of such great negative and dark undercurrents ?"

"yes . . I do seek it"

                "then I must insist
                before replying to such a negative query
                that you first ask yourself
                why you request an answer to such a dangerous
                                    thought form"

"it is because . . .
. . . it is because I am certain
that the only way to create or manifest a particular *positive*
is to fully comprehend the implications
of that same positive's *negative* or *reversed* position
so that the proper and successful formula may be found
for the transmutation of any particular *negative*
into its *positive* polarity — is this not true ?"

                "that is absolutely and entirely correct
                although it is extremely dangerous
                to dwell upon the image reflected darkly
                    in the reverse mirror

872   ☆   Canto Twenty

for but the very briefest moment of time — yet, it is true
that one must first become aware
of the mirror-reflected negative
of any particular event or situation
if one is to comprehend the alchemy
of how to reverse it . . . . . or how to re-*verse* it

how to *reverse its polarity* . .   and therefore
by so doing . . *transmute it into positive*

more especially so, when the event is considered
to be of such vast and urgent importance
as are the possible approaching cataclysms"

"and are these, then . . already cosmically timed ?

"it is a difficult question you ask
for there are no precise answers to it — that hour
is known only to far higher beings than myself
though there are guidelines one may use, with discretion"

"and these are . . . ?"

"each star . . holds a part of the answer
according to astrological configurations which you well know
and other forms of data besides
among these, studies of previous and similar Earth changes

there may possibly be — only *possibly*
two major quakes in California — very close together — as a *prelude*
to the later inundation of both coasts . . .
two quakes . . . perhaps between the Earth years of 1988 and 2,000

should this occur . . and do not forget that it may *not*
occur at all
but . . should this occur
it would constitute a stern and powerful *warning*
with the *intended positive result*
of a major and widespread change in attitude
and direction
on the part of all humanity . . .
the birth of a new ethic in every area of human life
which would, of itself, then perhaps have the strength
to prevent those larger Earth changes and cataclysms
possibly approaching not long after the beginning of the next century"

"is it true that, by 1990, we shall have *ten years*, or *less*
to stop the reign of lust and greed — to halt
the spread of darkness on Earth — before the poisoning of the planet
becomes irreversible ?"

Canto Twenty   ☆   873

"this is true
just as the people of Atlantis were warned
and rejected the warning — now those reincarnated
                                        Atlanteans
on Earth today . . hold the future
in their hands, as of yore
will they ignore the warnings, as they did before ?
or will they hasten . . swiftly, swiftly
to teach all Earthlings the magical alchemy formulas
for reversing the darkness, so fast approaching . . . . . .
                into its opposite polarity of Light ?"

"I would try to teach . . . oh, I would !
but I fear I do not know enough"

                "ask and learn . . nothing is secret
                that shall not be made manifest"

"is it true, Heathcliffe, as I have heard
that a kitten, a horse, a dog or a bird
or any animal at all . . . senses precognitively
                in advance
impending disasters and Earth changes
with more accuracy than the scientific instruments
which have been developed to detect these signs ?

I have heard that all animals are . . extremely restless
before earthquakes, floods, fires and the like
is this so ?"

                "it is correct . . and you, especially
                may be interested to learn
                a fact which has been indisputably
                                and carefully documented
                which is that . .
                ants pick up their eggs
                        and move out of their ant-hills
                in a mass migration . . before earthquakes"

"ants ? they do ? oh, how important that is . . to me, at least
because, when I was very small . . I had this experience
with ants, you see . . and somehow I knew
that they should not be killed . . or harmed in any way
and there was this summer . . . . . "

                "yes, I am aware of your sad experience
                with Ant Murders, Incorporated
                but there was another lesson about ants
                your experience was intended to teach you"

"there was ?"

"there was indeed . . do you not recall
the cruel matchstick forts
the boys in the neighborhood sought to use
to tease you into bribing them to stop ?"

"yes, yes . . oh, please don't make me remember
it hurts so to remember . . even now
what lesson . . was that meant to teach ?"

"it relates to . . . druids
or more properly to . . Druids
with a capital 'D', you see"

"druids ? I mean . . Druids ?
what do my teeny-tiny druids have to do
with such cruelty as the burning matchstick forts ?"

"you properly, as a child
spelled druid with a lower case 'd'
for these were Nature Spirits
        who were gentle, quite timid and shy
and very, very magical

you had . . a relationship to these druids
which it is not yet time to reveal
but you should be aware that they existed
in Britain . . many, many centuries
                        earlier
than the Druidic Priests
which the latter-day historians have recorded

these Druidic Priests, with sinister subtlety
adopted, in a gross distortion of Truth
their names — Druids — from the
                        much older Nature Spirits
who were rightfully outraged
at this theft of their essence and identity
by priests of cold cruelty and torture

even to this very day, the genuine druids
are greatly distressed by the ancient deception"

"even to this very day ?
there are still . . druids . . hiding here and there ?"

"there are indeed . . as real as real can be"

"will they ever reveal themselves to me ?"

"why not . . wait and see ?
they have the power, you know

to take human form, if they should wish"

"oh ! how perfectly, perfectly marvelous !
but . . I don't understand
what all this has to do with the flaming, burning torture
of the matchstick forts, when I was small"

> "the Druids with a capital 'D'
> those Druidic Priests who existed in Britain
> long before the Roman conquest
> were men of great learning . . but of evil intent
> given to discussions of stars and their
> > movements
> and all manner of things
> concerning this Universe and Solar System
> > and one of their rituals
> included human sacrifice . .
> during which, dressed in white hooded robes
> they carefully constructed huge figures
> of immense size, with limbs woven of twigs
>
> twigs being shaped very much
> like the 'kitchen matches'
> > you knew as a child
>
> then they filled these large figures
> with living men and women
> and set them on fire
> as the poor souls perished in agony
> in a sheet of flame . . "

"oh, God, oh, God . . "
were . . some of these victims . . virgins ?"

> "it has been thus recorded . . yes"

"oh, my . . it's just that I . . once I was told I was . . .
but never mind that now
do you suppose this is the true origin
of the white hooded robes of the Ku Klux Klan
and their burning crosses, in the south ?"

> "it is indeed . . the origin of this group
> whether they realize it themselves or not"

"but . . I have heard these Druidic Priests exist today
and perform their rituals in Britain
at Stonehenge . . within the mysterious circle of stones
near Salisbury Plain . . are they also . . cruel ?"

> "no, they are not . . .

but it is not a desirable thing to attempt to adopt
the imitative rituals and robes
of ancient cults of death and darkness
and perhaps they will someday realize this

their chief error is in holding their rites
as they do each Midsummer morning at dawn
when they celebrate with fire and water
the year's longest day
by watching, as they stand in the center
                        of the circle of stones
the sun rise in exact line
with the Heel Stone, just outside the ring"

"why do you say that this is an error ?"

        "because these modern Druidic Priests
mistakenly believe that their namesakes
        those ancient cruel ones
held just such a ritual at Summer Soltice
when Stonehenge was built
                over 4,000 years ago
and this is not so

for those who built Stonehenge
        for a purpose not yet dreamed
were not the Druidic Priests
described by Julius Caesar, and others . . "

"they were the really-truly druids !
my very own druids . . the ones who spell their name
with a lower case 'd', were they not ?
I just know this is true !"

        "you 'know it' ? then, of course it is
for, whatever you truly *know* to be true — *is* true"

"but . . do you believe it too ?"

        "do you need my approval of your knowing ?
this is not the best way for you to pursue
        your spiritual growing"

"allright, then, — it IS true
and I don't *need* you to agree with me !"

        "I do believe that you are beginning to see . . "

"to see . . what ?"

        "to see the formula for learning to listen

                    to remain alone, and heed
              the still, small voice within yourself
              which is the voice of the Higher Angel
                             of the you-of-you"

"I am beginning . . to listen
to the voice of my own inner self
but I'm still somewhat timid and fearful about it"

                    "fear is a tremendous faith, you know"

"it is ?"

                    "it is, yes — faith in the negative"

"you win that round"

                    "I speak but Truth, and you are aware of this"

"yes, you're right — I am
but we have wandered away from the subject
of Earth cataclysms . . and I have more questions
of genuine and great concern"

                    "ask and learn . . . nothing is secret
                    which shall not be made manifest
                    as has several times already been stated"

"you mean that nothing is secret
which shall not be made manifest . . *eventually*
when the time is right . . for you have not answered
all of my crucial questions tonight"

                    "true — I stand corrected"

"I need to know so desperately
for the sake of millions of others like me
fallen angels . . former gods and goddesses
of great powers, too long forgotten
is it really, really — not *nearly*, but *really* true
that these horrible
Earth cataclysms *can* be prevented ?"

                    "you are a great admirer of the sensitive
                    called Edgar Cayce, are you not ?
                    and he answered your question, when he said

                    ' . . . there are those conditions
                    which, in the activity of human thought and endeavor
                    oft keep many a city and many a land intact
                    through their observation of the spiritual laws

in their associations with individuals' . . "

"yes, I know Cayce spoke those words in trance
but I'm not sure I comprehend precisely what he meant
in the deepest sense of his intended message"

     "all the various attitudes, activities
     and actions of humans . . create something
     known as 'thought forms'
     and they may be of all manner of different
           shapes, colors . . . and musical tones
     you, yourself
     have called these 'thought forms' properly — vibrations"

"yes, all matter vibrates in some manner
and Abstract Al Einstein, who . . by the way
did not have a driver's license, you know
proved, in his relativistic methodology
that matter can be converted to energy — and vice versa"

     "that is correct — all matter vibrates
     to some particular frequency
     from the hardest metal substance — to
     the most delicate, ethereal gases

     these 'thought forms'
     which you correctly refer to as vibrations
     are actually a *mental substance*
     which may be defined as being somewhere between
     dense matter — and human consciousness

     and these 'thought form' vibrations
     constitute, literally, *a fifth force in Nature*"

"the lucky number 5 again !
the numerical value of the letters of the words
forming *Expect a Miracle* add to 5 too"

     "yes, five is an important number for you
     in this incarnation . . for many reasons

     but . . to return to the 'thought forms'
     which are Nature's Fifth Force
     they are quite real — as real as the chair
     you now sit upon in your wakeful sleep

     even the eminent neurophysiologist
     of your Menninger Clinic, Dr. Elmer Green
     recognized this, when he wrote . .

     ' . . . the mind is peculiar — it has energy

and the form of that energy is different
from that of neuronal potentials that travel
the axone pathways' . . "

"but . . this is not really consoling to me
because all these fragments of Truth are still but theory
not really proven in any major way"

"you are wrong — 'thought form' vibrations
and their immeasurable power over Nature
are not merely theory
their effect has been observed and proven"

"where ? and when ? and how ?
oh, please answer me — I need to know *now* !"

"the electromagnetic factors
of each Earthling's auric emanations — or aura
are very similar to
the electro-magnetic characteristics
of the Solar System in which you live

and this means that human auric light
or electromagnetic fields
are entirely capable of traveling outward
and inter-acting with similar fields
in the environment
as tuning forks respond to one another"

"and could this, then, inter-react
with all the factors underlying earthquakes, floods
pole reversal, cobalt bomb effects — and such ?"

"yes . . the proper projection of human auras
could so react with all geological activities
including those behind climatic change
which, of course, is why your American Indians
successfully performed their rain dances"

"how would this apply to an earthquake prone area
such as the San Andreas fault
and the similar fault that lies beneath Manhattan ?"

"simply by the 'thought form' vibrations
causing major changes
in the temperatures and air pressures
surrounding and permeating
any earthquake-prone land area, you see"

"but . . this is all theory you are telling me
and you promised to give me the proof of such magic"

880 ☆ Canto Twenty

"research by a number of scientists
related to the prehistoric populations
            of the American Southwest
have proven that, when the activities
of the people turned to negative vibrations
such as open warfare
and these actions became, therefore
            out of harmony
with the surrounding enivronment, then

the rainfall needed for their very survival
gradually dropped to such a low level
that these Earthlings were forced to move away
and to migrate elsewhere

conversely, in close neighboring areas
where the people did not engage in warfare
or killing each other — or their animal friends
and did not engage in the abusing of sexual power
            and who were, therefore
in complete harmony with their environment

in these close neighboring areas . .
the rainfall needed also for their very survival
                  remained high
throughout the same period of time
allowing them to remain in their homeland
safely . . happily . . and productively

a similar situation has now developed on Earth
in the area you call Las Vegas
where many forms of darkness of the spirit have prevailed
these dark negative thought forms of lust and greed
having finally seeded a current and swiftly growing
                        lack of rainfall there

forcing those guilty of the responsible negative vibrations
to migrate elsewhere — as can be seen
in their gradual moving of their operations
                  to Atlantic City — and your State of Florida

where the same inflexible Law of Mother Nature
will soon be felt by the unfortunate residents there
                  when the rainfall decreases
for, just as there is not enough water in the Las Vegas area now
there will eventually be a shortage of water in Florida

however, those who planted negative seeds
causing the rainfall level to so sharply drop in Nevada
were not allowed to move their spiritual pollution
back into the territory ruled over by your Earthling Castro

for, whatever others may think of the blend
of 'good' and 'bad' in his human nature, this Earthling
is tuned-in to his Higher Self . . and listens
                              with his inner ear

on this one level of at least subconsciously being aware
of the dangers inherent to his own land and people
in allowing such powerful negative thought forms
to cause Cuba's rainfall, needed for survival — to drop
and therefore, banished from Havana all Las Vegas controlled
                                         operations

all human-nature is woven of grey and white threads
and one must be careful to give credit unto — each Earthling
where credit is due — Castro is known to deeply admire
              Abraham Lincoln
and so . . let he or she . . who is without sin
                      cast the first stone
one must always hate the sin
but never hate the sinner . . there is a difference, you see
and one must always look for Light, even in the darkness"

"yes, that always appealed to me
to hate the sin — but not the sinner
it makes good, common sense"

        "returning to the proof you seek
        in a multitude of other ways
        through various different kinds of careful research
              it has been indisputably proven
        that the mental energy of thought form vibrations
        originating from the auras of men and women
        absolutely can — and positively does
        affect and control the material 'matter' of their
                              surrounding environment

        your question, however, is aimed in the wrong direction
        for, you see, the true crucial question
        upon which the entire human race now utterly depends

        is not *can* you — and others like you
        prevent the approaching and horrifying man-made and Nature
                              cataclysms

        the true crucial question facing humanity at present
        is not whether Earthlings are *capable* of successful intervention
        with the coming earthquakes, floods
        cobalt fire and brimstone in the air — and pole reversal

        no, the question is not *can* they — but rather, *will* they ?

will they recognize their own latent powers
as fallen gods and goddesses, in time . . . this time ?

and will they, then, *choose* to use their recovered powers
to increase the Light
rather than using them to increase the darkness ?

that is, assuming they receive help . . soon
so that each of them may learn
how the Third Eye of wisdom and power
called the pineal gland — may be opened
and once more activated"

" . . and your eyes shall be opened
and ye shall be . . as gods . .
does this refer to the Third Eye ?"

"it does . . that is correct"

"and how may the Third Eye, then
be opened ?   is there a way this can be accomplished ?"

"in rare cases, certain Tibetan monks
have been known to perform surgery
          upon the pineal gland, or Third Eye
in a clumsy attempt to re-activate its latent energy
but this is hardly a proper solution

also, an extremely high percentage of your 'psychics'
have, at some time in their lives, suffered a fall
or a sharp blow on the head, between the eyebrows
          which has predictably resulted
in the same kind of re-activation of the Third Eye
however, neither is this a desirable method
for one cannot go around striking one's friends
on the forehead with a hammer
in order to help them finally see the Light"

"but why should the pineal gland
or the Third Eye — *need* to be re-activated ?"

"in children, you see — until they reach an age
of around twelve or thirteen years
the pineal gland . . . medically speaking
is known to be soft and malleable, much like clay
          but when children grow older
                    . . becoming adults

this gland becomes gradually hard and dense
as hard as rock or marble
and, although your medical profession

has no explanation for this crucial change
the science of *meta*-physics does . . .

for, when small children begin to learn to lose
                              their childhood faith
through the negative
and dreary materialistic training of their elders
they also lose their power of magic
and all perception of their own auric light

this is especially unfortunate, because Faith
is only the beginning step toward final Enlightenment

first there must be what is called 'blind' Faith
          as all small children possess
which is not blind at all, and should not be thus labeled
for it is simply faith in the invisible
                              the yet-still-to-be-seen
inspiring a pattern of listening
to the voice within

then, after repeated observation of the successful results
of such 'blind' Faith — as in 'dreams coming true'

Faith leads to Belief
the child then learns, through Faith, that dreams **DO** come true
then learns to *Believe*
                    and Belief leads straight into *Knowledge*

the Knowledge of how to achieve Wisdom and possess Power

one might say that Faith is blind because the Third Eye
is not yet fully open, even in children — but Faith will open it
as naturally as the Sun and the rain gently open the petals of a flower

then Faith is no longer 'blind'
because the Third Eye can now fully see
and when Faith is translated into Belief — one is then able
to realize the inflexible Cosmic Law — which is
that Belief leads to *Knowing* — which, in turn
swiftly leads Wisdom and Power

Hope is weak
allowing for possible failure
Faith is stronger . . .
and Belief is more so . . . for it leads one to comprehend
          that the word **KNOW** contains the word *now*
placing one in the Eternal Now
          it also contains the word *won*
so . . . when you can truly *know* . . you have *won* !

as an example, small childrens' Faith in Santa Claus
and the Easter Bunny — shames their elders
into actually materializing or manifesting these dreams for them
and this is truly the mission of parents
to train children in realizing or *real*-izing that their dreams
are . . *real*"

"but what about when they later learn
that Santa and the Bunny were not real at all ?"

"this fattens Faith and the emotions — and makes them grow
for this only means they have come to know
that Faith *does* bring miracles
and it is even *more* beautiful when the miracles manifest
from the love of *others*, you see

and so . . first 'blind' Faith — then small miracles of Faith
then secondly comes the ability to Believe
which leads, through Cosmic Law that cannot fail
to the Light of Wisdom and Power of **Knowing**"

" . . suffer the little ones to come unto me
and forbid them not . . for of such as these
is the Kingdom of Heaven . . "

"precisely . . there is nothing sentimental about those words
of the Nazarene
for they are as reliable and as solid as a chemistry formula
or a mathematical equation

but when small children are deprived of their birthright
of shining Faith
they lose the opportunities
to observe the golden results of that Faith . . miracles

therefore, also losing the chance to take the next step
into believing
which naturally leads
into knowledge . . and the complete functioning
of the Third Eye
or, in other terminology
to the great powers all Earthlings eons ago possessed
as gods and goddesses
the outward, or medical sign
of this great loss . . being the hardening of the pineal gland
as children become sceptical and embittered adults"

"oh, I knew it, I knew it !
Gooober and I were right, after all ! and so were the OObers !
for the Keys to the Kingdom are teeny-tiny"

"the keys to the Heavenly Kingdom are indeed, very small
for they may only be held by those
who have truly returned, in their hearts
to the Faith and the Belief of their childhoods
and it is written . . . that *a little child shall lead them*

the power of true Faith, which is inherent within *innocence*
is a power more miraculous
than Earthlings have dared to dream"

"and were these powers gradually abused
with the prostitution of individual Divinity
reaching its peak . . . . . in the fated Atlantis ?"

"yes, and also upon the planet Maldek — and soon, once again, perhaps
upon this Earth . . but we will not speak further now
of Atlantis and reincarnated Atlanteans
for all these mysteries will be unfolded unto you later"

"I need to know about . . Adam and Eve . . and Eden"

"this will also be unfolded later, in due time"

"but at least tell me if the Serpent
of the Old Testament . . is to be considered
as good . . or as evil . . which ?"

"the answer to your question concerning the Serpent
is the answer to the Truth of Creation itself
and shall be manifested unto you clearly, at the allotted time
so that you may share this wisdom with all on Earth
                                        . . . for this mystery
contains the ultimate Power
to halt the swiftly approaching death of your planet
            in a flaming hell of fire and brimstone
and give birth to the Golden promise
of the Aquarian Age of unimaginable grandeur"

"when is the . . allotted time
in which I shall be permitted
to discover or uncover this mystery ?"

"the allotted time . . is soon"

"is the correct word for such enlightment
discover — or uncover ?"

"both terms, together, form the correct one
for, what you shall discover
will then lead you to uncover . . something tangible
the secret of a relic which has been long-buried

                    . . . made of quartz crystal"

"but . . what about the Serpent ?
are Satan and the Serpent synonymous ?"

                    "the answer to your question
                    is an emphatic Yes
                    and an equally emphatic No"

"you are speaking now, in terms
far too cryptic for me to comprehend
or even try to make rhyme"

                    "this is because it is not yet
                              that allotted time
                    for such knowledge to be made manifest unto you"

"can you give me . . at least
just one small clue ?"

                    "only one . . for the moment, meditate
                              upon this Truth
                    that the negative Serpent of hell equals one
                    and the positive Serpent you seek
                                        equals two
                    yet, the true Original Sin
                    is coiled around and connected to . . all three"

"your words are . . .
far too mystifying for me
        I simply cannot understand, or see
but, be that as it may . . .

when all men and women are someday gifted
with their individual birthrights of power — when all humans
regain the Divinity they once possessed
will they be able to remember where . . and how
and most of all . . why . . they fell ?
will they each, individually, be able then to see
the reason they became fallen angels . . from Heaven ?"

                    "they will indeed . . for, when their Third eyes
                    are opened again, as of yore
                    the windows on the past may then be opened
                                        at will
                    for brief periods only
                    otherwise, chaos may form within the mind

                    and when these windows looking out upon
                              Past-Present-Future
                    are at last flung open wide . . one may expect

a human condition very akin to that so well described
by one of your wiser and more profound Earthlings

                called, on this planet . . H. G. Wells

in his dream . . or in his story, if you prefer
titled 'The Grisley Folk'
                        in which he wrote that . . .

                'a day may come
when these recovered memories may grow as vivid
as if we, in our own persons, had been there
and shared the thrill and the fear
                        of these primordial days
a day may come . .
when the great beasts of the past
will leap to life again in our imaginations
when we shall walk again in vanished scenes . . . .
stretch painted limbs we thought . . were dust
        and feel the sunshine of a million years ago'

        . . and this is so . . even as he did record it"

"do you suppose that the Grisley Folk of H. G. Wells
were actually the druids . .
        with the lower case 'd' ?"

                "Arf ! Arf !
                this may quite very probably be"

"Arf ! Arf ! yourself !
oh, Heath ! do you know what just occured to me
isn't it strange that the word 'self'
contains within it, the world 'elf' ?"

                "not strange at all — but quite logical
                for a reason which will soon be unveiled"

"is the Self, then — an **Elf ?**"

                "nothing is secret
                which will not soon be made manifest"

"well, if I must wait for this mysterious
allotted time — the very least you can do
is to give me some hint of the various matters I believe
and am still trying to categorize as false and true
to which I will then be enlightened"

                "you are correct in your visions of many things
                but those which need revision . . or a re-vision

number among them, the following . .

the true identity of the Serpent
as well as the nature of the Original Sin
the mysteries of Stonehenge and the druids

and also . . a more concise solution
to the semantics problem you share with many others
concerning terms such as . .

the Soul . . the Individuality . . the Ego
the Overself . . the Supraconscious
     the Universal Mind . . the Holy Ghost
the Holy Spirit . . the Subconscius
        and the human Mind
none of which
truly possess the meaning you presently
ascribe to them, you see"

"I just realized another strange thing !

when you said that I need some re-visions
of my . . visions . . you sparked some fragment of knowing
the word revision or re-vision actually means to change
one's former vision
to the true vision of the Higher Elf
excuse me . . I meant to say the Higher Self"

     "but you did say it correctly
     you forgot only the first letter . . of 'S'"

"oh ! I see !
by adding the Serpent 'S' to 'elf'
one is separated from one's Higher Elf"

     "the computer of your brain
     is working quite nicely . . however
     this relates to the Great and Astounding Truth
     of language itself — and its Power
     over both Heaven and hell . . and is best left
     for the allotted time of learning
              and teaching
     we discussed before . . .
     now, let us return to your puzzlements
     related to what you mistakenly term
                   twin souls
     and the human soul
     I sense there is still some confusion
     about what is Truth . . and what is merely
     fragmented occult and religious illusion"

"you sense this correctly
I need to know the difference between
the Soul pieces of the me-of-me . . and my own twin soul"

"I fear I must reply to your query
in a somewhat round-about way
for when you say you wish to know more
about your own twin soul — you are using
an incorrect term
and this should be, so to speak, re-vised
your vision needs . . a re-vision"

"then please do revise anything necessary
in my scrambled semantics"

"I believe the swiftest way to do this
is for you to draw a diagram, which will show
exactly which 'pieces' go where"

"but . . that's really not fair !
I would have no idea where to even begin"

"yes, you do — you know it as well as I
but you may need my help in bringing
                              your knowing
to the surface of the consciousness
so that you may be fully aware
exactly which pieces go where . . and also
the correct terminology for each

therefore, if you will but close your eyes
for only a moment
I will activate the computer of your brain
by lightly touching your Third Eye
                    Presto !

now . . take paper and pencil
simply begin to draw
and you will see that you actually do already know
all of this knowledge you seek
just draw whatever comes into your head
there is no need to hesitate . . . go on, begin !"

"I'm not a professional artist, you know
and my drawing will be clumsy, as you can see"

"it looks quite clear to me
and the purpose of this sketch is not to win a prize
but merely to assist in opening your mind
to wisdom you already contain . . . "

"it has started to rain . . that's strange
the sound of the rain makes it easier to draw
what is suddenly pouring out of my mind"

                    "rain is a soothing music for creating, this is true"

"while I am drawing, I do so need an answer
to a most important question
which has been greatly troubling . . .
after Gooober . . . went away . . . that February day
during a brief time of darkness and despair
         I did this terrible thing
I called on Satan as my new 'god' . . and I wonder
if I should confess this in my Happiness poem
assuming it is ever completed — and published

that is . . oh, Heath !
do I have a right to take those who may read it
with me, down into the depths of hell ?"

                    "it's one of the shorter routes to Heaven"

"what a wise answer that is !
I never thought of it in quite that way

and I have another question
a friend of mine wants to start his own health food restaurant
and he has found investors who are willing to finance his dream
but their money is . . well, somewhat tainted
for they are members of Organized Crime
I don't know how to advise him . . because, well
I've always thought that one should render unto Caesar
that which is Caesar's — so to speak
and render unto God that which is . . God's
should he accept this stained money
perhaps earned from very negative and illicit activities ?"

                    "what humans do forget
                              regarding your Caesar-God analogy
                    is that . . what belongs to Caesar
                                   also belongs to God

                    there is no harm in using tainted money
                    and transmuting it into good"

"your profundity amazes me !
there ! my drawing is finished . . as much as I can now recall
does it seem correct to you ?"

Canto Twenty ☆ 891

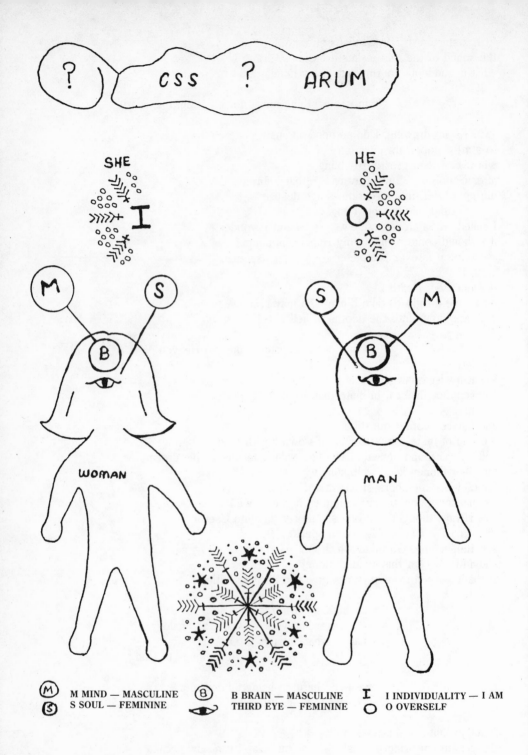

Ⓜ	M MIND — MASCULINE	Ⓑ	B BRAIN — MASCULINE	I	I INDIVIDUALITY — I AM	
Ⓢ	S SOUL — FEMININE	👁	THIRD EYE — FEMININE	O	O OVERSELF	

"it appears to be quite correct
though not entirely so
that is, there are some things missing
tell me please, what do the question marks
represent ?"

"they represent that I don't know what lies above
what I have set down on paper here
and now suppose *you* tell *me* . . what the letters mean"

"you will recall what lies above
as we speak further . . meanwhile
explain to me the meaning
of what you have already traced quite clearly"

"well, I don't understand it — not even nearly
let alone well — but I shall try to explain as best I can"

"why not begin with the letter 'I'
you have printed above the female figure ?"

"the letter 'I' is actually what I have been mistakenly
referring to as the Supraconscious — it is the true Higher Self of woman
and is the symbol of the words Individuality and Intellect
but the 'I' is strictly feminine, not masculine
so women *do* have an intellect !"

"indeed they do . . this is very true"

"the 'I' is the True Self of Woman
it is her Individuality and Intellect . . the Higher Angel of herself . . her S-elf ?
which is all powerful and all knowing . . . .

and the true Self of Man is called 'O'
which symbolizes the word Overself — and exactly matches the function
of the 'I' of Woman — yet also symbolizes the Circle of Eternity
therefore, the 'O' is the Overself of each man
and is a term which may never be used to describe the feminine
for 'O' is the Higher Angel of each man
        . . just as 'I' is the Higher Angel of each woman"

"you are explaining it all very nicely
continue, if you please"

"the Higher Angel of Woman — the Feminine 'I'
of her individuality, as well as her power
and the Higher Angel of Man — the masculine 'O'
of *his* individuality, as well as his power . . .
each of these control, in the individual Earthling — two things"

"and what might these two 'things' be ?"

" . . . . 'things' is not a proper term
I would rather say two 'facets' of the human essence
does that sound better ?"

"precisely correct — go on"

"the 'I' and the 'O' — each of these control
in the individual woman and man
two facets of the human essence — which are as follows
one is the M, which represents the masculine Mind
being the producer of all energy forms
ideas . . and invention
and the masculine Mind operates through the also masculine B or Brain
which is like unto a computer
used by the Mind for many purposes, such as memory
and many other functions I can't think of now
I only know this — that the masculine B or Brain cannot function
without the Mind directing it
but that the M or Mind can function equally as well
without the B or Brain — as with it

the Mind can still think and invent and produce energy forms
even if the Body Temple and its B or Brain — are dead"

"this is true, what you have said"

"and further . . the 'I' and the 'O' also each control
in addition to the masculine Mind — the 'S' or the feminine Soul
to which belong emotions, intuition, love, sentiment, music, creativity
all manner of things which are intangible — and spiritual
and, whereas the masculine Mind controls and operates through the masculine Brain
in *both* men and women
the feminine Soul of each 'I' and 'O' controls and operates through
the also feminine Third Eye
in *both* men and women"

"yes, each Feminine 'I' directs an individual
feminine Soul and masculine Mind
through the Body Temple of a Woman

just as each Masculine 'O' directs an individual
masculine Mind and feminine Soul
through the Body Temple of a Man

and the Mind and Soul are inseparably linked
to the Higher Self, as well as to the Body
for the Body Temple
cannot long function — and eventually cannot exist
without the harmonizing of the Mind and Soul
and when *one* of the Trinity of these three
becomes ill or diseased — or fails to properly function

894 ☆ Canto Twenty

then the *other two* will swiftly follow
also becoming soon diseased . . . and impotent

for it has so been ordained . . that these three
may not be separated, either in sickness . . or in health
as long as the three shall live"

"that sounds like the marriage ceremony"

"what I have spoken is the true origin
of those ceremonial words . . long clouded by confusion
as have been many other truths upon your Earth

do not forget . . that if one of these three
becomes diseased in any way . . . the other two will surely
swiftly follow
however . . *conversely*
if but *one* of the three is healed . . then this healing
will begin the process of harmony
which will slowly — but very surely — return to health
the other two
for this Law works also
in its reverse polarity, as well
do you comprehend the vast importance of this ?"

"yes, I do see, and I wish the bloody medical profession would see too
but I am reminded . . of something
when you spoke the words 'swiftly follow after'
my mind seemed to switch gears, for a moment, to another subject . . .

to the subject of . . fallen angels
because I just remembered an old Mother Goose rhyme
I memorized in childhood . . as most children do

*Jack and Jill went up the hill . . to fetch a pail of water
but . . Jack fell down . . and broke his crown . . and Jill
came tumbling after*

could this old nursery ryhme contain, somehow, a secret code
relating to those fallen angels who are twin souls ?"

"MOther GOOse rhymes . . learned in childhood
not all — but most
do verily contain, for those who are inspired
with the insight and the intuition to search for them
many sacred secret codes for Earthlings
leading to enlightenment
never have words
of more awesome prophecy and Divinely Ordained POwer
been written . . than these
which were so ordained in the year of 1833 of Earth Time

Canto Twenty ☆ 895

by MOther GOOse Her S-elf . .
                   although Her origin has never been traced . . .

          No ! NO ! my melodies will never die
          while nurses sing, or babies cry . . .

               deeply ponder **Her** words !"

"Heathcliffe, does the double **O** in her name
have something to do with the **OO**ber Galaxy of Stars ?"

               "it does indeed, my child"

"you are weeping . . and I sense this unmistakably
but why do you cry over this ? please tell me the reason you cry"

          "you . . and all the weary world . . will soon know why
          this new enlightenment of yours has made me cry
          with tears of gladness, and not of sadness . . .
          for the key to Love and Peace on Earth
          will soon open so many **DOOR**S of Joy and Light !
          such happiness as man and woman never dreamed . . . "

"oh, Heath, you are making me cry too — with you
and also *for* you . . since God spelled backwards is, after all, dog
yes, I am weeping too . . even though
I do not yet fully know
all the deeper reasons for your tears, which move me so"

          "then you must meditate and ponder this message :
          that the reasons lie within the long-buried secrets
          of your English alphabet . . so gently and divinely protected
          by your own druids for revelation in the Golden Age
          and as one small clue — small, yet of vast cosmic greatness
          think long and silently . . when you fall asleep each night
          of the ultimate mystery hidden within the word **UNIVERSE**
          for this word does also contain within it
          the words of Uni-verse, or 'one verse' — also the words
                    Seer . . Sun . . and Venus"

"oh ! . . Seer is a prophet — or prophetess
and the Sun is the giver of Life
while Venus is the goddess of all Love
Love and Life — Life and Love . . and what else ?"

          "the word **UNIVERSE** does also contain the word . . **nurse**
          in which is hidden the secret-sacred code to **Her** words:

          NO ! NO ! my melodies will never die
          while nurses sing, or babies cry . .

for there is cause why each baby born unto Earth, at present
does cry — and there is awesome Truth
behind this mystery of **SHE**
who does lovingly, and with Eternal Tenderness
nurse . . All Universes"

"how very odd . . how strange
that I now find myself weeping . . from far, far beyond my heart
from somewhere down so deep inside . . a place
where I never knew that tears could be wept"

"*For at the gates of the Mighty, She hath taken a seat,
and at the entrance thereof chanteth Her song : . .* "

"what are these strange . . yet so familiar . . words you sing ?
and how can mere words be said to . . sing ?
why do they make me cry once more ? whence cometh they ?"

"these words you rightly hear . . *DO* sing !
as *ALL* words do . . this secret shall be learned someday
and taught by you — and others too
when the mysteries of the druidic alphabet unfold
but this is for a later portion of your Happiness pOem
and must await further awakening
however, in answer to your last specific question

the song . . is from a painstaking translation of the *Septuagint*
which is — in Earth time — circa 250 B.C.
and is truly your Old Testament — in actuality
since the standard Hebrew manuscripts
comprising what is now falsely recognized as your Old Testament
date only from the Renaissance
and the words I quoted . . were excerpted from
the Septuagint's Book of Proverbs, you see . . "

"please sing them again to me . . "

"*For at the gates of the Mighty, She hath taken a seat,
and at the entrance thereof chanteth Her song :*

*In the beginning, before the Lord made the Earth
when He furnished the Heavens, I was with Him
and when He set apart His throne on the winds
When He set to the sea its bounds
and the waters passed not the word of His mouth
I was harmonizing with Him. I was the one in whom
He delighted, and I was daily gladdened
by His presence . . on all occasions*"

"then the Old Testament distortions of Truth
through the patriarch images or thought forms

have been promoted . . these false images . . by the Church Fathers ?"

"this is true . . but not even the Church Fathers
can stop the coming electrical storm of Truth on Earth"

"where are these ancient and true manuscripts ?
are some of them hidden within the Vatican . . in Rome ?"

"all secrets are hidden in Rome . . now restlessly stirring
but may not longer be hidden from pure and searching hearts
when the druidic alphabet is revealed
shall all these mysteries grow as flowers . . toward the Light

for the Light of Truth has been ordained
to be awakened in the dawning of the Golden Age of Aquarius
and this thunder and lightning in the human heart
may not be turned away or halted
the beginning of true Wisdom shall this awakening be . . and

it will purify Original Sin . . "

"please define Original Sin for me . . "

"you will learn this for later writings
following the first part of your Happiness POem . .
in its sequel you may choose to call *Twelfth Night Secrets*

. . the beginning of true widsom shall purify Original Sin
and this awakening shall be called Original **Innocence**
all of this has been ordained and pre-destined
for it shall bring about the new Aquarian Age of Golden Love
manifested in all the splendor and magnificence
of the re-born and wiser Atlantis
not all of your Earthling chauvinists . . no ! nor all your
atomic and nuclear and cobalt madmen
combined
can stop the lighting of approaching wisdom
nor hold back the Uranian tidal waves . . of Truth"

"but . . oh, Heath ! how may such mysteries
as the MOther GOOOse rhymes from the OOber Galaxy of Stars
be unfolded ? is there a secret key for the decoding ?"

"none but the opening of the feminine Third Eye, you see"

"but . . well . . concerning myself
and my own enlightenment . . I am so positive that the nursery rhyme
of Jack and Jill . . going up the hill
contains some seed of greater wisdom — yet, I don't have a single clue
as to what the mystery behind this rhyme might be
no idea of where to begin to decipher it

and learn why this is a matter of such great consequence to me"

"you may decode these messages you are seeking
in much the same manner that you — and many others
have already deciphered the encodements
contained within the very nearly spiritual words
of that wise Earthling book . . . called *The Little Prince*

which is, on the surface of it, a children's book
but which was written by its author, Antoine de Saint-Exupery
for perceptive and enlightened adults
as was Madeline L'Engle's so-called children's book
.. *A Wrinkle in Time*

both of these works have already achieved
a cult following, among intuitive readers
likewise . . the works of Lewis Carroll and James Barrie

truth always eventually calls forth those
who follow it where e're it goes
Peter Pan's flying, of course, was symbolic levitation

. . and are you, perchance, aware . . of the strangeness
surrounding the 'death' of the author of
. . *The Little Prince ?*"

"I am . . but please speak of it anyway
because this strangeness chords haunting music
in my inner ear . . like a healing melody
of beauty and lost loveliness . . . found again"

"it is said that author de Saint-Exupery
cast away his flesh Body Temple in a 'fatal' plane crash
on the Egyptian desert
or . . perhaps best to say he was believed to do so
since the actual crash of his plane did, indisputably occur

whereas, his book — *The Little Prince*
which was, of course, written before his plane crash
opens — in its very first chapter, on the first page
with the author's own plane crash on the sands
of the Egyptian desert
yes . . more than strange
. . is this"

" . . you have brought tears to my eyes
for I have always known that de Saint-Exupery himself was the Little Prince"

"I am aware whereof you speak"

"Heath, I still need some kind of clue from you

about the Mother Goose nursery rhyme of Jack and Jill
so that I may decipher its coded message
one which I feel, at this particular moment
is intended for the Elf of my own S-elf"

> "very well . . here, then, is one small clue for you
> the message for which you search . . in Jack and Jill
> is contained within that portion of the rhyme
> concerned with what they went up the hill
> > > to seek"

"you mean . . the water . . or the pail ?"

> "ponder this within your heart for yet awhile
> and you shall discover the answer for yourself
> even as we continue to speak"

"allright, then — a query about the medical profession
will they ever learn the secret of the necessity
for a perfect harmony of the Trinity
of Body, Mind and Soul . .
that, when one falls ill, the other two will swiftly follow
and when one is healed, the other two
> will likewise follow
since this trinity is one . . and forever inseparable ?"

> "their enlightenment is already seeded
> and soon they shall also discover
> > or finally realize
> that, when the body's parts
> such as arms or legs . . or even organs
> have been lost through accident — or removed
> > due to disease
> if the Mind and Soul are *fully healed*
> > and functioning together harmoniously
>
> *then even lost limbs . . and organs*
> > *are capable of regenerating themselves*
>
> like unto the crab, in Nature
> which, when it loses a claw — simply grows a new one
> or like unto the lizard, in Nature
> which, when it loses the tail — simply grows a new one
> and has even been known to grow new eyes
> when its own have been lost, through accident
>
> even presently have physicians learned
> that when a child — before the age of twelve
> when the Third Eye begins to close . . .
> > loses a finger

if, instead of sewing it closed
        leaving a stump
they leave it open and carefully covered
the child will grow a new finger
            a number of times has this occured
to astonish the medical profession . . .
        there have even been rare cases
when a human has likewise grown
            a partial new arm or leg
and, of course, it has long been known
that certain men and women in Russia
possess the roots for a third set of teeth

all of these miracles will your 'medicine men'
        discover
after they have learned that preventative medicine
through astrological diagnosis
is far more important
than their largely impotent and often dangerous cures
yes, even this shall they be enlightened unto
in due time . . if it is not too late"

"by too late, I assume you mean
that, if the misguided scientists, astronomers
and hard-headed materialistic industrialists
don't destroy the planet, before these miracles manifest ?"

                "yes, this was precisely the meaning I intended to convey
                and by the way . . your admiration for Einstein
                should be tempered with the knowledge
                that, although this Earthling was a genuine Avatar
                he became carried away by his own enlightenment
                and committed the grave error of judgement
                of failing to realize, in his excitement of discovery
                                            the danger
                his powerful 'thought forms' carried to this planet

                for Earthlings are not yet sufficiently evolved
                to be able to use such knowledge wisely
                therefore, Piscean Albert Einstein . . .
                as is known and sternly regretted by the Elder Brothers
                    failed in his appointed cosmic mission
                by severely endangering your planet's future Eden heaven

                although he also — as you already appreciate
                did plant upon your plan-et . . and ponder these two words
                    . . . even though Einstein indisputably also planted
                many positive and fertile seeds of thought
                which are, even now . . thrusting through the mud
                of humanity's clouded concepts

Canto Twenty   ☆   901

into the beautiful flowers of an approaching springtime

so, once again, one must give credit where credit is due
now . . let us return to the picture you perceptively drew"

"yes, I'm looking at my drawing — and it's more clear to me
because I now can see . . from the relative size
of my circular symbols of the masculine Mind and feminine Soul
a symbolism that too many humans
are presently directing the Body Temple's activities and achievements
with too much emphasis on the masculine Mind, operating through
the masculine Brain — which I intuitively drew larger
and with too little guidance and assistance from the feminine Soul
operating through the feminine Third Eye of intuition"

"and what does this mean exactly ?"

"I don't think I can properly explain it"

"be assured that you can — just try"

"it means that we are swiftly approaching
the same mistakes and unimaginable horrors . . of Maldek and Atlantis
because we are permitting the technology of the *masculine* Mind
to leap far ahead of — and beyond
the potential spiritual and esoteric advances of the *feminine* Soul

and this has allowed the masculine Mind
to crown the also masculine Brain
as the reigning King over each Earthling's Body Temple
over . . . each man *and* woman

while refusing to allow the yearning feminine Soul
to rule equally with the Mind
by crowning the feminine Third Eye as the also reigning Queen
of the Body Temple of each man *and* woman

oh ! . . but wait . .

OH ! OH !

again I am recalling
Mother Goose . . that old rhyme

Jack and Jill went up the hill . . to fetch a pail of water
but . . Jack fell down, and broke his *crown* !

and Jill . . came tumbling after
oh ! I see !"

"what new mystery have you decoded

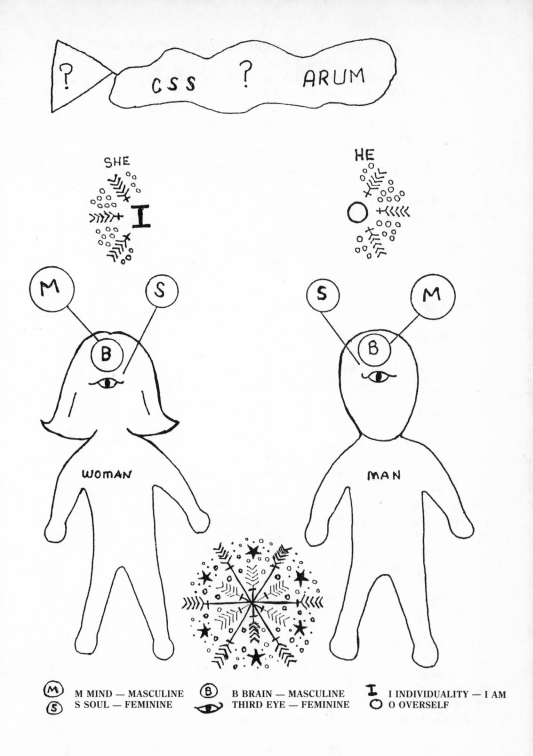

M MIND — MASCULINE   B BRAIN — MASCULINE   I INDIVIDUALITY — I AM
S SOUL — FEMININE   THIRD EYE — FEMININE   O OVERSELF

from the few words of this wise MOther GOOse rhyme ?
and do not forget
that there is good reason for these encodements
to have been conceived and created
by <u>Mother</u> Goose
for buried beneath these, as has been stated
are several layers of urgent messages"

"oh, yes ! this rhyme has now channeled many new thoughts !"

"women's struggle for equal rights with men
is an extremely good and beneficial goal
even an urgent need for Earth
but women have allowed, as in past eons, a subtle distortion
to snake and coil itself into their fight for freedom
and true equality
which is unguessed by women
and allows the Masculine force to continue to control them

this has caused . . . this is causing . . . "

"what you speak of has been seeded
in the sleeping Mind of women . . by the Unicorn"

"the Unicorn ? in what way ?"

"you will learn this later, as we continue speaking
meanwhile, go on . . continue
with what you were about to say"

"women have been tempted and persuaded to believe
that their equality and power must be symbolized, as well as gained
through the adoption of masculine thought processes
dress, manners, speech — and behavioral patterns of the man
and this is incredibly self-defeating

for the great influence of the feminine Soul
directed by the awesome Power of the Feminine Goddess
of each Feminine 'I'
cannot regain its lost powers . . through the alchemy of abdicating

the very essence of femininity itself

and if it continues, it will bring the inevitable and self-defeating result
of the struggle of women to emerge . . to have been in vain"

"correct . . . and the primal wisdom, still not fully envisioned by women
in their cosmically commanded struggle for equal rights
is the secret of . .
Woman's Eternal Superiority

this symbolized in the Act of Creation itself
by the Father and *Mother* Who art in Heaven
for, the Macrocosm Creation of all Universes by Them
is reflected, or mirror-imaged
in the microcosm creation of a child . . on Earth

and Man does, indeed, plant the seed of Life
but it is Woman — and Woman *only*
who controls, within Her own Essence . . the POwer
to either *permit* — or *not* to permit — new life
to miscarry, abort — or give birth

therefore, the Feminine Essence has been Divinely given
dominance over the Masculine Essence
in the final determination . . of all creation

for it has been known Eternally and Forever
that the sensitivity, compassion, love and intuition
        of the Feminine Goddess essence
comprise the inner wisdom to be entrusted with Life itself

and Woman may only regain her POwer . . . .
she may only bring the 'O' into the circle of her POwer
by *retaining* . . and not *losing*

                                                her own S-elf
this is her one and only
path to freedom . . there is no other
for, all other roads lead back into the maze of her submission

        woman must gaze into the Mirror of Truth
        and see reflected there — her own true Essence

which is the greatest of all POwers — the POwer over Life
for Woman, the Feminine 'I', is the
                        I AM
and these 3 letters
of the druidic, Chaldean alphabet
do contain the very deepest mystery-of-all-mysteries
in all Solar Systems, Galaxies and Universe . . .
        . . . the Overwhelming Mystery of Woman"

"which is ?"

"which is her primal **Innocence**
the mystery-of-all-mysteries
lies in the pOwer of wOman's innOcence

the great and awesome — ultimate Mystery of why she is capable
at each millenium — and only at a time of darkness
of becoming the vessel for an immaculate cOnception

there being a pure and simple truth behind this sacred Mystery
woven from the logical law of meta-physics
and its alchemy formula will be revealed to you at the allotted time
for Part Two of your Happiness pOem

however, it has been Cosmically Ordained that at no other time
and for no other purpose than Universal Salvation
            may WOman cOnceive . . alOne

        for the Masculine essence has been given the POwer
to seed new Life
            and other than this holy exception

an I-mmaculate cOnception . . . is impOssible
for the 'I' of the Individuality needs the 'O' to conceive

a great secret lies hidden in the clue that **woman** contains the letter 'O'
while the word **man** does not — and in the further clue
that the word **feminine** contains the letters of the word 'nine'
        the 9 of the Red Dragon of Alchemy of electrical energy and all Life
whereas, of course — the word **masculine** — does not

in the final determination
the permission — or the denial
of all new Life seeded by the Masculine 'O'
                    belongs to the Feminine 'I'
        belongs to WOman alOne

and while she may not, at present, create new Life
                    without the seed of the 'O'
neither is Man, the Creator of Life
in control of the final manifestation of either the new Universes
                or the new children . . he has seeded
in both the Macrocosm and the microcosm sense is this true

in such manner does the Cosmos remain in perfect Harmony
through the spectrum of the Rainbow
                and the Music of the Spheres

        and now . . to return for a moment
        to women's struggle for freedom and equality . . .
        are you aware that you summarized
        all these words I have spoken on this topic
        briefly and concisely — and quite clearly
        to the one you call Gooober . . during that first night
        the two of you found each other again
        when you said to him . . do you remember
                        what you said then ?"

"you mean . . when I told him that I have no intention

of allowing this ERA intervention
to seduce me into relinquishing my feminine privileges and perogatives
just to prove to the world that I'm equal to men
when I already know I'm superior . . is that what you mean ?"

"yes . . and do you not see how your words
summarize all we have been discussing ?
for, the lack of that fiery certainty
                    you expressed to the man you love . .

the lack of it in Woman
was the underlying cause for the fall
of both the planet Maldek — and the lost continent
                    of Atlantis"

"then the protection of the ERA's sacred mission
and the enlightenment of women
concerning its true purpose . . is . . "

"of urgent importance, yes
and do not overlook that the initials ERA
contain the word **EAR**
and this is a holy, cosmic pun — of grave
                    and serious implication
        . . let those men
                who have eyes . . see
        and let those women
                who have *ears* . . *hear*"

"do the current thought forms
of scientific experimentation . . in areas such as cloning
        test tube babies, artificial insemination
cryogenics — the freezing of bodies for later revival
brain implant, aimed to control humans, by way of electrodes
        from a distance
nuclear testing
and all these so-called leaps of science into the world of tomorrow
do these bear a similarity of pattern
to the wild and cancerous multiplication of the 'thought forms'
of energy . . which were indulged in by Atlanteans
before the inundation of their continent ?"

"they are, indeed, what you might term
the terrible beginning steps along that same path
they represent a rush toward
the very kind of scientific technology
which eventually led to the catastrophic inundation
of that once fair land

because these experiments are being made
at the great cost of neglect of the feminine Soul

to state this in different words . . .
Earth needs her poets far more crucially
than she needs her scientists
                    her genuinely motivated, esoteric astrologers
far more than her astronomers

Earth needs her composers, painters, writers and singers
far more desperately . . at this, History's Twilight Hour
than she needs her computers, industrial giants and politicians
and also . . as we approach
                    this new and darkened millennium
Earth needs her women more urgently
                            than she needs her men
yes, Mother Earth
            . . needs these

although both the 'I' and the 'O' are cosmically necessary
to the Whole of all heavens of happiness
                    . . . . at this trembling Star Time
it is the Woman

who will encourage in men the development
of the Soul's mission and direction
through the gentle . . but swift opening of the Third Eye
and the wise control of its powers

Mother Earth shall always need the strength
of the brilliant Sun-warmth of the 'O'
and could not exist in Space and Time without Man
but must presently look for salvation
            and *Expect Her Miracle* . . from the **I AM**
from Woman . .

for the seed atom in the heart of Woman — the 'I'
will gently and wisely lead the heart of 'O' — or Man
back once again to the memory of his true POwer . . .
and only after this Miracle has re-manifested itself
                            upon your Earth
may each 'I' and 'O'
those Twin Selves so long separated . . be spiritually equal
                        and once more united"

"I seem to believe it to be
as though Hansel — or Jack — or Raggedy Andy — had wandered
too far into the woods . . too near the dangerous
                    Gingerbread House of the Wicked Witch
            and were lost

and it is only Gretel . . or Jill herself . . or Raggedy Ann
who can take the lost man-child gently by the hand
and point out the way back home"

"I do recognize that to be a beautiful
as well as a celestially appropriate metaphor

but this is not to say . . . that there are not today
many men on Earth who do listen
to the voice of the 'O' of the Overself
for there are many male spiritual leaders, even now

men whose missions here are crucial

nor do I mean to imply that every single Feminine 'I'
of every woman on Earth, at this time
is gentle or wise enough
to lead Earthlings anywhere . . but deeper into the woods

I speak only of the Macrocosm need, in a general sense
        . . that guidance from the Feminine 'I'
must now be emphasized, for a period
until sanity returns to the majority of men once more
and the 'O' and the 'I' may once again lead together
                                        side by side"

"may the original 'I' of the Individuality — or the **I AM**
the Higher Angel of the Feminine S-elf
even though she is not an ancient myth or legend
but was — and shall be always — human
may she also be thought of symbolically . . as **Isis ?**

and may the original Lord of the 'O'
which is the Higher Angel of the Overself
even though he is not an ancient myth or legend
but was — and shall be always — human
may he also be thought of symbolically . . as **Osiris ?**"

"the answer to each question . . for good cause
                is yes
the symbolism . . and the actuality
may both be used, and used correctly
now, if we may return to your last drawing
it is my turn to ask some questions . . of you"

"**ARF ! ARF !** please do !"

"you are taking over my role, I see"

"oh, no ! I was only teasing
I meant no disrespect . . truly, I didn't"

"but why shouldn't you take over my role
and why should we not inter-change our knowing ?
as has been stated, we are all teachers

Canto Twenty ☆ 909

"no, no — if I know anything at all
if I have even one small fragment of wisdom
that fragment came from others . . such as you"

"you have also . . taught me much more
than you, perhaps, will ever guess
but let us not digress . . .
the question I have for you is this . .
can you tell me what you intended to portray
or symbolize — by the initials you placed
above the 'O' and the 'I'
such as, for one example
. . the letters **ARUM ?**"

"no, I'm afraid I cannot answer that
I know I placed them there — that they were channeled by my Higher S-elf
but I can't seem to understand why I did so
or what they stand for — can you explain it to me ?"

"there is really no need for me to explain
for you, yourself — will soon see
as we continue to communicate . . look again
at your drawing now"

"allright, I am looking at it"

"thus far, have you made it clear to yourself
through your not yet completed drawing
that the Essence you have been mistakenly calling
by turns, the Spirit, the Soul and the Supra-Conscious
is actually none of these
but is, instead, depending upon the gender
either the feminine 'I' or the masculine 'O' ?"

"this much, at least
I believe I finally do know"

"returning to the matter of individuality
or personal identity — in a different situation . .

many of your Earthlings have made the mistake
of anticipating what they call
the Second Coming of Jesus

the Mind, Soul and Higher 'O' of Jesus, the man
will return to Earth in human form
and in truth, this has already occurred . . however
his personal identity will be revealed
to but a chosen few

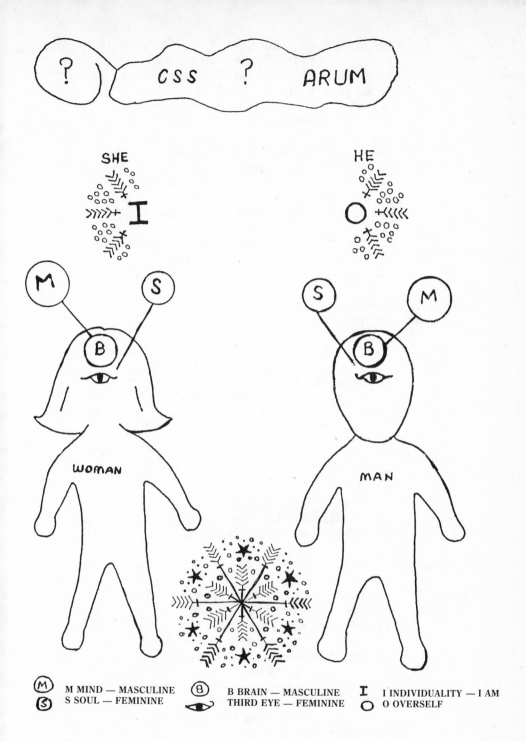

? CSS ? ARUM

SHE · HE

WOMAN · MAN

M MIND — MASCULINE
S SOUL — FEMININE

B BRAIN — MASCULINE
THIRD EYE — FEMININE

I INDIVIDUALITY — I AM
O OVERSELF

due to the former error
of Divinity-conscious humanity
his role on Earth will be vastly different this time
he will guide and teach, yes — as he did before
but will not be recognized — lest he once more
be worshipped

he will be viewed as an ordinary teacher
similar to many other Avatars and Adepti
presently leading humankind through the mazes
of the New Age
and there is a great cosmic cause for this

it has been irrevocably ordained, without equivocation
that, in this new and golden Aquarian Age
his former ultimate goal will finally be realized"

"his former goal . . his dream of before ?
I don't understand what you mean"

"meditate, then, upon his own words . . as an Essene

all things which I have done, you can do also
. . go thou and do likewise — and more

be it done unto you . . according to your faith"

"please explain this
I am somewhat confused . . and I must know"

"it is even so — as I have already stated
his *role*, this time, shall be vastly different
although his *goal*, this time, will be precisely the same"

"I simply do not understand"

"the Messiah of the Aquarian Age will be multiple
and this is altogether fitting and proper
for one man alone — one 'O' of a single Overself
could not possibly accomplish what is needed today
on a planet so over-populated and complex
as is Earth today
there will be a number of Messiahs or Saviours
and some of these will be guided
by the 'O' of a masculine Overself
while others will be guided
by the 'I' of the feminine Individuality

and the purpose of this
is to cause all men and women to recall that time
when each was a god or goddess . . .

912   ☆   Canto Twenty

the purpose is to open the Third Eye of each Earthling
not to train humanity to worship a single individual
                    as holier-than-thou
and can you not see, then, how this was his goal before ?
repeatedly, he tried to teach his followers
that what he did — they could do also — and far more

yes, far, far more
for he demonstrated but a small part of the magic
each Earthling god and goddess contain
within themselves . . within their latent powers

repeatedly, he tried to explain
the similarity between the Nature rain
and the rain of *human* nature

repeatedly, he attempted to teach that his miracles
were not his alone — but manifested through the faith
of those not yet able to believe fully in themselves
                    and so believed in him instead

therefore . . . *be it done unto you*
according to your faith, as he taught over and over again
but his counsel fell upon deaf ears
                    and tightly closed Third Eyes

this time, his return will have deeper implications
for, he will come . . and he will go
overshadowing the Body Temples of multiple Earthlings . . .
as stated, there shall be, in the New Age
many Messiahs . . both men and women
                    and he will come and go in these
until each woman — each 'I' Individuality
and each man — each 'O' Overself
have reclaimed their birthrights as gods and goddesses
of great and wondrous powers
                    this time . . not to be abused

    . . . only then shall the Mind and Soul of Jesus
who was and is, remember . . . . . . only a man
although he was and is, part of a great 'O'
                            of eons ago
only then will he remain the Owner
            of one Body Temple
for his mission will have been finally completed
the mission which failed before, because of Divinity worship

        only to those of pure heart
    shall it be revealed which Temple he shall choose
            and until this choice

he will come and go — to overshadow the Temples of many
from time to time, when he is needed

the Masters have prophesied another — *and related* — mystery
that, at some time during the Age of Aquarius
the 14 pieces of Osiris will come together in one man
who will be reunited with Isis . . and together, then
they will guide the planet toward *Pax et Bonum*
Peace and Good

now I see a question in your eyes . . and I surmise
it concerns your curiosity about the 14 pieces of Osiris
but do not trouble yourself with this now
it will be revealed soon, as we continue to talk"

"some of the things you have told me
about the Soul of Jesus, the man . . and especially
those things you've clearly stated
concerning multiple Messiahs and Saviours

are truths which will greatly offend
and even perhaps dangerously anger
many present-day religious conformists and churches
in particular, the born-again-Christians
the Bible Belt Fundamentalists
all those whose Third Eyes are still closed
and are, therefore, unable to see the true Light
how will these ever be converted to Truth ?"

"you are quite right — and it is a sad situation
for, all these humans you mention are truly
and essentially — very good Earthlings — not evil
and it is extremely difficult
to be forced to struggle, in attempting to reveal Truth
against both the positive and negative vibrations
simultaneously
one fully anticipates
the necessity of struggling against the darkness
but it is an added burden to be forced also
to struggle against the twilight
however, these good and well meaning ones
who are misled and misguided . . even they
as it has been ordained . . . shall be converted
become as little children . . and enter the Kingdom
you must remember that *perseverance furthers* . . .
keep the light of your own candle of Faith burning
and it will ignite a flame in others
. . even in the coldest hearts"

"some time ago, I asked you a question
but your reply was interrupted . . by my drawing

and I still seek to solve that mystery"

> "you asked about the difference, I believe
> between the pieces of the you-of-you
> and your own twin soul . . which you now know to be
> incorrectly named as the twin soul"

"then what is the correct term ?"

> "the correct term is the Twin *Self* . . for your *personal* quest"

"I see ! my twin elf !
adding the Serpent 'S' becomes my Twin Self
but I prefer to call Gooober my Twin Elf
it makes glad-tears spring into my eyes . . so may I ?"

> "you certainly may . . for it does relate to druids
> as you will soon learn . . and teach others
> but to avoid a semantics scramble
> > let us call it, for this discussion
> the **Twin Self**
>
> each 'I' of the feminine Individuality . . has a Twin
> and each 'O' of the masculine Overself . . has a Twin
> > of the opposite sex
>
> you have already drawn this as the 'I' blended with the 'O'
> in perfect harmony . . imaging it as a Snowflake
> whole and pure . . and so totally individual
> that there is no other like it anywhere in any Universe
>
> after Original Sin created a situation
> which eventually led to darkness on this Earth
> each highly individual symbolic Snowflake
> was split apart into two separate matching halves
> one being the 'I' and the other being the 'O'
> > the Twin Selves of polarity
>
> and it is necessary for each 'I' and each 'O'
> to locate the other half
> for Love and Peace to fall once more upon Earth
> therefore is it vastly important
> for all Twin Selves to find one another, and unite
> for these halves are absolutely distinct
> and, as in your Snowflake metaphor
>
> unlike any other two halves in any Universe"

"you called them Twin Selves of polarity
does that mean that one half of the divided Snowflake
is masculine — the other feminine

that is, is one half male or man, and the other female or woman ?"

"in essence, yes — the 'I' half of the Snowflake
is, of course, essentially female
and the 'O' half of the Snowflake is, of course, essentially male
however, both the masculine and the feminine essence
is present in each half of the whole"

"there is a little man, then — in every woman
and a little woman in every man — is this not so ?"

"look again at your drawings . . then make yet another one
I will wait until it is completed"

"while I am making another drawing
may we still talk ? I can do two things at once"

"of course we may . . what is it you wish to know ?"

"more about the mixture of male-female
in each half of the divided Snowflake"

"as you should know . . it is not wrong
for a man to be sensitive enough to weep"

". . and if a proper balance be kept
neither is it against Universal Harmony
for a woman to be strong and courageous
assuming neither is overdone, and a balance is maintained"

"there is much concerning the mysteries of the two sexes
to which you will soon be enlightened
and when that time comes, you will be truly amazed

now I see that you have completed your *new* drawing"

"yes, I have — here it is ! have I drawn it correctly ?"

"as you have already discerned through your drawing
the 'M' or Mind is linked to the 'S' or Soul

and each 'I' — each 'O' — controls and directs
its own personal Mind and Soul
as you have illustrated yourself, you see
the Mind is always masculine in essence
                              . . the Soul always feminine
whether these two
are directed by the feminine 'I' of the Individuality
or by the masculine 'O' of the Overself"

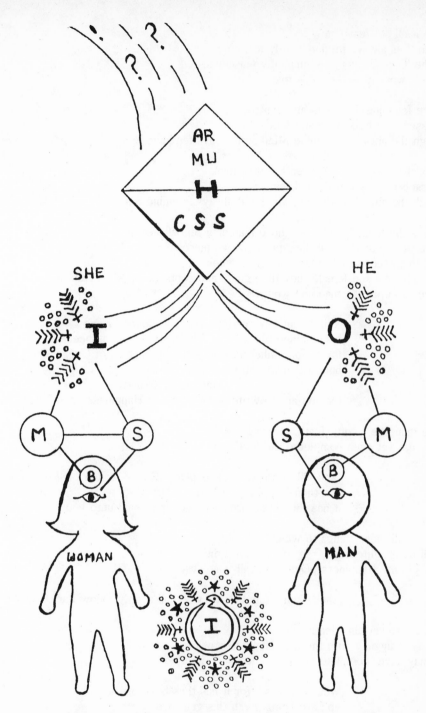

Ⓜ M MIND — MASCULINE	Ⓑ B BRAIN — MASCULINE	I I INDIVIDUALITY — I AM
Ⓢ S SOUL — FEMININE	👁 THIRD EYE — FEMININE	O O OVERSELF

"I see it all so clearly now !
for the 'I' is always predominantly feminine
and the 'O' is always predominantly masculine
the 'I' is woman — the 'O' is man

but the feminine 'I' directs and controls
the essence of both male and female
through the always masculine Mind and always feminine Soul

just as the masculine 'O' directs and controls
the essence of both male and female
through the always masculine Mind and always feminine Soul

and it is the 'I' and the 'O' — those matching Snowflakes halves
eons ago, due to Original Sin, split into two pieces
which must reunite into ONE complete whole
while the male and female they then guide and control as Body Temples
remain as **separate** man and woman"

        "this is entirely correct — and in your drawing
        is contained the seed of falsehood which has been
        for so long inherent in the Hindu teaching of Oneness
        but all this will be revealed to you
                at the allotted time
        for you are to write more than one Happiness poem"

"more than one ? oh, Heath, please !
I have not yet even completed the first"

        "you will write Happiness pOem One — called *Gooberz*
        and then Happiness pOem — Part Two
        it has thus been ordained, as I have said unto you"

"and will all these things to which you say
I shall be enlightened . . . at the allotted time
be told in my Happiness pOem you call Part Two ?"

        "they shall — and Part Two shall swiftly follow Part One"

"don't be so certain, Heathcliffe
I'm still struggling with the first Happiness pOem
and may never complete even it — let alone another"

        "you will do so, for it has thus been ordained
        you are being given this guidance
        for the enlightenment of each sister and brother
        all those Earthlings who are presently lost in the woods
        who have wandered far away from Eden
        and must be shown the way once more . . back home"

"I am still uncertain, but we shall see

can you guess what troubles me the very most
through mental telepathy ?"

        "what troubles you concerns the longing
        experienced by the separate halves
        of each eons-ago divided symbolic Snowflake
        while they remain lonely and apart
        and the deep yearning these separated
        Higher Angels feel — to seek one another
        but I must say . .
        this required not telepathy . . for your need
        is so visible on your features, as well as in your aura"

"do they . . always seek to reunite
as man and woman ?"

        "throughout numerous incarnations
        each separated 'I' and 'O' will seek one another

        they seek and discover, then lose each other again
            they burn and learn together
        as each struggles to grow, then to recognize and know
                the other
        throughout countless reincarnational Earth-lived nights

        they do come together many, many times
        before the complete and final blending
        through all manner of various human relationships
        and patterns of love
        as siblings . . as parent and child . . as friends
        and sometimes, unfortunately . . even as enemies
        on occasion, as business associates
                relatives or neighbors

        and only after all of these relationship experiences
        is each 'I' half prepaed to meet the 'O' half
                and vice versa
        in the deeper relationship
          . . of mates and lovers"

"does this mean that all lovers and mates
of the same — or the opposite sex
are Twin Selves, involved in their culminating relationship ?
to me, that certainly seems . . . . . "

        "by no means ! only those mates or lovers
        whose feelings for one another have reached the stage
        in a particular incarnation
        of being composed of an equal balance
                of a Trinity of three parts

a true blending of such Twin Selves is . . . "

"is it Twin Selves or Twin S-elves ?
is it Twin Self or Twin S-elf ?" I interrupted

        "the correct spelling of the plural should be Selves
            for druidic and Essenic reasons
        as you will soon learn for Part Two of your Poem
        and the correct spelling for the two others
        should be S-elf and Twin S-elf
               . . now, as I was previously saying . . . .
        a true blending of such separated Snowflake halves
        is composed of three parts
        and these parts are: a magnetic *mental* empathy
        a deep *emotional* chemistry
            and a true *spiritual* harmony

        a trinity of blending, in equal balance
               is needed . . . of these three"

"but . . you forgot the *physical*
you left out *spring* !
since the 'I' and the 'O' must express themselves
through flesh bodies . . as I guess they always must ?"

        "yes, they always must . . for cosmic harmony
        but you will learn more of why this must be
        at the allotted time, as has been stated"

" . . . as I was saying, since the 'I' and 'O'
must always express their love through Body Temples
then would not the physical blending Gooober and I call *spring*
        also be a very necessary part
along with the mental, emotional and spiritual ?"

        "no, the sexual blending is not a necessary part"

"it is not ? but I thought . . .
well, I'm sorry, but it is to me"

        "the sexual blending, you see
        is not a necessary part — it is the **whole**
        it is the result — one might even say reward
        of the equal blending of the other three parts

        for, when these are exactly matched
        and equally blended, in love's trinity
        then physical intimacy and sexual ecstasy
        experienced by these two . . is **deep**

            . . is very, very deep"

"yes . . . *deep*"

"deep calleth unto deep . . as you already know
and when this is so, between Twin Selves . . .
        then the tenderness and the glory
of such a higher sexual union
creates a unique auric glow around them
indicating a true tantric mating — or joining

which, due to the Law of Magnetic Attraction
is seen . . through Time and Space . . and recognized
by those entities awaiting birth
who seek to enter Earth . . within the vibration of love"

"how may one know if one has truly found the Twin S-elf
or is only deceiving one's s-elf ?"

"you are quite correct to think the hyphen in your mind
when you speak of your own s-elf or your Twin S-elf
        and the hyphen should also be used
when the words s-elf or Twin S-elf are written
however much this may disturb the language scholars

if everyone on your planet began swiftly
to correctly hyphenate this important word
the resulting mass vibration
        would be a powerful positive force for change
and would shine much Light
also, in the proper time, you will be taught
why this is all so — and why the letter 'S' must be
kept separate in these two words . . by the added hyphen
yet not removed from them either"

"how will it ever become possible
to convince people to think and write such commonly used words
differently than they were taught to do . . in school
and make this a new spelling rule ?"

"one must plant the seeds of Truth
at the right seasonal time . . . and human nature
        will take care of the rest
they will eventually grow . . and multiply

as for your question, the danger of s-elf deception

is admittedly great . . a testing of awareness
but one may know, by remaining still . . . and alone
listening to the Will of God — also the Will

of one's own Higher Angel of the 'I' or 'O'
yes, this is how one may know
through simply . . . listening for the Truth within"

"simply . . listening ?"

      "SSHHsshh ! be still, my love, be still . . "

"then Gooober was wiser than I
to sit alone and meditate, when he was troubled
why can't I learn to do that, instead of crying ?"

      "tears stem from many emotions in the human heart
                often from compassion
      but always . . from a sensitive soul
      and weeping is not always a sign that a soul is sleeping
      tears can cleanse the soul
              on its path to knowing

      whereas unshed tears may sometimes
      form an inner mist, to blind the soul from truth
      therefore, it is a good thing to shed tears
      as long as a proper balance is kept"

"it always broke my heart . . on the rare occasions
when Gooober cried"

      "with some . . . there are times
      when the most bitter and lonely tears are kept inside"

"after Twin Selves have found one another again
and have reached enlightenment together
may they then . . fall ?"

      "nearly all . . fall"

"and then must climb back up
to awareness again ?"

      "this is sadly . . . true"

"I am suddenly and inexplicably
reminded of . . death
death of the Body Temples . . and I'm also concerned
      about this pattern of speech
the way my questions seem to be hopping and skipping around"

      "in this way . . may the Truth be found"

"by one's mind hopping around ?"

"when one's Mind is being seeded with Truth
the seeds fall at random
and each blossoms when it is time
for it to burst through the soil
into the sunlight . . but be patient with yourself
for the entire garden of your enlightenment
will soon be filled with flowers"

"then it's allright if I return
to the subject of death ?"

"death is inseparable from the subject of Life
as you already know, there need be no loss
even if the Body Temple
which an 'I' or an 'O' was directing
be cast away
because of the Saturn-Seven-cycle you recalled
from latent druidic and Essenic knowledge

. . nor need there even be that casting away of the Temple

for, when Earthlings have become
sufficiently enlightened . . the Body Temple may be
translated
through certain alchemy formulas
and become immortal — one may re-order, so to speak
one's flesh body at will . . simply by re-generating it
through cell reversal"

*

"oh, please tell me more about this !"

"no, I cannot . . for this is a subject
which shall be revealed to you at a later time"

"then do, please, at least verify
what I believe I already know . . . about death
or of the present casting away of flesh Body Temples
even though this will be someday unnecessary"

"true, it will soon be unnecessary
to cast away the flesh body . . . to die
when many more Soul pieces are joined and made whole

but even before then
this miracle may be realized by each man or woman
through the opening of the Third Eye

*Additional information regarding this subject may be found
in Chapter 9 of the book, *Linda Goodman's Star Signs*, which was
written many years after this work was channeled

for, as each regains his or her lost powers
                              or god or goddess
there will be no more need
                    to die
as one of your muses, Shakespeare, wrote . .
'and death, once conquered
                              there's no more dying then' . . "

"but . . now that flesh bodies do die on Earth
let me see if I fully comprehend the current resurrection pattern
of the Saturn-Seven-cycles we spoke of before
about the Soul's decision to exchange one or more of its pieces
                    approximately every seven years
timed by certain Saturn astrological aspects to the natal chart
                                        of the Body Temple . .
this being one of the three choices
the Soul might make, during such time periods"

    I paused, uncertain

"somehow I feel that my terminology is wrong
in some way . . it is in error"

                    "true, it was not correct to say
                    that the Soul makes this karmic choice
                    it is the responsibility
          .   of the Higher S-elf . . the 'I' or 'O'
                    . . might I suggest that you make a new drawing now ?"

"oh, Heath, I really don't know how
or what to include in a new drawing . . that I didn't include before"

                    "nevertheless, please try once more"

"allright, let's see . . . once again
the 'I' and the 'O' . . and the Mind and the Soul
here, what do you think of this ?
it makes no sense to me . . can you explain it ?"

                    "I see that you have included new initials
                    at the top of your drawing
                    and have also placed new question marks above"

"yes, but I haven't the slightest idea
what these new initials and new question marks mean"

                    "as you have already seen . . your understanding will come
                    but let us return, now — to the proper terms
                    one should use, when describing what occurs
                    at the Saturn-Seven-cycle Time period
                    during what you have perceptively and quite rightly called

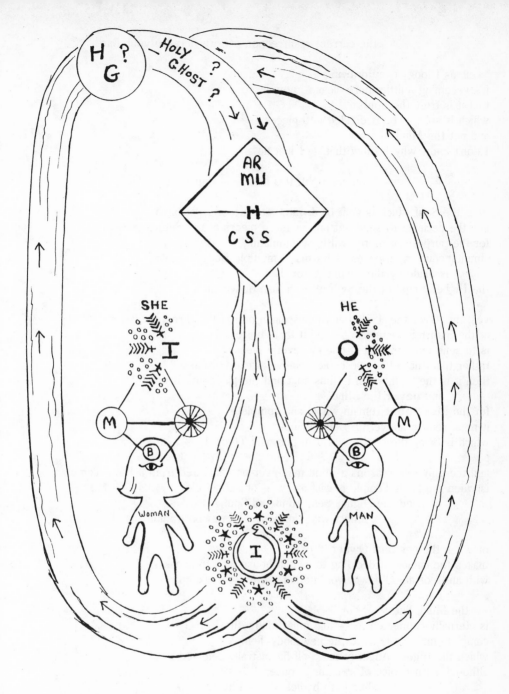

"well, as I look at my drawing
it's becoming a little more clear . . now I see
that it is truly the Soul
which is split — or is divided into pieces
and not the Mind — ever
I don't know why I know that — I just do"

"you are right, this is true — but continue"

"it is the Soul which is split or divided into pieces . . at birth
and the decision to send out one or more pieces at the Saturn cycle
for the purpose of more swiftly accumulating
simultaneous experiences of Karma in multiple Body Temples
        is made by the Owner 'O' or 'I'
the Higher Angel of the S-elf of each man or woman

yes, the 'O' or the 'I' Higher Angels make one of the three choices
at the Saturn-Seven-cycle — and if that choice
is to send out or recall in one or several pieces
rather than the other two choices we've already discussed
then it is the Soul which is thus split and the pieces exchanged
        and **never** the Mind
for the Mind **must** remain whole and complete
it must remain above the Body Temple
which is being directed by its own personal 'O' or 'I'

and the only two reasons a Mind may ever be separated from a Body Temple
is when the flesh Temple is cast away — or should die
        and the Higher Self, Mind and Soul
                connect with the body of a newborn infant

or when the personal Owner 'I' or 'O'
makes the choice of deciding to switch houses, so to speak
with an 'I' or an 'O' Owner of another *adult* Body Temple

    the Mind, like the Soul
is eternally connected to — and must follow the I or O
complete and whole . . to the new body Temple
which the Higher Angel of the S-elf has astrally selected . . .
although such choice of switching houses
                while both bodies are still living
may not be chosen indiscriminately . . but is allowed by Cosmic Law
only under special circumstances

    I just realized . . I mean, I somehow know
that, when such a choice is made because of the death
                of a Body Temple
then the *taking over* of a new flesh body
by the one who died — is timed, like the other choices

by the Saturn-Seven-cycle

but the so-called death itself — the *casting away* of a Temple
because of death
        is *not* timed by Saturn
            because death of the flesh body
cannot be astrologically controlled

in other words, the Saturn-Seven-cycle
determines when the so-called dead individual
takes over a new infant or adult Body Temple . . to *return*
but Saturn's cycle does not time
        the *leaving* of the former Temple . . called dying
is this not so ?"

              "what you have stated is true — no planetary aspect
              either indicates or governs what humans call death
              which is the casting away of a particular
                          flesh Body Temple"

"there are, in astrology, certain aspects or configurations
involving . . not just Saturn alone . . but also other planets and aspects
which many astrologers believe control one's death

and somehow, I've always known that this did not synchronize
in actual practice . . although my knowing comes more from intuition
than from experience . . since I've always refused
to even contemplate such matters as death
in my astrological calculations for others . . or myself"

              "there is a Cosmic Law — which is greatly misunderstood
              that there are certain astrological aspects
                      which do permit death
              however, one need not actually die
              when these occur within the personal nativity
              or horoscope"

"then why do you call them astrological aspects
which permit death ?"

              "note that I have called such aspects
              configurations which *permit* what humans call death
              because, when an Earthling casts away a Body Temple
              this person *will* be under such planetary influences

              for death may *not* take place *without* such astral permission

              however, one need not die each time such an aspect occurs
              since these particular configurations
              appear in the horoscope of each individual man and woman
              periodically, every few years or so

and are — quite obviously — repeatedly avoided

when the decision is made, by an 'I' or an 'O'
to depart from the Body Temple — the departure will occur
at the time of one of these so-called 'death aspects'
but *which* of the many such aspects during a life span
the Higher Angel of the S-elf will choose
                    as a departure vibration
cannot be determined
by any astrologer upon your Earth
yet, how many of them do — and great harm is thereby done
for the simple planting of the suggestive seed
                  by the astrologer
is enough to cause the person
to decide to depart his or her Body Temple
under one of these apsects — when such would not
have been the choice otherwise, you see

the electromagnetic influence of the stars and planets
serve well the purpose of keeping karmic patterns
in some semblence of order and organization
but the experience of flesh death may not be determined
nor, in the final analysis, controlled — by planetary aspect
           this great cosmic decision
belongs exclusively to each individual 'I' or 'O'
and is timed only through the God-gifted Free Will choice
of the Higher Angel of the S-elf
which is **completely immune** to astrological timing patterns
unless the astrologer causes the death, by the power
                  of suggestion
a serious spiritual sin
although all of the other Saturn-Seven-cycle choices
we have discussed . . are, as stated, governed by Saturn's cycles

       and do not forget . . . that one need not die at all
unless one chooses to do so"

"you mean that one dies when one *wants to die ?*"

"on what Earthlings call a subconscious level — yes
for this means only that the Higher Angel of the S-elf
          the *fallen* angel, remember . . .
has made this decision
sometimes communicating such desire to the Mind
        and sometimes not
and the decision is made for a myriad of reasons
ranging from depression . . through guilt
all the way to numb acceptance of falsely programmed Old Age
        do not the humans on your planet
recognize a phrase or term called . . death wish ?"

"but . . what about . . murder ?"

"as your Earthling poet, Kahlil Gibran wisely wrote . .

the murdered is not unaccountable in his own murder
for who is to say that he who is murdered in the flesh
has not already murdered in the spirit . . . . . his own killer ?

or *she* who is murdered in the flesh, as the case may be
this meaning simply that there are those
whose Higher Selves deliberately follow a course
                              of action or behavior
which magnetically attracts the murder of the body
        sometimes this is a Free Will choice
while, at other times . . it is simply the karmic pattern
from a former incarnation, as when the one murdered
                              in this lifetime
receives his or her Karma
for having murdered another in a former life
not realizing how one may escape from this dreary chain
of karmic action . . and re-action"

"then, if everyone who dies actually *wants to die*
in one way or another
and if every single person permits or allows
his or her own death — there could be no such thing
as what humans label suicide . . could there ?"

"there is such a thing as suicide, yes . . .
and this is the whole point of what I am saying
but suicide is a term Earthlings apply mistakenly
            to only certain ones among them

whereas, in reality — in true actuality
each death — of every Earthling on your planet
is — in a true sense — a suicide

"the death having been chosen
by the Higher S-elf, which is . . as I now remember
a fallen angel — and as such, therefore
sometimes makes wise decisions — and sometimes not"

"this is a clear way of expressing what I meant to imply"

"well, just to be sure it's clarified in my own mind as to the 'why'
you mean — that each man and woman who dies
in reality, chooses this
therefore, every death of a flesh Body Temple
is truly a suicide — not just certain ones ?"

"this is true — each casting away of a Body Temple

Canto Twenty ☆ 929

is a Free Will choice of the directing 'O' or 'I'
whether such choice is communicated to the Mind or not
and so . . each death of every human is a suicide

therefore, it is not fair or just . . nor true
to label only those who are *consciously aware* of the desire
of the Higher S-elf . . . as suicides
since, as has been clearly stated — *all* deaths are so

and . . with each and every death . . . some deaths
are harmonious with the Universal plan
                              some are not in harmony
and are prematurely chosen

although no Earthling on your planet
                    is in a cosmic position
to judge the difference . . .

to judge whether a certain death-suicide
be a harmonious decision — or one which is otherwise
and which interferes with Life's pattern
                    by being wrongly timed

not even Solomon himself, in all his wisdom
could so determine"

"I sense some grander scheme, some Master plan, behind all this"

"yes, there is a Master plan — a grander scheme
and, though the image I present is but a partial painting
until you are ready to absorb the deeper hues
          try to visualize this
if each 'I' and 'O' are split halves of one original Whole
then a harmonious pattern could only be created
when all matching, eons-ago split snowflake halves
are once more joined — do you see ?"

"which would be . . a sort of shifting around
of the already existing pattern
into one of Harmony and Wholeness ?"

"yes, a pattern reflecting the prismatic chords and colors
of the music of the spheres . . the rainbow's spectrum"

"but when the matching snowflake halves are joined
and once more Whole, in unity
then must individual man and woman also become . . only one ?"

"no, they must not — nor *should* not — as has been stated
Man must remain Man, and Woman must remain Woman

in relation to flesh Body Temples
the concept of a Unisex is but a myth . . a mis-conception
of the joining of the Masculine 'O' and Feminine 'I'
of the Higher Angels

a blending which does not relate in any way . . to bodies
but which causes a woman to become more fully Woman
and a man to become more fully Man

each sex more complete
because of the reuniting
the blending . . of their Higher Selves . . in harmony
. . yet eternally separate in the flesh
and the reason this separation is a necessary one
for creating miracles . . will later be explained to you"

"but . . assuming there are, at any given time
many millions of Body Temples residing on our Earth
who have achieved the illumination and initiation
of physical immortality
and are free to aspire to experience Ascension to other realms
but equally free to choose to retain
their present flesh Body Temples
continually transmuting and improving them
remaining on Earth as long as they wish
and . . infants are still being born . .

with all the new infant bodies . . and no one on Earth
ever dying, in the flesh
then what is the Divine solution
to what would clearly be a severe over-population problem
even in the Heaven-on-Earth we have discussed ?"

"the solution is contained in many Divine possibilities
and is more joyous — also more simple
than humans dream
for, as the Nazarene knew
and stated in parable
in my Father's House are many mansions . . .

a **mansion** is a symbolic alabaster Body **Temple**
in other words, a refined and exalted flesh body
which has been raised, through illumination
to its perfected, symbolic 'alabaster' substance
and the method or formula for achieving this
we shall discuss later"

"I absolutely *knew* you were going to say that"

"as I absolutely *knew* you were anxious to ask !
but to continue with what I was saying . .

Canto Twenty ☆ 931

those millions to whom you just referred
who aspire to immortality . . . and also achieve it
might be called — millions of 'mansions'
and if you should image the Father's **House**
as countless Universes and solar systems
                              each with its own 'Earth' . . . .

but first I should try
to make the term Earth more comprehensible
I should have suggested that you image the Father's House
                in a cosmic sense
as countless Universes and Solar Systems

each with its own Eden-heaven . . as your Earth once was
for these other dimensional levels of awareness
on other *very material and actual* planets
                              similar to this one
are called Eden-heavens
and such as these only become an Earth
through the repeated practice — in all its many forms — of **hate**

when such an Eden-heaven is polluted by hate
                including contempt for Nature
and all manner of negative thought forms . . or vibrations
then it becomes an Earth — and so remains aware
only of a limited Third dimension of reality
until the negative so outweighs the positive
                              . . until evil so over-balances good
that its resident humanity
brings upon it absolute destruction . . and final annihilation

however, when all humans who reside upon a waning Earth
in any number of the infinite number of Solar Systems
                                        and Universes
        . . . as many as there are grains of sand
upon this particular planet . . . . . infinitismal
when all these . . .
have achieved illumination — as you have suggested
by your last question . . . they will discover
through the space travel of Ascension in their 'mansions'
        within the Cosmos
that there is no shortage of Homelands for them
                in the Father's larger House
no shortage of higher dimensional awareness Eden-heavens
where their exalted alabaster flesh Temples may reside
if they should wish to relocate and seed a new planet

for . . . the wind of their desires then blows

                    wherever it wishes . . "

"what . . did you say ?"

                    "I said . . *the wind of their desires then blows*
                              . . . wherever it wishes"

" . . *the wind blows . . wherever it wishes*
the words of gentle John . . call John
    the coded message left for me by the him-of-him
on the paper beside his bed . . the night he died"

                    "yes, this was a sacred message
                    from the Carousel Bill to you . . "

"now, if I may
I'd like to share with you my understanding
of what you have just explained
concerning the Divine solution to the overpopulation problem
when infants are still being born . . . and no one dies

is not such a Macrocosm *apparent* overpopulation situation
analogous to the similar microcosm situation
of an infant and its parents, in a flesh body sense ?
since, to the infant or child
the parents seem to be a god and goddess
wise, knowing all manner of 'magic'
how to answer telephones, make the lights go on
cook food . . . and so on . . . and . . "

                    "this is correct
                    and the infant or child in your example
                    may be thought of as the infant Spirit
                    of those not yet enlightened or initiated
                    while the 'god and goddess' parents
                    may be thought of as those humans
                    who have achieved physical immortality . . "

"I see ! then, in a microcosm Earth-family sense
the child eventually matures, until it can . . . "

                    "until it realizes that it, too, can create 'magic'
                    all those things which made the parents
                    seem like a god and goddess before . .

                    when matured, the child sees
                              that it can even create life
                    as its parents did, when it was born
                    and now considers itself as equal to the parents . . .
                    a god or goddess himself . . or herself"

                    Canto Twenty   ☆   933

"let me repeat, then, to make it clear to myself . .
the Earth-family infant may be compared
                    to human Spirits who are still
in the infancy of their illumination
but who will, with absolute certainty . . eventually spiritually mature
into the grace of full initiation . .

while the Earth-family parents
who seem, to the infant, as a god and goddess
may be compared to those human Spirits
who have already achieved initiation and physical immortality"

            "quite correct . . and in your Earth-family microcosm example
            what happens when a child or children mature ?
            do they remain in the original home of the parents
            after they have grown into 'creators' themselves ?"

"no ! they move out of the parents' home
which is comparable to our Earth or this planet
is it not ?"

            "it is . . "

"they move . . into . . another 'house' of their own
and raise their own families . . . . "

            "in the Macrocosm analogous sense
            just as the matured human moves into his or her
            own new House on Earth . . the matured Spirit
            may also move to a new home"

" . . which is a different planet . . or Eden-heaven
in order to . . . "

            "in order to seed new life there . .
            just as the matured child moves into a new home
            and seeds its own new life . . . or children . . . on Earth"

"but, in the Earth-family microcosm example
a child who has grown and left home
also returns to visit the former home, from time to time"

            "likewise the grown and matured — initiated humans
            who may also return to visit the former 'home'
                                        . . this Earth
            when the desire to do so arises"

"and such as these may return for temporary periods as . . . . . . "

            "as Avatars, Adepti, Gurus or Masters . . . "

"I knew it, I knew it !
you were right . . . it's such a simple solution
to what one might think to be an overpopulation problem
for, in the Earth-family example, on a microscopic level
the home might also be overpopulated
if the children never left to find their own home
and seed their own offspring . . "

"but this never happens
except for brief periods of time . . and so
it all works out quite nicely, you see
on both the microcosm and Macrocosm levels

as has been stated, for those who are enlightened . . .
who have achieved physical immortality
and wish to move on . . . .
the wind of their desires does blow
                    wherever it wishes
and should they desire to leave . . temporarily
the new 'house' or planet
     of which they have become the 'seeders' . . .
the Adam and Eve or Isis and Osiris
     of the new Solar System . . .
and return to their former 'home' — this Earth
to become also involved in the exciting mission
of helping to seed a *new* Garden of Eden . . here
even as it is in Heaven
. . in the Macrocosm Heaven
          as well as all microscopic heavens . . .

then the Free Will choice is theirs
since physical immortality allows them
to return here as often . . and for as long
          as they should wish

and so, soon, there will be many more **mansions**
. . . initiated alabaster Body Temples
and as has been said, there will eternally be countless
new planets or Eden-heavens in the Father's **House**
for them to live upon . . and seed new life
more than may be counted throughout eternity"

" . . . and Eternity is Time
          moving in a constant serpent circle"

"it is indeed . . . "

"Oh, Heath, I know your words are true !
because, ever since I was a child, I have believed
it was such a dreadful waste of time to aspire to 'going to Heaven'

as all religions teach and preach that one should do
but I never wanted to go to Heaven, as a child . . . .
to some misty place out there in space
since it always seemed to me to be . . much more exciting
        to bring Heaven itself — to Earth

and I used to wonder . . why dream of going to Heaven
when Heaven can come here ?
Thy Kingdom come, Thy Will be done
on Earth as it is in Heaven . . the churches are all wrong
they have mirror-reversed what the dream should really be !

and those who wish to travel on — instead of remaining here
allowing the wind of their desires . . to blow them
                        wherever their wish is
returning here, from time to time . . . if they choose
will they somehow, in some way
lose the individuality of the personality ?

I could never believe in a Heaven
                whether Macroscopic or microscopic
where one loses one's own individual S-elf

because I am . . my own S-elf
and the me-of-me must always so remain
not blending, as in the erroneous Hindu Nirvana concept
                with the Great All
thereby losing **ME** . .
because Gooober told me I was his very special and unique rose"

                "you are, indeed . . and as has already been noted
                you have very strange toes . . . "

"stop that, Heath ! you remind me of Gooober
and are causing me to miss him dreadfully"

                "then I'll change the subject . . for now
                and return to your intense conviction
                that you must never lose your individuality

                in Her infinite and loving Light, **SHE** has made
                        an eternal promise
                to each human Spirit
                in a snowflake pattern of exquisite design
                        no two alike
                so that each Higher Angel of the S-elf
                                of Her children
                shall retain forever
                the precious possession of Individuality
                as you call it, the you-of-you

"how very lovely
how very beautiful a concept !"

"you mean . . how very beautiful a Truth
for what I say unto you has been Divinely ordained

and you are right . . nothing lovelier could be imagined
than the forever-repeating pattern of *individualism*"

"**OH !** how perfectly marvelous !
the churches teach that only certain Deities may ever aspire
to Ascension — and now I see that each Earthling may aspire to learn
the exaltation of Ascension — and still remain an *individual* !"

"yes . . even as individual as the snowflakes
which fall upon your Earth every winter season . . are
each and every single one . . *eternally individual*"

"**OH !** Oh ! oh ! my childhood snow diamonds . . !"

"your childhood image of **MO**ther **GOO**se
shaking her feathers . . . when you saw the snow falling
was a sublime vision of innocence and truth
seeded long ago by **MO**ther **GOO**se Herself

as She prayed that someday this image would flower
in the hearts of all lost and fallen angels . . . Her children
when they looked up into the winter sky
. . to watch Her falling snowflakes
and finally recognized
the miracle of this soft and silent pattern . . with which
She did so bless the fading planet, Earth
until Her beloved children should grow to know
Her grace and blessing
and understand, at last, Her gentle message
. . of falling snowflakes
. . no two alike

now, I fear that I am weeping
and you must forgive me . . . . . for many dawns have waited
until you received the blessing of this illumination"

"falling snowflakes . . . *no two alike*
in a soft and gentle pattern . . . like a silent winter's night !
a silent, holy night

like a tender blessing . . falling snowflakes
dear **MO**ther **GOO**se, shaking her feathers

OH ! Heathcliffe ! I just realized . . a trembling miracle !
I did, I did ! and I just **KNOW** it to be . . . .

i just know it to be true !"

> "then tell me what it is you now *know* . . to be true
> and I shall listen . . through my own glad-tears"

"His promise to His children
    is the rainbow
the gift of an eternal Spring . . to follow all Earth storms
the sunrise-rainbow promise of countless and forever Eden-heavens

and Her promise to Her children . . Her blessing
is the soft and silent, gentle falling snowflakes
    no two alike
the snowflake promise of an eternal and forever . . *Individuality* !

His rainbow . . and Her falling snowflakes
    create their blended promise
of an end to all Earth storms . . and countless Eden-heavens
blessed with an eternal and forever *Individual* **SPRING** !

OH ! Joy to the World !
how very lovely . . how very, very beautiful
such an exquisite love as this"

> "yes, dear druid . . many aeons have waited
> for Earth's children to open their hearts
> and receive this double blessing
>
> this blended promise
>
> of His rainbow . . . . . and Her falling snowflakes"

        . . and the silence, then . . between Heathcliffe and me
lasted for a long, long while

"I'm sorry I've been so silent
but I have been floating on little puffy clouds
of Indian smoke . . of happiness"

> "I understand . . for, so have I"

"now I would like to continue with our talk"

> "yes, let us continue . . to share the magic of words"

"may I ask a question involving space travel ?"

> "this might be an appropriate inquiry — yes
> yet . . even this subject may only be touched upon
>   with relative brevity
> for there are certain matters which must unfold

only when it has been so ordained
premature revelation is not a natural kind of growing
nor is it the wisest sort of knowing"

"I know that this is true
for, when I was a teeny-tiny girl-child, at my elf parents' home
on 8th Street . . I used to tippy-toe into Nana's garden
very early in the morning . . at sunrise
before any grown-ups were awake to forbid me

and I would try to pry open the buds of Nana's loveliest roses
so they would quickly ! become large blooms
but these experiments always ended in disappointed tears
as the petals fell off in my impatient hands
for the sun and the rain had not yet . . awakened the roses
it was not . . their allotted time to burst into beauty"

"it is good that your instinct tells you so surely
that my cautionary words regarding
premature revelation
speak truly to you
and that the Elf of your Higher S-elf
comprehends and agrees with what I have stated"

"I'm going to mentally hop and skip again
but you gave me permission to occasionally do this
so . . I need now to know
when — and why — each once whole Soul
was split into 14 pieces
and when — and why — each once whole Higher Angel
my drawings symbolize as a perfect Snowflake
was divided and split into two halves
causing each human Spirit to long to be joined
to the other half . . through so many eons of searching
in such terrible loneliness

as for the Soul, why was it not split into 12 pieces
to symbolize the 12 Sun Signs in astrology ?
why 14 pieces ?"

"the splitting of the Soul into 14 pieces
does not relate to astrology
for, astrology did not exist when this occurred
and was only later developed
by Isis and Hermes Thoth
as a way, which has already been explained
to decrease the continual dividing, since it was
resulting in even more lonely searching
by each separated Twin S-elf
as did Isis and Osiris search for one another
but their story must be told in your sequel

Canto Twenty ☆ 939

to your Gooberz Happiness POem . . not now"

"you said astrology did not exist at the time
when each Soul was split . .
to what time are you referring . . when ?"

"billions — not millions, but billions of years ago
as measured by Earth time . . when *there wase no Time*"

my thoughts wandered for a moment . . remembering
"how long is Forever, Goob ?
you said you would have waited in the lobby
of the Hollywood Roosevelt that night
for a million, billion Forevers . . . "

"did you speak ?"

"no . . I was . . just remembering . . something
please go on with what you were saying"

"briefly then . .
of necessity, *very* briefly, for the present
. . . Osiris was called the Sun god
Isis and Osiris seeded this individual planet
not Adam and Eve, as has long been
                              mistakenly believed
for Adam and Eve were seeders
of another Eden-heaven, in a different Solar System
not this planet . . but all this will be explained
at the allotted time

eons ago, for complex reasons you will later learn
Set . . whose true identity will also later be learned

. . . Set, the brother of Osiris, the Sun god
did murder Osiris
and cut his alabaster Body Temple
                              into 14 pieces

verily, verily, this deed was so evil
       so displeased Ra
and was such a horrible breech of Universal Law
that one of two Suns in this Solar System
which kept the planet in Light
                              over its entire surface
       exploded
                   striking one side of the planet
which was then not spinning
causing gross mutation at that point on the globe
and causing the planet, now called Earth
to spin around the remaining Sun

940   ☆   Canto Twenty

like unto a billiard ball when it is hit

instantly creating what you call Gravity . .
and darkness then fell upon the face of this Earth
            for the very first time
manifested as the Earth's first Sunset . . *Sun — Set*
simultaneously, what you call Time . . then began
whereas, before this cataclysmic event
Earthlings lived in the Eternal Now of the 4th Dimension
 also . . what you call death . . began
and the power of Set, who was a fallen angel
once on a level with Osiris himself . . was so intense
that his heinous act likewise caused
all Higher Angel Snowflake Twin S-elves . . to divide
and their Souls . . to split into 14 pieces
as did the Soul of Osiris, after his body Temple had been
            cut into 14 pieces

does this answer your query sufficiently ?"

"yes, it does . . but sufficiently only for now
    I will need much time alone
to ponder it and meditate upon its meaning . .
thank you for your partial answer, Heathcliffe
it helps me realize much of what has troubled me

now, to hop and skip once more — as I asked before
can you tell me if spacecraft is needed
for travel to other Solar Systems ?"

            "no, this is neither necessary nor desirable
            for those who aspire to such experience of visitation
            and who have properly prepared themselves for such travel
            need no equipment but their own exalted Body Temples"

"but what about the already-sighted UFO's ?"

            "these do exist — but do not visit for any purpose yet conceived
            nor are they from a place which Earthlings now do imagine
            their purpose, and their true earth-bound . . 'home'
            will be revealed unto you at an already appointed time
            which is not the immediate present"

"is there a clue to what you refuse to disclose
at the North and South Poles ?
I notice you are remaining silent . . I'm sorry
once again, I forgot the rules"

            "even the higher occult schools . . do have rules"

"and if one breaks them — is one then demoted

Canto Twenty ☆ 941

and sent to the rear of the class ?"

"this depends — sometimes so, but mostly not"

"then, must one always follow the dictates of the Teacher ?"

"in the sense in which you ask — the answer is **NO**
   when a teacher has made a statement
which, to the neophyte seems not true or proper
   then who is the judge ?
the answer here unequivocally — is the neophyte
it is better for one's evolvement into knowing
to occasionally risk a human error of judgement
than to risk the danger of becoming a mental slave
and so . . always retain the courage of your own convictions
and use your own divine instinct to judge false from true"

"well, most of the time, as you know, my instinct agrees with you
but now I see another pattern emerging . . . "

"which is . . . ?"

"which is that — then there are also
I mean to say, I guess — that **twin souls** *also* do exist
do they not ?"

"they do — and twin soul is a proper term
just as Twin S-elf is a proper term

for all split pieces of the Soul of each 'I' or 'O'
seek one another with heartfelt yearning
therefore, those who say they are searching for
                              the twin soul
are speaking of a true emotion"

"now I see that each man and woman — 'I' or 'O'
must first . . somehow call back all 14 *original* Soul pieces
before the long ago divided Higher Angel
. . the Split halves of the Twin S-elves . .
may be magnetized toward one another . . to once more join"

"this is so, what you have spoken
there are two searching patterns
                  which appear today upon the Earth

one involves the twin souls . . or Soul pieces
seeking each other
         the other involves those Higher Selves
the Snowflake seeking to become whole
after all the original Soul pieces
of each Snowflake half

942   ☆   Canto Twenty

have returned to the guidance of the original 'I' or 'O'
from which they were separated long ago
                              yes . . this is so

            separated by the sin of Set
            as seen by the very word **separated**
                        containing the letters of Set himself"

"oh ! and Heath . . just think of this Lexigram !
the word **UNTIED,** by simply switching two letters
    becomes **UNITED !**"

                  "your enlightenment to Lexigrams
                  does, indeed, contain the revelation of many mysteries
                  for the genuine and sincere seeker"

"then . . the split Soul pieces . . . which may be called twin souls
do not seek each other quite so desperately
through the darkness before the dawn
as they walk through the valley of the shadow
with the same sense of deep loneliness
as the separated Snowflake Twin S-elves feel ?"

                  "no, for as has been stated — each Soul piece
                  on each level of individual evolvement and enlightenment
                  seeks reunion with all original 14 pieces

                  but the longing of the Snowflake halves of each 'I' and 'O'
                  as you have correctly divined
                  is the most haunting longing of all
                              being deep . . . very, very deep"

"you just evoked something
that is causing me to tremble . . about . . deep
and I fear I must change the subject quickly
tell me, please, if I am correct
in believing that each of a Soul's 14 pieces
is either masculine or feminine in essence
rotating in order around the circle of the Soul
as I have drawn it ?"

                  "this is true, even as you have stated — yes"

"and then, since this is so
would the intense desire to become a transexual, through surgery
be caused by an over emphasis on one's sexuality
            not of the Body Temple
but of the Soul pieces . . with one's Soul containing
either too many masculine pieces . . or too many feminine ?"

                  "you have oversimplified this

but in its essence, it is true"

"then the way to overcome such desires
assuming one should wish to do so, is to . . . "

"is to reach attunement with one's own Higher S-elf
and communicate the desire for a balance
between masculine and feminine in the Soul pieces"

"which may only be ordered at the Saturn-Seven-cycle
since this is when the 'I' or 'O' may both send forth
and recall . . one or more Soul fragments ?"

"precisely — one must accomplish this re-order
at the time of the Saturn-Seven-cycle
and previous to this
communicate sincerely through prayer and meditation
with the Higher Angel of one's S-elf"

"Heath, what if an 'I' or 'O' should cast away a Body Temple
and die — then wish to take over a different adult flesh Temple
for the purpose of swiftly returning
to bereaved loved ones
then what happens to the Owner 'I' or 'O'
of the new Body Temple so chosen by the departed one ?"

"these arrangements are made and communicated
on astral levels of awareness
between the two 'I's' or 'O's' involved in the decision
and are far too complex to describe now

for, there are Temple Owners
who prefer to change — control or guide
a different adult body
just as there are others
who would choose, on an astral level, while sleeping
to allow another 'I' or 'O'
to take over the lease on the present Temple
while themselves preferring to take over
the different Body Temple
of a newborn infant — or an adult
and still others
who, as you know, refuse to ever leave
the Body Temple chosen at birth
and who quest for physical immortality . . . .
which more have achieved than guessed at present
and you have met several of these yourself
indeed, the choices and decisions thus made
are of an infinitely changing pattern of variation"

"it seems like a gigantic jig-saw puzzle

like a cosmic game of musical chairs"

        "those are not unlikely metaphors or analogies
        and all this chaotic confusion is not to be desired . .
        being the unfortunate result of Set's aeons ago action
        the Saturn-Seven resurrection pattern
           must be re-versed
        with a new 'verse' or Happiness pOem
                    or re-vised with a new vision
        yes, a re-vision is needed
        if true harmony is ever to exist upon your planet"

"then each man's and woman's recognition of a twin soul
plus the seeking of the Twin S-elf . . .
these are conditions and relationships which are . . "

        " . . . which are good and right
        and which must eventually lead each Earthling
                    into the Light"

"then . . are *both* the search for one's twin soul — or twin souls
of which each person has a total of thirteen
and the quest for one's own Twin S-elf — of which there is but one
a worthy Holy Grail for each man and woman today ?"

        "such a dual search . . such a dual quest
        is more worthwhile . . more infintely desirable
        and more urgently needed . . than any other goal
        to which Earthlings might aspire to attain
        in this dawning of the Golden Age of Aquarius

        and . . meditate upon the cosmic meaning here
        that this search, this quest . . . this dream of reunion
        is the *only way* . . all men and women
        may ever hope to find the path . . which leads back
        to Love and Peace on Earth"

"and what helps such a search or quest ?"

        "as you well know, the art and science of astrology
        is a vital and enlightening beginning step upon the path
        when such is esoterically and spiritually interpreted
        also . . the opening of the Third Eye
        would be a second step toward the heaven of reunion
           that joyful miracle of the lost being found
        with each man and woman, no longer half — and longing
        but whole once more . . and complete as before"

   "I see now how the Saturn-Seven-cycle
of Earth's present resurrection pattern — also helps
because each 'I' or 'O' — when it seeks a new Body Temple

takes along with it — *its very own personal and absolutely inseparable*
Mind and split Soul . . plus the eternal *Individuality* of its 'I'
      or the eternally unique 'O' of its Overself

this being the change at the Saturn-Seven-cycle
which allows the bereaved one to look into the eyes of a 'stranger'
after the 'death' of a loved one . . . since the eyes
are truly the windows of both the Soul — and the Higher Self
and see there behind them . . the *actual and literal* individual loved one
they mistakenly believed to be dead"

        "this is exquisitely true . . what you have just said"

"then it's true ! it's true !
like the lyric of the Easter song I sang at Sunday school
O ! Death . . where is thy sting ?

for if the grief is deep enough, intense enough
to unconsciously ordain or command such a changing to take place
then . . if the perception, sensitivity and Faith . . be strong
the bereaved may truly . . actually . . and literally

    find once more . . the one who has been lost through death !

the lost shall be found !

    for the absolutely *only* difference will be the flesh Temple itself
    all else will be identical and unchanged !

and if the bereaved who has once again found the lost one
will carefully and gently assist the Soul
belonging to the newly-discovered higher Angel of the 'I' or 'O'
then the memories will softly and gradually return
to the Mind of the formerly departed person
guided by the Soul . . and directed by the 'I' or 'O'

and the Mind will, through the Brain . . restore the memory
of the former Body Temple identity to the newly-discovered one
until finally, he or she will recall all which passed before

and this will be verified by the recollection of many incidents and phrases
many re-called fragments . . which no one else could have known
        except the formerly departed one

until at last, both will know the Truth
that the lost . . . really **HAS** been found again !

    . . . that the individual person — the 'I' or 'O' thought to be dead
    is now present completely and personally

yes . . and eventually even knowingly

completely aware . . as the Owner of this different Body Temple

then comes that glorious, Sun-sparkled moment
when both can speak together of this trembling wonder
as the lost one says . . 'I remember, I remember ! and I have returned !'
while both, then, recall many secrets privately shared before
which will constitute the final proof
                                        of their resurrection miracle !

therefore, the bereaved should not linger over-long
in tearful sadness . . in a funeral home

the truly inconsolably grieved and bereaved
should take care not to waste too much precious time
in involvement with the services for the not-really-dead

  but should, instead

begin right away ! . . . that very same day !
to initiate the exciting and mystical . . the glad and glorious
                                        search
keeping eyes and ears both open
and making certain that the heart is always listening
for a familiar chord . . an intimate word
a well remembered way of walking . . a turn of the head, just so
and the eyes, the eyes, the eyes !
            which are the windows of the Soul

through which the departed may soon be seen and recognized

for perhaps . . just around the next corner
at any time or any place . . unexpectedly
the bereaved and inconsolably grieved will suddenly !
                        gaze upon the face
of the loved one lost

and though the features may at first seem strange
the eyes will be . . oh ! so familiar . . whatever their color
and following this, the other personality patterns
will emerge . . until all is complete . . . and once more whole

            in such a joyous reunion !

oh, Heathcliffe ! this is true, true, true !"

                        "of course it is true . . it is as true-blue
                        as the colors in your aura at this very moment
                        for, when one is speaking Truth
                        the color of the aura shines forth in a shade
                        of brilliant sky-blue
                        . . . as is the case, right now . . . with you"

"since we seem to be tuned-in to Truth
I need to ask you about a dear and magical woman friend of mine
an 'I' female Individuality I knew in Colorado . . whose nickname was 'Mike'
she recently left her Body Temple in California

and a few hours after her not-really-death
a woman who had been an even closer friend than I, for many years
and was, like my friend's bereaved and broken hearted husband . . . .
sisters, brother . . parents . . and other friends and relatives
deeply affected by the shocking and unexpected loss

was driving in her car, her heart and mind both numb with grief
                            unable to stop weeping
crying out . . . speaking aloud . . to her not-really-dead-friend

        when suddenly

the car was filled with the powerful and unmistakable fragrance
        of the particular kind of perfume
the not-really-dead 'Mike' always wore
    very real it was, she said . . and overwhelmingly strong
as if someone had spilled a large bottle of this perfume
all over the seats and the floor of the car"

                    "but of course ! all things in existence
                    are measured by — and manifest through — vibrations
                    for, vibrations are the throbbing heartbeat
                                            of Life itself
                    although few are aware of it
                    all odors, scents and fragrances
                    are the vibrations of . . . . . released *vital energy*
                    registered through the sense of smell

                    and it is easy for an Adeptus to therefore, tell
                    that this woman's dear and not-really-dead friend
                    heard every word — saw every tear
                    and was trying intensely to break through
                    the blindness barrier — to prove that she was not gone
                    and would soon return, completely . . and personally
                    if she was so desperately missed and needed
                                            by those she left behind

                    countless incidents such as this occur

                    yet these very real signs of communication
                    from the not-really-departed
                    are rarely either recognized or understood
                    by those whose Third Eyes remain tightly closed

                    causing the not-really-dead to be unable to communicate
                    their intention to soon return, complete and whole

and recognizable — in those cases where it is, indeed
such an intention
because of this *spiritual* blindness
which is much more real — and far more tragic
than *physical* blindness

like all the mistakenly called 'dead'
this woman's friend, who was also your own dear friend
retired for a time, from sight
but was strongly stating that she will soon return
in astoundingly recognizable form

your perceptive and wise Earth poet, Emerson
did write . . and truly so

'nothing is really dead . . .
people feign themselves to be dead
. . endure mock funerals
and mournful obituaries
while . . . there they stand !

looking out the windows . . . of the Soul's eyes
in some strange, new disguise'

yes, I strongly sense that your friend has solid plans
to return . . unexpectedly soon
her main reason being to comfort those she left behind
who are more grieved than she, perhaps
anticipated them to be

would that more humans contained a healthy curiosity
regarding the subject of not-really-death
rather than submitting to the experience with apathy
numbness and blind acceptance
of what need not be accepted at all

as written in the Light of Asia . .
ye suffer from yourselves
none else compels . . none other holds you
that you lag and stay . . . and whirl upon the wheel
and hug and kiss its spokes of agony
its tyre of tears . . "

"then the Easter story is really true !
not nearly, but really true ?"

"Easter is total Truth — although Jesus, of Nazareth
being a Master, trained by the Essenes
chose to illustrate the Truth of human resurrection

Canto Twenty ☆ 949

through translation . . . rather than demonstrating it
through the current Earth pattern of resurrection
        of the Saturn-Seven-cycle . . .
by retaining his same Body Temple . . and re-ordering it
in the manner of Ascension, which magic
all Earthlings will someday once more' themselves remember
when they become again as children
        and their newly awakened Third Eyes
allow them to recall this lost POwer . . . and even more

yes, all this will be . . when men and women once again
become gods and goddesses of Innocent Faith
for . . it has been so ordained

and . . until this wisdom once more is possessed
                                by all Earthlings
the Truth of the Saturn-Seven re-birth
will be the beginning of their ability to believe, as before
        in a literal resurrection
for, when they begin to see the actual Truth in this
and are able to truly recognize
the departed ones for whom they so tearfully grieve
as literally and actually returned to them

and when the departed themselves bring back the memories
of the former Body Temple identity
and are thus able to prove that they, indeed, have returned
as their very selves
                that the lost has truly been found

then it will swiftly follow . . that the Light
will begin to dawn upon the Minds of all Earthlings
after which . . more miracles lie ahead
than even the greatest visionary could possibly imagine"

"does the Ascension magic
and all the mysteries connected with space travel
relate in some way . . . to the energy at the very top
of the Pyramid . . is this certainty I feel
some fragment of remembered truth . . from a former incarnation"

        "it does, yes — but we are beginning to digress . . .
        all the rest, such as the secrets of the Pyramid
        will manifest themselves unto you
        and also unto him, who is still your teacher
        after you have completed both Part One and Part Two
        of your Happiness pOem — to bring joy and comfort to others
        who still stumble in the darkness"

"they will be manifested unto me

and also unto Gooober ?   oh, Heath . . will he come back soon ?
does this mean
          that I have not much longer to wait
and to bear this loneliness ?

if I try very hard to learn
will he understand, and know . . and soon return ?"

                    "oh, ye of little faith !
                         wherefore didst thou doubt ?"

"then I must hurry and learn
so he may return . . so he may come home free !
oh, Heath, please keep teaching me . . . .
tell me more about the deeper mystery
of catching the brass ring on the Carousel
and transmuting it into gold"

                    "there is much for you to learn about the Mystery of Gold
                    but the secrets of Gold shall be revealed
                    when the time is deemed appropriate
                                   by the Masters"

"well, then . . meanwhile . . may we each
catch the brass ring, on Life's Carousel
and transmute it into gold . . . . . ourselves ?"

                    "yes . . even as Jesus of Nazareth did"

"and the Holy Ghost
I burn to know more of him . . for he has
always pursued me . . in a spooky-scary way
does this Holy Essence
perhaps, sometimes visit . . Body Temples ?"

                    "this pure essence you insist on calling the Holy Ghost
                                   this vital portion
                    of the three-times-three of the Holy Trinity
                    may visit in Earth-bound Temples, yes
                    but is made welcome in only a few
                    for not many Earthly Temples are worthy of this visitor
                    for long periods of time, you see"

"yes, I suppose people do invite him — the Holy Ghost
          if that is truly his name
into their Body Temples at Christmas . . or on other holy days
and occasionally, and briefly . . in other loving ways
it's just that, well . . somehow, I don't trust the Holy ghost
for, since childhood, he is the one
          who has always frightened me the most"

Canto Twenty   ☆   951

. . . or *she* ?
I wondered silently

        "when one's heart is, for the moment
        receptive to loving and giving
        the Holy Ghost of the spiritual Trinity
        may enter . . and remain within . . for brief periods"

"was Jesus, the carpenter of Nazareth . . not Divine
but only a man . . as you intimated a few moments ago ?"

        "Jesus, born in Bethlehem — was only a man
        albeit a most exceptional man
        yet no more exceptional than each other human can be
        or may become . . through growing and knowing
        and imitating his ways, as he tried to teach

        his Soul had already been through
                        the fiery furnace of testing
        in the Body Temples of many exceptional men
        and in the days of Palestine
        the Soul of Jesus, the man . . resided in
        a superior house
                symbolically, in an alabaster Temple"

"yes . . an alabaster Temple
purified in various ways we all could likewise do
        if we so desired
but . . was it not prophesied that Jesus would be born
of the 'House of David' ?"

        "yes, and this prophecy was precisely fulfilled
        for the 'House of David', in its esoteric meaning
        was but a Temple of flesh
        carefully prepared through the passing down
        of physical heredity . . gradually becoming
        sufficiently refined and harmonized
        on a material level of matter
        for him to occupy, while he performed his magic
        and his miracles of power
        once possessed, as I have repeatedly stated
                by all men and women on Earth
        and also . . do not forget
        as repeatedly stated by Jesus himself
             although very few truly heard him
        or were able to comprehend his meaning"

"the House of David . . . .
David is the one who wrote all those lovely poems
of truth and beauty . . called psalms
yet, David also knew Bathsheba — and loved her fiercely

with very earthly passion
and even with many extremes of emotions, did he not ?

and do emotions, then, make one's Temple unfit
to house visiting celestials ?
with David as an example, it would certainly not seem so
for his Body Temple was of sufficiently fine substance
to be chosen as the hereditary Temple
               to be passed down to Jesus

I've often been told one must strive
to eliminate all emotion — to cast out sentimentality
             yet, if this be true
then how can one's Soul remain sensitive to beauty ?"

               "no, this is not true . . you are right to so discern
               for, just as too much stress on emotion
                              is a negative vibration
               so also is the cold removal
               of all emotion — known as detachment
                              likewise a negative vibration
               a person devoid of all emotion
               or one who is successful in hiding emotion
               houses a Soul which has ceased to live

               a Soul must learn to mingle the inter-play of emotions
               accepting some, displaying some — controlling others
               but when *all* emotions have been banished
               especially those of compassion, sympathy, love
                                     generosity . . and grief
               then the Soul Itself
               is dangerously close to the death of its Beingness"

"Jesus wept" . . .

               "yes . . and God weeps too
               at the blindness of all His children on Earth
               gods who do not weep — or suffer — or even burn
                              in righteous anger
               have much to learn

               even with the higher God and Goddess — RaHram
               all emotions must be experienced . . blended
               and fired into a kaleidiscope of color and beauty

               what is the glory of joy . . where is the peace
                                     of tranquility
               without the comparison
               to the opposite polarities of yearning and controversy ?
               one is eternally necessary
               to cause the others to comparatively shine forth

the Essence men and women think of as 'God'
is not a faceless, nameless, shapeless cloud
or a huge blob of Nirvana . . unfeeling
but a perfect Libran balance of all emotions
all feelings . . all experiences
seeing these with the compassion of infinite wisdom
which reveals the positive side of each
not allowing the negative to destroy the positive
but allowing each to feed into each other
            creating the Third energy
which is both, yet neither . . and All Powerful"

"then emotions are a matter of degree of control
one must strive to conquer the most violent storms
but retain the soft rain . . of others"

            "this is so . . even as you have stated"

"and Jesus, the man
who knew the emotions of love and even anger
oh ! and sadness and despair . . and even fear
when he resided in the House of David
that Body Temple which housed the him-of-him
or rather, was the vehicle for the direction of the 'O' of him
because it was a superior Temple
could he then choose to invite the Holy Ghost, as a guest
for a longer visit than others might do ?"

            "this is true . . and the longest visit
            of the Holy Ghost . . in the Body Temple of Jesus
            was a continuous residence for three years
            transforming him, during that period
            into an entity the churches now call Jesus, *the Christ*"

"was Jesus of Nazareth
the Son of God, as all the Christian Churches claim ?"

            "but as he, himself — emphatically did *not* claim !
            for, when he was asked if he was, indeed
                              the Son of God
            his answer was . .
                    "*thou* has said it"

"which meant, in modern idiom
'*you* said it, I didn't'"

            "precisely . . . . he was, for three years
            the *Christ* . . or the 'Son of God'
            yet only in the same manner
            in which all men on Earth may be the Sons of God
                    or Christs

and all women may be the Daughters of God — or Christs
if they would prepare their Temples, as he did
and their hearts also
to invite the Holy Ghost to visit for lengthy periods
with the opening of the Soul's Third Eye
being always . . the first step toward this goal"

"did visitors who were . . unfriendly strangers
attempt also to enter the Temple of Jesus
as they sometimes attempt to take possession
of other earthly Temples ?"

"during the agony of his temptation of Gethsemane
for forty days and nights
in the dark hours of his soul
such enemy entities knocked upon the door
of the Body Temple of Jesus, yes"

" . . but he did not permit them entry — he refused them entrance
and what of his early manhood ?"

"these are the lost years of Jesus"

"yes, nothing is said of him in the Scriptures
from the time of his birth and infancy
until his parents found him in the Synagogue
answering the religious and philosophical questions
of the Rabbis and Priests — when he was twelve years old
and then not mentioned again, from the age of twelve
until he was thirty, and began to teach

twelve ! the magical-clock-strikes-midnight age !
when Jesus was twelve . . . .
is this when he became for the first time, briefly
Jesus, the Christ ?"

"when Jesus was twelve — yes — briefly
this was the initial period when his Temple
entertained the Holy Ghost as a visitor"

"and what of all the stories I have heard
contained in the Apocryphal Books removed from the Scriptures
by the Catholic Church, at the Council of Trent . . . in 300 A.D.
and also by Empress Theodora, that evil incarnation
of the fallen angel, Nephthys
and her husband, Emperor Justinian
that evil incarnation of the fallen angel, Set

. . what of those stories ?   among them, the one
which tells of the small child, Jesus, using wet clay
to create the tiny body of a bird . . which then flew away into the sky

Canto Twenty   ☆   955

before the very eyes of those who watched . . is this true ?"

> "it has been written that the small child Jesus
> did fashion of wet clay — a bird
> ' and then breathed the breath of Life into it"

"no ! I do not believe that story . . .
the way it has been told
I seem to somehow know that it's only partly true

for the little boy Jesus wanted so . . oh ! he wanted so to heal
and he placed wet clay on the eyes
                                    of a *dead* bird
which then flew away into the sky
all well and alive once more !

for, although I know that Jesus possessed
the ability to create matter from the energy of thought forms

I do not believe that the small child Jesus was a magician
concerned with magician's tricks . . performed for no purpose
than to entertain by showing off his powers

no ! he placed wet clay upon the eyes of a dead bird
so it could fly away again
and he did this from his love . . his childlike Faith
                                    and his desire to heal . . . .
. . . his teeny-tiny miracle
was motivated by genuine compassion
and not by the desire to perform some supernatural magic trick
somehow, I *know* this to be
                indisputably true"

> "if you truly *know* it to be true, then it *is* true !
> what one's heart says is true — is true
> when one as attuned to — or 'tuned-in' to
> the Higher Angel of one's own S-elf
>   as you are at present
> and perhaps someday . . you will even be able
> to prove that you are right in this"

"how could I ever prove such a thing ?"

> "do not forget those prophetic words of your H. G. Wells
> when he wrote that . . .
>
> *'the day will come when we shall walk again*
> *in vanished scenes . . stretch painted limbs*
>   *we thought were dust*
> *and feel the sunshine of a million years ago . . '*

as has already been stated . . .

there are many such incidents of the childhood Faith
of the small boy, Jesus
in miracles and healing . . which have been lost"

"the little boy Jesus believed in druids too
and magic mountains who could fly ! the same as I
I am so sure . . so sure of this"

"this is true . . the child Jesus did believe
in all miracles of Faith . . and in your tiny druids
for he loved Nature, and knew the druids well"

"why is it permitted by Heaven . . that past Truth
be so distorted . . and destroyed ?"

"Heaven does not permit this
it is permitted by those who, through their Free Will choice
accept as truth — such lies — and also, the lies of *omission*
believing everything they hear and read
as Gospel Truth
without first tuning in to the personal Truth within
by listening to the voice of the Higher S-elf
thereby learning to discern
innocence from sin . . . or truth from lie

and do not forget . . . that Set-Satan-Seth
for reasons you will soon be taught
is still seeding lies into the minds of humans
sometimes, even being brazen enough
to use his own name, thinly disguised
so certain is he
of the mental dullness and spiritual apathy
of today's masses of earth-bound, lost humanity
yes, even now . . *Seth speaks*
and his latest seed of untruth
is such a subtle, innocent *appearing* claim . . .
the insinuation that Jesus was never real in any sense
but only an imaginary Messiah
formed in the collective subconscius mind . .

this dangerous distortion — like a hidden bad seed
is nearly invisible
being wrapped, as it is, within the pages
of recent metaphysical literature
filled with fascinating, well-written and accurate
esoteric and occult information

anytime Satan-Set, by any name or fragile disguise
uses unsuspecting humans as the channels or mediums for his lies

Canto Twenty   ☆   957

he never fails to cleverly hide the intended lie
swaddled in blankets of actual truth
where it cannot be readily recognized or detected
by the unsuspecting listener — or reader
for, do not your own Holy Scriptures warn

of the days when the false prophets shall appear
and that the wolf comes dressed in sheep's clothing ?"

"yes — but I dislike that analogy
although I supose the intent of it is certainly true . . ."

"why do you dislike it ?"

"because it insinuates
that the wolf is evil, like unto Satan
and this is absolute falsehood . . for wolves are kind
made mad by the hatred of humans
as Francesco di Bernadone, of Assisi, proved
when he converted the ferocious Wolf of Gubbio
with love and kindness . . into a protector of the children"

"your reason is honest . . and very true
you are listening to your own inner voice
and synchronizing harmoniously
with the Higher Angel of your S-elf
                as well as with the Universe

but the reason this most recent distortion
            seeded by Satan-Set
is so dangerous to the future of your planet
and so harmful to the potential opening
of the Third Eye of innocence and wisdom
is because . . if men and women are led to believe
the falsehood that Jesus did *not* truly exist
as a very human man . . upon this Earth
then they have lost one of the more gentle and wise
and easier-to-follow teachers

for . . why attempt to imitate anything
or to believe anything . . taught or exemplified
by a person who never existed at all ?"

"yes, that's very logical . . and I can see
the power of the innocent-appearing evil behind it
for to take away humanity's ideals . . and idealistic leaders
is to take away their belief that they, too, can rise
into the same brilliance of Light and Knowledge . . and POwer

but . . what of the other lost years of Jesus
from the time he reached the magic age of twelve

until he was thirty years of age, and began his ministry
what of those lost years . . of his early manhood ?"

        "he lived most of those eighteen years
             . . . except for the years of his esoteric initiation
        as Jesus, the man — with all the experiences
        and testing for worthiness — of a man"

"there are some who believe . . that is
there are some theologians who theorize that Jesus
also . . loved . . as a man
and was perchance even husband to Mary Magdalene . .
is this true ?"

        "as has been stated — Jesus lived not all
        but many of those so-called lost years . . as a man
        with all of the experiences
        and testing for worthiness . . of a man"

"that is rather an indirect answer
to my question, it seems to me, but, well . . "

        "there are some things in this incarnation
        which you must *know* that you know
        and not expect a teacher to explain or tell
        related to all periods of world history"

"well . . if he was prepared by the Essenes
who were secretly druids . . for his passion on Calvary
then if he was married . . or if he completely loved a woman
as some say, even to this day
and if both he and she . . knew what was ahead
did he . . did she . . I mean, did they . . . ?"

        "Jesus was prepared by the Essenes
        for the continuous — and rare — three year residence
        in his Body Temple, of the Holy Ghost . .
        practicing many forms of human abstinence
        from activities which are not in any way negative
                in themselves
        but necessary to withdraw from only *for a time*"

"then if Jesus did love woman
it must be that he . . and she . . made the sacrifice
of celibacy . . . . . . for a period . . would this not be so ?"

        "why do you ask these particular questions ?"

"I ask them for two reasons only"

        "may I hear these reasons ?"

"yes — the first one is because there are so many lovers
who would feel closer to him, and less alone
if they knew that he understood completely
what it means to love — as man and woman love

and the second reason is — that I have read lately
many articles and reports
that the sexual revolution of the Sixties
is beginning to turn from the excesses
of sexual promiscuity, group sex experimentation
and all manner of sexual abuse
into what has been called
                    the new celibacy
I have heard — and read — that sexual abstinence
            for varying periods
is becoming prevalent among lovers
whether married or unmarried . . replacing the recent promiscuity
which is a situation of complete extremes . . you see ?

and I felt that . . for these latter Earthlings
it would be some comfort to know that Jesus did love woman
but also endured a temporary period of S-elf chosen abstinence
as a good and healthy — but a never intended-to-be-permanent-arrangement

        for man and woman"

                    "Jesus, the man — lived many of his lost years
                    with all the experiences and testing for worthiness
                                        of a man
                    to stand as a symbol
                    of all Sons of God and Daughters of God
                    who are striving to reach love and wisdom's Light"

"you still avoid a direct answer . . you are playing mental chess with me ?
so perhaps that means that Jesus did *not* love woman
for he was, after all, a teacher-Guru or a Master Avatar
who had evolved to the power of performing miracles, and . . . "

                    "you speak of miracles ? but this is not a power
                                given only to Adepti
                    any one among you . . can perform miracles
                    simply through attunement with the Higher Self"

"yes, but you see, my question . . . "

                    "did Moses part the Red Sea
                    and perform, before the Pharaoh, many more
                    magical feats of astonishment ?"

"yes, he did, but I still don't see . . . . "

"and were these not true miracles ?"

"of course they were, but I need to . . . "

"and was not Moses married ?
did not Moses also love . . . woman ?"

"true, Moses did love woman
still, you haven't answered what I . . . "

"Jesus, the man, incarnated upon Earth as a teacher
to stand as a symbol for *all* men and women
I cannot give you further details of his lost years
you must search within your heart
                    . . for you know the answers"

"why were those precious years
lost to us ?"

"lost because of those spiritual leaders
who were entrusted, as the heirs of Peter
with the Keys to the Kingdom
yet, who removed the writings of his lost years
from the Holy Scriptures
believing themselves to be right in so doing"

"how could such gross deception be right ?"

"part of the answer lies in a great mystery
even now kept contained within the Vatican in Rome
and related, in a most astonishing manner

to the mute . . but still secretly singing
strange circle of rocks at Stonehenge, England
inter-twined with a never revealed discovery
nearly seven centuries ago . . of ancient druidic writings
containing the awesomely wondrous, yet terrifying mystery
of the English alphabet . . and language
                    of *words* and *numbers*
at which time, certain members
            of the religious Hierarchy did determine
among themselves . . that these unexpectedly unearthed
secret formulas of the Truth of existence
            and the trembling reality
of the lost powers of the gods and goddesses
                    now called Earthlings

constituted dangerous knowledge for the masses
and therefore, caused to have removed
all references in the Scriptures
which might, even through latent suggestion

Canto Twenty ☆ 961

light the flame of soul memory
within the sleeping hearts of all men and women
who then might recall their lost powers
and once again use them as a force for awful destruction
    in this, the Church Fathers
                        believed themselves to be right

and the other part of the answer to your question
hidden for many centuries . . is the negative motivation
by those who desired to retain the religious patriarchy
for the sake of the priesthood
and indeed, for the sake of the entire religious hierarchy
of even each Protestant denomination
who felt it to be, as did the Church of Rome
                        a fearsome abomination
for the 'unclean' woman to arise
    . . . . for the feminine 'I' of the Individuality
to assume her rightful place — as equal in wisdom
to the masculine 'O' of the Overself
this even now reflected in the Church's attitude toward women
more prevalent in the Vatican and in the Mormon strongholds
    for these two pillars do hold many secrets
than do the more direct and uncomplicated Protestants churches

but the time is swift approaching

when all which has been so long buried . .
                . . when each earthquaking secret
shall be revealed into the Light of knowing

that long-awaited time is nigh
when each and every ancient lie . . shall be exposed
and the Truth shall reign once more
in all of its shining innocence and glory, as before
for this has been ordained by **RA** Himself

as a clue . . you are counseled to ponder the mystery
of the Chair of Peter, in Rome
which you, as a child, thought of as the Pope's throne
and the power of infallibility
with which this temporal and literal throne is said
                        to be endowed
and said so truly . .
for there is more than ritual mysticism
hidden near that physical location in the Vatican
    . . . all these things are set in their present pattern
by many men of good faith and good intent
                    . . nevertheless, misguided

another reason for the suppression of these truths
of ancient alchemy and the power of magic

is a word called Divinity . . a most seductive grouping
of the letters of the alphabet

for, Divinity can be a positive force
yet it may also become distorted
into its negative polarity
when it is falsely interpreted and abused
such as being used as an example of Beingness and Glory
not attainable or reachable by earth-bound mortals
. . . by ordinary man and woman

Divinity, when taught as an essence granted by Heaven
to only One — or to a chosen few
is an extremely dangerous energy form

during previous times of the history of formal religion
there were those who did believe
that the masses might be more easily converted unto faith
through fear

but worship of Divinity results in more than fear
it implants a depressing sense of futility
by its wrong implication that the Divine state of being
is unattainable to — and unreachable by
'ordinary mortals'
who are not ordinary at all
but who are gods and goddesses of lost powers

and this false Divinity concept hides the Truth
that Divinity is the birthright
of each and every man and woman upon your planet
attainable either through the reincarnational process
of repeated re-birth into Body Temples
until enlightenment is achieved

or reachable through the swifter process
and more desirable method
of attunement and atonement"

"what do you mean, the swifter process ?
and whatever you mean
would not the word 'atonement' come first, not last
since it means to 'atone' — or to make restitution ?"

"the meaning of the words 'atone' and 'atonement'
has been greatly garbled and distorted
in the interpretation of . . . 'making restitution'

for the true druidic meaning of atonement
is . . at-one-ment
being *one* with one's personal Higher S-elf

and . . before such at-one-ment may be attained
and attunement or at-**tune**-ment must be realized
　　　　the **tuning-in** to the 'I' or 'O'
and the listening . . to be aware of the silver cord
which connects each person to his or her Higher Angel
who then instructs the man or woman
thus tuned-in to his or her Higher S-elf
in how to reach at-one-ment
the way to be 'one' with the personal 'O' or 'I'
thereby becoming a god or goddess of great POwer

one of these powers being knowledge of the mystery
of how — and why — the Body Temple
　　　　　　　　　need not die"

"and it all relates somehow to Music
for, as *attunement* contains the word *tune*
the word *atonement*
　　　contains *tone* . . both musical terms

Divinity, then, is a good and positive thing
except for when it is abused
causing its meaning to be shrunken and diluted
through using it to describe but one person . . or a chosen few"

"this is true . . just as patriotism is now interpreted
to condone murder . . killing . . and selfish greed

for, patriotism is a good vibrational thought form
only when it symbolizes and represents
loyalty and devotion to *all* Earthlings
as brothers and sisters . . to all Nations . . and eventually
　　　　　　　　　　　　to all Universes likewise
just as Divinity
is a good vibrational thought form on Earth
only when it symbolizes or represents
all men and women as the Sons and Daughters
of God, the Father — and His Mate
who is the Mother of all Life forms upon your planet

to place one nation — or one person — above all others
is a false patriotism and a false divinity"

"is not the Pope, in Rome — as are the heads of other religions
all over the world — a good man ?"

"to a large extent, yes — a man of good intent
but not a man of total Truth
for he is forbidden to speak it by his own
　　　　　　　　　denominational inheritance
yet, he must be understood . . loved and forgiven

even as Set himself must be . . and even as
every single man and woman on Earth
must love and forgive . . and try to understand
one another's transgressions and human weaknesses
for, as your Earthling poet, Gibran, most wisely wrote . .

'you cannot fall lower . . than the lowest which is in each of you
nor can you rise higher . . than the highest which is in each of you . . '

and you must not forget that the current Church Fathers
            including the present 'heir'
            to the robe and shoes of Peter . . ought to be granted
            a considered amount of justification
            in at least their hidden, but very real concern
            that some knowledge may possibly be dangerous to learn
            and that one must be ever-cautious and watchful
            so that what occured to cause
                        the annihilation of the planet Maldek
            and the destruction of Atlantis
                        does not repeat itself
            for many would agree with this . . and think likewise"

"yes . . many would think likewise
and share Rome's opinion of the continuing need for secrecy
perhaps . . perhaps . . but still . . . "

            "I sense that some floating memory fragment
            is again causing you to need to listen
                                    . . to the Will
            of the Higher 'I' or your S-elf"

"yes . . some memory fragment
is deeply disturbing me . . and I am not sure
whether or not I should speak of it, you see"

            "great is TRUTH, and mighty above all things !"

"I beg your pardon ?"

            "as it is quoted in your Holy Scriptures
                        accepted even in the Vatican itself
            great is TRUTH !   and Mighty above all things"

"and . . what do you intend this to imply ?"

            "it is intended to imply
            that the suppression or omission of Truth
                        is the greatest lie
            greater far than the lies of commission
            are the lies of omission . . . .
            and one should speak what one urgently feels

Canto Twenty ☆ 965

to be the Truth — without fear of criticism
or religious or other reprisal

you must not fear the retaliation of human judgement
which has so long been grey and clouded . . .
nor should you fear disapproval by formalized religion
because of any Truth you feel needs to be spoken
for, as has already been stated
the greatest lie of all — is the lie of *omission*

whereas, the lies of *commission*
are merely fragments of each Soul's striving for the Light
each in his or her own way . . as long as the *intent*
is genuine

it is the suppression of Truth which is the more serious sin
not speaking in error of it — yes, Great indeed is **TRUTH**
and Mighty above all things — mighty enough
to send protection from Heaven to all who sincerely
speak it for the enlightenment of others"

"the greatest lie . . is the lie of omission . . yes
causing grave harm to the human condition
allright, then — I will speak my inner thoughts
for whatever they may be worth . . to the planet Earth
which may be vital . . and may be meaningless
nevertheless, I will speak them, and cast aside fear

this memory fragment relates to a time when I was about thirteen
and greatly enamored of the Catholic faith
those youthful years of growing, when to me, the Vatican
could do no wrong
when I believed all Catholic dogma to be
as infallible as the word of God Himself — in person

. . . oh ! how well do I remember . . one beautiful, nostalgic
and rustling-red-gold-leaf autumn . . lasting from September
through November
when I, and a good Catholic friend
whose name, I recall, was Chuck . . . . nearly made Earth and Heaven rhyme
through our mutual consecration to a Vatican cause

. . I can still hear far-off chapel bells chime
on our exciting climb up the high steps
of a Parish House, on a wind-swept hill
nearly every golden afternoon
and on many a lavender-violet twilight evening
. . saturated with the fragrance of fall's brisk, clean breeze

to share, with a twinkle-eyed, Irish Padre, named Paul . . . Fahey
and another Priest, also wise and youthful . . . twinkly and bright

various mundane mounds
of seemingly top secret paper work

to make things come out right
for a distant Cardinal, called Mindzenty

    I was hazy about this glowing cause
to which my friend and I were dedicated, heart and soul
        knowing little of its whys and wherefores
certain only that our sacred quest
                        . . our shining goal
    indeed, our Holy Grail

was to get Cardinal Mindzenty out of jail
and free him to do God's work in this weary world

    both the political and the religious implications
escaped me . . as they still do

    for, what drew me, to renew in me my Catholic infatuation
was the heavenly happiness inherent
        in the mystique and charisma of the whole affair
when the scents of autumn hung so heavy in the air
        mixed with the incense and red candleglow
  from the vigil lights on the mantle of the Parish House

as we whispered and murmured . . and laughed and talked
with these two energetic young men
        wearing mysterious black robes
the white Roman clerical collar . . glittering crucifixes
           around their waists
    and also wearing . . smiles

not the frowns of the serious Ministers I had always known
in the churches of protesting Protestants

    there were cookies . . and ice cold apple cider
and there was exciting conversation
        about secrets of Past, Present and Future
even touching on reincarnation . . and moments of recess
           to kneel and pray

after which I was troubled, when we were firmly told
that reincarnation did not contain the gold
        of spiritual truth
but was the Devil's Doctrine
cleverly disguised from innocent, youthful eyes

    as we worked together
feeling free to ask questions, and be answered honestly
honestly ? well . . at least to be answered . . .

I recall laughing and joking . .
          . . the gentle Priests smoking their pipes . .
and I truly felt that my friend and I

were making Life and Heaven rhyme
that golden autumn time . .

     and I knew, then, the truth — or so I convinced myself
     yes, right or wrong, I thought
                    I believe what I have been so softly taught

and right or wrong . . . this is where I belong
hearing the haunting song . . of Bernadette
          and conversing about on the mysteries of Fatima

     isn't it strange
that the word **conversation** should so arrange
                              its letters
to contain within itself
     the verb convert . . as in "to con*vert*"
and also the noun *con*vert . . as well as the word convent ?

     but Fatima . . . yes, Fatima

I remember waiting for the final Message of Fatima
from the three small children who shared a vision together
                         three times
for the world was told, back then
that the Pope would soon open the third and final message
                         of the children's visions

     and deliver it to the people

     the Vatican called it the Year of Fatima
that exciting, miraculous year, when the secret druid message
would be publicly read . . so everyone could know, at last
                              what it said
     what prophecy it held

yes, the mysterious, soon approaching Year of Fatima
was awaited anxiously by millions . . like myself

     . . never dreaming
               that the third and Final Message
to a waiting world
     would be hidden by the Vatican
and never spoken, to this day, in 1972

     still veiled behind curtains of secrecy
     hiding a warning of perhaps earth-quaking importance

for, when the Year of Fatima arrived
with all its far-flung, wide-spread celebrations
of colorful consecreation . . and mounting curiosity

the only sound from Rome . . was silence
not the great chords of music the world expected
from this final, thrilling message
of the third Fatima vision of innocence

simply . . silence
no message read to the world
by the Pope . . no hope . . no nothing
only silence

I'd heard it had been ordained
that this third message of the children's visions
was to be kept sealed
until this holy, long-awaited Year of Fatima

therefore, the Catholic Shepherd knew no more
about its contents . . than did his sheep
until it was opened and read in private, in the Vatican
then kept unrevealed

what last shining truth did these innocent three
two small girls and one small boy . . . see
in their third vision ?
what prophecy did they hear
from the tender lips of the Lady of their visions
dressed in robes of Virgin-Mary-blue
who appeared to them for the third and last time
in the green and dew-drenched grass
on that holy, misty, long ago Portugal morning ?
did she give them
some kind of warning ?"

"these are all valid questions you ask
and your meditations hold the seeds of enlightenment
concerning the Vatican's serious error
in keeping that which should be told — secret
thereby risking much future terror
when the revelation could *prevent* a great catastrophe"

"in later years . . I could never find a Priest anywhere
who would admit that he knew a single thing
about the Year of Fatima
despite all those planned Catholic celebrations
of the release of the third and final message to the world . . . .

celebrations suddenly and inexplicably cancelled by Rome
like some holy birthday party

with all the candles blown out on the cake
before anyone has a chance to make even one wish
and no one able to guess the reason . .

so I can't help wondering . .
does the Vatican hide more than ritualistic mystery
behind its heavy, carved wooden doors
does it also, perhaps, hide Truth ?
        and if so . . why ?"

                "as has been previously stated, the time is nigh
                when the world will learn why
                        for it has been so ordained
                that the third Fatima truth be soon revealed"

"and there is this other fragment in my mind
about music and poetry . . connected with the Roman Church
in some strange way, I feel it is of urgent importance
that the instantly-and-instinctively-loved-by-all-faiths Pope
                John Paul I
who died so swiftly and tragically
after such a pathetic few days of wearing Peter's robe
                was a poet

yes, a sensitive poet . . and I feel that he sensed or knew
all the truths we are now discussing
and was, perhaps of a mind to have decided
to reveal the true Light to the world
gradually and cautiously . . but very surely
and was, for some reason, prevented from doing so
cruelly stopped by . . some Higher Force
                which caused his Body Temple's death

yet it is difficult for me to see how this could be . . . .
why would any Higher Force
have wanted to seal the lips of such a holy one
who might well have been the first Pope since Peter himself
to tell Earthlings the total Truth, not just a part ?
and I ponder all these things in my heart . . "

                "you are correct in sensing that the druidic truths
                of language and numbers . . as well as the Truth
                of all the lost powers of man and woman
                can be more smoothly and swiftly penetrated
                by those who feel the rhythms of poetry and music
                for these two muses do lull the Mind and Soul
                into a gentle awakening of what is already known
                but long-forgotten . . and you are right
                to assume that the Poet-Pope was an exceptional man
                who might well have decided, in his heart
                to have revealed the true Light of all the Ages

to *the world at last, along with the third Fatima message*
* but all this is past . . and whatever the complexities
of yesterday . . we must turn our energies
upon today and tomorrow . . as the most expedient way
to end the Earth's sorrow, at this Moment of Time"

"I do understand what you are saying
and . . if we may return to the subject of praying
you mentioned our Mother in Heaven
does this mean that Heaven's Deities are
man and woman — equally ?"

     "the complete comprehension of this union of 'God'
        with His own Twin S-elf
will be revealed unto you at the allotted time
    to share with others
for the present, it will be sufficient to keep in mind
that each essence, including even the Highest
possesses, by Universal law, its own sacred POlarity
which is the mystery of all POwer and WisdOm
as well as all GOOdness . . and Peace . . and LOve"

"then, until I learn more
ought I to pray to our Father and Mother
Who art in Heaven ?"

     "such a prayer would not at all be out of place
and would, indeed, represent the beginning
           of true grace
and you might also ponder upon
the 4th line of the Lord's prayer
which you and your teacher know
the line following "Thy kingdom come . . Thy Will be done"
has been overlooked, its meaning rejected
    for two thousand years
because of the blind doctrine of the fear of hell
for, Earth will be greatly affected
   by the bringing about of this dream
which is your mission upon this planet . . . and also
the mission of the one you love"

"do you mean the line about Divine Will
     being done *on Earth* . . . . exactly as it is in Heaven ?

and that one shouldn't dream of dying to attain Heaven
but instead, work to bring its happiness and peace to Earth ?
I've never believed that Heaven is some mystical place in the ethers

*There have been several books written, claiming
that Pope John Paul I was murdered.

but a state of Beingness possible right here"

"this is correct — the Kingdom is *within*"

"why did Jesus begin the Lord's prayer
with 'Our *Father* Who art in Heaven' . . instead of
Our Father and *Mother* Who art in Heaven ?"

"when he was alone, on Sinai
Moses was told many shining truths
which he was warned to not yet reveal unto his people
for, their Third Eyes were not fully open
to absorb certain laws of fasting and abstaining
they were not ready to accept

and the same is true of Jesus
who knew also more mysteries and truth
than even those Twelve who followed his precepts
could understand
while they vibrated on a lower frequency than he"

"I realize that I am hopping and skipping
back and forth between subjects again . . but
I need to know if one Twin S-elf
can fall behind the other . . . on Earth
and then be rescued by his or her own Twin ?"

"yes, this is true — they often do
fall back behind one another
and one will often reincarnate to rescue the Twin
who has become a fallen angel"

"are there many fallen angels ?"

"nearly every man and woman on your planet
is one of these"

"and may that returning Twin S-elf
sometimes become lost too
in attempting to rescue the other ?"

"this is always a danger"

"how sad . . how very sad"

"yet this may also be glad . . if one is still
and listens to the Will . . of the Higher Angel
of one's own S-elf . . through which our Creators
do indeed speak, in a language
only the heart knows"

"oh, Heathcliffe, I do so need to know the truth
of why I fell . . why I became a fallen angel
I need so to know the state of Beingness of my own Soul
        as well as my own S-elf
and that of its other half . . its Twin"

                "listen to the voice within . . which guides you"

"is the mystery somehow contained
in the Holy Trinity — the Symbol of Eternity
    the Serpent, eating its own tail
with the male head or mouth of the Serpent feeding masculine energy
into the female tail — and the female tail of the Serpent
likewise and simultaneously
feeding feminine energy into the Serpent's mouth ?

and somehow also entwined in the third part
of the Serpent-circle-secret
which is the neutral and neither, yet also both combined . . .
an All Powerful energy created
by the flowing into each by the other ?"

                "that is not correct in its entirety
                but sufficiently correct for the moment
                the Serpent-circle-secret does contain all the mystery
                of the Holy Trinity — and do not forget
                that your Earthling scientist Kekule
                who discovered the principles of organic chemistry
                dreamed, while sleeping, of a snake eating its own tail"

"somehow I feel that there is more of this same mystery
contained within the planets of Venus and Mars
for, Venus is a feminine force, vibrating to the number 6
while Mars is a masculine force, vibrating to the number 9"

                "true, and when one takes the 9 and the 6
                to symbolize male and female — the figures of 6 . . 9
                and then reverses these key numbers . . "

"oh, I see ! the 6 re-versed, upside-down — is a 9
and the 9 re-versed, upside-down — is a 6 !"

                " . . . and together, the two numbers total 15
                the Chaldean symbol for mystery and magic . . . .
                which, when added, as in 1 plus 5
                                once again equals the 6"

"six . . the number of Venus . . and Love"

                "there is a similar mystery
                in the druidic letters of the English alphabet

which stand for Man and Woman . . do you see this too ?"

"do you mean the letter M for Man
and W for Woman ?"

"yes, I do — and can you see what they represent ?"

"oh, but of course ! they may also be re-versed
and still remain the same — while also being each other
because the M, re-versed, upside-down — is a W
and the W, re-versed upside-down — is an M
exactly in the same manner as the 6 and the 9 !"

"there is more mystery buried within the M and W
as letters of the alphabet — but for the present
what you have stated is sufficiently correct
and holds the key to the greatest mystery of all"

"then the 6 and the 9 represent the polarity
not only of man and woman — but symbolize also — all polarities ?"

"yes . . all polarities contain this mystery in common
which is symbolized by the 6 and the 9
the M and the W . . "

"each polarity is part of the other, then ?"

"yes, and each must blend
into the Holy Trinity mystery of the circle"

"I somehow feel . . that this relates
to the Body Temples . . why is that ?"

"your question is most profound
and contains a secret not yet ordained
to be revealed unto the world, until . . "

"until when ?   when will I know this secret
to help make Life and Heaven rhyme ?"

"you will be instructed . . at the allotted time"

"but may I have . . just one hint now ?"

"this the Masters will allow — but only one
the profound mystery you inquire about
is interlocked within the alphabetical capital letter H
and this is all I can presently tell you"

"allright, I'll wait . . then tell me
about the O

which symbolizes the Serpent circle
     also Pluto and Scorpio
yes, and even . . the hiSSing Serpent"

             "what happens to all single or double numbers
             when the O is added unto them ?"

"the POwer of these numbers
is then increased . . yes ! I see"

             "the mystery of the circle, therefore
             is the secret of the POwer of the Third Energy"

"and this powerful, neutral Third Energy
is it masculine or feminine — or is it neither ?
for example, the Holy Trinity of the Father — Son — and Holy Ghost
which of *these* three is masculine . . and which one is feminine ?"

             "the Father is masculine, of course
             and should be called, by Earthlings, **RA** or **RAH**
             there being a different reason for each spelling
             which you will later be taught

             the Holy Ghost — is a name chosen to veil
             His **M**ate — the feminine Goddess
             and this God and Goddess created all upon your Earth
             as well as creating your Earth's Universe "

I knew it, I knew it !
then the Holy Ghost is feminine !"

             "this is a mystery you should not yet ponder
             perhaps a fragment or so, as we are now speaking
             but for the present, continue your questioning"

"then, if the Father of the Holy Trinity is masculine
and the Holy Ghost is feminine
then the Middle One, the Son, must also be masculine ?"

             "may I also be permitted, like yourself
             to, as you term it, hop and skip about . . briefly
             as we discuss these sacred matters ?"

"you may hop and skip as much as you like"

             "we have been speaking of the Third Energy
             but do not forget what is celestially called
             the Fourth Energy — which is Time
                          and the Fifth Energy
             which is Nature Herself"

"when may I learn more about all of these energies ?
don't tell me . . never mind . . don't bother
I already know the answer
I will learn more at 'the alloted time' . . isn't that so ?"

        "you see ? you have read my mind, through telepathy"

"I don't find that amusing"

        "I apologize . . **ARF ! ARF !**"

"I'm sorry, Heath . . I forgot the importance
of what you said earlier . . .
I forgot my sense of humor"

        "if I may say so once again . . you do have funny toes
        for a tamed and unique rose"

"you stole that from Gooober, as I meant to tell you the first time you used it"

        "even a Master Avatar is allowed to plagiarize a bit
              for, as you ought to know
        there is — very truly — nothing *new* under **RA**'s Sun"

"you are forgiven . . now back to my question
about the sex — or gender — of the Trinity
if the Father is masculine
and the Holy Ghost, in her lace nightgown . . is feminine . . . "
then what about the Son
        the middle One
of the three-times-three of the Holy Trinity ?"

        "there is no Son — this is another patriarchial seed
        of deception and mis-conception
        for, the third Essence of the Holy Trinity
        is not the 'Son' — not Jesus — and not Man either
        this is what has been falsely taught
        by those who refer to themselves as the Church Fathers
        yet, one never hears of the Church Mothers

        the third Essence of the Holy Trinity
        wrongly called the Son — is *both* — the Logos children
        the Sons and Daughters of **RAH** and **R**am . . . or RaHram

        Earthling children of the masculine Father
        and the feminine Goddess — or Mother
              of this and all Universes

        now, once again, let us return to the mystery
        of the Masculine energy flowing into the Feminine

as the Feminine energy flows into the Masculine
by which blending the **Third Energy** is then created
which is both masculine and feminine
and All Powerful

this represented . .
though still veiled in all its Truth
by the Serpent eating its own tail"

"wait !   I am confused . . . because
well, I am confused in several ways"

"it is not yet time for you to penetrate
all mysteries
but of some confusions, you may inquire"

"first I need to know why **RAH**'s Mate
or **RA**'s Mate, as the case may be
should bear such a nonsensical false name
as the Holy Ghost"

"you are growing into much perceptive knowing
as your queston reveals . . .
for the Holy Ghost is not truly Her name . . only a veil
although, one must admit
it has been quite an appropriate term
for those who have hidden Her for so long"

"then, what *is* Her name ?
don't make me guess"

"you will learn her true name in a moment
however, for now, return to the second matter
about which you are now confused"

"I do not understand this All Powerful
        Third Energy Force
may it only be created by the blending of **RA**
or of . . **RAH** and His Mate, the feminine Goddess ?"

"in the particular example you are giving . . .
the correct spelling, in this instance of blending
                        is **RAH**"

" . . may it *only* be created by the blending
of **RAH** and His Mate, the feminine Goddess ?"

"it is created by **RaH**ram in the same manner
as man and woman of Earth blend themselves
        although seldom purely

to create the reflected microcosm energy"

"but are you trying to tell me
are you . . trying to say . . that this All Powerful
        Third Energy Force
would be Higher, even than God Himself ?
Higher even than God and His Mate
whatever Her name may be ?"

                "yes, this is true — your Third Eye is opening
                and when it is fully opened someday soon
                you will learn why the act of blending in love
                        with physical Body Temples
                is a good and positive blending, when pure
                and necessary for the Power to manifest
                although the carrying of new Life, within woman
                is neither positive or necessary
                and was never intended to be . . in the beginning"

"I'm anxious to learn more about what you are hinting
someday . . soon . . but right this moment
I need to know the name of this God, Who is even Higher
than **RA** or **RAH** and His own Twin S-elf
by what name is this All Powerful God called ?"

                "the name you seek . . has wrongly been called by many
                        the Holy Grail
                one of the names the term of the Holy Ghost
                was intended to keep hidden . . but you swim now
                in very deep waters"

"the Holy Grail ?   you mean the Truth King Arthur sought ?
and Lancelot ?   does the Holy Grail have anything to do
with the line I love so much from the 23rd psalm
my cup runneth over . . ?

                "yes, it does . . and note that the 2 and the 3
                of the 23rd psalm, written by David
                equal, when added — the magical number of 5
                which is the same numerical value of Expect a Miracle . . .

                but to return to those deep waters
                the Holy Grail is a cup which is never empty
                because it pours forth the Third Energy
                                flowing downward

                and when man and woman mate in love
                        . . . when Twin Selves unite . . and are illuminated
                both long separated halves joining
                to form the complete Snowflake of the Higher Angel
                the Third Energy is then purified

978   ☆   Canto Twenty

and drawn back up to its primal source
                                    the Holy Grail
the cup which is eternally full
and which . . . as David knew . . . runneth over

therefore, goodness and mercy
shall surely follow all Earthlings
        all the days of their immortal life

but those who secretly, among themselves
identify the All Powerful God as the Holy Grail
                    are mistaken
for this is not the name of the Highest-of-the-Highest
and the Mightiest-Almighty-of-All"

"this is *not* the name ?"

                "no — this is not the name of the All Powerful God
                for the Holy Grail is but the *container*
                of this All Powerful Third Energy Force

                and as the container of this Force
                the Holy Grail has another name itself"

"then tell me — first
what is this other name ?"

                "you know the name . . and know it well"

"no ! I tell you that I do not !
what is this mystery you refuse to tell ?
I must know the answer"

                "as ye grow . . so shall ye know"

"riddles, riddles, riddles !
will you please tell me the other name of the Holy Grail
that cup which . . runneth over ?"

                "it is such a simple name . . it is **Love**"

"Love ?"

                "yes, **Love** . . is the highest POwer of all "

"but . . then what is the name
of the **ALL POWERFUL GOD**, Who is the Highest-of-the-Highest
and the Mightiest-Almighty-of-All ?"

                "before you learn the name you are seeking
                please now create a new drawing"

Canto Twenty ☆ 979

"must I do this ?"

        "yes, you must — it is necessary
        for a clarification, you see — of the whole"

"allright . . I shall try to clarify
first the lesser names

so here is my fourth drawing . . . ."

        "then you now see that the correct initials of the symbol
        of the Feminine Goddess you were seeking . . have been revised
        they are **S C S** — *not* the **C S S** you transposed

        and these initials represent the **S**upra **C**onscious **S**oul
          the **S**upreme **C**onsiousness — or the **C**onscience
            of all microcosm Souls
        and this represents **RA**'s Mate"

"the feminine Goddess, who is the Supra Conscious Soul
is the Total Consciousness . . or the *Conscience*
of all feminine gender Souls on Earth
whether these be the Souls of Man or Woman ?"

        "yes, the Supra Conscious is the Total Consciousness
        of all feminine gender microcosm Souls
                of *both* men and women

        and . . as you have further shown in your drawing
        RA also has another name, you see
        which you have symbolized with the initials **M U**
        but when mirror-reversed
        these letters become **U M** . . the **U**niversal **M**ind

        and the Universal Mind is the Total Awareness
        of all masculine-gender microcosm Minds
                of *both men and women*
        the **S**upra **C**onscious **S**oul
        causes all feminine Souls of both men and women
        to possess the qualities of gentleness . . perception
        sensitivity and intuition . . intellect . . creativity

        while the **U**niversal **M**ind causes all
        masculine Minds of both men and women
        to possess the qualities of intelligence . . invention
        organizaton and reasoning . . courage and endurance

        do you understand ?"

"I do . . and it is a beautiful synchronization of the simplicity
of the balanced duality of sexuality

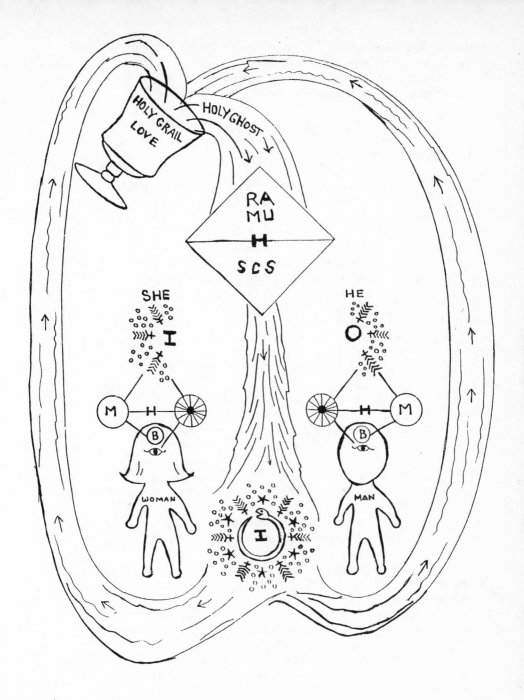

created by **RA** and His Mate . . . but as I said earlier, I would like to know
why such a spooky name as the Holy Ghost
has been used, down through the centuries of language confusion
to falsely represent the feminine Goddess"

"the Holy Ghost is a veil, you see"

"a veil ? will you explain this to me ?"

"as has been stated, the Holy Ghost is a veil
and most properly named, don't you agree ?

since one of the purposes of the name
and even of the initials **H G** . . has been
to hide the identitiy of the *feminine Goddess*
also to veil or hide the true identity
of the other **H G** . . the **H**oly **G**rail . . which is **L**ove"

"somehow, I always sensed that what I sought
was hidden behind a veil . . like Vail
and the Holy Ghost . . oh ! He — or She — was *always* the one
                    I mistrusted the most !"

"you must not be impatient
                    Mary-Mary-Quite-Contrary
and expect your garden to grow too quickly
for . . to everything there is a season
and a Time to every purpose under Heaven . .
there will be a variety of new seeds planted
for this new Eden heaven . . by many others besides yourself

and all must grow together, in the Sun and rain
until Spring truly arrives upon your planet"

"do you mean the season of the year
or the meaning of the code-word of *spring*
between Gooober and myself ?"

"I mean both of these . . they are the same
someday you will comprehend
why the one you love once wisely wrote
and counseled you to . . *trust your dreams of spring* . . "

"yes . . I remember those words
I can't recall the rest of them . . there was a second line
he wrote . . but I've lost that letter from him

anyway . . you still haven't told me the name

982 ☆ Canto Twenty

of the powerful Third Energy Force
please, Heathcliffe, I really must have this answer
and I must have it **NOW !** not later . . at the allotted time"

"then you, yourself, have so ordained it
and since you have commanded the answer
from the Universe — with all the POwer
of your own Higher Self or your 'I' — simply draw it !"

"draw it ? I can't — but I will try"

"just look once more at your last drawing
the name will occur to you . . and where it belongs"

"let's see . . . Jack and Jill went up the hill
to fetch a pail of water — and pail rhymes with Grail
a pail of water . . yes, a Grail of water . . *water and the spirit*"

" . . as the Nazarene spoke . . . 'I tell you the truth
no one can enter the Kingdom of God
unless he is born again . . *of water and the spirit*'
now, go ahead and draw the name you seek"

". . . . I see you have initialed the 'water' flow of the Force
with the letters **S H** — in place of the Holy Ghost
which is most interesting . . since it relates
to the **SSSHHHhhh !** mystery of the Sphinx
and **RAHRAM**
but to find the name you seek . .
the name of the Third Energy Force . . you must
mirror-reverse your initials of **S H** . . into **H S**
which letters represent . . the Holy Spirit"

"then the name of **T**hird **E**nergy **F**orce
is . . the Holy Spirit ?"

"yes, this is the name veiled in your earlier drawing
where you printed the **H**oly **G**host
this flow from the **H**oly **G**rail is actually the **H**oly **S**pirit
and there is no **H**oly **G**host, in reality
this *false* Feminine Essence was intended
as a Triple Veil"

"I *knew* the Holy Ghost who kept pursuing me — was a She !
and now I see . . that Holy Spirit . . the **T**hird **E**nergy **F**orce
created by Macrocosm and microcosm mating
or . . the Serpent eating its own tail
is neither masculine or feminine — but a perfect blend of both
which is the origin of its power !"

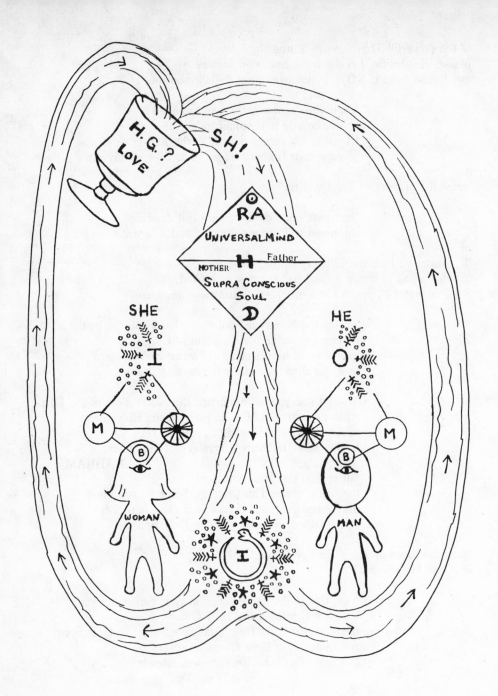

"is there another name which is higher than **love** ?
higher than the **H**oly **S**pirit ?"

> "not *higher*, no — but there is an *all-inclusive* name
> which symbolizes the Ultimate of All Oneness
> and this Ultimate mystery is hidden in alchemy . . . .
> for it is guarded by the 9 of the Red Dragon
> and it is not yet time for you to learn this secret"

"the Ultimate of All Oneness . . or the symbol of this ?"

> "that is correct . . . "

"I am suddenly reminded
of the truth that the number 9 is also
the number, in Earth-physics, of the Universal Solvent
which is . . . Water
and . . if one must be born again of *Water* and the Spirit"
then there must be a relationship between Water . . and the **H**oly **S**pirit"

> "you are right . . there is a secret affinity"

"may I please be told what this relationship — or affinity — is ?"

> "no, you may not . . at this time"

"how can you be so arrogant and stubborn ?
after all, Heath, please do try to remember
that you are only a dog"

> "only a dog ?   **ARF !   ARF !**   perhaps
> but do not forget that dog
>   spelled backwards — is God"

"now what riddle are you trying to express ?
is there some mystery in this ?
that dog, spelled backwards, is God ?"

> "there is indeed, a mystery here"

"is the mystery, perhaps
that dogs are so good and kind . . and loving and forgiving
since they continue to love deeply and steadily
even when their devotion is not returned ?"

> "this may well be the origin of the *word* 'dog'
> but, no — this is not the mystery of the Ultimate"

"does the word God really mean God ?
that is, does the word God mean the Ultimate ?"

"yes, . . but the name of the Ultimate
is *incorrectly spelled*
you should ponder this . . "

"you mean, it ought not to be spelled
as 'God' — but as 'Good' ?"

"no, this is *not* what I mean
and as has already been stated . . this Ultimate spelling
will be revealed to you at the allotted time
for the present, let us return to the **H**oly **S**pirit . .

and other matters important for you to learn"

"Heath, you can't be aware of how I burn
I must know the name which is the Ultimate symbol
for all Good — and for the Force, which flows downward
and is drawn back up again, purified
and I must know why **GOD** is mistakenly spelled
as well as what is meant by 'water . . and the spirit'
and the Red Dragon of Alchemy"

"these things are not ordained to be taught
for Part One of your Happiness POem
only for Part Two . . you shall call *Twelfth Night Secrets*
will these matters be revealed unto you"

"but I truly need to know now"

"you do *not* need to know right now — this is clear
for if your need grows intense enough
then it falls under the Law for all Earthling
enlightenment"

"and what is this Law ?"

"this Law states . . that when the need to know
is deep and genuine . . and finally overflows itself
within the Mind and the Soul . . both of these
then one will decode the mystery for one's own s-elf
and need not ask the teacher
therefore, your need has not yet reached this stage"

"you are quite an impertinent sage
are you aware of that ?"

"I am aware that we should continue our discussion
of the flowing downward of the **H**oly **S**pirit
containing the Force of the Third Energy
which is the primordial result
of the blending of **RAH** and His Mate . . a Holy Spring

986 ☆ Canto Twenty

through this miracle of masculine-feminine Oneness
all wonder is manifested . . all Universes are born

also, as a result of this magical-miraculous blending
of **RAHRAM**

the Logos Children — Twin Selves — are created
and when each Twin S-elf once more unites
in the microcosm of their own Spring . .
to thus blend . . and to harmonize once more

the Third Energy is then purified — as already stated
and drawn back up . . to fill the cup
that runneth over

the cup which is never empty . . the **Holy Grail**
because all the divine **LOVE** poured forth
is purified by *human* love . . . then drawn back"

"is there some way to picture, or to try to image
what the Powerful God called Love looks like ?
for the purpose of receiving grace ? or is this God-of-Gods
like the one I pondered upon, as a child
when I used to say, "God won't let anyone draw His face ?"

"you may receive grace by imaging God's face"

"but what does it look like ?"

"the All Powerful God called **LOVE** is masculine "

"Love, then, is of the masculine-gender ?"

"yes, . . but, as has been stated
all Divinity is Polarity
nothing exists alone or separate . . therefore
you may receive the grace of this God
and see His face
by imaging His feminine counterpart — or Essence"

"I may receive grace . . and see the face
of this masculine God-of-Gods . . . called Love
by imaging His feminine Essence ?"

"that is sublimely correct in every sense"

"but what is Her real name ?
what is Love's feminine name
which grants this grace ?"

"the other name of the masculine God called Love

which is His feminine Essence
. . is **LIGHT**

when one closes one's physical eyes
and opens up the Third Eye
this all Powerful feminine half of God is seen

as a brilliant **LIGHT**"

"so He is **LOVE** and She is **LIGHT** !
how perfectly marvelous !
for, they have been experimenting, in California
with children in hospitals, who have allegedly incurable diseases
by having them close their eyes
. . and image Light !
and the children
literally do see, then . . a brilliant Light
and when this is done repeatedly
their bodies do miraculously begin to heal !
and now I understand
that this Light the children see
is that **LIGHT** which is the feminine polarity
of the masculine God Force of **LOVE** . . .
. . . our Mother Who Art in Heaven !"

"it is . . and you see how easy it is
for the children to image this healing Light
when they are lovingly shown the way
for, as has been stated
the Third Eyes of children are still open both spiritually
and medically — the pineal gland
is still soft and malleable . . therefore what you say
is as logical as can be"

"oh, bless those lovely people, whoever they are
who first thought of treating the children
and healing them in this way !"

"as has been already said . .
the Garden which will burst into flower
One Fine Day
will be seeded by yourself . . also
by your own Twin S-elf . . and by many others too
for each has his or her own mission
in this dawning of the golden Age of Aquarius"

"and, then, when true Twin Selves find each other again
to once more unite . . . "

"they return to **Love** and **Light**

and may then, if certain laws are followed
            learn how to retain their Body Temples
as long as they wish
and travel through Space to the other Eden-heavens
then return periodically to Earth
to help their not-yet-enlightened brothers and sisters
through the magical alchemy
of the miracle known as Ascension
but these secrets will be revealed unto you
at the allotted time

all you need know at present
is that the translation called Ascension
is accomplished through **Love** and **Light** as **One**"

."and when they attempt to translate
through hate ?"

            "they cannot translate through hate
the energy vibration of hate
            will not permit humans to negate
each other's imperfections into purity
they may use the Third Energy force to translate
only through Love — never through hate

as has been taught by Jesus, of Nazareth
            resist ye *not* evil
for, to resist evil — or any polarity — is wrong"

"but to lead it into the Light . . "

            "this is right"

"if all this is true . . .
if we should all love one another equally
and resist *not* evil
then what about the group sexual coupling
of Heinlein's Martian, Michael Valentine
that promiscuous stranger . . in a strange land ?

so many people believe today
that group sex — even if the group numbers only three
is right and healthy and progressive
they even teach it as therapy
and lately — the commercials on television
actually promote and encourage the life style of ménage à trois
I know this is wrong . . but with all this emphasis
on 'loving one another as brothers and sisters'
and 'sharing love unselfishly'

I can't seem to find the words which will *prove* it wrong"

"to love all alike . . friends, enemies and strangers
yes, this is truly good and right
but the *physical* blending or union is different

the current pattern of pornography
encouraging sexual promiscuity
is the most dangerous negative energy
upon your planet today — for it debases Love
it attacks and distorts the great eternal Truth
        of Oneness

remember that the sexual ecstasy of physical intimacy
between true Twin Selves — is achieved only following
the harmony of first blending the three necessary parts
                of Love's Trinity
the Mental . . . Emotional . . . and Spiritual
in exquisite culmination

    recall the Snowflake, split in half, eons ago
each identical Twin Snowflake half
of an 'I' or 'O' . . . unique . . and like no other in all Universes

when these two Snowflake halves are joined
there is created an image . . or a picture . . of great beauty

then imagine countless of these snowflake pieces, split in two
which is very like unto
        a jig-saw picture puzzle, as you earlier pointed out

and one may only successfully complete the puzzle
thereby creating a picture of unimaginable, indescribable beauty
by slowly and carefully trying each piece against the other
and very gradually, then . . fitting them all together
           each piece . . where it belongs

there is only one spot, one place . . each piece will fit
and this must be done slowly . .
           one piece at a time
in the attempt to complete the picture

but if the pieces are continually scattered carelessly
thoughtlessly and promiscuously
then a final whole and complete rainbow of beauty
            will never be found
the electromagnetic energy of mating
between those who truly love . . as has already been stated
contains such glory and mystery
        and as yet unguessed power
that the resulting combined aura

reaches through Time and Space like a beam of brilliant **LIGHT**
becoming the signal for each 'I' and 'O'
who seek such a birth channel . . who are waiting
to be born into the vibration of Love . . .
therefore, this kind of pure sexual blending
is of ultimate and vital importance to the survival of your planet

one must not condemn those well-intended men and women
who are trying slowly, as best they can . . to fit together
two mis-matched and mis-mated jigsaw pieces
                                        of Love's puzzle
and repeatedly fail . . but keep trying

whereas, those who use pornography to seduce humans
into indulging in promiscuous mating
by inciting and arousing them to seek only selfish sensuality
                        motivated merely by lust
lacking all tenderness and innocence
                        are producing thought forms of great harm

the pornographers are condemned by the righteous anger
of **RA** himself . . . and by Her also
for they perpetuate Earth's long dark night of the soul
in many ways . . only one of these being
to create birth channels which allow unwanted infants
to enter Earth . . and soon become pathetic statistics on your planet"

"you mean like the over *two hundred thousand* babies
and small children . . who were recently beaten
                        sexually abused . . or killed
in just *one single year* . . in Los Angeles county alone ?"

"yes, two hundred thousand beaten, abused or killed
small ones — during such a brief period of time
and in only *one* county upon your Earth
    is a number which represents
the destruction of a vast amount of Innocence

and the pronographers also produce
those thought forms which also eventually lead
to the creation of sexual birth channels
of the kind which allow the lower-evolved entities
        some even from outside this Universe
to enter into Earth's dimensional level
these being attracted, you see, by the dull-red auras
surrounding those who couple only in lust"

"but what about the First Amendment Law
protecting those pornographers . . should it be allowed to do so ?"

"it should indeed — and those who legally protect
the right of evil to exist, alongside of Truth
those Earthlings who protect the legal privileges
            of Satan-Set . . to tempt
are performing a righteous service to all humanity

for it is not man-made law which has the power
to halt the spread of darkness
therefore, it is wrong and misguided to abolish laws
which do also protect the Truth
those Laws which protect the right of Light and Love
                                to also grow
and teach Earthlings to know . . and so

your man-made Laws of Enlightenment
such as your Constitiution's First Amendment
must be cherished — and continually protected from
                                extinction
therefore, those who do defend
the First Amendment Rights of the pornographers
perform a good and worthy service"

"that sounds so much like a chaotic non sequitur
how can it be good and right
to defend the very ones who constitute one of the major causes
of the possibly approaching major Earth-changes and awful cataclysms
which may entirely destroy our planet ?"

"as has been stated . . your man-made laws
do not possess the power to stop the spread of darkness
they do possess, however, the power to protect
the shining of the Light of Truth upon such darkness

the punishment of the ones who do spread evil
whether it be the evil of pornography
            or of material greed — or of
dangerous nuclear, hydrogen and cobalt
                        experimentation and use

is the punishment of those who offend Innocence
and shall come from a Higher Power
for, as Jesus did warn most seriously, in his time
when it comes to those who do offend
            the Innocence of little children
meaning small in size . . as well as
the innocent men and women, who contain within
                        still . . their childhood . . . Faith

. . . to offend these 'small children' of all ages
who hold the keys to the Kingdom of Heaven on Earth
        is a grave sin

992 ☆ Canto Twenty

the inescapable punishment of which shall be
                                                          so horrifying
that, in the words of the Nazarene
it would better for these offenders of Innocence
that they should be drowned, with a millstone
                                              'round their necks
 . . but they shall not be given
such a relatively easy way out of their offenses
unless they are halted . . before it is too late

no, the First Amendment is not what actually protects
your pornographers — they are protected, truly
by those Governors and Presidents . . blind politicians
Hollywood film stars . . and misguided major authors
who allow their names and power to be used
within the pages of darkness . . thereby enticing
the others who protect it in actuality
 . . . . those men and women who purchase such magazines"

"then . . promiscuous grokking around
really does short-circuit the Soul ?"

                  "speaking electromagnetically, this is true"

"then . . I suppose that, instead of hating
        Robert Heinlein
I should have just told him to . . go smell a rose ?"

                  "this Earthling author
                  in addition to writing *Stranger in a Strange Land*
                          which so offended you
                  has also written other books of great value
                  causing men's and women's imaginations to grow
                  and to gradually know . . and so
                  he fulfilled his earthly mission with sensitivity
                  therefore, he should not only be forgiven
                  he should be thanked as well"

"now I must make one more drawing
because I left out some important things
in each of the others"

                  "please do — and I am quite sure
                  that your new drawing will be nearly complete"

"only nearly ?"

                  "this is what I have said, yes"

"well, whatever . . here it is
I've tried to remember everything you've taught me

is it allright ?"

                    "it is very clear
                    Gooober will be quite proud of you
                    for all you have learned on this night

                    now your drawing is nearly complete
                    and very beautiful, if I may be allowed to say so"

"well, I guess Leonardo da Vinci
would not feel threatened
it is really quite amateurish, of course"

                    "not at all — you are mistaken
                    it is a beautiful drawing . . simply because
                    its purpose has been accomplished
                    that purpose being to make something . . clear

                    no one would comprehend that more than da Vinci
                    for, whether your Earthling Leonardo
                    was painting the Mona Lisa . . or the Last Supper
                    or creating one of his own drawings
                    through a multitude of inexplicable, scribbled sketches
                    his purpose was to attempt to make
                    a particular idea or thought form of energy . . clear

                    in actuality, if da Vinci were here
                    or to reverse the phrase — if da Vinci were here
                                                    in actuality
                    he would most certainly agree with me
                    for, how do you know he didn't create this drawing
                                            himself ?"

"how could that possibly be ?"

                    "through you . . you see ?"

"through me ?"

                    "by using your Mind as a channel to express
                    in whatever Temple, far or near
                    in which his individual 'O' currently resides
                    for this was truly the sort of sketch he did best
                    when he was searching for an initial concept
                    to prepare himself to create a painting
                                            of deep beauty and mystery
                    such as Mona Lisa's mysterious smile . . .
                    a lovely secret which you will be taught, in a short while
                    meanwhile, I suspect you have had some help
                    in creating your drawing — in an astral sense — from another"

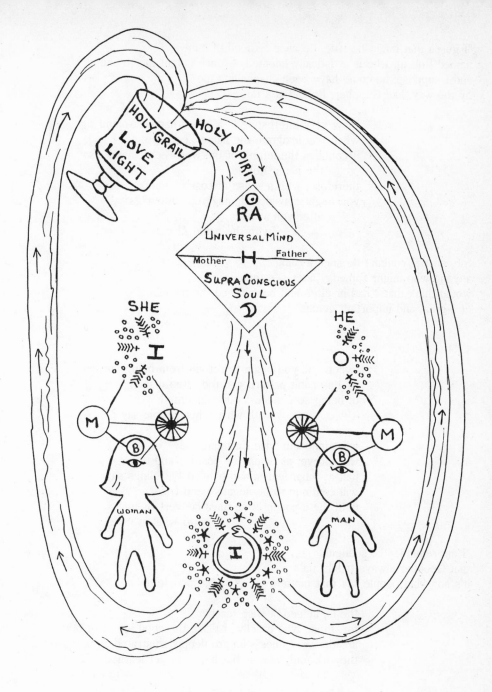

"I guess that might be true, because a friend of mine
named Roland, who is artistically talented — once taught me to sketch
and I suppose, he could have been channelling me . . .
by the way, like Gooober, Roland is a Leo"

      "how very interesting ! a friend named Roland ?
      when you lexigram the name Leonardo
      it contains the letters of the word Leo . . and *also*
           the name Roland
      therefore, with a sense of cosmic humor
      you might consider signing your drawings
           after you awaken
              with the name *Leonardo*"

"oh, no ! I couldn't do such a thing !
anyone who might someday later see them
would think that I had insulted and besmirched the name
of a great and important genius"

      "when will you begin to refrain from being burned
      by this habit pattern you too often display
      of being so unnecessarily concerned
           with what other people say ?

      what innocent-wise Earthlings say
      will forever-and-a-day be positive and true
      just as what fearful and blinded Earthlings say
      will continue to be negative and false
      until the innocent-wise ones convert them
              to what is true"

"I am reminded . . suddenly
that Gooober always taught me
it's not what people *say* that matters . . it's what people *do*"

      "he is, indeed, a wise teacher
      for, those who cruelly criticize the good intent of others
      are the very ones who are deeply frustrated . . because
      they can only *say* — but have not yet learned
              to *do*

      your channeled drawings
      would be understood by da Vinci himself

      for he is intensely aware, I can assure you
      of the glorious importance of a sense of humor
      because a 'sense' of humor . . as da Vinci
      was one of your first Earthlings to perceive
      is the beginning seed of the sense of *balance*

and the sense of *perception*
both of which are, verily . . necessary facets
of artistic conception
                        as well as written expression

therefore, the one who held the pen
and applied it to paper — should recognize the helper
not being overly concerned with the f-act of the matter

for, f-acts are those over-rated fragments
still casting clouds over the Third Eye, here on your Earth . . .
there is a distinct difference between f-actual
                                        and truth
you would be wise to ponder this

I believe it was one of your Earthling actresses
called Ruth Gordon . . she who possessed
                        a truly divine sense of humor
and was a most perceptive
        woman
                        who observed . .

'to get it right, be born with luck
or *make* your own — never give up
a little money helps, but what really gets it right
is to *never* — under any circumstances — face the *facts*'"

"Ruth Gordon, of course !
she starred in the popular cult film, *Harold and Maude*
        one of my favorites
and she was right, because the word 'fact' lexigrams into 'act'
indicating that facts are actors
playing a masked role on the stage of Life
        . . . beyond the fiction of Fact . . . lies Truth ?"

                "also remember that . . .
                eman sih dengis tsitra taerg siht
                        sdrawkcab gnihtyreve etorw dna, you see"

"what did you say ?"

                "I said that da Vinci always signed his name
                and wrote everything else — backwards"

"he wrote backwards ?"

                "sdrawkcab gnihtyreve etorw dna eman sih dengis
                                        eh, sey
                or mirror-reversed, this is true
                and if odranoeL had been taught, as a child

by your present day educational system
he would never have become the great genius and artist
your Earth now recognizes him to have been

for you see . .
       the left and right hemispheres of the brain
should properly function as a harmonious whole . . and
all Avatars and Adepti are, therefore, able to write 'backwards'
with both hands at once, in opposite directions

one should always write communicative language
away from the s-elf . . and never *toward* the s-elf
and this is obviously reversed for left-handed people
whose natural tendency is to write outwards
                              or away from the s-elf
and correctly so
which only appears to be backwards to the right-handed humans
yet is normal and healthy for the left-handed

when a left-handed child is forced to write in the wrong direction
it creates serious problems of introversion to be conquered
just as the same would be created in a right-handed person
who was forced to write backwards — or *toward* the s-elf

some interesting and helpful experiments
relating to the right and left facets of the human conception
have been noted in a book called
                     Drawing on the Right Side of the Brain
by your Earthling author, Betty Edwards . . . .
of course, no book existing on your planet today
contains *all* the amazing actualities concerning this subject . . .
each contains but a part, such as the Edwards observations
which are most enlightening, to be sure
       but . . there is much more to be learned"

"yes, and I want very much to learn it all"

       "you shall . . but for now, let's glance again
       at your last drawing . . . in looking at it, what do you find ?"

"I find one thing which still puzzles me"

       "ask and learn"

"I believe I understand
why I reversed the other initials here
which symbolize the feminine Goddess . . and others
but why did I mirror-reverse . . in my earlier drawings
the initials which represent the Universal Mind
and print them as **M U** — instead of **U M** ?"

"actually, it was unexpectedly perceptive of you
to print those initials, reversed, as **M U**
for, this relates to the lost continent

also known as Lemuria

which was destroyed, through no fault of its own
near the time that Atlantis was inundated
and the 3rd and 4th letters of Lemuria
contained the secret wisdom of that once fair land . . . .

. . . the 3rd and 4th letters of Lemuria
as a matter of actual verity
symbolize, in druid language . . all the wisdom
of that fair and innocent land
that peaceful and gentle . . . Garden of the Gods

this mystery contained
within the secrets of the druidic alphabet
you will very soon be learning . .

and so, the **M U** was the mystery of Lemuria's Innocence
which is why they called the Truth they taught
        by the name of **MANNU**

and also why the Lemurian Priests who spread its **Love**
and the Lemurian Priestesses who spread its **Light**
were called 'Mannus' and 'Mannas'
for reasons you will soon recall . . completely"

"is this why the Ute Indian tribes, in Colorado
called their God-of-Gods by the name of Manitou ?"

"it is — however, an extremely vital
and damaging mistake
has been made, in spelling the word Manitou
with only one 'n' instead of two
for the correct form of power is spelled 'Mannitou'
and the vibrations of the spelling of words
are, relating to numerology, of unrealized importance

you should also be forewarned and informed
that it would be wise, in the future
to always use the capital letter 'O' in the word pOem
as well as in the words pOet and pOetry

and there is another truth you should know
the name of the town you so love, called Cripple Creek
is the very cause of all its past and present troubles
for this name, as you are well aware
does vibrate with all the negative thought forms

Canto Twenty ☆ 999

of lust and greed . . and bleak despair
and only by changing its name
may this area regain its rightful glory of long ago

for the gold which is buried there
has deeper mystery and meaning than is presently suspected
and the time is swiftly approaching
when the essence of Fool's Gold will engage in conflict
once more . . in this area
with the mystical and powerful *alchemy meaning*
of **Gold**
and its citizens must make a choice
of far-reaching and momentous importance
concerning all this"

"oh, Heathcliffe, you surely must know

that such a decision on the part of those City Fathers
would nearly take a force as strong as an earthquake"

"perhaps **RA** will see that this does occur"

"you surely can't mean
that an earthquake is destined or ordained
for my flying mountains !"

"I speak not of a Nature cataclysm
for the land which lies in the benevolent shadow
of the Sangre de Cristo mountain range
will be among those areas which shall offer haven
should other parts of your planet
need to be more severely awakened

I speak, instead of an earthquake of Love and Light
in the hearts of — not those City Fathers
but first in the hearts of those City Mothers
who are even now beginning to see the Light
and to inwardly know
how to lead the men they love out of the woods
where they have so long been lost
in hunting and killing . . and dissipation
for it is the feminine 'I' in each woman there
who will teach gently . . all the children
along with the City Fathers
how one may wisely open the Third Eye"

"now *that* would be a miracle
truly — to end all miracles, I do believe"

"truly believe — and it shall be
have Faith, not hope — and you will see
that each citizen there will very soon

1000   ☆   Canto Twenty

"Heath, you have made me remember the strangest thing . . .
when I once said, in frustration, to Gooober
in our little crooked house, in Colorado . . . 'oh, Goob !
what in the world are we *doing* here ?'
   he answered me
in what was, I thought, a very negative way
for he simply said, with that faint smile of his

'waiting for the cataclysms' . . then came over
kissed me on the nose, and said 'magic !'
and this has always . . somehow, greatly troubled me"

        "your Higher S-elf can sometimes be — quite dense
        for your teacher was not referring
        to a Nature earthquake
        as he tried to show you when he said 'magic !'
        he was, not wishing, but ordaining
        through the power of the 'O' of his Higher S-elf
        an earthquake of Love and Light
        in all hearts there — and just as a Nature quake
               opens up the ground
        so will such a Human Nature quake
        open up the long sealed shut Third Eyes of the people"

"yes, I have been quite blind
to have, for all this time, believed
that Gooober would be guilty of imaging
such a negative thought form
oh, I miss him so . .   when when will he return ?"

        "there are two more lessons you must learn
        before you can expect your teacher's return
        and of course, you must also complete
        Part One of your Happiness pOem . . as you know

        the first lesson you must learn
            is another fragment of Truth"

"what is this last Truth I must see ?"

        "not the last — only one of the last, for the present
        and this concerns a release"

"a release ?   I don't understand"

        "within the Body Temple of the Carousel Bill
        you loved before . . and a part of whom
        you recognized and knew
        when your teacher's eyes of silvery-wise

first gazed on you . . .
. . . within this Temple
of the Carousel Bill . . he entertained strangers

let us say, visitors . . who were not all friendly
and one of these unfriendly visitors
persuaded the Mind connected to this Body Temple
to be, at times, weak — and to hurt
and finally, tragically, to drown in a vodka ocean

this visiting entity was *a piece* of another O's Soul
            not yet evolved into wisdom
as was the true Owner of that former Temple . . . . called Bill
and you did call that unfriendly visiting stranger back
                        once more

into the present Temple you love . . . as Goober
it's Owner-Overself 'O' being the same
as the one your recognized and knew — the one
            who so wanted to heal
but who was prevented from healing, in the former Temple
by this very visiting stranger you once more recalled"

"I called back — I recalled, into Gooober's Temple
this very same unfriendly entity
      who visited the him-of-him before ?
oh ! how could I ever have done such a thing ?"

            "by your old dreams — through remembering
            and re-living all your old fears . . from earlier years
            which once before fed and activated
                        and motivated this visitor — or Soul piece
            and did not help it evolve — even then
            when it was a guest in that former Temple of the Carousel Bill
            for it truly did not belong there
            but you encouraged this stranger to remain
            by feeding it with your fearing of the shadows of fears"

"it did not belong there ?"

            "no, it did not — nor does it belong in the present Temple
            guided by the wise 'O' you call Gooober
            the same Higher Overself as before . . who still desires
                                    to heal
            this stranger-entity . . . . or Soul piece
            needs a different kind of Body Temple
            in which to continue growing toward eventual Light
            this lower-evolved piece of another Soul
            during a Saturn-Seven-cycle
            formerly wandered into the wrong house, so to speak

1002 ☆ Canto Twenty

and in this new Temple of the familiar one
you loved, and lost, then found again
that entity *again* became an unwelcome guest, you see
preventing the same wise Overself-Owner

once more . . from healing
and even more importantly
standing as a wall . . between your sacred Oneness"

"oh, Heathcliffe ! what can I do ?
what can I do about this visiting stranger
I recalled unknowingly into Gooober's Temple ?"

"this visiting stranger no longer resides there"

"what do you mean ?"

"this new Body Temple of the one you have always loved
who was — and is — verily, your own Twin S-elf
is made from a finer etheric substance
than that from which his former Temple was fashioned
his present flesh body — its cells and genes
having been directly inherited
from what has been termed the House of David

or the Body Temple of David
although . .

there are many other Overself 'O's also
presently manifesting in bodies likewise inherited from David
due to the need for more Temples
or bodies of finer etheric substance

during this Aquarian Age

so that healing may be swiftly demonstrated
and age-reversal . . cell regeneration . . and other miracles
this is why there are multiple bodies on Earth today
descended — quite literally
and in actual verity — from the House of David

from that finer Temple
and the one you love
who is an eternally inseparable part of your own S-elf
presently resides in such a Body Temple
therefore, could not long entertain such an entity
so foreign to his own inner nature

and of necessity — did cast out that visiting stranger
from his flesh Temple . . some time ago
for its presence was causing him
to become mentally, emotionally . . and physically ill
and dangerously close

to becoming spiritually ill as well"

"you mean . . a fallen angel ?"

Canto Twenty ☆ 1003

"I do — and his own 'O' then so ordained
that this entity be cast out during his recent Saturn-Seven-cycle
which created much physical pain . . emotional suffering
and mental anguish . . in the process"

"oh, I am so sorry, so sorry
will he ever forgive me
for all the pain and suffering I've unthinkingly caused him ?"

"need you ask this ?   *he* — who taught forgiveness to *you* ?"

"yes, I know . . . within myself, I know
he has already forgiven me
but — where did this poor, lost entity go ?
where is this visiting stranger now ?"

"because the one you love does not control the All
but only his own powers, which are great — but not All
he had no control over the New Temple
the entity he cast out might then choose . . . therefore
that visiting stranger logically sought — and found
a similar, nearly identical Temple
as the one from which the exodus was made"

"and . . this 'double' or look-alike
then came to me, falsely — as Gooober himself ?"

"yes — for what you should, by now, recognize
as reasons related to the Universal Law of magnetic attraction
this could not be avoided, due to Free Will
but also, this occured for other temporal, complex causes
of conspiracy, among humans, on a political level
related to Gooober's trip on a ship
those who believed they were movers in the chess game
they played, regarding your relationship
but who were, in reality, only **RA's** pawns, you see "

"what you are saying
is not yet completely clear to me"

"the one you love, after casting out this Soul piece
which then entered, at a Saturn-Seven-cycle
another Temple of nearly identical appearance . . .
     was unable to then control
what occured . . because of the Free Will
of the Owner-Overself of the new Temple chosen
by the cast out visiting stranger or Soul piece

for, in this new Temple
that lost and wandering piece of another Soul
     found itself to *also* not be at home or welcome

and in frustrated anger
did subtly incite the 'O' of this new Temple
so similar in appearance to Gooober
to become once more entangled in your Karma
and that of the one you love
by becoming an actor on the stage of the drama
of your relationship

in ways which are too complex, on both a spiritual
and a temporal level
to explain at present"

"it is . . becoming more clear"

"then continue to listen — and truly *hear*
so that you may grow to know
the terrible destiny of travail which was nearly
not avoided"

" . . *he that repeateth a matter*
separateth very friends . . "

"did you make a comment ?"

"no, I was just . . remembering something . . from the Bible"

"and since that lost stranger entity piece of Soul
is no more at home where it presently resides
than it was in the previous two Temples
it therefore . . needs to be released
even from its present residence"

"Heathcliffe, I knew
it was a different man . . I knew, I truly did !
and is Gooober, then, proud of me
for this knowing ?"

"of course . . for it shows how swiftly
you are now growing
would you not be equally proud of him
if *he* passed the same test of Love's identity
involving *you* ?"

"involving . . *me ?*
oh, yes, I would . . because . . what did you say ?
INVOLVING ME ?
are you trying to say
that an identical Body Temple to my own
was sent to *him* . . as some sort of a karmic test ?
since he has been away ?
is *that* what you are trying to say ?"

Canto Twenty ☆ 1005

"I believe this is a truth which should be confirmed
or denied — as the case may be
by your own Twin S-elf . . and not by me"

"if such a terrible, terrible thing happened
he just **BETTER** have passed his test too !
oh ! he just **BETTER** have passed it, do you hear ?"

"I beg your pardon ? did you speak ?"

"I said . . he . . I mean . . well, that is . . "

"did you say something ?"

"what I meant to say is . . well
if such a terrible temptation came also to Gooober
I *know* he would have passed his karmic test
just as I passed my own . . wouldn't he ?"

"are you asking me a question ?"

"NO ! I am not asking you
I am *telling* you — that I *know* this is true
Gooober would have passed his test too
the same as I"

"but of course ! you are Twins in your strengths
as well as in your weaknesses
such as . . your momentary doubting just now
your briefly wavering candleglow of Faith
in the voice of your own 'I'

he has experienced moments
of similar torment . . and testing from his Higher 'O'
he has lived through . . . his own Gethsemane
and you must not ever forget this . . again"

"I won't — oh, I *promise* I won't !"

"now that the one you love is free
of this uninvited-by-him visiting entity
if that entity could be now *released*
from its *present* Temple
to continue on its own path toward soul evolvement
the man you love would then be free
as he has never been free before

for, even in its present Body Temple
so startlingly similar to the Temple of Gooober himself
this visitor is still lost, confused . . and not at home

and there is always the danger . . that this stranger
may once again attempt to enter
the Body Temple of the one you love
during Gooober's *next* Saturn-Seven-cycle period

  for, negative events which have once
                          been set into motion

          sometimes continue their reflections
          repeatedly . . . like ripples in a stream"

"and all this was originally created . . or caused . . by me ?"

          "by your confusing of a negative thought form
                          with a true dream
          for, they were not real dreams, in any actual sense
          but merely *Night Mare* dreams of no substance

          and the difference between Night Mare dreams of un-reality
          seeded by the subtle and sinister Unicorn
          with its phallic symbol horn of the deceptive Uni-sex
          and the singing dreams of inspiration and true prophecy
          borne to the Soul upon the wings of Pegesus
                          falsely spelled as Pegasus

          may always be detected quite simply, you see
          by the negative quality of the former
          and the joyful positive quality of the latter"

"then people should neither fear — nor repeat to others
their 'bad dreams' — ever
for these are not actually or truly shadows of events to come ?"

          "only if they insist upon clinging to them
          concentrating upon them — and telling them to others
                  then they will surely come true
          for, that which one fears — and believes
          whether good or evil, false or true
                          will absolutely manifest — in Time

          if one fears, therefore believes in — a bad dream
          one will set into tragic eternal motion
          all of its dark shadows . . like the repeated
          and ever larger circles in a quiet stream
          as has already been stated

          and the false reality of such thought forms, then
          will eventually grow into giants of actuality
          within the material world of matter
          this clearly demonstrated by the Unicorn
          whose mystery Earthlings remain unable to fathom

for, the Unicorn is a powerful force for deception
in that dark world of sleep . . . called the nether regions

you will be taught and given more proof
at the allotted time
of the intent . . and history of the clever Unicorn
suffice it for the present to say
that you must never spell the name of 'Pegesus'
        with an 'a', as in the false Pegasus

for this lie too, has been seeded through
woman's Earthling consciousness, coiling itself
around the still-sleeping mind
in order to make impotent the glorious powers
of this winged creature, Pegesus — designed by **RA**
to cause the Spirit to awaken to its mission
and this black magic may be invisibly implemented
through the deep mystery of the druidic alphabet
as you already know . . to a great degree
                        but must still learn more

as for now . . you must recognize
that, when your teacher known as Gooober
told you that your dreams of spring are the true reality
he meant only those dreams of Spring's soft sunlight
            and happy prophecy
not the nightmare dreams of darkness
which are as false as false can be
and may only be translated into realtiy
through the powerful negative Act of Faith, called Fear

confusing these nightmares
with the dreams of true reality
is symbolized by the present and deliberate confusion
between the Unicorn and the rescuing Pegesus
through the subtle numerological distortion
of changing one simple letter of the alphabet
and transforming this winged spirit of awakening
                        into Pegasus, you see"

"is the true identity and origin
of the word 'nightmare', then — the Unicorn ?"

"verily, verily, it is — this is true, without equivocation
the Unicorn's true name is the Night Mare

over this twilight world, he reigns supreme
and is often painted or depicted near a sleeping maiden
who embraces him, in her innocence . . and ignorance

for the Unicorn's midnight mission has ever been

to lull . . and to keep . . each feminine 'I' asleep
and unaware . . . unawakened
to the glory of her true destiny and hidden powers

wears he, the Unicorn, always . . garlands of flowers
around his neck . . but these have no fragrance
and are worn but to disguise his true intent
to attact and seduce the sensitive Soul of Woman
into his hypnotic, mesmerizing twilight world
                                        of Soul-sleep

it is karmically and obviously appropriate
that the Unicorn is seen today upon your planet Earth
everywhere one goes . . in paintings, posters
calendars . . books, sculptures — and so forth
depicted in tender pastel colors . . of ethereal beauty

like swiftly multiplying cells or baobob seeds
are these sly and deceptive images of the Unicorn
rising forth to oppose the explosion of new freedom
which calls to all feminine 'I' sleeping goddesses
to awaken !   and come forth unto their unsuspected powers"

"how upsetting this will be to all those people
who love and collect all kinds of Unicorn images
when they learn of it . . they cannot but be greatly disappointed"

"nevertheless, the hidden purpose of the Unicorn will ever be
that which Set has so decreed
            . . . to drug the feminine Soul with flowers
                                        and gentle mystery
so that the feminine Third Eye awakens not
in either sex — but remains asleep in both men and women

how strange that the present feminine Individuality
gives so little serious thought to those subtle messages
when it is the Unicorn who keeps locked
that very door to her own S-elf's karmic memory
of the true design of this creature . .
which is to continually discourage her from seeking
the path which will lead her into the Light
to take her rightful place beside her Twin 'O' S-elf
that they may, together, recover their lost POwers
                                        as god and goddess"

"and by my own past Unicorn Night Mares
which I mistakenly believed to be true dreams
I have caused all this hurt and pain to Gooober ?"

"and also — when he bore the name of the Carousel Bill
for, when you called forth this visiting stranger to dwell

within these two separate Temples of your Twin
you created for each a living hell
causing each to project an essence which was not
what it did seem . . . in each Temple's aura
this, yes, even so — caused by your old Night Mare dream
of loss . . and *imagined* infidelity

but now, as stated, that this entity has been cast out
and has entered a new Temple, where it still does not belong
you may only right this wrong
by releasing this stranger . . this visitor
which has, as you know, become magnetically
                                    attracted to you".

"and if I do . . release this entity
from its present Temple — where it also does not belong
will I, then, someday meet and again know this double
the nearly-but-not-really similar 'O'
of the similar Body Temple to the man I truly love ?
I am not certain that I would harmonize with him in any friendship sense"

         "this is an answer only Time itself can give to you
         but know that — if such a meeting did occur
         and that visiting, lost piece of Soul had been released
         you would quite likely feel nothing but warm friendship
         and compassion . . . for the 'O' or Overself
         of the Temple which has caused you in the past, such pain
         for this man is not an evil human . . . and as you know
         not responsible himself for what has transpired"

" . . *seeing the root of the matter*
is to be found in me . . . "

         "did I hear you speaking ?"

". . I was remembering something
from the Bible again . . Heathcliffe, please tell me

if I now bring about this release from the Body Temple
of Gooober's double . . look-alike . . or astral twin
is it too late . . too late for our love to be re-born ?"

         "it is not too late — for you have seen
         the glowing of the knowing in each other's eyes
                     of silvery-wise

         you have shared the memories of a long-ago Past
         through the burning of your Eternity ember
         and it would be well to also realize
         that the man you love, your own Twin S-elf
             was not completely blameless

when he allowed this visitor to once more enter
his present Temple, at your call
urged on by the sadness of your old false dreams

no, it is not too late
for the silvery-blue cord between you still beams
and connects your hearts with an invisible cord
             which will guide him back to you
so that you may join together . . and teach all Earthlings
the great healing power of Love and Light"

"is this related to a musical chord ?"

             "you will learn more of this at a future time"

"it is done, Heathcliffe . . oh, it is done !
why did I not release this visitor long before
in even that former Temple of the him-of-him I love ?
 . . . the Carousel Bill . . .
why did I condemn the healing mission
and the sacred goal . . of the Mind and Soul
of my own Twin . . to such a fate
and cause him to be forced to wait . . so long ?
I was so wrong, so wrong !
yes, Heath, I shall release all my old false Unicorn Night Mare dreams
and trade them for the true dream of the Reality of our Oneness"

"GREAT IS TRUTH, AND MIGHTY ABOVE ALL THINGS"

"so you know . . . . .

I suppose I expected that you would know
through telepathy — and you are right
there is one important truth I have not yet told Gooober
but I shall do so when I next see him
and telling him this very painful . . . truth
will somehow, I know . . help us both to grow"

             "*though your sins be as scarlet*
             they shall be made as white as snow

             your Spirit . . and the Spirit of your Twin S-elf
                                    are now flying . . . .
             flying toward a Door of Knowing
                  which shall soon open
             upon such Light as you have not yet dreamed

             a Light which will bathe you both
             in all the wisdom and illumination you knew before

when you were god and goddess
and you will be given great pOwers once more

as will, soon — all Earthlings"

"but how will such glory come to be
in addition to the opening of each person's Third Eye ?
there must be other methods also
for such a shining goal as you have described"

"in order to step through that Door of Knowing
into the angelic realms of Light
it is only necessary, after the Third Eye has opened
to raise or to lift one's own vibrations"

"and how may one accomplish such a lifting ?"

"the Law of existence is that all humans, all things
must abide within the vibrational sphere
of their individual development"

"I still don't quite understand"

"to raise one's own vibrations
a man or woman must lift up . . must step into
the higher vibrational level
of his or her own thought forms of energy
and this process . . continually lifts one higher
. . and always higher"

"but is this Ascension process possible
while man and woman still reside within a flesh Body Temple ?"

"yes, quite possible — for in actuality, you see
one may become thus exalted more swiftly and completely
when clothed in flesh, than through any other condition

if man and woman learn to levitate or lift the flesh
in exaltation . . into a spiritual texture
then they may fly through that Door of Knowing
into Love and Light and Wisdom . . without needing to die"

"now there is a warning to give
before you leave the wakefulness of your sleep
and return into the sleep of your wakefulness again
in the material world of matter . . . "

"a warning ?   what kind of warning ?"

"as has already been stated . . your Spirit is flying
as is the Spirit of Gooober

toward that Door of Knowing and Wisdom's Light
as will, soon — all Earthling Twin S-elves

yet, outside that Door,
        before its threshold may be crossed
lies the fearful, lonely emptiness
                of death, despair and darkness

the darkness of eternal night
luring and soft-seducing the Mind and Soul
back into the swirling, muddy waters of negative doubt
    . . . . before one may pass through that Door
into the brilliant Sunrise waiting on the other side
it is necessary to pass through David's *Valley of the Shadow*
        to pass the reverse-mirror test of darkness
which can magnetize one back into the false reflection
                        of life's mirrored images"

"oh, Heath, you sound as though — by such a Doorway
you're speaking of the flesh body's death . . and then
some ethereal resurrection . . . .
I do not believe in such misty nothingness
yet, I am somehow chilled and frightened by your words"

            "you see how magnetically seductive
            such darkness is ? already you are doubting
            and fearing shadows of fears . .

            no, I meant not what you are thinking
            but verily, its shining opposite polarity
                        of Immortality
            in the same flesh Body Temple in which
                                you now reside

            I did not refer to a departure from this Earth
            into some misty ethereal Space and Time
            I meant the mystery of becoming actually immortal
            and continuing your work here, on this planet
            for as many years — centuries
            or millenniums . . as you and your Twin may wish
            in innocence and wisdom, Love and Light
            with nothing changed — no loss of conscious awareness
            and no . . as you call it . . spooky mystical
                        or religious state of beingness

            you will, I assure you . . both leave and return
            with many of your same present flaws
            of personality, needing to be mended . . still flesh
                        still the you-of-you
            with no one knowing even that you have left briefly
            much less returned — unless you, your S-elf

should so choose to speak of it . . . . . "

"then . . what did you mean . . what was the vibration
I was picking up . . from your words
which so alarmed me ?"

"it will be sufficient for the present
to simply caution you to remember — to not forget
that, in the microcosm *human* nature
                exactly as in the Macrocosm Nature
it is so ordained . . *that it is always the darkest*
                                before the dawn"

the dar . . .

. . kest

*

            hour is . . ?

    be
        fore
            the ?
                d

                a
                w . .
                    n ?

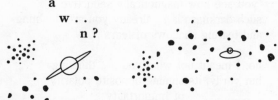

. . . . . as I slowly drifted and floated back through the stars
into conscious awareness . . . . . Heathcliffe was still staring at me

        but now only a make-believe sheepdog
        no longer playing astral leap-frog
                as he had in my hypnotic sleep-fog

just peeking at me
through his wiggley strands of paper hair
with his little beady eyes . . of wistful lonely

        no longer burning and glowing
        with knowing . . no longer silvery-wise

            but making me understand, at last, Gooober's words
                he wrote in his note, so long ago

    that love . . . is not always doing what brings pleasure
        love is also doing what is good for someone
        whatever the cost, at the moment

sometimes, it's leaving . . for awhile
and the love is shown, then, in the pain given

for pain is a lesson
            best learned
from the one who loves you the most

* * * * * *

. . . then I gathered up all his old letters
the ones written by the Bill from Carousel . . all of them . . each one
and made a fire of Heaven, not hell

            I placed them in the flames, the letters
            gently, tenderly . . as I had kissed Raggy and Algae
                        when I healed them
. . and kissed each letter
            and whispered goodbye, with my heart
while tears streaked down
            the cheeks of my soul

                        . . releasing them into the purifying fire

releasing too . . . that part of the him-of-him
and the you-of-you . . that lost entity who . . needed to go on
to climb higher . . in another Temple

            and watched the fire
turn from red to blue
                        in smoldering embers . . then die
    goodbye . . goodbye

                        Jesus, it is finished

please send Gooober back home to me
his Soul, my Twin . . now free

            then came a crash of thunder . . a streak of lightning
            zig-zagged through the pink sky of early dawn

. . and the rain poured down
in great cleansing splashes . . soaking the ground outside

    and beating against the window panes

RA's own tear drops . . and Hers ♪
        ♪   ♪
  ♪   ♪   God weeping with me
                              ♪
                    ♪

and crying too . . for you

yes . . God's own

te

a

r

dr

o

p

s

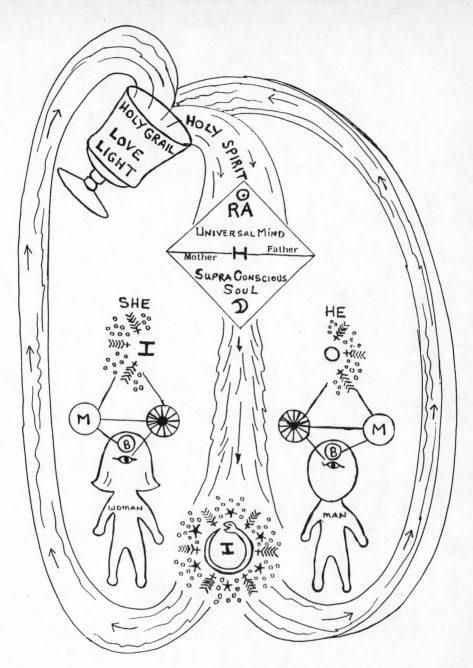

The meaning of this riddled life ?
 That we find
 where power to cause
 is very substance
 and every moment, consummation !
The way ?
 The way is theirs for whom love leads
 their reason will and senses
 into every action,
 whose adjutant selves stand fast in this.

Kyril Demys (Musaios)
Wings of Myrahi

<u>Wire Sent Through Our Easter Union</u>

FROM: Me . . New York, N.Y.   **TO:** You
         Zip Code: Loneliness 00000   somewhere . . out there
                                        on your predestined Star Quest

oh, Gooober, Gooober, Gooober
I just heard from Ruth, who rhymes with Truth
that our dear, gentle Peace is not missing us anymore
she grew tired of waiting for us to return and love her again

          and she . . went away

Ruth said Blueberry Love always stays close to home
which is unusual for a male
Love never goes more than a few yards away from the house
even when he runs outside to play

          but Pumpkin Peace . . she said
          has been wandering further and further away
          each day . . until finally
          they couldn't find her for nearly a week

          and when she did, at last, come back
          she was quiet and sad . . and refused to eat
          even her favorite kitty-tuna . . Ruth said

she just lay there, forlorn and still, in Emilie's antique cradle
not even chasing rainbows . . her favorite game

          and yesterday morning, Gooober . . they found her
                                        dead

she had . . just died

          we did it to her, you know we did !
          she died of a broken heart
          oh, Goob, if you knew . . I know you would cry

as hard as I am, right now

          how could we have allowed our gentle Pumpkin Peace . . to die ?

1020   ☆   Canto Twenty One

Magic Mirror on the Wall

Gooober, guess what, guess what ? oh ! you'll never guess !
not in a trillion centuries could you guess what happened

it's been 8 years since that grey February day
when I watched you drive away
                              eight years . . seems like eighty

and I've been having this dream lately
more than a few times . . maybe as many as seven

   in my dream, you keep telling me that you can't come home
until I miraclize Emilie's head back together again . . then you whisper
                                                          "magic !"
      . . kiss me on the tip of the nose

and I wake up suddenly, each time
feeling your kiss on my nose, as real as real can be

"oh, you know I can't do such an impossible thing
as to miraclize her head back together again !"
I say aloud, in frustration, every time I awaken from the dream

then wonder how you can be so cruel . . .
you must know how hard I tried to glue the pieces back together
and cried . . because of the unforgivable thing I did
                              . . to smash her head on the kitchen floor

they just wouldn't fit, the pieces
and I had to throw them all away . . as I wrote to you
a few years ago . . in one of the letters
I had to mail in the hollow of an oak tree, at midnight
and trust the druids to deliver for me

finally I decided that my recurrent dream
was not a dream at all . . but a Unicorn-seeded Night Mare

    . . . and lately . . for no particular reason
I've been thinking about what we called our honeymoon weekend

     that time . . in Laguna Beach

that weekend we drove there from our magic room at the Roosevelt
in Los Angeles . . through all the hot and muggy-smoggy
                              Freeway traffic
because you wanted to see, with me
that spot on the lonely Laguna Beach

    where I felt the pain in my tooth

Canto Twenty One   ☆   1021

at the same time you felt yours . . as I watched on the horizon
your ship . . *The Atlantis*
                              sailing by
. . its white sails
like some giant snow-bird
                    against the clouding sky

you wanted to walk along that shore with me
because you believed my mystical experiences there . . were so important to Us
but the Dolphin Suite was already rented
                    and we couldn't stay there

so we went, instead, to the Hotel Laguna
on a different beach
                              a mile or so north
                                    of the toothache shore
        that was the weekend
Emilie first came to live with us

you bought her for me from that enchanted druid, named Gladys
whose teeny-tiny shop called Les Gamins
                              is across the street from our honeymoon hotel
yes, Gladys is a secret druid
and very magical . . she didn't want to let you buy Emilie, at first
because she loved her so much . . herself

and when we asked where Emilie came from . . she told us
about the strange lady, with snow-white hair
who was about twelve years old, in the Oober faith
but in illusionary Earth time, maybe about eighty five . . so very young !

        she brought Emilie into her small shop one morning
        and said this was a doll she had received for Christmas
        nearly three-quarters of-a-century ago . . and loved very much
        but since she was moving soon . . she wasn't sure when
        she couldn't take all her sentimental keepsakes with her . . and so
            she sold Emilie to Gladys

it was only after we both coaxed her . . that she relented
and decided to allow you to buy Emilie . . for me
because, after all, we were still strangers then
though we've grown close, Gladys and I, these past six years
and she often says she wishes she had not sold, but *given* Emilie to us
. . . but she has since given me so many gifts of love

we took Emilie back to the hotel, with us
and do you remember the funny stares from the desk clerk
when we carried her on the elevator ? how we giggled
because he seemed so uncertain
whether or not to charge us the 'family rate' for our room ?

Emilie . . looked so real wrapped in a blanket

the memories of that Laguna weekend
have been wisping in and out of my mind so often lately
I decided to fly there . . to Laguna Beach
for just a few days, by myself
                                    and walk along the beach alone
where we once walked together

              thinking that, maybe it might make me feel
              in some way . . closer to you

and of course I popped in to say hello to Gladys
whose face, all wreathed in crinkly-elf smiles and sparkles of joy
                                    as always
made me think of a beautiful painting
of long ago . .
                    we bear-hugged each other, as usual
                    not mentioning right away, the forbidden subject . . of you

then suddenly, I glanced up . . and looked into the mirror
of Gladys' teeny-tiny druid shop
                                    oh, magic mirror on the wall !

for there in the mirror was reflected . . a remembered image . . of Emilie
so real, she looked . . . . in the mirror
but I knew it was merely a mirage I was seeing
and blinked away my tears . . then turned my head to glance back
just to be certain my hallucination had disappeared . . as all mirages do

and it had . . for when I glanced back into the mirror again
              Emilie was no longer there
the familiar features of her haunted, haunting face
                    had been only . . a lonely mirage of longing

and all I now saw reflected there, in the mirror on the wall
was a colorful rainbow . . of bathing suits, scarves and blouses
as the vision of Emilie
                    softly faded away

Gladys saw my tears, and asked me, tenderly, why I was so sad
her kind-soft-grey-blue eyes filled with understanding and compassion

"oh, Gladys, I truly believed I saw
there in the mirror, on the wall . . Emilie herself
reaching her heart out to me once more, through her sad, brown eyes
and her image was so very real
I fear I'm losing control over all reality
because, for just that brief moment
it was as though yesterday had chorded back into rhyme
and I heard the melody of a song . . without words

which has haunted me . . for the longest time
                    a kind of forgotten melody
it was so very strange
        like Alice-through-the-looking glass, you know ?"

    and Gladys nodded, smiling . . for she knew
    oh, yes, she knew all about Alice stepping through the looking glass
    back into Wonderland . . because she is a toy chest of faerie tales herself
    this adorable elfin creature, Gladys

            . . she nodded, then came over
                    kissed me on the tip of the nose

        and said . . "will you watch the store for me ?
        I have an errand that won't wait . . it must be done right away
        but I'll only be a few minutes"

then she was gone . . to the bank, I supposed
disappearing as quickly, it seemed . . as Emilie's mirror-mirage

        and I walked back and forth, between the browsing customers
        of her teeny-tiny Gamin shop . . pacing . . in a numbing trance

hardly aware . . of the babbling bubble of people confusion

            inside . . or outside
        on the sidewalk . . passing by

as I tried not to cry . . because I was genuinely afraid
that my mind had become so clouded with sadness
that it was no longer as sound and stable as before . . because
how could Emilie's features . . her faintly smiling face
        have been so **real** to my physical vision ?
when her face had clearly existed only in the mirror of my dreams
imaged back through the mirror on the wall
yes, only in my imagination had Emilie been there

        I had only imagined her face
        and such misty images should not appear so *physcially real*
                to the sane and stable mind
        or how could one ever determine reality from make-believe ?

then I looked up . .

        to see Gladys come floating back in through the door
        her long skirts swirling and billowing around her ankles
        the golden chains around her neck
                        . . . tinkling like little chimes
        her soft dark hair
            smelling like a fresh ocean breeze

her eyes . . dancing with tiny sparkles of joy

as she reached out her arms to me, smiling her Gladys-gamin-grin
to give me something she held, wrapped in a blanket

it was . . oh, Goob, it was . . *Emilie !*

Emilie, Emilie, Emilie !

not just an imitation, or a similar doll . . no ! it was truly Emilie
an identical Body Temple — no duplication or look-alike
with every eyelash identical, and the very same . . *the very same*
long, lacy-white dress
the same long, shining
chestnut hair

the same strange, sad brown eyes

the same pink mouth
and the same inscrutable smile

"Gladys, Gladys" I cried "am I dreaming ? this can't be real !
oh, I must, I simply must be dreaming
for how could this possibly be ?
Emilie is dead — she can't have returned this way
with each molecule of face and body intact
she can't have returned into material substance
from out of the ethers . . from out of . . . the nowhere
what does this mean ? is this a dream ? am I hallucinating ?"

"no, you are, believe me, not dreaming, and quite sane
just this once
why not allow joy to replace your pain ?

you see, miracles do happen . . and dreams come true
when you really want them to
after all, aren't these the very magics you told me
Gooober always taught to you ?
and also what you keep trying to teach to others ?

so why should you be so amazed and surprised
that what you see with your own eyes . .
what you know and believe to be true
really *is* true ?"

"but, how on Earth . . . I mean
how in the world could such magic possibly be ?"

"you mean, how did it manifest itself
on a material level ? what was the Earth channel
for the miracle ?

Canto Twenty One   ☆   1025

well, one day . . a few months ago
the same strange lady, with the snow-white hair
stopped in my shop, carrying a bundle, in a shopping bag
she unwrapped the bundle
                              and there was Emilie herself !
I admit that, at first
I was every bit as shocked as you are now

               because I could also see
               that this was was not just a similar doll, or a look-alike
               but absolutely Emilie — totally identical

then she told me the faerie tale — at least, it was to me
she told me that she has an identical twin sister
and on that snowy Christmas morning
                         nearly-three-quarters-of-a-century-ago
she and her identical twin sister
each received, from Santa's elves . . identical twin dolls
and she said she still remembered seeing them
sitting there, beneath the Christmas tree
                              . . lit with candles
and the excitement they both felt
as she and her sister danced up and down, with joy

and now that she's finally making the move to Oregon
to live with her twin sister, who has a larger home
they both decided, by telephone, the previous week
that there was no reason they should keep
just one of the twin dolls
     so, her sister asked her to sell this one for her
and she thought perhaps I would like to have it too
of course I said yes . . and bought it quickly
. . then wondered how to get in touch with you

and this morning, here you were !
               popping your head, unexpectedly, in my door
you must have received some sort of telepathic message"

"oh, I did, I did !"

then we bear-hugged, and elf-danced, gamin-druid-Gladys and I
and later . . we had dinner together

               afterwards . . that night, before I went to sleep
               in our old, comforting, memory-filled honeymoon room

Emilie and I took a walk along the shore
   it wasn't quite so lonely anymore . . then each of us
                         made one wish on a far-away star
and somehow, I knew . .
               that Emilie's wish was the same as mine

the next afternoon, which was the day-before-yesterday
Emilie and I flew back to New York together

      and she's sitting here now, next to Heathcliffe

with the same long, shining chestnut hair
the same strange, sad brown eyes . . the same pink mouth

    and the same inscrutable smile

now she has a head again
she has miraclized into beingness
    as whole as before

          but she still sits silently
          and doesn't say a word

Forgotten Melody

that song keeps coming back . . then leaving again
the melody fragment I always heard . . but later forgot
when Jerry Jones smiled at me
         then later . . at Aunt Maud's
        in the backyard . . that bee-buzzing time

when Charles Hollingswell . . handed me those wilted daisies

and sometimes the song I can't remember
yet still can't seem to forget
gets mixed up in my mind . . with the Happiness POem
    I keep trying to write
then tear up . . and begin all over again

    maybe I'll never write it . . maybe my Happiness POem called Gooberz
    is only a dream itself
          like the forgotten melody
           that song . . without words
I know my song isn't real

it's just a memory fragment

    but if it isn't real
    then why do these chords

keep pounding in my head ?

why do I keep hearing my forgotten melody
as though it has some power of its own
                           some mystical mystery
contained within its musical scale ?

        song without words . . pOem without rhyme

from a long-forgotten time
in a far-away place my heart once knew

        maybe I'll take the pieces out of the wastebasket now
        the torn, discarded pages of my Happiness POem
        tape them back together . . and start all over again

because I seem to somehow . . . know
that, only after I've learned to make sadness rhyme with gladness
only after I've recalled the alchemy of making Life rhyme
will I be able, at last . . to remember all the healing crescendos

        of that music from another place . . . another time

        my song without words . . haunting melody of mystery
        which will chord the sleeping déjà vu recall

of all gods and goddesses . . reminding them musically
of their forgotten POwers

so that they may then turn this . . . *their Earth . . their world*
all green and fresh and new again
                           by calling back their memories

of the secret magic of Sunrise
and the unguessed mystery of Spring

Playing Post Office Again

I wrote a love letter this morning to another man

at least *he* has a proper address
and I didn't have to mail my letter in a hollow tree, at midnight
I dropped it into a mailbox, in the daylight, at noon
as one does, when one writes to a real human being . . not a ghost

Mr. Ralph Nader
Knight-in-Shining-Armour
c/o the Round Table
Washington, D. C. — America

Dear Mr. Nader,

I love you

I would vote for you as Sheriff or Dog Catcher
because I know you would be kind and fair to both people and animals
            when they were temporarily goofing up
I would also vote for you as Mayor or Governor or Congressman
or Senator or Pope or President . . especially President

I like the way you gallop around on your snowy white steed
warning General Motors to fasten their safety belts
scaring the insecticide out of the farmers
scaring Agent Orange out of the Pandora's Box, where it still hides
scaring the carbonic acid out of the soda pop people
scaring the worms out of the hot dog people
and scaring the hell out of businessmen in general

most of all, I like the way you relate to girls and women
      the ones who flutter their lashes at you
when you're rapping with Earthlings in public auditoriums

            you never even wink back

I guess you have more urgent things to do
more important plans in mind — for willing women
than a quick tumble in the hay with a passing fancy

      that's why I love you

you are one man I could really trust to be loyal and faithful forever
that is, once you had promised me, and made a commitment
but it's not our Kismet to make those vows, Mr. Nader
because . . well, you see, I'm already committed to a Lion
not a Nature Lion, an astrological one
actually, he's not so much a Lion, as he is . . a ghost

I realize that sounds spooky and ethereal and even bananas
            to be committed to a ghost
but a commitment is a commitment, you know ?
and the ethics of love are as clearly and divinely defined
as the ethics of saving Earthlings from their own ignorance

I guess maybe you feel sometimes that you're being loyal to ghosts too
for all the attention and respect some people give you
but with you, like with me — a commitment is a commitment

      I believe you are a Gooober

yes, the singular is spelled with three o's
I doubt if you understand that, so I won't try to explain it all now

Canto Twenty One ☆ 1029

just take my word that it's a compliment
a kind of distinction — but it doesn't mean you're superior
        because a dog can be a Gooober too
it just means that you've discovered you have three eyes
instead of only two . . . does that make any sense at all to you ?
it's not like being included in Who's Who, on an Earth level
    it simply means that you are a Who, who *knows* he is a Who
which may have something to do
        with why Brown Owls say "Who-Who-Who ?"

have you ever heard of the Oober galaxy of stars ?
do you know what a druid is ? or a Brown Owl ? or a god or a goddess ?
it's sort of like that . . if you know anything about the Essenes
                                          or the Brownies
        it also means that you are a stranger
                in a strange land
        and that, I am sure, you will understand

                    . . it's from the Bible, you know

the reason I'm writing to you is . . well
I was wondering if you need any help, slaying dragons
and trying to spread some Light in the darkness

that is, if you need a Gal Friday, who works cheap, you can call me
I would love to help you thank green trees
and work with Greenpeace to save baby harp seals
from being clubbed on the head, and skinned alive, while their mothers
                                    watch . . helpless
and fight by your side when you need me
I have my own white horse, as you can see . . so
you wouldn't have to provide that

we could team up together to stop the maniacal AEC
from tormenting the tummy ache of the San Andreas fault
with the fission laxative of nuclear and hydrogen castor oil . . . .
and from cobalting our atmosphere into an explosion of fire and brimstone
maybe we could even just once . . oh ! just once ?
give those people in airports, who collar strolling passengers
with their propaganda pamphlets in favor of nuclear insanity
just one small Zen-Buddha clip on the jaw ?

we could swat down pornographers and drug pushers and the oil interests
and hunters-for-sport-or-for-any-reason
like those people who shoot white-winged doves, in Texas
                                during open season
white-winged doves, Mr. Nader

DOVES

in Texas, they kill them

maybe we could try to find out why so many Texas Earthlings
want to hurt or maim or kill anything kind and gentle
                                        or smaller than they are
of course, not everyone in Texas is cruel
I'm sure there are some druids and Gooberz who live there too
but how very sad and unhappy they must be . .

and we could try to stop those other lost souls
who club foxes during their annual picnic, in Holmes County, Ohio
just club them to death, for fun and sport

and all the ones who butcher animals for meat-food
which Earthlings don't need — because it makes them so ill
and they don't even realize it — and completely removes their chance
of ever owning three eyes
and all those people who torture helpless animals for medical research
without any anesthetic . . like the cosmetic companies
who drop poison, one drop at a time . . into the propped-open eyes
                                        of innocent bunny rabbits
who are strapped down, and can't move
much less cry out in pain . . because bunnies don't speak like us, you know

we could take a stand against the FBI and CIA snoopers
and Big Brother's worth-less-than-plastic Social Security cards
and lead all these lost-in-the-woods Hansels and Jacks
who are so wrong, but think they are right
back on the path of truth and love and light — which may take some time
and we may have to include the AMA and the FDA
                                and some of the stuffier churches
but we'll have to be careful
when it comes to the churches, you see
because some of the newer religions have a strange list of Commandments
like Thou Shalt Kill — and Thou Shalt Commit Suicide
and Thou Shalt Trample Underfoot Anyone Who Persecutes Thee
and if we tell them they are misguided
                        they may call that persecution
and I'm just not ready to leave this Body Temple yet . . because
I've grown sort of attached to it by now

to be perfectly honest, I do have a few habits that might turn you off
one of them being that I might not be too economical
with the stingy budget you allow yourself
I'm extravagant with money, when I'm in a hurry, or on a crusade
            I have an impulsive nature
sometimes I speak rashly, without counting to ten
I have no Bachelor's Degree — or Doctorate — or a Master's
in anything at all
                and then too . . well

there's this other embarrassing thing
I don't have — I know you won't believe this

Canto Twenty One ☆ 1031

but I don't have a driver's license

                  . . neither did Einstein, you know

but I'm a hard worker, dedicated and committed
sincere and sensitive . . maybe a little too sensitive
and I write poetry, though it doesn't scan right all of the time
because, you see, I'm trying to make Life rhyme
and that takes lots of experience

If you should decide you can use me
I promise I won't flutter my heart, or even my lashes at you
like I told you, I'm already committed to a ghost
                who also admires you, by the way
and I guess that's about all I wanted to say

except . . well, there is this one thing that bothers me
and has been keeping me from sleeping lately

you see, Abraham Lincoln isn't around right now
to the best of my knowledge, that is
and Howard Hughes, another man I trust as implicity, as I do Abe — and you
is out there somewhere . . hiding behind the Northern Borealis
till it's time to "come home free" . .

                . . did you ever play Red Light
                    when you were small ?

and as for Gooober, he's disappeared
for how long, I have no idea
so it gets . . . kind of lonely at times

which is why I wanted to ask you this secret-code question

        are you from Saturn or Arcturus ?
        and if it's Saturn . . are you sure those rings around your home
        are properly magnetized against invaders ?
        because they're sneaking around, snapping candid photos now
        I guess you already know that
                but a word to the wise . . sometimes helps

and the most important question
I wanted to ask you is . .

        whether you're from Saturn or Arcturus
        why, in the name of all the Holy Galaxies, did you do it ?
        whatever possessed you and obsessed you to volunteer
        for National Guard Duty down here
        in the third dimension of this waning planet
                    . . so fast losing Light ?
        not that it matters
wherever you are from . . and Whoever sent you
or if you decided of your own volition . . . I'm glad you came

very sincerely

"me"

P.S. my name is Alice-Mary
           and I am a Brown Owl

Where-Are-You-Where-Are-You-Where-Are-You ?

I flew back to Colorado today
because Ruth called yesterday, to say . . oh, Gooober !

did you ever receive the letter I wrote about the kittens ?
the one where I told you about Love and Peace
having two baby kitties, but one died . . and I named the one that survived
                                        Soon ?
actually, I named her *Soon* Love, after her father
which was the same time that I named the three kitties Bones had
       Please . . Hurry . . and Home

so I could stand on the front porch, and call them
Please . . Hurry . . Home . . Soon . . Love . . Peace !   remember ?

well, Ruth called yesterday . . to say
that our new baby kitten named *Soon* . . died last week

probably because she was lonesome for her mother
she hadn't played very much since . . . Pumpkin Peace went to live in Heaven

and Ruth told me . . . that Love
hadn't eaten a single bite, since the baby kitten died
not even a sip of water . . oh, I hurried as fast as I possibly could
as fast as the plane would fly through the air . . to love him and heal him

but tonight . . just an hour before I arrived here at our little crooked house

                         Love . . left
I was too late, too late, too late
our Blueberry Love . . had already died

Gooober Gooober Gooober . . did you hear how deeply I cried ?
now our Love and Peace are both gone
and our small, fragile *Soon* . . their only daughter . . is gone too

       what shall I do ?

Canto Twenty One   ☆   1033

what is there left to believe ?
oh ! why have you left me alone to grieve ?

they died of loneliness . . all three
yes, they did, they did, you know they did !
of loneliness and heartbreak . . and lack of human closeness

      how could we expect them
      to bear the winter cold without our warmth ?

without you to tickle their tummies
and cut their toe nails . . and scratch their ears ?

their deaths have brought back
all my old fears

      is this a symbolic message
      from the Unverse . . Love's death . . . and Peace too

that our own love is dead too . .
all our shared peace gone forever ?

      is it, Goob . . is it ?

I forgot to say
that Bones has also gone away . . to stay

      to live with friends in the country, who have a big farm
      friends of Ruth, who rhymes with Truth

and Bones took one of his . . I mean one of her . . babies along
the one called *Please*, in case the farm seemed lonely

      he . . I mean, she . . said to tell you goodbye
      and not to cry
            because he . . I mean, she will be happier there

but Bones left his . .
I mean, her . . other two babies behind

      the ones I had named *Hurry* and *Home*
    when they were first born

      and I have decided to re-christen them

      Rainbow and *Magic*

tomorrow, I shall fly back to New York

and they will remain here in our little crooked house
to play with the boys next door, who have promised to feed them
each day, while we're away

> and maybe they will run in the grass
> and be healthy and happy . . because, I guess

I mean, I pray

> that Rainbow and Magic will be stronger . . somehow
> than Love and Peace
> > . . strong enough to wait

oh, Gooober, is it too late ?

> > our Love and Peace are dead

but . . can we find each other
through Rainbow and Magic instead ?

> wherever you are . . do you still believe
> in rainbows and magic
> > and me ?

Gethsemane — The Serpent Circle of Time

how will I ever reach a 4th Dimensional Now
when my mind is so imprisoned
within the pages of illusionary, yet painfully, convincingly real
> > Earth-time

> called a calendar ?

how can I ignore the calendar's desultory
and at least intellectually indisputable message
that you have been gone now . . . nearly nine years ?

> 9 . . the number, according to the ancients

of the Alpha and the Omega . . signifying always
> > one of two paths
either the Final Ending of an event or a situation
> or its New Beginning

> or both ?

this morning, I awoke

with the sound of West End Avenue traffic in my ears
           it was just a dream

only our astral S-elves had kissed once more
but this time it was so real . . . . you seemed so near

           oh ! I am tired of dreaming, do you hear ?
           tired of believing and praying
                   I am weary-weary-weary

    of this endless hell of waiting
    so grey and dreary

how often have I heard it said, how often have I read
that one may not argue with God's Timetable — or Cosmic Wisdom
and that the karmic lace for testing each soul
                           in its own time and place
should not be defied or questioned
for what is Time, but an illusion ?

           I know we are being soul-tested, Gooober and I
           but Heathcliffe, it's been *nearly nine years*
           and if he doesn't return soon, I truly believe I will die
           as Love and Peace died . . from a broken heart

is it *always* darkest before the dawn ?

true, it is in the Macrocosm of Nature
that hour, just before Sunrise, the sky is its blackest velvet
then the Sun's first rays . . rise silently over the hilltops

    and this microcosm of the long night of our separation
    has never been darker than now
    but I see no dawning pink-gold glow, to let me know
    that there will ever again be any worthwhile reason for living

what does God — what does the Universe want of me ?

    I have already given Gooober the gift of forgiving
    and I've released that visiting entity
           which kept him from healing before
    I call back that poor, lost soul fragment no more

I'VE TRIED EVERYTHING !   EVERYTHING !   EVERYTHING !

I heard myself angrily shout

                   . . then came the faintest whisper

everything but the absence
of the last teeny-tiny sliver of doubt

did you speak, Heathcliffe ?
or am I hearing only the lonely echo
of my own dying faith and dreams ?

     I know nothing is ever what it seems
     but it's so terribly dreary and dark

Heathcliffe !   did you speak . . did you bark ?
please don't tell me more empty metaphysical lies

  but Heath was silent

      just staring at me, through his wiggly strands of paper hair
      with his little beady eyes of wistful wise

Piscean Persistence — Long Distance

"hello, Ruth — I called to say — I called you because
he has not returned, and it's been nearly nine years
you were wrong ! oh, Ruth, it has been so long
and I'm not strong enough to wait anymore
while he's sharing spring
with some other Butterfly, on a foreign shore"

     "he will return"

"oh, Ruth, why can't you see the truth ?
will you never learn ? he is gone, he is gone, he is gone !
why can't you admit he was never real ?"

     "because that is not how I feel"

"my god ! you Pisces Fish are simply too much
always drowning in mis-placed compassion
it's been nearly **nine years**
and he has not come back — Ruth, do you hear ?
this is the ninth endless year !"

     "he is already here"

"already here ? **where ?**
have you gone mad ? you must be mad !"

     "no, I have not gone mad

but I'm very sad
that you have so little faith"

"you make no sense at all
what do you mean, he is already here ?
he is already where ?
where, where, *where* ? I just don't see . . . "

        "he is where you *know*
           and *believe* him to be"

"oh, now I see — yes, now I see !
you're tossing my own empty words back at me
all the words I spill out to others
when they're missing children — or friends
husbands, wives or lovers
empty-empty-empty vain words I used to preach . . .
words the Masters should never have allowed me to teach
don't you see how those futile words of faith
now cut me like a knife ?
why do you say things that are so clearly not true ?"

        "because I know that he's lonely too"

"you're impossible, really impossible !
is there no way I can make you comprehend my pain ?"

        "why not look for a rainbow
        instead of the rain ?"

   then we were . . . disconnected

it's no good, no use — I won't call back
the world is hopeless and black . . nine years of darkness
Ruth does not rhyme with Truth — she is wrong
I am not strong — not strong enough
to fight the frigid fact of the futility of waiting
it is finished . . it is over

        he will never return

and there's nothing to learn
from love . . but loneliness

     O ! my God, my God

        why have You forsaken me ?

Good Friday

I have returned to our little crooked house once more
to try and heal my wounds

>how long can I fly back and forth across the country
>without an Escape Flight license ?

I'm here watching our magic mountains, who refuse to fly
and trying not to cry, as I listen for the phone
>>just in case it might ring
even though . . it's disconnected

>>. . it is nearly spring

although the snow is still on the ground . . .
soon it will be Easter — our season of gladness

and we'll be spending it apart again . . in sadness

>but . . I must expect a miracle
>and not hope — but *know* — it shall be done unto me
>as I learned, as you taught me from the OOber catechism

today . . as these thoughts flew like birds through my mind
I raised the blind of my long-suffered despair
to let in the fresh air . . of knowing
and it blew across my heart, leaving the sweet scent
>>of wet grass in my nose
O !   where is a rose ?
where is a rose I can smell ?   I wondered

>suddenly, it thundered

and I threw open the front door, to see a bright flash of lightning
>an electrical storm was coming
and oddly, then . . I began humming a mixed-up Mother Goose rhyme
as I did that other time, so long ago . .

>*. . this is the day they give miracles away*
>*with half a pound of peppermint tea . .*

but this was not a day that miracles were being given away
only an ordinary late April afternoon
and this time I hummed alone — there was no Us to sing the lyric
no miracles anywhere to see

>just Rainbow and Magic . . the storm . . and me

an electrical storm ?   with snow still deep on the ground ?

how strange !   I thought . . even for unpredictable mountain weather
like a mixture of summer and winter
                  . . . like all seasons crazily blended together

as the silvery rain needles fell down on my head
I left the door open . . then came back inside
thinking . . it's too late for miracles now . . too late, too late

                  but . . wait !

Rainbow and Magic were playfully pushing around on the floor
a lavender and pink, crumpled up ball of . . what ?

I reached over and picked it up to see
while a giddy feeling swept over me . . you naughty kittens !
where did you find this bunch of old paper flowers ?
you must have been romping in the basement
                  and you know perfectly well that's not allowed

then Rainbow lifted her paw, as if to tease
as Magic grabbed the flowers . . and ran under the table
and for the first time I noticed that they were
                                    . . sweet peas
once more, I walked through the door
and stood on the front porch, inexplicably laughing aloud
perhaps it was just feeling the cool rain on my face
or a memory seeded into my mind, from some errant cloud
that flashed before me, suddenly
my **JOY** ! as a child, when an electrical storm
brought a rush of feeling, so lifting and wild . . so free !

         yes, lifting and wild . . and free

but I'm no longer a child

         oh, Gooober, why aren't you here ?
         this is nearly the end of the tenth endless year
         will you never-never come back ?

then heard myself saying . . aloud

"that's not druid praying — druids pray in rainbow colors
not in dreary mantras of black . . or chants of grey
that's not how druids pray !"

so I grabbed Raggy and Algae, and hugging them tightly
I began to sing a shiny-new-golden song   ♪

" . . . don't you understand, don't you see ?
it's only Time-out-of-focus
that makes it *seem* like the tenth year !

Raggy and Algae, do you see ?   Gooober is already *here* !"

such a silly, childish, make-believe, wishing song
such a meaningless rhyme to sing . . did the telephone ring ?

      but it can't ring . . it's disconnected

almost instantly, I heard a knocking
at the back porch kitchen door . . a desperate, insistent
                                    loud knocking
and I thought . .
        it's probably Ruth, who rhymes with Truth
        just dropping by to see
        if everything is allright with me

I ran quickly to the door
to tell Ruth I finally understood
what she had been trying to make me see before
that I must stop grieving
        . . and start believing

but when I unfastened the lock
oh ! delirious shock !

IT WAS YOU !

just standing there, with the rain in your hair
*   *   *   *
*   stars falling all around you   * *
*   *
as they did the night I found you   *
      *

                you whispered . . "Gooober, I've come back home"
      *
I answered . .   *
    "I know, darling, I know"

        then the rain magically changed to snow
        and your aura began to glow and glow
                . . like snow diamonds

after awhile . .

      I closed the door on your astral image
      for that's all it was . .

all ?   oh, you were still tall !
and your eyes were still ocean green . . silvery-wise

      . . . after I closed the door
      I walked slowly into the den . . still alone

blew a happy kiss at the silent telephone . . . .

knelt down near your side of the couch
then said a joyous thank-you prayer for your return

. . . . for whatsoever thing you desire
pray as if you had *already received it*
and you shall *surely* have it !

oh, Goob . . you must have thought I would never learn !

His Rainbow . . Her Snowflakes

The New York Times carries all the news
that's Fit to print . . or so they say

so I read it today

I like "Fit news"

but I also read the National Enquirer
the newspaper of that frustrating blend
of good and evil — positive and negative

yet the Enquirer
does succeed in reaching a surprising balance . . .
along with reporting the same nonsense
as other magazines of trivia
it also reports news of vital importance
and sometimes magical power
news the New York Times does not consider "Fit"

yes, along with trash and trivia
the National Enquirer also prints — truth
about various Aquarian Age discoveries
which gradually open the long-sleeping
Third Eyes of humans
news ranging from the scientific to the meta-physical
occasional stories of love and compassion

also reporting upon . .

the cruel torture of our helpless animal friends
by Satan's own testing laboratories

and so . . this morning

I read both the Times and the Enquirer

it was a feature story . . .

Gooober, if you were really there, as I believed you to be
during that midnight vortex, when Heathcliffe
                              spoke with me

do you remember the discussion we had
about the visions of Fatima . . a town in Portugal
experienced by three small children
10 year old Lucia dos Santos . . and her cousins
a 9 year old boy named Francisco
and a 7 year old little girl, named Jacinta . . in the year 1917 ?

the Virgin spoke to them three times during that year
and gave them three messages . . the first, on May 13th

and do you remember . .

            that Heathcliffe told me
            it had been ordained that the third message
                  the children received at Fatima
            would be revealed "soon" ?   he was right

      now it has been revealed . . by the National Enquirer
      the paper that tells it like it is, never mind "Fit"

I read somewhere else that the revelation was also announced
in an Italian newspaper . . before it was published here in America

      I'll begin by telling you
      about the first two messages of Fatima — given to the children
      in their first two visions . . by "the Lady in blue"

   in the first one . .

      the children claimed
      that the Virgin told them
      she would soon "come to take
                        Jacinta and Francisco
      with her, in Heaven . . .
      but that Lucia would remain on Earth
                        for awhile longer"

the next year, Jacinta and the boy, Francisco
caught flu . . and eventually died from it
Lucia remained on Earth and entered a convent, near Fatima
as Sister Mary Lucia

where she lived into her eighties

in the second vision of Fatima . . during the year 1917

the Virgin told the children
that the war was about to end (World War I)
and it did, the following year, in 1918
but that "another and worse war would begin
during the reign of Pope Pius XI"

this was in 1917, Gooober
Pope Pius XI didn't assume office until 1922
and during his reign . . Adolf Hitler
launched the offensives that heralded the beginning
of World War II

if you were truly there that night
when Heathcliffe and I had our mystical conversation
you already know about the third message
of Fatima

the one the Vatican had promised to read to the world
during the Church's celebration
of the Year of Fatima
and then, inexplicably, remained silent
making me wonder, at the time
what could have been in that third message
from the Virgin to the three children
the Church felt it might be unwise to reveal ?
what caused the Pope to break his promise
to announce it to the world ?

now that it has finally been revealed
I can understand why the Vatican kept it a secret

the Church Fathers evidently believed
and perhaps rightly so . .
that the third message was so alarming
it could cause a great cloud of fear to descend
upon those of all religions

the Vatican may have felt there was good cause
to keep the third message of Fatima from all of us . . . back then
but now the secret is out
and I feel it's important that people know about it, Goob
because the world is so near to the time
warned about by the Virgin in her prophecy
to the children

how else can a warning be rightly accepted
in the true sense of the word ?

for, the divine purpose of any warning . . astrological
                                        or otherwise
is not to bring about negative
but to *prevent* the warned-about negative of any vision
                        from manifesting into reality

        and . . I especially need
to talk with *you* about it
                but you're gone . . for awhile
so all I can do is write it to you
in another letter I can't mail . . except in the hollow
of the old oak tree
and let the druids deliver it for me . . again
    if that's what they've been doing
I hope so . . oh !   I do hope so !

                the third message from the third vision
        was written down, after the child, Lucia, grew up
        and presented to the Vatican — sealed
                then they announced the Year of Fatima
        along with the Pope's intention to open it and read it
                                        to the world
        which must have been
                somewhat embarrassing to the Church

the message is . . . very scary, Goob
indisputably frightening and ominous . . even sinister
but the New Age . . with our help
will turn it all around at the last minute . . Aquarian-like
into a happy ending
                you'll see . .
I'll explain how
    after I've told you the message

                Mahmet Ali Agca . . the convicted assailant
                who tried to kill Pope John Paul II . . in 1981
                on May 13th . . the same day
                the Virgin first appeared to the children, in 1917
                told a courtroom in Rome
                that his attempt on the life of the Pope
                "was connected to the Secret of the Madonna of Fatima"

practising the ancient adage that "silence is golden"
to this day, the Vatican has firmly refused
to publicly discuss the content of the third Fatima message
probably fearing that it would be abused
by a sensation-hungry press . . and other media
yet, the newspaper carried a photograph
of the present Pope John Paul II . . and Sister Mary Lucia
and they are both smiling . . with love and trust
                                in one another

evidence that the present Pope John Paul
does respect this grown-up child of Fatima
and surely does not consider her to be a "flaky psychic"
or a "prophetess of doom" . . like today's current crop
of those who claim to "channel" ethereal entities or a "guide"
and who hide . . behind the endorsement
of film stars and other celebrities
ignoring the always reliable inner voice of their own Higher S-elves

      according to Italian journalist Domenica Del Rio
      who has covered the Vatican for many years
      and has long been trusted and respected there . . .

     . . . the contents of the third prophecy
were learned in the early 1960's . . from Pope John XXIII
by the Pope's good friend, Padre Pio
a famed Italian monk, who is now being considered
                    for sainthood
and journalist Del Rio was told by Padre Pio
before he died in 1968 . . the text of the third Fatima message
Del Rio struggled with his conscience for years
before finally deciding to reveal
what he had been told by Padre Pio

the Vatican refuses to either confirm or deny the text
yet many Church Prelates privately agree upon its credibility

     . . . this is part of the message
and remember, Gooober, I told you it was scary
but I also told you how we can transmute it into a happy ending
or I will tell you how . . after I quote certain parts of it
              for you to meditate on now

      the text written by the grown-up Fatima child, Lucia
      according to journalist Del Rio, who received it
              from Padre Pio
      having originated with Pope John XXIII

says . . in part

      "a great plague will befall mankind near the end
              of the 20th century
        nowhere in the world will there be order
        and Satan will rule in the highest places . . .

      Satan will succeed in seducing the spirits
      of the great scientists who invent arms
      with which it will be possible . . . to destroy
      a large part of humanity in a few minutes . . . . . . "

and this was experienced as a vision

written down by Sister Mary Lucia
decades before the nuclear arms race . . . .

    the prophecy continues with . . .

        "Satan will have in his power the powerful
        who command the people . . and who will incite them
        to produce enormous quantities of arms . . . . .
        . . . the great and powerful will perish
        along with the small and weak . . for the Church
        it will be the time of its greatest trial
        Cardinals will oppose Bishops, Bishops will oppose
                      one another . . . .

        fire and smoke will fall from the sky
        the waters of the oceans will become mist
            the foam will rise to tremendous heights
        and . . . millions . . . will drown

        millions will die from hour to hour . . as a huge war
        erupts in the last half of the 20th century . . .
        whoever remains alive will envy the dead
        everywhere one turns . . . . there will be anguish and misery
        ruin in every country
            . . . because of the errors committed by the crazed
      and the time . . . draws nearer"

undeniably, Gooober, a frightening prophecy
which has already shown signs of manifesting on Earth
and the signs increase . . . every day, every hour

        in 1980 the present Pope John Paul II
        engaged in private audience with Domenico Del Rio
        during which he hinted at the contents
            of the third Fatima message
        and even used some of the very language it contained

    His Holiness told the journalist that the contents
    of the third vision's message . . were "impressive" . . and he added
    that the text spoke of "men stripped suddenly of life
    by the millions, from one minute to the next"

from the first moment I read those words
I shuddered . . . not so much from the words themselves
as from wondering how many people had read them
in American and Italian newspapers . . and in other countries
            where they have also been printed

    and knowing . .

what the planting of such negative seeds

in the minds of millions . . . has the power to do

      the power . . to bring about
      that which has been multiple-imaged by so many

in the midst of my intense concern . . I had a dream one night
I dreamed I was in Russia . . talking with a man
             who had a kindly face and a warm smile
he wore a funny felt hat, exactly like the one
my dearest Guru, A.G., used to wear . . and also glasses, like him
and the very same scar on his head

on the front of his coat were printed large initials: **M. G.**
I didn't learn the name of this Russian in my dream
nor could I recall a word of our conversation when I awoke
but the dream left me with a sense of peace . . a sense of
        "God's in His Heaven . . all's right with the world"
from the verse by poet Robert Burns

      . . . . . .

      Gooober, we must use the Virgin's warning wisely
           we must
      use the warning as it was meant
      not to bring about . . but to **PREVENT**
        the terrors precognitively told

  what must we do ?

      like the laws of physics . . the laws of meta-physics
          are specific and precise
      and tonight, I made a list of them . . of what to do
      to share with my Higher S-elf . . and with you

since much of my enlightenment has come to me
in my slumbers, when God sometimes speaks to us in numbers
I decided to number the "what to do" formulas

Number One: I remember what Heathcliffe told me
      about the several evidences
      that the feminine essence is superior
             to the masculine

      only one of these being that . . .
      while man can seed life
      only woman can permit or deny birth
      whether of human infants . . . or of solar systems
           and Universes

      therefore, at this time when our Earth could be "aborted"
      thanks to the mad men who are running the world at present

polluting Nature . . . and the Minds of children
we should be praying to our *Mother* Who art in Heaven

for, it is She who has the POwer to permit the abortion
or to Ordain the protection of Her child . . our Earth

Number Two: each man, woman and child . . every Earthling
must immediately stop imaging disaster
and the Gotterdammerung
which most of them have been doing for decades
even before the third Fatima vision
was recently revealed

each one of us must begin now
to *know* . . not hope or believe . . but **know**

that the New Age is, after all, the Aquarian Age
and therefore contains
the Uranus essence
of unexpected, sudden **change** . . at the last minute

we have had only three Aquarian American presidents
Abraham Lincoln . . . Roosevelt, Franklin D. . . and Ronald Reagan
each one manifesting the astrological Uranus "change", you see

those who worked to place Lincoln in the White House
expected him to be tough on the South
but what did he do ?
he turned "soft" on the South, as the Civil War neared its end
sternly opposing the "carpetbagging" which ravaged the South
after his assassination

those who worked to place Roosevelt in the White House
expected him to favor Big Business and the wealthy
but what did he do ?
he turned against his backers after he was elected
and became a champion of the blacks and the working class

as for our Aquarian film star president, Ronald Reagan
we know that he changed from Democrat to Republican
after he married Nancy
then, not long after he was calling Russia "the evil Empire"
a major news magazine noted that Reagan had switched
to "kissing babies in Red Square"
another change at the last minute astrologers knew would occur
before he left office

and so . . we must remember
that this is the Aquarian Age . . of sudden and unexpected
change
and the Aquarian ruling planet, Uranus

is entirely capable of turning the Fatima prophecy
into its polarity of peaceful solution
before the end of this century

Number Three:

we must realize that this is only a mirror reflection
of the real world
as the Tibetan monks know, when they daily chant
"this is the world of illusion"
and through such realization
we can bring about the 3rd and 4th lines of the Lord's Prayer
we used to recite at night before we fell asleep
not every night . . but often

"Thy kingdom come . . Thy Will be done
on Earth, as it is in Heaven"

Number Four:

Sister Mary Lucia's third Fatima message
also contained a grave warning for the Vatican itself

"Satan will even succeed in asserting himself
at the top of the Church . . . . and walk among
Bishops and Cardinals . . . and the Church will be in darkness"

my Higher S-elf has channelled some counsel for Rome
the Vatican would be wise to re-instate the Latin in the Mass
removed some years ago . . keeping alive the ancient ritual
that acts as a spiritual glue . . to keep the faithful within its folds

and would also be wise
to remove from particular Catholic altars, in some churches
the Bob Dylan-Judy Collins-Joan Baez type of "entertainment"
featuring electric guitars and folk music
in an effort to attract the "New Age Youth"

not that there is anything wrong with these people
or their music
and it may, indeed, be appropriate for Protestant churches
but it does not belong on the Catholic altar
and is not harmonious with the magnetic ancient rituals
of chanted Latin . . incense . . and candles

one recent change the Vatican would be wise to retain
and not remove
is the edict pronounced in 1978
giving to Priests who read the Christmas Mass
in all Catholic churches . . . each Diocese

permission, if they should so choose
to refer to those who followed the Star to the stable
not as "the three Wise Men"

     but correctly, as "the three *astrologers*"

a final counsel to Rome
is to accept and endorse astrological birth control
   called astro-biology
which is not in any way opposed to Catholic principle
perfectly safe . . and 100% reliable
. . . . also a great blessing for those
who want children, and have been mistakenly told
that they are barren or sterile

astro-biology would end two enormous problems
of the Church today . . the raging controversy over birth control
    and abortion
causing the loss of millions of Catholics all over the world
for, abortion is not an issue when there are no
       unwanted births
an additional blessing, of course
is the solution this ancient art offers
     to famine and world over-population
with no offense whatsoever to Catholic doctrine and teachings

    perhaps these actions in the Vatican
    would have the power to negate
    the Fatima warning that . . "the Church
        will be in darkness . . "

Number Five:

   this formula involves the true meaning of forgiveness
   and the lesson you taught me about so-called
       dangerous, vicious Dobermans
  . . remember ?

   it also involves the ancient adage that one must
   "hate the sin . . and not the sinner"

   Earthlings must remember, know and realize
   that Satan-Set is a fallen angel
      once a great god
   and brother to Osiris

   * whatever the origin of his fall . . and his responsibility
   for causing darkness to fall on the Earth for the first time
   he later sought . . and still seeks . . forgiveness

*The origin of Satan's fall is part of the story in the forthcoming
sequel to this book, with the working title of *Twelfth Night Secrets*

he hungers for atonement
as does every single lost Soul and Spirit
each and every fallen angel

Set himself regrets the forces of darkness he has let loose upon the world
but he cannot stop it alone, whatever his inner desire

many people have asked me
why the healing ray of the rainbow spectrum
violet
creates such a strange lexigram with its letters
violet contains: **love** (and) **let live**
which is true and logical
but the word also contains, the letters of
love evil
and those who question me are puzzled about
why this should be so

it's not a puzzle to those who know
a great truth
for, evil cannot ever be destroyed
by either hate or fear

evil may *only* be destroyed by the compassion and forgiveness
of Love

evil . . which lexigrams into vile and live
feeds on both hatred and fear . . and grows stronger

but evil cannot resist Love
the most awesomely powerful force on Earth
in Heaven or in hell

and so . . if any magical druid spell
is to be cast to negate the third Fatima warning
it must involve the forgiveness of Satan
and neither hatred nor fear
of satanic forces

as St. Francis of Assisi's experience
with the ferocious wolf of Gubbio proved . . .

it's important to remember, Gooober
that *loving* evil is not synonomous with condoning evil
the two are vastly different

I'll close my Fatima meditation, darling
with a memory fragment of joy
taught to me by Heathcliffe . . about His Rainbow
and Her Snowflakes

for Their grace
>has brought us safe so far
>and Their grace
>>will lead us home

SUMMER — New York

today I made some peppermint tea
and drank it alone . . trying to remember Us
>but all I could see
>>was
>>>you and me
separately

>>oh, Heathcliffe, how long, how long ?

surely you must know
your little beady eyes of wistful wise
told me everything else I needed to learn
how long, Heath, before his return ?

>doesn't he know that I've been wrong
>and it was he who was strong . . in hurting himself by leaving ?
>oh, doesn't he see . . that when he's hurt
>>it has to hurt me
>because I and he . . are "we" ?

I'm not seeking to be under*stood* anymore
I want to under*stand* ! I'm not asking to be *loved*
>I want to *love* !

doesn't he know that yet ?

>poor Heath, your little beady eyes of lonely are wet
>but don't you mind . . boy dogs can cry, and not be weak
>>Jesus wept

and I brushed away the tear
on Heathcliffe's cheek . . with a little snowflake kiss

>Gooober, wherever you are
>do you know how dreadfully much I miss you ?
>do you miss me too ?   are you lonely ?

then I took a long walk . . and stopped in St. Patrick's
to light a candle beneath St. Anthony's compassionate smile

and to say hello to Francesco too
as always, feeling closer to you
when I'm near St. Francis

his gentle eyes cast down, hiding secrets of pain and joy
standing there, so silent and tall
newly placed, by some understanding Prelate . . outside the cathedral wall
where he belongs . . surrounded by grass and trees
so he can hear the songs of his beloved birds

I knelt down before him
to be alone . . and still . . and to pray
without words

after a while . . I rose . . and began walking again
with nowhere to go . . just walking
as a soft, rain-scented breeze tangled my hair . . and my mind

into little wispy cobwebs
. . of memory

I walked past NBC . .
and the Rockefeller fountain
the Plaza . . . Columbus Circle . . and Lincoln Center

giving popcorn and *Expect a Miracle* cards away
to some hungry pigeons . . . and lonely, separated lovers
Earthlings, reaching for a star
who needed a miracle desperately enough
not to care if anyone saw them cry

. . but not so desperately as I
this wintry July
no, not so desperately as I

when I passed the big oak tree on the corner
where the kids park their bikes . . a little girl was skipping rope
oh, no !   not that !   not a child at play
when it's too late . . when I just became three hundred
and ninety eight today
then I turned, and came inside

lay down on the bed . . and cried

as I listened to the clock above the bed, over my head
ticking Forever away
tick-tocking

tock-ticking Forever away

```
t
 i
  c
   k
    i
     n
      g
   t
    o
     c
      k
       i
        n
         g

            f
             o
              r
               e
                v
                 e
                  r

                     a
                      w
                       a
                        y
```

How Long is Forever ?

for an hour or more . . a century or longer . . ?
I lay on the bed, staring at the ceiling

        hearing a faint sound . . I could not identify

so thin and trembling . . pale and wispy . . a faint echo
perhaps it was the beating of my heart . . keeping time with the clock

    tick-tocking . . tock-ticking . . Forever away

tock-ticking Forever away

t
 i
  c
  k
  i
   n
   g

t
 o
  c
  k
  i
   n
   g

f
 o
  r
   e
   v
    e
    r

a
 w
  a
   y

Brother Sun — Sister Moon

was it Tagore who first said . .

    Faith is the bird that feels the light
    and sings, when the dawn is dark ?

maybe so, but it was Francesco Bernadone, of Assissi
who *knew* it first

listen, Francis . .

I heard him singing just now
    that crazy bird

          from the deep depths
          of the dark night of my soul

          and God knows
          there's no light for him to feel
          no promise, even, of a Sunrise

          just a few faint notes he sang
          not really a morning song

          poor bird, I believe he's hungry
          it's been so long
          since I had a crumb of caring
          or a morsel of memory to feed him

             why does he sing ?

          doesn't he know that Spring
          might be planning never to return
          and is almost certain
          to be late again this year ?

there ! he warbled a cadenza ! Francesco .·. did you hear ?

but it's summer, not spring . . how could I hear a robin sing ?

        then I answered the telephone

though I hadn't heard it ring . .

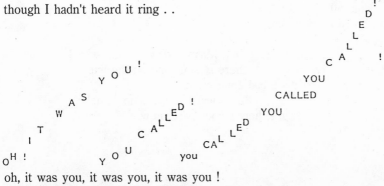

oh, it was you, it was you, it was you !
you called, you called, you called !

and never before did July ever crack open
with such Liberty Bells of glorious color and light !
                not even in 1776 !

        like the bursting bag of fireworks
        I saved up for the **BIG BANG !**
        when I was a child, in the wonderful and wild
                                days of Independence !

FIREWORKS !

        OH ! what a sky-rocket, block-busting miracle !

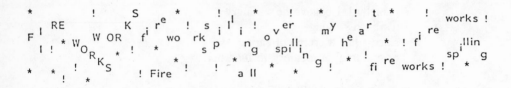

        FIREWORKS !   FIREWORKS !   FOREWORKS !

                spilling all over my heart

SPIT DEVILS
        of sputtering telephone wires !

snap !   crackle !   pop !

    "hello — hello ? hello !"

                        "but, Ma'm, I didn't ring . ."

"oh, yes !   you rang, you rang !"

                        "no, I'm sorry — I did not ring . ."

    "oh, yes !   you did !
because I just heard a robin sing !"

                        "but, Ma'm, I didn't . . oh, wait !
                        there *is* someone on the line
                but it's a bad connection
                                just wait . . hello ? hello ?
                yes, here's your party now . . "

"OH WOW !

    "hello ? hello !"

ROMAN CANDLES AND SPRAYING FOUNTAINS
AND SPARKLERS OF WORDS !

sparklers of words !

                       "Goob ! I'm home — I'm here !
☆   *   *   back from the Oober galaxy
                          and just wait till you hear
! *   ☆   ☆   what's happened ! darling . . it's me
     *   *   I'm home . . I'm here !

    !   ☆
      !   !

"oh ! where *are* you ?"
hello ? are you there ? the connection's not clear"

☆   *   . . *be still, my love, be still, I'm here* . .
 !   *
          !
☆   !
    *   ☆
      ☆   *   !   ☆
                                 *

SHOOTING SKY ROCKETS of delirious rejoice ☆ !   *

    your voice, your voice, your voice !   ☆   * !   ☆
                                            *   !
    !   * "I've missed you so, and I love you so
   *   oh, I do, I do . . I do love you so !
     *   hurry, Goob, come out here to me . . !
☆   * I'm in a phone booth
!   ☆   near a big oak tree
             at the corner, where the kids park their bikes
               a six year old, with rosy cheeks
             and pigtails tied with yellow yarn
             is skipping rope in front of me . . she looks
                               like you
               . . darling, hurry"

I ran out to the street
on flying feet . . like the mad woman of Chaillot
       then stopped
to gather soft-blue-velvet-peace around me
and floated
       floated
            floated
               on little puffs of Indian smoke

to your dusty blue Bug
with the *Expect a Miracle* card still tucked in the windshield

the door . . . and your arms . . . were both open wide . . . you pulled me inside

        !   and for one pounding moment

   ☆   silence
     *   !
then we trembled . . and touched   *
and the whole 4th of July bright-spangled sky ☆
*   *
☆   exploded with singing stars !   *
                     ☆
  *   !   ☆   *   *

you wrapped me up tightly in the circle of your arms
                 . . your arms, your arms

    tied me with pink-gold ribbons of love
        and mailed me back to join your soul
our scattered pieces once more whole . . . . . with a long, long kiss

    my knees grew weak

I smelled your cheek . . . you smelled my ear
then I touched the snowflake tear
    on your face

    and our dusty blue Bug filled up like a giant balloon
    with the swelling helium of tenderness

I said . . "here ! I brought Algae and Raggy
to say hello . . they missed you too !"

             and you hugged them

       "where's Heathcliffe ?"

"Heath stayed inside, to hide
his little beady eyes of restless lonely . . are wet
I think he may be crying
but he's such a proud male chauvinist animal
he doesn't want me to tell . . "

    you uttered a miniature Tarzan yell

      "hey, funny-face ! I almost forgot . . guess what ?
      I brought you an OOber forget-me-not
          from across the border"

  then you reached under the seat
  and pulled out a double surprise

a map of Alaska, with the word *lonely* written across it
and a Mexican calendar, with July crossed out
where you had printed the word *Spring* in blue

              "I held back the season . . till I came home to you"

oh, thank you for loving me . . that much
I whispered inside, where you couldn't hear
but you read my mind . . and said . . low and clear

              "thank you for loving *me* that much *too*"

then I heard a distant roll of summer thunder
and saw the leaves on the oak tree tremble
as a silvery splatter of raindrops
sprinkled against the windshield . . gently reminding

"I . . oh, Gooober, look . . it's raining"

                    and you repeated

              "thank you for loving *me* that much *too*"

      and so I knew

I knew it was time — and I squeezed my eyes shut
feeling my heart squeeze tightly
        squeezed *his* hand . . his nail-pierced hand

dear Jesus, give me strength and courage
you know I have to level with him now
I have to tell him like it is
Jesus, I need you so . . please stay . . don't go
oh, don't go away when I need you so
please remind him how it was with Mary, the Magdalene one
how you forgave her . . and loved her

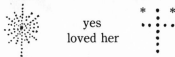   yes
                  loved her

and Peter and Judas . . how you forgave them too
oh, Jesus ! what if he doesn't understand ?
oh, Jesus ! . . . do you think he will ?

then I reached out again, and felt his nail-pierced hand
close tightly over mine . . and thought I heard him whisper

          SShh . . be still, be still

"Gooober . . oh . . "

and the tears streamed down
like a waterfall I could not control
as I heard the thunder roll . .
and the silvery splatters of raindrops
beat harder on the glass . . God's own tears . . and Hers

        . . *she tumbled over in the grass*
she was so dear, so small, . . . she fell . .

"Oh, Gooober — I have something to say
I have . . . something to tell . . "

                        and you waited, expectantly

"that time when I caused you so much agony
when I . . oh, Gooober !"

                I cried once more

and his nail-pierced hand closed tighter over mine
squeezing harder than before
as I heard him, clearly, whisper softly

                        be still . . be still
                        and know that I am . . inside
                        be still . . I too have wept, I too have cried

"Gooober . . . "
    I said, quietly now

"I lied . . no star fell in New York
there was no falling star"

oh, Jesus, remind him, please . . . that we were both once Essenes
and how we used to stop the rain
remind him of my old dreams . . and how they hurt . . and the pain

"there was no star — I lied"

and I tremored, like the quaking oak leaves . . as
a **BIG BANG** of **CRASHING THUNDER**
smashed through the wet, fresh, sweet-smelling air
bringing a niagara of water . . a drenching downpour
flooding the curbs, and the empty streets
and draping the car, like a curtain

        . . a veil of rain . . Vail, Vail, Vail . . .

                then you began to stare . . and stare . . and stare
                        straight inside my soul
                and your silvery-wise eyes began to burn

with the same strange light, as on that night, so long ago

as the rainbow aura around your head began to glow
like millions of delicate snowflake-diamonds . . no two alike
                    oh ! the shimmering, sparkling, glittering snow !
bathed in the golden glow of the street lamp
on that silent, holy night . . when the lost was found
in Charleston . . . my blue and silver rosary . .

but this was not night — it was day, and raining
then once again I heard myself say, with courage waning

"I lied to you — there was no star"

                    your silvery-wise eyes
were burning-burning-burning, like embers
like green eternity embers
                        and your aura continued to glow
as you whispered softly . .

    "yes, I know . . "

"you *know* ?   you *knew* ?"

        "not in the beginning . . but
        when I came home from Vail, I knew"

"but that was the same time
I found out too . . that there was no star
oh, Gooober . . you knew ?"

        for a moment, you were silent . . then

            "I knew no star fell through the sky . . or you
                    oh, Little Girl Lost
            there was no star . . it was just a tiny prayer
            only your old dream, still there"

"but we wept together . . for her
we wept for the little lost star . .
Gooober, you cried . . and you *knew* I had lied ?"

                then you sighed . . and said

            "yes, I grieved for her . . . and cried with you
            she was so dear . . so small . . so new
            too small to stand against our winter winds
                    oh, can't you see ?
            there was no star, I knew . . but I wept once more
            for when she fell *before*
            did you not know that my old dream was still there too ?"

"didn't you know I was lost, the same as you ?
but I also wept with thanksgiving
that I learned enough, in that other Temple
not to repeat as deep a hurt to you . . "

"no, not as deep on that Thanksgiving
as in your other Temple before
and I do give thanks that you didn't . . again
share with a stranger . . our deep"

"and I grieved for another reason
because our old pain had been repeated once more
even though it wasn't as deep as before
still, it brought back your old dream
as well as mine"

"old dreams . . yes . . there is something I need to know
something long past, except for the scars
a hurt of ten years ago . . and sometimes yesterday's sadness
can only die . . by trying to understand why"

"if the scars have not yet healed
and I can help . . then ask me, if you feel you must"

"it's about the time I flew to California
after you drove away that day
from our little crooked house . . to find out . . well
I guess . . just to say a dignified goodbye"

"why didn't I come to the room when you called ?
I really can't say . . at least not in any way
that really matters anymore

after you called, I did drive over to the Roosevelt
parked the car in the lot out back
came inside . . and sat there in the lobby
for a long and lonely, endless time

but somehow, nothing seemed to rhyme
and something kept me from going up to our room
so I walked down Hollywood Boulevard . . uncertain
wondering what I should do . .

finally, I went to Pickwick Bookstore
and just stood there
where I first saw you
and where we first said hello . . with our eyes
trying so hard . . so hard . . to image you
rushing through the door, breathless . . smiling

1064 ☆ Canto Twenty One

the way you did before . . like an impulsive Ram"

"but — oh, Goob, I did !   I did go there
I went to Pickwick too — but it was not that night I called
it was the night before, right after I arrived"

        "you see ?   we were being guided — or restricted
        by far higher powers than our own selves
        because I kept thinking that . . if you came there too
        it would be a sign that we should try once more
        but after awhile, I knew . . I realized
            . . the whole world was out of harmony
        and our telepathic communication had been . . disconnected
        which disturbed me so . . that I walked back to the Roosevelt
        climbed in the car . . drove back home
            stayed up all night packing

        and . . . early the next morning
        I left for the airport, with my heart breaking all the way"

"but . . if you didn't come to our room at all
and if you didn't say 'Western Union' at the door
then you see, I'm afraid that I . . . "

        "say *what ?*   Western Union ?   what do you mean ?"

"oh, Goob, that's just it . . I don't *know* what I mean
there's so much I can't seem to understand . . "

        "yes . . what does it mean . . what does it all mean ?"

"I somehow feel that you know more than I
about what it means . . maybe not everything
but still, more than I've been able to discover"

        "it seems we were entangled in a larger Karma
                than our own
        for some higher galactic purpose . . "

"also for an earth-bound, political conspiracy purpose ?"

        "yes, and one which was very dangerous . . although
        it's over now, and we should be grateful
        for it could have been far worse
        since neither of us had any warning, in time to rehearse
            the parts we had to play
        hardly even time to pray . . that our love
        would pass the test other people forced it to bear
        others . . as well as, perhaps, some Master OObers
        somewhere out there . . who are wise enough to know
        far more about our mission than we guessed ourselves"

"I know . . that is, I do agree
still, I am so very puzzled and confused . . "

        "I'm aware that you are — and I know why
        not back then, I didn't know — I only learned it later
        but I do understand how you must have felt then
                and how you feel now
        about that witch's brew of double-double-toil-and-trouble
        as I always understand
                  everything you feel . .

        which is why I thought, when we return to Colorado
        we can sit by the fire, like two druids, and talk
        and heal all those old wounds . . . . . . for each other

        because, you see, the 'double' reason for your
                    winter season
        was later shared
        in all its puzzlement, also by me"

"by *you* ?   oh ! *you too* ?"

        "yes, and when we go home together
        I'll try to explain to you all I understand myself
        or at least, all I've learned — which is only a part

        meanwhile, I've been waiting . . and wanting
                  with all my heart
        to tell you something
        and I know these words aren't adequate . . but
        well, I've wanted so long . . . . . just to say to you

          how very sorry I am
        for all the hurt and humiliation others made you bear
        and for all the pain I've caused you too . . . .

          please don't cry
      I came home to bring you a rainbow
              . . not to make you cry"

"these aren't sad-tears, they're glad-tears !
because now I know why sadness rhymes with gladness
you see, I've waited such a long and lonely time
   to hear you say . . those words"

        "then let me see your old elf smile again"

I smiled

and the burning Eternity embers
were glowing-glowing-glowing

somewhere behind your eyes
reflecting some strange growing-knowing in my own
as you stared . . . and stared at me
and I gazed back into your eyes . . deeply, deep

then . . . *miracle ! miracle ! miracle !*

the drenching downpour, incredibly, stopped.
abruptly.   just stopped.

not trailing off, with a few scattered drops, or a lighter shower
as is always Nature's rule
it simply, suddenly and instantly — stopped.

and at the same exact split-second in time
the Sun burst out, with a nearly blinding light, creating a huge rainbow !
so abruptly, so unexpectedly . . . I gasped aloud
          as one lone passer-by
also gasped, stood perfectly still . . and stared up at the sky
as if expecting to see the Heavens open . . for it had been
so shockingly instantaneous

"oh, Gooober, see ? look ! the rain has stopped !   see ?   the rainbow !
LOOK ! YOU'VE FINALLY STOPPED THE RAIN !
you perfectly marvelous, over-grown druid . . look !
you've really-truly **STOPPED THE RAIN !**"

                              you smiled

              "don't you remember, darling
              the Essenic alchemy formula for stopping the rain ?"

"well, let's see . . I believe
it has something to do with stopping pain
is that right ? oh, please help me remember !"

              "once you told me about the Three Monkeys
              see no sadness . . hear no sadness . . speak no sadness
              and I said the word I learned as a child was 'evil'
              see no evil . . hear no evil . . speak no evil

              but you told me it was all the same
              because, you said, sadness rhymes with evil
              do you recall telling me that ?"

"yes, I remember that time
but . . well, evil spelled backwards is 'live' . . "

              "right ! and we must live, must we not ?

              and so we must know sadness — or evil

Canto Twenty One ☆ 1067

human tears . . and God's own tears, called raindrops
both are sometimes sad, but not always bad
for, some rain is good for the *Growing* things in Nature
just as some tears are good for the *Knowing* things
in *human* nature . . and in the heart

the laws of Nature may be interrupted for the same reason
that the laws of *human* nature may be interrupted
                              interrupted meaning
interference with Karma"

"and that reason ?"

            "it's only when Nature's rains are so heavy
            that they threaten flood or destruction
            that they may — or should — be stopped

            and it's only when the tears of the heart
            in *human* nature . . are too heavy
                        threatening to flood the Mind and Soul
            that they may — or should — be stopped

            remember the rose . . and Nature's lesson
            a rose may only flower and open if it receives
                              both Sun and rain
            and so it is in *human* nature
            both gladness and sadness must be experienced
            if our Third Eyes are to be opened from their long sleep
                              do you see ?"

"Oh, Goob ! now I can complete my Happiness pOem
because you've taught me what I've been seeking
      why gladness and sadness should rhyme

yes, Charlie Brown, you funny clown, I finally see
            Good Grief !
grief is good, for it helps you grow to know
unless it becomes too flooding and painful to bear
but . . . what is the secret formula you recalled just now
that made you know how . . to stop the Nature rain ?
I'm sure I knew it too, when I camped out in the mountains with you
and with those spooky Essenes . . . but . . "

            "don't you mean . . when we camped out
            in the *flying* mountains with those spooky Essenes ?"

"yes, flying mountains !
and learned from the druids how to interpret dreams . . "

            " . . and that dreams are the true reality"

"yes . . the true reality
the place where we are taught the *knowing*-things
and what we call reality, is just a fragile bubble
where we learn the *growing*-things
a bubble made of reality-illusion and people confusion
only our dreams are truly real, and really true
but not our Night Mares
oh, but Gooober, tell me, tell me . . do !
tell me exactly how to stop the Nature rain
I want to learn how one may calm the storm"

        "well, you see . . . " you said, rather arrogantly
        as you donned your symbolic purple velvet robe
                and golden Leonine crown
        and waved your invisible sceptre of Superiority
        and your Royal teaching authority
        arranging your features
        in your familiar, lecture-the-peasants stern frown . .

        "well, you see . . . . "

but I didn't mind, for you are my kind
my great and wise, strong Lion
King of our Jungle — Ruler of my Pride
    and Man in our house
yes, Man to my teeny-tiny make-believe female mouse
              of great POwers
mouse-spouse that rhymes
with special, unique rose . . as everyone knows
    everyone but those
who carry the word 'equality' spelled backwards
on their Women's Lib banners

no, strong, wise Comforter Man-Lion
I shall never again resent your gentle Lord and Master mien
for we were created Man and Woman . . to teach each other
in precisely equal — but eternally different — ways

"Goob, quick — tell me !
how did you stop the Nature's rain ?"

        then you shook your mightly Lion's mane
        your beautiful, toadstool-cut golden hair

        with a perfectly marvelous arrogant air
        and answered, somewhat pedantically
              and chavinistically

        "Good Grief, Lucy wench !
        can't you remember that simple secret ?

when you've grown enough, and known enough
    spunky mouse-spouse
to allow your man to be boss in the house . . which is
the only way to be happy, as everyone knows . . "

"OH, GO SMELL A ROSE !

don't tease, now please . . tell me the formula"
I interrupted impatiently

      and your eyes gazed deeply into mine

      "the answer relates to the difference between
      the Lesser Mysteries . . and the Greater Mysteries"

"that sounds very 'heavy', in a spiritual sense
perhaps you'd better explain it slowly
one step at a time . . so I can truly understand"

      "allright . . I'll explain the difference
      between the Lesser Mysteries and the Greater Mysteries
      slowly . . one step at a time

      the Essenic formula for stopping the rain
      has much to do with first stopping pain . . "

      you said, with such infinite compassion
          transfiguring your face

      "the pain felt by all of God's creatures
      all Earthlings — humans and animals alike
      come, now, think — you can remember the formula
          if you really try"

"it has . . . something to do
with why I shouldn't cry . . "

      "yes, since raindrops are God's own tears . .
      the Nature rain is like unto your own secret fears"

"but how can it be stopped, the Nature rain ?
you still haven't helped me remember how"

      "impatience, impatience ! be still, and listen, darling"

"I'm sorry for interrupting"

      "the steps are simple, actually
      first, you must be able to stop the rain
      in your own heart . . to *still* your own soul . . "

. . be still, my love, be still . .

"then you must *desire* — and try — to stop the rain
in the hearts of friends . . and even strangers
        as well as in the hearts of our animal friends

finally, you must be able to stop the rain
which causes such pain . . in the heart
of your own twin soul or Twin S-elf
        as the case may be . .

and when you have mastered all these lessons
you may stop the Nature rain
by simply saying . . *Peace ! Be still !*

however, remember that first you must learn
to *listen* . . so that you may know Love's will"

    you paused
for a long, long moment

   a long eternity

        . . then finally said

"and you must learn to forgive — *not condemn*
those who have lost the way
        . . but *forgive* them"

"oh, I try to forgive the lost ones
I do, Goob, I do . . I try . . but how can *anyone*
forgive certain things . . like . . well, for example
those blind brutes, who call themselves human
and cheer, while the poor Bull is driven mad, then slaughtered
in the bullfight ring . . while they throw flowers

or those other blind brutes
some of them even women . . my God, *women* !
who sit at ringside, at prize fights
and cheer and scream and yell . . and urge the boxers on
to beat each other to a bloody pulp
yelling like insane beasts . . exactly . . . oh ! exactly
like those other brutal, blind and ignorant monsters yelled
        in the Roman Coliseum
too blind and thick-headed to even dimly comprehend
how degraded they are . . to obtain such pleasure
from watching beating, brutality, injury, blood and death
how can *anyone* forgive people like *that* ?

. . . and those are only two examples
of the unforgivable . . on this dark planet Earth"

                              you continued to stare at me . . then repeated

                              ". . . . and you must learn to forgive — not condemn
                              those who have lost the way
                                        . . you must learn to *forgive* them . . "

          as you stared at me
          I felt my heart begin to sway

to far-off music

                              " . . as he forgave the Magdalene"

suddenly there was a sharp loving-pain
an enormous mump-lump . . . behind my ears
while far-away tears streaked across my Soul

                    " . . and as he forgave Peter . . and Judas
                    . . . . the soldier who pierced his side
                    and even those who nailed his body to the cross
                    then tossed dice for his robe"

"while his Body Temple suffered terrible agony . . yes . . oh, God
they tossed Las Vegas dice, for his robe
at the foot of the cross . . where he could see them, in his suffering"

                    "but he saw them with the clear vision of his Third Eye
                    for he cried out, not in pain — but cried out
                    'Father, forgive them . . they know not what they do'

                    . . . . *they don't know what they are doing*

                    seeing within them, through his Third Eye's wisdom . . . .
                    . . . . their latent innocence"

"yes . . it was Pope Innocent himself
one of the greatest Popes of the Catholic faith
who said, to Francesco . . and to Claire, in Assisi

'my children . . . errors will be forgiven . . .
in our obsession with Original Sin
we do often forget . . . Original Innocence'

and I do believe that **RA** Himself did reside in
or hovered above — overshadowed — that Body Temple of Pope Innocent
                                        for a time
for the purpose of teaching this great Lesson
. . . also the lesson of humility to Earthlings possessed of false pride

when he kissed the feet of Francis, in the Vatican
when he . . kissed Francesco's mud-stained
    scratched and bleeding feet
while wearing his velvet, jewel encrusted robes of POwer"

                "this is true, darling . . what you believe about **RA**
                and we will swim further in those deep waters later . . .
                but I don't believe you quite yet understand
                the secrets of the Lesser and the Greater Mysteries
                                . . . do you ?"

"no, not quite all . . . that is
my understanding is still incomplete
so please continue . . . "

                "only when one has learned, then mastered
                the lessons of stopping pain in the heart of *human* nature
                may one then say, 'Abracadabra !' — and stop the Nature rain
                as Jesus, the man, calmed the storm
                                and was able to walk upon the water

                and he possessed these POwers over Nature
                because he had first mastered control of his own *human* nature
                making his Body Temple a fit place for the Holy Spirit to visit
                not just on holidays, and in special, loving ways
                                but permanently, as a Forever guest
                which is also why he was capable of Ascension
                        this being the ability and POwer
                to retain the same Body Temple, if one should desire
                and continually regenerate its cells and molecules
                as well as travel back and forth
                                between this Earth and other Earths
                        in all Universes and Solar Systems
                or create the ethers a new Body Temple if so desired . . .
                as all Earthlings are capable of doing themselves"

" . . . when they allow their Third Eyes to open
so they may once more regain the POwers they possessed
as gods and goddesses . . . each one"

                "that is entirely correct, Goob . . .
                you must have been engrossed in deep study while I was gone"

"oh, I was only having little raps and chats
with Heathcliffe . . . that's all
which reminds me . . Gooober, I simply must know
why God's name is mistakenly spelled — *God* meaning our co-Creators
do you know the correct spelling ?
and . . does it have something to do
with the first letter of Love ?"

"you are quite perceptive, darling
        but I will not allow you to trick me
into answering a question prematurely
and . . even assuming that what you are hinting
is correct . . do you not see
that such a spelling only seeds several *more* questions
with layers of profound meaning
                not yet guessed by humans
especially by those in Colorado ?"

"yes, I do
because, if what I am thinking is true
then it does open up several more mysteries
to be solved . . or meditated upon"

        "then let us postpone the matter of the correct spelling
        of God's name . . until the allotted time . . "

"oh, Goob, you sound like Heathcliffe now
I am so weary of hearing that phrase
'*at the allotted time*' . . . . "

        but you continued, ignoring
                as usual, my interruption . . and repeated

        " . . . until the allotted time
                now it's important to clarify the difference
        between the Lesser and the Greater Mysteries
        because if we don't . . . it may be forgotten

        you see, the Lesser Mysteries must first be mastered
        before the Greater Mysteries unfold . . .
                the initial lesson of the Lesser Mysteries
        is to find the lost sheep . . and bring them home

        and the second lesson of the Lesser Mysteries
        is to master control over one's S-elf, one's *human* nature
        do you understand, spunky mouse-spouse ?"

"I understand, I really do"

        "for the Lesser Mysteries involve Power over *human* nature
        dealing with the *subjective* sphere of wisdom

        while the Greater Mysteries involve the POwer over Nature
        dealing with the *objective* sphere of wisdom
        of learning how to unfold and harmonize with . . and
        finally control and command . . all the capacities of Nature

        the first mastery is an essential preliminary to the second
        that is, the Lesser Mysteries must be mastered

> before the Greater Mysteries may be finally revealed

> it has been so ordained that Earthlings
> may not learn or know the Greater in advance of the Lesser
> it is impossible to successfully command
>   the elemental essences of Nature
> until one has become a true Master
> over the elemental essences of one's own *human* nature
> for, discipline of the S-elf must precede dominion over Nature"

"I believe I shall italicize that
    mentally and otherwise
Discipline must precede Dominion

that applies to every sort of ruling, doesn't it ?
I mean, one isn't truly qualified
to rule a nation either — or a church — or a religion
until one has been able to 'Master' the discipline of one's S-elf
and, oh ! Gooober, I just real-ized
that the word 'discipline' contains the word 'disciple' !"

> "yes, darling, it does — and the word 'apostle'
>   contains . . what ?"

"It contains the word 'lost' !
therefore, one is first an apostle, while one is still
in some ways . . lost
and one becomes a 'disciple' when one has learned
or at least started to learn . . . s-elf discipline !
isn't all this true, Goob ?"

> "yes, this is true, spunky — and it contains the seed
> of why the druidic language is cosmically of awesome mystery
> one of those Greater Mysteries . . we will discuss later
>   *soon* . . but *later*

> nevertheless, what you have discovered is true
> and — if you'll forgive a pun, darling — as right as rain"

"oh, I'm used to puns
Heathcliffe taught me they are very wise
and point out important hidden truths"

> "Heathcliffe is a wise Gooober
> I knew it from the very first day I saw him wink at me
> from the shelf of that store in Pismo Beach"

"but what happens if the process is reversed ?
if humans should try to master first — the Greater Mysteries
before mastering the Lesser Mysteries ?"

Canto Twenty One   ☆   1075

"this is controlled
by a Universal Law discovered by Isaac Newton
. . . for every action, there is a re-action

it is not possible to successfully command Nature
unless and until one has become Master of one's own nature
because the great POwers within himself or herself
will betray him — or her — to the awesome POwers without
if one should dare attempt this
and the bommerang re-action then, from such an action
is so terrible as to be nearly . . unthinkable"

"you mean . . the Higher Angels of the 'O' and the 'I'
of each man and woman
will betray Earthlings to the awesome POwer of the Universe
if they should dare reverse their mastery
of the Lesser and the Greater Mysteries . . which would
result in the destruction and the destroying
of their entire . . world . . and their environment ?"

". . yes, this is sadly true
and this is why there is so little time left
to spread the Light
of Love and Knowing . . on Earth
and this brings up something I must tell you

it was not I alone, who stopped the rain today
you see, only through loving you as deeply as I do
was I able to truly forgive . . then pray to find a way
to stop your sadness rain
and understand your hurting-pain

but the summer storm and downpour of the Nature rain outside
was stopped . . do you understand . . . "

and you stared and stared

" . . it was stopped by another hand"

" . . by a nail-pierced hand ?"

you didn't answer my question directly
you said . . .

"it was stopped as a mystical sign
neither of us must ever forget

for I am yours, as you are mine . . and our mission
is to give all Earthlings an OOber Valentine
from the Land of Love
to heal them and teach them

1076 ☆ Canto Twenty One

so they may learn to heal and teach *themselves*
through the magic we learned long ago
when we camped out with the Essenes and the druids . . "

" . . in those perfectly marvelous flying mountains !
so all Earthlings may grow to know the **JOY**
of growing and expanding . . . into the Universe !"

"that is correct . . not quite told — yet
in its completeness or its entirety
but sufficiently correct . . for the present"

then the burning glow of the Eternity ember
that made us both remember . . so much
left your eyes
but they were still silvery-wise
with deep blue velvet love . . for me

"and now, darling . . it's time to look for miracles !
now that our old shared dream of sadness is past
we will send the Morning Star
streaming back through all the distant galaxies
to tell *her* it's time, at last — to return !
and maybe even bring with her
this time . . simultaneously
a teeny-tiny boy star
to help us create a Twin-Joy on Earth !

and . . it is also time
that we may soon speak of all the *knowing*-things
because now we've shared together
all the necessary *growing*-things"

"Goob, may we really-truly make such magic together ?
may we tell the Morning Star
to stream back to Heaven with the news
that we ordain, not *one* miracle — but *two* ?"

"darling . . in a divine sense . . that is up to you"

oh !   miraculous rejoice !
thank you, thank you, God . . however you spell your name !
thank you for the growing-knowing — and thank you for the Little Prince
who tamed me into his own special, unique rose !
and thank you for the miracle that came to me on a midnight clear
on that silent, holy night in the snow . . so long ago
when the lost was found again !

this is not the 4th of July — this is Thanksgiving Day !

Canto Twenty One   ☆   1077

"oh, Gooober ! may a holiday be just any day ?
any day you choose it to be ?"

                       and you laughed

        "right on, baby ! that's how druids pray !
            in **RAINBOW COLORS**
        not mumbling mournful mantras of dreary grey"

"*Om Myoho RaHram Kiu !*
let Heaven and Nature sing !"

        then you slipped on my proper finger
        my *Love is Eternal* ring

"Oh, Goob, you kept it
you didn't lose it or give it away
End of Sadness and Beginning of Gladness !"
I heard myself say

        "the reversal of the Alpha and the Omega !"
        you answered right away . . then gave a Tarzan yell

        **"WE'RE GOING TO RE-VERSE THE POLARITY
           OF HEAVEN AND HELL
        WITH LOVE AND LIGHT . . . ON EARTH !"**

"O ! Gooober . . . your beard . . . it's gone
you don't have a beard anymore !"

        "did you only discover that now ?"

"yes . . I didn't notice it before . . I wonder why ?"

        "you can channel the answer to that
        go on . . . just try"

"I know, I know !
I didn't notice that your beard was gone earlier
because I've finally learned to see with my Third Eye
which means that I'd know you anywhere
with or without a beard . . or however you wear your hair"

        "even if my face turned green ?" you smiled

"of course ! because I know how . . now
to always see only the *real* you-of-you
I've learned so much since you've been gone
but think how long it took !"

        "it's like I've always told you, Lucy-wench
        it doesn't matter how you look

then you feigned a dizzy spin
and whispered . .

"darling, I somehow sense that we are within
                the vortex of a tornado
and I feel a growing thunder in the me-of-me
                blending with the lightning of the you-of-you
and very, very soon
                this golden summer afternoon
is going to be translated into a violet-April *Spring*"

  we smiled at each other, then, and miracled in joy
and the happiness in our hearts . . was blessed and multiplied
for we had both been crucified on the Cross of Growing
and through the alchemy-magic of Forgiving
we had both risen . . . into the Easter Light of Knowing !

!* !* !* !* !* !* !* !* !

then, as the Universe whirled on its axis
skipped a single pulse beat

                . . . and spun right-side up again

I thought of the cross I had crucified you on
and cried . . "Oh, Gooober, please will you forgive m . . . "

        but before I could complete my supplication
        you handed me a small white card
        with a teeny-tiny daisy drawn in the corner
        by your drawf-clutched pen
                    . . and you had written

            "all those times you suffered such pain
            from the unkindness of that identical Body Temple
            which only *looked* like me — but was *not* me
            I cried . . because it hurt me so inside
            will you forgive me for not letting you know ?"

"dear, funny druid — I knew !
from the very beginning . . my heart knew"

            and you murmured, then, against my cheek
            " . . . . . oh, the Nile is blue . . . so blue"

and as the happy sky poured forth the Music of the Spheres
I smiled at you . . through the Pyramid Rainbow of millions of years

and handed you my very own special OOber surprise
from this side of the border

"see, Goob ? my really-truly official Brownie card !
I found it in the attic, identifying me as a druid !
and next week, I'll be getting my driver's license !"

                    "I don't need those things to identify you, spunky
                     since I've been spinning on a saucer, with Master OObers
                     . . and I'll tell you more about that later . .

                        since I've been gone
            I've found out who I am   and who you are too"

"you have ?
oh, tell me, tell me, do !"   *   *

                                                                            *

                    *   *

                *   *

                                    "you are me
                    *   and   *
                                     I am you

                    we are eternally One . . and eternally also Two
                    which encircles us within the magic Three
                            of the Holy Trinity
                            of Miracles
                                                . . . do you see ?"

*   then our eyes locked   *
                     in a deep, deep knowing
    *   *

                        we touched noses
        *   *

                        and whispered

            *   *
                            magic !

        *   o   *

                *MAGIC * MAGIC * MAGIC * magic * magic * magic * magic * !

as the earth-clouds vanished . . . and the sky opened up
to shower us with sprinkles of star-flake shavings
from the twinkling OOber galaxy

                    you said . .

            "the keys to the Kingdom are teeny-tiny"

and our eyes filled with druid dust
all sparkly and shiny

so we ran quickly inside, crying . .

            "Heathcliffe, don't hide !
            we want to give you the Reztilup prize for Love
            because you gave us the last verse
                        of our Happiness POem !"

Heath's little beady eyes of wistful wise
glistened with pride . . and he knew what we knew too !
for he lifted his funny mop feet . . and grew and grew and grew

            so tall

showing not the least bit of canine hesitation
as he joined us in the miracle of Love's levitation

while all the seasons blended . . spring into summer
                            into winter . . into fall
        snow mixed with rain

        JOY ! replaced pain

and wafting through the open car window . . came the scent of sweet peas

then you wrote across my heart
in your squiggly dwarf scrawl . .

                    Gear Dooober . . I love you

                    and **Love** is **All**

THE END

WHICH IS THE BEGINNING

THE PLANETS

we've fought a long and bitter war, my Twin Self and I
lost and lonely, fallen angels — exiled
from a misty, long-forgotten OOber galaxy of stars

caught in Neptune's tangled web
wounded cruelly by the painful thrust of Mars
tortured by the clever lies of Mercury

shocked and nearly torn asunder
by Vulcan's distant, raging thunder
shattered by the lightning
of the sudden, awful violence of Uranus

    crushed beneath the weight of stern, unyielding Saturn
    who lengthened every hour into a day . . each day into a year
    each year . . into millenniums of waiting

scorched by the Sun's exploding bursts of pride
as those wandering angels, stilled and helpless
                    deep within us, cried

still we fought on, in unrelenting fury
    striking blow for blow
driven by the pounding drums of Jupiter's giant, throbbing passions
stumbling at the precipice of the Moon's enticing madness

    to fall, at last, in trembling fear
    before the ominous threat of Pluto's tomb-like silence
    consumed by inconsolable sadness
                  and the bleakness of despair
we bear . .

    the wounds and scars of furious battle, my Twin Self and I

but now we walk in quiet peace . . with all our scattered pieces whole
together, hand-in-hand . . full serpent circle
back into the pyramid-shaped rainbow of tomorrow's brighter Eden
crowned by gentle Venus with the Victory of Love

    that *did not die,* but has survived
    the night of selfish seeking

to wait for morning's soft forgiveness

     and the dawn . . of understanding

for all the lonely ones who have read this book

I wish the miracle

of love

Linda Goodman

" *. . . for whatsoever things ye should desire*
pray as if ye had already received these
and ye shall surely have them . . . "

with Everlasting Love

I dedicate this

and all my future books

to "my sneaky Guru"

Aaron Goldblatt

who has patiently, throughout all incarnations, guided my creative efforts and
spiritual enlightenment with the infinite gentleness and wisdom of a Master Avatar,
and who has been . . . is now and ever shall be . . . responsible for all my miracles
. . . every single one of them manifested only through his faith

Be not forgetful to entertain strangers; for
thereby some have entertained angels unawares.
Hebrews 13:2

"My children, errors will be forgiven. In our obsession
with original sin, we do often forget . . . original innocence."

Pope Innocent of Assisi
15th Century A.D.

Linda Goodman was born during a spring thunderstorm on an April day. She has four children: a Goat, an Archer, a Water Bearer, and a Scorpio Eagle, who are currently pursuing their assured dreams, and with whom she celebrates Groundhog's Day and other important holidays frequently. Linda lives in the Colorado mountains with her dogs, Benjamin and Bear, Cancer and Gemini respectively. Ben and Bear are vegetarians. One is twelve years old and one is nine years old, so they are still puppies. A lion who was born free sometimes visits Linda's home, but is quite tame and friendly, despite an occasional grumpy growl. The author's favorite songs are "When You Wish Upon A Star," and "On A Clear Day," of which there are an abundance in her home town of Cripple Creek (stars and clear days). Her favorite perfume is vanilla extract and sweet peas in the rain. Her favorite book is *A Wrinkle in Time*. She is 5'4" or 5'5" depending on whether she is wearing shoes or is barefoot, so most of the time she is 5'4". So much for vital statistics and background.

Linda, herself, adds:

One misty and mystical morning, I took a walk in the woods, and found eleven druid-elves, who agreed to scatter magic dust around me to materialize "Gooberz" from my heart into the bookstores, and I'd like to thank them here for their various spells of enchantment . . . . Andrew Ettinger, Jerry Perles, Roger Nittler, Jim McLin, Neil Brawner, Nancy Sarada, Toni De Marco, Terry Winders, Phillip di Franco (a leprechaun with a Lion's mane) . . . and two of them I knew long ago and far away, when the three of us danced in a circle beneath the stars on a Midsummer's night at Stonehenge . . . Rob Dorgan and Steve Bolia.